ALL *AGAINST* THE LAW:

The Criminal Activities of the Depression Era Bank Robbers, Mafia, FBI, Politicians, & Cops

BILL FRIEDMAN

ALL *AGAINST* THE LAW:

The Criminal Activities of the Depression Era Bank Robbers, Mafia, FBI, Politicians, & Cops

Copyright © 2013
by
Bill Friedman

Published in 2013 by
Old School Histories
www.OldSchoolHistories.com

www.AllAgainstTheLaw.com

ISBN: 978-1494958138

TABLE OF CONTENTS

Table of Contents

THE PURPOSE, ORGANIZATION, & SOURCES FOR THIS BOOK

WHY THIS HISTORY?

Here for the first time is the complete story of the careers and lives of the four successive Public Enemies Number One who were the most dangerous machinegun toting Midwestern bank robbers of the early Depression years - John Dillinger, Baby Face Nelson, Pretty Boy Floyd, and Alvin Karpis with the Barker brothers. Besides being complete this presentation is wholly different from previous histories because for the first time the newspaper article accounts of these gangsters' activities are included. These were written by reporters from interviews of the eyewitnesses at these events, police and detective descriptions of the handling and findings of their investigations, and the trial testimonies of both the criminal cohorts and also the people who harbored these killers during their long fugitive manhunts. These facts were merged with the FBI agents' internal reports sent to the Washington Headquarters that frequently admitted or confirmed their misconduct, as well as the many other documents used by previous crime historians. All this information combines to present the first complete timeline of these criminals' actions and personal lives as each fugitive alternated between hiding in a safe haven and staying on the run often just ahead of determined lawmen. Just as a movie is made up of many individual pictures that are flashed one after the other to produce the action, the many individual facts collected about each of these incidents create a dramatic step-by-step flow that produces an incredibly exciting and fast-moving adventure story.

Interspersed throughout these Public Enemies Number One manhunts is the transformation of the Federal Bureau of Investigation (FBI) from an accounting department of government money into a national police and detective agency. This is by far the most penetrating story of how J. Edgar Hoover took this group of politically-appointed accountants and attorneys, who by law could not carry guns or make arrests, and turned them into a full-fledged criminal detective agency. Hoover's leadership of the FBI has been discredited by numerous previous scholars, but this book goes much further in presenting how poorly-trained the agents were in police and detective procedure, the lack of respect they had for individual liberties and rights, and their total disregard for the safety and well-being of the civilians who unintentionally appeared in their paths.

Previous historians have usually described the actions of Hoover's FBI as like Keystone Cops or repeatedly referred to agents' actions as "inexplicable." But Hoover's agents' behavior was the direct byproduct of their Director's leadership and training procedures. After the reader learns the capabilities and values of Hoover's agents, their actions are neither funny nor baffling but instead very predictable. As each confrontation develops the reader can sense how the situation can go terribly wrong as these courageous but ill-prepared early agents headed into what would likely become another botched raid or else produce disastrous results for the lawmen or innocent civilian bystanders caught up in the lines of fire.

The mismatch between the skills of Hoover's early agents and the killers they went after could not have been more stark. These untrained agents went after the most aggressive and dangerous killers in history. These were not the typical variety of criminal who tries to escape when pursued by the police. Whenever these killers started to feel trapped or pressured, they would turn about face and run on foot out in the open, or whirl their car around as they floored the accelerator, charging their pursuers while blasting away with their machineguns. All this aggressive determination made Dillinger, Nelson, Floyd, and Karpis and the Barker brothers dreadfully successful at killing more policemen and FBI agents than any other American outlaws. Not only did each of these gang leaders and a number of their followers successfully escape multiple pursuits, but many also broke out of jail or prison along the way. Against these hard-driving shooters, Hoover's agents faced repeated failure and disaster. It seems inconceivable any of this could have happened, but every word presented here comes from either the victims, eyewitnesses, local police officials, or the pursuing FBI agents' official internal reports.

Hoover's mismanagement of the FBI was revealed in major exposés by the nation's newspapers and magazines from early in his career and after each of his agents' botched raids and other misdeeds. Not only did other federal and public officials regularly harpoon his actions in the press but some also lampooned his agents' more ridiculous performances. Hoover's underhanded, often illegal, tactics against his critics; his occasional fights to survive his malfeasance in office; and his frequent shredding of Americans' most cherished Constitutional protections and denial of individual liberties are detailed as they occurred in the course of these Public Enemies Number One manhunts. Few Americans today are aware of how Hoover became an unaccountable malevolent fourth branch of the federal government totally outside the brilliantly-conceived checks-and-balances system created by the Founding Fathers to prevent just the type of actions he specialized in during his 48-year tenure.

These incredible manhunts cover the first 11 chapters, and then the Kansas City Massacre is solved in Chapter 12. While the public is well aware of the St. Valentine's Day slaughter of seven gangsters in Chicago, the Kansas City Massacre was the more shocking crime of its time, resulting in the deaths of four lawmen and the wounding of two more. Half of these six victims were FBI agents, and it led Congress to create a national police force by arming agents, giving them the power to arrest, and making it a federal crime to kill a federal agent. From early in the Kansas City Massacre case, Director J. Edgar Hoover decided that Pretty Boy Floyd and his partner were two of the three shooters, and he made their capture a cause célèbre. Crime historians ever since have argued about exactly who the three killers might have been.

The thorough cold-case investigation presented in Chapter 12 not only identifies for the first time who the three shooters actually were but it also finally reveals their motive. It first proves that no one who has been suspected up until now could have been involved. To accomplish this the history of Kansas City's political structure and Mafia gang organization are presented. Kansas City suffered from the most unique political/criminal power structure in the country. The Mafia leader was the lieutenant to the city's dominant political kingmaker, and in return for delivering the vote in the Italian neighborhoods, he was given the authority to select the Chief of Police and his detectives. The state legislature tried to stop this affront to justice by having the governor appoint a five-man Police Commission to control the city's departmental hirings. This action just led Kansas City's Mafia chieftain to expand his political sphere of influence across the state to elect puppet governors who appointed the Police Commissioners of his choosing.

The last four chapters (12 through 15) cover the complete history of the Kansas City political dynasty of the three successive Pendergast family members alongside the five consecutive Mafia leaders who were referred to in the press as "political leaders" rather than gangsters. The crowning achievements of this political/criminal machine was putting Kansas Citian Harry Truman into the U.S. Senate with stuffed ballot boxes and then getting him nominated as Vice President of the United States.

The final chapter is a shocking political exposé about the only President in history who sold out to organized crime. The entire chapter concerns Harry Truman's tenure in the White House, but it strictly covers the many interactions he continued to have with Mafia leader Charles Binaggio. Their mutual political hijinks, antagonisms, and intrigue are staggering. This Kansas City Mafioso headed the First District Democratic Clubhouse on Truman Road, and when he was slain there the nation's papers carried photos of his body sprawled beneath a five-feet-high enlarged portrait of President Truman. The next day Republicans got up in both the U.S. Senate and the House and directly accused the President of having ordered his hometown political henchman to kill the Mafioso. This whole period in the White House is beyond mind-boggling.

All the events in this story tie together one after the other, and some key figures are also linked to the Nevada casino industry where I spent my entire career. This book opens in Nevada when Reno was its largest city, and Bill Graham and Jim McKay where the biggest casino operators both before and after gambling was legalized in 1931. Baby Face Nelson was a doorman and occasional bouncer for this duo before going into bank robbing. Graham and McKay were also the state's biggest Prohibition violators. In the *Golden Hotel,* the state's largest, they operated the most popular casino, and they developed an effective but very illegal tourist-marketing program to bring in high-rollers during the Great Depression. They offered an emporium of services for criminals who used guns to steal money or conned their victims. This drew financial criminals in large numbers from across the country. One service was to hide fugitives on the run in this isolated town protected from police interference. In the weeks to months before the FBI took down Dillinger, Nelson, Floyd, Karpis, and Fred Barker, all enjoyed the safe haven provided by Graham and McKay.

This book closes with the career of Kansas City's fifth Mafia leader, Nick Civella. He financed a new wave of hidden underworld casino owners on the Las Vegas Strip through the Teamsters Union Pension Fund, as the original pioneer gangsters, who had earned their initial fortunes during Prohibition and built the Strip, reached retirement age and sold out. In between the beginning and ending of the book, Mafioso Binaggio, who was shot to death under President Truman's portrait, had planned to become a major investor in the *Thunderbird Hotel & Casino* on the Strip before Ben Siegel had begun construction of his Fabulous *Flamingo* gambling resort, but the most unusual of circumstances disrupted Binaggio's plans. Other links between the Kansas City Mafia and the Nevada casino industry during this era are also presented.

THIS HISTORICAL PRESENTATION'S UNIQUE FEATURES

A history is a chronology of events, but when multiple incidents occur at the same time, it can be difficult for the reader to clearly focus on any specific topic. Thus each chapter section in this historical presentation follows a single gang or individual and takes each issue one at a time to its conclusion. This makes each event or subject much easier to follow and view in its entirety.

To further make the storyline clearer and easier for the reader, only the names of key participants and dates are presented in the text. The names of people who appear briefly in a single incident are listed only in the endnotes to be available for historians without cluttering, complicating, or slowing reading of the text. These people's roles are clearly identified in the text according to their relationship to the event. For example "an eyewitness" or "his girlfriend."

Dates in the text are replaced with the length of time in days, weeks, or months between pairs of related events to make the time frame clear. The date of every major event is presented in the source notes, and the key dates for related events are listed in chronological order to create clear historical timelines.

The information contained in this text was found in a variety of sources, which are identified in the extensive endnotes to assist historians interested in further study or to confirm the accuracy of their use in this text. For every quote, the name of the person who said it and the source where it was found are identified either in the text or in these notes. Quotes taken from gambling-industry pioneers who contributed to my research are listed as "my interview."

Facts contained in most consecutive sentences in the text are from different sources, so a complete documentation would require a book much longer than this one. The simple but effective solution when dealing with newspaper reports was to not identify the specific sources when it was obtained from the following six daily newspapers from 1930 on - the *New York Times,* the *Chicago Daily Tribune,* the *Los Angeles Times,* the *Las Vegas Review Journal,* the *Las Vegas Sun,* and Reno's *Nevada State Journal.* Additional valuable sources for this book were two more daily newspapers from 1923 through 1950 - the *Kansas City Star* and the *Kansas City Times.*

In addition to these newspaper sources, many documents were used, and each is identified either in the text or the source notes. They include FBI internal reports, Congressional hearings, legislative and court records, books and magazines, federal and state government departmental records like the Missouri Secretary of State Archives & Records, and unpublished documents. In the text these are cited by type – for example, "in testimony before the U.S. Senate Kefauver Committee."

THE EXTENSIVE NEWSPAPER RECORDS

Newspaper reports are primary source material for biographies about politicians, business leaders, and criminals, and for law enforcement investigations as well. The U.S. Attorney in Chicago who successfully directed the IRS investigative team that prosecuted Al Capone and his lieutenants for income-tax evasion, George E. Q. Johnson, testified to a Senate Judiciary Subcommittee on April 2, 1932 about the importance of newspaper articles in building these cases. He explained, "I made up a card index. Newspaper men have amazingly accurate information. It was rather astonishing. It was not evidence, but it was very accurate information as to who the gangs were and the leaders [and their activities], so I had a newspaper man make a card index of all the gangs, taking it from newspaper stories." This was his principal source material to identify and locate the criminal associations and financial holdings of Capone and his lieutenants.

In an era when many newspapers specialized in publishing organized-crime exposés, their articles were a useful law-enforcement source tool. For example, from the 1920s through the 1980s, about half the pages in the FBI files of members of organized crime were reproductions of newspaper articles. (I did not study the FBI files after the 1980s because they were no longer relevant to the Nevada casino industry.)

Nevada's early gaming controllers depended heavily on press reports to determine if casino license applicant's should be granted a license. During the 1940s through the 1960s, Nevada knowingly licensed illegal casino owners and executives from other states for two reasons. First, Nevada had no home grown operators, so the newcomers were the only experienced and knowledgeable casino managers available. Second, a high percentage of casino dealers and executives in that era were accomplished slight-of-hand cheats. Thus casino officials had to be very knowledgeable or their operations would have gotten ripped off. Legitimate businessmen who were licensed in this era had a high-rate of quick bankruptcies after opening because of employee theft. The goal of the early gaming controllers was not to keep experienced illegal casino operators out, but "to determine the good hoods from the bad hoods." Nevada wanted licensees who had been involved only with the crimes of gambling and Prohibition, not those who had committed crimes of exploitation or violence. To accomplish this, they depended on interviews with crime reporters in the cities the applicants came from. The first Nevada Gaming Control Board Chairman, Bob Cahill, told me, "Newspapermen were a very important arm of my law enforcement program. There were the out-of-state newsmen. Every town has a reporter who specializes in hoods and syndicated crime. I got more information from newsmen than from official law enforcement agencies. They have access to information the police do not have through personal acquaintance with the criminal element."[i]

I studied the microfilms of six archived daily newspapers from five key cities. I read the relevant articles in a total of 123,200 newspapers from the following years.

- The *New York Times* - 1910 through 1959 (50 years)
- The *Chicago Daily Tribune* - 1910 through 1959 (50 years)
- The *Los Angeles Times* - 1920 through 1949 (30 years)
- The *Reno Gazette-Journal* (it was the *Nevada State Journal* until its merger with the *Reno Evening Gazette*) - 1931 through 2006 (76 years)
- The *Las Vegas Review-Journal* - 1931 (the year Nevada legalized casinos) through 2006 (76 years)
- The *Las Vegas Sun* – its first edition on July 1, 1950 to the final edition on September 30, 2005 (55 ¼ years)

The *New York Times* is an exceptional newspaper that had a liberal editorial page but employed both top liberal and conservative reporters to obtain balanced news coverage. Its articles gave in-depth analysis of most issues and included much historical information. The *Times* is a researcher's dream because its articles often lead to other sources and related issues and individuals.

The *Chicago Daily Tribune* was staunchly conservative, but the publisher valued law and order and honest politicians more than its political agenda. Thus, this paper led the fight to topple Al Capone and exposed Republicans as readily as Democrats when it found them to be corrupt. It endorsed Democrats against the worst-offending Republican candidates and elected officials.

The *Los Angeles Times* during this era was a huge research disappointment. It carried sparse coverage of Prohibition and illegal gambling in Southern California, even though casinos operated openly in Los Angeles and Palm Springs. The *Los Angeles Times'* articles did not list all the facts from police reports, and often did not list the address or even the city where illegal casinos were busted or having legal problems. Its reporters did almost no research, so unlike the other five newspapers, which frequently exposed the activities of major criminals in their communities, the *Los Angeles Times* produced almost no crime exposés during the 1920s through the 1940s. At least part of the reason can be found in the paper's political agenda. It endorsed and supported the most corrupt politicians and DA's during this period. It even editorialized in news stories on behalf of the crooked officials who protected the serious criminal element in the Los Angeles metropolitan area. The *Los Angeles Times* contained some useful information, but unfortunately buried much more.

The three Nevada newspapers effectively covered the casino industry and its leaders in Las Vegas, Reno, and Lake Tahoe. They also reported on the strength of the economies, market trends, and state politics, including actions and decisions by the state legislature and the city councils, courts, and state and gaming control authorities. Each newspaper had an aggressive investigative reporter who specialized in the gambling industry and politics. (There were four excellent ones until the merger of the *Nevada State Journal* with the *Reno Evening Gazette,* when it was reduced to three).

Activities that occurred primarily in Kansas City, Missouri are presented in the last four chapters of this book. The *Kansas City Star* and the *Kansas City Times* for the years 1923 through 1950 were critical for this history. Fortunately both newspapers had excellent investigative reporters who provided much of the raw material available for the city's political and criminal history. The knowledgeable and exceptionally helpful staff at the Kansas City Public Library provided the multitude of critical newspaper articles and many of the biographies produced in-house about the city's political and criminal figures. In recent years federal and state government agencies have placed many of their historical records on the internet, and the endnotes list the numerous sources that were drawn from.

It is important to note that reporters sometimes write inaccurate information because some of their sources lie, and reporters sometimes present incomplete or distorted information because press deadlines occasionally require them to submit articles before fully completing their investigations. Thus, my research of many other types of documents was invaluable in confirming, correcting, and expanding upon these newspaper reports.

CHAPTER 1

CASINOS, BABY FACE, & DILLINGER

RENO & THE MIDWEST BANK ROBBING BUSINESS

Four machinegun-toting bank robbing gangs of the 1930s Depression Era became infamous as Public Enemies Number 1. All had strong ties to a pair of Reno, Nevada casino owners, Bill Graham and Jim McKay. They met working in the mines of the great Tonopah, Nevada silver and gold boom in the center of the state. Early in Prohibition they moved to Reno, the state's largest city, and became the vice lords. They became the principal illegal importers of fine liquor. A few years later they opened the town's only legally licensed brothel, a sprawling 80-room house of joy that operated around the clock. As the state's top Prohibition violators they controlled the police department which dutifully shut down the many small illegal brothels owned by competitors.

Next Graham and McKay expanded their vice menu to include illegal casinos. They increased their monthly bribery payments to Reno's Police Chief and the Washoe County Sheriff to not only ignore their Prohibition activities but to turn a blind eye as they became the illegal gambling kings of Reno and Lake Tahoe. They had the state's largest illegal casino, the *Bank Club,* in the basement of the state's largest hotel, the 250-room *Golden* in the heart of downtown Reno a half block from the train passenger depot. Its hotel rooms and three fine bars were the hangout and meeting places for the state's cattlemen, mine operators, politicians, and men traveling on business. Graham and McKay also had the elegant *Willows* nightclub where the wealthy partied nightly in their finery, several speakeasies with one or two gambling tables each for working men who felt out of place in the more upscale *Bank Club* and *Golden Hotel,* and the *Cal-Neva Lodge* at the North Shore of Lake Tahoe for affluent San Franciscans who owned summer homes in the forest surrounding the lake.

In that era tourism was still a minor industry in America except for resorts that were within a horse and buggy's ride from major cities. However the nation's style of living was undergoing dramatic changes and this was affecting criminal behavior as well. The assembly-line and mass manufacture of automobiles opened up travel to many Americans. The federal government built the country's first hard-surface transcontinental highway in the middle of Prohibition and Reno was situated along it. This meant for the first time criminals were mobile. It allowed them to easily strike at wealthy victims in surrounding states and quickly leave the jurisdiction of local law enforcement. In a few key cities criminal support groups developed to hide and protect fugitives on the run as they planned their next crimes. The invention of the Tommy Gun made robbers and kidnappers far more dangerous. The country's law enforcers had to adapt to these developing crime trends. They had to learn how to trail suspects on the move and keep people associated with them under surveillance. Lawmen had to develop expertise in the new phenomenon of car chases and machinegun battles. No federal law-enforcement agency had authority over this new breed of machinegun-toting criminal on the move and no centralized agency existed to assist local lawmen to communicate with each other about these vicious criminals' activities and travels.

UNIQUE CASINO PLAYER-MARKETING PROGRAMS

Reno's *Bank Club* was Nevada's largest and most outstanding 1930s casino operation. During the Great Depression when the state still had little tourism and the country was in desperate economic times, the *Bank Club* had an amazing amount of business around the clock because Graham and McKay created marketing programs like no other legal or illegal casino in history. Long before Nevada would become a tourist destination, their gambling joint attracted America's Depression-era financial criminals in droves.

It was well known by the town's people that many major criminals visited Graham and McKay at the *Bank Club* and nearby bars where the pair regularly bought rounds for the other patrons. Still no one feared Graham and McKay. They were well liked because they were nice guys who treated everyone with respect and helped those in need. They always lived by their word and their handshake. Finally they protected Renoites from crime by strictly imposing a condition on visiting gangsters. They ordered, "Stay clean during your stay in Reno. Women and children must always feel safe walking the streets." Under their watch no thug ever broke this rule.

But there was another side to Graham and McKay. From the *Bank Club* they offered a full-service emporium for financial criminals from across the nation. They gave living money to criminals fresh out of jail, or who had gone busted, until they reestablished their careers, and they loaned money to criminals to buy the equipment needed to commit upcoming crimes. They laundered bank robbery cash loot and kidnapping ransoms through their casino cages and bars in small quantities to a multitude of winning players who cashed out chips. They stored criminals' ill-gotten cash stashes in their casino cashier's safety-deposit boxes. They also hid fugitives on the run with false identities and protected them from local police harassment. For each of these and other diverse services they charged a fee, a share of the take, or a discount on laundered funds in return for clean greenbacks. Locals may have wanted to believe Graham and McKay's criminal associations were innocent friendships, but these were profitable crime relationships to feed the pair's craving for larceny and greed.

In addition to assisting the nation's financial criminals, they ran their own criminal enterprises. Graham was the mastermind, financer, and biggest bettor of a large horserace fixing ring when racing was the nation's most popular spectator sport. The ring members were ultimately convicted but Graham was never charged because none of the leaders, who were the only ones who knew Graham was behind it, would testify against him.

For more than a decade Graham and McKay made Reno the country's swindling capital. The financial euphoria of the Roaring '20s stock-market boom made the greedy and gullible among the wealthy especially vulnerable. Con men nationwide ran their own scams but Graham and McKay made these frauds possible. They financed these stings for 15% of the proceeds. They supplied con men the large cash bankrolls they flashed in their schemes, and paid their travel expenses to Reno. While the con men were in Reno, the pair guaranteed that the police would not act on victim complaints against unidentified out-of-state con men who used temporary unknown aliases.

Graham and McKay took the fake bookmaking operation depicted in the 1973 movie *The Sting* a big step further. Some popular con games required having a bank cash the victim's check so the con men could run with the cash and yet the check would quickly clear the victim's account before he or she could return home and stop payment. Graham and McKay had a legitimate state-licensed bank in an out-of-the-way location and its sole purpose was handling such fraudulent transactions. The pair introduced con men to an official at this legitimate bank who did not ask their sucker embarrassing questions about why he or she was doing such a risky kind of transaction. Graham and McKay also validated the victim's signature to rapidly convert negotiable securities into cash, lent the bank the cash to purchase the victim's securities, and placed the stolen cash in their casino cashier's safety-deposit boxes until the con men were ready to leave town or gamble at the *Bank Club*. These easy-money crooks usually gambled away more than another 15% at the popular faro or crap tables.

Con men brought victims from all over the U.S. and Canada to the Graham and McKay bank sting operation. Since the bank mailed the victims' securities to New York for resale through legitimate channels that had no idea the bank was acting improperly, these frauds fell under the jurisdiction of U.S. Postal Service inspectors. When they finally brought their case against Graham and McKay, a large number of victims were ready to testify that their loses totaled many tens of millions in the spending power of today's dollars.

The first two trials of Graham and McKay ended with hung juries because the pair was rarely seen at the bank by the victims. For the third trial the federal prosecutor had more con men become state's witnesses, and the pair was easily convicted. Graham and McKay were sentenced to 9 years and served a little more than 6 years in Leavenworth Penitentiary before being paroled. Five years later, with the support of their powerful Nevada political allies, both received full pardons from President Harry Truman. Graham and McKay resumed operating their *Bank Club* before Nevada began licensing its legal casinos. The two owners had unacceptable backgrounds because of their felony fraud convictions and involvement with prostitution, but the Nevada Attorney General established the "grandfather" protection concept at the very beginning of state licensing. He took the position that state gambling-control authorities could not apply rules or regulations retroactively on earlier improper behavior or revoke existing licenses based on newly passed standards.

THE BABY-FACED KILLER

Graham and McKay developed a close working relationship with Lester Gillis who would later become infamous with the nickname Baby Face Nelson. He grew up in Chicago and became a street gang member before his teenage years. At just 14-years old, he was convicted of car theft and sentenced to two years at the Illinois State School for Boys near St. Charles, 40 miles west of Chicago. He was a model inmate, surprising based on his later adult record, and paroled, but just five months after his release he was caught driving the car of another person and was sent back to the School for violation of parole. Again a model prisoner he was paroled 10 months later. This time it was only three months until he was returned for parole violation. His conduct was exceptional so he was made college captain, or monitor, over 75 other wayward boys. Paroled after nine months at age 17, he headed for Reno where he worked at Graham and McKay's *Rex Club* bar as a doorman and occasional bouncer even though he was a diminutive 5-feet-5 133-pounds.

During Prohibition Graham and McKay bought their booze from a rumrunning gang based in Sausalito, California, a small town on the other end of the Golden Gate Bridge from San Francisco and nestled on the bay shoreline. This gang downloaded imported fine liquor from freighter ships in secluded coves to trucks waiting on the beach. They distributed their inventory to many destinations in the northwest. Nelson soon went to work for this gang riding shotgun for their liquor convoys.

Nelson had a wanderlust and occasionally moved between three cities - Sausalito, Reno, and Chicago. When he returned to his hometown, he found Al Capone's gang had become deeply involved in the new crime of labor racketeering. Caponites forcibly took over a number of unions through threats of violence and the murders of a number of officials. Some union leaders lined up armies of bodyguards to fend off the gang's killers and Nelson became one of their hired guns protecting their lives. While in Chicago he married his young girlfriend when she became pregnant, and she often accompanied him in his travels, waiting for him at their abode during his crime escapades.

After three-and-a-half years working out west Nelson returned to Chicago. He branched out on his own by partnering with two other men in 10 major bank robberies and jewelry thefts, stealing a total of $135,000 [This equals $1.9 million in today's buying power]. Their violent crimes included kidnapping a jewelry-store employee to use as a hostage while driving away from a robbery. They later threw him from the car. Three of their jewel robberies were home invasions. In each they terrorized up to eight adults and children as they used adhesive tape to bind them. Chicago detectives finally became interested in the trio's activities probably from information supplied by a snitch who was arrested and wanted to get a lighter sentence. After a one-month investigation and surveillance of the trio, detectives swooped in and separately arrested the three simultaneously.[1]

Nelson was the first to be tried. He was identified as one of the bandits in the Hillside State Bank robbery by two employees and one of his two cohorts who turned state's witness. In addition police had found a revolver in the home of the third accomplice that he had stolen along with the cash from the bank. This associate pled guilty because he was a fugitive on the run from a life term in Ohio for murder. Nelson was convicted and sentenced to one year to life.

Just two weeks after Nelson arrived at the Illinois State Penitentiary at Joliet, a search of his cell block turned up 10 saw blades. The prisoners had already started cutting a square opening in the metal plates in the back wall of the shower room to gain entrance to the corridor on the other side that was lined with unbarred windows at street-level. The warden was convinced Nelson was the prisoner responsible for arranging to have the blades smuggled in.

Eight months into his confinement, a prison guard transported a handcuffed Nelson to Wheaton, Illinois, 25 miles west of Chicago, for trial in the Itasca State Bank robbery of $4,600. He was convicted and received a second one-year-to-life sentence. In a blinding rainstorm the prison guard escorted the convict back to Joliet Penitentiary by train and then a taxi. In the cab outside the prison gates Nelson suddenly produced a gun and pushed it into the guard's side. Nelson ordered him to remove the handcuffs linking the two men and turn over his gun. Nelson trained his gun on the cabbie and ordered him to drive a distance from the prison before forcing both he and the guard out. It was later assumed that as Nelson was being escorted off the train a seated passenger slipped the gun into his overcoat pocket.

Nelson spent the rest of his life as a fugitive on the run moving frequently from city to city. He only stayed for long periods in Reno and Lake Tahoe protected by Graham and McKay and in Sausalito with trusted friend John Paul Chase as the two road shotgun for Prohibition convoys. Nelson was still unknown to the public even in Chicago where the newspapers had barely mentioned him despite his many dramatic and terrifying robberies. Instead John Dillinger was about to grab the nation's headlines and go down in history as the country's most notorious bank robber. Dillinger and Nelson would soon be introduced in Reno at the *Bank Club* when both hid out under the partners' protection. Nelson then joined Dillinger's gang and through these misadventures Baby Face quickly rose from obscurity to become the country's second most villainous bank bandit.[2]

DEFIANCE WITHOUT PURPOSE

To understand why John Dillinger and Nelson paired up it is necessary to begin with Dillinger's early criminal career. He came from a well-to-do family in contrast to most robbers who grew up in inner city poverty. Dillinger's father was an Indianapolis, Indiana grocer and then moved his family 20 miles southwest to became a farmer near Mooresville. The son's values differed greatly from his hardworking father. John lacked goals and self-discipline, was a very poor student, and hung out with bad friends. When it came to work he only occasionally took odd jobs. A close adolescent friend said of Dillinger years later, "I never thought he was a mean guy, but he used to carry a book with him on Jesse James. Jesse James got to be his idol. I knew then that he was headed for trouble." At age 20, a young high school girl jilted John and he decided to get away by joining the Navy. Three weeks after completing basic training he rejected his regulated life and went AWOL. After being captured he was given 10 days in solitary. Upon his release from the brig it was only a short while before he again went AWOL. The Navy listed him as a deserter and he returned to his father's farm to live.[3]

From childhood Dillinger rebelled against societal norms, and his defiance grew every time his wayward activities were hindered by legitimate authority. One night the deserter and his ex-convict friend 10 years older got to drinking and decided to steal some money. They hid in an alley in wait for a 65-year-old local grocer who walked his receipts home each evening for deposit in the bank the next morning. After the grocer passed the alley Dillinger quickly ran up behind him, struck the back of his head with an iron pipe, and reached down to the prostrate man to steal his $555 in cash. The victim identified the pair and both pled guilty. Because Dillinger had brutally and needlessly assaulted a defenseless senior he drew a stiffer 10 to 20 years in Indiana's Pendleton Reformatory.

There Dillinger sought the company of the most hardened bank robbers, tried to escape twice which led to another year being added to his sentence, and violated the rules including fighting, destroying property, and gambling. When he applied for parole, the reformatory head declared he was an unruly prisoner. When Republican Governor Harry Leslie studied Dillinger's record he concluded he was an incorrigible criminal unfit for release to the normal world. The Governor denied parole and ordered him transferred to the hard-core Michigan City State Penitentiary to serve out the remainder of his term. Dillinger's disobedient behavior continued and he was found in possession of a razor blade. Dillinger became close to four dangerous long termers – John Hamilton, Russell Clark, Charles Makley, and Harry "Pete" Pierpont. He plotted a scheme with them that after his release he would break them out in order to form a super bank-robbing gang. They agreed that if he freed them they would join his new gang.

The Great Depression election of 1932 was a Democratic tide that swept in a new Governor, Paul McNutt. Dillinger's father enticed 169 neighbors, including the victim who his son had bashed with the lead pipe, to sign a petition for John's parole on the basis he was a fit subject for rehabilitation and was needed on the family ranch. The Governor was building a powerful political machine so he took up this cause led by citizens from Morgan County where he was from. The Governor had a false record of Dillinger's criminal and prison activities submitted to the Parole Board. It defended the convict by pointing out that this was his first offense, but it left out the viciousness of the crime and his long-term troublemaking behavior in prison. It claimed the two perpetrators' sentences were "inequitable," but they accurately reflected the degree of each one's culpability. The submission did not include two letters from law enforcers. A deputy warden at Michigan City Prison opposed parole because Dillinger was "a dangerous criminal." The Governor's false report said the presiding judge at his trial supported clemency when his letter said exactly the opposite and recommended a "careful investigation" of his record before making a decision. Most striking was the Governor's violation of the state's prison-system rules which prohibited parole and required the maximum term be served by convicts who had attempted to escape. McNutt's two newly-appointed flunkies on the Parole Board approved his release while the legitimate and experienced member abstained from this outrageous travesty of injustice. The Governor's undermining of proper and responsible law enforcement would quickly lead to terrifying robberies and tragic murders and woundings of Indiana citizens and lawmen, and it would cost tax payers a huge amount to right this wrong as the law tried to capture and incarcerate him again. But at the time Dillinger was paroled after serving 8 ½ years no one had an inkling of the pending horror McNutt had unleashed on his fellow citizens.

Upon his return to Mooresville the 29-year old Dillinger acted like a reformed man. He thanked the neighbors who had signed the parole petition, visited the elderly victim he had assaulted, and even attended church with his family. After a few days of this playacting he disappeared. Three weeks after his release from prison, he began obtaining the funds needed to break out his long-time prison friends. He stuck up an Indianapolis Haag's Drugstore for $10,600. He followed this with robberies of a tavern and three Indiana banks in Daleville, Montpelier, and Indianapolis for a total of $29,100. He also spread out his field of operation outside Indiana by hitting banks in Bluffton, Ohio and Farrell, Pennsylvania.

Three months after Dillinger was paroled he initiated the key phase of his plan. At midnight he walked up to the high wall of Michigan City Prison and tossed three pistols over it. Before his friends arrived at dawn to pick them up an unrelated convict found and turned them in for good favor with the authorities. Officials suspected another prisoner was behind the attempted breakout, put him in solitary, and assumed the incident was closed. Dillinger soon mailed a box of thread containing three more pistols to the prison shirt factory. Guards watched as his convict friends examined the contents and told them it was the standard delivery. Ten dangerous prisoners used these guns to take a group of unarmed guards hostage. Then Dillinger's four chosen inmates forced a sheriff visiting the prison to drive them in his patrol car out to freedom. The other six prisoners compelled the kidnapped guards to surround them like they were being escorted outside the prison walls for transport to another facility. When the six convicts reached the gas station across the street they hijacked a driver's car and sped into obscurity.

Indiana Governor McNutt was guilty not only of improperly pardoning Dillinger but also making this astounding prison escape possible. He took office with an overwhelming Democratic legislative majority of 91 to 9 in the House and 43 to 7 in the Senate. He used it to pass the Executive Reorganization Act eliminating more than a half century of legal restrictions imposed on the governor's appointment of officials and his influence over state agency policies. He used his new power of "at the will of the governor" to oust his opponents in both parties from state jobs and to require state employees to pay 2% of their salaries to the Indiana Democratic Party slush funds in order to keep their jobs. He gave exclusive beer distribution franchises to his largest campaign contributors. He had the legislature keep local officeholders, who were predominantly Democratic, in office an extra year by postponing the 1933 municipal elections under the guise of a cost-saving measure. He distributed the state's 75,000 Depression-era federal Works Progress Administration jobs to his political supporters. While local governments had always been responsible for identifying welfare needs and distributing relief, McNutt's administration took control of all government chartable giving to needy Hoosiers. By eliminating all checks and balances, power was concentrated in just the Governor alone leading opponents to refer to him as "Emperor McNutt of Indiana."

The staffs of Indiana's prisons had always been hired based on qualification and ability with no regard for political affiliation. But the new Governor quickly implemented the spoils, or patronage, system by replacing the knowledgeable warden and 69 of the experienced 120 guards with political appointees totally untrained in prison control. This led to systematic laxity including changing the routine in the Michigan City Prison shirt factory. Instead of having the contents of incoming packages examined and approved by guards they transferred their work load to the prisoners. This is why Dillinger and his cohorts knew their gun-importation tactic would work and that the 10 convicts would be able to march out the front gates while McNutt's unsuspecting guards looked on blindly to all the violations of proper policy.

In response to the uproar over this appalling prison breakout, the Governor announced he would appoint an impartial commission to investigate. Instead he had his political hacks on the Prison

Board of Trustees issue a report whitewashing his irresponsibility. Incredibly the only prison official fired by the Board was the Republican deputy warden who had publicly opposed the release of Dillinger and then dared the administration to really investigate the causes of this massive breakout of dangerous criminals. During each of the next two election campaigns McNutt opened investigations regarding Dillinger's parole and the prison escape but he let the inquiries fade away after election day.

After the Michigan City Prison escape Dillinger failed to reunite with his friends because of an incident four days earlier. Police in Dayton, Ohio were sitting surveillance outside the boardinghouse where Dillinger's girlfriend lived. The detectives were watching for the fugitive bank robber when he visited her for an afternoon tryst. Two detectives armed with a machinegun and shotgun burst into her room and a surprised Dillinger slowly raised his hands. In her room the detectives found a large stash of cash, half a dozen automatic pistols, and maps of Michigan City Prison. Dayton police escorted Dillinger to the Allen County Jail in Lima, Ohio to face charges of having robbed the nearby Bluffton Bank of $2,800.

The Lima jail was built on the back of Sheriff Jess Sarber's home. Three weeks after Dillinger's arrest, three of the convicts he had sprung from the Michigan City Prison waited until evening to walk into the county jail and announce that Indiana authorities wanted him returned. When the Sheriff asked to see their credentials the three quickly drew revolvers and one explained, "These are our credentials!" as he fired a bullet into the Sheriff's abdomen. The shocked Sheriff asked "Why?" as he fell to the floor. The sound of the shot attracted a deputy and the Sheriff's wife. The desperadoes locked the pair in cells and released Dillinger. The quartet left the Sheriff bleeding out in a pool of blood while his distraught wife was trapped behind bars unable to call anyone for help or comfort him as he passed on. On the quiet street outside, the fugitives jumped unnoticed into their car and fled home to Indiana. Chicago was the Midwest's biggest city, and the next day its newspapers would begin the saga of John Dillinger with his bloody jail escape.

The first item on Dillinger's agenda was to obtain guns so his new gang could pull off the planned bank robberies. During the next 10 days the gang barged into two police stations to steal their arsenals of machineguns, shotguns, pistols, ammunition, and bulletproof vests, and they also hit their first bank, the Central National Bank in Greencastle, Indiana for $75,000. The public was shocked by this reign of criminal terror that included one dead sheriff and another lawman kidnapped from a police station during a weapon robbery. They released him along their getaway path. In response Governor McNutt stationed 700 National Guardsmen at the state's armories, an empty gesture since the gang already had an abundance of machineguns and vests. Next the Governor placed 70 sheriff deputies and police officers, 560 National Guard members, and American Legion Post shotgun details in 44 secret locations to quickly respond to robbery sites. This was a waste of manpower since they would have arrived after the desperadoes were gone. These special deputies should have either staked out the banks or else stood in their doorways to discourage the bandits into leaving the state. FBI Director J. Edgar Hoover refused Governor McNutt's request to involve his agents in the multi-state hunt for Dillinger except to offer fingerprint identification assistance. Then Hoover's boss, U.S. Attorney General (AG) Homer Cummings, told him to investigate the murderous escape, but except to order agents to conduct a few frivolous interviews to create a flimsy record of having followed orders, he even ignored his demands. Escalating events would soon force Hoover to yield on his resistant attitude.

Dillinger moved into a Chicago apartment with Michigan City Prison fugitive Pierpont and their girlfriends. Dillinger lived a quiet life but he went out in the evenings. He saw movies three or four times a week and preferred gangster films. He was clearly unconcerned about being recognized despite his picture in the papers because he had a friendly easy-going personality that belied his defiant and violent nature that only surfaced when he was challenged.

Dillinger developed a serious skin infection on his face so he arranged an after-hours doctor's appointment through a former prison acquaintance, but this man informed police of the time and location. Dillinger arrived after dark, parked facing south, and left his girlfriend in the car to wait for him. Four unmarked police cars with 16 Chicago Detectives and Indiana State Troopers parked in the same block so they could surround his car as he pulled out. Three detective cars parked at the other end of the block. They faced north toward the front of his car so they could block off every lane of the street and prevent his escape. The fourth parked a few cars behind Dillinger's also facing south so it could be turned sideways behind him to prevent his backing up. One of the three facing detective cars was parked on the same side of the street as Dillinger's and as the fugitive returned to his car this illegally-parked car made him feel uncomfortable. As he got close to his car, he quickly leaped in, turned on the ignition, and sped away from the curb in reverse until he reached the end of the block. Once in the intersection he turned backward into an intersecting lane before shifting into forward and speeding east. The four detective cars tried to catch up as officers fired a fusillade of bullets but Dillinger out drove them and disappeared from sight. His abandoned bullet-riddled car was found the next day. Five days after this narrow police escape in Chicago, Dillinger and five accomplices robbed the American Bank and Trust Company in Racine, Wisconsin for $27,700. Each outlaw forced one or two hostages to lead them out the exit to their car as human shields from police bullets. Before fleeing the robbers wounded one patrolman. Three weeks later, Dillinger and two cohorts rummaged the safe deposit vaults at Unity Trust and Savings Bank in Chicago, looting them of $8,700 and much jewelry.

A month later Chicago Police issued a new list of 21 Public Enemies. John Dillinger was now Number 1 followed by 11 of his gang members and Baby Face Nelson. For the first time it included few Capone mobsters even though the gang was still active but low-profile since Scarface had gone to prison. Three evenings after this Enemies list was issued the same six bandits robbed a New Year's Eve celebration on the outskirts of Chicago at the Beverly Gardens Roadhouse which featured taxi dancing. It led to a dramatic shootout against seven policemen that resulted in the wounding of two participants on each side before the gang successfully made their escape. That was the day Chicago gave orders for police to shoot bank-gang members on sight.

Two weeks later Dillinger, Hamilton, and Pierpont drove up to the First National Bank in East Chicago, Indiana near closing time. Pierpont remained in the driver's seat idling prepared for the getaway. Dillinger and Hamilton stepped out and briskly walked in the bank door where Dillinger pulled a machinegun out of a trombone case and barked, "This is a stickup. Put up your hands, everybody." A bank official pressed the silent alarm to the police station a block-and-a-half away. Dillinger lined up the more than two dozen employees and customers while Hamilton robbed the tellers' cages. A patrolman from the station walked in with his pistol drawn, but Dillinger got the drop on him, forced him to drop his gun, and had him join the lineup. A bank vice president described what happened next. "That machinegunner, who the police say is Dillinger, is a terrible man. While the second man was getting the money he glanced out the doorway and saw other policemen congregating. Instead of appearing frightened he called out to the money gatherer: 'There's been an alarm and the police are outside. But don't hurry. Get all that dough. We'll kill these coppers and get away. Take your time.' When [$20,000] had been collected the pair made [VP Walter] Spencer join them. Using him as a shield they walked out the door." Detective William O'Malley stood at the door with his revolver to block their escape, but afraid of killing the banker he remained motionless as Dillinger pushed the hostage slightly away to spray his machinegun killing the lawmen. The two bandits then used the banker as protective cover as they dashed across the sidewalk to the car. The seven policemen hiding behind parked cars and in storefronts on both sides of the bank's front doors were also limited by the human shield. As the two desperadoes jumped into the car they pushed the hostage back, and as the driver pulled away the police opened fire wounding Hamilton several times including once through his bulletproof vest. Detective O'Malley was 43 and left a wife and three children. By the time their abandoned bullet-riddled and blood-stained car was found, the gang was on its way to a western vacation in warmer weather.[4]

Dillinger's robberies were terrifying and bloody. His gang deliberately forced innocent people in harm's way as shields. But as horrible as his crimes were many hard-working American families had bigger concerns. They were suffering the overwhelming hardships of the Great Depression, and in their desperation and hopelessness they viewed banks as the villains by taking good people's life savings through mortgage foreclosures on homes, farms, and businesses. These people viewed outlaws and especially Dillinger, who brazenly took what they wanted at gunpoint, as folk heroes. At the safe distance of their homes, the public did not understand from newspaper accounts how murderous he was. Beside this, people liked Dillinger's image of chivalry by never harming the female hostages he seized and always letting bank customers keep their wallets as he liberated the banks' money. In addition, he had a jaunty manner, trading quips with tellers and customers, and making his personal signature an athletic leap over the tellers' window even when an open gate was close by. As an Indianapolis man stated in a letter to a newspaper editor, "Why should the law have wanted John Dillinger? He wasn't any worse than the bankers and politicians who took poor people's money. Dillinger did not rob poor people. He robbed those who became rich by robbing the poor. I am for Johnnie." There was one other aspect of the appeal of these serial bank robbers. In the gloom of the deepening Depression, their crimes, pursuits, and escapes became escapist distraction like a continuing Saturday matinee serial. That is why these gangs sprang up in the rural Midwest and were primarily in seven states – Illinois, Indiana, Iowa, Minnesota, Missouri, Ohio, and Wisconsin. For the most part only the press in these states sensationalized and glamorized their exploits whereas today bank robberies get scant attention unless a victim or perpetrator is seriously injured.[5]

Despite his cold-blooded violence, Dillinger became the quintessential Depression-era folk hero to any because of the audacity of his escapes and police-station raids and for his likeable nature. He had fine people skills. He was never known to talk tough or say a bad word about anyone. This allowed him to go out regularly to dinner, movies, nightclubs, and sporting events without attracting attention or recognition. He seemed to pay no attention to the people around him and talked and laughed a lot with his companions. Dillinger later told a reporter, "Those were exciting times. We moved from house to house [in Chicago, Indiana, and Wisconsin], rented one, stayed a few days and moved on when the neighborhood got hot. But we used to go to the downtown theaters whenever we wanted to." [6]

Dillinger had an easy smile and wink. He seemed to be eternally cheerful and enjoy life. He always joked with his law-enforcer captors and welcomed the townspeople who wanted to meet him in jail. He was courteous, almost gallant, even when pointing a gun at innocent people. But in his final bank robberies the pressure of pursuers was crushing in on him and another side showed. The man who seemed to so easily roll with the punches became seriously focused on getting the job done and then getting safely away any way that would work. Some photos of him reveal chilling eyes and a menacing nature.

After the East Chicago bank robbery, Dillinger drove west to Reno where he frequented the *Bank Club* and met Baby Face Nelson who had been laying low in Reno and Sausalito for three months. Their hook up was likely prearranged as Nelson had partnered with two of Dillinger's closest associates on two bank robberies before departing the Midwest. In the first Nelson was with

Michigan City Prison fugitive Tommy Carroll who for the second robbery also brought in parolee Homer Van Meter. It is very likely these two cohorts told Dillinger to look up Nelson in Reno to get a safe house under the protection of Graham and McKay. The two outlaws partied openly in Reno for four days, Nelson with his wife and Dillinger with his girlfriend. The two machinegunners also made plans to join forces and partner on some future Midwest bank jobs that would make them the most notorious killers of their time.[7]

A WOODEN GUN

Dillinger wanted an extended vacation in warmer weather so he drove with three associates he had broken out of Michigan City Prison from Reno to Tucson, Arizona. Charles Makley and Russell Clark had rooms at the Congress Hotel. They went out with their sweethearts and when they returned firemen were fighting a fire at the hotel. The pair panicked because the two suitcases they left in their rooms were filled with many thousands of dollars. They offered a fireman at the scene a substantial sum to carry out their bags but this unusual offer caused him instead to alert nearby policemen who took both into custody without a shot being fired. Dillinger always blamed them for offering the firemen too much money. He later told a reporter, "If the saps had made it only a couple of bucks, we'd still be safe and happy."[8]

In one of their two hotel rooms, police found a slip of paper with two addresses. Squad cars went to both of these homes unaware more fugitives were lurking in town. As Harry Pierpont walked up to his residence police arrested him. When Dillinger returned to his abode, he walked up to the porch and inserted his key into his front door lock. From their hiding places in the shrubbery, 15 policemen and deputy sheriffs charged. Dillinger whirled around reaching for the machinegun sticking partially below his coat but facing overwhelming firepower he meekly submitted to handcuffs. In one day the local lawmen arrested four heavily-armed fugitives without firing a shot, but until the fingerprint checks came back they had no idea who they were or how violent.

Immediately upon being placed in the Pima County jail, Dillinger became friendly and agreed to let Tucson residents come in and take a look at him. During the five days Dillinger was there more than 10,000 men and women walked by his cell and he greeted them pleasantly. He also shrewdly urged them to vote for Sheriff John Belton in the next election even though Belton had captured him. The Sheriff observed that Dillinger never wasted energy hating people or doing anything that was not necessary.

Three states got into an intense competition for the extradition of the four wanted men, and Arizona split them up. It sent the three who had killed Sheriff Sarber during their break-out of Dillinger to Ohio for trial. Pierpont was electrocuted, Makley tried to escape and was shot to death, and Clark got a life sentence. Ohio also wanted to try Dillinger but Indiana won the politically-charged extradition tug of war. It wanted to try Dillinger for murdering Detective O'Malley during the bank robbery two weeks earlier. The prosecutor had 10 bank employees and customers prepared to testify as confident eyewitnesses against him.

Dillinger's transfer to the Crown Point, Indiana Jail created a festive scene. Dillinger still in his street clothes accommodated reporters by admitting many of the crimes he had committed. In the foreground middle of a newspaper photo, Prosecutor Robert Estill is shown standing between Dillinger and Sheriff Lillian Holley. The Prosecutor had his arm wrapped behind Dillinger's neck and had his hand holding the far shoulder of the man who he planned to execute. At the same time the Prosecutor was looking to his other side with an expansive grin at Sheriff Lillian Holley because of their successful capture. The Prosecutor was roundly criticized for his unprofessional conduct and voters ousted him in the next election.

With all the talk about the Prosecutor's inappropriate conduct, no one ever mentioned Dillinger's confident smirk nor his pose in the photo. The killer had his arm resting on the prosecutor's nearest shoulder with his hand hanging in front. He had his four fingers bent like they were holding a gun handle with his trigger finger poised to fire. The desperado seemed to display very different future plans from all the law enforcers surrounding him.

A disreputable attorney, Louis Piquett, visited Dillinger in jail to become his counsel. Then he met in Judge William Murray's chamber to hear the Prosecutor's request to confine Dillinger at the more secure state penitentiary at Michigan City. Piquett wanted Dillinger to stay in the jail where he was so he baited Sheriff Holley by questioning whether she and her jail were up to the job of holding Dillinger. She proudly claimed she had made the County Jail an armed camp safer than the state penitentiary which was why she had twice rejected the warden's offer to have him returned there. The Judge sided with the Sheriff by lying that the statute gave him no authority to order a transfer unless Dillinger's life were endangered by mob violence, but as a Grand Jury Report later stated the Judge "could and should have ordered the transfer" for violation of parole. All the while that attorney Piquett sat in front of the Judge toying with the Sheriff's pride, he had the County Jail floorplan tucked in his pocket. It had been given to him by Dillinger who wanted it passed to his girlfriend along with directions for his former prison pals to break him out again.

Five weeks after Dillinger's capture he and the other 14 prisoners in his cellblock were doing their morning exercises in the corridor between the cells when the 64-year-old repairman and turnkey, Sam Cahoon, pulled the lever opening the gate into their wing and walked in carrying the soap for the inmates weekly showers. Dillinger suddenly shoved a gun into the old-man's ribs and ordered him to turn over the keys he carried for repairing the cell-door locks. Along the only exit hall from the cellblock was the warden's office where guards were drinking morning coffee. Dillinger had to overpower these guards to escape but he had the advantage because guards always entered his cellblock unarmed, and the floor level of his annex was four feet higher than their hallway blocking their view of him lurking beside the entrance gate. Dillinger directed the elderly janitor to call out the name of Deputy Sheriff Ernest Blunk, the in-house fingerprint expert, and then walk back from the gate deeper into the cell block corridor to focus Blunk's attention. This led the Deputy to walk past Dillinger who jumped behind him and shoved the gun into his ribs. Dillinger ordered Blunk to call individually the Warden and then each guard by name for assistance in the cell block. As each responded in turn, Dillinger locked him in a cell along with the other prisoners except for Herbert Youngblood, an African-American, who had agreed to join Dillinger's escape to avoid a murder trial.

When the Warden and all the guards in the exit hallway had been jailed, Dillinger and Youngblood ordered Deputy Blunk to guide them out of the jail. The trio headed directly to the now uninhabited jail office where Dillinger grabbed from the arsenal two machineguns, pistols, and ammunition and split them with Youngblood. The trio then proceeded through the kitchen. When Deputy Blunk had followed Dillinger's order to close the cell doors in his cellblock, he pushed the lever to close them but not the second one that locked them. This allowed the guards to quickly push their cell doors open, but they continued to be imprisoned in the corridor behind the locked cellblock gate. The Warden's apartment was on the other side of the wall and he called out to his wife through a peephole. She ran down the stairs to get help from all the armed lawmen surrounding the building, but when she opened the kitchen door, she faced a man in prisoner's garb holding a machinegun. He said, "Oh no sister, you won't stop Dillinger now." Dillinger locked the Warden's wife and a woman employee in the laundry room down in the basement. Then he took the eight guards, whom the pair had encountered and disarmed along the way, back up to the second floor cell area and locked them up.[9]

The two desperadoes now prepared to escape the building with their hostage and guide, Deputy Blunk, leading the way. He did not want to get in the middle of a shootout so he warned the pair that the Sheriff had a large contingent of guards encamped at the front entrance laying in wait in case Dillinger's cohorts tried a frontal assault to spring him. Thus the trio had to take a circuitous route to avoid encountering them. To understand this phase of the desperadoes' brazen escape path, it is necessary to picture the layout of the six buildings on that city block. Three buildings faced west onto Main Street, and the three buildings behind them faced east on South East Street. On Main Street the Lake County Jail was on the right-hand corner, and adjacent to it in the middle was the Criminal Court Building followed by the Main Street Garage on the corner of the alley to the left. On South East Street a small car garage was attached behind the Jail Building, and the other two structures were home's surrounded by yards.

Thus the two fleeing escapees headed to the Jail's car garage with Deputy Blunk taking the lead. Both Dillinger and Youngblood held a machinegun in both hands ready for action. The trio exited the Jail Building from the side door on the south side and walked alongside the wall in the enclosed courtyard toward the back of the building until they reached the Jail's garage side entrance and entered. Two cars were parked inside, but Deputy Blunk told the fugitives the keys for both were sitting back in the Warden's office. With no transportation the two desperadoes decided the Main Street Garage offered the best chance for escape because they knew the keys would be in or near the vehicles.

The pair had Deputy Blunt lead their escape out the Jail's garage front entrance. The trio walked out the door and turned left along the South East Street sidewalk. What a sight it must have been with the two fugitives brashly carrying their machineguns in the open poised to kill as they marched down what immediately turned into a residential neighborhood. After walking past the first house the trio turned left to walk through the yard separating the two homes, and then they turned right behind the second house to walk to the alley. There they turned left to enter the rear side door of the Main Street Garage.

Six employees and customers were inside, but none offered any resistance when the two machinegun-toting fugitives burst in. Youngblood kept his weapon aimed at them as Dillinger asked the garage mechanic which car was fastest. He pointed out Sheriff Holley's personal car, a V8 Ford. Dillinger ordered Deputy Blunk to drive and he settled into the passenger seat while Youngblood and the mechanic sat in back. Each escapee laid his machinegun on his lap aimed at the kidnapped hostage sitting next to him. Then they audaciously drove out the Garage's front entrance in the Sheriff's car onto Main Street with just the Criminal Court Building separating them from the Lake County Jail at the other end of the block. Thus the escapees turned in the opposite direction to the right, or north, away from the Sheriff's encampment of law enforcers extending out into the street.

As soon as the fugitive's car pulled out of the Main Street Garage and turned onto the street, one of the just-released hostages, a mail-truck driver, ran out the same door but tore in the opposite direction over to the guards stationed in front of the Jail to inform them a breakout had just occurred on another side of the building. The mail driver then ran to the Jail's front door to warn the deputies inside but Dillinger had locked it along with all the other doors on his escape route. Thus the mail driver began running along the side of the building to find another way in, when he heard the locked-up jailers yelling to be liberated from behind barred windows on the second floor.

Dillinger warned Deputy Blunk to drive slowly and carefully along less-traveled side streets and gravel roads. Meanwhile the Warden called and alerted Chicago police and a huge number of officers scurried to cover every access road into the city. It should have been easy for them to nab the approaching Dillinger, but they were given an incorrect car license-plate number. The Warden had told a deputy to subtract one number from the license on a specific one of the two cars in the jail garage. The deputy did what he was told except that he chose the wrong car's number to subtract from. Thirty miles out of Crown Point the escapees released the two hostages to thumb rides as the two fugitives drove blithely on to Chicago where Dillinger met with his waiting attorney Piquett and girlfriend. Dillinger got $300 spending money from his lawyer and headed with his girlfriend to her sister's apartment. Along the way, he dropped Youngblood off at a streetcar with $100 and his thanks.

How did this fiasco occur? To start with Holley had been appointed Sheriff in memory of her husband after he was killed in the line of duty. The building was secure for its time, but investigations by a Lake County Grand Jury, the state Attorney General, and the U.S. Justice Department found not one person on the Sheriff's staff was qualified to handle a dangerous criminal. She employed three relatives as deputies, other deputies had criminal records, and the jail was manned largely by trusties meaning the prisoners policed themselves.

For Dillinger's incarceration Sheriff Holley had made the jail look like an armed fortress with a minimum contingent of 35 deputy sheriffs and Farmers' Protective Association volunteer guards toting machineguns outside to repel an attack by the high-profile prisoner's criminal associates. Unfortunately not one had any tactical combat training and worse all were in the front of the building. Not a single guard was posted on the other three sides. It would have taken no more than one or two guards on each side to fire a warning shot to easily recapture Dillinger if he had tried to escape through a different door or a window. The Sheriff, Prosecutor, and Judge all acted unprofessionally in this case and proved themselves to be unqualified to hold any law enforcement position.

U.S. Attorney General (AG) Cummings lambasted the situation and ordered all federal prisoners transferred to a proper lockup. He pointed out that a competent Arizona sheriff had captured Dillinger and it was Sheriff Holley's policies that had made his escape possible. The AG said, "The negligence of these people may ultimately result in the death of some person who is trying to capture Dillinger or who runs afoul of him." His warning of pending consequences was prophetic as Cummings' Justice Department investigative unit, the FBI, would pay the heaviest toll. But the developing tragedy would begin with local police. Two weeks after the duo's escape, a sheriff and two deputies trapped Dillinger's fellow escapee Youngblood in a small grocery store. He killed the sheriff, wounded his two deputies, and shot the unarmed proprietor's son in the shoulder. That is when the wounded young man reached down, picked up the sheriff's pistol laying on the floor, and fired two bullets into the fugitive killing him.[10]

Ever since Dillinger pulled off his implausible escape, crime historians have speculated how he was able to take control over the guards. By assembling all the available facts, the events of that fateful day can be explained for the first time. Prisoners were allowed to have a safety razor, and Dillinger used his to whittle a wooden slat from a washboard into the shape of a revolver grip. To this he attached the razor's tube-shaped handle to look like a gun barrel. He finished by blackening his toy replica with shoe polish. After Dillinger escaped, guards searched his cell and found the broken washboard under the mattress and wood shavings scattered on the floor under the bed.

A replica of the original carved wooden gun is on display to the public at the John Dillinger Historical Museum in Hammond, Indiana. It shows how pathetically unrealistic Dillinger's toy gun actually was. Yet the warden and each captured guard saw the gun he held that day up close and all of them always swore it was real. It is not possible that all were so frightened they saw what he told them to see, for two reasons. In the year before and after Dillinger's escape, major criminals in other prisons used the toy-gun routine and in every case the threatened unarmed guard recognized it was a fake, took it away, and charged the convict with attempted escape. Furthermore Dillinger's captive lawmen saw his gun several times. After each was locked in a cell, they were no longer being threatened and observed Dillinger bring in each additional guard for lock up. Everyone who faced Dillinger in the jail swore the revolver he pointed at them was larger than the crude-carving he displayed as he departed the cellblock. Deputy Blunk was alongside Dillinger throughout the ordeal of subduing every guard and watched his every move. He maintained Dillinger used a .45-caliber automatic pistol to threaten the guards, and did not produce the wooden gun until they were all jailed so he could grandstand with his captives to humiliate them. Indiana Attorney General Philip Lutz and head Chicago Police Detective Captain John Stege always maintained they were convinced Dillinger had a real gun that day.

This raises the question of why Dillinger bothered to carve the toy gun if he had, or thought he was going to get, a real one. The answer is that only a tiny number of jailers and visitors were in a position to slip him a gun in jail and whoever considered doing it knew he or she would have been intensely investigated because of the inevitable scandal that would result from the infamous prisoner escaping with a real gun. Thus to get assistance Dillinger had to make it appear that he used a toy gun, and he accomplished this by openly whittling, finishing, and showing his wooden gun to the other prisoners in his cell. He bragged that it was his ticket to freedom, but they just laughed at his ridiculousness until he walked out the door. After his escape the Sheriff and other elected city officials did not want to admit they let him smuggle in a gun, and besides they actually believed his cleverly-crafted deception that he was carrying a carving that day despite what every locked-up jailer said to the contrary.

The only way Dillinger could have come into possession of a real gun was for someone to have smuggled it in, and the likely suspects are his four visitors and a few members of the jail staff. Three visitors were on Dillinger's payroll and committed felonies to meet his every need while he was a fugitive. These were his attorney and two of his employees - his investigator and his gofer who was a former convict and listed as an "alibi witness." Dillinger's girlfriend was also a loyal pawn who always did his bidding. The lady Sheriff swore all four were thoroughly searched and she double checked the girlfriend herself, but her statements rung hollow because of her total lack of leadership – she allowed every other accepted jail procedure to be violated during her tenure so what confidence can anyone have in her statement that she handled the searches properly? [11]

However, since it is possible the visitors were correctly frisked, the primary suspect in this case becomes the elderly jail repairman. Sam Cahoon's drunkenness occasionally resulted in his own jailing during which he continued his trustee duties in prison garb. A former judge described Cahoon as "irresponsible and incapable of holding a jail job" but the elderly man was given responsibility for guarding the most dangerous man in the country. Cahoon single-handedly created the opportunity for Dillinger to escape by violating the absolute rule to never unlock the cellblock door when the prisoners' cell doors were open and they were mingling in the corridor. This transgression is particularly noteworthy because this was the first morning during Dillinger's month-long stay that he joined the other inmates in the corridor as if he might have known what was about to happen. Cahoon followed this grievous violation with a most peculiar statement overheard by the other prisoners. After Cahoon called Deputy Blunk into the cellblock, Cahoon said, "Johnny, I can't go through with it." Dillinger then forced Cahoon into a cell and ordered Blunk to call in the Warden and the other guards. Cahoon's odd statement did not relate to anything going on with the escape and it certainly sounds like he was backing out of a plot with Dillinger. Remember one of the jail staff gave Dillinger a copy of the floorplan and the old repairman knew where it was stored. [12]

Dillinger's capture in Tucson appeared to change his attitude toward the world. From childhood he may have rebelled against authority but his easy capture in Tucson made him feel foolish. When he was hauled into the Tucson Police Station, he was visibly shaken and enraged. He cried out, "My God, how did you know I was in town? I'll be the laughingstock of the country. How could a hick town police force ever suspect me?" From that moment on Dillinger was contemptuous of lawmen and relished embarrassing them. His Crown Point Jail photo op a few days after his arrest with the Prosecutor has always been interpreted as part of his fun-loving ways, but it was the beginning of his new campaign to demean law enforcers. Unbelievably his main concern during the escape was humiliating his guardian captives. After grabbing a machinegun from the jail's arsenal he wasted valuable time walking back down that long hallway to the cells to show off his toy gun to the Warden and guards. Grinning and tapping it on the cell bars to rub it in, he announced, "Just wanted you boys to know I did it with my little wooden gun." Once he returned to the bank robbery-killing business, he posed for a photo in a suit and hat with a dashing stance and a machinegun in his right hand and the wooden pistol in his left. He mailed this photo to a newspaper for national publication. At the same time, his easy-going polite attitude during bank robberies disappeared as his attitude toward employees and customers turned serious and became more threatening and violent over time.[13]

While hiding out in St. Paul, Minnesota Dillinger put his girlfriend on a plane to visit his home and deliver some robbery loot to his dad and give his sister a letter along with the wooden gun. He wrote with great braggadocio about his escape and he viciously disparaged the police. He pointed out it was worth 10 years of his life to disgrace the coppers like that. He told his sister that he wanted her husband to keep the toy gun forever. Except for feeding his ego, this letter's only purpose was to try to authenticate that he used the play gun in his escape to continue to humiliate the lawmen and to increase the toy gun's value at auction for his family.

In his fervor to disgrace lawmen, Dillinger even penned a short note to car-baron Henry Ford. He wrote "I want to thank you for building the Ford V-8 as fast and as sturdy a car as you did, otherwise I would not have gotten away from the coppers in that Wisconsin, Minnesota, case." In the two months since escaping from the Crown Point Jail, Dillinger had split his time between driving Ford V8's and Model A's. Ford felt restrained from publicizing this letter because it told how his product helped the desperado beat "the coppers," possibly offending one of Ford's big markets - police departments. Ford Motor Company covered up the existence of this letter for three-quarters of a century, while replacing it with a fraudulent letter that has been used in the company's V8 publicity ever since. The scam letter extols the car's virtues in words that sound more like a salesman or a brochure than a hardened thug and make no mention of evading coppers. "You have a wonderful car. Been driving it for three weeks. It's a treat to drive one. Your slogan should be, drive a Ford and watch all other cars fall behind you. I can make any other car take a Ford's dust."

Dillinger also sent the FBI Director several taunting postcards, but J. Edgar Hoover never revealed what the gangster wrote him. The public was shocked and outraged by the jail's lack of security allowing Dillinger to escape and local, state, and federal officials including Hoover's boss, the U.S. Attorney General, lambasted to the press the incompetence of the Sheriff, Judge, Prosecutor, and guards. This outcry and the fugitive's derisive postcards to the Director would finally bring the FBI into the hunt for Dillinger.[14]

Chapter 2

THE FBI DEVELOPS INTO A DETECTIVE AGENCY

GENESIS OF A NATIONAL POLICE FORCE

When the machinegun-toting bank robbers became a scourge in the Midwest during the early Great Depression years, the United States had no national police force. Thus this story is not only about these brazen bank robbers' careers, but also how their violence led the federal government to establish a nationwide police force that would ultimately subdue these outlaws. The Federal Bureau of Investigation (FBI) began as a small Justice Department detective agency in 1907. It investigated violations of a few unrelated federal laws, and its primary responsibility was auditing the handling of federal funds.

The FBI's brief-case carrying investigators had a peaceable jurisdiction. Agents were not permitted by law to carry guns or make arrests. They had to solicit the aid of local policemen or sheriff's deputies to make arrests and raids. The agency was denied this authority because many in Congress feared a secret police force could threaten American civil liberties. The FBI's Director hired most agents in each state's field office based on the recommendation of one of the state's U.S. senators who used these appointments to reward political supporters. Thus many agents became guilty of corruption, dirty partisan politics, or gross violation of innocent citizens' civil rights, everything Congress had feared.

This all changed in the middle of the Roaring 20s, when U.S. Attorney General (AG) Harry Daugherty was forced to resign because of scandals over his actions in office that had nothing to do with the FBI agency under him. Newly-appointed AG, Harlan Stone, fired the FBI's Director and took personal control over the agency. He promoted J. Edgar Hoover from his assistant position to Director which was an odd decision because Hoover was as culpable as anyone for the agency's illegal actions. AG Stone clearly did not trust Hoover because he ordered him to stop the agency's spying on individuals' political opinions and also prohibited the new Director from conducting any fact-gathering investigations of possible violations of federal law without Stone's personal authorization. Stone said, "When a police system passes beyond these limits, it is dangerous to the proper administration of justice and to human liberty." Stone remained in this office for a year until the day the U.S. Senate confirmed him as a Supreme Court Justice.[15]

Congress and the public continued to fear that a national police force could become an independent malevolent secret Gestapo. Thus Congress would not let the Department of Justice have its own investigators but instead forced the AG to borrow agents from the Secret Service which was under the Treasury Department. Congress explained in hearings why it separated the detective force from the federal prosecutor's office. Congress feared Justice Department agents could become a secret police carrying out the dictates of the President or AG to snoop into the private lives of citizens by collecting scandal and gossip. If the agents were under the authority of the AG, there would be no oversight because the agency might hide its activities from Congress. As Democratic Congressman J. Swager Sherley (Kentucky) wisely observed, "I recall no instance where a government perished because of the absence of a secret-service force, but many there are that perished as a result of the spy system."[16]

Ironically everything Congress feared later came to be, but not quite the way they expected. The lawmakers feared a malicious and dishonorable president or AG might do these things but never considered the possibility that the agency's Director might become so powerful that he could dictate to presidents, Attorneys General, and Congress, all of whom were supposed to oversee him. But this is exactly what would occur as J. Edgar Hoover made his agents' primary effort the collection of embarrassing and damaging information about politicians, their supporters, and any citizen whose views he disagreed with. However Hoover did not start this way. When he was appointed FBI Director he was fully aware the AG and Congress were skeptical about a federal police force so for the next decade he worked in obscurity and avoided any publicity or scandal.

Soon after Hoover became FBI Director, he opened a fingerprint repository and identification laboratory and then offered fingerprint and ballistics testing free to the country's local law enforcement departments. Hoover built his image with the claim he had the world's most professional and scientific police force but the facts prove otherwise. While the accuracy of DNA testing has been thoroughly studied by the scientific community and rigid standards have been established, the validity of fingerprint comparisons has never been tested by scientists. Even the basic assumption that fingerprints are unique has never been proven. In fact "From a statistical viewpoint, the scientific foundation for fingerprint individuality is incredibly weak," according to renowned forensic scientist Henry C. Lee. No objective procedural standards exist as they vary between fingerprint examiners and between legal jurisdictions around the world. Not one of these different techniques has been scientifically studied to determine its accuracy percentage. On the contrary, experienced examiners over decades of proficiency tests have serious failure rates often over 50%. Despite no supporting evidence whatsoever, the FBI's text on the subject is named *The Science of Fingerprints,* and its website erroneously states "fingerprints offer an infallible means of personal identification."[17]

In discussions of fingerprints one important fact is rarely considered. It is a simple procedure to take a photo of a person's dusted fingerprints from any object or a fingerprint card and then plant a perfect set of that person's latent prints at a crime scene. This can be done by a perpetrator who can photograph someone else's prints from something they touch, or by an unscrupulous cop who has access to copies of most citizens' fingerprints.

Congress slowly gave the FBI authority over additional types of crime. Three months before Prohibition began, Congress made transporting a stolen vehicle across a state line a federal offense. Until that time, robbery had always been treated as a local crime, but the availability of the automobile allowed robbers to commit crimes across state lines. Crooks often used recently stolen cars so their license plates were not yet reported to police. Then they sped home because jurisdictional limits made it difficult for states in which crimes were committed to search for and extradite offenders in other states. More than a decade after passage of this law, the administration wanted the FBI to begin pursuing the proliferating bank-robbery gangs. If these gangs had not used stolen cars to cross state boundaries to commit their crimes or to flee, the FBI would not have had jurisdiction over these criminals.

During the first quarter century of the FBI it was not responsible for enforcing any type of violent crime with the exception of the flight of a felon or witness across a state line in an effort to avoid either prosecution or giving testimony. In these cases, agents had local lawmen do the actual apprehension. Then thirteen years after enactment of the stolen-car law, there was a rash of highly-publicized kidnappings for ransom early in the Great Depression. The nation was shaken when the 20-month-old son of aviator hero Charles Lindbergh was kidnapped. He paid the ransom, but two-and-a-half months later his son's body was discovered. One month after that Congress passed a law giving the FBI authority over abductions in which either the kidnapper or victim crossed a state line. This was the first type of crime that would put the FBI in the national press limelight.[18]

TRAGEDY AT A TRAIN STATION

Nine months after passage of the Lindbergh Law, President Franklin Delano Roosevelt (FDR) took the oath of office after winning election by promising to solve the country's Great Depression economic crisis. Just three months into his term a single crime greatly broadened the focus of his administration from just the economic calamity to include the escalating violent crime problem. This one crime led his newly appointed AG to launch a national war on crime which caused a drastic change in the FBI's mission.[19]

The incident involved Frank "Jelly" Nash who was a hard-core criminal. He was convicted of murder at age 26. He had shot a man who was his confederate and friend in the back to avoid splitting their $1,000 take from a store robbery in Sapulpa, Oklahoma. After serving five years he was released early and joined a bank-robbery gang. While holding up a U.S. postal train in Okesa, Oklahoma he assaulted a mail custodian and was sentenced to 25 years at Leavenworth. Over time he earned the staff's trust. Seven years into his term the guards had him run an errand alone outside the prison but he did not return. Nash went back to robbing banks while making a good living as owner of a Chicago Prohibition beer and slot-machine joint. Two months after Nash walked away from Leavenworth he assisted seven of his convict pals to escape from Leavenworth. Six months later he assisted another 11 prisoners to escape from Kansas State Penitentiary.

Two years after Nash had escaped, the FBI arrested two of his close bank-robbing associates as they played golf in Kansas City, Missouri. They revealed Nash vacationed each summer with his wife and young daughter in Hot Springs, Arkansas. The town was made a safe haven for organized crime members and bank robbers by crime boss Dick Galatas. His White Front Cigar Store was a Prohibition beer and bookie joint and hangout for visiting criminals. Since Nash had already visited that summer FBI agents had to sit on this information for almost a year until early in the next summer when they staked out the saloon. When the unarmed agents spotted Nash they enlisted the aid of the McAlester, Oklahoma Police Chief. As fugitive Nash strolled with beer glass in hand from the backroom pool room to the bar in front, the Chief captured him at gunpoint.[20]

Upon Nash's capture, his wife Frances ran to local gangster Galatas for help in arranging his escape from FBI detention. That afternoon Galatas flew her and the couple's daughter to the farm of Herbert "Deafy" Farmer five miles south of Joplin, Missouri. Deafy was nicknamed because of his deafness. He was a well-traveled confidence man who offered a hideout for Midwest hoodlums and fugitives on the run. At Farmer's home that evening Frances called her husband's best friend, Verne Miller. He had formerly been a policeman in Huron, South Dakota until he was elected sheriff. Then he was convicted of embezzling his office's funds and sent to prison. Upon release Miller used his proficiency as a machinegunner during his Army duty to become a bank robber and to ride shotgun for major Prohibition gangs in New York City and Chicago. He was also reputed to be a hit man for these gangs but was never connected to any specific killing. Whatever crimes Miller had committed they were clearly profitable because he and his wife lived large as they enjoyed leisure and golf in a fashionable Kansas City, Missouri residential area.

The night of Nash's arrest FBI agents transported him by train from Hot Springs to Kansas City and from there they planned to drive him back to Leavenworth Penitentiary an hour away to complete the long sentence from which he had escaped. A corrupt Hot Springs detective notified local crime leader Galatas that Nash would be arriving by train in Kansas City the next morning, and Galatas passed this information onto Miller in Kansas City. Arrangements were quickly made for three shooters to free Nash from the custody of the FBI agents and armed local police detectives. Then Miller proceeded to the Union Railway Station to scout the layout.

Escorting Nash on a Missouri Pacific passenger train from Hot Springs were two FBI agents and an armed local police chief. Waiting for their arrival on the Kansas City Union Railway Station platform were two more FBI agents and two Kansas City police detectives. The plan was to sit the prisoner in the front passenger seat of the agents' car with three law enforcers sitting behind him in the backseat and one driving and to have this car followed by three officers in the detectives' car. On the train platform the seven peace keepers surrounded the handcuffed prisoner and walked him to their two cars parked in the public lot, but four goons were already lurking in position poised to attack. One kept the getaway car engine idling in readiness, while the other three holding machineguns knelt beside cars behind and on both sides of the officers' parked cars. Two FBI agents and the police chief settled behind the prisoner in one car, a third agent was about to get into the driver's seat, and the other three officers prepared to take their seats in the trailing car. At that moment the gunmen on both sides quickly raced towards them blasting away as the third leapt up on a car running board, extending out a few inches below the bottom level of the doors on both sides, and fired down on the agents' car from behind. The withering rat-tat-tat of spraying bullets lasted no more than a few seconds. The helpless quarry inside the car were unable to defend themselves. The prisoner and police chief were killed instantly; one agent was critically wounded by three bullets; and another agent was miraculously unscathed by the deadly fusillade that riddled the car. A third agent next to the driver's door lay prostrate on the ground from mostly head wounds. The three men standing outside the other car were supposed to protect them, but they were the first targets. The dead bodies of two detectives lay on the ground, and the fourth agent was shot in the left arm as he instinctively fell to the pavement too. When the shooting subsided, he jumped up, grabbed a shotgun from the detectives' car, and futilely fired at the escaping killers' car as it roared out of the parking lot. The agent and dozens of stunned bystanders had not gotten the car's license number.[21]

This carnage of four dead peace officers and the wounding of two more, one critically, shocked the nation and became known as the Kansas City Massacre. Even though the lawmen failed to shoot a single attacker, the outraged public heaped little blame on Hoover and his self-proclaimed scientific methods. After all FBI agents were prohibited by law from even carrying weapons. However Congress had already given Hoover's agents the responsibility of accompanying law enforcers in arrests of violent criminals so the Director should have given his brief-case-toting accountant and attorney staff training about strategic and safe arrest procedures, effective protection of witnesses and prisoners, and the best tactics to survive gun fights as both agents and the Nash went down unnecessarily that day. For this Hoover should have been fired for gross incompetence and malfeasance because he failed to prepare and to train his agents in even the most basic elements of combat methods and safeguards.

Hoover should have had his agents study the Capone gang's horrific decade of successful Chicago machinegun killings during the preceding Roaring '20s, as well as the current rash of Midwest machinegun bank robberies, to be well versed in the best ways to handle such clashes. Then his agents could have prepared a simple and easy way to avoid any bloodshed at the train station that day. The moment after the train pulled in, the officers' two cars should have driven up beside the train car the prisoner was in so it shielded the automobiles from the passenger platform. The officers could have quickly transferred the handcuffed prisoner from the passenger car to the two automobiles and whisked him away on a circuitous route to disappear long before any criminal associates standing on the platform could have been able to return to their car and give chase.

Not only did Hoover's agents use a reckless strategy but they tragically bungled it. After three law enforcers and the convict were seated in one car, the remaining four lawmen were focused on getting into their car seats when they should have been on alert looking in all four directions for a pending attack. The correct procedure would have been for two FBI agents to accompany the prisoner in one car and another agent drive the second car behind them. The other four should have walked beside their slowly-moving cars with the three local lawmen armed for action, just like standard Secret Service agent policy accompanying the president, until they got through the parking lot and beyond any possible ambush site. Then the four could have jumped in and quickly sped away. Their inapt actions made the three aggressive, brutish plug-uglies look like tactical geniuses.

The shooters train-station Massacre plan began to unravel immediately. As soon as radio stations began broadcasting the first news bulletins about the horrific slaughter of lawmen, a Joplin woman called police about a suspicious conversation she overheard the day before. She had eavesdropped on the party telephone line she shared with Deafy Farmer who had helped Nash's wife. Just five hours after the Massacre, police raided his home, but all the conspirators who planned the plot had already taken off for safer locales. Joplin police notified the FBI about Deafy's possible involvement and agents obtained his home phone records. He had made many calls to one Kansas City phone number leading agents to raid the home. The owner was long gone, but an agent dusted the empty beer bottles in the cellar and other items for fingerprints. These latents identified Miller, and neighbors confirmed from his picture that he owned the house, although he lived there under an alias. The FBI made him its most wanted man.

Deafy Farmer soon returned home where agents were waiting to arrest him. Other agents tracked Nash's wife to a relative's home in Illinois. Both admitted making phone calls to plan what was intended to be Nash's escape, but neither knew where Miller was or who his accomplices were. The case went cold almost immediately and remained so for quite some time. In the interim, the Kansas City Massacre led to dramatic changes in the FBI's mission and authority as agents turned their focus to other interstate bank-robbing gangs. Ironically between the time of the slaughter and Farmer's arrest days later for conspiracy, he had participated in committing a major kidnapping with one of these other bank-robbing gangs headed by Alvin Karpis and the Barker brothers. The FBI had no idea Deafy was involved with this abduction so while he was out on bail for making phone calls to assist in the Massacre, he again joined the gang in a second terrifying kidnapping.

A GOVERNMENT WAR ON CRIME

As a result of the Great Depression's crushing unemployment, armed robberies and thefts skyrocketed. When the violent bank-robbery gangs appeared in the Midwest, the public viewed them as a new type of criminal scourge, but they were really the final phase of that era's escalating crime wave. As this crime problem escalated during Republican President Herbert Hoover's administration it caused some citizens to hold anticrime rallies criticizing the government. Even though Herbert Hoover's leadership had this political weak spot, Democratic presidential candidate Franklin Delano Roosevelt (FDR) campaigned against him primarily on the pressing economic crisis. The challenger did not talk about the gloom and doom the electorate was feeling, but instead projected a buoyant, optimistic attitude to offer a sense of hope. FDR did not explain how he was going to solve these problems until his first inaugural address when he outlined in broad terms how he hoped to govern. In this speech he tried to keep the very real economic problems in perspective by reminding the American people that the nation's "common difficulties" concerned "only material things."

This was a time when the American people were afraid of a number of societal forces that were out of their control. In addition to serious unemployment and economic worries, they faced radical proposals to change the collapsed capitalism system, a possible spillover from the decade-and-a-half old Bolshevik Revolution in Russia that began as a workers' protest and morphed into Communism, union organizing, moral values that were drifting from traditional Puritanism, and a crime wave from new breeds of gangsters – Prohibition's large organized gangs, kidnapping gangs, and brazen bank robbers who seemed to relish shooting it out with police. These forces caused an underlying dread that the economy and society were disintegrating and the government could no longer control the country's destiny. This crisis of confidence was illustrated by a multitude of Hollywood gangster films between 1928 and 1933 that made the criminal the hero and led to the disrespect for law enforcement or the government, and a wave of censorship against excessive violence on the screen in the newly-introduced talkies.

This general fear the people were feeling was acknowledged by Roosevelt in his first inaugural address, but he focused his discussion about Americans' basket of fears on the most pressing issue, the economic collapse. A grim President said, "Let me assert my firm belief that the only thing we have to fear is fear itself - nameless, unreasoning, unjustified terror which paralyzes needed efforts to convert retreat into advance. ... Only a foolish optimist can deny the dark realities of the moment. ... This nation asks for action, and action now." He finished by framing the struggle as a war, "I shall ask the Congress for the one remaining instrument to meet the crisis – broad executive power to wage a war against the emergency, as great as the power that would be given to me if we were in fact invaded by a foreign foe."[22]

From the beginning of FDR's administration, newly-appointed Attorney General (AG) Homer Cummings studied ways to mount a drive against organized crime. While mindful that Congress and the public were concerned about a federal police force becoming a secret police Gestapo, he was also aware that citizen outrage over escalating crime was unsettling the nation. While the administration wrestled with solving the national economic crisis, the U.S. AG wanted to launch a war on crime to make citizens feel safer in their beds at night. He had the insight to understand that the sensational headlines about machinegun-toting robbers made it seem like dangerous crime was escalating out of control but this was really a political crisis exasperated by a bundle of fears. The AG wanted to initiate a successful war on crime to confirm to the people that government could indeed solve problems and protect them. Then three months into FDR's term, the horrific slaughter of peace officers in Kansas City shocked the nation. It occurred one year after the Lindbergh baby kidnapping, and these two cases dramatized the nationwide breakdown in law enforcement especially with the wave of Midwest kidnappings and brazen machinegun-bank robberies regularly making the headlines.

In this alarmed-public atmosphere, the AG made the Massacre in Kansas City the rallying cry to sell his idea of a war on crime to the public. This event caused the President to quickly embrace the AG's proposed crusade against crime in order to achieve an obtainable victory for his New Deal agenda while at the same time the administration dealt with the more difficult and protracted economic crisis. After six weeks of quiet in-house preparation by the AG, FDR went public, ordering a war against crime and instructing his Attorney General to take appropriate action. Three days later AG Cummings announced he was marshalling federal forces to launch a nationwide war to drive organized-crime gangsters, kidnappers, and bank robbers into prison by utilizing a new federal police force. In reality this campaign amounted to nothing more than changing the names of a few federal law enforcement agencies and upgrading the Justice Department's FBI agency to division status.

AG Cummings designed his war on crime to create a sense that the government could stabilize the society and protect its citizens. It started as an aggressive publicity campaign with the AG's tough rhetoric getting him quoted in the front pages of the *New York Time's* in 335 articles during

1933. This amount of print was particularly impressive because he was in office for just nine months that year, and he conducted his campaign against crime only during the final five months. The AG's frequent and vociferous rhetoric promoting his crusade made him the nation's leading anticrime protestor, but his top cop, FBI Director J. Edgar Hoover, made no effort to go after either organized-crime gangs or machinegun-toting bank robbery gangs. Hoover did honor Congress' mandate under the Lindbergh Law for the FBI to go after the limited number of high-profile kidnappers who crossed state borders. Otherwise Hoover and his FBI agents did not try to confront a real criminal until seven month's into his boss' vaunted war on crime.

For example three months after the U.S. AG declared his war on crime, Indiana Governor McNutt publicly asked FBI Director Hoover to assist in the manhunt for John Dillinger and the three men who freed him while killing the Sheriff. Hoover refused to get his agents involved despite his boss's declared war on violent criminals. Three months later, President Roosevelt made the war on crime a centerpiece of his second State of the Union Address. This put the FBI in the press spotlight, but Hoover still made no effort against bank robbers or organized-crime gangsters. FBI internal memos make clear that Hoover viewed the Dillinger case and other gang activities as potential quagmires that might take extended periods of time to solve and could result in unacceptably-high failure rates for his highly-polished FBI image.

Even though it would be a year after the Kansas City Massacre before Congress would pass AG Cumming's bill to remove the legal clause prohibiting the FBI from carrying guns and making arrests, this atrocity against lawmen had caused Hoover to buy his agents an arsenal of pistols and some machineguns. However agents' use of weapons was still a felony, and Hoover avoided taking risks throughout his career. He routinely covered any action that might be questioned by others with a memo to file blaming someone else as responsible. Since the FBI needed guns and the ability to make arrests in order to carry out the announced war on crime by the AG and the President, it is highly likely the Director got at least their verbal blessings to proceed. The only protection Hoover really needed was the AG's verbal authority because as head of the Justice Department he had sole power to prosecute or not prosecute an FBI agent for possessing or using a weapon, and it was in his purview to either turn a blind eye to the practice or else to defend it as justified under certain extraordinarily threatening circumstances.

Hoover distributed these guns to every FBI field office across the country but he gave no directions to his SACs (special agents in charge) on how to train their agents to shoot. This was a serious omission because the vast majority of Hoover's pencil-pushing accountants and attorneys had never seen a real gun let alone fired one. At least one SAC had local police instruct his agents, but most offices offered no meaningful training. Some told agents to grab a gun from the office arsenal and learn on their own, while others took their agents out into the woods to shoot at makeshift targets with no tutoring from expert marksmen. Hoover had armed his agents without giving them a clue about the strategies and tactics of a shootout, what it was like to face gunfire, how to determine the most protected and commanding cover from which to shoot in a gun battle, or the importance of first escorting civilians out of the line of fire. Soon they would learn all of this from bad and failed performances by going up against the most aggressive machinegunners imaginable.

The Director had not only failed to train his accountant and attorney agents for armed battle, but he had not instructed them in the most rudimentary police patrolman practices such as how to make arrests and how to chase speeding getaway cars. He had not tutored them in critical detective techniques like covertly trailing suspects, keeping them under surveillance surreptitiously, conducting stealth stake outs to determine if suspects were or were not in the buildings agents planned to raid based only on conjecture, or developing underworld informants to generate leads.

His brief-case toting accountants and attorneys simply had no idea of how to go about finding Dillinger, and if they were to have encountered him, they lacked the basic skills needed to effectively pursue let alone capture him.

After all Hoover had no background in police or detective work, never bothered to learn anything about his alleged profession, and never hired experts in these areas to lead or train his staff of young college graduates. An administrator in any field is rarely an expert in more than one specialty and often times people are put in leadership positions because of their administrative skills with little or no knowledge about the field. Administrators excel by employing the finest expertise in every specialty and making sure these department heads effectively train their staffs. As an administrator J. Edgar Hoover was a complete failure in training, preparedness, and operating policies. His only contribution to leadership was to make sure that when his agents unnecessarily died in combat that their suit slacks were sharply creased and their hair well trimmed and properly combed. Dress code and grooming was detailed in his many manuals.

Crime authors have typically said Public Enemies Number 1 were creations of the press that arbitrarily selected them out of a whole bunch of bank robbing gangsters of that era, but these gang leaders stood out and warranted headlines because of their gutsy daring. Rather than try to elude lawmen, all repeatedly charged, blasting away with their machineguns while either running out in the open or driving cars at them. They became famous because the press wrote about one incredible police and jail escape after another. These killers earned their reputations because of their mind-numbing audacious actions. Unfortunately the skills Hoover's agents needed to be able to capture these determined armed fugitives would be learned mostly at the cost of funerals of fellow agents and the toll of wounded and terrified innocent civilians who got in the way of the agents' errant gunfire. John Dillinger, Baby Face Nelson, Pretty Boy Floyd, and Alvin Karpis and the Barker brothers built their reputations by being dreadfully effective at killing more FBI agents and policemen than any other American outlaws.[23]

J. EDGAR'S WAR AGAINST DEMOCRACY

FBI Director Hoover ruled as an absolute dictator keeping his men in fear of him. He remained in Washington as his SACs ran the investigations from field offices across the country. They had to send him memos about everything they and their agents did, and the Director remained omnipresent by firing off frequent memos at anything he disliked, expressing his angry, hostile, threatening temperament.

Hoover was obsessed with his agents' clean and neat appearance and proper demeanor about which he wrote a shelf of rules manuals. When entering and exiting the office, agents had to sign in and list the time. If an agent was just one minute late he was required to fill out a long explanation form. The SAC had to issue a disciplinary memo to the agent and an apology to Hoover explaining why this happened. A second tardy could lead to suspension. Former FBI clerks of that era reported to the press that curt tongue-lashings were administered for the slightest of reasons and discharges for relatively unimportant offenses were not uncommon.

The Director's whole focus was on his agent's dress and grooming codes, the proper placing of dots on reports, and punctuality. Totally ignored was teaching the newly-armed agents proper police and detective procedure, and instilling a respect in them for civilian safety and civil liberties. The basic police role of protect and serve was a seriously missing component of Hoover's FBI as his sole concern was the successful capture or assassination of public enemies, no matter how unnecessarily bloody, and the proper handling of the press interview afterward. For the Director, a sharp crease in the trousers, trimly-cut hair, and being on time no matter how demanding the case load meant far more than knowledge, competence, professionalism, and integrity. Hoover was all about form and not substance, all about public imagery and not accomplishment or effective law enforcement. Military personnel refer to his style of ineffectual-leadership as "a cluster fuck!"

Hoover's first move for political power was asserting control over hiring policies with his boss. When AG Cummings was planning to launch his war on crime, Hoover only opposed one item in the FBI-reorganization plans. He vehemently fought absorbing the Treasury Department's Prohibition enforcers (Prohis) who were soon to be eliminated with the ending of the Noble Experiment. The AG wanted to quickly expand the number of FBI agents by absorbing employees Congress had already authorized for another department. But Hoover argued the Prohis were no more than armed and dangerous high school dropouts compared to his elite group of bright young lawyers and accountants who carried briefcases instead of guns. Hoover knew he would never be able to intimidate and control these experienced law enforcers like he did his young recruits recently graduated from college.

Victory in this first power fight led Hoover to initiate behind-the-scenes political battles with individual elected officials over hiring policies. He started opposing Senators' demands to hire their political allies and supporters as agents. The Director wanted sole control to hire what he called "competent" and "qualified" men when he actually meant those men who would give him strict obedience and absolute loyalty, making them in every sense of the word droids. The FBI would soon become an important crime-fighting division in the Justice Department, and then the Director would quickly drive out those agents who did not conform to his rigid obediency requirements.

In the interim, Hoover took advantage of the ties of some his politically-sponsored agents. The former confidential secretary in the Chicago FBI Office wrote, "In return for Director Hoover's consideration of the sponsors of his appointees, there was the reciprocal arrangement of the sponsors considering him. It was well known that Mr. Hoover had a neat and handy catalog of his employees and their influence. I wrote many of the letters requesting that influence be directed in his behalf when there was a growing feeling of uncertainty about his reappointment under the Democratic regime."[24]

FBI records reveal Hoover had a strict mold that his agents had to fit. He hired men with law or accounting degrees between 25 and 35 years old. Every agent was a European-American man, and a disproportionate number were southern as Hoover was a staunch segregationist. He hired few with law-enforcement experience. These were almost all southerners. Specifically excluded from employment were African, Asian, Hispanic, and Native-American men, and all women.

In Hoover's training schools, anyone showing a capacity for original thought was automatically rejected. The direction of every investigation was centralized under Hoover's personal oversight through his SACs. Achieving the correct balance between centralized oversight and field-level initiative continues to plague the FBI to this day.

Hoover's tyrannical management style, secret and improper use of authority, and penchant for publicity were first revealed by an investigative reporter in a *Collier's Magazine* article just three weeks after AG Cummings announced his war on crime and the important new role he was giving the FBI. The reporter wrote, "There is a serious and sinister side to this secret federal police system. It had always been up to its neck in personal intrigue and partisan politics." But it had since become the Directors "personal and political machine. More inaccessible than presidents, he kept his agents in fear and awe by firing and shifting them at whim; no other government agency had such a turnover of personnel."

Hoover would fight a long public battle that involved hearings and court cases to become the only federal official whose employees were not monitored and protected by the civil service law or a union. "This meant that he could hire or fire, promote or demote, anyone he chose, without having to justify his actions or have them subject to review." He maintained this unique, unlimited, arbitrary power to intimidate and threaten his agents into total submission, conformity, and silence until the day he died. His agents never served the people or the elected government. They survived only by bowing to and appeasing the Director's every whim. Former agents reported that the first rule of the FBI was "Do not embarrass the Director!" Unfortunately, this reporter's early revelations did not set off alarms with anyone in power. Neither the AG nor the President realized how ill-suited Hoover was to lead America's secret-police force in a democratic society. They could have quietly fired him then before he would become more powerful than any president or other elected official in this country's history.[25]

Hoover's primary strength was his mastery of publicity. As the *New York Times* said in its long obituary for the Director, "As Some of the men closest to him volunteer, Mr. Hoover's primary genius might well have been publicity. ... Mr. Hoover never held a news conference. The closest thing to a mouthpiece in the press was not a political pundit or a crime reporter but the late [syndicated gossip columnist and national radio broadcaster] Walter Winchell, who traveled with an F.B.I. escort and carried an item about "G-man Hoover" almost every day. The making of the Hoover folk hero, in which Mr. Winchell played a large part, was undertaken purposefully in the early thirties – long after the director's quiet administrative mastery had established him securely [in power]."[26]

The author of the early *Collier's* article also exposed Hoover's total self-aggrandizing control over FBI public relations. "The director's appetite for publicity is the talk of the Capital, although admittedly a peculiar enterprise for a bureau which, by the nature of its work, is supposed to operate in secrecy. Although Mr. Hoover issued strict orders against publicity on the part of his agents, he was never bound by them." The author went on, "In appearance, Mr. Hoover looks utterly unlike the story-book sleuth. He is short, fat, businesslike, and walks with a mincing step ... He dresses fastidiously, with Eleanor blue as the favorite color for the matched shades of tie, handkerchief and socks ... A little pompous, he rides in a limousine even if only to a nearby self-service cafeteria."[27]

The "mincing step" comment was to alert the country that Hoover was a closet homosexual which made America's top cop subject to blackmail by anyone threatening to expose him unless he handled criminal investigations as they ordered. The Director retaliated against the reporter by launching a quiet investigation into his private life. This dirt was secretly supplied to favored newspapermen who confidentially let their source be known to other members of the press. This illegal and outrageous misuse of his police power frightened off the whole journalistic corp, and later television newsmen, from writing and speaking out about this aspect of the Director's life until after his death. This illegal and anti-democratic abuse of power should have led to immediate dismissal because it laid bare that the FBI's primary job was to investigate for dirt on politicians, their supporters, bureaucrats, and activists in order to silence and control them with threats of exposing the raw material maintained in official but inappropriate files. All this made Hoover's FBI exactly the opposite of everything it should have been.

The author of the early *Collier's* article also disclosed detailed information that the goal of Hoover's FBI was not fighting crime but digging into the private lives of prominent politicians including even President Herbert Hoover. A year after Director Hoover's death the man who had been third in the FBI's chain of command, Assistant Director William Sullivan, stated in a newspaper interview that Hoover "was a master blackmailer." He went on to describe how the Director's system worked. "The moment he would get something on a senator he'd send one of the errand boys up and advise the senator that we're in the course of an investigation and we by chance happened to come up with this data on your daughter. But we wanted you to know this; we realize you'd want to know it. But don't have any concern; no one will learn about it. Well, Jesus, what does that tell the senator? From that time on the senator's right in his pocket." Two years later

Hoover's congressional liaison, or chief blackmailer, testified to U.S. Senator Church's Committee that it was his duty "selling" hostile congressmen on "liking the FBI." No matter how inappropriate the conduct of any elected official or bureaucrat, Hoover never offended the powerful as long as they did his bidding. The Washington press heard these rumors whispered so frequently they gave up paying attention to his desecration of democratically-elected government in America.[28]

The Director used his secretive, often illegal methods, to observe, harass, and blackmail not only political leaders but also activists, dissenters, and the rich and powerful. As a result of the secret files amassed by Hoover, he become America's chief blackmailer, so people of influence held the FBI and the Director as sacrosanct as apple pie and never criticized either. The few individuals who courageously spoke out against his anti-democratic operation because of their passionate belief in individual civil liberties, freedom, and justice were assailed by the Director as "professional do-gooders, pseudo-liberals, and out-and-out Communists." However these citizens' only offense was respecting and defending the most basic tenants of the Constitution of the United States. While those who stood up to the Director paid a terrible price personally and professionally through his desecrations of the principles of the U.S. Constitution and the American justice system, the Congressmen who were Hoover's biggest supporters very likely had the dirtiest professional and personal background reports filed away about them, making them the worst officials in the political system.

The mass of official FBI documents written by Hoover and his Boys during his reign, which have been publicly-released, confirm the Director was the chief archivist of "other people's filth," as publicly stated by an anonymous FBI agent four years before the Director's death. But Hoover's misdeeds were leaked by the press throughout his 48-year leadership of the FBI from soon after AG Cummings's reorganization of the agency for his war on crime. A number of historians have used the FBI's records to write entire books exposing Hoover's horrific leadership, but what we know about his wrongdoing may be only the tip of the iceberg. Hoover kept the records of all his inappropriate, often illegal, investigations of politicians, personal enemies, the rich, the influential, and celebrities in secret Official and Confidential Files separate from the General Files. These blackmail files were so voluminous they had to be stored in filing cabinets in several secure areas of the FBI Building.[29]

The Director required his agents in Washington to intensely monitor the activities and behavior of the nation's leaders. Agents were required to submit a written report every time they received a derogatory rumor from contacts and informants or overheard it on wiretaps and bugs whose use he justified under the guise of "national security." Hoover wanted information about immoral or criminal activities especially homosexuality, heterosexual affairs, prostitutes, or alcoholism. Hoover had the files on the Congressmen, White House aides and visitors, government employees, and governors all placed in one group of cabinets. These sensitive folders were deceptively labeled. For example the file containing President Richard Nixon's misconduct in office was labeled "Obscene Matters." This allowed the Director to deny to Congress that the FBI maintained files on its members in its central-records system. It also allowed his few lieutenants to quickly pull the files of Congressmen to evaluate how cooperative each would be with various facets of Hoover's political agenda.

All these blackmail files were accessible only by the Director, his secretary Helen Gandy, and his lieutenants. Gandy went to work as Hoover's secretary six years before he was promoted to the Directorship, a position she held for 54 years until his death. Upon Hoover's passing, Richard Nixon demanded the secret files, but Gandy and the lieutenants lied to the President of the United States by denying their existence. Then this band of coconspirators spent the next two months at the government's expense shredding most of them.

Three year's after Hoover's death, a U.S. House subcommittee investigation exposed the shredding. The former secretary, and Hoover's lieutenants who were involved, claimed these were the Director's personal files, but all were government records resulting from official investigations whether or not obtained legally. Yet none of these enemies to American democracy, and to the right of the public to know, was charged or prosecuted with this most heinous assault on Constitutional freedom and safeguards.

The still-existing documents clearly show Hoover's personal agenda. They prove he operated the FBI as a tool to influence public opinion and national politics by furthering his conservative political philosophy and judgmental moralism. His actions were in complete opposition to his official and public claims of his FBI's professionalism, political neutrality, and respect for the law and the rights of privacy. Today the FBI continues with its struggle to gather vital criminal and terrorist information without compromising national values of democracy, civil liberties, and basic freedoms.

Chapter 3

DILLINGER THWARTS THE EARLY FBI

THE FBI JOINS THE FRAY

With this background about Director J. Edgar Hoover's untrained and unprepared college-boy agents, we return to Dillinger's flight from the Crown Point, Indiana Jail using his alleged wooden-gun charade. His break-out was blasted by local, state, and federal officials causing several local police agencies to go after Dillinger and make him the country's most hunted man. Dillinger drove to Chicago, dropped off his accomplice, and got spending money from his attorney Piquett before driving his girlfriend to her sister's apartment for the night. The next day the wanted man and his girlfriend quietly rented an apartment in St. Paul, Minnesota.

That evening Dillinger's new pal, Baby Face Nelson, was driving through St. Paul's twin city of Minneapolis when another car bumped his fender. The young hot head went ballistic, decided the other driver was reckless, took chase after the man's car, and forced his vehicle up on the sidewalk. The unarmed family man tried to run from the psychopathic killer but he fired twice killing him.

Two days later Nelson joined Dillinger's gang to rob a Sioux Falls, South Dakota bank of $46,000. This was Dillinger's first crime since escaping from the Crown Point Jail and his gang had become more dangerous. Its robberies were bloodier and they began to perilously target bank employees and customers as well as pedestrians walking along the sidewalk. At this robbery a cashier pushed the alarm button, and when a motorcycle cop pulled up outside to park, Nelson sprayed four machinegun bullets through the window killing him.

Hoover was about to make a decision to finally join the pursuit of Dillinger but the fugitive's bank robbery three days after his escape was not part of the Director's consideration because it would be quite some time before his agents would learn Dillinger and Nelson had committed it. The Director was always the last to learn such things because his secret police had yet to develop a single underworld informant even though the mass criminality of Prohibition had just recently ended and organized-crime gangs had been proliferating across the country for a decade and a half.

Hoover's great reluctance to go after Dillinger was overpowered by a combination of negative press stories regarding the FBI. The fugitive's alleged toy-gun escape had finally produced headlines about a Midwest bank robber in newspapers across the nation causing a huge public outcry. In addition, Hoover was suffering from bad press over a couple ongoing cases. The Kansas City Massacre case had gone cold, and Hoover had charged the wrong people in the William Hamm kidnapping case leading a Federal Jury to quickly and correctly acquit the defendants for lack of evidence. If the Director sat Dillinger out, there would have been no reason for his agency to exist. Hoover realized saving his job depended on getting the fugitive. Since bank robbery was not yet a federal offense, Hoover justified taking action because Dillinger had stolen the lady Sheriff's car during his Crown Point Jail breakout and driven it across state lines.

On the day Hoover made his decision, he wrote two internal memos that illustrated how he not only managed by fear but also documented outright lies in the files to make his closest and most loyal subordinates scapegoats if Congress should ever criticize the Director's own mistakes and oversights. The memo to his assistant criticized his Chicago Office Special Agent in Charge (SAC)

Melvin Purvis. Hoover wrote for the files, "Last evening I had occasion to call Mr. Purvis at Chicago to inquire of him what steps had been taken in the Chicago Office toward bringing about the apprehension of Dillinger, and much to my surprise the Chicago Office has done practically nothing in this matter." In reality the lack of FBI action against Dillinger had been under the specific orders of the Director. Then Hoover penned a memo to Purvis, "In talking with you last evening, I gathered that you had practically no underworld informants or connections which your Office could contact in the event of an emergency arising. ... I am somewhat concerned." Again it should be noted that it was Hoover's policy for the FBI to take no action against armed criminals and to not bother to teach agents police and detective procedures.[30]

The morning after firing off these two memos, the Director wired every FBI Office SAC to "give preferred and immediate attention" to the Dillinger case. Hoover also told his favorite SAC, Melvin Purvis, to take command of the search. Purvis was a small-town lawyer who Hoover hired because of the intercession of a U.S. Senator. Such employees usually lasted only as long as their sponsors remained in power, but the Director took a special liking to Purvis. Five years after he joined the FBI, Hoover made him the SAC of the second-most-important field office, Chicago.[31]

Purvis was slight of build and hardly five feet tall. Photos show him being towered by other agents. He was from the south, was a segregationist who referred to African's as "darkies," and had a cocky air of self-importance referred to at that time as Southern privilege and is now called a sense of entitlement. Hoover's memos with the young man contained personal comments not found in the Director's memos to other subordinates. Hoover would mention his SAC's attractiveness to women and even remark about how appealing his various facial features were. It is unmistakable that Hoover was infatuated, but Purvis dated women and eventually married. Despite a fondness expressed in their correspondence, the two men's massive egos and desire for personal publicity would lead to an enormous clash. The Director may have been the boss but he gave orders in the obscurity of his command center at Headquarters, while his SAC was the action-figure who daringly faced off with and fought criminals out in the field, making him far more interesting and glamorous to the press and public.

Purvis directed his agents to put out maximum effort, but after weeks of questioning everyone they could think of who might know about Dillinger's whereabouts, all the SAC had learned was that the fugitive's long-time girlfriend was named Billie Frechette, location unknown. Despite such an inauspicious beginning, the FBI's hunt for Dillinger would become its most important case. It would turn a regional crime-wave phenomenon into a national problem and thus validate the Roosevelt administration's campaign for a strong federal law-enforcement agency.

While the FBI's early crime-fighting efforts continued to be inept, the agents had become a more-determined band of secret police because of the Kansas City Massacre. This horrific slaughter of lawmen not only led AG Cummings to instigate his war on crime, but it also convinced the FBI Director and his Chicago Office SAC to change the rules of engagement against machinegun-toting bank robbers. The AG's mandate was to apprehend violent criminals, but Hoover and Purvis reinterpreted this directive into a drive to slaughter them. From here on, when confronting violent desperadoes, agents would shoot on sight whether fired upon or not. Unfortunately wanting to shoot someone and being qualified to do it are very different things as the FBI agents' lack of training and preparedness was about to demonstrate. Agents were about to take on the most aggressive and reckless killers in history. When lawmen pursued these machinegun-toting desperadoes, they turned and charged their hunters, spraying fire at anything that moved.

Meanwhile Dillinger and Nelson were also hard at work. A week after their first robbery the gang hit a Mason City, Iowa bank for $52,000. When the bank president saw the men entering were armed, he ran into his office and as he locked the door, robber Homer Van Meter fired through the door wounding him. As the gang fled the bank a pedestrian on the sidewalk was shocked at the sight of machineguns and froze. Since he was deaf he did not understand Nelson's verbal commands and the impatient goon blasted away, killing him. From a third floor window an elderly judge saw the escaping gang and shot at them with an old revolver hitting the shoulders of both Dillinger and Hamilton but neither was seriously wounded.

In both the South Dakota and Iowa robberies the gang forced terrified bank employees, customers, and passersby to be human shields against police bullets. These petrified citizens had to stand on the gang's getaway car's side running boards and front and back fenders. These hapless people had to find a way to hold on to the moving vehicle to balance themselves on their precarious perches. All the while they faced the thugs' machineguns aimed at their bellies. These terrifying escapes lasted for up to 30 minutes before the gang finally released their shields beside the road and sped away. After the second robbery with Dillinger, Nelson took off for his Reno safe haven, and days later he would become the prime suspect in killing a witness who was set to testify against casino partners Graham and McKay who protected him there.

During the month after Dillinger's Crown Point Jail escape with the supposed toy gun, Purvis and the FBI failed to learn anything about the gang members' whereabouts or that they had committed the bank robberies in South Dakota and Iowa. Had Purvis placed the Dillinger farm under surveillance the agents would have seen his girlfriend arrive to visit the fugitive's father, and then they could have easily trailed her as she went directly back to the desperado's arms.

A BREAK IN THE CASE

FBI records say the break in the Dillinger case came when the manager of the Lincoln Court Apartments in St. Paul called about two tenants, a Mr. and Mrs. Hellman. The couple stood out because they were observed to have an unusual pattern of behavior. They were secretive, warily glanced at and studied their surroundings, used only the back entrance, and had frequent guests. Because of this suspicious pattern two agents were dispatched to the address with no other information about who these residents were.

The two agents were carrying pistols but this was still prohibited by federal law, so they enlisted the assistance of a St. Paul detective to question the couple and officially make an arrest if necessary. One agent waited in the car as the other agent and the detective walked up to the apartment. At that moment Dillinger gang lieutenant Hamilton walked out of the building with his girlfriend and another girl on their way to breakfast. The trio walked right past the agent sitting in the car. He was observing the entrance but failed to recognize this wanted fugitive.

When the other agent and the detective knocked at the apartment door they had no idea that Mr. and Mrs. Hellman were actually Dillinger and his girlfriend. She opened the door and claimed her husband was not at home. When they insisted on talking to her, she said she was not dressed and quickly shut and locked the door while telling them to wait a minute. She ran into the bedroom and woke up the country's most-wanted fugitive. The two lawmen stood patiently at the closed door for nine minutes while the couple dressed and Dillinger loaded a suitcase with money as he tried to figure out what to do. This is when gang member Van Meter entered the building by way of the back entrance. The instant he entered the floor with their apartment, he saw two men standing at their door. Composing himself, he continued walking casually right past them. The agent waiting patiently at Dillinger's apartment door thought the man who walked by him looked familiar, and as Van Meter disappeared down the front stairs the agent realized who he was and took chase. The agent caught up with the fugitive in the front yard where the two faced off guns in hand. It was a wild shootout with both emptying their pistols but missing each other. At that moment gunfire erupted inside the building distracting both agents and Van Meter was able to flee on foot and escape.

When the shots rang out in the front yard between Van Meter and the agent, the detective was still waiting patiently at the apartment door. He and Dillinger both immediately reacted to the outside gunfire. The detective stepped aside from the door towards the front of the building a moment before Dillinger sent a machinegun burst through the apartment door barely missing him. A ricochet bounced back hitting the fugitive just below the knee. Ignoring this wound, Dillinger quickly opened the door, held the gun out pointing it down the hallway, and fired blindly. Fortunately the detective had already run towards the front stairs and had leapt into an alcove before the volley roared past him. As soon as Dillinger stopped firing, the detective armed only with a pistol retreated lickety-split down the front stairs. Dillinger and his girlfriend ran out the apartment door into the empty hallway and headed in the opposite direction toward the back exit and tore down the stairs. While the fugitive stood guard she backed the car out of the garage. Then he quickly took over the steering wheel and drove them to Indianapolis.

The two agents and the detective remained waiting in front of the building entrances, so they knew the shooter in the apartment had not escaped that way. They rounded up a bevy of police and headed back upstairs where this assault force stood strategically at the empty apartment's door for two hours before boldly storming in. The agents still had no inkling about the identity of the apartment tenants who had been shooting at them until they searched the premises and found photos of Dillinger and confirmed his fingerprints.

With yet another FBI raid a failure, J. Edgar Hoover was embarrassed and enraged. He made getting Dillinger his top priority. It was now clear his survival as Director likely depended on it. But then he made two counterproductive decisions that weakened his agency's ability to accomplish his primary directive. He reemphasized to his agents that the FBI only allowed police to join federal raids when extra manpower or equipment was needed. The ego-driven Director wanted all the glory of the kill for himself. However his agents were so new to handling weapons and so inexperienced in handling pursuits, he should have understood that they needed trained police officers backing them up to make sure the job got done. This point was brought home to him at that time when he learned that some of the Chicago agents who were leading the search for Dillinger had never fired the machineguns the Director had distributed to them. His reaction to this revelation was his second incomprehensible decision. Instead of doing the obvious by setting up an effective and intense training program focused on shooting skills, making arrests, and conducting tactical assaults, Hoover simply assumed that his accountants and lawyers would become marksmen and qualified policemen on their own without expert direction. It is a rather incredible dichotomy that the Director unofficially turned the FBI into a heavily-armed police force at a time that federal law still specifically forbade agents from carrying or using weapons, but then failed to train them in handling the weapons and in doing the basic police work he had now illegally assigned them.

Two days after the Dillinger raid the apartment manager's husband was cleaning his former unit and called the FBI to report that its agents had overlooked a scribbled apartment address, possibly one of Dillinger's visitors. The next day three agents went to the apartment address written on the note and found the African-American building owner cleaning. She told them the former renter would be returning to pick up a suitcase he had left. The lead agent ordered the woman to wait behind the door, answer it when the man knocked, hand him the suitcase, and signal if this was the former renter. He stationed an agent inside the front window near the door and gave him the order that upon seeing her signal he was to "shoot him" through the glass. He repeated the order "shoot him" even though they had no idea who this man was or if he had ever committed a crime. She was terrified and protested being there, but the lead agent forced the woman to act as a human shield to protect Hoover's finest.

She somehow overcame her panic and opened the door, handed the man the case, and signaled to the agent standing at the nearby window that he was indeed the renter. That agent immediately opened fire bursting out the glass and fatally wounding the guy with the suitcase in his hand. From a hiding place and without offering any warning or identification, the FBI blew this man away, in the back, with no idea who he was.

The FBI tried to cover up its agents' cold-blooded murder-by-cop with false written internal reports, but these contained similar verbiage creating serious doubt their legitimacy. For example every agent used the phrase "a menacing gesture." While the Director required his agents to detail each incident, in these they all suddenly gave nothing more than a vague hint of what occurred. In addition it is inconceivable that an unarmed man walking away from lawmen, whom he had no idea were present, could have made any kind of threatening gesture in their direction. Of course the agents left out the fact they shot him in the back. This cover-up was so rotten that one of the agents who wrote the phrase about seeing an unexplained menacing gesture also wrote in the same report that he never had a view of the victim.

The FBI always claimed to carefully check the facts put into its reports, but these accounts incorrectly listed the African apartment owner as a maid which denied both her business and social standing in the community. The FBI was never known to put a European-American civilian into harm's way, but the lead agent was from Lynchburg, Virginia, and he forced this woman to risk her life to protect these incredibly cowardly and depraved agents.

It turned out the victim was a Dillinger gang member, Eugene "Eddie" Green. He survived, delirious in the hospital, for 10 days before dying. An agent intimidated the doctors and nurses to allow him to remain alone in the room with the victim while he questioned him. The agent pretended to be a doctor and tried to get the confused victim to reveal the identity of the members of Dillinger's gang and its structure. When the victim refused to answer his questions the agent-doctor denied the suffering man pain killers until in desperation he finally talked. This was the first time the FBI learned they exchanged gunfire at Dillinger's St. Paul apartment with Van Meter and that Hamilton had walked right past the surveillance agent.[32]

Five days after Green's assassination, the nation's most-wanted fugitive and his girlfriend showed up for a large day-long family reunion at the Dillinger farm. That evening the pair headed for Chicago but a little way from home he parked for a moment on the side of the road and got out. The FBI still had no surveillance in place at his father's farm but two FBI agents were driving toward it to make a random check. This was a futile waste of time because without seeing the visitors entering and leaving they could get no idea of who was or was not there. As the agent's drove past the man standing near the car they studied him but concluded he was not the most sought-after man in America.

The day after the family reunion Dillinger's girlfriend sought out an acquaintance in Chicago to find a place for them to stay. He said he would try to find a spot and asked her to meet him at the Tumble Inn that evening. The acquaintance happened to mention who he was helping to a friend and the friend immediately informed SAC Purvis. Under the watchful eyes of a dozen FBI agents, Dillinger parked down the block from the Inn and his girlfriend walked in. Two agents were parked in a car near Dillinger's and another agent decided to check out the driver. He walked along the sidewalk within a few feet of his car but did not recognize Dillinger nor notice the machinegun in his lap. The girlfriend later said Dillinger thought she was taking too long and walked through the tavern to make sure she was alright. Coincidentally that was the very moment agents physically grabbed her and took her into custody. Seeing this, Dillinger turned, sauntered out, and drove off into the night past the parked surveillance agents. She was sentenced to two years in federal prison for harboring the desperado.

Five days later Dillinger and Van Meter concealed machineguns under their overcoats and then brazenly walked into the Warsaw, Indiana police station to steal guns and three bullet-proof vests from its arsenal. Three days after this Dillinger accompanied Hamilton as they visited Hamilton's sister at her Sault Ste. Marie, Michigan home. She cooked dinner and cut their hair. Even though the FBI now knew the gang members' identities, Hoover had still not directed surveillance of their families. A neighbor of Hamilton's sister notified Purvis' team that the two fugitives were visiting, but by the time agents and police raided her home the next day the fugitives had been a couple hours on their way in an unknown direction. Hamilton's nephew told a reporter, "Dillinger had been wounded in the right leg and limped. My uncle had a wound in the shoulder. They were not feeling any too good, but you can bet they are ready to shoot it out with anybody. They both had on steel vests and they said they'd keep them on the rest of their lives." A little over a year later Hamilton's sister was sentenced to three months in jail for harboring the two fugitives overnight.[33]

During the seven weeks since Dillinger had walked out of the Crown Point Jail, he had successfully robbed two banks with Nelson and looted a police station's arsenal. In contrast the FBI had developed four leads about the fugitive's possible location. The agents raid on his St. Paul apartment was a fiasco, they arrived late at Hamilton's sister's home, and they failed to recognize him twice as he passed by nearby agents searching for him. As the frustrated Director and Chicago SAC waited and hoped for another lead to develop, Dillinger and his gang, including Nelson, decided to take a quiet vacation and stay out of sight.[34]

A QUIET VACATION

Dillinger's gang had spent seven active weeks that included a jail escape, a jail-arsenal robbery, violent bank robberies, apartment shootouts, and close calls. The gang members decided to go on a secluded vacation at a fishing resort in a pine forest. Dillinger, Hamilton, Van Meter, Tommy Carroll, and their girlfriends were joined by Nelson and his wife at the Little Bohemia Lake Lodge near Mercer in northern Wisconsin. The first floor of the small building was popular with locals for drinking, dancing, and dining. The second floor and the nearby cottage contained sleeping rooms.

Two days after Dillinger and Hamilton said goodbye to his sister, the fugitive guests unpacked at the lodge. Then they announced to the owner-managers that they were the Dillinger gang and displayed their guns. They kept the owner, his wife, 8-year-old son, bartender, and busboy under close watch so they could not notify authorities or inform local customers. The owner said, "They mingled with the other guests as calm and unconcerned as if the whole nation wasn't hunting for them." The rest of the time the fugitives played poker, strolled in the woods, and conducted frequent target practices nearby, something the FBI agents should have done more of.[35]

The owner wrote a note explaining they were prisoners of the nation's most-hunted man and rolled it up among the cigarettes in a pack. Early the next morning his brother-in-law stopped by from his nearby residence and the owner handed him the pack. The brother-in-law called Chicago's Federal Building but a guard said no one was in on Sunday. A friend of the brother-in-law was able to reach a U.S. Marshal he knew in Chicago. He contacted the home of SAC Purvis who called the brother-in-law's friend. Purvis wanted all the glory for the kills so he warned the two men not to tell local authorities and he promised to bring enough armed men for a raid that night. This was a terrible decision that Purvis made solely for self-aggrandizement. This capture was so critical to FBI Director Hoover's career that he flew his Assistant Director Hugh Clegg to back up Purvis.

The SAC and 20 agents flew into Rhinelander on a chartered plane and drove the 50 miles to the Little Bohemia Lake Lodge. These agents were accountants and attorneys who had no training in strategic assault tactics and little if any experience firing weapons. Even though the agents were totally lacking in field expertise and experience in mortal combat, Purvis failed to contact any local police or residents to learn about the unfamiliar territory they were entering in the dark of night or to determine where the desperadoes were situated. The agents simply drove into the resort's woods with car lights off and no plan but to rush in shooting machinegun-toting bad guys to death.

Their arrival set the dogs to barking, but since these pets announced every incoming car no one inside was alarmed. As agents walked toward the building three local workers concluding two hours of beer drinking walked out the front door and began to drive out. As the car approached the agents hiding in the dark one called out "government man," but the car's radio drowned this out and the surrounding darkness hid the agents' presence from view. The agents decided the workers were fleeing despite being warned so from three directions machinegun bullets ripped through the car hitting one man in the head and body killing him instantly. The driver jammed on the brakes, jumped out, and ran. A moment later agents riddled his empty seat with bullets. He still got wounded in the right arm and cut in the arms and face by flying glass. The other passenger was shot in the neck, shoulder, arm, and hip but recovered.

The gunfire slaughtering innocent civilians alerted gang members who sprung into action. They grabbed weapons and prepared to jump out the second-floor rear window but agents rounded the corner of the building and opened fire. Dillinger returned a spray of machinegun bullets. The agents ducked and stayed hidden so long the four gangsters were able to jump and disappear into the darkness before the agents looked up again. The fugitives spotted other agents who were standing between them and the garage housing their three cars so they turned and ran through the woods. The agents surrounding the resort building assumed the bank robbers were still cowering inside so Purvis set up an all-night siege as the family with the young boy, employees, and the gangs' three women inside lay on the floor terrified. At daybreak Purvis launched a tear-gas bomb and machinegun assault against the building as all the unarmed civilians inside screamed out begging not to be shot. Purvis had the advantages of surprise and overwhelming numbers, but his entire haul consisted of a shot-up lodge, three terrified girls the gang had left behind, and dead and wounded civilians.

Dillinger, Van Meter, and Hamilton, all toting machineguns ran a mile to another small resort, woke up the residents, and commandeered an employee's car. They made him drive 40 miles and then left him beside the road in Park Falls, Wisconsin. The resort owner telephoned local police about the kidnapping and the employee's stolen car number. At a bridge over the Mississippi River 20 miles SE of St. Paul at Hastings, three deputy sheriffs were cruising and observing license numbers for the employee's car. Upon spotting the car the fugitives had hijacked they took chase and attempted to pull them over, but Dillinger blasted through his vehicle's back window. A wild high-speed gunfight ensued for the next 17 miles. On a sharp curve, Van Meter made an abrupt right turn onto a dirt road. At that moment a truck entered the highway from a side street and the deputies had to slow down. The lawmen passed the truck but by the time they got to the curve the fugitives were out of view so the deputies continued on. The fugitives waited until the deputies passed them and were out of sight, but they now knew that the St. Paul police were patrolling the city's entry roads and knew their license number. They drove back to the road, parked it across the lane to block the next car, and forced out the couple and their baby before tearing on toward Chicago. During the high-speed chase Hamilton had been seriously wounded in the lower back and died two days later. Dillinger and Van Meter quietly buried him in an empty parcel of land. Eight months later Van Meter's girlfriend revealed to authorities for the first time that Hamilton was dead. His body was later dug up for identification to close the case and was then reburied in a more appropriate site.[36]

While the other fugitives were jumping out the resort's window, Nelson ran out of the nearby cottage, fired a pistol at Purvis' feet, and disappeared into the darkness of the woods. His agents gave chase but tripped into ditches and became entangled in a barbed-wire fence. Nelson stumbled through a mile of underbrush in the dark for a half hour until seeing lights from the Birch Lodge cabin. He walked in the unlocked door with his automatic pistol in hand. A neighbor observed the home invasion and reported it to local police. They in turn called a local constable who was at a nearby resort. He had joined up with two FBI agents who were patrolling in search of the fugitives.

The trio of lawmen sped to Birch Lodge and pulled into the driveway behind a car preparing to pull out. It contained Nelson with the couple sitting inside as hostages. The agents yelled for everyone to get out. Nelson leaped out of the passenger's seat and charged the trio with his machinegun blazing. The lawmen were sitting ducks. The agent in the passenger's seat was the one who a half-hour earlier had shot to death an unarmed innocent civilian who was heading home from Little Bohemia. This agent had a machinegun in his lap but it appears he was in shellshock and unable to fire after having killed an innocent man. He ducked his head behind the agent in the driver's seat, and then he jumped out of the car tossing the machinegun as he ran. Nelson shot the unarmed fleeing agent three times in the neck killing him, pumped five slugs into the constable, and dropped the other agent with a bullet that bounced off his skull. Nelson then leaped into the agents' rental car and drove off to connect up with his fleeing wife. He left the couple badly traumatized but unharmed.[37]

Along the highway Nelson soon passed an oncoming car with four FBI agents who were arriving somewhat late for the raid. They had made the long drive from St. Paul because they feared flying. As they drove toward Nelson's oncoming car, the four failed to recognize him. They continued on to their Little Bohemia Lodge destination where the civilians lay frozen in terror on the floor of the perforated building in the eerie silent darkness.

The heartbreaking result of the FBI's inept and blundering raid was the murders of both an innocent civilian and the agent who killed him, and the serious woundings of two civilians headed home, a constable, and an agent. In their internal summaries agents reported firing on six cars in the vicinity of the Little Bohemia Resort in the night darkness with absolutely no idea who was in them. Not a single car contained a fugitive. Thus if these vigilante agents had known how to aim their guns they would have committed the most horrific slaughter of innocent civilians in history, all without any justification and from an ambush in the cover of darkness.

The most disturbing aspect of this tragedy was that it was totally avoidable. Purvis could have easily guaranteed capture of the fugitives without any risk whatsoever to a single civilian. The only escape routes from the Lodge were over three bridges. Purvis could have solicited the aid of local police departments to put up an impenetrable road block near each. A team of agents and policemen could have waited around a curve behind a solid wall of police cars blocking escape. The unsuspecting fugitives would not have seen the barricade until the last moment and then had to screech to a halt. Their retreat would have been prevented by lawmen hiding in ambush behind trees on both sides of the road in back of the fugitives' three cars.

Hoover may have routinely fired off blistering memos about agents being a minute late for work, but he remained curiously quiet about this disaster. He had hired both of the raid's leaders, his Assistant Clegg and SAC Purvis. Scapegoating anyone at the top of the command would have ultimately fallen back on him. One of the agents who had followed Clegg and Purvis on that fateful raid, St. Paul Office SAC Werner Hanni, wrote a memo to the Director condemning the handling of the tragedy but never sent it. This memo was found on his desk by Clegg who surprisingly added it to the FBI files while punishing Hanni for putting the truth in writing. Hanni was relocated to Omaha, Nebraska to refrain other agents from criticizing the FBI. Participant Hanni had written,

"[There] does not appear to exist any good reason whatsoever for Dillinger and his accomplices making a getaway. It was quite evident that the raid was fully staged with a lack of organization, and lack of knowledge and judgment cannot be concealed. The writer himself and those accompanying him to Bohemia proved to be tripped into a regular death trap. No preparation appeared to have been made, in spite of the fact that a chart of the locality had been furnished prior to proceeding there. Had it not been for the fortunate good treatment accorded the motorist who flashed a spotlight right into the writer's face, four more agents would, undoubtedly, not be here today."

On that horrible evening, Purvis lacked any semblance of leadership or planning. Hoover's FBI could have learned from this SAC's mistakes but instead of improving they simply copied his blunders in future clashes against the country's infamous bank robbers. These raids were disorganized and undisciplined, and utilized but one strategy - charge in shooting to kill. They were always done in great haste without bothering to determine whether the target was present at the location or where he might be situated at the site. The safety of innocent civilians and the lawmen was never a consideration. J. Edgar Hoover's FBI became the textbook example of the ultimate in lack of law-enforcement professionalism as it repeatedly produced the most ineffectual arrest and capture raids imaginable.

BACKLASH TO A DEBACLE

Word quickly reached Washington that the disastrous Dillinger Little Bohemia raid resulted in every fugitive escaping while leaving behind a carnage of lawmen and civilians. Criticism was intense and immediate against the FBI's "criminal stupidity" in its search and raid techniques. That morning AG Cummings met privately with FBI Director Hoover. The details were not revealed but Justice Department officials reported it was "a sharp exchange of words." While the Democratic administration castigated its own agency, two Republican U.S. Senators blamed the catastrophe on bungling by the FBI and stated, "More detectives and fewer politicians" is what the FBI needs. The Michigan Department of Public Safety Commissioner denounced the FBI for failing to cooperate with local authorities because they wanted to take sole credit for tracking down the outlaw and this probably cost the capture of Dillinger. Local citizens living around the Little Bohemia Resort signed a petition addressed to the Department of Justice in Washington demanding the removal of Purvis. It protested the "irresponsible conduct of federal operatives in such a stupid manner as to bring about the deaths of two men and injury to four others." The document sadly noted that not one victim was a gangster. It also assailed FBI agents for failing to seek aid from anyone living in the vicinity because everyone would have advised preventing the fugitives' escape by barricading the three nearby bridges. Social commentator Will Rogers wryly commented in his syndicated column, "Well, they had Dillinger surrounded and was all ready to shoot him when he came out, but another bunch of folks came out ahead, so they just shot them instead. Dillinger is going to accidentally get with some innocent bystanders some time, then he will get shot." In regards to the FBI's stellar capture of a wife and two girlfriends, Rogers said the problem was Dillinger always managed "to keep at least two women ahead of 'em."[38]

Making matters even worse, as Purvis had arrived at Little Bohemia to conduct the raid, Hoover had called reporters into his Washington Headquarters to proudly tell them Dillinger was surrounded and could not get away. Hours later subordinates reported the devastating results to the press corp. The Director was humiliated and Purvis disgraced.

The *Chicago American's* headline called for local SAC Purvis to quit or be ousted. The *Chicago Times* editorialized, "Government authorities…have made [the Dillinger manhunt] a farce-comedy – except that it has turned to tragedy in killing innocent bystanders rather than the hunted desperado." The *Chicago Tribune* described outrage coming from every direction. Based on its sources it bluntly stated, "Because of the criticism which is gathering around him, Hoover's dismissal is regarded here [in Washington] as inevitable unless he succeeds in putting an abrupt close to Dillinger's career." From unidentified FBI officials the *Tribune* made the stark prediction, "Federal agents probably will kill John Dillinger on sight, taking no chances on trying to capture him alive, it was admitted here tonight." It concluded, "Officials would not admit tonight that any order had gone out to federal agents to kill Dillinger on sight. But it was freely admitted that agents are keyed up to shoot Dillinger as soon as they see him, and that nothing is being done to restrain the agents or to caution them that Dillinger should be taken alive if possible." This attitude that the FBI could salvage its reputation only by killing Dillinger was reflected two weeks later in a *Time Magazine* article in which Assistant AG Joseph Keenan said, "I hope we will get him under such circumstances that the Government won't have to stand the expense of a trial." The FBI, which was still constrained under federal law from carrying weapons, had disintegrated into a shoot-'em-up, renegade, vigilante posse.[39]

While condemnation of Hoover and the FBI swirled around Washington, the President and Attorney General immediately took advantage of the disastrous news to hype their anticrime bills and push them through Congress. The AG had recently submitted his 12 Point Crime Program to Congress after incessantly promoting his war on crime publicity campaign in the press for eight months. Congress incorporated the AG's law-enforcement recommendations into 21 separate bills. These bills were already headed for speedy passage in the Senate, but the House Judiciary Committee placed them on hold because of concern about their infringement on state rights. On the morning of the announcement of the calamitous Little Bohemia raid, FDR called the Committee's Chairman, Democrat Hatton Sumners (Texas), to the White House for a conference. The Chairman emerged from the President's office to announce he would report the bills out of Committee "tomorrow."

That afternoon after the President's meeting, AG Cummings went to Congress to testify before Sumners' Committee pleading for passage of his anticrime measures. He gave a two-pronged pitch. First he incorporated the threatening image of John Dillinger roaming the countryside. Dillinger became the most infamous of the bank robbers in large part because of the AG's publicity-campaign for new laws and then Hoover making the take-down of Dillinger the center stone of his law-enforcement achievements in his books, speeches, and publicity for the rest of his career.

The AG's second position actually took advantage of the FBI's terrible performance. He claimed it demonstrated the agency needed wider jurisdiction and the right to carry weapons and make arrests if it was going to have a chance against Dillinger. This was disingenuous because none of these laws corrected the FBI's lack of training and incompetence that alone were responsible for the debacle. The AG's position ignored a pertinent fact that no one in the administration, Congress, or the nation's press bothered to address. In the Little Bohemia raid of the night before agents had violated federal law just by carrying weapons, and they acted with depraved indifference when they fired machineguns at numerous unidentified innocent civilians.

The AG asked for more power under the law and a much larger appropriation for the FBI to hire additional agents and to buy new cars and some airplanes. The FBI's car pool was made up of vehicles confiscated from runrunners during Prohibition and many were in dilapidated condition. He wanted more cars and new models "that can go as fast as the devil." The FBI had 400 agents and 600 clerks and other support staff. "We need about 200 more. The trouble now is that the men work on one job and when a hurry call comes they have to drop everything and go to that."[40]

Many politicians and state and local lawmen countered the AG's pleas with complaints about the FBI's go-it-alone policies and "pathetic lack of cooperation" with local authorities. The most vocal was Senate Anti-Racketeering Committee Chairman Royal Copeland, a New York Democrat. He told reporters there had been "a pathetic failure of cooperation between federal, state, and local authorities" in the Dillinger case. Instead of authorizing a reward for Dillinger, the Senator said, "If they would send for some of the New York troopers and put them on the trail they would catch him." Unfortunately for the nation, the political momentum was against replacing Hoover's unqualified, unprofessional, and law-violating leadership.[41]

Two days later the House Committee approved two of the anticrime bills. In less than two months President Roosevelt would sign all 21 bills which passed with little opposition. These new laws lifted restrictions preventing FBI agents from making arrests and carrying arms by instead authorizing them to do both, along with allowing them to execute warrants. The laws made federal crimes out of the offenses of killing or assaulting a government agent, robbing a federal bank or state-chartered member bank of the Federal Reserve System or federal insurance, racketeering in interstate commerce, crossing a state line to commit a crime, and interstate transportation of stolen property. Amendments strengthened the interstate felony fugitive pursuit law and the interstate Lindbergh Kidnapping law.[42]

The bills also appropriated funding for 400 more FBI agents, doubling the number in the field, planes, and new cars, a few armor-plated. Some of the new agents Hoover hired were to give some balance to his school boys. They were experienced tough street cops mostly from the south who did not improve either the FBI's lack of professionalism or disrespect for citizens' civil rights. These anticrime laws birthed a national police force, the forerunner of the modern FBI.

AG Cummings bills targeted those crimes that were the easiest to solve and that received the greatest publicity. He wanted high conviction rates and loads of press credit. Specifically he wanted authority over kidnapping and bank robbery. What he did not want was to saddle the Justice Department with local crimes that were committed by the politically-protected organized-crime gangs like the Mafia. He wanted a success record of combating and defeating celebrity criminals who had become symbols of the crime problem, while refusing to take responsibility for those crimes that were impossible to eradicate and would have held him accountable for the growing crime problem. He wanted to be able to say he had incarcerated the worst criminals and the local police would have to explain their continuing crime problems.

AG Cummings' policy about federal legal jurisdiction was adopted and adhered to by Hoover for the rest of his career. The Director fought behind the scenes with Congress against every proposed expansion of the FBI's authority, but he went further than the AG who stayed away from local organized gang's crimes. During Hoover's half-century directing the FBI until the day he died in office, he repeatedly swore that no Mafia criminal organization existed in the U.S. He spewed this falsehood to eight Presidents and 17 Attorneys General, who were his bosses; to Congress, which funded his agency; and to the American people, who entrusted their safety and security to him. As organized crime developed and flourished in America's big cities with the advent of Prohibition, Hoover relegated his national secret-police force to the sidelines, where they remained missing from action for four decades under his leadership. He continued to keep his troops busy with his personal agenda of political espionage, and a few high-profile kidnappings, to make it appear he ran a legitimate police agency. All the while these large gangs moved from Prohibition to muscling control over many unions and plundering from massive numbers of workers, businesses, and consumers. The FBI was the only law-enforcement agency in the country with the power and authority to nip the development of organized crime in the bud, but the Director single-handedly prevented the agency from doing its job. The record of Hoover's FBI fighting serious crime could not have been more dismal. As one high-ranking organized crime leader said to this author in an interview, "Wasn't J. Edgar Hoover a wonderful man!" As he said this he had a huge smile from ear to ear with fond memories of America's top cop. I sat there trying to absorb this disturbing incongruity.[43]

During the two months following the Little Bohemia raid fiasco, the AG pushed through his anticrime bills but the FBI remained a national laughingstock. Purvis was having a hard time finding out where in the world Dillinger was. He was also drawing blanks on Nelson, and the Kansas City Massacre case remained cold. Not only the reputations but likely the jobs of Purvis and Hoover depended on the FBI taking down Dillinger which remained their top priority.

Chapter 4

THE HUNT FOR DILLINGER

LIFE & THE LAW AFTER BOHEMIA

After escaping the FBI's raid on the Little Bohemia Resort, Dillinger and his two cohorts stole two cars in their travels to Chicago. The trio arrived in the evening after the President and his Attorney General (AG) had spent the day rallying Congress on their anticrime bill package by lambasting the most-wanted fugitive. The desperadoes first order of business was to steal Illinois license plates from a car parked in front of a residential home to replace the legitimate Minnesota plates on the stolen car they were driving.

A week later Chicago police found the car abandoned. The rear window had been removed in preparation for fending off police pursuit. In the car were matchbooks bearing the name of the Little Bohemia Resort proprietor. The car seats were stained with blood and emergency surgical kits were strewn on them. Dillinger and Van Meter had used them to try to save Hamilton from the gunshot wounds received during the long highway chase and shootout with Minnesota deputy sheriffs. The next day Hamilton succumbed, and Dillinger and Van Meter buried him in an unmarked vacant parcel. More than a half year later Van Meter's girlfriend would reveal for the first time that Hamilton was dead and where his body was located. After burying Hamilton the two surviving fugitives went their separate ways with Dillinger remaining in the Windy City and Van Meter moving on to St. Paul.

The fugitives appear to have abandoned the car several days before it was found because three nights after their arrival in Chicago, Dillinger and two women had dinner at a restaurant and then departed by taxi. The waiter recognized him from his newspaper photos and called police as soon as the group left but the trail went dead. The restaurant was located in the Town Hall district where Dillinger had lived in a hideaway a half year earlier.

Meanwhile the FBI was searching the Twin Cities in Minnesota for Dillinger because agents in the Little Bohemia raid had mistakenly thought the cash they had found at the resort was part of the ransom paid for kidnapped St. Paul banker Edward Bremer. Even though agents soon learned the cash at the resort was not part of the ransom, they continued to assume without basis that Dillinger was part of the kidnap gang operating out of St. Paul. When Chicago reporters asked SAC Purvis if Dillinger could be in Chicago, he said it was possible but doubtful.

Dillinger quickly reestablished contact with Baby Face Nelson. A week after arriving in Chicago the pair were driving with three associates through Bellwood, Illinois at 1:40 a.m. Three local policemen were in a car stopped at a red light. As the light turned green the outlaws Ford V-8 sped right by them. The police gave chase and reached speeds up to 76 mph. Two-and-a-half miles into the race, Dillinger turned off his car lights thinking he had outdistanced the police pursuers. He stopped at a gas station and ordered the attendant, "Give us some gas in a big hurry." As the man pumped gas, the police car pulled up. Two of the policemen jumped from their car and ran toward the speeders. One policeman later described what happened. "I was about to step over the gas hose which was already in the tank of the car when someone jumped out of the front seat with a Tommy machinegun in his hand and said, 'Stick 'em up.' I recognized Dillinger and thought the jib was up for me." While Dillinger held the two patrolman at bay, Nelson leaped from the driver's seat and ran to where the third policeman was still seated in the patrol car and ordered him out. The officer later explained, "I couldn't shoot. My own men were in the way." The outlaws disarmed the policemen and lined them up between the two cars. Without provocation Dillinger suddenly swung his machinegun and knocked one officer to the ground with the muzzle. The desperadoes then sped off with the gas hose still in the tank, pulling over the whole pump. The police recognized Dillinger even though he had shaved off his mustache and was heavier especially in the face. The fugitives' maroon car was muddy and dusty as if it had been over country dirt roads.

Three days later the Justice Department charged all of Dillinger's known gang members with a federal crime. In addition to the outstanding interstate transportation of a stolen car against Dillinger, prosecutors indicted him, Nelson, four other gang members, and four women for conspiracy for having sheltered each other from the law, the only federal statute applicable to their crimes. At the same time Chicago SAC Purvis had agents intensify their search for Dillinger in St. Paul, while the fugitive remained living in the Windy City where Purvis was headquartered.[44]

Four Dillinger gang women remained in FBI custody. Nelson's wife and two gang members' girlfriends were grabbed at Little Bohemia two weeks after Dillinger's girlfriend was arrested in a speakeasy. In both raids agents were after Dillinger and he escaped leaving the women behind. Agents interrogated all four women. They offered no useful information but newspaper reports of their questioning led to more embarrassing comment about the FBI as it led to the circulation of a cynical joke - "The FBI may not always get its man, but it always gets his women."

A month after the Little Bohemia fiasco, Nelson's wife and the other two gang members girlfriends pled guilty to harboring the gang. The Wisconsin federal judge gave each a one-year sentence and then suspended these in favor of 18-month probations. This was at the request of SAC Purvis who had six agents trail the women in case they returned to their men. At the hearing, Nelson's wife was anemic and too weak to stand. Her weakened state did not stop her three days later from ditching the agent following her in a movie theater. When Tommy Carroll's girlfriend slipped her surveillance, FBI Director Hoover was fed up with SAC Purvis ineptitude so he sent top aide, Inspector Sam Cowley, from Washington Headquarters to the Chicago Office to take charge of the Dillinger case. Less than two weeks into Cowley's command, agents lost Van Meter's girlfriend who quickly rejoined her fugitive man.[45]

A week after the Little Bohemia debacle SAC Purvis told the press that Dillinger had likely died from wounds inflicted at the resort raid. Purvis said, "We are still looking for him." He added that the FBI had been "unable to confirm reports that he is dead in Wisconsin." "No one has reported seeing him and no reports have been made by agents on the case."[46]

A month later Purvis announced he was "convinced" that Dillinger was dead. He said his agents were searching for Dillinger's grave and believed it to be in southern Indiana. Purvis revealed that his investigators had talked with an Indiana doctor, who had dressed Dillinger's wounds a week after the Wisconsin shooting battle. This doctor said he bound up three wounds, anyone of which, he declared, "might have been fatal." The doctor said three men brought Dillinger into his home. After treatment, the men drove back toward southern Indiana. No record exists about Dillinger being badly shot up during this or any other period in his criminal career so this doctor apparently misidentified as Dillinger another criminal he was forced to treat with serious wounds.[47]

Five days before Purvis all but declared Dillinger dead, two East Chicago, Indiana detectives were on late-night patrol. Their route took them through the barren region along the old Gary Macadam Road which had some industrial plants surrounded by swamps. At the time the officers were pulling out from the police station to begin their route, a plant watchman noticed a large sedan with four men parked on this road. Fifteen minutes later the watchman again looked where the sedan was parked, but it was gone. Near where it had been the detectives' car sat in the middle of the road. Both officers were in their seats riddled with machinegun bullets. Each had been killed instantly from eight or nine bullets to the head and neck. The two detectives were married and had a total of nine children.

No evidence proved Dillinger was there but the scene certainly fit his modus operandi. In reconstructing the scene, it was obvious what had happened. The detectives drove up towards the front of the parked sedan and pulled beside it to question the men why they were there. Since both detective's weapons were holstered, the response must have been immediate machinegun fire from car window through car window. The killers were likely fugitives or they would have submitted to the questioning and gone on their way. Strangers rarely drove this area because it was easy to get lost on the seldom-used roads. However Dillinger and Van Meter knew this section of town because it offered numerous isolated hideouts. Another weak piece of evidence fit Dillinger being on the road that night. A man resembling the fugitive collided with another car in a hit and run in Indianapolis a few hours earlier and the crime-scene road lie in the path to Chicago. In addition after the Detectives were shot, a large sedan was seen speeding through Whiting headed toward Chicago. Whiting lay between this road and the Windy City.

The day after the cold-blooded murders of these two detectives, the five states of Indiana, Illinois, Ohio, Minnesota, and Michigan each anteed up $1,000 to make a total reward of $5,000 for the capture of Dillinger. A month later AG Cummings offered a $10,000 reward for Dillinger and $5,000 for Nelson. This reward officially made Dillinger Public Enemy Number 1 and the most sought-after criminal in the country.

The AG authorized the reward under the year-old federal reward law that said the AG may, at his discretion, award only a part of the money promised if the criminal is killed in the capture. This proviso was written in at the AG's request because he declared to Congress he much preferred to dispatch criminals through the courts rather than at the point of a smoking gun. Thus Cummings' reward offers did not include the famous phrase "dead or alive." Obviously the AG and his FBI Director could not have disagreed more on this issue.

For a two-month period, Dillinger was not known to have committed a bank robbery. Witnesses placed him at a couple of robberies but other evidence about the fugitive's whereabouts around those times draws these reports into question. Of course he may have committed one or more robberies during which the terrified witnesses were so shaken up they focused on the deadly machinegun barrels instead of the desperadoes faces. All we know for certain is this was the longest time period during which no confirmed robberies were reported.[48]

WHICH BANK ROBBERIES?

Van Meter and Dillinger had met in prison. Van Meter's first conviction was for car theft in Aurora, Illinois, and a year later he was convicted of a train robbery in Gary, Indiana. In both cases he was sentenced to reformatories, but in Indiana he was removed to the more hardcore Michigan City Prison just like Dillinger. Here they met and plotted their war on society. Van Meter was paroled four days before Dillinger by Indiana Governor McNutt's Parole Board. From then on the two partnered in bank robberies until the gang vacationed at the Little Bohemia resort. After escaping the FBI raid the two fugitives remained in contact but it is unclear whether they committed any more robberies together.

During the next three months Dillinger cannot be definitively linked to any robbery, but he never went that long between heists before. In contrast Van Meter clearly remained active. Five days after escaping from the Little Bohemia FBI raid, Van Meter led four men in a $6,900 robbery of the Villa Park Trust and Savings Bank in Villa Park, just west of Chicago. This robbery went without incident, but a week later his gang robbed the Fostoria, Ohio First National Bank of $13,990. It was a terribly bloody affair. This led local police to conclude it must have been Dillinger, but their conclusion was based on ignorance about the various bank robbers' modus operandies. Wanton shooting like this one was actually the trademark of Baby Face Nelson not Dillinger. In addition, the victims to the robbery were divided about whether or not it was Dillinger they saw. Thus this robbery is a textbook example of how difficult it is to determine which crime each desperado was guilty of.

The unique layout of the bank entrances caused the robbers to take unusual actions. The bank's main entrance was situated in a building down a hallway lined with retail shop entrances on both sides like a mini-mall. These stores also had front entrances facing the side streets on both sides of the building. Near closing time three men entered the street entrance of the Orwig Drug Store. Their topcoats were slung over their arms covering two machineguns, an automatic pistol, and muslin sacks to carry their loot. When the trio reached the bank lobby, the two machinegunners pulled out their weapons and yelled "Stick 'em up!" as they fired bullets over the cashiers' heads. They ordered the seven employees and six customers to line up in front of the bank counters. The Bank President got real close to the face of one machinegunner. Because the President was a little slow in lining up the robber grabbed his apparel as he forcibly shoved him into the lineup tearing his shirt.

A bizarre scene occurred right after the robbers' entered and let go their spurt of gunfire. A bank VP was working at his desk on the mezzanine-floor which had a large opening overlooking the bank below. He walked over to the edge of the balcony and looked down to see what was causing the percussive explosions. A bandit with a machinegun ordered him to come down, but he replied "No thanks" as he returned to his desk. He appears to have gone into a state of frozen denial because he sat there without attempting to call police. None of the three gunmen fired warning shots upstairs or went up to bring him down, making this one of the most unusual robbery interactions in history.

Just before the bandits entered, a cashier had left her teller's window to go to the back of the bank. When she heard the gunfire she ran out the bank's back door to the police station to notify the elderly Police Chief that the robbery was in progress. The 69-year-old Chief and a patrolman ran into the bank's main hallway via the O. C. Harding Jewelry Store. One desperado saw them, rested his machinegun on the bank President's shoulder, and fired at the two officers who desperately tried to get into the elevator, but it was stopped up on the second floor so they could not get the doors open. Trapped in the open hallway both lawmen returned fire as they dashed back into the jewelry store, but a bullet hit the Chief. It crushed a rib and went through a lung causing him to collapse into a chair. He ordered the patrolman to go to the station and bring a riot gun. The Chief was rushed to the hospital where he was listed in critical condition and died.

When the two or three gang members in the double-parked car at the bank's side entrance heard the gunfire, they sprayed machinegun fire all around to discourage any citizens or approaching lawmen from joining the battle. Three civilians were hit. A retired policeman was shot through the leg; a farmer received a serious back wound; and a bystander was hit in the foot. A number of people sustained bullet scratches and others had clothing pierced. There were many near misses as shaken people after the robbery proudly showed where the bullet holes were and where they had been when they penetrated. Some people had just stepped out of what became the line of fire. Bullets hit buildings, crashed through windows into offices, and punctured cars and tires up to a block away. At least three people took up protective cover and fired back at the shooters' car. More than 150 shots were exchanged outside. Inside the bank building up to 50 shots were fired. A cashier was hit in the back, but the bullet was partially deflected by a suspender buckle so its penetration stopped about one inch deep.

When the robbers had collected the loot they kidnapped two employees as hostages, a female bookkeeper and a male assistant cashier. The kidnappers first started walking the hostages down the main front hallway but they saw a crowd had assembled outside the building's entrance door. They returned to the bank lobby and left through the drug store and its outside exit door where their escape car idled. The two hostages were forced to stand on opposite running boards. The man stood on the passenger side with a machinegun rammed into his belly. The driver held the girl's wrist tightly inside the car as he prepared to pull out. A local sign painter with a sawed-off shotgun had taken an advantageous position against the banditos car. He planned to hit all the robbers when they got in it but he knew he would have hit the human shields too so he stood helplessly by as they took off.

Almost 150 trains came through Fostoria daily and they blocked all but one escape road that had no tracks. This was in a northwesterly direction and was the one the bandits used for their getaway. The kidnappers dumped roofing nails out a back window to deter pursuit and reached speeds of 70 mph as the two human shields desperately tried to hang on to the door posts. Two miles outside of town the car slowed to almost a stop and the two captives were ordered to jump. The pair dusted themselves off and were taken to town by a passing cattle truck. The 20-year-old girl was hysterical, but the 40-year-old man contained his emotions. He appeared to handle the situation much better, but soon afterward he died of natural causes. Townsfolk always believed the traumatic horror of the experience contributed to his early death as a relatively young man.[49]

The eyewitnesses in the bank robbery were divided about whether or not it was Dillinger. He was identified as one of the two machinegun desperadoes inside the bank by the two hostages and an assistant cashier who was threatened by the bandits. The two kidnappees agreed with the cashier's conclusion, "It was Dillinger without a question. He had red hair, but no mustache." In contrast, Bank President Emerine, who was one of the victims lined against the wall by the man thought to be Dillinger and many other witnesses said none of the bandits resembled the fugitive. From about the time of this robbery for the next two months, half a dozen Dillinger look-alikes were arrested or almost shot by overzealous police.[50]

This robbery demonstrates just how persistent myths can be even when people personally know better. Reminiscing decades later were two eyewitnesses who were outside the bank to this robbery-kidnapping. Amazingly both spontaneously remembered what a considerate robber Dillinger was despite what they had seen that day and how much their fellow townspeople had suffered. Fostoria historian Paul Krupp was an objective news reporter of events as they occurred, but he later penned these fabricated impressions about the past. He wrote, "Dillinger was never a vicious killer, as opposed to some of his gang members. Many times he averted killings by members of the gang. Whenever his associates did kill during holdups, Dillinger was reported to have said, 'Why did you do that?' Dillinger often bragged that he could rob a bank without harming anyone. He was always pleasant to the teller and cashiers when asking them to hand over all the money." A local resident who was 16 years old at the time later told a reporter, "He was not a bad guy. He never seemed to be trying to kill somebody." He said this despite his personal loss. That day his band had parked and was walking toward the bank while the robbery was in progress. They were there to pick up their drummer after work. He was the bank's assistant cashier who was kidnapped as a shield and died soon after the ordeal, possibly because of the extreme stress.[51]

Two months after the bloody Fostoria, Ohio bank robbery, four bandits heisted the Merchants National Bank in South Bend, Indiana. It is possible that Van Meter was joined by Dillinger, who was identified by three witnesses, and maybe also Nelson because the gang's wanton violence increased. This and the previous robbery were committed by the same gang because the same license plates were used on the getaway car in both, but again the eyewitness reports about Dillinger's involvement are conflicting.

As the robbers entered the bank, the leader identified as Dillinger fired several shots from a pistol into the ceiling. The other two robbers were carrying machineguns. Then as they were leaving with $29,890, one desperado needlessly shot a bank VP in the hip and a cashier in his leg. Out on the sidewalk the trio shoved its way through cowering pedestrians. A traffic policeman at the nearby intersection started firing his pistol but he was killed by a spray of machinegun fire. This same shooter then sprayed the cars and pedestrians in the intersection. A motorist sitting terrorized in his stopped car was shot in the eye, and a metal manufacturer walking by was shot in the abdomen. He was reported near death at the hospital in the last available report. A number of other innocent citizens said they had terrifying close brushes with bullets whizzing by them as they walked, or bullets bursting into their cars.

The robbers finally got into their waiting idling getaway car in front. As it roared from the curb, a patrol car with two officers took pursuit raking the desperadoes with bullets and shattering their back window. The robbers returned a fierce attack of their own and escaped. One of the two pursuing patrolmen said he had shot the getaway driver who had slumped over in his seat, and then his companion in the passenger seat helped the driver move over while he took control of the wheel. The patrolman said definitely that the second driver was Dillinger, but this identification is brought into serious question by the following information.

After the desperadoes escaped the patrolmen tracked the sightings of the gang but their route became bizarre. The fugitives' course makes no sense no matter where the robbers' home base was, and if it was Dillinger it is even harder to understand because their car veered away from Chicago where the gang had doctors on call ready to treat them. Chicago was less than 100 miles from the robbery in South Bend, but half way between the two cities at the southern tip of Lake Michigan, with Chicago laying to the north, the robbers instead turned south. They drove 70 miles to a spot where they had previously parked another car about two-and-a-half miles north of Goodland, Indiana. They switched vehicles which was observed by several boys. These boys saw four men, whereas some bank-robbery witnesses thought there were two or three shooters, waiting in the getaway car in addition to the three who went into the bank. The abandoned car was bullet-riddled and had a blood-stained front seat. The boys said two of the banditos were obviously wounded and the four headed west toward the Illinois state line in the other vehicle. However at some point the two wounded men had to have acquired a separate car because they reversed direction and headed northeast 125 miles to North Webster, Indiana. It is impossible to make sense of wounded men acting like this especially if it was Dillinger's gang. They first went southwest instead of northwest to Chicago and then backtracked to within 50 miles southeast of the robbery site where they started from. From the robbery scene it would have been less than a two-hour drive to Chicago, but after the noonish robbery the two wounded robbers took this circuitous route of over 12 hours to arrive at their destination after midnight on a Sunday morning when every doctor's office in the small town was closed.[52]

Dr. Leslie Laird was asleep in his home on the main street when he was awoken by pounding on his door and a man calling out for a doctor. The doctor described his experience: "I went to the door and the man said a friend of his was waiting at my office, a block down the street, and wanted me to dress a cut on his arm. He said they had been in an auto accident. I got dressed and went with the man. I saw that his companion had been shot twice in the left arm, below one elbow. They forced me to treat the wounds as a precaution against tetanus, and after I had dressed them the man who was not injured asked for some cocaine. I told him I didn't have any cocaine, and that is the last thing I remember until about an hour later, when I came to and found that I had a gash on the back of my head and a bruise on my forehead. Apparently they struck me with the butts of their guns. I tried to telephone the sheriff but couldn't get the operator. The phone was dead, so I went to the restaurant across the street." The thugs had cut the phone wire.[53]

The Kosciusko County Sheriff went to the doctor's office to find it ransacked by the criminal patients in an apparent search for narcotics. The robbers had taken bandages and medical equipment with them. As an aside, none of Dillinger's gang was ever associated with illegal drugs which only a small percentage of the population used back then as America was an alcohol-consuming culture. In addition after their deaths Dillinger and his associates were autopsied and no evidence of drug use was found for any of them. Dr. Laird was emphatic that neither man fit the description of Dillinger or looked like his photographs. In fact they did not fit any of the available photographs of Dillinger gangsters. In comparing the two eyewitness reports, the patrolman saw the desperado he believed to be Dillinger only at a distance while in a gunfire-filled pursuit, whereas the doctor was able to study the two patients faces up close for half an hour.[54]

Information about the two abandoned getaway cars makes this case even more confusing. The getaway car from the South Bend bank robbery had no license plates. In contrast the second car that the four switched into at Goodland was found later the next day in Columbus, Ohio about 275 miles southwest in the opposite direction from Chicago. The stolen plates on it had also been used in the Fostoria, Ohio bank robbery two months earlier. This connection between the two robberies would have been extremely helpful information if there were absolute IDs of who participated in either one of the robberies, but much question remains about who the shooters were in both.

For Dillinger and his associates the traveling south and east away from Chicago after the South Bend robbery make no sense. Van Meter was living in St. Paul, 400 miles further northwest from the heist than was Dillinger in Chicago, making his residence far further from where the bank robbers actually traveled. Based on witnesses at the Fostoria robbery, Van Meter was the more likely leader than Dillinger in these two robberies, and if either he or Dillinger was involved, it is probable that Baby Face Nelson joined because both robberies were viciously bloody affairs that were his trademark. Ironically South Bend police announced their prime suspect was Dillinger because of the ruthless spraying of machinegun bullets and the gang's dramatic getaways. This was a misinterpretation of the possible suspects' modus operandies. This brutality fit Nelson and dramatic getaways were a staple of all the robbers in this book and a key reason for each becoming Public Enemy Number 1. In addition these two crimes had a glaring characteristic not found in any other robberies attributed to either Dillinger or Van Meter. In both crimes two or three men sat in the idling getaway car prepared to spray the entire neighborhood. It is interesting to note that whatever criminal acts Dillinger was committing during the two months encompassing these two robberies, Chicago SAC Purvis expressed confidently in press interviews that the fugitive was already dead from the Little Bohemia raid.

THE DEVIL'S DISCIPLES

Two men made Dillinger's crime spree possible. Indiana Governor Paul McNutt manipulated his pardon with a false criminal record and undermined the state's prison policies allowing him to aid his gang to escape. Then shortly after Dillinger was extradited from Arizona to the Crown Point Jail in Indiana, corrupt Chicago lawyer Louis Piquett made an unsolicited visit to the well-healed bank robber's cell to offer his legal services. First he helped Dillinger escape by daring the lady Sheriff, and challenging the Judge, to keep the defendant housed there rather than in the penitentiary which allowed his client to escape with his alleged toy-gun. Then hours after Dillinger's escape attorney Piquett met with his fugitive client to hand over cash so he could hide out. Finally following Dillinger's flight from the FBI raid at the Little Bohemia Resort, Piquett arranged to harbor him and arrange for other people to supply his every need.

Piquett assigned the investigator who worked in his office to handle everything Dillinger wanted. The fugitive would telephone the investigator and tell him to meet privately at ever changing designated locations around the Windy City. The investigator passed messages and cash from the desperado and his gang members to their girlfriends. He also acted as the contact man between Dillinger and the other people Piquett arranged to harbor and assist his client.

A week after escaping from Little Bohemia, Dillinger telephoned the investigator and told him where and when to meet. At that time Dillinger told the investigator to have Piquett get hold of a reliable plastic surgeon to give him and Van Meter face lifts to change their appearance and to alter their fingerprints with acid. Piquett knew of two doctors who would operate on the fugitives, and he made the payoffs to them.

To hide Dillinger and care for him during his recovery from the surgery, Piquett chose acquaintance James Probasco, a 67-year-old man who had been arrested several times in the previous decade for receiving stolen goods but never convicted. Piquett had known him for 20 years and knew he was in bad need of money to keep his Howard Street saloon afloat after the repeal of Prohibition. Probasco lived alone in a home that was out of the way. The investigator made the arrangements for Dillinger to have the procedures performed there and then to live there until he recovered enough to again venture out in public. It took two weeks for Piquett to make the arrangements with the two doctors, and another two weeks for the investigator to set-up having the procedures performed.

Six days after Dillinger underwent the scalpel and acid application, Van Meter used the same doctors to try to conceal his identity. He had a facelift and also had a tattoo of an anchor, scroll, and the word "hope" on his left arm blanked out leaving a dark blue splotch on his skin. He dyed his naturally chestnut hair black. After the surgery, Van Meter convalesced at a friend's home in Calumet City and then resided in St. Paul with his girlfriend.[55]

For two weeks after his surgery, Dillinger stayed holed up at Probasco's house and then he started venturing out in public again. The facelift had altered his features slightly and removed a prominent scar, a mole from his forehead, and a dimple from his cheek. Dillinger also dyed his reddish-brown hair jet black, and had grown a small, carefully trimmed mustache also dyed black. He completed his simple disguise with wire-rimmed glasses. The fugitive introduced himself to people as Jim Lawrence, a Board of Trade clerk, who spent money freely if not lavishly. On one of his outings, Dillinger/Lawrence met Polly Hamilton Keele, a waitress at the S&S Café, and they became quite enthralled with each other.

Dillinger wanted to move out of Probasco's home and asked Polly if she knew of any accommodations. Polly had previously been one of the girls in a Gary, Indiana brothel and became close friends with the madam, Ana Cumpanas, who went by the name Anna Sage. Three weeks earlier Anna had found out that Immigration agents were investigating her status to determine if she should be deported to her native Rumania for prostitution convictions, so she moved from Gary to Chicago. Polly, who had earlier left prostitution to marry a Gary, Indiana policeman, had divorced him at the time her friend Anna moved and went to Chicago too. Polly knew Anna could use extra cash from a renter. Dillinger moved into Anna's apartment where her 23-year-old son from a former marriage also resided.

Anna's son, Steve Chiolak, later told Chicago police about their life together. Dillinger continued the nightlife pattern he had enjoyed before the surgery. His favorite evening out was at the movies, but the foursome also made the rounds of cafes, nightclubs, and dance clubs and had beer parties at home. Dillinger was fast with his wallet and paid all the bills. He had always acted inconspicuously when out in public and appeared to be comfortable when surrounded by many strangers. But the surgical procedures seemed to give him even more confidence as he started engaging in afternoon activities in view of even larger crowds. He started attending Chicago Cub's baseball games at Wrigley Field. Piquett accompanied the fugitive to at least one game but FBI records indicate no surveillance was placed on either Dillinger's attorney or the investigator who was the fugitive's gofer. Dillinger also liked visiting theme parks.

Steve declared he never had a suspicion that Lawrence was Dillinger, and there is no indication that his brothel-madam mother or Polly knew either. After Polly dated Dillinger for a few evenings, she moved into his room at Anna's, but she kept her hotel room paid in advance to maintain her independence. She was rarely seen visiting her hotel room during this period, but when she was, she was always in the company of a man with glasses and a black mustache. For the first three weeks of their courtship, Dillinger picked Polly up after work each evening. At this point he persuaded her to quit her job so they could spend more time together. He gave Polly a diamond ring and she gave him a ruby ring.

The foursome enjoyed a fun and easy life. But two weeks after Polly quit her job, Anna received an upsetting letter from the Immigration and Naturalization Service. It told the immigrant her appeals to remain in America were denied and a warrant for her deportation had been issued. The world of the 25-year U.S. resident was shattered. This is when she saw a picture of Dillinger in the newspaper and recognized he was her renter using the alias Lawrence. She quickly realized that her knowledge of the fugitive's whereabouts might be an effective bargaining chip to cut a deal with the Immigration Service to obtain citizenship and stay in the country. The next day she sought advice on how to proceed from her close friend Detective Sergeant Martin Zarkovich of East Chicago, Indiana. Years earlier the two had become friends. This was before he joined the force and while she was a prostitute in a brothel in that city. When the establishment's owner died she took over the operation until she moved to Gary nine miles away. Anna displayed photographs in her apartment of she and Zarkovich socializing together. His wife had divorced him 13 years previously and she later said it was because he was "too friendly" with the madam.

After Anna moved her brothel operation to Gary, Zarkovich entered the East Chicago police force. This was in the early Roaring '20s when East Chicago police and elected officials prided themselves by profiting from allowing the city to become one of the wettest spots in the nation and to feature wide-open brothels and casinos. In the next few years Zarkovich was indicted three times for corruption but he avoided conviction because the politicians and judges were in cahoots and rewarded him for helping keep the city wide open to liquor and vice by promoting him to Chief of Detectives. Then Zarkovich became a central figure in a large Federal Prohi sting. Following a seven-month undercover investigation the Prohis arrested 136 East Chicago residents. Heading the list were the Mayor who was a practicing physician, the Police Chief, and Chief of Detectives Zarkovich. These officials were charged with conspiracy to allow the manufacture of moonshine and the smuggling of legitimate liquor onto the shores of Lake Michigan from Canada. The Mayor was still under indictment three months later when the citizenry reelected him because a majority appreciated his efforts to keep a ready supply of booze available. Two months later the Mayor took the oath of office for his second term and the next day went on trial with his coconspirators. In the prosecutor's closing arguments he contended that East Chicago and its sister community of Indiana Harbor had long been in the grip of crooked officialdom. The Federal Jury found them guilty of conspiracy and they were given the maximum sentence of two years in prison. It turned out that the prosecutor could not have been more accurate about the corruption of local officialdom because after his release Zarkovich rejoined the force and quickly rose to his old rank of Sergeant Detective.[56]

In an incredible coincidence Anna's friend Zarkovich just happened to be the person who was most determined to bring down Dillinger. Six months earlier during an East Chicago bank robbery Dillinger had machinegunned to death Zarkovich's detective partner William O'Malley. At that scene O'Malley had stood outside the bank with his pistol drawn waiting for the desperadoes to come out, but when Dillinger walked out he was shielded by an innocent banker. The Detective was afraid of hitting the civilian so he stood motionless. This did not deter Dillinger who mowed him down. The killing of his lifelong friend and working partner caused Zarkovich to develop a burning obsession to get Dillinger. In order to devote full time searching for the fugitive, Zarkovich took a furlough with the consent of his superiors and for months paid his own expenses because departmental funds were short. This allowed him to focus his hunt based on the Lake County Grand Jury investigation of the escape of Dillinger from the Crown Point Jail in hopes of picking up the fugitive's trail. Zarkovich was invited to assist in the case and given free reign by his friend, State's Attorney Robert Estill, who along with Judge William Murray had great respect for the Detective's ability.

When Anna informed Zarkovich she knew where Dillinger was hiding out, the Detective's most fervent wish was answered. She explained that in return for turning over her information she wanted a deal with the Immigration Service to remain in the country. Zarkovich went to his superior, Captain Timothy O'Neil, to discuss how to handle the situation. Dillinger was in Chicago out of their jurisdiction, and the local police had no influence to help Anna with her deportation problem, so the two Detectives took her to a meeting with SAC Purvis and Inspector Cowley in a car on a secluded road to negotiate a mutually beneficial deal.

The FBI was under enormous pressure to get Public Enemy Number 1. In the three months since the Little Bohemia fiasco the agents' nationwide search for Dillinger had not yielded a single person who had sighted the fugitive, and Purvis had told the press that he was "convinced" that Dillinger was dead from wounds inflicted at the resort raid. These corrupt Detectives also wanted to cut themselves in on the deal by offering to let Purvis and the FBI take all the glory in return for their sharing the reward money with Anna whose only goal was citizenship. Purvis readily agreed because he needed the triumphant kill to help make up for his previous raid blunders. Inspector Cowley backed up his local SAC Purvis who with Cowley's approval promised to help Anna with her immigration problems and to permit the Detectives to join his raiding squad to qualify for the reward money. The Chicago police were not informed of the FBI's plans even though this was their jurisdiction.

Anna told the lawmen that Dillinger was staying at her apartment, and he was planning to take Polly and her to a movie the next evening. She said she would wear a bright orange dress to make it easier for agents to spot the trio on the sidewalk walking up to the theater. Amazingly Cowley, who headed the Dillinger investigation, did not put any surveillance on her apartment fearing it might scare the fugitive into fleeing. He put total trust in Anna coming through. This was a bad strategy. It would have failed if Public Enemy Number 1 decided to move on in the next 24 hours, which hunted fugitives often did, or Anna failed to come through out of fear or for any other reason. Besides agents could have raided the apartment with no risk of injury to civilians unlike their plan of trying to take him on a busy public street. As it turned out, Anna did telephone Purvis late the next afternoon that the trio would be walking to a nearby theater to see its evening feature.

A GANGSTER MOVIE BECOMES TOO REAL

The next evening Inspector Cowley and SAC Purvis along with 10 agents and East Chicago Police Captain O'Neil, Sergeant Zarkovich, and two detectives arrived at the Biograph Theater. Purvis sat in his car parked a few feet south of the theater. Cowley strategically posted the other 14 men to cover every theater exit, to line the sidewalk on both sides of the theater entryway, and to stand on the sidewalk across busy Lincoln Avenue to block off the three possible front entrance escape routes.

Soon Dillinger accompanied by two women walked up. The trio had come out of an alley that was a shortcut from the women's apartment. This alley was just three narrow two-story shops to the right of the theater. The lawmen assumed that would be the route Public Enemy Number 1 would use after the movie.

In addition to his simple disguise of hair and mustache dyed jet black and eyeglasses, that night Dillinger added a straw hat. He also had on a white silk shirt, a gray tie flocked in black, lightweight gray summer trousers, and white canvas shoes. He had no coat and the lawmen later said they saw no pistol bulge in his shirt or pants pockets, inside his belt lining, or at his ankles as he walked the sidewalk to and from the theater and his clothes brushed against his body. Every FBI agent and the four East Chicago detectives observed him carefully as he entered and left the theater because their lives depended on knowing what they were up against.

One of Dillinger's companions that night would forever be known as "the woman in red." Anna wore the bright orange dress so she would be easily recognized by agents, but the marquee's neon light altered it. Later she said, "That night when they got Dillinger, I was wearing an orange skirt and a white blouse. The dress may have looked red under the light, but it was more yellow than red. I still have it." Dillinger purchased tickets and the trio went inside to see *Manhattan Melody,* a crime melodrama featuring Clark Cable and William Powell along with Mickey Rooney in one of his early child performances.

That summer evening it was still around 100 degrees. Late in the film, all the men in black suits loitering around the theater began to concern the ticket cashier. She told the manager she thought there was going to be a holdup. He agreed and called the Sheffield Avenue Police Substation. Three Chicago patrolmen, two in street clothes because of the change in shifts, rushed over to the theater and questioned the men hanging around in suits. The agents flashed their federal badges and intimidated the patrolmen. The agents warned them not to interfere with their business and did not tell them that Public Enemy Number 1 was inside. Just then the two-hour entertainment feature concluded and the crowd starting emptying onto the sidewalk.

The two groups of lawmen surveyed all the audience members as they left the theater. Finally Dillinger and the two women came out. He had his hat and glasses on and was smoking a cigar. He seemed at ease. The trio turned left in the direction from which they had come. After the trio passed by the FBI agents standing in wait, they followed but walked faster to close in right behind him. The action follows in the words of SAC Purvis who related this story to reporters immediately after the confrontation. "I was standing in the entrance of the Goetz Country Club, a tavern just south of the theater. When he walked by, he gave me a piercing look. Just after he went by and was midway of the next building, a National Tea Company store, I raised my hand and gave the prearranged signal. [FBI reports say he lit a cigarette.] Dillinger went on, perhaps another dozen feet, and stepped down a curb to the mouth of an alley. My men, at least five or six, were closing in on him. I had thought it impossible he could have a weapon concealed and the plan was to seize him, pinion his arms, and make him a prisoner. However, the men were instructed to take no chances. Becoming suspicious, Dillinger whirled around toward the men closing in. He was facing, I believe, toward the dark alley when he reached for his pistol. And that was when the shots that killed him were fired. Four altogether were fired. Three took effect."[57]

Actually Dillinger was hit four times, his hat brim was pierced once, and two innocent women passersby were wounded. A 45-year-old woman walking into her residence next door to the theater was struck in the left leg, and a 27-year-old woman passerby was grazed on her left side. The agents had fired as the fugitive turned into the alley where they knew he was headed. If they had waited just one second longer until he had stepped fully into the alley, no civilians would have been in their line of fire.[58]

Purvis continued his narrative with a defense of his actions. After restating that Dillinger put up a fight, he painted himself as the brave special agent in charge who interceded to protect everyone. "He saw me give a signal to my men to close in. He became alarmed, reached into a belt and was drawing the .38 caliber pistol he carried concealed when two of the agents let him have it. Dillinger was lying prone before he was able to get the gun out and I took it from him." Purvis sole purpose in talking to the press was to make himself a hero. He did not even bother to mention that two innocent women had been wounded or how they were faring because their bloody injuries would have stained, and drawn attention away from, his valiant account.

The many eyewitnesses to the slaying gave accounts that were consistent with each other, but all were very different from the interview by Purvis. A number of witnesses had unhindered views. All said Dillinger was unaware of the agents approaching him from behind and they saw the fugitive make no threatening gesture towards them. No witness saw Purvis or any other agent reach down and take a gun from Dillinger's hand or belt.

Anna Sage later testified in Federal Court about the moment of the shooting. Her testimony was similar to the eyewitness' statements and very different from Purvis'. She told the Judge, "When the picture was over the three of us walked out. Dillinger was between us. Polly and I each took one of his arms. [As we passed the lawmen] I saw Mr. Purvis from the corner of my eye. He was coming toward us. I saw Zarkovich. I thought: 'Now they are going to arrest him, and I stepped aside. In the same second I heard shots. There was Dillinger on the sidewalk, dead." She testified she clung to Dillinger's arm until a split second before he was shot to death and confirmed Dillinger had no chance to react. She also testified that on that 100-degree evening, "Dillinger had no coat on. I never saw him carry a gun [that night]." All the gunfire came from behind so Anna had no idea who did the shooting.[59]

In piecing together what really happened at the Biograph that night, Anna's testimony, the eyewitnesses' statements, and the agents' internal reports all said the lawmen waited until Dillinger passed them before they quickly walked up behind him to blow him away. Chicago homicide detectives pointed out that powder burns surrounding Dillinger's fatal head wound meant the shooter had to be within a couple feet behind the fugitive when he fired. The autopsy added final confirmation to all these statements. Coroner's Physician J. J. Kearns found three of the four Dillinger wounds were minor with two grazing him and the third tearing a "superficial" hole. It was the first bullet that instantly staggered him and was fatal. This one struck him directly from behind in the back of the neck, smashed a vertebra, tore through the spinal cord, cut through the lower part of the brain, severed two sets of arteries and veins, and passed out through the right eye. Dillinger was unaware he was hit because it was immediately lights out. From the moment Dillinger was shot he was paralyzed and brain-dead which explains why no witness saw Dillinger have any reaction as he fell forward. No bullet hit him from the front which would have been the case if he had turned to fire. Thus this mass of evidence all puts the lie to Purvis' claims, both in his interview and later in his book, that the shootings were justified because Dillinger reached for a gun and turned to use it on them.

This overwhelming evidence also puts the lie to another Purvis claim, the one that he took a gun away as Dillinger tried to pull it out. Dillinger's body did not have a weapon in the clothing when it arrived at the Coroner's. Yet no one at the scene saw Dillinger attempt to pull a gun nor see anyone else reach over to take a gun from the body. This makes it doubtful that Dillinger was packing that night. Even Purvis' statement at the interview about a gun is suspect. Purvis said, "He saw me give a signal to my men to close in. He became alarmed, reached into a *belt* and was drawing the .38-caliber pistol he carried *concealed* when two the agents let him have it. Dillinger was lying prone before he was able to get the gun out and I took it from him." Purvis started the sentence by saying it was in "a belt" and later in the sentence added it was "concealed" as if he realized that having it in his belt would have made it exposed and his assassination team would have been criticized for not having seen it. Purvis' statement is ridiculous because if it was in his belt the entire gun would have been exposed, and if it was tucked inside his pants but over his belt the large handle would have been exposed in view of every lawman there.[60]

Purvis displayed a gun at his press conference, but he refused to turn it over to the Coroner or homicide detectives for examination even though this was a Chicago shooting case. The next day at the Coroner's Inquest the autopsy doctor presented his findings. SAC Purvis did not appear, but Inspector Cowley repeated his SAC's big lies of the evening before. Cowley testified under oath, "[Dillinger] was approached by one of the agents. He drew a gun and was shot and killed." It was clear that Hoover's official intimidated the Coroner because he was allowed to weave his story without interruption or questions. Despite the FBI's pride in covering the details, Cowley failed to present Dillinger's alleged gun at the inquest to prove that he was indeed a threat.[61]

The Inquest Jury quickly found that the unidentified FBI agent who had killed Dillinger acted in a "justifiable homicide." The Jury then concluded its ruling by heaping praise on the FBI that bore no relationship with reality because Inspector Cowley's perjured presentation was not questioned by the Coroner. "The government agents are to be highly commended for their efficient participation in the occurrence, as shown by the fact that there was no further loss of life in the capture of a man of this type." This respect for life statement by the Inquest Jury totally ignored the tragic fact that the FBI had wounded two innocent women passersby just hours before and they were still being treated in a hospital. Next it was FBI Director Hoover who perpetuated SAC Purvis' lies about Dillinger drawing a gun on the agents. The Director testified to this as fact under oath to Congress and then wrote this in his books.[62]

Both Hoover and *Chicago Tribune* publisher Colonel Robert McCormick were arch political conservatives, but after the Coroner's Inquest this newspaper wrote an in-depth scathing editorial about the FBI's unprofessional conduct in killing Dillinger. Among the numerous criticisms were, "Dillinger was shot instead of being seized. It cannot pass notice that two women also were shot and by mere good luck not seriously wounded or killed. … [Mr. Cowley] was granted a power of censorship and he refused to make the complete statements which a legal record of a man's death would require. For reasons of state a detailed explanation was withheld. The coroner and his jury, much impressed by the event and also by the authority of the federal agents, were satisfied with an incomplete record. … Mr. Purvis, controlling the information, used his position to censor even the legal proceedings required for an account in the case of death from other than natural causes and can be charged with suppressing information in order to enhance the prestige of the federal manhunters, cover up the defects of his contingent, glorify the Federal Department of Justice …."

In Purvis' interview with reporters after Dillinger's assassination, the SAC told a number of other serious lies to cover up his grossly inappropriate official actions. He falsely said the presence of the East Chicago, Indiana policemen at the scene was due partly to coincidence. In reality Purvis had brought in local police from another state who had no authority in this jurisdiction, while at the same time refusing to tell the three local patrolmen who arrived on the scene just before the assassination that Public Enemy Number 1 was inside. One of these local lawmen told reporters that Purvis' failure to inform them of what was happening came frighteningly close to costing him his life. The patrolman said that after the shooting was over one of the FBI agents said to him that he was a very lucky man. He quoted the agent's words, "When we got the signal you were close to

Dillinger. You looked like Dillinger and I was about to shoot you when the other fellows let loose and killed the right man."[63]

Purvis could not seem to mend his lying ways. Two years later his book *American Agent* added a new wrinkle to the Dillinger assassination. He claimed he started the action by yelling out "Stick 'em up, Johnny, we have you surrounded." Purvis never made this dramatic claim in his many press interviews, and it does not appear in any FBI memo by Purvis or any other agent present at the scene. No witness reported hearing it. On the contrary every witness expressed surprise and shock when bullets suddenly rang out on that quiet, peaceful evening. Purvis himself contradicted this claim in his interview right after the shooting with, "I raised my hand and gave the prearranged [silent] signal."

Official FBI reports have always stated that its agents fired all the shots that evening. They had to maintain this position for two reasons - Hoover and Purvis wanted all the credit for the killing, and the East Chicago, Indiana detectives at the scene had no law-enforcement authority in another town let alone another state. However Chicago police detectives and newspaper investigative reporters always doubted these FBI reports. They steadfastly expressed the belief that East Chicago Sergeant Zarkovich fired the fatal shot. Unfortunately they never revealed the reason for their confidence, but they lived just 20 miles north of East Chicago along Lake Michigan so it was easy for them to talk to those detectives who were witnesses at the scene about what actually happened that night.

It is noteworthy that when AG Cummings arrived in Chicago the day after the shooting, he praised SAC Purvis' leadership and immediately told the reporters, "And I extend my congratulations to Captain Timothy O'Neil, Sergeant Zarkovich, and other members of the police force of East Chicago for their cooperation and friendly assistance." In addition Hoover, who never shared credit with anyone no matter how deserving, did send identical letters of commendation and thanks to East Chicago Captain O'Neil and Sergeant Zarkovich that ended with expressions of "highest esteem and best regards." While it is possible both the AG and the Director were simply complementing the local police for locating Dillinger's whereabouts, both Hoover and Purvis continued to maintain the FBI located Dillinger through their agency's great detective work.[64]

About three-quarters of a century later the 38-caliber service revolvers of Zarkovich and Captain O'Neil were sold at separate auctions. They were billed as the weapons that fired two of the bullets that killed Dillinger. While this is certainly an interesting development, no specific evidence was provided at the auctions that proved that one or both East Chicago detectives shot Public Enemy Number 1 that day. If either indeed fired the fatal shot, it means every FBI agent missed the fugitive's vitals from very close range due to Hoover's failure to institute marksmanship training and courses in arrest, assault, and combat tactics.[65]

Immediately after the killing, dozens of squads of Chicago policemen rushed to the scene. Purvis continued his lies by saying the local police had been kept in the dark about the presence of Dillinger in the city because the fugitive had only been there a few days. In reality Chicago police had been on the hunt for Dillinger because they wanted to take him alive and persuade him to talk about his crimes and his associates while the Director and Purvis intended to assassinate him.

With the FBI having the advantages of overpowering numbers and surprise, it certainly seems like it would have been easy for agents to have taken him alive. After all within the previous 10 months both the Dayton, Ohio and Tucson, Arizona police had seized Dillinger without resistance or the firing of a single shot. The fugitive always surrendered to an overwhelming police presence. Besides he almost certainly had no weapon that evening.

Both AG Cummings and his underling Hoover had been under tremendous pressure from the press to stop Public Enemy Number 1 so they were overjoyed when they were notified of the assassination. The Director rushed to his office and told the assembled reporters, "This does not mean the end of the Dillinger case. Anyone who ever gave any of the Dillinger mob any aid, comfort, or assistance will be vigorously prosecuted." He described Baby Face Nelson as a "rat," and mentioned targeting Homer Van Meter. Agents could now focus on getting these two fugitives.[66]

The AG smiled in elation as he told reporters it was "gratifying as well as reassuring. The search for Dillinger has never been relaxed for a moment. He has escaped capture on several occasions by the narrowest of margins." Later that day the AG stepped off a train in Chicago as he traveled from Washington to Hawaii. He was welcomed by Purvis at the train station and they had dinner together. The AG continued his praise of Purvis and the FBI but he also said the exact opposite of what the papers were reporting - "What has happened is an illustration of the success that can be accomplished by concentrated effort and fullest coordination between federal and local authorities. To bring about that sort of friendly and helpful cooperation is one of the cardinal points in our movement to suppress crime."[67]

When Dillinger was assassinated the country was fearful the economy might collapse and frightened by the many cultural changes going on. AG Cummings used the killing as evidence the administration could make the country safe from public enemies and to rally support for the New Deal agenda. While the AG was trying to unify the country, Hoover hyped the slaying to start building public confidence in his personal leadership of the FBI.

Purvis' many lies glorifying his actions with reporters led the newspapers to turn the gallant G-Man commander into a national hero. Purvis was now more famous than the Director. Good publicity was the counterbalance desperately needed for the FBI's sorry raid performances so Hoover traipsed his new hero before the country. Inspector Cowley stood for photos with Purvis and the AG at the railroad station. The next day Purvis flew to Washington for photo ops with the Director.

All the time Hoover was seething at his SAC's public egotism and was planning to banish him from further contact with the press. Cowley had always scrupulously avoided the press so no one was aware he was over Purvis in heading the Dillinger detail. Cowley continued to work with this kind of anonymity, and Hoover ordered his Inspector to make sure that Purvis never be involved with another high-profile case. However, fate sometimes steps in to overturn the best laid plans.

Three days after Dillinger was killed, his sister gave him a "decent Christian funeral" at her home. The ceremony began with a quartet singing, "God Will Take Care of Him." The minister's talk did not include mention of the desperado's character or career. The funeral was planned by relatives as a quiet and respectable affair, but the presence of thousands of curiosity seekers, photographers, and planes overhead turned it into a spectacle. As 40 policeman watched, the throng braved the scorching sun at the funeral service at his sister's home and then stood in a downpour of rain for the burial at the cemetery. The killer's 70-year old father, John Dillinger Sr., had been much troubled by his son's crimes, but with a shaking hand he wiped the moisture from his eyes.

Just days later Dillinger's father opened a vaudeville act between movie presentations at an Indianapolis theater. The poster-board signs on the sidewalk in front contained bigger print than for the film on the marquee. They proclaimed, "ON STAGE IN PERSON! JOHN DILLINGER SR. AND MEMBERS OF HIS FAMILY." The presentation included Dillinger's brother, sister, half-sister, and nephew. It may not have been exciting entertainment but at least a banner across the theater's entrance advertised it was "Healthfully Cool."

Dillinger's elderly father soon had another job capitalizing on his son's notoriety that would last two years. He was employed by his son's former victim, the owner of the Little Bohemia Resort, and his family who had been held captive while the gang partied. Many residents in that area of the country saw pictures in their newspapers of the badly shot-up lodge and made a trip to visit the scene. The owner left the bullet holes untouched and preserved the shattered windows by putting another pane of glass behind each one. The former lounge absorbed most of the FBI's assault fire and it looked like a sieve with upwards of 100 bullet holes. It was named the Bullet Room and converted into a little museum exhibiting the belongings the fleeing desperadoes left behind in their suitcases. Displayed were coats, shirts, neckties, toothbrushes, and a tin of laxatives. Dillinger's father became the museum's curator who answered visitors' questions about his son and their family life.

BETRAYED BY THE DIRECTOR

Returning to the Dillinger shooting scene, both women companions were horrified by the unexpected gunfire right behind their ears and Dillinger falling dead in front of them. The two women ran down the alley to Anna Sage's apartment. Then Polly raced to the restaurant to say goodbye, spent the night in her hotel room, and left town the next day to stay with her parents in Fargo, South Dakota. Polly's identity came out because her ruby ring was on Dillinger's finger and her photo was in the back of his watch, but she never surfaced publicly after that. Anna said she changed her orange-yellow dress and then joined the crowd in front of the theater. Its possible she actually dumped over a Lake Michigan pier a machinegun, pistol, and bulletproof vest that Dillinger may have kept locked in a closet. These items were found two days later by a swimmer, but they were never confirmed to be the slain desperado's.

SAC Purvis, FBI Director Hoover, and even the East Chicago detectives kept silent for a long time about who the $15,000 in rewards for the capture or death of Dillinger was going to and who the informant was, but the *Chicago Tribune* got the full story except for Anna's name the day after the shooting from someone in the East Chicago PD. This source reported its detectives had located Dillinger and were to receive the reward. The paper had everything but Anna's name and it soon got that although the FBI continued to refuse comment. Less than three months later AG Cummings authorized a $5,000 reward to be split between Midwest Detectives O'Neil and Zarkovich. The AG said he was withholding the remaining $5,000 because Dillinger had been killed instead of captured. In reality he quietly gave the rest to informant Anna. The $5,000 offered by Indiana and Minnesota were given to Dillinger's sweetheart Polly Hamilton Keele who was never aware she was living with Dillinger or that he was being led into a trap until the FBI's guns barked.[68]

A month after Dillinger's killing the Immigration Service ordered Anna's deportation to her native Rumania and she appealed. She had been convicted four times for operating a brothel. She had her political clients get the Indiana governor to pardon the most recent two convictions in Gary, but she had forgotten about the earlier two in East Chicago and Indiana Harbor. It was these two that Immigration was using as its basis for deporting her.

The Director made no effort to keep the pledge to assist her to stay in America that had been made by both his SAC and Inspector. The FBI did quickly make an official request for a stay in the deportation order as long as they might need her testimony, but then the FBI notified Immigration officials it was "no longer interested in the case." She appeared before a Federal Judge who listened to whether or not the FBI had failed to keep its promises to her. This was the first time she had spoken in public and the world learned of the FBI's broken promise to her. She also testified that the two high-ranking FBI agents who led the assassination had promised her that Dillinger would not be killed.

Two of Anna's four brothel convictions had been pardoned by former Indiana Governor Harry Leslie. After her testimony she publicly appealed to current Governor Paul McNutt for a pardon on the other two convictions. He refused to pardon her for minor offenses even though she had put her life in jeopardy to bring down the country's Public Enemy Number 1. What made the Governor's decision so disgusting was that he single-handedly made possible Dillinger's bloody crime wave by presenting false documents about him to his appointed Parole Board and by undermining professionalism in the staff at the state prison.

A Federal Judge heard Anna's appeal of the deportation order, and Purvis to his credit told the truth under oath in contradiction to the Director. Purvis testified he indeed made the promise to her and fulfilled it by recommending that the deportation proceedings against her be dropped, but his superiors, meaning Hoover, would not accept his recommendation. He said, "She did furnish the information which led to Dillinger's capture, and I for one am not ungrateful, and I sincerely believe that some step should be taken to prevent her deportation. Had she not furnished the information it is entirely possible that many other brave officers, and even private citizens, employees of banks and others, might have been killed before Dillinger could have been apprehended. I did inform her that I would bring to the attention of the appropriate officials in Washington her actions in aiding the government in this respect, and that I would recommend that some step be taken to prevent her deportation if possible." He also said, "I believe personally that she ought to be allowed to stay in this country because she performed a service that ranked among the highest needed by the country at that time." The Judge also had East Chicago Sergeant Martin Zarkovich testify on her behalf about hearing the FBI agents' promise to Anna. Hoover insisted in Washington that no deal had been made to permit her to remain for betraying Dillinger, and the Director kept Inspector Cowley unavailable so he would not have to corroborate under oath the truthful testimony of Purvis and Zarkovich.[69]

After lawmen Purvis and Zarkovich gave their glowing defenses of the heroic immigrant woman wrongfully denied in her fight for citizenship, Anna publicly appealed to Governor McNutt to pardon her on the two old brothel convictions to permanently put an end to the Immigration deportation proceedings against her. McNutt refused her request. The Governor may have been guilty of improperly pardoning numerous vicious criminals including Dillinger and of destroying Indiana's professional prison system allowing many more to escape, but he did not want on his political resume that he pardoned a small-time brothel operator no matter how justified his actions. McNutt may have been a liberal New Deal Democratic politician while Hoover was an arch conservative law-and-order Republican, but the two men combined to ruin Anna's life because both public officials were devoid of any sense of ethics, concern for justice, or interest in making the public safer. The only thing McNutt and Hoover cared about was their public image no matter how many innocent people they hurt in striving to make themselves look good.

When Governor McNutt abandoned the immigrant woman who had made such a valiant contribution to her adopted county, the deportation hearing resumed. After hearing all the testimony, Federal Judge John P. Barnes declared "nowhere in any statute is authority for the FBI to tie the hands of the Secretary of Labor. … Assuming what you say is true, the court would not be justified in overturning the judgment of the Secretary of Labor." Six months later the U.S. Circuit Court of Appeals upheld the Judge's ruling by saying, "Nowhere is there any authority given to a public official to grant a favor to an alien who seeks privileges in the face of the statutes." With this she abandoned her fight to escape deportation as an undesirable alien. Before boarding the train to leave the country she told the press she had been in the country for 27 years since she was 17 years old. She had no living relatives in her native Romania and had no idea what she would do when she got there. She concluded, "I wish they had only let me stay. That was what I wanted … not the $5,000 reward I got for helping get rid of Dillinger."[70]

In Anna's case Hoover violated a basic tenant of American jurisprudence. The goal is to convict the person most responsible for a crime occurring. For example in a contract-murder the prosecutor tries to convict the person who instigated or paid for it. To accomplish this federal and local prosecutors regularly let the actual murderer go free in return for state's-witness testimony that is needed to convict the initiator. In Anna's situation, she had brought down the country's most dangerous killer, put herself in harms way, and potentially saved many lives. But Hoover would not free her even though her brothel crimes were victimless, meaning both parties involved were consenting, and magnitudes less egregious to society than a murder.

A year and a half after Anna's deportation, Hoover repeated his lies about her in his new book *Persons in Hiding* by saying, "Anna Sage sold out Dillinger for $5,000, which was paid her. She was made no other offers of reward of any kind." When a cop lies, justice is denied in that case, but it also undermines the whole system because people lose their trust in the police and become reticent to assist or cooperate with law enforcers. This was the result of Hoover's breaking Anna's sentencing deal promised by his top officials. This highly-publicized episode laid bare to the underworld and the nation that Hoover was a dishonorable cop who did not keep his word. Thus not a single organized-crime figure turned state's evidence for the FBI in the next quarter century as this terrible crime scourge expanded unabated across the nation. Interestingly the first gangster to turn state's witness after Anna's case was Mafioso Joe Valachi. However he did not flip for Hoover's FBI but instead sought out U.S. AG Robert Kennedy for a deal he could rely on. Valachi then gave first-hand eyewitness testimony in nationally televised Senate hearings about the existence of the powerful Mafia gangs in many major cities and revealed to the public for the first time the blood oath that initiated members take. Exposure of this reality did not deter the Director's continued lies that no such thing as the Mafia existed in the U.S., nor his ongoing refusal to prosecute organized-crime gang members. What a horrible price America paid in so many ways for having Hoover as the Director of America's secret police force.

Hoover tried to mitigate the publicity from Anna's truthful assertions about the FBI breaking its promised sentencing deal. The Director went to great expense and effort to keep Anna out of sight and silent about his deal-breaking treachery until the Immigration and Naturalization Service was prepared to deport her. Hoover dispatched top aide Inspector Cowley to keep her hidden from the world during the two months her appeal worked its way through the Federal Courts. Cowley held her captive under false pretenses. He scared her by claiming that Baby Face Nelson had vowed to kill her and was offering a reward to obtain the secret of her hiding place, but he magnanimously extended FBI protection to repay her for services rendered in leading them to Dillinger. Most of the time Cowley babysat her in a Detroit hotel room and then he took her to visit her relatives in California. During this period the Director refused to acknowledge the requests of reporters for validation of the rumors that Sage was the Dillinger informant. Instead of fighting crime, Hoover had this top aide waste two months stifling the Constitutionally-protected free speech rights of a woman who had made such an important contribution to the country's crime-fighting enforcement and in the process likely saved Hoover's job.

It would have been easy for the Director to have requested the Immigration and Naturalization Service to drop the case against her for the valuable services she was contributing to the country. This course of action would have also eliminated wasting two months time of Inspector Cowley and the agents involved in squelching and babysitting Anna. But Hoover refused to keep his officials' promise because he found her morally repugnant. In his peculiar value system he was highly repulsed by promiscuous heterosexuals and he disparaged woman in general. These personal values having nothing to do with the law or justice led him to break his officials' promise to Anna that was not only inappropriate but a serious disservice to his country's interests. Hoover's values are documented in a case later that involves an informant who the Director found disgusting because he liked to chased women. As will be seen Hoover's unprofessional perverse response in that case created far more disastrous consequences for America than the ending of informants against organized-crime.

Hoover's stock in trade was the lie and the cover-up, and he did not care how many innocent citizens he hurt in the process or how badly he impacted their lives. For example, a week after the Little Bohemia fiasco, the FBI intimidated the Coroner's Jury to rule that civilian Eugene Boiseneau was accidentally killed by FBI agents "in the act of trying to apprehend the Dillinger gang." The FBI offered no monetary compensation to the family for its agents' wonton and unjustified slaughter of this innocent man riding home from the resort, not even funeral expenses. To make matters worse six months later the U.S. Controller General ruled the government could not pay the hospital expenses of three innocent civilians wounded by FBI agents in their hunt for Dillinger. These included the other two innocent men in the car with Boiseneau at the resort and one of the two women hit with a bullet near the Biograph Theater the night Dillinger was assassinated. The Director pressured the Controller General to avoid admitting the FBI errored by blasting away with gunfire at innocent civilians in both cases.[71]

A DETECTIVE IN TROUBLE AGAIN

Five years after Zarkovich participated in the Dillinger assassination, he was promoted again to East Chicago, Indiana Chief of Detectives and eight years later was appointed Chief of Police. After serving for four years, Zarkovich, the Mayor, and other high-ranking city and police officials were indicted by the Lake County Grand Jury with malfeasance and misfeasance in office for allowing the notorious Big House Casino to operate in East Chicago. This prosecution was a reflection of the national reform movement against wide-open illegal casinos as the U.S. Senate Kefauver Committee held hearings across the country that led to the shut down of almost every casino except those legally licensed in Nevada. In Lake County, Indiana a new Prosecutor was elected on a reform ticket against illegal gambling and prostitution. He soon permanently closed the Big House and went after the city and police officials who had protected its operation. A vicious legal battle developed between the idealistic Prosecutor and the totally corrupted and megalomaniac Lake County Criminal Court Judge. He used contempt actions to stifle the free speech of the Prosecutor and the Grand Jury and then he banned the Prosecutor from appearing in his court. The Indiana Supreme Court later slapped the Judge's wrists and prohibited such improper actions in the future.

In a dramatic scene in the courtroom the Prosecutor accused the Judge of recently taking a vacation with Zarkovich while he was under indictment for a case pending in the Judge's court. The Judge retorted, "I was not only with the Chief a couple of weeks ago, but I hope he will spend a couple of more weeks with me at my cottage in Eagle River, Wisconsin. Chief Zarkovich is a long time friend. I consider him the best and most upright policeman I have ever met. I would rather associate with him even though he is under indictment than with some of the fellows [the Prosecutor] has been with." While Zarkovich was under indictment, he was demoted from Police Chief to Captain of the Traffic Bureau. Even though the Judge quashed the indictment against Zarkovich by quoting legal authority he did not possess, the former Police Chief resigned two weeks later after serving 30 years on the East Chicago police force at age 56. In the election six months later, the voters returned the Judge to office again, but they defeated the law-and-order Prosecutor who had shut down the illegal Big House Casino.[72]

Incidentally, this was this same judge who 17 years earlier had blocked the prosecution of the Crown Point jailers who were charged with assisting Dillinger escape from the Crown Point Jail. It was also this Judge who had ruled that Dillinger could remain in the County Jail instead of being transferred to the State Prison by totally misquoting his authority under the law. This unlawful action made possible all of Dillinger's shootouts and killings that ensued.

DEFENDING THE INDEFENSIBLE

In the days after Dillinger's slaying, the FBI arrested his attorney's investigator and the two doctors who had performed the fugitive's plastic surgery. All three quickly confessed to assisting Dillinger and explained that the medical procedures were done at the home of James Probasco. That evening agents swooped in on his residence and scooped him up. They took him to the local FBI offices on the 19th floor of the Bankers' Building for interrogation. The next morning a man was walking through Rockery Court, the space between the Bankers' and Rockery Buildings. At that same moment the prisoner plunged 19 stories to his death splattering right beside the stunned pedestrian.

A Coroner's Inquest was held that afternoon. The mood of the questioning was dramatically different from the whitewash at the Dillinger inquest three days earlier. In that one the Coroner was clearly intimidated by the FBI agents and gave them free reign to testify as they wished. In marked contrast the Deputy Coroner assertively questioned FBI officials about the unusual circumstances of the death of the 67-year-old Probasco. Not mentioned at the hearing but simmering in the background were the accusations and rumors from recent Chicago cases about FBI agents violently interrogating prisoners.

For example three months before Probasco fell to his death, the FBI held a former Illinois legislator, John J. "Boss" McLaughlin, on a kidnapping charge and questioned him in these same conference rooms. The defendant told reporters that he had not told the agents anything despite a vicious beating and being dangled by his arms outside a 19-story window. He made the same charge in a Chicago Federal Court when he appeared at his hearing for extradition to St. Paul, Minnesota to face trial on the kidnapping charge. The defendant's wife also sent a telegram containing these accusations about outrageous FBI misconduct to Assistant AG Joseph Keenan in Washington. It is important to note that this charge of being dangled out the window came before rather than after Probasco's plunge to his death.

At the Probasco Inquest the official FBI storyline was that two agents had taken the elderly prisoner from the room they were holding him in for fingerprinting, returned him to the room, and left him alone for three minutes before he somehow flew out the window. The FBI testimony never explained why one of two did not remain with the unrestrained prisoner especially since they admitted two loaded shotguns were left leaning against a wall in plain sight. He could have easily used one to kill or subdue both agents on duty and escaped.

At Probasco's death inquest Inspector Cowley was the first witness. The suspicious Deputy Coroner came at him with tough and repeated questions about whether the FBI ever used the third degree in interrogations, and Cowley consistently denied such tactics were ever used. This was blatant perjury as FBI internal memos in other cases of that period reveal FBI Director Hoover personally ordered the use of these tactics on a case-by-case basis and numerous Chicago agents had carried them out.[73]

Then the Deputy Coroner started questioning what might have happened in that room just a few hours earlier to cause a prisoner's death. Since every FBI employee denied being with the defendant, no one could be sure so the discussion became speculative. Inspector Cowley dismissed the possibility of Probasco falling out accidentally because the window sill was three feet above the floor. On the other hand Cowley testified, "I found a chair up against the window sill, indicating he had stepped up on it to the window." Cowley said this was strong evidence of suicide, but he failed to explain how the chair would have helped. There were only two ways Probasco could have gone out the window of his own volition – head first or feet first. If he had dove out head first, the chair would have actually been an impediment that distanced him from the window meaning he would have had to generate much more forward thrust to make it out the opening. If he had gone out feet first, he would have had to stand on the chair, put one foot out the window, sat down on the sill, pulled the other foot out the window, and then pushed off. But he would have had no reason to stand on the chair because this would have raised his buttocks way above the level of the sill. From this raised position it would have been almost impossible for him to lower his bottom to the ankle level of the foot he was standing on so he could direct his free foot out the window and then try to sit on the window sill with his balancing foot now behind him. Such difficult acrobatics are especially inconceivable for an elderly man. It is clear Probasco did not use a chair in a suicide meaning that Cowley made up the chair prop thinking it would support his contention of suicide without first having thought through the full implications of taking this fabricated position.

Falsehoods often have the unintended consequence of leading the liar into taking a position that he then realizes he does not want to be in. This is what happened to Inspector Cowley and his agents who testified at this Coroner's inquest. Cowley first claimed the chair implied the prisoner committed suicide, but this put him and the other agents in a tenuous position. If the elderly man had given any indication that he might be suicidal or emotionally unbalanced in any way, the agents would have been culpable of depraved indifference by leaving him alone in a room near an open 19th-story window with loaded shotguns at hand. Thus Cowley immediately watered down the possibility of suicide by stating, "It does not seem likely he would have taken his life to escape 18 months imprisonment."[74]

One of the two agents who had been in the room just before Probasco went out the window was the next to testify. Agent R. D. Brown further weakened the FBI's suspicions about suicide by testifying that Probasco was downcast but did not seem on the verge of suicide.

However, it was the absence at the hearing of the second agent who had been with the prisoner just three minutes before his death that raised serious questions. Cowley's explanation for not having Agent Morris Chaffetz present was unsatisfactory and suspicious. The Inspector testified Agent Chaffetz was unavailable because he had other work to do that afternoon. But the FBI had no more serious responsibility under the law than trying to solve a suspicious death of a prisoner while in its agents' custody. This hiding of Chaffetz raised just two possibilities - the Agent had refused to perjure himself like the Inspector and Agent Brown did, or Agent Chaffetz was so distraught over having unintentionally killed a man by letting him drop out of a window that he was unable to testify. Questions about Agent Chaffetz's failure to appear are magnified by the Director's peculiar disciplinary action against him at that time. FBI internal memos state that Agents Brown and Chaffetz together left the defendant alone, but Hoover issued a two-week suspension for this infraction to just one, Agent Chaffetz. Not only did Hoover rarely suspend agents, but the Director did not take actions that would leave such blatant injustice in the official record. Thus it is all but certain that this suspension was punishment for Agent Chaffetz refusing to perjure himself at the Inquest like Inspector Cowley and Agent Brown did.

Agent Charles Winstead inserted another alleged fact into an internal FBI memo, but the way this information was handled further damages the claim that Probasco committed suicide. Agent Winstead's memo said that after he and other agents arrested Probasco, they searched his home and found a suicide note penned by the prisoner. This memo went on to say that Inspector Cowley therefore ordered the defendant watched all night while he remained alone in the conference room. If such a note had actually existed, it meant that the Inspector's direct orders were violated. In addition it was FBI custom to either attach this note to the report or at least quote it to make clear exactly what it said. In addition Inspector Cowley would have presented it at the Inquest to prove his case for suicide rather than suppress it and keep it secret. It is telling that only one agent mentioned such an important piece of evidence in his report and also that he failed to document what it said. Such major deviation from established and enforced policy reeks of an attempt to cover-up an involuntary manslaughter.

At the Inquest, the testimony of Inspector Cowley and Agent Brown presented no evidence that Probasco committed suicide or that he was suicidal. On the contrary their testimony made clear the two agents on duty abandoned all proper safeguards of holding a prisoner in an office including leaving him alone in a room with loaded shotguns. At the Inquest and in internal memos agents made inconsistent and incomplete statements about the incident and they clearly manufactured false evidence with the chair being at the window and the missing suicide note. The only conclusion that connects the facts contained in the agents' Inquest testimony and internal reports is that the two agents dangled the prisoner out the window trying to get him to cough up information about Dillinger and his gang that he did not possess. In the process agents lost their grip hold on him. Remember a prisoner in a different case claimed three months earlier that Chicago agents had dangled him by the arms out the very same window.

The Coroner's Inquest Jury returned a verdict of suicide because no evidence was presented to refute the agents' testimony. At Probasco's funeral three days later, his sister declared he was not despondent and did not kill himself. She also accused the arresting FBI agents of treating him roughly in front of his house. That very day the *Chicago Tribune's* editorial said, "The strange death of Probasco while in custody of federal agents needs a lot of explaining. The bad man is dead, but a great deal of suspicion lives after him."[75]

Two months after Probasco took his dive from the 19th floor, a similar accusation was made against FBI agents in another case. Hot Springs crime boss Dick Galatas filed in Federal Court a motion to suppress coerced confession statements he had made. This was the man who tried to help Frank Nash's wife by freeing her husband from FBI custody which led to the Kansas City Massacre. After fugitive Galatas was finally apprehended by agents in New Orleans, their internal reports to Headquarters state they badly beat him up because they were convinced he could solve the whole lawman slaughter case, but he actually knew nothing about the crime or who the participants were. Next the prisoner was flown to Chicago where agents chained him in the FBI's 19th-story offices where Probasco had taken his dive. Agents' reports to Headquarters said they administered a more vicious beating. Then Galatas said the threats seemed far too real. He asserted agents' warned him, "I'll use the necessary tactics to get what I want. … If you are found dead in the streets, the same as others were found, no one would ever make inquiries." Then he was drug to the open window and told, "You are a long way up and you won't bounce when you hit bottom." He did not accuse these agents of dangling him out the window. Agent reports to Headquarters from both New Orleans and Chicago confirmed a "vigorous physical interview" was used, but these reports were not available to the Judge.[76]

The agents' incriminating internal reports in this case were contained in the FBI's files for Galatas' involvement in the Kansas City Massacre. Its very possible that similar examples of vigilante agents' violent attacks against prisoners could exist in other cases' internal memos during this era. These may have yet to be researched by crime historians, or they could have been found but never connected with each other to show how extensive these practices were. Remember after Hoover's death his closest subordinates conspired in a massive cover-up by devoting two months to the shredding of the most damaging or incriminating files, those that were hidden from the rest of the FBI hierarchy in special locked rooms with very limited access.

PROSECUTING THE HARBORERS

When the investigator for Dillinger's attorney and the two doctors confessed to FBI agents that they had harbored the fugitive, all agreed to testify that Piquett was the ringleader in the plot to conceal Dillinger and Van Meter from FBI agents. All were hoping for a deal and the doctors wanted to retaliate against Piquett who had promised them $10,000 for the surgery but paid them just $3,000. Six months after Dillinger was assassinated, Piquett went on trial for harboring him. Piquett testified in his own defense with a string of lies. He maintained everything he had done was legal and proper for an attorney representing a client. He added he was trying to get the fugitive to surrender at the time he was killed. The Federal Jury found him innocent shocking every one who followed the case. Five months later, Piquett was tried for harboring Van Meter and the attorney could not use the defense that this killer was a client. This Federal Jury found Piquett guilty. He was sentenced to the maximum two years for harboring Van Meter and was later denied early parole.

Early in Piquett's career he had put himself through law school by working as a bartender. After passing the bar, he continued to pour drinks until notoriously corrupt Chicago Mayor "Big Bill" Thompson, who completely sold out his office to Prohibition gangster Al Capone, had Piquett appointed a city prosecutor. When Thompson left office, Piquett opened a criminal law practice. Four months after Piquett was convicted for harboring, the Chicago Bar Association disbarred him. After he was released from prison he returned to bartending.

Piquett's three associates who pled guilty and testified against him received lighter sentences. The doctor who performed the surgeries was sentenced to one day in the custody of the U.S. Marshal, but he was remanded to Leavenworth Penitentiary as a parole violator to finish serving 18 months of a previous term for a narcotic law violation. The doctor who assisted as anesthesiologist was given a suspended sentence. The two doctors had spent about eight months in jail while they were waiting to appear as witnesses. Later during World War II the anesthesiologist worked for the Army Medical Corps in the Pacific rising to the rank of major. A year after returning from the War he fatally shot himself in the right temple in his sister's home. His family said he had been "nervous and highly strung" since leaving the service.[77]

Dillinger's early girlfriend Billie Frechette served a two-year sentence for harboring. She later married and had children. Dillinger's last girlfriend Polly Hamilton married a Chicago man.

THE REST OF THE GANG

Returning to the night Dillinger was killed, Van Meter decided to blow town and drove with girlfriend Mickey Conforti from Chicago to St. Paul. In this case FBI Director Hoover's belief that women were often the key to locating male suspects proved to be true. Dillinger was fingered by a woman, and a month later Van Meter would be undone by a woman although inadvertently. It was Mickey's relatives who became suspicious of Van Meter's weary nature and reported their concerns to St. Paul police. Two weeks later the police investigation disclosed the fugitive's identity. An unidentified informant notified police of the fugitive's plans for that day. Police Chief Frank Cullen and three high-ranking officials sat in a car at a busy intersection near the center of St. Paul waiting for Van Meter to walk into a car dealership. The intersection was filled with motorists because University Avenue was the main route connecting the city to its twin, Minneapolis. Upon seeing the fugitive get out of his car and walk towards them, one officer leaped from the car with shotgun in hand and commanded him to surrender. Instead, Van Meter swiftly drew a pistol, shot twice, and ran across the street into an alley with the pursuing police shooting at him. At one point officers had to hold their fire to avoid striking a woman pedestrian who came between them. When the police entered the alley they could see it had a dead-end with Van Meter facing them. The fugitive started shooting again, and the police fired more than 50 shots from shotguns and machineguns. Van Meter was hit by more than a dozen slugs before falling down dead in the muddy alley. The St. Paul police said they intentionally did not invite the FBI to this gunfight, kind of as repayment for the FBI recently excluding the Chicago police from the assassination of Dillinger.[78]

Three of the convicts Dillinger helped break out of the Michigan City State Penitentiary in Indiana were convicted in Ohio for killing Sheriff Jess Sarber as they freed Dillinger from the Lima jail. All three went to the Ohio State Penitentiary at Columbus. Charles Makley and Harry Pierpont used a toy gun to attempt a break out. Makley was killed by prison guards and Pierpont was wounded. When Pierpont had recovered a month later he was walked to the electric chair. His eyes were bloodshot from numerous crying jags during the previous few days. He refused assistance entering the room, kissed a crucifix, handed it to a Catholic priest, and sat down with a sardonic smile. The third convict, Russell Clark, served 34 years of a life sentence before he was paroled to die of cancer four months later.[79]

Chapter 5

THE SEARCH FOR PRETTY BOY FLOYD

HUNTING THE KANSAS CITY SUSPECTS

The FBI's hunt for Dillinger took four-and-one-half months. During this period the Kansas City Massacre investigation remained inactive because the FBI had no idea who the shooters might be. FBI Director J. Edgar Hoover had markedly different interests in pursuing these two cases. In the Dillinger case the Director had steadfastly refused to join the hunt during the five months between the time Indiana Governor McNutt requested federal assistance with the murder of Sheriff Sarber during Dillinger's escape from the Lima jail, until mounting Washington political pressure caused Hoover to feel insecure about keeping his job unless he not only joined the hunt but took the lead. In contrast in the Massacre investigation, Hoover immediately assumed the lead because one FBI agent was killed and two others were wounded. The Director did this without having any legal jurisdiction in this case since Congress did not make killing or assaulting a federal agent a criminal offense until almost a year after this horrific slaughter of four lawmen.

Just days after the Kansas City Massacre, the FBI's investigation dried up because the two initial suspects had disappeared from sight and agents developed no other leads. The two missing suspects were Hot Springs crime leader Dick Galatas and Kansas City organized-crime associate Verne Miller. Agents had no idea where in the world either was, but Miller's wife, who used her maiden name Vi Mathias, had absconded with her husband right after the slaughter was broadcast on radio news reports. Agents pursued the only lead they had to the couple, Vi's parents, who were raising her daughter at their Brainerd, Minnesota farm. Agents from the St. Paul FBI Office started intercepting the parent's incoming mail and a month later hit pay dirt. A gift arrived for their young granddaughter and agents traced its mailing origin to a novelty shop in Lake Placid, New York.

Agents went to the shop hoping to pick up Vi's trail. Hoover called such a hunt a *cherchez la femme* meaning *find the woman*. He preached to agents that a criminal's weakness was often a woman and she could be trailed right to him. Fortunately, a shop cashier remembered the gift's purchaser and the description fit Vi. In addition she had told the cashier that she was on vacation and mentioned her next destination. The agents stayed one step behind her through several northeast states and Montréal, Canada. At every stop she chatted about her next destination with salespeople and hotel employees. During the chase agents lost track of her three times. For example in Atlantic City, New Jersey a hotel employee reported she had gone out to lounge on the beach. Surveillance agents put on bathing suits and reclined on beach chairs while scanning the mass of sunbathers looking for her. Unbelievably they selected chairs right next to hers. They failed to recognize their blonde subject because she had dyed her hair dark.

Then in Newark, New Jersey a lone agent picked up Vi's trail and found she was traveling with a couple. He got the couple's identity and residential address from a hotel registration clerk. When the trio got into a car he followed until the couple dropped her off at a hotel. The agent assumed she was checking in so he followed the couple to see if they were headed to Miller, but when the agent was confident they were returning to their Manhattan apartment, he went back to the hotel. At the front desk he asked for Vi's room number, but he learned she had loitered in the lobby for 20 minutes until she was sure no one was tailing her. Then she walked out and rushed to embrace Miller, the real target of their cherchez. In the front of that hotel her trail dried up.

For the next three months the FBI learned nothing about the whereabouts of the two Massacre suspects or Vi. Then a frustrated agent went back through the limited information agents had collected about the case. That is when he recalled that soon after the slaughter, the Chicago FBI Office SAC (special agent in charge) Purvis, who ended up taking the lead in the investigation way back when he was still in Hoover's good graces, had obtained the address of Vi's best girlfriend, Prohibition nightclub waitress Bobbie Moore. Agents went to that address which was for the Sherone Apartment Hotel and presented the manager photos of both women. She confirmed Bobbie lived there and Vi had rented a separate apartment under an alias three months earlier which would have been when she had ditched the FBI's cherchez.

Agents rented an apartment near Vi's to observe those entering and leaving her apartment. They observed her apartment door and the nearby hallway by keeping their apartment's door slightly ajar and from an air vent into the hallway. They also tapped her phone. Five days later a man who resembled Miller showed up at Vi's door. Agents telephoned the Director who ordered them not to raid the apartment until they obtained a positive ID. The next night agents observed the couple walk out of the apartment and down the hall. The moment they positively IDed the subject as Miller, 10 eager agents tried to get through the open apartment door at the same time. They jammed and blocked each other as Miller ran down the stairs towards the building's front entrance. Purvis had placed machinegun-toting agents on the roof of the next building, but no agent in the surveillance apartment remembered to signal them through the window that Miller was on the move. Thus the agents on the roof did not alert the agents posted in parked cars at the front and rear lobby entrances.

Six agents were lounging inconspicuously in the lobby as Miller entered from the staircase. He slowed to a normal but hurried walk to avoid attracting their attention. Miller knew agents were pursuing him on the run not too far behind, but he kept up his controlled hasty pace until he got out the front door. At that moment Vi's girlfriend drove up and he leapt into the passenger seat. He quickly turned back towards the chasing agents as he pulled out a pistol to fire two shots. Two agents returned pistol fire as pedestrians dove for cover. Then a state trooper fired two bursts from his machinegun. The spray exploded the car's rear window, the only damage done by all the shooting. The cool-headed waitress sped down side streets until she ran into a dead-end. The moment she realized her mistake and came to a stop Miller thanked her, jumped out, and without identifying his destination ran in search of safety.

One FBI internal report about Miller's escape fiasco criticized the Director's decision without mentioning his name. This is probably the only agency document that ever disparaged Hoover and it was scathing. It attacked his order to agents not to raid the apartment and it also condemned the 20 agents for their lack of coordination, their allowing the subject to escape despite covering every route, and their failure to have cars positioned to pursue the waitress' fleeing car.

This shameful escape fiasco led to public scorn of the Director. He was desperate to find Miller and put the bloody Massacre case to rest. The only lead was the two women in Miller's life, his wife and her girlfriend. When Miller had bolted from his wife in the apartment hallway to run down the stairs to freedom, two agents had grabbed her. Two days later her waitress friend had surrendered to the FBI. Agents interrogated them separately for long hours. The agents began by threatening them with prison for harboring the suspect and later ratcheted up the pressure by warning each one that the welfare of her child was at stake. Both women expressed extreme worry about their children's futures but neither provided any useful information about Miller's possible whereabouts. This is almost certainly because they had no idea.

Miller had several places to turn. His shooting skills and tight lips were highly respected by the leaders of a few major Prohibition groups and bank-robbing gangs with whom he had close contact. Because of Miller's silence about his criminal activities, the FBI only knew about his friendship with Louis "Lepke" Buchalter. He was the labor and industrial racketeer who dominated the large New York City garment industry. Right after the Massacre Lepke and his wife Betty had welcomed Miller's wife Vi as a guest in their luxurious apartment and Lepke presumably hid the fugitive somewhere nearby. Then the Buchalters took Vi along when they went on a two-week vacation during which the FBI lost her trail three times. During all this the FBI had no clue of Miller's whereabouts, and there is no indication Miller contacted Lepke again after his narrow escape from FBI agents at Vi's apartment.

Miller's escape from the FBI's horribly-botched raid at Vi's apartment would ravage efforts to solve the Massacre case. The fugitive seemingly vanished for the next month until his nude body was found in a drainage ditch on the outskirts of Detroit, Michigan. Someone used a hammer to smash his forehead repeatedly, strangled him with such strength it crushed his Adam's apple, ripped off his clothes, and mutilated his body. Such brutality and disrespectful retaliation means someone was really incensed over a personal affront. Miller went from being the long-time darling of some of organized-crimes top leaders to dangerous enemy overnight making one scenario likely. He escaped the FBI apartment raid carrying little cash so he was desperate for funds. He lacked any leverage to demand funds from a Detroit gangster to finance his run from the law except by threatening to talk if captured. Whatever the reason for his spiteful murder, the news was devastating for Hoover. As the Massacre's presumed mastermind and lead shooter, Miller was the only person who could have identified the other two shooters with certainty.

By coincidence the day before Miller's body was discovered, four FBI agents questioned his friend Lepke Buchalter at his attorney's Manhattan office about the missing suspect's whereabouts. Lepke was forthright about entertaining Miller's wife Vi as a guest in his apartment after the Kansas City Massacre and then taking her on a vacation with he and his wife. The gangster also identified the times the two couples had socialized over the years. The FBI's summary of their questioning contained a few interesting quotes by Lepke. He told the agents, "No one will have anything to do with Miller now," but Lepke himself had protected the fugitive's wife while knowing the FBI was in pursuit. He added "If Miller shows up in New York, you will know about it." The agents focused on whether Miller might be "bumped off" in the next month, and they observed in their report that he "gave a knowing smile and said he didn't know about that but he coyly offered to make some inquiries around town."

The agents interpretation of Lepke's statements was that he knew Miller had been bumped off. This is almost certainly true but not for the reason the agents thought. Remember that Hoover and the FBI always swore that organized crime and specifically the Mafia did not exist. Thus agents had no clue how organized crime gangs were structured, interacted, or operated so any interpretation by them would have been totally ignorant conjecture. In contrast to the FBI, every American schoolboy during Prohibition and for decades after was able to name every major Mafia gang leader across the country.

In reality the Jewish Lepke was an associate of the nation's largest Sicilian Mafia gang. This New York group had 20 times more shooters than any gang in Detroit. In addition Al Capone's gang had half the shooters of the New York gang, and under successive leaders, the Chicago gang always allied with and backed up the New Yorkers. Killing anyone under the protection of the country's biggest gang would have set off a war that would have inevitably resulted in the wiping out of the small Detroit gang. Thus Miller's killer would not have acted without either requesting Lepke's permission beforehand or else notifying him immediately afterwards that his wanted buddy had threatened to break the code of silence and testify to send both Detroit and New York gang leaders to prison. This would have justified the elimination of Miller no matter what friendships or protection he enjoyed.[80]

FLOYD BECOMES ENSNARED

Miller was murdered almost a half year after the Kansas City Massacre, and the FBI still had very limited information about the crime's genesis, all developed within days after it was committed. Agents knew that right after they had taken prison-escapee Frank Nash into custody in Hot Springs, Arkansas, his wife had gone to the city's crime leader Dick Galatas for assistance in freeing her husband. Galatas in turn flew her to the home of confidence-man Deafy Farmer in Joplin, Missouri where she telephoned her husband's best friend, organized-crime associate Verne Miller. He lived in Kansas City where the FBI was transporting Nash the next morning on his way back to prison. This was the totality of the Director's knowledge.

Within days after the horrendous slaughter the FBI had arrested both Deafy and Nash's widow, but neither had any information about how Miller had arranged and carried out the crime. The FBI's only other suspect was Galatas but he had vanished as a fugitive. Besides it was dubious that he knew anything more about how Miller had pulled off the crime than the two coconspirators already under arrest. The only link FBI Director Hoover ever had to the men who had committed the crime was Miller and he was now dead. Hoover was beside himself. He desperately needed to learn the identity of the other two shooters to quell public criticism over the FBI's recent raid fiasco at Vi Mathias' apartment, but every clue had been exhausted.

The Director always assumed that Miller was the lead shooter, but in fact the FBI had no idea whether Miller had led the attack, turned it over to someone else to direct it, or notified a major organized-crime leader who also liked Nash and assumed control of the situation. If Miller had simply passed word about both the prison-escapee's predicament and the FBI's transport plan, he would not have known anything more about who the shooters were than the two arrested coconspirators who were known to have forwarded information until it finally reached this unknown ringleader.

For the next three months the investigation went nowhere. Then the FBI lab belatedly examined a possible clue that had been ignored for nine months. For the first time it compared the latent prints found on the beer glasses that had been impounded after the FBI's raid on Miller's home just days after the Massacre. One print was a match to Adam Richetti, partner of Oklahoma's most notorious bank robber - Charles "Pretty Boy" Floyd. Hoover soon launched an extensive manhunt for Floyd but this effort seemed rather futile because no lawman or press reporter had heard about the elusive fugitive's possible whereabouts during the previous four months.

Hoover's manhunt suffered from two glaring legal flaws that everyone seemed to ignore because of the hysteria over violent-crime that seemed to be sweeping the country. First no evidence existed to implicate Floyd. Second the FBI had no jurisdiction in the Massacre case because the shooters had not broken any federal law. The shocking slaughter did generate political pressure on Congress to make the killing of a federal agent a crime, but this was passed a year after the slaughter and two months after Hoover started his hunt for Floyd. Ironically the law's passage did not give the FBI jurisdiction in the Massacre case because the Justice Department cannot retroactively prosecute a crime committed prior to the passage of a law. The Director did not let mere legal technicalities like lack of authority and no evidence impede his determined search for Floyd. Since agents had no grounds to arrest Floyd and the Justice Department had no authority to prosecute him even if he was guilty, Hoover's orders to get him meant the Director had turned his secret-police force into an assassination hunting party.

During the five-and-a-half months after the FBI lab matched a fingerprint of Floyd's lieutenant Richetti on Miller's beer glasses, agents picked up no word about the possible whereabouts of either bank-robbing partner. Then underworld intrigue in Kansas City where the Massacre occurred created a possible break in the case. It began with the murder of the city's Mafia boss Johnny Lazia. Police never identified his killers, but Lazia's successors soon went after small-time criminal Michael "Jimmy Needles" La Capra, nicknamed for his drug addiction. Hoover and crime historians have assumed based on the timing that it was vengeance over Lazia's killing, but Kansas City investigative reporters maintained it was because he was demanding a larger share in the profits of unspecified rackets of the gang.

Needles escaped the gang's first attempt on his life and stayed on the move. He was driving with two female companions outside Argonia, Kansas 250 miles southwest of Kansas City, Missouri, when three gang members caught up with his car. The Mafiosi's car pulled up alongside his car and blasted away at Needles. Mercifully the shooters' car ran off the road and stalled. Even though no one in Needles' car was injured the terrified man backtracked 20 miles to the police station he remembered passing in Wellington, Kansas. He ran inside the Sumner County Jail to turn himself in even though he was not wanted on any criminal charge.

At the same time Needles was pleading to be taken into custody, Kansas Highway Patrolmen stopped to assist a stalled car on the highway. When they saw the shooters' weapons, they arrested the men and apparently gave them a pretty-good working over. The Patrolmen knew nothing about a shooting having occurred and they locked the three Mafiosi in the cell next to Needles'. One can only imagine the threats these thugs hurled at their trapped prey through the bars separating them. Facing his contracted killers must have been the ultimate horror imaginable for the petrified Needles. He called for officers to help him, explained his plight, and demanded they notify the FBI that he would tell them a saga about the Massacre in return for obtaining federal protection. In the meantime police transferred Needles to an isolated death cell intended for convicts awaiting execution which was probably imagery that only intensified his morbid fears. For his own protection police held him on a technical charge of illegal transportation of a stolen car.

When Needles talked to the police about the Massacre he said Floyd had led the murderous trio. Since this fit in with the Hoover's unsupported supposition, he dispatched agents to interview him. They visited Needles' isolated cell where he was so panicked they had a hard time understanding much of what he said. He told them a second-hand story that he claimed was told to him by his brother-in-law, a Lazia Mafioso. He spewed out a fantastic tale that tied in the Director's chosen cast of characters for the Kansas City Massacre – Floyd, his partner Richetti, Nash's friend Verne Miller, and Kansas City Mafia boss Johnny Lazia.

Needles' yarn contained all the facts that had been released in the newspaper accounts of the crime. It also contained elements that could not be verified at that time but would later be proven untrue as additional evidence surfaced. For example Needles said during the Massacre shootout Floyd was wounded in his left shoulder by a ricochet from one of his own bullets and extensive loss of blood forced him to visit a physician. However not one of the many Massacre witnesses reported seeing any of the three shooters act like he had been wounded. More importantly the autopsy after Floyd's death found no scar on his left shoulder from an old bullet wound or other injury.

There was also a huge inconsistency in Needles' tale that should have set off warning alarms to a good detective. Needles claimed Miller chose Floyd and Richetti as shooters because Mafia boss Lazia was afraid the heat from Kansas City detectives would be too great after killing local lawmen. But then Needles totally contradicted this contention in his fable by saying that after the horrific slaughter the supposedly worried Lazia harbored and partied with the pair of shooters for two days before personally escorting them out of town. If Lazia was actually too fearful of being involved, he would have never have associated with them afterwards and instead ordered them to immediately get out of his town.

Hoover missed the significance of this glaring inconsistency in Needles' story but he worried about the informer's veracity because he did not trust junkies. The Director wanted confirmation from the plot's other participants and his first target was Miller's wife, Vi Mathias. Three weeks after Needles squawked, she was paroled from the Milan, Michigan, federal women's prison after serving a year's sentence for harboring her fugitive husband. The FBI had no legitimate grounds to go after her because she had served her time for the only crime she had committed. She was now innocent of any federal crime, but Hoover never not let technicalities like innocence get in his way.

As Vi Mathias headed from the prison for a long-awaited reunion with her daughter and parents, three FBI agents kidnapped her because they had no grounds to arrest her, took her to a Detroit apartment, and held her prisoner. She was kept totally isolated from outside contact and without access to an attorney for 11 days. It is unclear how much the agents tortured this helpless terrified woman, but they reported in internal memos how they berated and threatened her around the clock. She gave them nothing because she knew nothing about her late husband's criminal associates.

It is important to note that while Attorney General Cummings package of anti-crime bills allowed the FBI to arrest suspects for the first time, it also required agents to have a warrant unless they had reasonable cause to believe the suspect would escape if time were taken to obtain a warrant. In addition it required agents to quickly take an arrested prisoner before a Federal Judge or U.S. Commissioner. In Vi's abduction, agents committed four serious violations of the law and the Constitution of the United States. Agents failed to obtain a warrant even though she was not an escape threat; they took her into custody with full knowledge she had not committed any federal crime and they could not charge her with anything; they did not take her before a committing officer to approve the arrest and set bail; and they denied her the right to an attorney. Since agents knew she had not committed any federal offense, Hoover had degenerated his secret-police force into a domestic-terrorist gang preying on innocent American citizens.

Four days after kidnapping and imprisoning Vi Mathias in a Detroit apartment, agents finally got a lead on the only known Massacre plotter who had not been apprehended, Hot Springs crime leader Dick Galatas. Immediately after the Massacre he had gone on the run and he had remained a fugitive from the FBI for 15 months. For a while he had hid out in Reno under the protection of casino operators Graham and McKay, and then he had become a paint company's southeastern distributor based in New Orleans. One day he interviewed a job applicant who realized that he had seen the businessman's picture in the current issue of *Liberty Magazine* along with his real identity. Immediately after the interview the applicant informed the U.S. Attorney who had the FBI arrest Galatas that afternoon.

Hoover ordered the same isolation-and-no-lawyer treatment for Galatas as he had approved for Vi. Like her he was imprisoned in an agent's apartment and he was abused. A memo by the Director to his assistant said, "I stated [to Inspector Sam Cowley] that I intend to have Galatas held by our Division until we are able to obtain some information. We know he is the key man and he may clear up many doubts in our minds and may confirm some of the information already in our possession." In this case, Hoover's Gestapo-style storm troopers not only resorted to terrifying threats but also added vicious torture. The code word for cruel pain in FBI memos was a "vigorous physical interview." A Hoover assistant in the Washington Office then ordered a New Orleans agent to "go to work" on Galatas because "he is yellow and, of course, there is a way to deal with people like that." "What we want is a good vigorous physical interview." After three agents worked Galatas over, they sent this memo to Hoover: "Subject Galatas was brought to the office after dark and was kept there until shortly before daylight. The interrogation was continuous and vigorous."[81]

In Federal Court Galatas filed a motion to suppress coerced confession statements he made about trying to help Frank Nash's wife free her husband from FBI custody because of the agents' Inquisition-style torture techniques. His motion described what Hoover and his agents meant by the term a "vigorous physical interview" that they proudly mentioned in their internal reports. After intensive brutal interrogation at the New Orleans FBI Office, Galatas was transported to the Chicago Office where the agents of Purvis and Cowley were more experienced with such interview tactics. Galatas claimed he was kept handcuffed to a chair and never allowed to lay down or to sleep and given little food. Agents used their fists, kicked him, and battered him with rubber hoses to the face, base of his neck, and ribs until he was unconscious. His life was threatened with statements like "If you are found dead in the streets, the same as others were found, no one would ever make inquiries." After threats like this he was actually stood up against the office's window sill, and his head pushed forward and down through the window opening to force him to look at the sidewalk 19 stories below. As he was held in this position he was told to contemplate his death as they threatened to shove him out. The imagery must have been powerful indeed as this was the same window that the agents had dangled and then dropped 67-year-old James Probasco just two months earlier. At least the agents seemed to have learned from accidentally killing one suspect not to dangle defendants out the window anymore. Galatas presented these complaints at trial, but no one including the Federal Judge wanted to believe they lived in such a nightmarish secret-police terror state. Unfortunately the Judge had no access to the FBI internal reports admitting the agents' guilt.

Galatas' claims were confirmed in general a year later by the former confidential secretary to Chicago SAC Purvis in two *Chicago Tribune* articles. She said the agents "had heard about the 'third degree' and tried to use it without knowing how. Their attempts were stupid and useless. They picked the wrong men to hit and got little information for their pain." "I sometimes saw the bruised knuckles of agents who had used more primitive arguments with refractory [stubborn] prisoners."[82]

During the FBI's torture sessions Galatas readily admitted everything he knew but he had no idea who Miller's cohorts were. Despite holding Galatas and Vi in isolation and uncomfortable cramping positions for long periods, bombarding them with terroristic threats, and administering intense pain, the FBI learned absolutely nothing about who the Massacre shooters were. Hoover had been unable to obtain any evidence whatsoever about the involvement of Floyd and Richetti in the horrific slaughter, but this did not stop him days later from falsely announcing to the press that the FBI had identified the pair and Miller as the assassins in the 16-month-old Massacre case. He reassured the public that his agents were conducting a "vigorous" search for the two bank robbers who were still alive.[83]

WHO WAS THIS PRETTY BOY?

FBI Director Hoover now had his troops focus on the search for Charles Arthur "Pretty Boy" Floyd, but the country, except for Oklahoma, knew nothing about this bank robber who the FBI had just thrust into the national spotlight. History has recorded Floyd to be the FBI's next targeted Public Enemy Number 1, but the Justice Department never applied this designation to him nor offered a reward for him. When Dillinger was killed this unsavory title was transferred to Baby Face Nelson because rewards had been offered for both Dillinger and Nelson after the Little Bohemia fiasco, and Nelson was still on the loose roaming the countryside.

When little Charley Floyd was 7-years old his parents were poor Georgia farmers who moved to Oklahoma looking for better opportunities. He was raised on tenant farms that made small profits. He worked arduous hours with his family in the cotton and corn fields until he was 16 when he hit the road to become involved in minor crimes and with bootlegging at the beginning of Prohibition.

At age 21 he robbed the $11,929 payroll at a Kroger store in St. Louis, Missouri and five days later local police took him in for questioning because they were suspicious about his new clothes and car. Upon searching his residence they found cash still in the bank's wrapper so they arrested him for the first time. He pled guilty and received a five-year sentence in the Missouri State Penitentiary. From the time he was released from prison he partnered with experienced Kansas City criminals in robbing banks.

Late in his prison term Floyd's wife had divorced him for desertion and taken custody of their four-year-old son, but during the rest of his career he occasionally lived with his former wife and son. The son later said his dad was a wonderful father who showered him with gifts.

A year after his release, Floyd robbed the Farmers and Merchants Bank in Sylvania, Ohio. He was soon arrested in Toledo, Ohio 10 miles southeast and was sentenced six months later to 12 to 15 years. While being transported by train to the Ohio State Penitentiary he leapt out the window and spent the rest of his life on the run as a fugitive. He returned to Oklahoma and organized a gang to continue robbing banks. He introduced the machinegun and bullet-proof vest to Oklahoma's bad men.

When Pretty Boy hit a bank he grabbed not only the cash but also the records of outstanding loans and mortgages. In addition he gave food and cash to the struggling people living near his home. This charity to the needy was probably intended as bribery to encourage them to keep their mouths shut about his location. It was a time when banks were foreclosing on many local homes, farms, and businesses, so the local newspapers turned Floyd into a legend with the dispossessed and downtrodden dust bowlers of the Great Depression by portraying him as a modern-day Robin Hood. This media hysteria led witnesses to report seeing him at bank robberies in which he was not a participant so he was credited with many more robberies than he actually committed.

Five months after escaping custody on the train, Floyd and an associate were walking along a sidewalk in Bowling Green, Ohio when the Chief of Police and a Patrolman recognized the fugitive. As the officers approached it turned into a running gun battle until the two fugitives reached their car, jumped in, and sped off. The Patrolman slid behind the wheel of his car, while the Police Chief jumped on the running board, and the chase was on. The gun battle continued during the pursuit until the Patrolman was wounded and slumped over the steering wheel. The 29-year-old Patrolman died a week later. Bowling Green charged Floyd with murder and issued a wanted-dead-or-alive poster.

Back in his home state of Oklahoma, Floyd robbed two banks in one day in the cities of Castle and Paden. These robberies led the insurance companies to double their rates for covering bank cash. This increase in expenses led the Oklahoma State Bankers' Association to request Governor William Murray to call out the National Guard to hunt the fugitive down. Instead the Governor offered a $1,000 reward for his capture, and a year-and-half later the states of Oklahoma, Missouri, and Ohio were offering a total pot of $6,500, mostly for the killing of policemen in their states.

During a two-month period Floyd became notorious by escaping unscathed from two wild car-chase shoot-outs with Tulsa, Oklahoma police. In one Floyd wounded a detective leading Governor Murray to appoint the former McIntosh County Sheriff as a special investigator to track him down. Three months later this bounty hunter traced Pretty Boy to the farm of his father-in-law near Bixby. The special investigator led a posse of officers in a midnight raid on the farmhouse but they did not find him so the investigator dismissed the raiding party. However he remained suspicious that Floyd was hiding in the darkness so he remained. The fugitive and his bank-robbery partner Earl Birdwell were indeed there but they had heard the raiders approaching and had hid in silence. As the officers drove off, the pair quietly got into their car. Suddenly Birdwell turned the ignition and floored the accelerator. As the pair sped away Floyd exchanged machinegun fire with the lingering lead investigator killing him.

Less than two weeks later, Floyd and Birdwell robbed the Stonewall, Oklahoma First State Bank. A group of irate citizens carrying guns gathered outside, waiting for them to walk out so the pair of killers kidnapped two cashiers to use as shields in their successful escape. Outside the city limits they viciously beat and left the two cashiers beside the road and then kidnapped a passing young woman driver for a shield in her car. These atrocities led citizens in six counties to organize posses to hunt them. The pair continued to rob banks and their kidnapping of cashiers became part of their routine. They were becoming increasingly more violent.

Six months later Pretty Boy even robbed the bank in his old hometown where his family and former neighbors kept their life savings. He, Birdwell, and a cohort heisted $2,530 from the Sallisaw State Bank. The three desperadoes carried machineguns but did not fire. When Birdwell yelled an order at a farmer, Floyd said, "Don't hurt Bob, he's my friend." One of the desperadoes guarded the front door and corralled every passerby while his two accomplices grabbed the cash from the cashier tills and vault. As the trio left they kidnapped an assistant cashier and as they roared past the edge of town they shoved him out of the car. A half dozen citizens, some of whom went to school with Pretty Boy, recognized him.

While some people who were suffering from the Great Depression looked up to bank robbers as heroes, many other citizens were incensed about the theft of their life savings. Some took up arms. This is what occurred three weeks later when Birdwell robbed the Farmers' and Merchant's State Bank in Boley, Oklahoma, a segregated African-American village of 800 people. Birdwell had two comrades with him but not Floyd. One henchman was African-American so he could case the bank for the two European-American partners without standing out. As the robbers stormed in the front door, the cashier jumped into the bank vault. As the bank's white-haired president stood facing the muzzle of Birdwell's pistol, he defiantly pulled a hidden alarm and the fugitive shot him dead. With the sound of the retort, the cashier burst from the vault with a rifle returning fire and killing Birdwell. The gunfire turned the angry townspeople into vigilantes who rushed toward the bank with the town's policemen. As the European robber ran out the door towards the getaway car, a hail of bullets from the mob gravely wounded him. He was followed by the African who raced through gunfire to the car and drove down the street as bullets perforated the vehicle. He slumped dead in his seat as the car bumped into the curb. The townsfolk proudly surveyed their courageous wipeout of this violent robbery gang. The next day Governor Murray congratulated the cashier "for keeping your head in the face of danger" and offered condolences to the bank president's family. On the day after that the Governor announced a $500 reward for anyone killing a bandit in the act of robbing a bank. He gave that reward amount to the cashier who killed Birdwell and signed a commission making him a Major on his administrative staff. Courageous citizens in other towns also took up arms against these violent predators.

Floyd was not with Birdwell when he faced the vigilante citizens' wrath because this man whose blazing machinegun had made him the terror of the southwest had tired of life on the run. He gave up robbing banks and dropped from sight by hiding out with relatives. Days before Birdwell was killed, Floyd took his wife and young son, Jack Dempsey Floyd, named after the world heavyweight champion boxer, to a movie theater. The ticket taker told them the mystery film was too lurid for a small boy and turned the fugitive and his family away.

During his retirement Floyd most enjoyed assisting women family members in the kitchen baking fresh pies. When local police arrested several of his relatives, Floyd headed to the safe haven of Reno under the protection of casino operators Graham and McKay. For a time he lived there quietly and occasionally visited their gambling places.

Eventually Floyd returned to robbing banks with Adam Richetti as his new partner. Dead-or-alive rewards for Floyd's capture were posted in Oklahoma, Missouri, and Ohio for bank robberies and murdering peace officers. While Floyd and Richetti were driving through Bolivar, Missouri their stolen car needed repairs so they drove into a garage. They got out of their car, machineguns in hand. One ordered the mechanics to go to work while the other lined up the bystanders against a wall. At that moment the Sheriff happened to walk in and they disarmed him. When the repairs were completed, the desperadoes kidnapped the Sheriff for use as a shield during their 120-mile journey northwest to Lees Summit, Missouri. As the trio approached the city the fugitives released the Sheriff unharmed. This put the fugitives 20 miles from Kansas City in the evening, as Verne Miller was making plans for early the next morning to pull off the horrendous Massacre of lawmen at Union Railway Station. This is when Richetti presumably had a beer at Miller's home. The two fugitives likely turned to the organized-crime associate upon arriving in town to obtain his protection for them by corrupt local police detectives.[84]

AN ASSASSINATION TEAM AT WORK

It was not until nine months after the Kansas City Massacre that the FBI's lab identified the fingerprint of Floyd's bank-robbing partner Richetti on the beer glass at the home of the chief suspect in the slaughter, Miller. This is when FBI Director Hoover launched a search for Floyd and Richetti but the Director did not publicize this manhunt to the press because agents had no evidence Floyd had ever committed a federal crime. The investigation was beginning from ground zero because in the nine months since the night before the slaughter both desperadoes had seemingly fallen off the face of the earth.

The FBI's manhunt during the next two-and-one-half months was fruitless. No one called into the FBI the suspected whereabouts of Floyd, not a local police department, a newspaper reporter, or underworld source, because Hoover's FBI remained imperious, cooperating with no one and communicating with no one, thus leaving the FBI without resources except for blind luck. In most cases Hoover's FBI waited for a citizen complaint or a lead in a newspaper article, and agents spent a lot of time reading newspapers. While Hoover almost never initiated an investigation of an organized-crime figure, occasionally inquiry was requested about a specific crime by the Justice Department from the U.S. AG or U.S. Attorneys or from heads of other federal agencies. Thus under Hoover over half the documents in every organized-crime leader's file are newspaper articles because the FBI lacked direct resources, unlike nation's police department detectives who develop dependable sources from investigative reporters and underworld figures.

Even though Floyd had successfully eluded detection by anyone for almost a year, he was worried for his life. He knew if captured he faced the death penalty for killing local policemen, and he may have been afraid the FBI had targeted him for extermination. At this point Floyd had an emissary convey to Hoover an offer for his surrender if the Director would guarantee him immunity from execution. Hoover explained in internal memos to two assistants how he twice rejected the fugitive's offers to drop the death penalty. The Director told Assistant Ed Tamm, "I suggested, in this connection, that [Blake] make it clear that orders are out to kill Floyd on sight, and if he doesn't surrender in short time, he will no doubt be killed by our men." Five days later the Director reaffirmed his intentions to assassinate the fugitive in memos to Assistants Tamm and Pop Nathan with "we are going to kill him if we catch him."[85]

Hoover's decision was wholly irresponsible and nightmarish. It guaranteed that if Floyd felt cornered by anyone his only option was to charge them machinegun blasting away. The Director ensured a fatal confrontation with the dangerous killer, putting his agents and local lawmen in maximum danger of serious harm. His decision kept the frightening killer at large robbing banks at will and in the process terrorizing employees and customers facing machinegun barrels, kidnapping human shields, and shooting civilians in his way. Hoover totally disregarded the lives and safety of America's lawmen and innocent civilians, instead putting all at maximum risk, making the FBI Director the opposite of everything a police commander should be.

Four months after rejecting Floyd's surrender offers, the FBI still had not obtained a single clue as to Floyd's whereabouts. This led Hoover to take his assassination threat to the press to apply more pressure on the elusive fugitive to shoot it out with his agents. The Director told reporters in slightly veiled language what his reply was to the offers of surrender by Floyd's emissary - "He killed one of our men and he must take the consequences. Moreover, we don't deal with gangsters." This vengeful, wild-west shoot-'em-up approach kept the perilous killer at large and everyone who encountered him potentially in harms way, all in violation of the Director's oath to protect the public and to arrest the bad guys. Hoover's shoot-to-kill assassination witch-hunt was made more outlandish because he still had no jurisdiction in the case and no evidence implicating Floyd with the Massacre except for junkie Needles' nonsensical second-hand story.[86]

It was now seven months into the FBI's fruitless search for the fugitive with nary a single lead about where he might be, mainly because agents still had not put his family members with whom he lived under surveillance. Then two-and-a-half weeks after Hoover made his public veiled assassination threat, the Director tried to ratchet up the pressure on the fugitive further by announcing to the press that Floyd was one of the shooters in the 16-month-old Massacre case. This was of course still without any substantiation beyond Needles' questionable story that Kansas City FBI agents passed on to reporters as gospel. These agents also said they believed Floyd had slipped away from the FBI's New Orleans' raid that captured Richard Galatas and his wife, and the fugitive was now fleeing to his native Oklahoma.

Actually Floyd was not in either Louisiana or in Oklahoma. A day after the false announcement by Hoover and the Kansas City Office that Floyd was a participant in the tragic slaughter, a huge break finally came in the hunt for the Pretty Boy, but it was made by a local Iowa sheriff's unit rather than any FBI action. This sighting of the fugitive meant the inevitable confrontations the Director had set in motion were about to occur as many lawmen and civilians would soon face Floyd's gunsights and blistering gunfire.

Floyd quietly surfaced on a McIntyre, Iowa farm where he and two associates paid the farmer to allow them to do some pheasant hunting. When one of the trio told the farmer their leader was Floyd, he notified the Iowa State Bureau of Investigation. A carload of deputy sheriffs responded quickly to the call and surprised the fugitives who ran to their car and tore off. The deputies pursued at high speed exchanging gunfire. Floyd drove one country rode after another searching for an escape route when he ran into a dead-end. Recognizing his mistake he hung a squealing Ueee and floored it directly at the approaching deputies' car. In the resulting game of chicken the criminals blasted machineguns as the lawmen emptied their pistols. No one was hit as the deputies slowed and swerved out of the way, but by the time the deputies turned around and regained momentum the fugitives were safely out of sight. That night the FBI took charge of the investigation from local deputies but the agents failed to pick up Floyd's trail. The case had again gone cold.

A week later Floyd and Richetti robbed a bank in Tiltonsville, Ohio and continued to run. The next day outside Wellsville, Ohio, Floyd skidded on wet pavement into a telephone pole. The two fugitives had their girlfriends, who were sisters, drive the car into town to be repaired, while they awaited their return on the hill beside the road. It afforded them a good view over the surrounding terrain. The next morning, a resident found it peculiar that two men should be sitting there on blankets and called the Police Chief who deputized two men. The trio wearing street clothes had no idea who they were walking towards, but Floyd realized they were law and opened fire shooting the

Chief in the ankle. The two fugitives ran in different directions and the wounded Chief somehow pursued Richetti on foot despite his wounded ankle. The lawmen kept up with Richetti and when the fugitive turned to confront him his gun misfired forcing him to surrender to the determined Chief who had him dead in his sights.

Floyd's machinegun had misfired when he had confronted the Police Chief so the fugitive tossed it as he ran to the road. He pulled out a pistol to force an oncoming driver to stop and get out of his car and the fugitive drove toward Lisbon, Ohio. On the outskirts of town he saw a roadblock checking cars so he hung a Ueee and took off. Deputy sheriffs at the roadblock saw his car turn and jumped in a patrol car in hot pursuit. This became a wild high-speed shootout. Even though Floyd was driving he was still able to shoot a pursuing deputy in the shoulder. All of a sudden Floyd jumped from his moving vehicle and ran into the nearby hilly woods where he disappeared from sight. While the deputies mounted a massive search, a local policeman identified the fingerprints of the man, who the wounded Police Chief had captured. When the policeman realized it was Richetti, he notified the Cincinnati, Ohio FBI Office about who they had arrested, making it likely the fugitive they were chasing on foot in the vicinity was the Pretty Boy.

Ironically Hoover had banished his publicity-crazed SAC Purvis from the Chicago Office because it was the FBI's main operating theater against the Midwest bank robbers. Hoover had sent him to the quiet Cincinnati FBI Office to get him out of sight of the press. Even though Purvis may have been the SAC Hoover most disliked and distrusted, he was now the FBI's senior agent in Ohio so Purvis now led the hunt for the highly-publicized fugitive. Hoover ordered his SAC to charter a plane with 19 agents to join the local police hunt. Upon arrival Purvis divided his agents into five cars to patrol the area where Floyd was last seen.

During the night Floyd had walked eight miles through the undergrowth. The next afternoon he approached an isolated farmhouse. The widowed owner prepared him a meal for which he insisted on paying her $1, and her brother and his wife agreed to drive him to the nearby village of Clarkson where he could board a bus for his destination of Youngstown, Ohio. In the meantime the owner's brother-in-law out in the apple orchard had sighted Floyd as he exited the woods covered with twigs and needles and walked towards the farmhouse. He quickly called East Liverpool police seven miles away.

The Police Chief and three patrolmen were searching the area in a patrol car when their office notified them of Floyd's likely location. As they headed to the farm, the FBI car carrying Purvis and three agents just happened to encounter the patrol car and flagged it down to find out how the search was going. The FBI followed the police posse because it had a possible location. As the two carloads of lawmen drove up to the farm, the brother and his wife were settling in their car's front seat. From the backseat Floyd ordered the brother to drive behind a nearby tall corn crib. Frustrated by the brother's slow speed, Floyd called him a "son-of-a-bitch," pulled out a pistol, jumped from the car, and crawled under the corn crib. His quick changes of direction indicate he was unsure of how to escape the eight lawmen. Moments later he leapt out, went toward the car, and then sprinted across the pasture toward the wooded hills two football fields away. He ran zigzagging as the lawmen jumped from their cars. Purvis yelled, "Let him have it!" and the lawmen blasted away with two machineguns, shotguns, and pistols. He was hit 14 times in the back and once in the side before he fell on his face, got up on his knees, and fell again dying minutes later surrounded by the police and agents. Floyd had a pistol in his hand and one in his inside shoulder holster both fully loaded and unfired.

It is important to note that if Floyd's machinegun had not malfunctioned the day before while escaping from the Police Chief, the carnage of lawmen at this scene could have easily rivaled that of the Kansas City Massacre due solely to the FBI Director letting him continue to rampage at will. As it was Floyd wounded a police chief and a deputy sheriff in separate incidents the day before his assassination. On the one hand Hoover left the nation in harm's way of a dangerous killer by refusing his offer to voluntarily surrender to a life sentence, and on the other he directed his agents to hunt and kill him even though the FBI had no legal jurisdiction in the Kansas City Massacre case and no evidence against him in that or any other crime.

While Hoover publicly agitated the situation with inflammatory and threatening rhetoric towards Floyd that made violent confrontation inevitable, the Director's agents failed to get a single lead about the fugitive's whereabouts during the seven months between the time the lab identified Richetti's fingerprint on a beer glass and Floyd's assassination. Local police departments were responsible for every discovery of the fugitive's location. It was purely coincidental that Purvis and his agents encountered a local police car on its way to capture Floyd. While Hoover and Purvis took all the credit for the fugitive's assassination, this was strictly a local police effort that the agents accidentally stumbled upon. The FBI's only role in this long-time hunt and takedown was to follow and backup the local police car that finally cornered Floyd.

Fittingly the last meal for the condemned man at that farm house had included freshly baked pie. He died at age 30 leaving behind a widow and young son. Floyd's body was returned to the Oklahoma hills, where he was laid to rest at Akins Cemetery. A crowd estimated at more than twenty thousand made it the largest funeral in Oklahoma history. Fourteen years later the brother of the state's most infamous bank robber still lived in their hometown of Sallisaw, Oklahoma where Floyd had once robbed the bank. Despite Pretty Boy's infamy, his brother was still able to be elected Sequoyah County Sheriff.

Less than a year later, Adam Richetti was tried in a Missouri court for the murder of one of the Detectives in the Kansas City Massacre, one of the four lawmen killed that day. The trial was a sham. The FBI's long investigation had produced no circumstantial or forensic evidence and not a single eyewitness. The only real evidence the FBI could supply to the local prosecutor was opportunity - Floyd and Richetti were in Kansas City the night before the slaughter and Richetti knew Miller, the man who the FBI assumed led the murder team. However agents were never able to find any evidence implicating Miller as being at the slaughter either.

The FBI had interviewed dozens of witnesses at the Massacre parking-lot scene but not a single one identified Floyd, Richetti, or Miller as one of the three shooters who was blazing machineguns that day. Even the internal reports of the three surviving FBI agents confirm they were unable to describe any of the three which is amazing considering police officers are trained to recognize distinguishing facial and body features. FBI internal updates discussing the status of the case reveal the three agents were still unable to remember anything about the culprits until they took the witness stand at the trial. Then they suddenly became confident that Floyd and Miller, who were deceased and unable to give alibi rebuttal, were two of the shooters. The third agent was the strongest prosecution witness because he now remembered Richetti's face. Either these three agents had the most coincidental and miraculous recall epiphanies in judicial history, or all committed blatant perjury to frame this defendant who will be shown through new evidence to almost certainly have been innocent of this crime. The jury convicted Richetti on these FBI-manufactured identifications and he was sentenced to be hanged. By the time he was executed three years later the state had converted its method of execution to the gas chamber where he died still righteously proclaiming his innocence. Not only did Hoover's FBI execute two men who were innocent of committing this crime, but by falsely closing the case they let the actual perpetrators get away totally free.

Eight other people were charged with conspiracy for making a series of telephone calls to attempt to rescue prisoner Frank Nash from federal custody resulting in the Kansas City Massacre.

Two of the defendants were freed for turning state's witness, and the jury convicted the other six who were sentenced to the maximum sentence of two years in a federal penitentiary. This was an unusual trial. While prosecutors invariably cut deals with murderers to obtain testimony against the instigator who planned or financed the plot, in this case the woman who initiated the plan and the widow of the prime suspect were set free to testify against those who simply conveyed messages between the two state's witnesses and alleged ringleader Miller.[87]

Immediately after the Floyd assassination, Purvis quickly called a press conference to boast about his exploits. In his usual fantasy-hero style he falsely implied his gun barked first. Three months earlier at the Dillinger-killing scene, Purvis' braggadocio had led Hoover to order his subordinate to keep his mouth shut about future cases, but with the first opportunity his errant, incorrigible SAC was at it again. Hoover was furious and he erupted the next day when Floyd's assassination story in the *New York Evening Journal* carried the banner headline - *And Again Melvin Purvis Triumphs*. Washington Headquarters quickly wrote and teletyped a statement to the press about Floyd's killing that gave all the credit to the illustrious Director. Purvis dutifully issued this press release with dispatch. Hoover quickly sent written orders to every SAC that established a monopoly by Headquarters on releasing all future case information. Two nights later, an FBI official at Headquarters reached Purvis at his Chicago home and told him to not return to his office and to not tell anyone he was back in the city. This allowed the Director to issue his fictionalized accounts of the Floyd killing to writers who sought different angles for additional feature stories or for film or radio dramatizations. Since Hoover was the only source for facts about cases, reporters either wrote what the Director gave them verbatim or they were cut off from all information about the agency's future cases.

By muzzling every regional FBI office from commenting on arrests, all announcements became the sole domain of the Director. He argued that he was the only one qualified to handle these because statements made at the scene without Headquarters' analysis led to false reports. However, the few times Hoover was in on future arrests, he immediately pontificated to reporters about his successes without benefit of Headquarters' analysis. In doing so he used the same bravado and dishonesty about his personal contribution that he so condemned Purvis for doing.

Floyd has gone down in history as the second of four successive Public Enemy Number 1 Midwest bank robbers brought down by the FBI, but Floyd never held this title. Neither the FBI nor the Justice Department ever designated him as Public Enemy Number 1, issued a reward for his capture, or obtained an arrest warrant for him. On the contrary, from the moment Dillinger was killed three months earlier, Baby Face Nelson became Public Enemy Number 1 because the Justice Department had offered rewards for both gangsters two months after the Little Bohemia fiasco.

Many newspapers attached the title to Floyd in stories announcing his assassination because Purvis in his braggadocio right afterwards made the false claim to reporters that he had just killed Public Enemy Number 1. This counterfeit label was only applied to Floyd that one day, as FBI agents immediately focused attention on the actual title holder, Nelson, who had remained elusive since he escaped the FBI's Little Bohemia botched raid a half year earlier. The search for Nelson is rejoined again in the next chapter.

All pertinent facts developed about the Kansas City Massacre by the local police, the FBI, and the press at the time, as well as crime historians since, have been presented here. However, there were a multitude of relevant facts available that no one until this research project realized related to this case. They are assembled and analyzed in a thorough cold-case examination, and they reveal for the first time who actually ordered the Kansas City Massacre and who the three shooters really were. This cold-case is presented in Chapter 12 after the FBI finally brings down all the machinegun-toting bank robbers. This cold case is presented separately because the real Massacre culprits also participated in a completely different, but most significant and incredible, part of American criminal and political history that concludes this book.

Chapter 6

NELSON STILL ON THE RUN

BABY FACE AFTER LITTLE BOHEMIA

After the assassination of Pretty Boy Floyd, the FBI focused again on Baby Face Nelson. Following the FBI's Little Bohemia raid fiasco Baby Face made his escape separately from John Dillinger and his two other henchmen. He first walked a mile to the Birch Lodge where he killed an FBI agent and wounded another agent and a constable. Then the fugitive stole the car belonging to the Lodge owning couple and he roared off disappearing into the darkness. As the night went on, the FBI and police expanded their dragnet assuming that he was getting ever further away. In actuality he drove 20 miles east and took an out-of-the-way unpaved road where his car stalled in mud.

Knowing that law enforcement at all levels was still searching for him in the immediate area he decided against returning to the highway to try to thumb a ride from what might be an oncoming lawman. Instead he backtracked west by foot in the darkness through the woods and brush. He trekked more than 10 miles until he encountered Lac Du Flambeau, a lake named after the nearby Native American reservation.

There he stumbled upon a tarpaper shack where an elderly Indian couple lived. Nelson passed off his disheveled twig-covered appearance by claiming he was a game warden who had lost his way and needed lodging. The old man made a meager living tapping the surrounding maple trees, but he welcomed the fugitive into his humble abode. Nelson rested and waited four days in hopes all the law in the area that was trying to find him had moved on with their search. When he felt safer he went to the nearby little village of Lac du Flambeau and stole a rural mail carrier's car. The wanted man drove first due south and then west 140 miles to Greenwood, where he abandoned the stolen vehicle. Next the fugitive hopped a ride with a farmer who drove him 27 miles southeast to Marshfield, where Nelson bought a used car. The car dealer realized who his customer was because Nelson unwittingly tipped his hand. The dealer had a good quality used model that was identical to the mailman's stolen car that everyone was watching out for, and when the fugitive totally rejected considering it, the dealer waited until his customer was out of sight and called police to report the sale. Having wheels again Nelson was soon out of Wisconsin to points unknown.[88]

For the next three months the FBI heard nothing more about the fugitive's whereabouts. The FBI's primary focus was not on Nelson but on Public Enemy Number 1 Dillinger until agents killed him. With Dillinger's death U.S. Attorney General (AG) Cummings officially designated Nelson as the country's new Public Enemy Number 1, declared him a "rat," and ordered a widespread FBI search. Other authorities made public statements that Baby Face was "kill crazy." Nelson was now the only living criminal with a federal reward posted for his capture with $5,000 on his head. To avoid meeting the poster's capture prophesy, Nelson started moving through a variety of cities staying only a short while in most. He only felt safe and hid out for any length of time under the protection of Graham and McKay in Reno and in Tahoe City. This tiny village was nestled in the trees along the California shoreline of Lake Tahoe 11 miles southwest of Graham and McKay's

Cal-Neva Lodge casino. The Tahoe City constable later confirmed, after seeing a picture of Baby Face, that he had lived there following the date of the FBI's Dillinger assassination.

As usual FBI Director J. Edgar Hoover's agenda was different from that of his boss. While AG Cummings may have made Public Enemy Number 1 Nelson his top priority after the FBI killed Dillinger, the Director made Pretty Boy Floyd his agents' primary target thinking the desperado might have been involved in the Kansas City Massacre. Besides for the next three months nothing more was heard about Nelson. Then local police and agents killed Floyd, and the FBI finally centered its attention on Baby Face. The Director had let his case languish for six months after the Little Bohemia raid debacle even though Nelson had murdered an unarmed FBI agent.

Hoover remained totally frustrated in his efforts to silence Purvis with the press. After the Dillinger killing and Chicago SAC Purvis' braggadocio to the press, the Director banished him to Cincinnati where there were no high-profile manhunts. Then Floyd showed up in the area, and Purvis just happened to follow the local police cruiser searching for Floyd that ended up slaying him. Right after the killing Purvis gathered the press to brag about his glorious exploits, but all his presentation accomplished was to reveal that he was completely out of the loop with both Headquarters and roving Inspector Cowley who headed all public enemy cases. When Purvis stood before the cameras he should have known it was inevitable the press would ask one question, but he was totally unprepared for it. A reporter asked, "Who is the new Public Enemy Number 1?" even though the press knew Nelson had held this title officially for the last three months. However Purvis was now standing on quicksand because he had no idea what the AG or the Director were planning to say about future Public Enemy designations. Thus he replied, "That would be hard to say. We still have plenty of work to do." No answer could have made it more clear that Purvis was no longer in the chain of command. Exiling Purvis to a distant outpost had not shut him up, so Hoover returned him back to Chicago under the thumb of his chief aide in the field, Inspector Cowley, who sequestered Purvis away from future action. The Director thought he had finally hushed up Purvis but the best laid plans sometimes do not work out.[89]

Nelson was the antithesis of Dillinger and Floyd who both achieved folk-hero status during their short-lived bank-robbing careers. Even though they pointed machineguns at terrified citizens during these robberies, they could be charming and polite, and typically only fired when trapped by the law. In contrast Nelson in a few robberies callously laughed as he sprayed his machinegun fire about and he shot at people who were not interfering with his escape. His hyperemotional, wild-eyed, maniacal appearance in some robberies earned Nelson the deserved reputation as the most violent Depression-era machinegun-toting outlaw. Its possible he was truly tetched, but its also possible he was simply emulating the craziest villains in Hollywood's earliest gangster films, a genre that sprouted up during this Midwestern machinegun bank-robbery era. In marked contradiction to the evil persona of Nelson when carrying a machinegun, he traveled on his fugitive runs accompanied by his wife, Helen, and they acted like an ordinary couple. This is why his whereabouts remained unnoticed for so long. The couple sometimes even took their two small children along giving a whole new meaning to the concept of family man.

Nelson took the FBI's killing of Dillinger in Chicago as a sign it was time for him to flee town. He loaded up the car and took off with Helen for the far west to visit the cities where he had worked on and off during the final eight years of Prohibition. He contacted old associates for help in finding residences that reduced the couple's visibility. He began at his old rumrunning base of Sausalito. One of his former bootlegger bosses directed him to a cousin, Louis Parente, in El Verano 45 miles north of San Francisco. The cousin had a sprawling country inn in the wine country aptly named the Parente Hotel. When Nelson moved there, he was joined by his two closest associates, Joe "Fatso"

Negri who had driven the gang's whiskey-laden truck, and Johnny Chase who rode shotgun along with the Baby Face.

The fugitive left Parente's and spent the next two months traveling the back roads of Nevada visiting tiny cities south of Reno. Baby Face and Helen were joined on their trip by an entourage of six. These were Chase with his new girlfriend, former waitress Sally Backman, Fatso Negri, and Jack and Grace Perkins of Chicago along with her child. Nelson wanted Grace and her child on his mad dashes across the country purely as a shield to divert suspicion. If a lawmen noticed him he would be in the company of two women and a child which did not fit Baby Face's profile. The group traveled in three cars. Nelson with the two women and child, Chase with his new-found love, and Negri taking along Jack Perkins. All used aliases and it is unlikely any of the proprietors where they stayed had any inkling they were catering to Public Enemy Number 1.

The first long stop of two weeks was at David Wally's resort at Wally Springs 52 miles south of Reno. The group then drove southeast more than 100 miles to Walker Lake and to Hawthorne, 12 miles south of the Lake, where they stayed a total of three weeks. The woman owner of the Walker Lake resort later testified, "They used to have gay times there. Why, I remember one night I had to go and warn them not to make so much noise because they might wake up the sheriff. That was the sheriff of Tonopah, you know. He was sleeping in another cabin with his wife and baby." The sheriff was visiting from the adjacent County of Nye, and the woman owner probably used the ruse of wakening a lawman to quiet the group down. It worked better than she expected because Public Enemy Number 1 did not want a shootout that would announce to the nation's lawmen where in the world he was hiding out, so the entourage quietly called it a night.[90]

Between destinations, the group slept in auto camps or outdoors on the natural desert under blankets during the comfortable summer and fall nights. They often prepared food along the roadside beside their cars. They occasionally ate in restaurants, but Nelson never went in with the group. They brought him a takeout meal, a chore usually handled by Grace.

Three weeks after the killing of Dillinger, Nelson's 66-year-old mother and 31-year-old sister held a press conference at the mother's home where the sister and her husband also resided. The two women announced that Chicago police had been watching their home. His mother, a Belgium native said, "They needn't think he'd be so dumb as to come here. We have not heard from him. We offered to speak in the hope that he will read the story, where he is, and know that we're standing by him." Nelson's sister was raising not only her six children but also her fugitive brother's 5-year-old boy and 4-year-old girl.[91]

Three months before this family press conference, Helen Nelson and the two gangsters' molls who the FBI had captured in the Little Bohemia raid pled guilty to harboring Dillinger, and a Federal Judge had given each a one-year sentence and then suspended it in favor of 18-months probation so the FBI could trail them back to their fugitive men. It took Helen three days to ditch her surveillance. In the press conference Nelson's mother and sister revealed Helen returned to his family's home, spent time with her children, and soon disappeared again, leaving the young ones behind. However both mother and sister denied they had seen Baby Face for two years. Months later the sister's husband revealed to local authorities that the fugitive had returned to his mother's home after escaping at Little Bohemia. Nelson was staying there when his wife snuck away from her FBI surveillance and rejoined him. It is curious that Hoover - a man who preached that a cherchez la femme was a criminal's weakness, and a man who lived with his mother until her death when he was 43 years old - never seemed to consider that a criminal would return home to visit his family or to have a soft place to land when in trouble. As usual the Director had not directed agents to place the family home under surveillance when Nelson visited even though his young children were being raised there.

At the family's press conference, Nelson's sister picked up her 13-month-old baby girl and said. "The federal men have told us they want to take my brother alive. I know what treatment they would give him. They say they want to learn a lot he knows. But I hope they never take him alive. The mother agreed, "So do I. Of course, I hope he keeps on escaping from them. But I don't see how he can go on much longer. I don't see what hope he has." His sister added, "He must have to pay heavily for protection everywhere. It's dreadful to think of his being hunted always." While their upset and contradictory feelings gave some insight into the impact of Nelson's behavior on his family, this press conference seems to have served just one purpose – mother and sister warned Baby Face he could not return home again or there would be a shootout at the house. This warning also applied to Helen who would face violation of probation and a new charge for harboring. This would have made her the first woman in history to be charged with harboring two successive Public Enemies Number 1, first Dillinger and then her husband, Baby Face.[92]

It had been four months since Nelson escaped the Little Bohemia raid fiasco, killing an agent on the way out, and the FBI was still without a lead as to his whereabouts. However about the same time that Nelson's mother was holding her press conference, San Francisco SAC E. P. Guinane learned for the first time that Nelson's disappearances from Chicago were often to the west coast. He got the information in a circuitous manner from the wine country to the north. Hotel proprietor Louis Parente told his visiting niece in passing that the country's most-wanted man had stayed at his resort. She returned home to Oakland and told her husband, a police detective, and he immediately forwarded the information to SAC Guinane across the Bay. Unfortunately the niece had heard about Nelson's visit three weeks after he had departed from the inn. Agents called upon Parente who told them what he knew about Nelson's closest pal Johnny Chase. He gave the agents their first information about Chase having a new girlfriend and that roly-poly Fatso Negri was Baby Face's other trusted friend. Agents also learned Nelson was driving a Hudson, but none of the employees at the inn had noticed the license number. The FBI notified police departments in the locales that Chase was known to frequent about his newly discovered associations and the Hudson.

This was fortuitous timing for the FBI because Chase and his girlfriend Sally Backman had recently separated from Nelson's party in Nevada and returned to Sausalito. Soon the city's Police Chief recognized Sally walking along the sidewalk, picked her up, and turned her over to the San Francisco FBI Office for an intense debriefing. She remained silent for two days before opening up. By the time she decided to turn state's witness against the other Baby Face harborers her knowledge about the whereabouts of Chase and Nelson was stale.

San Francisco SAC Guinane forwarded to the Chicago Office Sally's information about the locations where she had stayed with Chase and Nelson. Inspector Cowley assumed Baby Face would eventually return to his native Windy City where his children lived with his sister, and among his known haunts Cowley felt that a nice resort inn northwest of Chicago was the most likely place he would visit. Thus he had Sally flown to Chicago to see if she could visually identify the resort. She remembered the tiny city had an inn, two small lakes, and an iron bridge, and Nelson's contact there was named Eddie. Cowley assigned Agent Charles Winstead to drive her on a tour in hopes she would recognize the site. The pair traversed Lake and McHenry Counties that were between the northern border of Chicago's Cook County and the southern rim of Wisconsin. Agent Winstead and his prisoner asked local authorities along the way if they recognized the resort from her description. A deputy sheriff realized that Nelson's group had been at the Lake Como Inn in Lake Geneva, Wisconsin 75 miles northwest of Chicago, and he even knew the handy man was named Eddie. Agent Winstead put Sally on a plane and then interviewed Eddie and the owner of the Inn. To avoid harboring charges, both told everything they knew about Nelson's visit including that he was planning to return during the upcoming winter season.

To take advantage of this possibility Cowley assigned Agent Winstead and a partner to settle in a cottage at the resort graciously supplied by the owner. The two agents acted like tourists as they staked out the public areas waiting for the possible return of their prime target. With the agents sitting in wait, the trap was laid, but its success or failure would depend on whether the antsy Nelson would return to the comfort of old haunts or seek out new settings.[93]

A CROSS-COUNTRY PURSUIT

Two weeks after San Francisco SAC Guinane learned about Nelson's stay in the wine country, Baby Face, Helen, and Negri planned to meet up in Reno with Chase who had dropped his girlfriend off in Sausalito. The trio returned from Walker Lake to Wally Springs to cut more than half the distance off the planned trip to Reno, and there they waited for a message from Chase that he had arrived in Reno and at which location they should meet. They searched the *Reno Evening Gazette's* personals to find the information - "William Fields - Mother is very sick and keeps asking for you. Go home, Brother Bob." While the quartet were regrouping in Reno, SAC Guinane's agents eventually talked to someone who knew the model of Chase's current car, its license number, and the alias he had registered it under. Guinane's Office had previously sent Nelson's photo to police departments in the cities Chase was known to have visited and hit pay dirt. Reno Police Chief J. M. Kirkley later described receiving Nelson's photo. "I saw Baby Face in Reno about October 1. I identified him from photographs sent my office. I called San Francisco Department of Justice headquarters immediately. Shortly after that, the San Francisco office telephoned me to look for a car with a New York license, registered to J. Hogan, who was in reality, Chase. Baby Face was living in Hawthorne then. We spotted the New York car on the street. We had orders not to pick it up. I saw the car again the next night. Nine Department of Justice agents flew into Reno when I telephoned them. Next, we found the New York car in a local garage. It was watched for two weeks, with the hope that Chase would show up to claim the car. All this time we were in continuous contact with the Department of Justice."[94]

A number of local Reno businesses accommodated the financial-criminal clientele attracted to town by Graham and McKay. These felons were the most affluent tourists visiting town during the Great Depression, but many of the local businessmen may never have suspected these well-heeled customers were using aliases to cover their true identities. The casino partners sent players who needed car servicing to Frank Cochran's Air Service Garage that was located a short walk from the *Bank Club*. The garage was located on South Virginia Street two blocks south of the Truckee River bridge with the downtown casino hub on the north side.

After Police Chief Kirkley confirmed by telephone that he had seen Chase's car, San Francisco SAC Guinane and eight of his agents flew into town that evening. The agents went to Frank Cochran's Air Service Garage and searched Chase's vehicle to find a powerful array of weapons in the trunk. SAC Guinane later testified in the Nelson harborers' trial that the hunt was reaching its height. He showed photos of Nelson and his associates to Cochran and Fatso Negri to confirm the suspects had recently been there, but both men falsely denied ever having seen the men. To elicit the garage owner's cooperation in bringing down their most-wanted man, SAC Guinane took Cochran into his confidence. Guinane later testified, "I told him all about the case. I told him that Chase and Nelson had been associated in running rum between Sausalito and Reno. Then I told him how we intended to put our automobile in the garage opposite Chase's. Our car was loaded with camping equipment to make it look like a tourist's. The hood was left open so it would look as though it was being repaired." He continued his story at the trial. "Two of our agents and Police Chief Manuel Menotti of Sausalito, who knew both Nelson and Chase, were left in the garage. Police Chief J. M. Kirkley of Reno aided in preparing the trap. I asked Cochran to let us know if anyone telephoned about Chase's car, which we had traced to Reno from New York, and to signal us by adjusting his tie if anybody came in to inquire about it." In addition to the agents stationed inside the garage, SAC Guinane positioned others at nearby locations to keep the entrances under surveillance while waiting for Chase or Nelson to come to retrieve the car and its arsenal.[95]

SAC Guinane may have needed the garage owner's cooperation in setting up this trap, but he failed to consider that Cochran might be in cahoots with the dangerous criminal. No agents were assigned to watch his home. Cochran did dutifully report, but it was to Baby Face he supplied his information. Years earlier Nelson had made arrangements to check with Cochran at his home to get the all-clear nod that no law was around before returning to pick up the various cars he kept at the garage. When the FBI arrived in Reno Nelson had been laying low at Wally Springs. Driving a car the FBI had yet to identify, he returned to Reno and checked in with Cochran at his home. The garage owner warned the gangster that his garage was swarming with agents and he even supplied the FBI vehicles' license numbers to the Baby Face. In the same time frame another local lawman was talking to Cochran. Washoe County Sheriff Russell Trathen visited Cochran's home and confided he would like "to get Nelson, because it would help in the coming elections." Cochran listened stoically so as to not tip his association with this targeted criminal. The Sheriff was defeated.[96]

With the law bearing down on Nelson he was determined to retrieve the valuable difficult-to-replace major weapon cache. He directed his associates to maintain close watch of the garage to learn the agents' surveillance routines. Agents were camped next to Chase' car; a ring of agents watched the garage's entrances; and at a wider perimeter the lawmen were unknowingly surrounded by the forces of Public Enemy Number 1. Cochran had become suspicious that agents were watching his house so the next meeting with Nelson, Chase, and Negri was out on the lonely Virginia City highway near Reno. Nelson was furious over his seized car and weapons. He brashly made the decision to surprise the FBI agents and have his gang members charge en mass spraying machinegun fire at everyone in their path. Cochran later testified, "He was pacing up and down the road with a machine gun strapped to his shoulder. He said he was going to get the stuff. I told him not to, that it probably would make trouble, and someone would get killed." Nelson's shocked associates were eventually able to chill him out. A week later the hot-head repeated his threats to get the car at all costs, but Cochran warned how many agents were in wait. Nelson replied, "I know it. I've been in to look them over. I don't care how many of them there are. I've a good notion to go in there and clean them all up." He was eventually cooled off again. Then Nelson settled on leaving town with his associates to avoid all the law-enforcement heat boiling up in Reno.[97]

When Reno Police Chief Kirkley held his press conference describing how he had helped the FBI in its hunt for Public Enemy Number 1, he said the local newspapers had for some time agreed to cooperate with peace officers by remaining silent about the fact that well-known criminals bobbed in and out of town. Since Kirkley never arrested a major felon visiting town, it is likely that this was a clever way to keep reporters from questioning why all the big-time desperadoes came and went seemingly unmolested.

Nelson's goal was to head in the direction of his native Chicago, but he took a leisurely trip with layovers at isolated locations where he remained until he sensed the law might be closing in on him. His first and longest stop was at Wally Springs. During his stay the Sheriff in Gardnerville seven miles to the southeast visited Wally's three times asking the cook if she had seen a Hudson. She had seen Nelson's car but she said no because she thought his Hudson was a Plymouth. Baby Face and Helen moved on to Walker Lake while Chase and Negri went to Fallon 60 miles north. After a few days they reconnoitered at Walker Lake and the foursome continued toward Chicago in the Hudson and a Ford Truck that Chase had bought with Nelson's money to throw off lawmen searching for them, since a sedan had always been the type of car they drove. The Hudson's transmission conked out near Durango, Colorado, and Negri waited for it to be repaired while the other three continued on to Chicago. To avoid detection in cities where Baby Face's picture might have been in the local papers, they put Chase up in a hotel each night, and the couple slept in the truck in isolated spots despite the cold November temperatures. After arriving in Chicago, Nelson and Chase stole a new Ford V-8 sedan from a Chicago dealership. Negri had arrived in town first, ditched the Hudson that law enforcement was searching for, and obtained another vehicle. The next day the gang planned to regroup. Negri later testified while using Nelson's long-time alias with his associates of "Jimmy Burnell." "With Clarence Lieder, I loaded a car with ammunition and license plates. We were to meet Jimmy in the country and waited all day. Jimmy didn't show up though. We drove back to town." Nelson, Chase, and Helen were headed to meet with Negri when the trio ran headlong into lawmen. It was about to become Baby Face's longest day.[98]

DESTINATION CHICAGO

On their way to regrouping with Negri, Nelson with Helen and Chase first stopped at their safe-haven resort at Lake Geneva. They were looking to find handyman Eddie and arrange accommodations for the whole gang to relax, party, and make future plans. However the FBI's effective detective work had resulted in stationing two agents as tourists at the resort awaiting for the possible return visit of Public Enemy Number 1.

On what was about to become a very long afternoon four separate pairs of agents would encounter the fugitives in their stolen new car, but each duo in turn would seriously blow its assignment. These compounded failures by eight agents all resulted from FBI Director Hoover's failure to teach his detective staff the fundamentals of police work or to give any rudimentary training. His agents were mostly accountants and attorneys who had learned nothing about marksmanship, arrest techniques, tactical combat, strict adherence to proper procedure, or safeguarding the civilians they had sworn to protect.

Arriving at the Lake Como Inn, Baby Face, Chase, and Helen drove around looking for Eddie. Standing in front of the resort conducting their stake out was Agent Winstead and his partner. The unsuspecting trio pulled up to the two men and asked if they knew where Eddie was. Both agents realized they were talking to the dangerous killer. If they had whipped out their pistols they could have easily arrested or killed the unprepared and seated fugitives. But when the two agents had left their room on duty earlier that day they had not bothered to pack their guns. All the agents could do was tell the trio no and watch them drive off back toward Chicago. These agents later had to testify to this lapse in protocol under a defense attorney's cross-examination. As soon as the car disappeared from view, the two agents telephoned the Chicago FBI Office to report the fugitives were headed their way. At least they were able to supply the license-plate number. It was now 2:30 in the afternoon and the confrontation was soon to begin.

Inspector Cowley immediately swung into action. He advised two agents in the Office that Nelson was driving towards the Windy City from Lake Como on the Northwest Highway southeast. He directed them to intercept the fugitives by heading northwest and watching for the oncoming license plate. At that moment another pair of agents reported into the Office from a Chicago apartment. The Inspector also dispatched them in the same direction. Then Cowley told Agent Herman Hollis to join him in the hunt in a third car. SAC Purvis wanted to accompany them, but the Inspector made it clear he was to remain in the office. Police do not like wearing armored-plated vests because they are hot and uncomfortable. The temperature was not an issue on that late November winter day, but Cowley and Hollis decided to ignore procedure and leave their bulky vests behind. Adding to the agents' lack of preparedness, Inspector Cowley had always been a desk jockey and never bothered to qualify with any type of weapon at the gun range. The three pairs of agents were now on patrol on the same Highway in the same direction heading towards the oncoming fugitives.

At 3:50 p.m. the fugitives were on this Highway outside Barrington about halfway between Lake Geneva and Chicago. The first two agents to leave the Office drove past Nelson's shiny new car in the opposite direction but failed to recognize that the driver was the man they were searching for, or that his license number was the one they were looking for. Reporters learned this soon afterwards when they overheard a conversation at a public telephone by one of the two agents calling the Chicago FBI Office. When the agent heard what had transpired since they had been searching on the Highway, he exclaimed to the Office, "Good God, we must have passed that car 10 minutes before the shooting."[99]

At 4:00 p.m. the pair of agents who had called into the Office from an apartment saw a Ford V-8 coming towards them on the other side of the grassy median divide that separated the two lanes of busy traffic in each direction. As the Ford went past they saw half the number on the license plate and it matched. The agents hung a Ueee and pulled in behind Nelson's car. As the agents confirmed the complete number was the one they wanted, Nelson pulled his own Ueee to head in the opposite direction in an apparent attempt to escape from this fast pursuing car. However immediately after Baby Face past the agents' car, he hung a second Ueee and began his own hot pursuit of the agents. Chase later testified what transpired next, but he referred to Nelson by his gang's alias of "Jimmy." "Jimmy, who is a fast driver, caught up with them. Jimmy told them, 'Pull over,' and he said to me: 'They may belong to the Dago syndicate in Chicago. Put the gun on them.' He told me to shoot. I said, 'What for? I have no reason to shoot any one.' Helen cried: 'For God's sake, don't shoot.'" The agent in the passenger seat later testified "Both cars were going southeast. Nelson drove up beside us and yelled, 'Pull over.' The man in the back seat had a Winchester repeating rifle trained at our heads, completely covering us. Then [Agent] McDade speeded up. We ducked our heads. Three shots were fired at us. I turned around in the seat and fired back with my automatic pistol, aiming at their windshield. We traded shot for shot, going 75 miles an hour. I reloaded my clip as we got to the west limits of Barrington. The Ford appeared to be gaining on us. We went on to Palatinc. Then McDade and I got out and hid in some tall grass, waiting for the Ford. A Ford passed, but it was not the same one." Chase continued his testimony with, "They speeded away and then started to shoot at us. Jimmy took his revolver and began firing with his left hand [out the window], the other hand on the wheel. Helen cried out that she was shot. Jimmy said: 'Do we have to be killed before we can shoot any one?' Then I put a gun to the windshield and fired through it." The windows on both cars exploded but Helen had not been shot. The only difference in their testimonies is both sides claimed the other side fired first.[100]

The two agents' decision to speed ahead more than five miles and hide in wait is inexplicable. As aggressively as these bank-robbing goons charged when confronted, their efforts were always intended for escape, whether it was to take out the lawmen, or to make them cower long enough to burst free. As soon as the fugitive's car was out of sight, it was all but certain they would turn in reverse, or more likely turn on a side street and take a very round-about out-of-the-way route to their intended destination. Not one of these murderous police-escape artists was ever known to charge ahead into any situation they thought might be a possible police trap.

When police are well ahead of oncoming violent offenders, they do not lay down beside the road hiding in tall grass, but set up a road block to stop their progress and take them into custody. These two agents' strategy had multiple serious flaws. The fugitives were approaching at high speed. By the time the agents recognized their vehicle and opened fire, they would have had almost no time before the escapees would have been out of accurate firing range. In this tiny time frame the agents would have had the difficult task of trying to hit desperadoes racing at high speed. Also busy traffic would have been passing the fugitives' vehicle in both directions putting many civilians at risk. Thus the agents strategy had almost no chance for success and great likelihood of wounding or killing innocent people. Fortunately the fugitives did not continue on because the so-called trap these two agents had set up was a potential cluster fuck of civilian carnage at an horrific magnitude.[101]

Interestingly, the agent who was driving admitted during cross-examination by a defense attorney that when the fugitive's car pulled beside them and Chase had the rifle trained on the two Agents, Chase could have killed them but did not fire a shot. The agent was asked if he drove away from the desperadoes as quickly as possible and he testified, "So would you!" which caused a burst of laughter that caused the Judge to quiet the court.[102]

The car with Inspector Cowley and Agent Hollis was just minutes behind the FBI car that reversed direction and got into the shootout with Nelson. All of a sudden Cowley and Hollis were amazed to hear a gunfight and then see the high-speed battle roaring down the Highway towards them. As soon as the shoot 'em up went past, Agent Hollis hung a Ueee and tried to catch up behind Nelson's fast-moving car. The desperadoes were so involved in the shootout with the agents in the car in front of them that they were unaware the second FBI car had reversed direction and taken pursuit behind them. Then one of the pistol shots from the agents' car in front blew a gapping hole in the fugitives' gas line next to the fuel pump disabling the motor. As it slowed, the lead agents' car continued to roar out of sight and they went on to take their grass-covered shooting-gallery position miles ahead.

The fugitives realized they were having engine trouble and were relieved to see the lead agents disappearing from view. Chase later testified, "We went on down the highway and suddenly I heard a ping and the sound of broken glass and saw our back window had been hit. There were two men following us in a Hudson. 'We're going to get murdered,' I cried to Jimmy."[103]

As this new gunfight passed alongside the fields outside North Side Barrington Park, an unsuspecting local resident closed in behind the FBI car as it slowed along with Nelson's car. The man later said, "I hear a lot of cracking noises. It took me half a second to discover it was gunfire. I jammed on the brakes, backed my car right into a field, jumped out and ran like hell. Shots were buzzing around my ears, and I flopped down in the mud. I got up and ran to get farther away and somebody shot at me again." When Inspector Cowley saw a man running from another car, he assumed he was with Nelson and sprayed him with machinegun fire twice even though the FBI had no reason to believe another vehicle accompanied Nelson that day. Fortunately for this innocent civilian, Inspector Cowley had no experience firing or aiming guns.[104]

As Inspector Cowley showered the fleeing civilian, Agent Hollis pulled alongside the desperadoes' car to try to force them off the Highway. Nelson was approaching the Park's dirt road entrance on the right but still going too fast to turn easily. Baby Face attempted the turn but veered to the other side of the entry road running over the curb onto the overgrowth 50 feet from the corner. Agent Hollis pulled back into the Highway's right lane and screeched his brakes as he went past the corner about 50 feet before stopping over the curb in vegetation.

Three gas stations were lined up in a row across from the Park entrance road and about a dozen employees and customers became alarmed at the sound of Inspector Cowley shooting at the running civilian and then Agent Hollis' screeching brakes. The stunned people dropped to the ground and watched in astonished horror as bullets peppered the brick wall of one filling station and pierced at least one parked car. These witnesses later completed local police reports and several testified as to what happened next.

Chase testified, "They had fired several times when we pulled in about 50 feet off the Northwest Highway. The other car stopped on the Highway. Jimmy told me to pass the big gun from behind to him. I did so and he started firing at the men in the Hudson. I got out on the right side of the car." A woman witness said, "A woman got out of the gang car which had slipped half into a ditch. She ran down the side road a few yards and then threw herself flat in the ditch." Then she added, "All four men were using automobiles as shields at first." When Nelson first fired through his driver door window he was very vulnerable because bullets turn door metal into shrapnel. When the two agents and two fugitives battled away using their car hoods for protection, the part of their bodies covered by the engine block was shielded by a thick mass of impenetrable armor. The fugitives finally hit Inspector Cowley in the stomach and chest. He fell backwards mortally wounded but a vest would have stopped both bullets from penetrating his flesh. Before being hit Cowley had first put seven machinegun bullets into Nelson's stomach and chest, but the gangster appeared unfazed. The reckless and impulsive Baby Face still rushed out into the open towards Agent Hollis with his machinegun ablaze. Hollis fired back with his sawed-off shotgun hitting Nelson with 10 slugs up and down both legs but all the witnesses said he did not act wounded at all though hit 17 times. When Hollis had emptied his shotgun he ran away across the Highway firing his pistol backwards. He was within arm's reach of a thin telephone pole when Nelson felled him with shots in the left side, back, and base of the skull tearing away part of his head.[105]

A witness testified about the continuing action. "[Nelson] ran toward Hollis shooting. Chase was firing from his car. Hollis fell in a ditch on the [far] north side of the road. Then Nelson ran to the ditch, dropped his gun and looked at Hollis [to confirm he was no longer a threat]. Nelson motioned with his hand to Chase that he was going to get in the [FBI's] Hudson. He got in this car, backed it to the Barrington Park entrance on the south side of the Highway. Cowley was lying in a ditch on the south side of the road near a telephone pole. Nelson drove the Hudson to where his [crippled] Ford was stalled and Chase transferred guns from the rear of the Ford to the other car. Chase got behind the wheel and Nelson sagged in the front passenger seat. The woman ran from the weeds and jumped into the rear of the car and they sped off." Other witnesses added a few details. Chase had been shot once in the leg and he had obvious trouble walking while the seemingly invincible Nelson with 17 wounds kept right on charging, walking, and driving. Neither fugitive appeared to have had any idea where Helen had gone and were preparing to drive off without her when she ran up and jumped in the backseat amidst all their high-powered weaponry.[106]

As the fugitives pulled away the action turned to one of the gas stations. An off-duty and unarmed highway policeman had been gassing up when the gunfire erupted, and he and the attendant hit the ground like the other witnesses did when the shooting started. When the fugitives settled into the FBI's car, the witnesses started getting up and the attendant handed the policeman a rifle. He fired several shots in vain as the fugitives headed northwest away from Chicago. The civilian who Inspector Cowley had tried to machinegun down had taken sanctuary at this station, and he, the policeman, and attendant went to check the condition of the prostrate men. The targeted civilian later testified, "We saw Hollis lying dead. Then we saw Cowley and at first I started to cuss him out, but he motioned me to get down and listen to him. He was mumbling incoherently. Then we found a card in his pocket which identified him as a government agent." When the defense asked, "Didn't you blame Cowley for the Shooting?" the witness replied, "I talked wildly when I first saw him. After all I had just escaped being shot." The witness explained that he had lost his watch and fountain pen in his flight from the shooting. When asked, "Are you going to sue the government for the pen and watch?" he replied, "You don't expect me to sue Baby Face Nelson for them, do you?" The policeman said Cowley whispered, "I'm a federal officer. Help me but take care of my partner first." Unfortunately Hollis was already dead. An ambulance rushed Inspector

Cowley to the hospital. The two agents who had sped ahead from Nelson's pursuit were still lying in wait in the tall grass a few miles away where they heard none of this deadly gunfight.[107]

The moment the Chicago FBI Office received word of the shootings, SAC Purvis hurried to see Cowley in the hospital. After spending a little time with the gravely-wounded Inspector, Purvis held a press conference even though he had learned nothing about the day's events. He could not have given a more vacuous presentation because his goal was not to deliver relevant information but simply to stand in front of the amassed reporters and their cameras. Purvis started with a lie. He said earlier that afternoon he was going to accompany Cowley in the patrol car to the shooting scene but another matter held him at the office. Remember the truth is Cowley had banished him from the hunt. Then Purvis said, "I am reasonably sure that Nelson and a confederate were the men in the fight, but I don't know, and I have no details of the chase leading up to the shooting. Also, I do not know where the other agents were at the time." By other agents he was referring to the pair overheard by reporters on the public telephone at the hospital saying to the Chicago Office that they must have past Nelson's car without recognizing him 10 minutes before the shooting. After Purvis delivered his nonsense to local papers he telephoned reporters in other states with really whopping lies that contradicted his press conference. The SAC claimed he had rushed to Cowley's deathbed, obtained a deathbed identification of Nelson, and taken "an oath in Cowley's blood" to avenge him. This preposterous grandstanding story was accompanied with headlines in papers like, "If It's the Last Thing I do, I'll Get Baby Face Nelson." Remember only minutes before, after allegedly having talked to Cowley, Purvis told Chicago reporters he only thought the shooter might be Nelson. Three days later SAC Purvis had a subordinate agent testify at the Coroner's Inquest that just before Cowley died he whispered in Purvis' ear, "Nelson - we got him." However the agent who testified was never with Cowley in the hospital so Purvis had to have been the source who gave this false information to the agent who then submitted this bogus information at the inquest to get the SAC's name in the paper one more time.[108]

Four months after the shooting, the Doctor, who had operated on Cowley in a vain effort to save his life, testified in court as to what actually happened in the Inspector's room, exposing Purvis' many falsehoods about talking to Cowley. The Doctor acknowledged Purvis was in the room before the surgery but made it clear the SAC never had an opportunity to talk to Cowley as "He was conscious but suffering from shock." From the moment Cowley arrived at the hospital he was incapable of saying anything to anyone.[109]

The morning after the shootouts the articles began appearing, and Purvis' totally false press pronouncements became the last straw for the Director. With two dead agents laying on slabs in the Morgue, Hoover as usual was focused on his own publicity image. The Director had Inspector Hugh Clegg immediately fly to Chicago and take over leadership of that Office. Hoover then wrote a memo to file for his records detailing his orders to Inspector Clegg. He wanted Purvis away from the hospital, reporters, the office, and any other public place.[110]

Hoover wanted to fire his incorrigible press-hound, but he was afraid of public reaction because Purvis' false statements to the press after the Dillinger, Floyd, and Cowley killings had made him Public Hero Number One. Hoover was also afraid to demote Purvis, but he isolated him from the rest of the staff and made his life uncomfortable trying to pressure him to resign. Purvis never talked to the press again while an FBI agent. A week later the Director had an agent give the following unattributed statement to the *Chicago American* - Purvis "is incapacitated by overwork and is on sick leave. ... Insiders do not expect him to return to the command of the Chicago office." At the same time Hoover was planting this seed of Purvis' demise with the press, Attorney General Cummings publicly banned everyone in the FBI from giving out information about major cases. The AG also denied that Purvis would resign or be transferred but he failed to mention his loss of authority over the Chicago Office. As usual the Director got the AG to relent on this order so the Director along with the AG could take over the authority to comment on any case. However, Hoover continued the AG's ban on any other FBI official talking to the press without his prior approval.[111]

When Cowley's Doctor testified he also said the only time his patient spoke after the surgery was upon recognizing his wife at his bedside. He said, "Hello, sweetheart." Cowley passed 10 hours after the shooting. Cowley was 35-years old and Hollis was 28. The two deceased agents were married with small children. Both had been attorneys rather than law enforcers before joining the FBI. When told of her son's death, Cowley's mother said, "That's just what I expected. He expected it, too. He knew of his precarious life and had planned to leave it and set up a law practice but he never did." Hollis' graveside service in a stinging snow in Des Moines, Iowa was raw with emotion. His widow sat calmly with her small son at the edge of the grave as last prayers were read, but as the casket was lowered into the grave she leapt up screaming, "Take me with you; O, take me with you." Then she collapsed and had to be carried to a waiting car. After the service ended, Hollis' parents remained. They had not spoken to each other in years, but they stood together in their mutual grief.[112]

THE FINAL SEARCH

The FBI put out an APB for its car that Nelson had stolen, and all agents and local police departments instituted a major manhunt for the escaped killers of the two FBI officials. Washington Headquarters issued orders to shoot Nelson on sight while imposing censorship on all official information about events that preceded the battle.

At the crime scene the Lake County Sheriff examined Nelson's abandoned stolen car. In addition to the blown-out fuel line, the two agents fleeing Nelson's car had punctured the radiator causing the car to boil over. Its back seat was heaped with a half dozen rifles and machineguns, several boxes of canned foods, three suitcases containing men's clothing, two battered men's hats, several cans of motor oil, and six sets of license plates from as many states.

Returning to how the fugitives escaped from the shootout scene, Chase later testified he was transferring their guns to the FBI's Hudson when Nelson told him, "'Drop everything and take me to the priest.' I asked him where Helen was and he said he didn't know. I got behind the wheel and then she ran up and jumped in. Jimmy moaned: 'I'm done for.' Helen was crying." Baby Face and Helen had met a Catholic Priest at a Long Beach, Indiana resort a year earlier. The couple was using aliases, and they and he took a liking to each other so the Priest had invited them to visit him when they were in the area. The Priest lived with his sister in Wilmette 25 miles east of Barrington. Chase and Helen knocked at the Priest's door and asked him to take in the badly-wounded Nelson, but the priest refused to allow anyone in the house. He offered to drive his car and lead them to a hospital. Chase's testimony continued as he started following the Priest's car. "I told him [Nelson] we were going to a hospital. Jimmy said: 'Turn around. I know a place to go.' I drove to the house directed, parked the car in the rear and two men came out and took Jimmy in. One of the men said: 'You'll have to get that car out of here.' I told him I would if he would come with me because I didn't know my way about. With this man driving ahead, I drove the car to a road I think was 41A. Just as I crossed some railroad tracks the car ran out of gas. I got out and left it there. I asked a man who was passing how to get to Chicago. He directed me to a railroad station. I got on the train and went to Chicago." Police found the FBI's stolen vehicle the next day in Winnetka five miles north of Wilmette.[113]

Back at the two men's residence, Helen had placed her husband on a hotel blanket because he was bleeding profusely from 17 wounds, seven in his torso and five in each leg. She removed the soaked clothing from his blood-stained body, and bound a piece of cotton cloth around his abdomen to try to plug up a gaping wound. This was the fatal damage as it caused internal hemorrhaging.

These wounds resulted from 50 machinegun bullets fired by Inspector Cowley and 10 shotgun cartridge discharges by Agent Hollis. Both FBI agents had died without knowing if they had hit or killed Public Enemy Number 1 who had taken their lives.

The morning after the shooting, as it was going on 7 a.m., Nelson died with his face badly contorted. Helen and the two men wrapped his unclad body in the blanket and dumped it and his blood-soaked clothes about two-and-a-half miles apart in suburban Skokie (then Niles Center). This was six miles from Winnetka where the stolen FBI car ran out of gas. His body was left in a dry blanket in a recently rain-soaked grassy ditch on a parkway at the entrance to St. Paul's Lutheran Cemetery so authorities knew what time it had been dumped. Nelson had grown a small golden-colored mustache. In addition three finger tips on the left hand had been filed in an apparent effort to change their texture just as the little finger tip of the right hand appeared to have been treated with acid.

Minutes later Helen anonymously called undertaker Philip Sadowski who had previously buried her mother and a sister. The undertaker called the police about the strange call and they found the body at the location described. As requested Sadowski conducted the funeral at his parlor across the street from St. Mary of the Angels Catholic Church by offering a few prayers, but no priest attended to wish his soul well. His family was there but not his wife who had already been picked up at her parents home by agents for harboring her husband.

At the conclusion of Inspector Cowley's funeral a reporter asked his widow how she felt about her husband having killed his slayer, Baby Face. She replied, "I am thankful for that. It makes me very glad. I know that Mr. Cowley felt keenly that he would like to accomplish that job. Knowing that he is dead, I can feel sure that Mr. Cowley would not have felt that his death was so useless."

Nelson established an ignoble record of killing the most FBI agents in the line of duty, three. Baby Face was Public Enemy Number 1 for 128 days, from the FBI's assassination of Dillinger until he and the two agents caused each others' deaths in that park. He died at age 25 appropriately branded the "most desperate criminal" of his time. The two men who were charged with him in his first arrest for a series of Chicago bank and jewelry robberies told police then that he was "a killer at heart" who they always feared. He had a quick trigger finger, was merciless, and shot in the back two of the three FBI agents he killed. He had an insane hatred of "coppers and G-Men," the public's title for FBI agents when they started carrying guns.

Nelson was not known to have committed any heists from the time he escaped the FBI's bungled Little Bohemia raid for the final seven months of his life. A number of victims in different robberies thought Baby Face might have been one of the gunmen, but in addition to their uncertainty other victims at these crimes were adamant that he was not one of the banditos. Prohibition had ended earlier that year so shotgun jobs on liquor convoys had become an obsolete profession. Unlike most financial criminals who blow their cash fast, Nelson lived unassumingly, and he was known to stash his spoils with trusted associates. Fatso Negri later testified in his Baby Face harboring trial that Nelson had instructed him to fly to Reno and tell associate Henry "Tex" Hall to get the loot from the robberies Nelson had left for safe keeping with Tom "Tobe" Williams, a Vallejo, California hospital manager, and give it to Hall's employer, Jim McKay. Robbers and con men routinely placed their ill-gotten gains in *Bank Club* casino cashier's safety deposit boxes during their Reno stays. The FBI was never able to locate Nelson's hoard, and not one of his associates ever spent like he had it. Could Graham and McKay have ended up with the remaining balance?[114]

While Nelson may not have pulled a robbery for over a half year, Chicago's Chief of Detectives believed he was planning a major holdup for the day before what turned out to be his funeral. It was to have targeted a Chicago Loop department store's daily average $150,000 bank deposit. Without warning upwards of a dozen desperadoes were to have blasted away in wild west fashion to terrorize and control the employees and customers. From the moment the Detective Chief heard about the plans a week earlier, he had machinegun-toting detectives accompany the bank messenger to discourage such an attack that would have put so many civilians at risk. This police protection was given while the store turned its cash transfers to an armored-car service. It is certainly possible someone was planning such a robbery, but it does not fit in neatly with the time line of the arrival of Nelson, Chase, and Negri in Chicago. Chase and Negri never mentioned it but then it would have made them look even worse with law enforcement and also with their criminal associates if they had revealed their names and intent.[115]

In a seven-month period, FBI agents killed three notorious public enemies – John Dillinger, Pretty Boy Floyd, and Baby Face Nelson. Within months or weeks before each one's death all three were seen in Reno or Lake Tahoe under the protection of Graham and McKay. These were just a few of the dangerous looking strangers observed by casino pit executives, local players, and reporters at the gambling tables of the *Bank Club* and *Cal-Neva Lodge* casinos.

CLOSING THE CASE

Two days after Nelson's deadly shootout with the FBI, agents captured his widow at her parents home. Six months earlier she had pled guilty to harboring John Dillinger at Little Bohemia, and she had been given 18-months probation at the request of the FBI in the hope she would lead agents to her husband. However three days later she ditched their surveillance and rejoined her husband's fugitive run. At that time the Federal Judge revoked Helen's probation and ordered her arrested for having violated probation, and the agents now acted on this outstanding warrant.

A week after her capture, a Federal Judge gave Helen a year's prison sentence at the Women's Federal Reformatory in Milan, Michigan for violation of probation by associating with gangsters and failing to report to her probation officer. Now she faced at least a charge for harboring her husband and possibly also as an accomplice in the killing of the two FBI agents, meaning she would never see her children again. She quickly gave up the name of her husband's partner in the shootout and agreed to be the state's star witness against him. With this information the FBI intensified its efforts to capture Chase.

With maximum time allowed for good behavior Helen was released after almost 10 months, but she was transferred to San Francisco to await trail for harboring her husband. Three months later, an African-American woman prisoner pressed a rabbit's foot into her hand for luck as she prepared to plead guilty. The Federal Judge granted her probation because she had turned in Chase and had been prepared to testify against him if needed by the prosecution. At 22 she reentered the straight life from which she had come. She raised the couple's two small children and spent the rest of her life working in a Chicago factory.[116]

On the day of the deadly shootout the FBI had two dead agents and no idea who Nelson's killing partner was. Agents had no reason to suspect Chase more than any of Nelson's many other associates. Besides law enforcement had not heard anything about Chase's whereabouts since he had dropped off girlfriend Sally in Sausalito, and his background did not fit the gangster profile. He had no police record except one arrest for drunkenness so authorities had no fingerprints of him and no photos to show to witnesses. Chase had held legitimate jobs until riding shotgun during Prohibition, and the only other crime he was known to have committed was harboring Baby Face. It was not until Chase started carrying a machinegun to fight side by side with Nelson on his fugitive flight that he became a major public enemy.

With no special reason to suspect Chase, the FBI would likely have looked elsewhere, but agents had quickly arrested Nelson's wife and she informed them that Chase was the couple's traveling companion and was the other shooter in the killing of the two agents. Her information placed him in the Chicago area on that fateful day, and an investigation established that soon afterwards an employment ad in the Windy City attracted his interest because it was for car drivers to Seattle, Washington. This job would get him back to the west coast, but he had to register with the police for a chauffeur's license under an alias and was photographed. This would be the only photo of him ever taken by law enforcement and it would be his undoing. He drove west to Seattle as a chauffeur and then hitched rides south to Mount Shasta, California near the Oregon border.

The San Francisco FBI Office had already called upon each of Chase's known associates and warned them that if they had any contact with him and failed to report it they would be facing harboring charges like those brought against the confederates of Nelson, Dillinger, and Floyd. Chase tried to borrow money from employees he used to work with at the State Fish Hatcheries. They reported his presence to local police. One month after the Chicago shootout, the Mount Shasta Police Chief recognized Chase from his photo thumbing on a highway. Unarmed he gave no resistance, but his braggadocio came out while being fingerprinted. He told the Chief if he had had a pistol "there would have been one less policeman around here."[117]

The next day Chase was transported to Chicago for trial in the murders of Inspector Cowley and Agent Hollis. He rode in a stateroom on the Overnight Limited train wearing leg arms and guarded by six agents. Again FBI Director Hoover's undisciplined boys ignored the Constitutional and statutory requirements. They failed to take him before a U.S. Commissioner or Judge for both just-cause arraignment and approval to remove the prisoner from one federal court district to another, similar to a state extradition proceeding. In addition the FBI was prohibited by law from transporting prisoners interstate as this was reserved for U.S. Marshals, and examples would soon develop that illustrated how inept J. Edgar's FBI could be at moving prisoners between locales.

Chase was the first person tried under the year-and-half-old federal statute making the slaying of a federal agent while on duty an offense punishable by the death penalty. It was passed as a result of the Kansas City Massacre. Because Nelson's widow was prepared to testify against Chase, he readily admitted he was at the shooting scene but his whole defense was that he had not shot anyone. The state's witnesses were the people at the gas stations across the street, and the two agents who had run away and hid in the grass. Chase was the only defense witness. After four hours the Federal Jury found him guilty of murdering Inspector Cowley but recommended mercy with a verdict of "Guilty without capital punishment" meaning automatic life imprisonment. Three U.S. Marshals took him manacled hand and foot on the Overland Limited to Alcatraz Island Prison.

Within a few months of Chase entering Alcatraz, he claimed he had watched Nelson kill Reno bank manager Roy Frisch more than a year before, and that he could locate the body buried in the desert. Frisch was to have been an important witness in the mail fraud swindling trial of Reno gambling kings, Graham and McKay, who were Nelson's former bosses and his safe-haven protectors when he later became a fugitive. Because a key federal prosecution witness had been killed, U.S. AG Cummings ordered Hoover and his agents to investigate and try to find the manager's remains. The FBI transported convict Chase to the Hawthorne area where he and Nelson had hid out while on the run. Chase had great familiarity with the isolated back roads, but he would suddenly become confused about the route or forget what the precise location looked like. In addition Chase damaged his credibility by giving agents a different motive for the killing on different occasions. Each of the two stories earned him an escorted tour of the desert before the FBI concluded the lifer simply wanted a couple short vacations from the Rock. A cold case investigation of Frisch's disappearance in the next book in this series about the history of the Reno gambling industry solves this mystery, and neither Nelson nor Chase had anything to do with the crime even though both were definitely in town at the time it was committed.

Two decades into Chase's sentence a court motion was filed on his behalf demanding an immediate trial on the indictment charging him with Agent Hollis' murder or else dismissal of the case. Six months later a U.S. District Judge dismissed the pending indictment for lack of a speedy trial making Chase eligible for parole. His requests were routinely denied for 11 years until he was finally paroled after serving almost 32 years in Alcatraz and Leavenworth. Freed at age 64 he worked as a janitor for the next six years until dying of cancer.[118]

The day after Nelson's deadly shootout with the FBI, agents began arresting 17 persons for harboring him in flight which carried a maximum penalty of two years imprisonment. The FBI's statement reflected Hoover's homosexual hatred of women by stating that the outlaws could not have operated on such a deadly scale without the aid of their "contact" women so agents would relentlessly bring these women to punishment. The FBI's statement also falsely attacked the Federal Judge who suspended Helen Gillis' sentence to make it possible for her to assist Baby Face on his fugitive run, when the suspension was given at the request of the Director and it was his inadequate training of agents that let her so easily escape their surveillance.

Of the 17 persons charged by the FBI, Fatso Negri and Chase's girlfriend Sally Bachman pled guilty and became the prosecutions star witnesses against the seven who were finally tried for harboring Nelson. When Negri was pressed at trial to fix a date of when he had met Pretty Boy Floyd, he testified, "before Pretty Boy was killed." Ten days after Chase was convicted this Federal Jury convicted four of the seven harborers including Reno garage owner Cochran and casino employee H. O. "Tex" Hall. Despite assisting Nelson to ultimately murder two FBI agents, the Judge did not impose more than a year on any of the four convicted. One of the three acquitted was Mrs. Grace Perkins who rode in the Nelsons' car with her baby although her husband had pled guilty before the trial.[119]

THE SILENCING OF PURVIS

Seven months after the deadly Nelson shootout, Purvis announced his resignation. Instead of leaving quietly he held a final FBI press conference. He claimed his reasons were "purely personal," but he was clearly unprepared to answer any questions. He denied rumors he had "had differences" with the boss. Reporters pointed out to Purvis that Director Hoover's name was used by the FBI office in every city when reporting arrests of criminals except in Chicago where Purvis' name was used. His reply was "Frankly, I'm glad to get out of here," and then he refused to talk further. A year after his resignation, an in-depth article claimed his ouster was forced - "Where discharges would bring unfavorable reaction Hoover is said to force resignations. It is a well known fact that Melvin C. Purvis, one-time head of the Chicago G-men, who by a series of exploits for a time threatened to eclipse Hoover in the public eye, found relations so uncomfortable that he resigned." Purvis' banishment from public contact by Hoover was confirmed in two other articles by the former SAC's confidential secretary, Doris Lockerman. She wrote, "The Dillinger hunt made him a hero with the public and strengthened his hold on his men. His reputation increased after he led the chase in which Pretty Boy Floyd was tracked down and killed. It apparently increased too much for the pleasure of his superiors in Washington. They saw to it that he got no assignments which would put him in the public eye. He spent most of his last six months in the service interviewing applicants for jobs as agents." The SAC also filled out personnel reports and stared into space as he received demeaning letters from the Director over trivial infractions such as being unavailable by phone or being late in getting the latest Chicago newspapers delivered to Headquarters. In another article Lockerman wrote, "I watched the machinery turn which made a public hero, and saw that hero forced into a partial decline and eventual resignation because his publicity became so great that it seemed to threaten the job of his boss in Washington, J. Edgar Hoover." In the few speeches Purvis gave after leaving the FBI he devoted most of his time going into details about his supposed killing of wanted criminals rather than discussing the goals, policies, and procedures of effective law enforcement.[120]

Soon after leaving the FBI, Purvis opened a private detective agency, but Hoover had enough influence with local law enforcement to prevent any cooperation, putting him out of business. But even the Director could not constrain Purvis' unbridled penchant for publicity. Less than a year after the SAC left the FBI, Hoover was incensed when Purvis established himself again as a highly-publicized detective. This time it was in cartoon adventure scenarios on the backs of Post Toasties cereal boxes and in large newspaper ads in the Sunday newspaper comic sections. These ads were the width of a page and a third of its height. Each ad contained a cartoon story of "How America's Ace 'G-Man' captured a notorious criminal." Each weekly ad began, "Mervin Purvis, formerly the ace G-Man of the Department of Justice … who directed the capture of Dillinger, 'Pretty Boy' Floyd, 'Baby Face' Nelson, and scores of other public enemies. Mr. Purvis reveals here the methods used in capturing desperate criminals." Each adventure was supposedly taken from the confidential files. Post Toasties simply changed the face of its four-year old cartoon character, Inspector Post, who held a secret operator's badge for his Junior Detective Corps, with the face of former star G-Man Purvis who held a G-Man shield for his Melvin Purvis Law and Order Patrol. Purvis organized Junior G-Men for Post Toasties. These young boys sent in two box tops to become an official Melvin Purvis Junior G-Man with a badge, handcuffs, and a secret code. This gig lasted more than a year. At the same time he landed a radio detective job announcing the children's show *Junior G-Men.*[121]

Months into these two public-relations jobs Purvis autobiography, *American Agent,* was published in 1936. He was surprisingly modest about himself but glorified his alleged exploits. He was the hero in these adventures starting with Dillinger. Purvis avoided mentioning his two bosses – Hoover and the slain Cowley - or his own demotion. Hoover was so infuriated that he falsely changed Purvis' voluntary resignation to termination "with prejudice" meaning it was for bad conduct. The Director turned his gossip-collecting forces to seeking out scurrilous information on his former SAC until his FBI file became as thick as those for the criminals he had hunted. Their mutual animosity had grown into a personal war between two egocentric, mean-spirited, petty, childish bureaucrats fighting for imagery instead of protecting, serving, and respecting justice, truthfulness, or any other ideal. Ironically Purvis' book became a best-seller while Hoover's first book *Persons in Hiding* written by a ghost-writer two years later about many of the same cases languished in the stores. However Hoover's book did lead to three separate G-Man movies.

Purvis left the limelight while serving during World War II. He returned to South Carolina where he was involved with a small local radio station. Then he became the announcer for the G-Man radio show *Top Secrets of the FBI* that was not sanctioned by Hoover. He was presented as "The Former Ace Agent of the FBI" and also his lifelong calling card "The Man Who Got Dillinger." "Purvis's announcing style gave the show its only suspense: he stumbled repeatedly over his lines, sometimes pausing eerily in mid-sentence as though he could not quite believe what he was reading," according to the remembrances of historian Richard Gid Powers. Meanwhile Hoover continued to abuse the power of his office to frustrate Purvis' career, especially with law enforcement whenever possible including blocking his opportunity for a federal judgeship in 1952.[122]

At age 56 Purvis had inoperable cancer and was depressed. His wife was gardening at their home when she heard a shot fired inside. She ran to find her husband's body with a bullet through the jaw from a .45 automatic that his fellow agents had given him when he resigned. The FBI, and most people, labeled it a suicide but some argued that he may have been trying to remove a jammed bullet. This possibility actually worsens Purvis' professional memory because anyone experienced with shooting does not point a gun at their face especially one they know is loaded.[123]

Chapter 7

IMAGERY VERSUS LAW ENFORCEMENT

COMPETING ANTI-CRIME CAMPAIGNS

While the FBI was hunting and killing three successive leading Public Enemies, AG Cummings continued his aggressive newspaper and radio-news War on Crime. He ratcheted it up five weeks after the John Dillinger assassination by hiring the *Brooklyn Eagle's* Washington correspondent to direct the Justice Department's crusade. Then weeks after the killing of Baby Face Nelson, the AG held a Conference on Crime attended by law enforcement officials from across the nation. The AG explained to these lawmen that his high-powered publicity campaign against crime was to turn the public's respect for, or need for, law enforcement into the ultimate crime-fighting weapon. The AG believed public opinion had to support law enforcement, and the public needed to believe the FBI was invincible if it was going to be able to deter crime such as the rash of kidnappings.[124]

At the same time, the AG enlisted Hollywood's imagery to promote his anti-crime campaign. In the first five years of talking pictures, Hollywood spewed out a succession of gangster films which made the criminal the hero. These created disrespect in many people against law enforcement or the government. Complaints by police chiefs, religious groups, and the public about the content of some types of films led Hollywood movie producers to voluntarily establish a self-imposed censorship code. Enacted after the killing of Nelson, one of the bans prohibited gangster films because of excessive violence. However the AG's PR man interceded and successfully convinced Hollywood's producers that they should allow an exemption for films whose hero was the Justice Department's G-Man (this nickname for the FBI's detectives became popular when Congress permitted them to carry guns). He pointed out that this would not only raise strong public support for law enforcement but it would also benefit the producers' bottom lines.

Ironically the first person to benefit from the loosening of the censorship code was SAC Purvis. He entered negotiations with a Hollywood company to make a film glorifying his career in tracking down and assassinating Dillinger and Pretty Boy Floyd. And how speedily Purvis acted. Just four days after Floyd's slaying, an indignant AG announced that the Justice Department would not approve such a script. The AG said, "Those things are not in accord with our ideas." Purvis' attempt to establish himself as America's top cop further infuriated FBI Director Hoover, who was already outraged over his SAC's unauthorized self-aggrandizing press conferences. In this clash of gargantuan egos Hoover became determined to hush his incorrigible subordinate.[125]

The AG may have quashed Purvis' movie dreams, but in the next year, the AG's efforts to loosen the censorship code led Hollywood to release 65 G-Man hero movies with the most enduring being *G Men* starring James Cagney (1935). Ironically four years earlier Cagney had played a wise-cracking bad guy in one of the early major gangster films, *Public Enemy* (1931), and he brought this wise-cracking character back to life but this time as an attorney in the first film showing a G-Man at work. He went after Midwest bank robbers. This type of celluloid gun-wielding gangster was short-lived because the British Board of Censors complained that these exempted movies were nothing more than the same old violent films using a veneer of glorification for the G-Men instead of the gangsters. The Production Code Authority yielded and banned them again. From then on G-Men no longer chased gun-totting gangsters. The villains were racketeers, spies, Communists, and Ku Klux Klansmen until the code was relaxed to allow military combat in film so movies about courageous and victorious World War II battles could be made.

For a year-and-a-half after the Kansas City Massacre, AG Cummings tried to make himself the country's anti-crime hero by pushing Hollywood to cast his position as the action detective in the many G-Men movies, but Hollywood quickly learned only three elements were needed to satisfy the action-hero image the public enjoyed watching, and the desk-riding administrator in Washington D.C. was not one of them. They needed a villain who was a dangerous threat to the nation, a G-Man action hero who was a combination traditional detective and new-style gun wielder, and the man directing him in the field, the FBI director. Hollywood had accomplished something Hoover dared not try and Cummings could not stop. It had made a star out of the country's top G-Man while relegating his boss, the Attorney General, to public irrelevancy.

Cultures create heroes when they need strong people or institutions to stand up to perceived ominous threats. This was the case when the nation reached almost hysterical alarm over Midwest machinegun-wielding bank-robbing gangs early in the Great Depression. Statistics assembled later showed there was no spiked crime wave, but the newspaper headlines of the day reported a different story. Thus Hoover zealously adopted his boss's emphasis on anti-crime publicity and created and directed an enormous internal public relations machine inside the FBI that never mentioned the existence of either the Attorney General or the Justice Department, the man and the agency that supervised him. The publicity's function was to extol the exploits of Hoover's FBI and act as a personal propaganda machine to polish the Director's public image for honesty, patriotism, and professionalism.

Hoover did not believe the job of law enforcement was to ensure the safety of citizens, but rather to make them feel safe. As the horrors of organized-crime gangs were growing rapidly across the country, Hoover's FBI was devoted to public relations efforts rather than to crime busting. From the Director's point of view, the FBI's actual accomplishments were an irrelevancy. His primary focus was on creating the appearance of successful crime-busting rather than doing it. Although Hoover may have been the most ineffectual law-enforcement administrator in history, he certainly displayed an exceptional talent for showmanship and self-aggrandizement.

While every historian has recognized that Hoover learned the value of publicity from his AG boss, these scholars have ignored the important distinctions between their two positions' dissimilar responsibilities. The AG's job was to interpret the meaning of the nation's laws for the President of the United States to support the administration's actions and legislative agenda, set federal law-enforcement policy, and prosecute federal offenders. In contrast Hoover was a cop. His job was detective work to investigate and arrest criminals, but the Director failed to put out much effort doing this except in selected high-profile cases that enhanced his image as America's top cop. Hoover created a career out of publicizing crime fighting while failing miserably in his efforts to actually combat crime. He headed the federal version of the Keystone Cops with a huge publicity organization that rewrote history to cover up his untrained and unprepared agents' many shoddy performances.

The fact is Hoover spent his entire FBI Directorship trying not to be a cop. Throughout his career he quietly manipulated Congressmen, who he had blackmailed into serving in his hip pocket, to prevent passage of proposed legislation that would expand federal criminal laws requiring enforcement by the FBI. From his earliest days in power he lobbied Congressmen in backrooms to keep his accounting agency from being turned into a police force. Early on he saw the desire of some to have a national police force, and he was determined it not be his FBI. However the transformation began when he failed in his attempts to keep his bookkeeping Bureau from assuming responsibility for bank robbery and being given the authority to make arrests as part of AG Cummings massive anticrime push following the Kansas City Massacre. However Hoover never let Congress' mandates control him. Throughout his 48-year tenure the Director repeatedly made two false claims. When he did not care to enforce any federal violation he maintained that the law prohibited him from acting, while at the same time involving himself in any issue that concerned him despite the law giving the FBI no jurisdiction and in many cases actually prohibiting his detectives from acting.

AG Cummings had mounted his War on Crime to support President Roosevelt's New Deal agenda and to relieve the greatly over-inflated fears sweeping the country. The AG tried to develop a national law-enforcement policy and generate popular enthusiasm to support crime fighters. The Director joined his boss in trying to reduce the public's belief that crime was an ominous threat, but Hoover used publicity to try to make people feel safe in bed at night from criminals without bothering to really address the serious crime problems facing the country. At the same time the Director privately anointed himself moral and political custodian and dictator of the nation. He espoused his conservative political philosophy and judgmental moralism in his secret blackmail files. The Director tried to shape and guide public opinion to his personal, rigid, intolerant, peculiar values of "Americanism" that undermined the basic principles of individual liberty, democracy, and justice for all embodied in the U.S. Constitution. This blatant divergence between Hoover's public pronouncements and his personal values led the Director to covertly implement policies that were in stark contrast to his counterfeit claims of FBI professionalism, political neutrality, respect for the law, and concern for individual privacy rights.

The great turning point in Hoover's career status was the FBI's assassination of Dillinger. Until then Hoover's performance as America's top cop against the bank robbers had been dismal and he was held in disrepute by both Congress and the public. Dillinger's killing not only started to garner the Director some respect, but he forever proclaimed it to be his most significant achievement. He frequently bragged about it in his speeches and books as being the hallmark of his career. Even decades later when he was scheduled to give a 20-minute presentation to the House Appropriations Committee about his agency's coming year's budget, he instead gave a two-hour dissertation to the Congressmen by again glorifying the slaying. The Director did not hesitate to completely rewrite history to make Dillinger's assassination a classic crime-and-punishment story with himself as the hero. He left out the leadership of SAC Purvis, the debacle at Little Bohemia, the luck of Anna Sage stepping forward, Hoover's dishonorable refusal to keep his Bureau's promised deal with Anna, the wounded innocent bystanders at the Biograph Theater, and the lack of scientific investigative work by his agents. All these issues, including his agents' tactical sloppiness and overreaction, was ignored in Hoover's fabricated story line. The Director concocted his version to illustrate one point - Hoover always got his man by personally leading scientific analysis and professional police work.

Hoover only shared information about the FBI's activities with those reporters who accepted and regurgitated his fictional official account of the Dillinger story and ensuing crime-busting stories. Early on Hoover learned he had great power to manipulate the press because he controlled the only news about the FBI. He could modify or fictionalize the stories from his secret files, something he did frequently, because he was the only one who knew what they actually contained. To tighten his grip on the FBI's image he disseminated this information only to reporters who supported his version of the facts. He gave obliging reporters, who supported his FBI party line, scoops and supposedly inside information which was a priceless boon for investigative reporters and gossip columnists. Hoover identified these friendly reporters on an internal "Special Correspondents" list. They received unidentified leaks to enable them to write both positive stories about the FBI and to counter unfavorable articles by other reporters. As an additional motivation, "Almost every former SAC could, if so inclined, cite criminal charges which were dropped, or never pursued, because they involved persons known to be on the director's Special Correspondents list."[126]

In return for Hoover's extra-legal assistance and protection, the Special Correspondents' articles heaped adulation on the Director giving him a veneer of infallibility and invincibility. As his status grew with the public and he developed more blackmail material against Congressmen, Hoover won ever larger appropriations from Congress. Greater funding allowed him to expand his power base further by conducting many more blackmailing investigations of the rich and powerful. Syndicated columnist Westbrook Pegler crusaded for conservative policies and supported many of the Director's positions, but even this fellow traveler had to describe the FBI under Hoover's leadership as "the greatest deposit of personal dirt ever amassed."[127]

In contrast to the pampered treatment of Special Correspondents, Hoover relegated reporters, newspapers, magazines, and radio networks, who he deemed hostile because of derogatory comments about his leadership or his Bureau, to the "Not To Be Contacted" list. These media people were denied press releases and all other inside information including assistance with research and verification of developing stories. But Hoover had a much more sinister purpose for his enemies list. The Director vindictively tried to destroy the reputations and careers of anyone who insinuated anything but sainthood for him. For the slightest provocation, Hoover could target his agents to go after any American citizen. He directed investigations in search of damaging personal and professional information particularly sexual or criminal conduct. Hoover especially liked discrediting enemies by raising questions abut their loyalty and character. The Director used the secrets his agents uncovered to blackmail some of these offenders into ceasing to write about him. In other cases he released the private information to a Special Correspondent for publication or broadcast from a supposedly unidentified source. The resulting public humiliation was intended to teach the virtue of silence in regards to his lordship. He also supplied his Congressional supporters, who conducted witch-hunt hearings, with damaging accusations about people he disliked even though the evidence was at best trivial or frivolous. In some cases he encouraged other law-enforcement officials to consider prosecuting the nemeses. Whether this led to charges or not, the investigative process alone was most upsetting for the persecuted targets. A former FBI administrative assistant said of the Director, "If he didn't like you, he destroyed you."[128]

Hoover was not only successful in manipulating the news about the FBI, but he also occasionally limited what the public could hear and learn. The Director clearly did not believe in freedom of speech except for his Bureau's propaganda machine and personally harming those he disliked by planting disparaging information that was not only often unproven but many times had been proven untrue by his agent's investigations. Hoover trashed his oath to uphold the Constitution, as he devoted his half-century career to the distinctly un-American practices of repressing freedom of speech and suppressing the right to know to form their own opinion.

Hoover was known to be a paranoid personality who was suspicious of everyone. He trusted no one unless he had a collection of dirt to control the person through blackmail. He ordered agent investigations of everyone who came into his field of vision and this included his few friends and allies. He was always in search of leverage against anyone who might dare to challenge his authority. It did not matter how much someone had helped his career, the moment the Director found a flaw in them he quickly turned on them. In his files Hoover never expressed respect let alone admiration for anyone, but instead found serious fault or condemnation for each subject.

Two months after the FBI debacle at the Kansas City Massacre, and a year before the FBI assassinated its first gangster, Dillinger, Hoover created an internal publicity machine. He raged at the time, "If there is going to be publicity, let it be on the side of law and order," but he was also clearly attempting to rewrite his agency's sorry performance. Its goal was to promote the Director as America's hero in the rapidly-evolving cultural media. Hoover employed flamboyant free-lance writer Courtney Ryley Cooper to create the official myth by writing articles for distribution to friendly newspapers and magazines. Cooper churned out 50 feature-length articles in one year and then wrote the first biographical book about J. Edgar Hoover's FBI, *Ten Thousand Public Enemies* (1935) with an introduction by Hoover. It was released at the same time as Jimmy Cagney's *G Men* movie. Cooper's book projected the FBI's self-image to the public and this model was never deviated from in all future Bureau publicity, except the evil villain shifted to match the public's current perceived major-criminal fear – from gangsters to Nazi spies and then Communist subversion. Cooper's adventure stories about the agents' behavior fit the popular entertainment action detective, except his agents – in suits with trimly-cut hair and nondescript personalities - were always part of a team and all credit was given to Hoover and the agency rather than to the action hero risking his life in the field. Cooper's stories also presented Hoover as unifying American law enforcement which could not have more misrepresented the truth as he worked isolated from, and often in conflict with, local lawmen and other federal agencies.[129]

Cooper followed Hoover's admonition that it was not the FBI's job to rid the country of crime but rather to lead the police and public to fight crime. Hoover claimed the FBI's goal was to encourage public support for the law and to demand honest police, but his actions were the opposite of this objective. During his half century in office he never cooperated with local police or busted more than a handful of the many corrupt police units across the country even though this was one of the responsibilities Congress assigned him. Instead of making it the FBI's role to capture criminals, Hoover captured headlines.

Writer Cooper was given control of the FBI's tiny Research Division that had issued a few publications to local law enforcement agencies. With the name changed to the Crime Records Division it grew into the Bureau's most important section as it manufactured Hoover's image to the world. "In later years many critics of the Bureau, among them a few frustrated former agents, complained that Hoover's FBI was the servant of its public relations image rather than a master crime-fighting agency. Agents resented being made to concentrate on cases that would provide the headlines and statistics to support Hoover's claim that the Bureau was forever becoming more efficient and effective."[130]

Hoover tightly controlled the FBI's publicity in press releases, interviews with reporters, speeches to various groups, and books about him and the agency. Having mastered these it was time for the Director to turn attention to the entertainment field to expand and broaden the promotion of his personal image and his FBI anti-crime campaign to make Americans feel safe in their beds at night. He descended his reach upon the movie, comic book, detective magazine, and radio-drama industries. He advocated his formula G-Man action hero to all these media, but there was a problem. His formula had vast differences from the standard action detective. Audiences identified with action heroes who embodied cherished cultural fantasies – independence, self-reliance, and strength. Hoover rejected not only these traditional American action-hero qualities but also other relished ones such as rebelliousness, individualism, and anti-intellectualism. The popular pulp rogue-detective role was the antithesis of what Hoover projected. Instead the Director's formula was for his agents to be faceless, anonymous, scientific, and obedient to their boss's orders. Hoover wanted his agents to symbolize security, order, and subordination as much as being two-fisted crime fighters. From 1935 for the rest of his career, the Director fought with the American entertainment industry for control over the FBI image.

As the early talking gangster films became the rage, Chester Gould created a gun-totting detective comic strip, *Dick Tracy*. This was followed by other G-Man-style comic-book detectives for four years, at which time two independent detective comic books featuring FBI heroes were launched two months apart. The first was *G-Man* that used the popular rogue-detective theme and was published for the next 18 years. The second was *The Feds* that received Hoover's endorsement for following the FBI's organizational formula. It folded prior to its second anniversary. Before *The Feds* disappeared Hoover launched his own comic-book, *War on Crime*. Both of his comics followed the standard action-detective formula except for a single flaw. Hoover made the organization's role the central character. Their lack of a G-Man hero with a personality and individual heroics doomed them. The popular comic-book action heroes had no use for a desk-sitting leader unless he was the foil who the G-Man circumvented and outwitted in his roguish style. Comic books were the favorite fantasy-hero vehicle of the Great Depression, but the routine rules and regulations of the FBI did not produce epic adventures or valiant heroes. Hoover's efforts to civilize the action detective failed, but fantasy rogue special agents remained a popular genre. A frustrated Hoover launched a multi-year investigation of one such comic strip, *Special Agent X-9*, for being "subversive."[131]

During Hoover's early foray into comic books, he teamed with a successful radio producer, Phillips Lord. Predictably their *G-Men* broadcasts focused on the Bureau's organization and scientific investigations. Because of the Hoover entertainment formula, the episodes moved slowly, lacked action, and had no hero. The first show featured the assassination of Dillinger, but no matter how much Hoover had bragged about this great exploit he managed to make the show boring. After 13 episodes, the sponsors dropped it. Soon Lord was back on the air with another show with rogue cops, lots of action, and no FBI endorsement. *Gangbusters* became one of the most popular radio shows in history lasting into the early television era when radio drama disappeared from the scene.

Amazingly, Cagney's *G Men* movie changed the balance of power in the real Justice Department. Until this film exploded upon the screen, the media had made AG Cummings the nation's ever-present anti-crime crusader, but this film and the gangster genre that followed led the public to give sole credit to the subordinate FBI and embrace the Director as America's top cop. This allowed Hoover to start acting as an independent agency within the Justice Department and to free himself from accountability to anyone. Until AG Cummings launched his War on Crime in the difficult times of the Great Depression, many in Congress had expressed fear of, and blocked proposals for, a federal detective agency out of fear of the potential for abuses by an unaccountable secret police force. Little did any of these worried Congressional critics of the day realize just what a horrible force against justice, democracy, and individual liberties it would become under Hoover. Even when two major accurate exposé articles about Hoover's leadership of the FBI soon appeared, no action was taken to stop the Director's malfeasance and misconduct before he became so powerful no politician in the country dared stand up to him or interfere with his unconstitutional political harassment of people whose personal values differed from his. He had become an ominous independent political force, a covert fourth branch of government not prescribed by the U.S. Constitution. The first article was in *Collier's Magazine* described earlier, and the second was a *Chicago Tribune* article with some new points that follow.

FEMINIZATION OF MINCING

While the assassinations of successive Public Enemies permanently impressed the reputation of the G-Men on citizen and criminal alike, it was clear that FBI Director Hoover had not improved his feeble management style. A second scathing and detailed article about his leadership of the FBI and lifestyle appeared. The two articles were published three years apart and appeared at critical moments in the Director's career. The earlier *Collier's Magazine* article had appeared three weeks after AG Cummings had announced that he was launching a War on Crime. This later *Chicago Tribune* article appeared as Hoover was winding down his assault on the successive Public Enemies Number 1. Its author Walter Trohan was also demeaning and included additional disparaging information.

Trohan sadly summed up what legitimate law enforcement officials thought of Hoover and his agents. "To thoroughly disgusted colleagues in federal investigatorial units, who for years have followed a policy of strict anonymity in no less thrilling and possibly more successful games of hounds and hares with the criminal element, he is a Keystone cop and his men callow drug store cowboys with twitchy trigger fingers and a love of the limelight. These tried veterans look upon Hoover as a clerk who by plodding long enough in a bureau found himself one day in the role of detective and began to play the part. ... Hoover is not a police officer in training or by instinct. It is gravely doubtful whether Hoover – and this is said without disrespect – could single-handed track down the perpetrator of a crime in the scientific manner taught at his school. Some doubt that a single G-man could track down a criminal without the aid of local police." Hoover's later *New York Times* Obituary pointed out, "Even Chief Justice Harlan Fiske Stone, who had appointed the F.B.I. director in 1924, observed critically that 'one of the great secrets of Scotland Yard has been that its movements are never advertised.'"[132]

Local police departments complained that Hoover's agents revealed the identity of stoolies who were their best sources of information and they had to flee the area to survive. "Local police of many cities now refuse to have anything to do with G-men even in a government case until they are actually up to the arrest stage. Such departments, it is said, learned by bitter experience that the 'Boy Scouts,' while brave under fire, are not trained in police technique in the observation of suspects or the nursing along of informers. G-men, they say, make an informer a clam."[133]

Trohan's article pointed out that America's other federal law enforcers held Hoover and his boys in contempt for their lack of police training and investigative ability and for their shoot-and-brag approach to taking down suspects. Many other concerned people at the time decried the vigilante assassinations of Hoover's boys by pointing out that local police forces regularly arrested similarly dangerous criminals without violence and without serious risk to nearby civilians. Relevant criticisms were voiced soon after the shootout in Chicago in which Nelson and two FBI agents killed each other, especially since one of these agents had tried to hit and narrowly missed an innocent civilian simply because he was fleeing in terror from the gun battle. For example the Illinois Bar Association formerly stated that killing criminals was a dangerous practice "except in extreme cases. A police officer should seek the ends of justice rather than the end of a criminal. It is better to convict such men as Dillinger, Floyd, and Nelson than it is to kill them. It has a more corrective effect on the criminal element." Similar sentiments were echoed by the Chicago Crime Commission President, who was deeply involved in the effort that imprisoned the murderous Al Capone. He said when the legal system abandons due process and infringes on civil rights, no citizen, however honest, or innocent, is safe. He continued, "No pity need be expended upon criminals so killed; but the price paid in seeking to kill those outlaws was too high" in the cost to innocent civilians. He described a number of the deaths and close-call shootings of innocent civilians by FBI agents that are presented in this book as a price too great to pay when local police regularly brought in equally treacherous criminals with no risk to civilians or lawmen. "From my standpoint as a lawyer, I doubt whether that is the effective way to end criminals' careers. ... In my opinion, this practice belittles the government and shows a lack of confidence in the laws to curb crime and criminals. Let the law carry the criminal to the electric chair or to the penitentiary, rather than make a hero of him." Regarding the FBI's flagrant violations of established law, a local Circuit

Judge also stated, "The utter disregard and disrespect for the great institutions guarding human liberty, which have grown up during centuries of struggle for emancipation, is a more serious threat to social security than the depredations of the criminal element." Even a local resident in a Letter to the Editor three days after the Nelson deadly shootout opined "'Pretty Boy' Floyd, it is stated, made several overtures of surrender to the government, but the 'F' [federal] men preferred to slaughter him, and one can scarcely blame 'Baby Face' Nelson for shooting it out with the agents, especially when the orders were to kill him on sight. Nelson and the rest of the gangsters knew that they had but a slight chance to surrender even if they wanted to." Now two of Hoover's FBI agents were also dead at the hands of Nelson.[134]

In addition to all the criticism in the press, the Secret Service quietly began an investigation of the FBI's use of unnecessary and excessive force in the Dillinger, Floyd, and Nelson cases until Hoover made a strong protest with AG Cummings. He in turn went directly to President Roosevelt to stop the Secret Service from further inquiry.

Reporter Trohan pointed out that at Hoover's rare press interviews, he would have an agent telephone him, and then this fanatically secretive man would make tantalizing comments over the phone like "You found finger prints … What's the classification? … That sounds like … It is? … Good … Wire Chicago.' Or "You've got him surrounded? … Good! … Smoke him out … Call me when he's under arrest." Visitors would watch newspapers for days waiting for an announcement of some major G-Man arrest so they could tell their friends they were in the Director's office when it came down. But this was always a futile search until they realized America's top cop had punked them to make himself look important.

Despite Hoover's crushing personal attack on the first reporter, the fearless Trohan in the *Chicago Tribune* repeated the "mincing" remark but made it more pointed by adding two words at the end of its description. "Hoover walks with a rather mincing step, almost feminine." This type of walking was politely referred to in that era as being "high in the loafers" referring to a man tip toeing with the heels raised high because of being jabbed in the butt so frequently.

Trohan continued the article with Hoover's preference for the friendship of men with, "He has but few friends," and these three men all worked closely under him. "No women are among his intimates, for Hoover – and he would have every G-man be likewise – is a woman hater." Trohan tried to explain the Director's sexist position with "it may be due to his cardinal creed as a crime fighter, which is the traditional French phrase, 'Find the woman' (cherchez la femme). In every search for a criminal Hoover has directed operatives to look for woman associates of the malefactor. He was swift to recognize the oft proven fact that a criminal's weakness for women leads him into the arms of the law."

Hoover never participated in athletics during all his years of schooling, but he had started displaying a masculine image by attending sporting events. Trohan pointed out, "He can be seen at ball games, important football games, and boxing matches, always in a prominent seat, studiously oblivious of recognition. At such spectacles he always lets his office know where he will sit so he can be called out to announce to the press the capture of some desperado or other."[135]

Reporter Walter Trohan's *Chicago Tribune* article was scathing, but he did not indicate that Hoover had attempted to retaliate for it in his memoir *Political Animals: Memoirs of a Sentimental Cynic*. However it is still possible that Hoover launched a secret investigation that was never filed and never led to retribution because this author proved to be invulnerable to negative exposure. Trohan did say in his memoir that he and Hoover eventually became friends even though he continued to criticize the Director "when he undertook duties and performed actions I did not like." Trohan was the paper's Washington Bureau Chief through 10 presidents, and he made an observation about his lifetime of covering politics with, "From the lofty beginnings of police reporting, I descended into politics. My progress has been steadily downward ever since."[136]

It should have been obvious to anyone who observed FBI Director Hoover's lifestyle that he was a homosexual. He lived with his mother until she died when he was 43. He and his chief aide, Clyde Tolson, had been each other's only friend from before Hoover's appointment as Director. Both were lifelong confirmed bachelors who never dated a woman. Both had few women friends over their entire lives and their rare get-togethers with these women were in public at restaurants. Hoover did have one-time "dates" with a few celebrity women for publicity mentions in his pal Walter Winchell's syndicated gossip column to falsely counter the rumors about his homosexuality.

Edgar and Clyde were always together as they followed their rigid routine. They drove to work together and their offices were near each other. For lunch and dinner every day they shared a booth at restaurants. Then they spent a private evening together at Hoover's residence. At bedtime Tolson went to his residence. Most weekends they went to New York City on the subterfuge that it was their biggest regional office. In reality Hoover virtually never went to that office except to hold press conferences since the couple spent their weekends cavorting in the suite. Clyde was at Edgar's side for every Washington outing including White House affairs and sporting events. America's rich and powerful recognized and treated them as a couple, always including Clyde whenever inviting Edgar to dinner. The couple signed the thank you notes together. They also took their vacations jointly in shared suites all but a couple of years. In a 1943 letter Edgar wrote Clyde, "Words are mere man-given symbols for thoughts and feelings, and they are grossly insufficient to express the thoughts in my mind and the feelings in my heart that I have for you. I hope I will always have you beside me." Hoover got his wish. The two were buried in Congressional Cemetery within a dozen coffins of each other.[137]

Hoover went to great lengths to counter the reality he was a closeted homosexual. Hoover's publicist Lou Nichols said in an interview years later that the Director adopted the "tough cop" image while pursuing the bank robbers to counter the incessant rumors about his homosexuality. He said the killing and capture of four Public Enemies Number 1 "pretty much ended the queer talk," but it actually persisted for the rest of his life.[138]

Hoover also used a false and hypocritical public Puritanism to compensate for his private sexual preferences. In the 1950s he proposed a campaign to completely rid the country of pornography to protect all future children from ever being exposed to it. This was from a man who less than a year into his tenure as FBI Director created an Obscene file and sent a letter to all his SACs to forward him all seized pornographic films, literature, and printed material. Forty-one years later he sent another letter to all SACs warning them, "While this (obscene) material is in the office, it must not be shown to other personnel of the office who have no need to observe it. ... there should be no undue curiosity about such filth." Yet, he had a special screening room built in the basement of the Justice Department as well as a collection at home so he could proudly show his illicit pornographic films to his trusted associates and selected visitors from outside the FBI. If non-homosexuals were in attendance, he presented movies containing heterosexual sex scenes because they offered something for everybody as viewers could fantasize about the gender of their persuasion. Hoover also displayed photos in his home of his companion Clyde in a bathrobe, in the pool, and asleep, not exactly the kind of pictures professional colleagues take of each other. When Hoover died his will did not mention his six nephews and nieces as he left his estate of about $550,000 and his home that contained so many of their special memories to his lifelong escort. [139]

To further disassociate himself from homosexuality Hoover mercilessly went after others whether guilty or not. He made strong public statements about his hunt for "sex deviants in government service." To maintain his own proclivities, he hounded others sexuality and destroyed their lives. Not only did he go after other homosexuals but he planted false accusations by unidentified sources with favored reporters to devastate the careers of heterosexuals who disagreed with him politically. He got rid of homosexual FBI agents by threatening to expose them to family and friends unless they resigned. He always made others pay the price for his own guilty secrets like his homosexuality.

After the *Collier's Magazine* and the *Chicago Tribune* articles mentioning his "mincing step," there appears to be just one other article that dared allude to Hoover's sexual inclinations despite much gossip in Washington about the couples morning-to-night courting behavior. Four years later before World War II, *Time Magazine* carried an article about the Director that included the sentence, "seldom seen without a male companion, most frequently solemn-faced Clyde Tolson." An angry and frightened Hoover sent orders to "most vigorously" interrogate any citizen suspected of making such a slanderous statement about the Director until they clearly recanted and understood they were not to mention such a thing again. The agents had to write a report about such incidents. Thus legitimate citizens ended up with FBI files containing nothing but one report about a terrifying interrogation. Agents who delayed filing a report about such passing comments were chastised and threatened with termination for further offences.[140]

This is just one illustration of how the Director had agents spend massive amounts of time and attention on non-criminal activities in American society as Hoover used the FBI as his personal instrument to force standards upon the citizenry of the country that he personally failed to meet. America's top cop and his lieutenant constantly espoused law and order and morality rhetoric while nightly committing the sexual criminal felonies of homosexuality and sodomy. Their behavior indicates they committed hundreds of times more felonies on the nation's law books at that time than any criminal they ever went after.

Hoover hid the low priority he gave to crime-fighting with a massive publicity machine and by regaling Congress with scores of the number of crimes committed, the subjects apprehended, and the crimes solved. The FBI often inflated its numbers by taking credit for local police successes like in the recovery of stolen cars. The former head of the FBI's Criminal Division claimed in an interview that Hoover's statistics were "hogwash," and revealed about auto-theft cases, "In at least half, and possibly more of these, the thieves are arrested and the cars returned by local officials." Hoover's conviction rates were astronomical, often around 96%, because he cooked the numbers. He implied that these rates were based on the total number of investigations but they were actually his conviction rates based on the number of cases that were brought to court. Obviously Hoover pursued only strong cases to protect his vaunted statistics meaning he gave a free pass to a huge number of criminals who should have been tried. Since Hoover concocted the numbers on which the country judged him, it is not surprising that his record improved with each annual visit to Congress when he made his insatiable pitch for larger funding. Various government officials and scholars cast doubt on Hoover's statistics during this lifetime, but America's elected and appointed political leaders were too afraid of the blackmailer in chief to act against all his gross misconduct in office.[141]

It is interesting the *Chicago Tribune* published this second expose article on the management failings and values of tenaciously conservative FBI Director Hoover because Publisher Colonel Robert McCormick was a stanch conservative. However McCormick valued democratic ideals, effective law and order, and honesty in politicians more than his political agenda. Thus, he single-handedly led the fight to topple Al Capone and his paper exposed Republicans as readily as Democrats for corruption. The *Tribune* even endorsed Democrats against the worst-offending Republican candidates and elected officials. McCormick and Hoover gave a very different meaning to the term conservative, so McCormick was about the nation's strongest publisher in standing up to the autocratic, intimidating, and blackmailing FBI Director.

HOOVER THE MAN HUNTER

This book focuses on J. Edgar Hoover's second of five decades as FBI Director during the Great Depression in the 1930s. However Hoover's first decade of power during the Roaring '20s is relevant here because it shows his total disregard for the individual liberties and democratic principals embodied so nobly in the Constitution of the United States. Hoover's distorted leadership objectives for the FBI are grounded in the core of his personality of being a librarian. He devoted his career to amassing data about his fellow citizens and peculiarly mostly those who had violated no criminal laws.

His predilection showed itself soon after graduating high school when he went to work at the Library of Congress, the world's largest filing cabinet, where he learned the Dewey decimal system of classifying files. In the evenings he studied law and earned his degrees at nearby George Washington University so he could continue living with his mother. A month after America entered World War I the Selective Service Act went into effect requiring all men aged 21 to 30 to register for the draft. As will be seen when Hoover goes after the next set of Public Enemy Number 1 bank robbers, Alvin Karpis and the Barker brothers, he suffered from crippling cowardice causing him to search for a way out of joining the mass of American soldiers headed to France in defense of America. He learned Justice Department employees were exempted from the draft so he obtained a job as a clerk. In this position Hoover could continue his penchant for organizing data. He switched over from cataloging and searching for books to classifying and hunting men.

Hoover spent the rest of his career at the Justice Department where he focused on investigating the patriotism of others while failing to ever exhibit any himself. In addition to failing to assist in the war effort he never once bothered to vote although he influenced the outcomes of many elections by leaking confidential information that was often false smears about candidates with whom he disagreed. His most dreadful conduct was his frequent trashing of the most basic tenants of the U.S. Constitution, especially those protecting freedom of speech and individual liberties, those providing due process and fair trials, and those promoting justice for all.

A year after Hoover went to work for the Justice Department, the military became concerned that many young American men had not signed up for the draft. Hoover at age 22 headed the Justice Department's Enemy Alien Registration Section that cataloged foreigners from countries America was at war with. This is where Hoover first exhibited the two qualities he would most excel at throughout his career. He became a hunter of men and targeted for punishment those who shared his personal failings, in this case fellow draft dodgers. The young Hoover was directed to deal with the military's concern about draft avoidance and he teamed up with Clyde Tolson, who reported to the Secretary of War. However Clyde would soon become Edgar's assistant at the FBI and lifelong partner. For two days this tandem conducted federal raids in four cities. Their Gestapo-style raiders accosted at bayonet point every young man they encountered walking the sidewalk, riding street cars, frequenting retail businesses, or working in offices. The raiders demanded each produce either a draft-registration card or a birth certificate proving he was not of draft age. Few young men had yet learned to carry such documentation so the many violators were herded into temporary fencing without food, water, or toilets and penned up for as long as two days. Some of these corrals were so crowded that detainees stood squeezed against each other shoulder-to-shoulder and front-to-back despite all eventually soiling themselves. Hoover and Tolson terrorized between 50,000 to 200,000 young men with this horrifying and repulsive violation of their civil rights. The number is not more exact because Hoover later had most of the raid records destroyed. Not a single one of these abused detainees was found to have avoided the draft, but such total violation of innocent citizens' Constitutionally-protected rights, especially those dealing with probable cause, arrest warrants, and due process would become the standard operating procedure of Hoover and Tolson.

Hoover was just getting warmed up. In the midst of WWI the Russian Revolution overthrew the Czar to institute a communist society. This event led many dissatisfied American citizens to begin publicly uttering radical political statements that communism was needed to get workers a livable wage and safe working conditions. These statements attacking unrestrained exploitive capitalism unsettled the rest of the population. After two years of such negative political talk, U.S. AG Mitchell Palmer created a new Justice Department division, the General Intelligence Division (GID), to collect information about these radicals' activities. AG Palmer appointed Hoover to head GID which for him was like finding paradise. He was responsible for categorizing radical leaders, organizations, and publications. In a little over a year America's new librarian in chief indexed almost a half million names of political dissidents.

As public worry about radical talk and literature grew U.S. AG Palmer expanded Hoover's authority to arrest political radicals for expressing unpopular thoughts and ideas even though their expressions were non-violent and clearly protected under the U.S. Constitution's right to freedom of speech. The AG's office notified the U.S. Attorney in every state about pending raids and instructed them they should deal only with Hoover about them. On the selected day in 12 cities Hoover conducted his raids against the most fundamental principals of American democracy. Even though Hoover's ongoing investigation of the Communist Party USA proved conclusively that it was a legitimate non-violent political party, Hoover obtained 3,000 arrest warrants by falsely proclaiming to a Federal Judge that membership in this organization and expression of free speech regarding its tenants was a deportable offense. Hoover's ambition was to hunt men, and their guilt or innocence and their Constitutionally-protected individual liberties were totally irrelevant to him. Thus Hoover arbitrarily selected 3,000 alien names out of his vast index without a stitch of evidence that a single one was a member of the Communist Party USA. Then Hoover ordered his federal storm troopers to arrest not only the 3,000 innocent men named in the warrants but also anyone who was found associating with them if they had a foreign appearance. In addition he ordered his Gestapo force to grab anyone else they encountered in known immigrant hangouts who looked like they might be foreigners. This foreign-look order resulted in the arrests of another 7,000 people for the crime of existing. Hoover's storm troopers were unbelievably brutal. The nation's newspapers decried bloody beatings of arrestees with some thrown down stairs. This horrendous Nazi police-state anti-American operation would establish Hoover as the country's foremost anti-communist crusader for the rest of his career.

Of the 10,000 men so cruelly arrested, Hoover had no evidence that a single one had ever made a dissident statement, but even if they had radical political thoughts it was their right to peacefully speak them. The fact that all his targeted victims were innocent under the law did not stop Hoover from continuing to persecute them. He wrote the Immigration Commissioner for New England, Henry Skeffington, that allowing bail for these aliens to contact their attorneys, "defeats the ends of justice." A second memo requested all arrestees be held without a hearing even if there was no evidence against them just in case information about a radical affiliation might be developed by later investigations. Then without an Immigration hearing or any federal court due process action Hoover took it upon himself to illegally deport 249 of these innocent arrestees. Fuhrer Hoover ordered his Gestapo troopers to quickly load these arbitrarily selected victims on boats and to prevent them from contacting attorneys because he knew any federal judge would have immediately stopped his outrageously illegal actions. Hoover had these immigrants put on boats without winter clothing and without notifying their families they had been arrested or deported so all these families who had proudly come to join the land of the free had no idea why their loved ones suddenly vanished.[142]

The public was outraged at Hoover's storm troopers' barbarism and total shredding of Constitutional rights, so Hoover tried to scare Americans into supporting his action by releasing provocative radical literature that had no association with any of the 10,000 arrestees. He also started lying that he had nothing to do with the disgraceful operation. However Immigration Commissioner for New England Skeffington testified before a Federal Judge questioning the arrest procedures that the Justice Department's Hoover had total jurisdiction for these foreigner raids. Then Hoover's boss' AG Mitchell Palmer repeatedly told a U.S. Senate Judiciary Committee investigation that only Hoover could answer their questions about the raids because he had sole authority. In the face of these high-powered accusations Hoover kept up his big lie. In trying to explain away his hideous injustice and inhumanity, Hoover under oath committed perjury and undermined his boss by claiming he was only following orders. But Hoover had left a paper trail. At the very moment he was illegally placing the foreigners on boats for deportation, he sent a memo to his boss admitting, "no authority under the law permitting this Department to take any action in deportation proceedings relative to radical activities."[143]

All of Hoover's actions at GID were taken against fabricated domestic political radicals, but his actual goal was to stifle the country's dissatisfied labor force. Inflation was soaring while salaries remained low so workers were striking all over the country. In one year four million workers paraded picket signs in an incredible number of challenges to business ownership and management authoritarianism. Hoover made the blatant lie at one Immigration hearing that over half of the nation's labor unrest was caused by the Communist Party USA's agitation. With this proclamation Hoover found the scare tactic he would officially but falsely hurl at every dissent group for the rest of his career including the civil-rights movement of Martin Luther King three decades later. Despite Hoover's terrible disparaging of King's character for struggling for equality, the country would later honor him with a national holiday in his name.

Eventually U.S. AG Palmer came to realize that no domestic Red scare existed in America so he dropped the charges against every arrestee including those Hoover had illegally deported so they could return to their families in this country if they could acquire the passage fare. The AG also shut down Hoover's radical-foreigner mandate because of public outrage over the excessive police force against a nonexistent enemy. However Hoover unbeknownst to his boss continued quietly classifying many citizens into his radical lists even though he conducted no investigations and had no evidence against any of them. He also had agents keep a quiet watch on the activities of the Communist Party USA as he waited for the opportunity to use this trumped-up scapegoat to arouse public fear to stifle dissent and crush freedom of speech against opinions he disagreed with. It is important to note three things about Hoover's Red herring. The supposedly fearsome Communist Party USA decried by Hoover was made up only of American citizens and not any foreigners, it advocated changing the American political system by winning non-violently at the ballot box, and it never had more than a few dozen members. Hoover knew the true nature of the Communist Party USA better than anyone else because of his agents' constant surveillances of the members and trailing of the group's pathetically small legal funding sources. The Director expanded enormous manpower illegally investigating a legal and non-violent political party's membership, while he prohibited his agents from inquiring into or even monitoring organized crime as it flourished and proliferated its domestic terrorism, violence, and exploitation of businessmen, workers, and consumers across the country.

Four years after these unconscionable political raids, AG Harlan Stone promoted Hoover to be Director of the FBI. How Stone could have picked a man who had proven such contempt for the

U.S. Constitution to be America's secret police chief is a mystery. Stone must have felt some unease about his appointment because a month later he requested his new FBI Acting Director to review the applicability of federal criminal statutes to communist activities in the U.S. Then four months after that AG Stone's assistant required Hoover to respond with a memo admitting on paper his actions in the immigrant raids were illegal and unwarranted. Hoover's key line was, "It is, of course, to be remembered that the activities of the Communists and other ultra radials have not up to the present time constituted a violation of the Federal statutes, and consequently, the Department of Justice, theoretically, has no right to investigate such activities as there has been no violation of Federal laws." For the next 48 years of his tenure Hoover repeatedly made two false claims. He maintained that the law prohibited him from acting on any federal violation he did not care to enforce, while at the same time he involved himself in any issue that concerned him despite the law giving the FBI no jurisdiction and in many cases actually prohibiting his detectives from acting.[144]

From adolescence on Hoover led a very constricted life, letting almost no one into his narrow private reality. He never exhibited any capacity to learn, grow, or change from new ideas. Throughout his long FBI tenure he appeared inflexibly fixated on the values of his youth in his management goals and style; rigid and judgmental personal, religious, and political standards; and extremely limited interests. For example three years before his death he wanted to make mass arrests of all young men on the streets of America as possible Vietnam War draft dodgers repeating his horrific actions during World War I at age 22. In a memo to his six Assistant Directors, Hoover explained how he had complained to President Richard Nixon about the political composition of the U.S. Supreme Court. "I said the problem of the draft is a serious one and, of course, the Supreme Court says the police cannot arrest a person and take his fingerprints because if they do, they are violating the Constitution. I said that is an unheard of thing...[the] kind of thing we are getting, not only at the local level but at the Federal court level." Hoover was enraged that he could not arrest anyone at will without any probable cause. This is when he directed agents to seek out dirt on the "activist" Supreme Court Justices whose rulings tried to protect the civil liberties, free speech, voting rights, equal opportunity, health, and safety of the individual American citizen from the power and tyranny of big government bureaucracies and huge corporate entities. Hoover's goal was to eliminate these Justices so President Richard Nixon could install conservative Justices whose goal was to write out the key individual and personal liberties and protections guaranteed by the Constitution.[145]

No one seemed to realize Hoover's prime goal was to force on American society his Darwinian survival-of-only-the-fittest capitalism and his warped-Christian views. He presented his ideals in a 1939 speech in which he defined his view of democracy as the "dictatorship of the collective conscience of our people," meaning noncomformity was a crime. By making conformism the highest political virtue Hoover completely inverted the ideals of the Founding Fathers and the U.S. Constitution making him the ultimate Un-American. Hoover's statement is made even more frightening by the context of its times. Both Japan and Germany were rapidly building military planes, ships, and guns while finalizing plans for World War II. Imperial Japan had already brutally invaded and occupied Korea, Manchuria, and China, and was systematically exploiting their natural resources. The Japanese Empire had also proclaimed to the world that it was going to "free" the other Asian countries and Pacific Islands from European and American colonialism to assume total dominance and control over this vast region of the world. Adolf Hitler had preached to the German people they were a superior master race who were intended to rule the world, and just three months after Hoover's speech Nazi Germany invaded Poland to launch World War II. The dictatorial leaders of both Nazi German and Imperial Japan demanded absolute goose-stepping political and cultural uniformity in which no dissent was tolerated. The individual existed solely to serve the state, and the highest honor of citizenship was to give one's life for the country's leadership. It was in this world context that Hoover expressed his ideal that no dissent should be tolerated.[146]

Hoover tried to quell dissent and promote conformity by spending his career decrying both crime and communism as threats to cultural consensus, but he gave little more than lip service to combating either. Instead his secret-police activity focused on manipulating the truth in the media, blackmailing politicians to follow his agenda, and to conducting witch hunts of various groups that did not adhere to his rigid, intolerant standards. For example, Hoover's secret-police force supplied all the information for the McCarthy Committee communist witch-hunt that ruined so many innocent peoples' lives. Not a single one of the multitude of legitimate citizens targeted by Hoover and McCarthy was ever indicted for any type of illegal activity, and especially never for spying or disloyalty. They were simply pawns of Hoover's secret-police campaign to instill too much fear in the populace for anyone to speak out against his grand political agenda. The Hoover and McCarthy totally-false hyperbole about a dangerous communist enemy from within successfully produced pervasive but unwarranted fear among the American people during these sad years for the Constitution's democratic ideals.[147]

To a superficial observer Hoover led a circumspect life that was beyond reproach, but it is noteworthy that despite the massive investigative media analysis during his lifetime, and the vast scholarly historical research since his death, not one single person who worked for him or socialized with him was found who could remember his ever expressing or showing any empathy, feeling, or even concern for another human being. While he destroyed countless lives with his often illegal and reprehensible actions not a single person could mention this self-proclaimed Christian man once doing a good deed, offering a kindness, being forgiving or merciful, or mentoring anyone. In his entire life he only got close to two people and this was because he was dependent on both his mother and his employee who was always at his side to obediently and immediately indulge his every whim. Hoover's rare help to others was always to the rich and powerful, and then only when he was rewarded with a quid pro quo of greater value in return. His view of Christianity was that the super rich were the chosen ones given carte blanche to dominate and exploit everyone else, so his career was spent fighting politicians and government efforts that assisted workers, families, the elderly, the sick, the handicapped, the needy, the oppressed, and the downtrodden.

Hoover spent his whole career hidden from the rest of the world with Tolson in their office complex and love nest where the couple plotted to harm everyone they disliked and to destroy or overthrow everything they disapproved of about the rest of the country. In addition the restaurants the couple ate dinner at most frequently reported after Hoover's death that he typically downed six alcohol drinks before having the food served which fueled his inhuman pathology. It is a sad commentary that in studying the careers of the politicians, reformers, and police leaders who have spouted tough law and order rhetoric the vast majority have proven to be more corrupt than the people they condemned. Similarly the self-proclaimed patriots who attacked the loyalty of others have typically been found to be the citizens who were most devoted to furthering their self interest at the expense of their fellow countrymen.

Ironically the only good thing that can be said about Hoover is that his fixation on data collection and organization of innocent people's names has left historians with a rich reservoir of information about his extensive misconduct and evil intent. This despite his coconspirators - his secretary and closest associates - spending the two months after his death at the government's expense shredding what they considered to be his most detrimental and damaging government documents about him.

Utilizing this greater understanding of the Director's leadership we return to the Public Enemy manhunts. Five weeks after the FBI and local police had killed Floyd, and right after two of

Hoover's boys died while killing Nelson, Director Hoover selected his next target. It would be another Midwestern bank-robbing gang led by two of the Barker Brothers and Alvin Karpis. With multiple leadership, this gang developed more extensive tentacles and much more diverse criminal patterns. The Karpis-Barker gang would give the FBI far more fits than the previous three – Dillinger, Floyd, and Nelson - and prove to be the most difficult and elusive of this dangerous breed to track down and capture.

Chapter 8

BANK ROBBERIES & KIDNAPPINGS

BIRTH OF THE KARPIS-BARKERS GANG

One of the most vicious gangs of the early 1930s was led by Alvin Karpis and the Barker brothers. Each of the Barkers was a petty thief by his early teens and soon moved on to major crimes before all four brothers were killed by bullets. The family lived in Webb City, Missouri until the boys were teenagers, when the family moved to Tulsa, Oklahoma because the sons had so many problems with the police. Their father George eventually moved back to Missouri away from his outlaw offspring. Whenever the brothers were not in jail they lived at the home of their mother, Arizona "Kate" Barker. Just like her boys everyone called her "Ma." When all four sons were away in prison or on the run, Ma supported herself and paid their legal fees by boarding their fugitive criminal associates. It was a rather unpretentious hideaway lacking electricity and running water but having a well and outhouse.

Kate's favorite son was her youngest, Freddie. At age 25 a Kansas robbery landed him in the Penitentiary for five years. During his incarceration his three brothers fared poorly. Brother Herman tried to cash stolen bonds in Wyoming and as he was driving away a sheriff's deputy pulled him over. Herman picked up the gun on the seat beside him and killed the officer. A month later Herman stole supplies at a store in Newton, Kansas, and while escaping encountered a roadblock. He floored the gas peddle and opened fire. As he charged he killed one policeman but as Herman whizzed past the patrol cars, the other officers wounded him. Bleeding profusely he slowed down, pulled over, angled the barrel of his Lugar in his mouth upward, and used his last bullet to end his life.

During the same era brother Lloyd Barker received a 25-year sentence for postal robbery. After serving 17 years he was released and went straight. He managed a Denver, Colorado market. One evening he came home from work, opened the door, and his wife, Jean, blasted him with a 20-gauge shotgun. She told police she feared her husband was going to kill her and the children. A week later she pled innocent by reason of insanity. She was committed to Colorado Psychopathic Hospital for observation but further records about her case were unavailable.

The remaining two Barkers would become major gangsters. While Fred was in the Penitentiary he befriended fellow inmate Alvin Karpis. He was born Albin Karpavicz in Montreal, Canada, but he shortened his name as a teenager. When he was a young boy his Lithuanian parents moved him and his three sisters to Topeka Kansas. At age 16 he was convicted of stealing car tires and sentenced to 10 years at the State Industrial Reformatory at Hutchinson, Kansas. Three years into his stretch he and a fellow inmate sawed through their cell bars to escape. The pair remained on the run for a year until Kansas City, Kansas police pulled their car over. Their vehicle was packed with safe-blowing equipment. Karpis was returned to the Reformatory, but weeks later guards found him in the possession of knives. He was transferred to the Kansas State Prison where he befriended Fred Barker. Karpis was paroled a year later and Fred Barker months later.

The two parolees lived in Ma's Tulsa home. The pair soon committed a $5,000 jewelry robbery at Henryetta, Oklahoma. Returning to Tulsa, Freddie eluded police but Karpis was arrested. He spent three months in the County Jail until the judge sentenced him to four years in the State

Penitentiary at McAlester, Oklahoma. Then instead of transferring him to prison the judge inexplicably paroled him. Karpis and Fred again joined forces. Three months later the pair were in a garage in West Plains, Missouri, when the Howell County Sheriff walked in to question the newcomers to town about a robbery the previous night. Even though FBI agents later learned the pair had nothing to do with the robbery, the skittish Karpis was on probation and killed the Sheriff. The city charged the pair with murder so Karpis and Fred became fugitives on the run.

The fourth brother, Arthur "Doc" Barker, was soon released from prison. As a teenager Doc developed a bad criminal record. He was charged with car theft in Joplin, Missouri, and jailed for an attempted bank robbery in Muskogee, Oklahoma. At age 23 he was convicted of killing a St. John's Hospital night watchman in his hometown of Tulsa for which he got life. He was locked in Oklahoma State Prison but both Doc and his mother loudly proclaimed his innocence. After a decade of incarceration he was vindicated when a California-based thief confessed to the murder. Doc may have been proven innocent, but Oklahoma paroled him as an incorrigible criminal with the condition he leave the state and never return.

The Parole Board's evaluation of Doc as an habitual criminal turned out to be correct as he immediately joined his brother Fred in Karpis' gang. Alvin was the leader because he was an effective planner while both Fred and Doc were rather dim-witted. In addition, Doc, who stood 5-feet 3 ¾ inches high, was a problem drinker and remained bitter about his wrongful conviction for the killing of the night watchman.

The Karpis-Barkers gang committed robberies throughout the Midwest. Three months into their crime spree the gang was suspected of robbing the Third Northwestern National Bank in Minneapolis, Minnesota, of $20,000 cash plus securities. During their getaway they killed two policemen and a civilian. More than two years later this case would resurface in a most unusual way.

Shortly after this robbery, the gang leaders drove to Reno to spend the winter vacationing under the protection of casino operators Graham and McKay. Ma Barker traveled with her two sons cooking for them. She doted on her boys but Karpis was her "pet." She adored him despite his appearance. While every machinegun-toting goon terrified robbery victims, Karpis added a new dimension of scary to the experience. His face could have doubled for Boris Karloff's horror-movie villains, which earned him the nickname with his comrades of "Old Creepy."[148]

EXPANSION INTO KIDNAPPING

The Karpis-Barkers gang robbed banks for two years when Alvin decided kidnapping wealthy men could produce a greater cash flow. Karpis would later explain, "My profession was robbing banks, knocking off payrolls, and kidnapping rich men." His first target was Hamm Brewing Company Chairman William Hamm Jr. The St. Paul, Minnesota resident was 38 years old. One day he was walking from his brewery office to his mansion for lunch when two men approached. One of the strangers asked the other, "Is that him?" When the other nodded yes, the first firmly clasped Hamm's right hand as two other goons appeared from behind and poked guns in his ribs. They pushed him towards the car parked at the curb and into the backseat. They shoved him to the floor, slipped a pillowcase over his head, and sped off.[149]

Two hours later an anonymous telephone call was received by an official at the brewery. The caller informed him that they had Hamm and they wanted $100,000 ransom in small denominations - $5, $10, and $20 bills. The official was told delivery instructions would come later. The next day a taxicab driver delivered a ransom note to the official. At the same time a drugstore employee found a second note in a phone booth also addressed to the Hamm's official and took it to him. Hamm had signed both notes authorizing his bankers to pay the ransom and directed this official to deliver it but gave no location. The next day a third note was placed in the car of another Hamm employee. It contained detailed instructions about how the money was to be delivered, but that evening the official received an anonymous phone call with different instructions that were to be carried out immediately. The official was ordered to remove his car's doors and its turtleback hatch so the gang could see if a policeman was hiding inside and then attach a red lantern on its rear so they could easily identify his car approaching. Then he was to drive a specific highway without exceeding 20 miles per hour so police could not tail him without their second crawling vehicle being obvious to the watching kidnappers. The official was told he would drive by a car parked on the other side of the street that would flash its headlights five times to signal for him to drop the package with the ransom money on the road and continue down the highway at the same slow rate of speed. The official complied by leaving the package laying on the road as instructed and then returned to Hamm's home.

The Hamm family sat waiting desperately for their beloved one to return alive. The hours slowly went by in the overwhelming empty and silent home. A day past and then another. The next morning the gang took the blindfolded Hamm from their hideout and pushed him into a car. They drove until they neared the town of Wyoming, 30 miles north of St. Paul, and dumped their victim into a field. Having been restrained from moving for three days he struggled to a farmhouse and called his mother. She sent a car to pick up her still dazed son, and he was driven to his waiting family at the mansion.

A couple weeks after Hamm's kidnapping, Karpis and Fred and Doc Barker were at their St. Paul hideout when they received a warning that police were on the way to nab them so they hurriedly moved to another location. Alvin and the two brothers debated who might have turned them in to the cops. They decided it had to have been Ma Barker's second husband. A few nights later Fred Barker invited his stepfather to take a car ride and his pal Karpis offered to join them. A couple hours later almost 100 miles northeast of St. Paul at a lake near Webster, Wisconsin, the bullet-riddled body of Ma's current husband floated in the darkness. Later it would be discovered. This made Karpis and Fred fugitives from murder charges in two states, the first a sheriff in Missouri and the second a relative in Wisconsin.

A little over a month after the Hamm kidnapping, Fred Barker drove to Reno to turn over the hot Hamm kidnapping loot to Graham and McKay. They passed it on to winning players through their casino cages, and they gave Fred a discounted amount of currency bearing unrecorded serial numbers. He carried it in a suitcase and drove to a Long Lake, Illinois vacation cottage 55 miles northwest of Chicago. The other kidnap participants joined him there, and Fred distributed the laundered ransom cash. Two days later the Karpis-Barkers gang robbed the Cloud County Bank in Concordia, Kansas, and Fred who was recognized was charged with this crime along with the two separate murders.

A month after hitting the Kansas bank, the Karpis-Barkers gang robbed the postal service in South St. Paul, Minnesota. Two couriers guarded by two policemen picked up the Swift & Company payroll cash bags at the railroad depot, and then walked a block to the local post office where they added its cash receipts to their stash. As the quartet of couriers and guards walked back out to the sidewalk, gang members leapt from their car. The two policemen quickly raised their hands, but the robbers blew one's head off and seriously shot the other in the head while the two couriers jumped under nearby cars. One of the thugs stole a machinegun from the police car before the killers made off with $30,000. The two officers had a total of five young children.

Three weeks later four employees of the Federal Reserve Bank in Chicago walked two sacks of first-class mail from the post office to the Bank. Two cars drove up and robbers leapt to the street with machineguns and shotguns to surround the bank employees. After snatching the sacks containing negotiable securities and checks the bandits leapt into one car and sped off. In their haste they crashed into a car in the intersection of Adams and Halsted Streets and overturned. The accident attracted the attention of Patrolman Miles Cunningham who walked over to investigate when one of the robbers shot him dead. Then the gun-pointing desperadoes forced an oncoming motorist to stop and turn over his car so they could flee.

More than a year later, the FBI would raid Doc Barker's apartment and seize a machinegun that forensics would eventually tie into the killing of a policeman at each of the two previous postal-service robberies. The machinegun's partially-obliterated serial numbers identified it as the weapon stolen from a police car at the South St. Paul postal-receipts robbery. Two months later a ballistic comparison of a bullet taken from a telephone post near the South St. Paul robbery proved to be a perfect match with the bullets used by the bandits in the Chicago robbery and the shooting of the policeman in their getaway. This meant Doc Barker had murdered a policeman in two different states three weeks apart. These senseless carnages led to intense manhunts for the killers forcing the gang to flee to Reno and lay low for the next two months under the protection of Graham and McKay.

When the gang reassembled in St. Paul they started planning their second kidnapping. This time they targeted 37-year-old Edward Bremer. He was a successful St. Paul banker and his family owned Schmidt Brewery there. One morning Bremer dropped his eight-year-old daughter at the exclusive Summit Girls School and drove on toward his office. When he was a few blocks from where Hamm had been snatched, he pulled up to a stop sign. A car was parked on the cross street near the stop sign to his right. As he came to a stop, this car pulled into the intersection and turned to face his car front bumper to front bumper just as the car behind Bremer pulled up close to squeeze him in-between them. Two masked armed men ran from each car toward Bremer who tried to leap out but a pistol was thrust in his face. As gang members entered both front car doors, they tried to shove him into the middle of the seat, but Bremer put up a real effort to fight them off until they badly pistol-whipped his head. They threw him on the floor of the backseat of his car and strapped a pair of tape-covered goggles over his eyes. All three cars sped away unseen by any witnesses. Bremer's abandoned car splotched with much blood was later found in an outlying residential neighborhood.

Next gang members showed up at the doorstep of a doctor friend of Bremer, blindfolded him, and drove him five hours to have him treat the victim. Then they drove the blindfolded doctor to near his home. If it seems like the Karpis-Barkers gang, which would develop such a murderous record, seemed to take especially good care of their kidnap victims' health, it probably resulted from a clause in the Federal Lindbergh Kidnap Law that states the death penalty cannot be imposed on the perpetrators if the victim is "liberated unharmed."

Soon after Bremer was snatched, the gang delivered a ransom note to his wealthy contractor friend. It contained detailed directions to deliver the $200,000 ransom payment in $5 and $10 bills, but the vault at Bremer's bank had already been time-locked for the night so the plan could not be implemented that evening as ordered. During the next several days no further word was heard from the kidnappers as his family agonized over whether their loved one was still alive. After two-and-a-half weeks of chilling silence, Bremer's father, Adolph, held a radio and press conference appealing for his son's release. He offered a three-day period to negotiate in secrecy without police involvement. This was a fortuitous decision because the kidnappers had stopped communication because the initial non-payment caused them to suspect the contractor was working with the police. Almost immediately after the father's offer was broadcast, the gang delivered the final instructions.

The contractor friend followed these directions implicitly. He went to a specific street corner to find an empty, unlocked, parked car with the keys in the glove compartment along with an instruction note. He drove at 15 miles per hour until he stopped and waited for a specific bus that he followed 100 yards behind. When he spotted four flashlights on the left of the road near Zumbrota, Minnesota, he stopped and arranged several flashlights he had purchased in a prescribed pattern on the highway. Then he drove on and took the first right until he saw a parked car's headlights flash five times. He stopped, laid the ransom package beside the road, and drove on.

The family again began an anxious wait that must have seemed interminable. Two nights later three gang members drove Bremer to Rochester, Minnesota, 35 miles south of St. Paul, and pushed the blindfolded victim out of the car. After 22 days restrained without moving, he staggered to a bus depot only to find out he had missed the last bus for the Twin Cities. He took a train to Owatonna where it caught up with that last bus. After midnight he stumbled into his father's mansion unshaven, tired, and "very, very nervous." He crawled into his own bed where he could finally stretch out. The wounds on his head were close to healed.

The Bremer family members were the victims, but they looked bad in the newspaper stories about the kidnapping because AG Cummings criticized the father for having refused to cooperate with the FBI by secretly conducting negotiations with the kidnappers and by privately having the ransom delivered. This negative image grew after the son's release when he refused to identify his kidnappers. However the reality was very different from the appearance created by the AG's press conferences and publicity releases. Bremer's father was actually a personal friend and political donor to President Franklin Roosevelt who had mentioned the kidnapping in one of his weekly radio fireside chats. The fact is the father had worked in secret with the FBI who recorded the serial numbers on every ransom bill. The night the son returned he had refused comment to the FBI only because he was disoriented after being bound for 22 days and he was still experiencing horrible freight of the kidnappers. The next day the victim privately told the FBI he could identify two of the men because they were unmasked when they grabbed him by force. Agents had already showed him likely mug shots and had quietly begun a search for Karpis and Fred Barker.

While the AG was putting out misleading information to the kidnappers about lack of cooperation by the family, the FBI was already hard at work on the case. The first break came when Bremer's contractor friend returned from delivering the ransom package. He described the four unusually large flashlights laid out in a pattern to signal him to turn into a side road. Agents checked St. Paul stores that sold such lights and found a saleswoman who remembered selling four to a man. When shown mug shots of Old Creepy Karpis she identified him.

At the same time a farmer near Portage, Wisconsin discovered four empty five-gallon gasoline cans on a private unpaved road near his farm. He called the sheriff who turned them over to the FBI. Its laboratory found that one fingerprint on a can matched Doc Barker. The gang had brought along the filled gas cans when transporting Bremer because they could not risk stopping at a gas station where the attendant might see the blindfolded victim lying on the back floor.

Even though the local farmer and sheriff deserved sole credit for finding and realizing the importance of these gas cans, the FBI falsely claimed sole credit a year-and-a-half later. The Chicago FBI Office SAC D. M. Ladd, who had succeeded Purvis, spoke to the local Kiwanis Club about how agents had solved the Bremer case. What a whopper of a false yarn he told. "At about midpoint in the journey, which lasted approximately 12 hours, the contents of the cans were poured into the car and the cans were left by a gravel road. We computed the approximate distance a car could travel in 12 hours, found the approximate halfway point of the trip and drew a circle around St. Paul on a map. Agents found the cans after seven days. An examination of the cans revealed a fingerprint of Arthur "Doc" Barker, a leader of the gang." None of the listeners considered that it would have been near impossible during a lifetime of searching to find some empty cans on an unspecified private dirt road in an unknown direction more than 100 miles away.[150]

SAC Ladd's tale is interesting because the FBI could have used the investigative technique he described to solve an important set of clues about the apartment in which Bremer had been held captive for 22 days. Bremer had been blindfolded and bound in a dark room. Night and day relays of two guards sat behind him with the warning to not look around on pain of death. He absolutely obeyed the orders because he feared he might be killed and desperately hoped to be free again. Despite his awful plight Bremer focused every waking moment on the neighborhood sounds he could hear outside the window of the bedroom where he was held. He was only concerned with noises that occurred day after day, and he estimated the time each occurred by the amount of sunlight that seeped through his blindfold.

These are the sounds Bremer heard with what they turned out to be contained in parentheses. Every morning about 7 am he heard a grocer start up his truck and drive away (from a small frame shack across the alley). He heard children playing (at a grade school nearby a half-block to the north) and their shouts and laughter as they walked by to and from school. Church bells chimed four times a day (a block to the south). Switch engines puffed (at the Milwaukee Railroad switch yards two blocks to the east). Four times a day a factory whistle blew. (It was on top of the railroad roundhouse four blocks east.) Along with this whistle at noon a siren wailed with one short blast (when the town's telephone operator tested the fire siren in the city's business district to the northwest).

Agents could have quickly identified this location using the analytical technique described by SAC Ladd in his Kiwanis talk. The kidnappers had released Bremer in Rochester, Minnesota, and they had dumped the gas cans about half way on the trip in Portage, Wisconsin, 173 miles east of Rochester. Bremer remembered that they had not reversed course after dumping the cans so he knew he had been held about 173 miles further east. Bremer's perceptual ability while blindfolded and his memory were extraordinary. If agents had listened to him and applied his recollections to a map they would have deduced the kidnappers could have held him in only two small areas of the country. The kidnappers could not have traveled directly straight from the east because Lake Michigan was a huge blockade in this direction 84 miles away, which was just half the distance Bremer assumed they had driven. Thus the kidnappers had to have come from either the northeast or southeast approximately 173 miles. If agents had fanned out in all directions from the highway system in the northeastern tip of Wisconsin, and also to the southeast in the northern part of Illinois, they would have found the town that contained Bremer's house of horrors in a matter of days. It would turn out that Bremer was held in Bensenville, Illinois, 163 miles southeast of Portage. This made Bremer's recollection guesstimate of Portage being "about midpoint" of the trip off by just 6%. What a remarkable accomplishment for a terrified blindfolded victim, but agents did not bother with such a reasoned, scientific approach in trying to locate his dungeon. Instead agents randomly scoured towns in seven states trying to find the combination of facilities Bremer described hearing near the apartment. Thus it took FBI manpower almost a year to identify the town as Bensenville.

When agents finally found the town, they determined the specific apartment by triangulating or centering its location among the combination of facilities Bremer heard. This was nifty detective work considering that Bremer never saw the exterior of the building or its surroundings. All he saw during the short periods his captors removed the bandages covering his eyes were some elements in his caged bedroom - the odd wallpaper design, some fixtures, and a crack in the wall. He burned this image in his memory, and when agents took him to the suspected apartment almost a year after he had been snatched, Bremer confirmed it was the room of his horror.

When newspapers reported Bremer visited the apartment and positively ID'd it, fugitive Karpis and accomplice Volney Davis tried to discourage their kidnap victim from testifying against their associates who had already been incarcerated. The thugs sent death threats to Bremer who was guarded around the clock. The FBI was told by an unidentified gang member that the desperadoes had plans to shoot Bremer on a St. Paul street.

A month after Bremer's release, AG Cummings announced the Bremer kidnapping had been solved and specifically mentioned that the FBI was now working in "perfect harmony" with the Bremers. The AG said Karpis and Doc Barker had been linked to the crime through fingerprints found on a gas can thrown out of the car from which Bremer was released. The AG said the other members of the gang were known but this was not true. At the time the FBI believed the two suspects were members of John Dillinger's gang. When the Karpis-Barkers gang members heard why the FBI was searching for their two leaders, they had a doctor obliterate their fingerprints and Old Creepy got a facelift just like the Dillinger gang had done.[151]

The doctor who worked on the gang's fingerprints and did Karpis' facelift was Joseph Moran. He graduated from Tufts Medical College in Boston where he was an honor student. He opened a practice in La Salle, Illinois, but he was convicted of murder by abortion. He was paroled from Joliet two years later but was returned for a parole violation. He was finally freed a year later. While he was an inmate at Joliet, he was a respected physician who performed hundreds of operations on both prisoners and prison officials. Despite his successful surgeries in prison, the ex-convict could not obtain a license as a physician on the outside so he opened a medical practice for gangland criminals in hiding.

Moran accompanied the Karpis-Barkers gang when they moved from Chicago to Toledo, Ohio. There he became an alcoholic who liked to boast about his infamous criminal clients. A few months before he was indicted for assisting the fugitive Karpis-Barkers gang, he visited their hideout and a couple members took him for a ride. Three months later the mutilated body of a man his age was found strapped to a clump of bushes near a lonely road west of Toledo, but no identification was possible. Two years later the FBI had the body exhumed and sent the hands to the Washington lab for identification but this failed. A year later, a Toledo Federal Grand Jury indicted 10 people for harboring the gang at about the time Moran disappeared. Agents interviewed several of the defendants and their description of his appearance shortly before he disappeared matched the slain body. FBI agents in Toledo and Cleveland told reporters that the body was identified as Moran and indicated that Director J. Edgar Hoover would soon announce this. But the next day at Washington Headquarters, Hoover for unknown reasons denied that the body was the gangster surgeon. This was followed by an amazing breach of protocol by the Toledo agents. Hoover demanded total obedience, squelched agents from making internal dissent, and prohibited them from speaking to the press except as directed by Headquarters. Yet these agents contacted the local reporters again to override the Director's announcement by publicly reaffirming the body was that of the long-missing doctor.[152]

THE RANSOM-CASH TRAIL

Soon after Bremer's release from captivity, the local farmer and the policeman found the kidnappers' gas cans with Doc Barker's fingerprint, and Karpis and Fred Barker were identified by the kidnap victim. But the FBI had no idea where in the world any of the three were. With that the kidnapping case went cold for three months. Then a City National Bank teller in Chicago became suspicious about 10 $10 bills handed him by a customer. The teller proceeded to question the man and when his answers were unsatisfactory had him arrested. Then police interviewed this gambler and ex-convict and he quickly gave up two co-conspirators. He identified a fellow money passer as a Loop hotel bartender. The suspect also admitted the $2,600 he was carrying was Bremer ransom money and said it was given to him by John J. "Boss" McLaughlin.

McLaughlin had been a powerful but seedy Democratic political power on the West Side and a member of the legislature. During his tenure he obtained the release of many criminals from state prisons. Then he abandoned politics to join the dark side. At the time of this money-passing arrest he was out on bail pending a federal trial for possessing bonds stolen in a $500,000 Loop mail robbery a year-and-a-half earlier. At the time that indictment was issued two of his co-conspirators died. One committed suicide six hours before the indictment was made public likely out of fear of gang reprisal, and three days later the other was shot to death in front of County Commissioner Charles Weber's Prohibition beer distributing office probably to eliminate him as a potential witness. McLaughlin's main source of income had been a partnership in an illegal casino with North Side gangster Ted Newberry. That is until Newberry in a bid for power hired a Chicago police detective to kill Al Capone's successor, Frank Nitti. Nitti was seriously wounded but still able to figure out who had set him up and to order retaliation. Three weeks after the Nitti shooting Newberry's body was found on a lonely road.

McLaughlin was arrested for laundering the Bremer ransom cash five days after SAC Purvis' Little Bohemia raid fiasco against John Dillinger and Baby Face Nelson. FBI Director Hoover immediately had his chief assistant Harold Nathan fly to the Windy City and publicly take over the Bremer-abduction investigation. Hoover stated fingerprints proved the kidnappers were Karpis and the two Barker brothers, even though Karpis and Fred Barker had been identified by witnesses rather than fingerprints.

The night of the arrests of McLaughlin and his son the FBI interrogated the father in the now infamous 19th-story Bankers' Building after-hours dungeon for "vigorous physical interviews." The next morning while awaiting arraignment the suspect claimed to reporters that he had been tortured all night. He maintained, "They grilled me all night, and used third degree methods on me. They kept me prisoner in my home all Friday. Then all night they kept at me in Purvis' office. They never gave me a chance to sleep, and one agent hit me in the mouth and knocked out a tooth." Agents also threatened to drop him out of a window from the 19th story. McLaughlin kept his mouth shut through this horrible ordeal, and defiantly told the press he would win the case.[153]

For the next six months McLaughlin remained locked in jail because he was unable to put up the high bail. Exhorting with his blustery political style he continued to indignantly deny that he and his son were guilty. McLaughlin's 17-year-old son, John Jr., was the only leverage the FBI had against the old politician. Agents arrested Jr. in the Board of Trade Building where he was a messenger. He possessed $85 of the Bremer ransom cash. This was a small amount and he could have claimed at trial that he had no knowledge of its source which his father would have backed up. However it would have been difficult for the son to convince a jury of a legitimate reason for having hidden those bills in his hat band. Even if found innocent he would have carried the stigma of the trial for the rest of his life. Finally the old man cut a deal with the FBI. He confessed to dispensing $53,000 of the $200,000 ransom through two passers who gave it to Chicago banks and stores. Immediately after the father pled guilty the charges against his son were dismissed. Both money passers had been paid a substantial percentage of the money they distributed, but it was clear to the agents that McLaughlin and the two passers had not participated in the abduction. The two passers would get five-year sentences. Even though McLaughlin was considered more involved in the crime than the pair of passers because he had distributed the ransom cash to underlings, he was 68-years old and suffered from diabetes so he also received a five-year sentence.[154]

McLaughlin and his two Chicago ransom-money handlers knew nothing about the kidnapping gang so the case again went cold. After the gang had released Bremer, the leaders had moved their base from Chicago to Toledo, Ohio. There the doctor who had earlier worked on Dillinger gave Karpis a facelift and used a chemical process to eradicate or mutilate his and several associates' fingerprints. Gang members then moved on to Cleveland, Ohio, where Karpis took a job as a tuxedoed bouncer at the plush Harbor Club Casino. He and his girlfriend lived a quiet life for a half year. Then the girlfriends of the two Barker brothers and gang member Harry Campbell went out for the afternoon to enjoy themselves at a hotel bar. When the three women became drunk and rowdy, Cleveland police were called and took them into custody. They were girlfriends of gang members so the FBI also interrogated them but agents released them without putting tails on them. They immediately returned to their fugitive boyfriends. Fortunately before their release, police had elicited from one of the girls where they had parked their boyfriends' car. Detectives searched it and found two addresses written on a slip of paper. Late that night at 4:00 a.m. police raided one of the homes, but Karpis, Fred, Doc, and Campbell had already taken off with their girlfriends and Ma for Chicago. The gang leaders soon decided to part ways and all again disappeared from sight.

Karpis and his girlfriend, Dolores Delaney, stayed for a short while at the El Commodoro Hotel in Miami lolling on sunny beaches, going to races, and visiting nightclubs. Then they settled in Havana, Cuba, where his messages with the other gang members were forwarded back and forth through the manager of Miami's El Commodoro. Three months later a merchant in Havana, Cuba, gave a customer change with U.S. bills. The purchaser was a resident FBI agent and he recognized the bill's serial numbers were from the Bremer kidnap ransom. The agent began searching the city for the presence of gang members. While riding an elevator at one hotel, he just happened to stand next to Karpis. The agent failed to recognize the desperado, but Karpis realized the clean-cut man beside him was an agent. He quickly fled his Havana home with Dolores to the Florida hideout of Fred and Ma Barker.

Two months later the FBI arrested two men in Miami for having harbored Karpis for three months in Havana. At the same time America's secret police requested that Cuba's secret police incarcerate the American manager of Havana's Hotel Park View, Nathaniel Heller. The Cubans complied and held him incommunicado without the presence of an attorney for interrogation by two FBI agents. Since Heller had not committed any crime in Cuba and he was not charged with one, he readily admitted using Karpis' alias to lease a home, purchase a car, and exchange cable messages with associates in the U.S. For all three services the manager logged in the hotel's accounting books having received the standard commission because no Cuban laws were violated. Heller told reporters through the barred jail windows, "I have been denied the right to see my friends, family, or lawyer. I have been threatened by them. I have been treated worse than a murderer would have been treated." He said FBI agents told him during lengthy questioning, "When we get you to the States we'll make you talk," even though he had admitted everything and turned over all records and cables.[155]

The Cuban authorities' actions of holding Heller incommunicado and without charge indefinitely violated their Constitution and laws. Even though Heller had lived in Havana for several years and his hotel enjoyed an excellent reputation, the FBI applied pressure to force the government to deport him as an undesirable alien. American Embassy officials said they had not instituted extradition proceedings through regular diplomatic procedure and made it clear this was solely an FBI operation. Hoover's only interest was in enhancing his public crime-fighting image at home. Thus he did not care how negatively he impacted America's foreign policy relations by not getting approval from either the U.S. State Department or President Roosevelt. Cuba's *Ahora* newspaper attacked the U.S. for undue influence to deport Heller who had committed no crime in Cuba.

The FBI also presented evidence to a Federal Grand Jury in Jacksonville, Florida, to get Heller and five others indicted for harboring Karpis. Two days later without explanation the Cuban Government suddenly suspended its deportation proceedings that under its law should have freed

Heller but instead turned the American resident over to the FBI agents attending the hearing. It never came out what kind of gunboat-diplomacy threats were made against the small banana republic by Director Hoover. FBI agents said they were cooperating with Cuban authorities to conduct an intensive search in Havana for America's Public Enemy Number 1 but unbeknownst to them Karpis had been quietly nestled back in the U.S. for two months.[156]

The man who arranged the disposal of $72,000 of the $200,000 Bremer kidnap ransom in Havana was also charged in the Florida indictments. Cassius McDonald had been a lumber expert for the government until his father, a Chicago political leader, left him a large fortune that he then lost in the 1929 stock-market crash. This forced McDonald to become a consulting engineer in Grosse Point, Michigan that again made him wealthy. Before the indictment he had lived four years in Havana and operated a racetrack. After the indictment he continued to live in the safe-haven of Havana, but eight months later he visited his fine Detroit residence where FBI agents arrested him. Four months later he was convicted in St. Paul and sentenced to 15 years in Leavenworth Penitentiary. For four years his wife fought for his release until a Kansas City, Kansas Federal Judge ordered his release on the technical grounds that he was not represented by adequate counsel and he should have been granted a change of venue to Florida where he was indicted. It is interesting that the two big distributors of the Bremer ransom cash were a powerful Chicago politician and the son of another.[157]

GIBSON WAS THE FIRST TARGET

FBI agents kept secret their only solid lead in the Bremer kidnapping. When the three Chicago ransom-money lenders were arrested, two informed on a fourth man, Russell Gibson. Not only had he distributed part of the loot, but the others believed he had been a participant in the kidnapping. Five years earlier Gibson had been arrested for a $75,000 bank messenger robbery in Oklahoma City, Oklahoma but escaped the city's jail and remained on the loose. Gibson was indicted with Boss McLaughlin for the kidnapping money laundering, but this action was kept sealed because the FBI did not want to let the long-term fugitive know he had become targeted as a hunted man and drive him deeper underground.

In the meantime, FBI Director Hoover had made an important change in the leadership of the task force going after the machinegun-totting bank robbers. He had replaced the youthful attorney Purvis with the experienced Cincinnati Office SAC E. J. Connelley. He had combat experience as a first lieutenant in the First World War, and he had been an agent for 15 years. However he also had a tarnished FBI raid record. In Cleveland he had laid a trap for Karpis and Doc Barker, but the culprits had made a clean getaway. Unfortunately this would not be Connelley's last raid fiasco as the problems with Hoover's boys were built into the system by the Director's flawed leadership, failure to train, and lack of professional police procedures.

Three months after Connelley's Cleveland misadventure, the FBI was informed that the wife of suspect Gibson had been living with another couple in a Chicago apartment for two months. Agents set up surveillance of Clara Gibson and a week later Russell Gibson showed up. SAC Connelley waited until the following night to raid their abode. His contingent wore bulletproof vests and were armed with machineguns, rifles, and tear-gas bombs. SAC Connelley divided his 16 agents into three groups. One remained in the building's courtyard in the entranceway while another went to cover the rear exit. Connelley led the third group into the vestibule where he rang Gibson's second-floor apartment bell and shouted into the intercom, "Come on down, one at a time. The place is surrounded." Getting no reply, he led his group up the stairs to the second floor where they saw Clara coming out of the apartment to survey the scene. Upon seeing them she darted back inside and slammed the door. The agents ran down the hall and opened fire through the door but did not hit anyone inside. At the same time agents heard shots in the rear of the building.

When Connelley had barked over the intercom his command to surrender, Gibson had grabbed a machinegun, kissed his wife goodbye, told her and the other couple to surrender, and headed toward the rear exit stairs. At the bottom he ran straight into the waiting agents. He fired one shot, and the agents returned fire. An FBI bullet blew the weapon out of the fugitive's hand. As he stooped to pick it up, agents shot him in the back three times. The wounded man ran into a dead-end passage, turned around, and collapsed. He was rushed to the hospital dying but he refused to give up the whereabouts of Karpis or Doc Barker. The fatal slug was a .351-caliber bullet from a high-powered rifle that pierced his bulletproof vest and lodged in his right lung. At the Coroner's Inquest, Agent Ray Abbaticchio testified to firing this fatal shot. As an aside, a quarter of a century later Nevada's Governor would appoint retired FBI Agent Abbaticchio to be the second Gaming Control Board Chairman policing the state's casino industry. His long FBI experience did not prepare him for this responsibility. Many perplexed long-time Nevada leaders evaluated his leadership in this gaming control position as erratic or weird.

When the agents in the front courtyard heard the gunfire from the rear, they assumed a pitched battle was going on at Gibson's apartment so they ran to the side of the building and guessed which window was his. They machinegunned out the glass and then hurled three tear-gas bombs inside. Unfortunately they chose the wrong apartment. An innocent man was alone sleeping soundly and securely in the safety of his domain. From inside the apartment he had not heard the gunshots in the back of the building so he was blithely unaware of any commotion until the FBI launched its formidable assault against him. He awoke in the darkness to all hell breaking loose right on top of him – the concussive explosions were followed by the smell of a strange gas, difficulty breathing, and burning in his eyes and on his skin. Bewildered and terrified, he staggered through the darkness chocking from teargas onto the small balcony screaming, "I surrender! I surrender!" The spreading tear-gas fumes overcame many other families in surrounding apartments, forcing them to flee outside on their balconies or through the exits despite their overwhelming fright that the waiting shooters might blow them apart.

When all the gun-totting FBI agents arrived at the building and began surrounding it, a half dozen neighbors called the Town Hall Police Department. As always the FBI failed to forewarn local police about its assault plans. Several squads quickly responded to fight what they assumed was a violent Chicago gangland war. Police units faced off against FBI agents in both the front and back of the building in tense situations that came precariously close to producing a tragically deadly firefight. In the front, the lieutenant squad leader shouted, "We are police officers." His men were on the verge of opening fire when he ordered them to wait as he called out to the agents a second time and they finally identified themselves. Upon hearing the shooting of Gibson going on in the back of the building, three police sergeants ran from the front, saw the armed men, jumped behind available cover, and prepared to open fire against presumed gangsters as one agent finally cried out, "We're D. J. men!" (Department of Justice).

SAC Connelley had not even been announced publicly as replacing SAC Purvis in leading the FBI's fight against bank robbers, and he was already being blasted for the ineffectiveness of his raiding tactics and disregard for the safety of civilians. It is significant that Assistant Director Harold Nathan flew into Chicago from St. Louis that day to make the public announcement about the killing of Gibson. He was accompanied by SAC Purvis who obediently did not say a word and had not been seen in public since the Floyd killing six weeks earlier.

Townspeople were outraged and condemned the FBI for not warning police before starting the firefight, but Assistant Director Nathan lied to the press by saying he had no time to inform local police. The truth was the raid had been planned for 24 hours and the FBI never worked with other law enforcement agencies. Two days later at the local Inquest into Gibson's killing, Chicago Chief of Detectives John L. Sullivan brought up the FBI's counterproductive tactics. He testified Chicago police had sought Gibson for some time as the leader of a band of jewel robbers. During their investigation, they had located a previous apartment he was living at and put it under surveillance. Detectives knew Gibson was not at home and were patiently awaiting his return when they watched helplessly as FBI agents stormed up and raided the empty residence. Of course Gibson never returned. The Inquest Jury returned a verdict of justifiable homicide and awarded a commendation to the agents in the case. But it also issued them an admonition that in the future the FBI take greater precautions to insure the safety of innocent persons. The press asked the civilian, who was awoken by a machinegun volley blowing out his window and spreading tear gas in the darkness of his room, his thoughts about the raid, but he declined to condemn the FBI agents explaining, "I'm too glad to be alive."

As all the action was going on at the apartment building's back entrance and in the civilian's apartment, agents in Gibson's apartment arrested his wife and another woman who were overcome by fumes. Then the other man staying with them came down the front stairs unarmed and with his hands raised in surrender. This capture of Byron "Red" Bolton was the biggest break in the case as he would piece together the whole Bremer-kidnapping crime for the FBI and go on to become the star witness for the Federal Prosecutor. But returning to this momentous night of FBI activity in Chicago, it was just getting underway.[158]

GOING AFTER THE BARKERS

On the night the FBI fatally shot Gibson, other Chicago agents were quietly closing in on Doc Barker. A month earlier Ohio agents had learned Doc had married Mildred Kuhlmann in Toledo, and agents had been searching for him since. They got her girlfriend to give up Mildred's Chicago hotel room forwarding address. The Ohio Office called the Chicago Office and that night agents sat in the lobby observing as Mildred and another girlfriend checked out. When Mildred returned to her car agents tailed her hoping she would take them to Doc, but they got stuck in traffic and helplessly watched her drive out of sight. The agents returned to the hotel and studied Mildred's room telephone records and found she had called a local apartment. Agents put it under surveillance and were watching the building when they saw her walking along the sidewalk nearby. They followed her as she entered another building, the Surf Lane, whereupon they rented an apartment to continue their surveillance. Eventually Mildred walked out with Doc Barker to go for a walk. Two agents started following at a distance until the couple reached where three agents were hiding in wait. The trio jumped into their path and the unarmed Doc ran between two parked cars into the street until he slipped on the ice and fell face down. Before he could get up agents cuffed him. When searched he was asked where his gun was and he resignedly commented, "Home - and ain't that a hell of a place for it?"[159]

Agents documented in FBI files that they used "vigorous physical efforts" against Doc Barker for eight continuous days. The reports included an agent hitting him over the head with two books. Even FBI Director Hoover at Headquarters told the press that Doc had undergone "intensive questioning." Still Doc refused to talk about his brother Fred or Karpis.

Doc's nickname made him the most remembered of the Barker brothers, but this was a misnomer as he suffered from a low IQ of 81, as administered in a prison test. It was his poor memory that would lead to the next big break in the case. He had recently visited with his brother Freddie and Ma, and to make sure he could find them again, he had drawn a map of their hideout. Although the drawing was laying in the open in his apartment, agents inexplicably took three days to discover it. Almost a year after Bremer's kidnapping the FBI finally had a fix on Fred. Just as the FBI did not announce that Gibson had been indicted until agents killed him, it likewise did not announce the capture of Doc Barker for fear Fred would bolt. Agents illegally held Doc incommunicado, even denying him an attorney as they administered their ongoing torture regimen. At the same time other agents used his map to try to close in on his fugitive brother.

The map showed Fred and Ma Barker were hiding out in a rented house near the little village of Ocklawaha on the edge of the north shore of Lake Weir in central Florida, 115 miles south-south-west of Jacksonville. The village contained a few stores and one phone with homes scattered around the lake. Since the fugitive and his mother were using aliases, agents asked locals if any new comers had moved into the area. It took the scouting agents five days to identify their house. Freddie and Ma had been living there about two months. The newbies kept to themselves but locals observed they had a lot of company, mostly late at night.

Cincinnati SAC Connelley was again sent in to lead this assault. Unfortunately he again failed to develop a viable tactical plan. He simply followed Purvis' modus operandi of opening fire at anyone who moved. His agents wore bullet-proof vests and were armed with machineguns and tear gas. Shortly after daybreak they sauntered toward the house. Along the path they warned a few of the nearby residents of the impending danger. These people quickly deserted their homes, but about 200 parked cars of residents remained within view and gunshot of the targeted house. After surrounding all four sides of the house, agents took cover. Then Connelley called to the occupants to surrender, but he was answered with a spray of machinegun bullets from an upstairs window. Agents returned fire. The sleeping nearby residents were shocked by all this gunfire so near. Most ran outside before realizing what was going on, and then they hit the dirt in horror as they watched the nearby pitched battle. They described it as "like a war," and were prepared to run if the combat moved their way.

A bizarre pattern of intermittent warfare quickly developed. Machineguns would bark for 15 minutes and this would be followed by a long eerie silence. Then the tit-for-tat rat-a-tat-tat started anew. Witnesses said all the shooting came from upstairs and Fred Barker seemed to keep changing windows because the shooting would be from one side of the house and then from another. All the while agents stayed holed up in their positions. It should have become clear to the agents that there was only one person firing back. With 15 men SAC Connelley separated them in five groups with five in front, four in back, two on each side, and the final two keeping civilians from getting close to the front. This was effective placement of his forces because it covered the four sides of the house with most men facing the front and back doors. But agents should not have stayed dug in for six interminable hours. This is undoubtedly the longest record by far for one man without a hostage to have held off a SWAT team deployed on all four sides of a building.

It should have been obvious that the agents who were located at the entrance where the shooter was not firing from upstairs, could safely enter the house and move stealthily by advancing only when shots were being fired. The gunfire would have led them to the shooter's room, where he would have had his back facing the door. They could have burst in with guns aimed at his back while yelling, "Don't turn around!"

Instead of this reasonably quick and effective resolution, this one-man machinegun standoff lasted for six hours until around 11 a.m. and only then because shots stopped emanating from the house. Despite the ongoing silence agents remained entrenched behind protective cover. They had no way of knowing whether Fred was dead, had run out of ammunition, was taking a long potty break, or was waiting for agents to commence an assault. Then SAC Connelley came up with a solution to their quandary. They went to the nearby guesthouse where the home owner's African-American caretaker, Willie Woodbury, lived with his wife. This couple had been sound asleep in their peaceful setting until the first bullets burst out their windows causing them to dive under their bed in horror. Two armed agents brought the terrified Woodbury out from under his bed to the protected hiding place of SAC Connelley. He ordered the civilian to boldly enter the premises to determine if Fred was alive or dead. Connelley gave the petrified unarmed man the empty assurance that Barker would not shoot someone he knew. The SAC shared his fervent wish with Willie that as a civilian he might be able to talk the determined fugitive into surrendering. Willie was horrified by the directive but this was Florida that at the time gave African-Americans no civil rights of human existence. In addition most of Hoover's agents were southerners who the Director selected because they were staunch segregationists. These agents treated this civilian like he was a government slave and terrorized him into entering alone and unarmed to do their job, while these 16 spineless lawmen remained in hiding, too cowardly to go in en mass carrying machineguns and wearing armored vests.

Woodbury held a handkerchief over his mouth to reduce breathing the lingering tear gas fumes. Slowly with great foreboding he entered the quiet house. He called out Freddie's name and explained he was forced to come in by the agents outside. He heard no reply. He walked slowly through the downstairs rooms and then climbed up the bloodstained staircase. He gingerly looked into each of the four bedroom doors. Finally with tears running down his face he stuck his head out a window and hollered, "They both up here!" Connelley yelled back from hiding, "What are they doing?" "They all dead!" The relieved agents finally crawled out of their holes and entered. It is not surprising that all 15 agents escaped a six-hour shootout without injury because everyone behaved with cowardice in the extreme. Agents found Fred Barker sprawled on the floor with three machinegun bullets in the head and 11 more in a shoulder, and his mother lay dead from one bullet wound in the forehead.[160]

It is hard to believe that this was not the most pathetically ineffective law-enforcement action in American history. Agents said they fired about 1,500 rounds of ammunition into the house before finally hitting the lone suspect. Unbelievably he single-handedly held off 15 of Hoover's most qualified agents for six hours even though they had multiple points of entry and the barricaded suspect held no hostages that would have deterred or complicated an assault. While no military or law-enforcement tactical manual in the world recommends forcing unarmed civilians to check on the physical welfare of entrenched dangerously-violent suspects, these agents reached an unprecedented level of depraved indifference by forcing an innocent man to go inside. If the cold-blooded killer had still been alive, he would have almost certainly made Woodbury his human shield in front of a window to further complicate the situation and to create wholly unnecessary civilian tragedy.

Shockingly, this was not the agents only reckless violence towards civilians that day. Another incident occurred as agents machinegunned at everyone who they saw moving and without any idea who they were trying to kill. In the nearest neighbor's house to Fred and Ma Barker lived a mother and her daughter. Immediately after the shooting stopped the mother described to a reporter their harrowing experience with Hoover's finest. "It was like war. I was suddenly awakened by guns firing. I got out of bed, and as I stood up some bullets came through the closed door between my bedroom and the dining room and hit the head of my bed. I opened the door a crack and more bullets came through the window and hit the face of the door above my head. I looked out a window and saw the yard was full of men. I could see the blazes from the men's guns on the outside. There was a lot of rapid firing like machineguns. My daughter was in bed. I broke open the back window of our room and told her we had to get out. About that time some more bullets came smacking through the dining room window and hit the wall. My daughter and I climbed through the window and got down on the ground. We were going to run to my neighbor's house, about 50 yards back of our house. The house from which the bullets were coming was only about a 100 feet in front of my house. As we lay down on the ground for a moment we heard the firing coming louder. We got up and started to run to Mrs. Rex's house. As we ran some men yelled at us to stop. We did not stop. They began shooting at us. I learned later it was the federal men. We kept on running and they kept on yelling and shooting. They must have shot at us two dozen times. They didn't know who we were. It was still a little dark. Finally we got to Mrs. Rex's house. There appeared to be 15 or 20 agents. The shooting kept on all morning. Just before noon it stopped. We saw all of the federal men go into the house. Some of them came out in a few minutes. It was all over."[161]

The bullets that hit the woman's house probably came from Fred Barker shooting at agents, but the FBI should have cleared the adjacent homes before beginning their assault. The agents' failure to protect the obviously endangered civilians placed both mother and daughter directly in the suspect's close field of fire. Worse, that morning the agents posed a far greater threat to the lives of these female innocents than the murderer inside who was not intentionally targeting civilians. Had the agents been better marksmen with their machinegun sprays and injured or killed these women, Hoover would have been dismissed in disgrace and the FBI possibly disbanded by the Congressmen who were already disgusted with Hoover's boys' many irresponsible and dangerous acts towards civilians. Despite the atrocious misconduct of the FBI agents, the next day an Ocala, Florida Coroner's Jury returned a verdict that Fred and Ma Barker were killed "while resisting arrest" and the FBI agents had acted "in the protection of their own lives."

By now Hoover's intimidating leadership had silenced his boys. None dared speak to the press until he had obtained the Director's revisionist version of an incident. This was illustrated by Chicago SAC D. M. Ladd's "no comment" responses after the FBI's arrest of Doc Barker and then the killing of Fred and Ma Barker. The day after they were slain, the *Evening American* accurately reported that FBI agents had taken Doc Barker into custody eight days earlier at the same time they shot to death Gibson. When reporters questioned SAC Ladd about the accuracy of this report he answered, "I have no comment to make." The next day AG Cummings revealed that Doc indeed had been captured without resistance "at about the time" FBI agents killed Gibson. Even after the AG's public statement, SAC Ladd withheld comment saying that he had no instructions to make this information public. This illustrates his fear of making any public statement without the explicit instructions of Director Hoover because of the ignoble ending of the career of his predecessor, Purvis. Hoover had truly transformed the FBI into America's secret police force.

Hoover always tried to cover up his agency's misdeeds. To avoid admission of improprieties he also tried to prevent payment of restitution to damaged innocent citizens who were caught up in his agents' irresponsible shootings. However the ongoing national publicity about Fred's elderly mother being killed in a six-hour shootout kept the badly-riddled home in the public's eye. The image of this private home seriously damaged by agents compelled Congress to pass a $2,500 reimbursement to the property owner to repair the mass of bullet holes, even if this action was done two-and-a-half years after the fact.[162]

A DANGEROUS LITTLE OLD LADY

It was one thing for FBI agents to have slain Fred Barker, a fugitive kidnapper, bank robber, and cold-blooded killer who had opened fire upon them, but quite another to have blown away Ma Barker, an elderly grandmother whose only crime was harboring her fugitive sons. She was similar to the many family members of the other bank robbers who had harbored their blood kin and received one or two-year federal prison terms except in her case agents assassinated her. FBI Director Hoover desperately wanted to justify his agent's killing of her, but he faced a real quandary. Everyone who knew her said she was a devoted mother who lived with her sons, worked jigsaw puzzles during the afternoon, and listened to popular radio shows in the evening. Several of the gang members later said they never discussed their crimes in front of her. They almost always gathered at separate hideouts or gang meeting places to plan their crimes. When they did talk at the house it was amongst themselves while Ma was busy cooking in the kitchen or absorbed in a radio show in another room.

Hoover always backed up his public pronouncements with investigative information he alleged was taken from his FBI files, but his storage cabinets contained nothing about Ma Barker. Prior to turning her into a corpse not one agent had ever mentioned her name in an internal report, public statement, or Federal Grand Jury presentation. In the FBI's multiyear investigation and hunt for the Karpis and Barker brothers gang, the Director never instituted a search for her, not even a cherchez la femme to try to capture either of her sons because Hoover had no idea she had any contact with them. That fateful day of the prolonged shootout agents were only after Fred Barker. She just happened to be staying with her fugitive son. Hoover had spent his career disparaging local law enforcement agencies, but he now desperately needed one or more to say Ma was part of her sons' criminal activities. Indeed several Midwest police departments had spent years seeking the Barker brothers and Karpis for murders or bank robberies, but not a single local lawman ever suspected or believed Ma was involved in any of her sons' crimes.

As soon as the raiding agents saw that they had killed Ma along with Fred, they called the Director. He realized he was facing an about-to-explode public-relations disaster. Hoover's only strong talent was manipulating publicity, so he knew he had to immediately get out a story justifying the FBI's killings of a mother and son to be included in the nation's first newspaper accounts of the slayings. Hoover quickly called a press conference at his Washington FBI Headquarters to initiate the most colossal lying campaign of his career by vilifying Fred's harmless old and now dead mother. The *New York Times* lead article was typical in making her the chief villain. "Mrs. Kate (Ma) Barker who has been called the brains of the Barker-Karpis gang held responsible for the Mr. Bremer kidnapping. … She had been credited with having directed the Barker-Karpis gang in a number of bank robberies throughout the Middle West." This loathsome assassination of the truth by America's top cop involved monumental lies to cover up and falsify the evidence, and also unconscionable character assassination. This campaign was pulled off with totally false information.[163]

FBI Headquarters followed Hoover's lead by disseminating additional lies to fabricate the wholly-false grandmother-goon myth. The Director's first announcement proclaimed she died holding a machinegun in her hand with a portion of the ammunition drum exhausted as if she too had been firing at the agents. This was absolutely untrue as every civilian witness and all agent reports only mentioned one gun being fired from that house, but this falsehood was needed to profess she was an active participant in the gang. To further distance agents from the killing of the old woman, an official gave the papers an off-the-record supposition that either her son's last act was to mercifully kill her or she committed suicide upon seeing him killed. This set off the intended conjecture and rumors about how she died by the press and public, but it totally contradicted the forensic evidence at the scene. Fred could not have taken out his mother after he was shot because the three machinegun bullets to his head killed him instantly. Ma could not have committed suicide because agents and local police knew no gun was laying close enough to her body for that possibility to be even raised at the local inquest. Thus one of Hoover's agents had to have fired the single fatal bullet, but the Director prevented his highly-touted scientific crime lab from investigating this case because a comparison of the bullet in her body with each of the guns fired that day would have identified which agent had slain her, and because lack of gunpowder residue on her body and clothing would have ruled out suicide.

Hoover's fable about Ma's criminal genius became one his favorite stories. Two years after her killing the Director made her the centerpiece of his autobiography. He wrote, "In her sixty years or so this woman reared a spawn of hell…To her [her sons] looked for guidance, for daring, resourcefulness. They obeyed her implicitly." In a book 20 years later, he wrote "it has been said that Ma Barker trained her sons in crime;" "certainly she became a monument to the evils of parental indulgence;" and "there is hot-eyed, hard featured Ma Barker in a jealous rage berating her boys. Then she is the motherly individual smoothly settling details of the rent with an unsuspecting landlord for an apartment hideout." "Ma Barker and her sons, and Alvin Karpis and his cronies, constituted the toughest gang of hoodlums the FBI ever has been called upon to eliminate." The Director had finally elevated her to the "toughest" villain in American history. One interesting aspect of his incendiary attacks against her always rang hollow. During the Director's half century in office he always discussed each criminal's specific crimes. However every statement he made about her was not only a vague generalization but not one ever involved her in lawbreaking.[164]

Later some of the gang's members became state's witnesses, wrote autobiographies, and/or gave newspaper interviews. All scoffed at Hoover's assertions. For example Karpis wrote about Ma Barker's role in his life in his autobiography many years later. "The most ridiculous story in the annals of crime is that Ma Barker was the mastermind behind the Karpis-Barker gang. ... The legend only grew up after her death … to justify how she was slaughtered by the FBI. She wasn't a leader of criminals or even a criminal herself. There is not one police photograph of her or set of fingerprints taken while she was alive. ... She knew we were criminals but her participation in our careers was limited to one function: when we traveled together, we moved as a mother and her sons. What could look more innocent?" Another notorious bank robber of that era, who pulled some heists with the gang, observed in his autobiography, "The old woman couldn't plan breakfast" let alone a criminal enterprise.[165]

Chapter 9

WHERE IS OLD CREEPY?

THE FBI'S HUNT FOR KARPIS

When Alvin Karpis and his girlfriend Dolores fled Havana because of the FBI's presence, the couple spent the next month first returning to Miami's El Commodoro Hotel and then visiting the hideout of Fred and Ma Barker. Karpis and Dolores lived there under the aliases of Mr. and Mrs. Summer. Dolores did not feel safe in Ocklawaha, Florida, and she was well along expecting Alvin's baby so he put her on a train to Atlantic City, New Jersey with the girlfriend of Harry Campbell. He was a gang member who had helped abduct Edward Bremer and then sat guard over the restrained man in the apartment bedroom. Karpis and Campbell relaxed with Fred and Ma for another week and then decided to join their girlfriends in Atlantic City. The two fugitives pulled out of Fred and Ma Barker's home the day before the FBI conducted its six-hour morning raid killing Fred and his mother. By then Karpis and Campbell had stolen a car in Jacksonville, Florida and were driving to Atlantic City. Karpis knew well that he would become visible to every lawman on the east coast if the FBI learned his license plate number and broadcast it, so he frequently changed vehicles by buying some new ones and stealing the rest.

In Atlantic City the two fugitives' girlfriends had checked into a room at the small Danmor Hotel a half block from the Boardwalk along the beach. When the two wanted men arrived in town they rented an adjoining hotel room. The Danmor's guest parking was next door to the hotel in the Coast Garage. During the middle of their arrival night, an Atlantic City Patrolman noted a car in the Garage had a stolen Florida license plate. He telephoned this into the Detective Bureau and a detective in turn called the hotel's registration desk to find out the number of the room the driver was registered in. Three detectives were dispatched to the scene before dawn. The FBI APB announcing the license plate number had not mentioned Karpis' name and he had registered using an alias. Thus detectives had no idea they were about to encounter the man who had become Public Enemy Number 1, after the FBI killed Baby Face Nelson less than two months earlier.

One detective remained in the lobby to block the room guest from escaping while the other two detectives went to his fourth-floor room. They pulled out their revolvers. One detective stood behind as the other one leaned his shoulder forward and crashed into the door breaking it open. The two startled fugitives were sitting inside. Karpis was in a rocking chair near the far wall facing them with a machinegun in his lap while Campbell was sitting on the bed's edge also cradling a machinegun. The lead Detective barked, "Stick 'em up!" Karpis retorted, "Stick 'em up yourself, copper," while lifting the weapon from his lap to fire a spray at the two detectives. He missed them as they quickly retreated backwards into the hallway and out of sight while getting off one shot. They backed down the hall to a protected bend in the corridor and aimed at the open room door to prevent the occupants from escaping. Whenever either fugitive stuck his head out the detectives opened fire with their pistols to back him inside. Karpis played this standoff routine for a short while, and then disregarding the detectives' gunfire, he leapt out the door while firing a machinegun burst towards them. One bullet ripped through a detective's cheek. It left a deep gash but it was not life threatening. At that moment the two girlfriends tried to escape from the gunfight by running out of the adjoining room into the hallway. Another bullet from Karpis struck Dolores who was pregnant with his baby in the right leg. Both women immediately ran back into the room slamming the door behind them. After the two detectives exhausted their ammunition, one tried to plug the leaking cheek of his partner while still in the hallway bend. When these detectives stopped firing, the two fugitives backed down the hallway in the opposite direction toward a rear stairway. At the fire escape they scrambled down the stairs and then ran along the sidewalk toward the garage housing their stolen car. That frigid winter morning both fugitives were wearing bedroom slippers and an overcoat but Karpis also had on trousers while Campbell was in his underwear.

As the two fugitives approached the Garage's entrance they realized it was blockaded by three uniformed patrolman. When the three cops saw the two machinegun-toting fugitives approaching them, they opened fire emptying their revolvers. The fugitives returned fire as they charged the officers, and a bullet from one of their sprays struck a wall near a patrolman's head causing flying cement chunks to knock his cap to the sidewalk. The wanted men continued advancing and drove the outgunned uniforms to flee. The five shooters exchanged 200 shots resulting in damage to one officer's cap. Having taken command of the Garage, Karpis now stood guard at the entrance as Campbell ran inside and stole a local woman's car. This allowed them to take off in a car without a hot license plate, at least until the owner learned it was stolen and reported it to lawmen. As Campbell drove out the entrance, Karpis jumped in, and the pair fled into the snow and rain. The two fugitives soon returned to the hotel and circled it twice apparently trying to figure out how to rescue their girlfriends. Then patrol cars recognized the fugitives and closed in. This drove off the fugitives with police following in hot pursuit. The desperadoes kept making turns but they did not know the street layout. Twice they ran into dead ends at the Boardwalk facing the ocean ahead. Both times Karpis spun the car around as Campbell leaned out the window behind him in his underwear firing his machinegun. Then Karpis floored it directly at the pursuing police in an explosive game of chicken. Eventually the wanted men were able to lose their pursuers in the stormy weather.

Detectives arrested the two girlfriends in their room. The pregnant Dolores was not seriously injured, but she was taken to the Atlantic City Hospital. She had previously registered at the facility because she was expecting to soon give birth. At that time Karpis had told the attending physician money was no object. The Hospital released Dolores, and agents took the two women to an undisclosed location in Philadelphia, Pennsylvania 60 miles northwest. The girlfriends gave up no information about their fugitive boyfriends' destination.

The gunfight pursuits against these dangerous criminals on the streets of Atlantic City caused the Police Department to soon request authorization to purchase six machineguns. These car-chase battles also intensified the city's political debate about creating a training school for policemen, and about hiring recruits based on attitude and fitness rather than political influence.

For the two months prior to Karpis' escape from the Atlantic City Police Department, Hoover's boys had been searching for Public Enemy Number 1 in Havana even though he had been back in the U.S. the entire time. When the pair's getaway hit the news the Director's Office immediately launched a manhunt along the Atlantic seaboard as Karpis and Campbell sped west. The fugitives did not dare drive far in daylight as they assumed the license plate on their newly stolen car had already been broadcast to police, and the vehicle had a smashed windshield and four bullet hole punctures in the trunk that were telltale signs of their identity to any passing police car. The shattered window made for a rather chilly ride for two men wearing bedroom slippers and an overcoat. Karpis also had trousers, but Campbell was still in his underwear.

Even though they fled Atlantic City before dawn, by midnight they had traveled only 100 miles northwest. As they neared Sellersville, Pennsylvania the fleeing duo forced a car off the highway, commandeered possession of it, and forced the owner, a physician from a local hospital, to join their flight as a hostage. In the victim's words, "I was driving along Route 309 on my way back to Allentown State Hospital, after visiting my parents in Philadelphia when a green sedan forced me to the side of the road. A man got out of the car, pulled out what I suppose was a submachinegun and told me to get in the back seat. I didn't argue with him and did as I was told. This man took the wheel of my car and led the way. The other car followed. After a short drive, both cars stopped and we abandoned the green car. They opened my suitcase and tied my hands behind me with strips from my pajamas. Both men got in the front seat of my car and drove away very rapidly." The fugitives forced the Doctor to cower in the back seat of his car for 21 hours on a 350 mile journey west to 15 miles southwest of Akron, Ohio. They traveled at a slow pace because the roads were in bad shape. It snowed throughout the trip but the two fugitives had added the Doctor's coat and some of his packed clothing to the flimsy attire they escaped in. The Doctor continued, "Finally about 9 o'clock they pulled up behind the Grange Hall here, went in through a rear door, and fastened me securely with the belt from my overcoat and my pajamas [and gagged him]. It took me an hour or so to get loose, then I called the police. I was not able to tell them much except that one of the men was a little shorter than the other." The fugitives ditched the stolen Doctor's car down a lane near a resort section of the Lake Erie shoreline and walked toward Monroe, Michigan. They were observed abandoning the car by a rural postman. He took notice only because they left the motor running and he notified police. Karpis sometimes left the engine running in the cars he abandoned in rural areas in hopes that by the time lawmen found one of these cars it would appear as if he had run out of gas and possibly assume he was still nearby on foot when he was actually long gone in a newly stolen vehicle.[166]

The fugitives obtained another car and two days later entered a bank in Trivoli, Illinois. They pointed their machineguns at the employees and two customers, but there was a hitch. The time lock was set to keep the vault's door closed for 15 more minutes. The desperadoes held everyone prisoner as they waited patiently. Then the pair took $3,000 and sped away.

After hitting this bank the FBI had no idea where the desperadoes were for the next three months until they surfaced to commit their next robbery. Karpis had returned to the safe haven of Reno under the protection of Graham and McKay. In his earlier visits Karpis had left his car at Frank Cochran's garage, but Cochran had recently pled guilty to harboring Baby Face Nelson and had become a state's witness against the other harborers. While Karpis resided in Reno a machinegun was found dumped in the Truckee River that meanders through Reno. It had not been in the water long enough to rust. By the time this weapon was identified as belonging to Karpis, he was again on the move to points unknown. In addition to enjoying the hospitality of the casino partners in Reno and at Lake Tahoe, Old Creepy was also seen in Auburn and Marysville, California. The two cities are about 50 miles apart and southwest from Reno over 100 miles.[167]

THE BREMER KIDNAPPING TRIAL

One year after the Edward Bremer kidnapping, the Chicago FBI Office broke the case wide open with a stellar evening of activity. Agents in three separate actions went after five suspects. They arrested Doc Barker; they arrested Byron Bolton while fatally shooting Russell Gibson; and they arrested the two men who had set up the hideout where the gang held the kidnapped victim captive. One of these two was local farmer Harold Alderton who rented and lived in the four-room Bensenville, Illinois apartment where the victim was imprisoned for 22 days. The other was Elmer "Deafy" Farmer who owned a tavern that he had operated during the recently-ended Prohibition era. At his tavern the gang members rendezvoused and planned the kidnapping. It was a convenient five blocks from the apartment where Bremer would be locked away. Remember Farmer was the man who assisted the wife of Frank Nash in an attempt to free her husband after he was taken into custody by the FBI, an effort that led to the Kansas City Massacre. Two weeks after the FBI's triple Chicago arrest actions, a St. Paul, Minnesota Federal Grand Jury indicted 22 people for either participating in the kidnapping or distributing the ransom money.

At the very beginning of the Bremer kidnapping trial before the jury was selected, defendant Byron Bolton stepped up to the judge without legal representation to enter a guilty plea of conspiracy to kidnap, but he let his previous plea of not guilty to the actual kidnapping still stand. Both charges carried life sentences but by being guilty of only conspiracy, it gave the judge the leeway to reduce his sentence for becoming a state's witness. Bolton would become the prosecution's star informer. Once the trial began Farmer also pled guilty to the conspiracy charge and then testified against his associates too.

One of the men charged with handling the Bremer ransom money testified in his own defense. James Wilson swore he was innocent and testified he falsely confessed only after two FBI agents beat him so hard "they broke one of my ears." He complained about the all too standard vigorous interrogations. They "hammered a confession out of me in the 19th-floor office of the Justice Department in Chicago." He asserted that they handcuffed one hand to a chair while he wrote the statement with the other. The two agents denied his charges, but fellow Bremer kidnapping defendant Oliver Berg, already serving a life sentence in Joliet, Illinois Prison for an unrelated murder, testified he saw the statement written under duress. The judge had excused the jury from the courtroom so they could not hear the two defendants' testimonies, and then declared he doubted the prisoner was abused. No one wanted to believe America's secret police tortured prisoners and forced confessions, especially since the American government strongly condemned such practices by the secret police forces of foreign adversaries.[168]

In the Bremer kidnapping trial the prosecution had two state's witnesses. The Federal Jury convicted five defendants, but acquitted two money handlers because they were state's witnesses and had testified they did not know the hot money had come from the kidnapping. The Judge quickly sentenced Doc Barker and Oliver Berg to life imprisonment under the Lindbergh Kidnapping law. The two defendants who were involved in supplying Bremer's hideout bedroom were Alderton who was convicted, and Farmer who had pled guilty and become a state's witness. Both received the same 20-year sentence. The two money handlers received 5 years each. This Federal Judge did not give reduced sentences for those who pled guilty, which reduced the government's time and cost of prosecuting them, or for those who became state's witnesses and possibly made the convictions possible against the tried defendants. Had other Federal Judges employed such counterproductive sentencing standards, it would have led to much less frequent and much more costly criminal prosecutions. It's a simple justice-system concept – defendants do not cooperate with the prosecution when there is no sentencing deal. In the case of John Boss McLaughlin who headed the ransom-money distribution, the Judge gave him the same sentence as James Wilson who played a lesser role in dispensing the money. By giving both men the same sentence the Judge may have looked with favor on McLaughlin because he was a state's witness and/or suffered from diabetes at age 68. This was the first time Federal prosecutors tried not only the principals in a crime but every one with any connection to the perpetrators.

Throughout the trial Doc Barker was kept in irons. A week after conviction Doc Barker was transferred to Leavenworth Penitentiary. Three U.S. Deputy Marshals transported him by train from St. Paul to Kansas. They debarked two miles from the prison and walked five blocks to a bus station for the ride to the prison. During the walk the trio of Marshals kept the notorious prisoner in both handcuffs and leg shackles. They knew fugitive Karpis had recently spent four days in a Minneapolis apartment planning to free his pal from the St. Paul jail, but Karpis never attempted to crack into the well-fortified lockup. It was now 16 months after Bremer's kidnapping, and FBI agents continued to search for the nine remaining indicted fugitives, including Karpis and his cohort Campbell.[169]

LUCK OF THE HIGHEST ORDER

One Bremer kidnapper who had been indicted and arrested was unavailable to be tried with his accomplices. Volney Davis had been a long-time associate of Doc Barker. The two had spent 10 years in prison after the pair were incorrectly convicted of killing a night watchman in Tulsa. When another thief confessed to the crime Doc was paroled. For reasons that are unclear Davis was not paroled, but the Oklahoma State Prison granted him an eight-month leave of absence and then extended it for a year. On the specified date for his return Davis did not show, and Oklahoma listed him as a fugitive.

A year after being released from prison Davis joined Doc Barker in kidnapping Bremer. Davis watched from one of the two cars as the banker was abducted in his car. Then Davis delivered the ransom notes to the family while his six accomplices drove Bremer and the three cars towards the hideout dungeon.

Eventually the FBI apprehended fugitive Davis in Kansas City, Missouri. Then two agents took him, heavily manacled hand and foot, on a charted plane for Chicago. Early that evening the pilot was forced to make an emergency landing on a farm field near Yorkville, Illinois, 55 miles southwest of Chicago. The farm owner and his neighbor heard the plane circling overhead and went to the spot where they landed. They saw the three passengers climb out of the cabin and then the agents removed the prisoner's handcuffs and leg irons. Neither farmer was known to have had law enforcement experience, but both later commented to a reporter that they were confused why the agents kept restraints on the captive aboard the plane when he had no chance to escape and immediately after deboarding removed them as soon as the opportunity to run presented itself.

The farm owner drove the two agents and the prisoner to the Nading Hotel in Yorkville. One agent called the Chicago FBI Office about the situation from a telephone booth, while the other agent took the unbound prisoner into the bar and bought them both beers. The agent toasted the prisoner, "Here's to you." Davis cordially replied, "And here's to you," as he swiftly tossed the beverage into the agent's face, struck his startled guard with a staggering blow to the jaw, and ran crashing through the bar's glass window. Davis tossed off his glass-shroud covered overcoat and ran. The agent got up, drew his pistol, and shot three times, all misses. The two agents ran out and fired as the fugitive disappeared. Davis had the lead but he was unarmed while the agents with pistols drawn were in hot pursuit. As Davis ran as fast as could down the street trying to figure out a solution to his desperate dilemma, he saw a car ahead sitting in the street's driving lane with no one in sight. The owner had apparently left it while running into a store for a quick purchase. The car was poised in the right direction away from the trailing agents, the driver's door was open, the keys were in the ignition, and the engine was running. Davis must have been in total disbelief and joy as he jumped in, stomped on the gas, and headed for Chicago. The agents did not arrive at the site until after he had driven away so they were unaware he had secured transportation. For an hour they continued to desperately search the surrounding streets in vain, frantically hoping they would not have to call in their humiliating miscue.

Just 15 minutes after escaping, Davis sauntered into another tavern in Aurora. It was a place he used to frequent so he asked the owner for help. The owner noticed that Davis was not wearing an overcoat on that frigid winter day and his hand was cut. The owner later said, "Hansen [Davis] was in here from time to time last summer. He is the man called Davis in the circular. Hansen asked me for $10. I gave him 50 cents and some sandwiches. He asked me for a gun but I didn't have one.

Then he ran out and drove away." The car Davis stole outside the hotel bar was found abandoned the next morning near Wheaton, half way to Chicago. And so Davis was on the run making him unavailable to join his accomplices for the Bremer kidnapping trial.[170]

Four months after escaping from the FBI, Davis was driving a coupe with Georgia license plates in Chicago. He stopped at a corner and got out. Seven concealed FBI agents leapt out. Davis started to run but a single shot into the air halted him. No one expressed concern that when a bullet is fired up into the air, the force of gravity that slows it down then propels it ever faster back towards earth making it as dangerous a projectile as when it was fired. If it was justified to fire a warning shot it should have been aimed directly into the ground The FBI never told the Chicago police or the public about the gunplay or how the agents trapped him. A chastised and muffled SAC Purvis refused to "either affirm or deny" that it was Davis who had been captured. Director Hoover later announced that it was Davis who was seized in Chicago amid "a little unpleasantness" but he offered no details, not even about the gunfire.

A contingent of agents flew Davis to St. Paul in a chartered plane. From the plane, agents carried the heavily manacled prisoner to a waiting car and chained him to its floorboard to prevent another escape even though an overwhelming force had him subdued. They took Davis directly to the Federal Court where he confessed to his part in the Bremer kidnapping and pled guilty because of the strong witnesses presented in the trial of Doc Barker and his henchmen that had resulted in guilty verdicts two weeks earlier. Like the other key participants he was sentenced to life imprisonment.[171]

JUSTICE DELAYED, DENIED, OR BUNGLED?

At this point in the Karpis-Barkers gang saga, a two-year-old bank robbery moved to center stage. This unusual case graphically illustrates how difficult it is to accurately link a lawbreaker to all the crimes he has committed, and to also eliminate those crimes it was possible for him to have committed but actually had nothing to do with. In most armed-robbery cases the only evidence is eyewitnesses, but their reports are the most unreliable type of evidence so they are the main cause of innocent defendants being convicted. Eyewitness reports are problematic because victims go into a state of panicked terror when facing the gun barrels of menacing robbers. Their frightened reactions can cause them to error in two ways. Some witnesses focus on the guns while others look at the gunsils' faces without noticing anything about their features so they do not recognize the culprits when shown their photographs. Other witnesses develop hyperactive imaginations that falsely convince them they are facing the most famous desperadoes they have seen in newspaper pictures. Thus descriptions by multiple witnesses in criminal cases are usually inconsistent and often contradictory. Crime historians typically offer readers a complete list of crimes committed by each outlaw or gang, but these authors' lists invariably differ significantly from each other. In this research specific crimes were attributed to each criminal only if law enforcement concluded it had solid evidence or reliable witnesses. Thus the crimes listed in this book for each gangster should be correct but many lists could be incomplete.

Perpetrator identification problems occurred in the curious case of a robbery at the Third Northwestern National Bank in Minneapolis. Late that afternoon a stolen large black Lincoln was parked at a distance from the bank. Sitting inside were four to six desperadoes observing the bank's entrance. Just before closing time an armored truck they were expecting delivered $19,000 in currency. Right after it pulled away the banditos drove up to the front of the bank and charged inside. One carried a machinegun and the rest pistols. The leader barked, "Hands up!" The machinegunner ordered the 16 employees and customers to lie down as the other robbers scooped up all the cash in sight and placed it into canvas bags. When a bank teller explained he did not know the combination to the safe, the thug smashed a pistol into his head cutting a deep gash and knocking him unconscious. However before the teller was struck, he had stepped on the silent burglar alarm connected to police headquarters.

The robbers had cased out the routines of the bank employees and of the police patrols in the district. The banditos knew at this moment the evening police shift was about to head out from the station, giving them time to escape. However the police on the day shift were three minutes behind schedule and still near the bank when the alarm went off, so these two officers decided to quickly respond before going off duty. As their patrol car stopped near the bank's entrance the machinegunner inside fired through the bank's windows, blowing out the car's windows. The outlaws ran outside and the machinegunner charged the car firing a withering barrage. The driver slumped dead at the wheel riddled with at least 10 bullets. The other officer opened the passenger door with shotgun in hand but as he emerged he was hit in the back, abdomen, and leg. A citizen carried the officer to his car and drove him to the hospital. The patrolman lingered on the brink for two days before dying.

The gang members tossed the stolen $20,000 into their car and took off at high speed. They quickly realized they had a problem. Their own stray bullets had flattened their car's front right tire and punctured the radiator. The driver maintained speed as the tire shredded from the rim. He made it into Como Park where they had left a second car in advance. They switched cars so they would not be driving around in the one seen at the robbery. As they climbed into this second car, two men drove by and looked at the culprits standing near a car with no tire. The machinegunner blasted the car hitting the 29-year-old passenger in the head. The driver rushed his buddy to the hospital where he soon died.

Late the next night police got a big break in the case. One of the robbers lived in an apartment in the adjacent town of St. Paul and he went out to celebrate his big score. After becoming quite inebriated he returned to his apartment building but staggered into the unlocked door of the wrong apartment and interrupted people playing a game of bridge. When the host ordered him to leave the intruder drew his gun and threatened the man. Then he walked out and the host called the St. Paul police who searched the building. Officers walked into a nearby apartment where the drunken tenant tried to draw a gun. An officer quickly subdued him by cracking a pistol-butt on his head. In the apartment police found Northwestern National Bank wrappers containing $1,700 in cash and $10,000 in stolen securities. The rest of the robbery loot was never recovered.

At the police station the suspect was identified as Lawrence Devol. Many years earlier he had escaped with Karpis from the Kansas Reformatory. The pair fled together and were soon captured. After Karpis was transferred to the Kansas State Prison, Devol was not known to have had any further contact with him. Since Devol's release he became a fugitive wanted for the killing of one policeman and the wounding of another in different jurisdictions. St. Paul police called detectives in neighboring Minneapolis who took Devol into their custody and easily got the drunken partier to confess to machingunning the two policemen in the bank robbery, but he would not reveal who shot the civilian in the park. Minneapolis detectives admitted they "questioned rather severely" to get the apartment address of two of his associates who they arrested. In addition St. Paul police staked out Devol's apartment and when his brother returned home, they arrested him. All four suspects were ex-cons and had long police records.

Minneapolis detectives showed 15 witnesses who were at the bank robbery a lineup composed of the four suspects and two police officers all dressed in street clothes. Each of the four suspects was positively identified by three or four witnesses and neither police officer was identified by any of them. These eyewitness accounts were the primary evidence at trial. Devol gave police a signed confession that he was the leader of the gang and killer of the two policemen. Then he pled guilty and received a life sentence at hard labor. The other three suspects claimed they were innocent. Leonard Hankins was the first to stand trial. He was found guilty and also given life at hard labor. The remaining two suspects obtained lengthy delays before their trials. By the time they appeared in court some witnesses' addresses were no longer valid and other witnesses' memories had become tentative, resulting in jury acquittals for both.

Devol was incarcerated at Minnesota's Stillwater Prison. After three years at hard labor his personality turned violent so he was transferred to the St. Peter State Hospital where he was rendered harmless with sedation. Months later he led 15 other inmates in an escape from the criminally-insane ward. They used their fists to overpower the outnumbered guards. Asylum officials refused to give any other details about the breakout, not even the names of the other convicts.

For the next month Devol stayed on the move. Along the way he robbed two banks in Kansas. One evening he sauntered into an Enid, Oklahoma beer parlor. For an hour he drank by himself in a booth and then he signaled to a man and woman outside that they could come in. Devol apparently wanted to make sure that no one in the bar recognized him before having his associate enter, but the tavern owner, a former policeman, feared the customer's unusual signaling behavior meant a holdup was about to commence and called police headquarters. Two patrolman responded, approached the fugitive seated with his two companions, and told him to come with them. He replied, "Let me finish drinking my beer. I think I know what you want me for." His face lost its color and his hand trembled as he raised his mug and swigged the contents. As he sat his stein back on the table he used his other hand to whip out a .38 pistol and commenced firing. With the first shot one policeman collapsed at Devol's feet dead, and with the second the other policeman dropped a few feet away seriously wounded. Devol and his two companions fled running down the street in different directions, but the Assistant Police Chief and another officer soon arrived and took chase of Devol, all of them on foot. They caught up with Devol two blocks away. The fugitive leapt on a car runningboard and shouted to the driver that he was a deputy sheriff in hot pursuit of a felon. The driver had just started to roll as ordered when he saw the two uniformed officers in the rear view mirror running towards him. He hit the brakes and the escapee, standing on the opposite side of the car from the officers, whipped out his gun and opened fire shooting off one of the Assistant Chief's fingers. The two lawmen fired nine times killing Devol who slumped to the ground beside the car. The dead officer left a wife and two children. A civilian, who was an employee of an Enid foundry, had run behind the police to witness the criminal pursuit and paid for his curiosity with a bullet graze of his leg. One can only imagine how many times during his life he proudly showed off his scar administered by the slain killer and bank robber. Minutes later the officers arrested Devol's drinking companion who was the last of the St. Peter asylum's 16 escapees to be recaptured.[172]

It was at this point that the three-year-old bank robbery became one of the major miscarriage-of-justice cases in the nation's history. Remember Devol had pled guilty, two associates were acquitted, and only Leonard Hankins was convicted. He had appealed his conviction to the Minnesota Supreme Court which affirmed his guilt based on eyewitness testimony. The Court pointed out, "At least three are positive in their identification." Hankins also shared a unique similarity with Devol who had pled guilty to the murders. Both men possessed an identical "Colt 45-caliber automatic pistol fitted with special [customized] aluminum grips" and the weapons serial numbers had been chiseled off "not only in the same peculiar manner, but also by the same tool."

The Court's well-reasoned decision sounded like case closed, but two months after Hankins lost his appeal to the Minnesota Supreme Court, new evidence surfaced that indicated he might indeed be innocent of the crime. This occurred when a fugitive, Jess Doyle, who was wanted for passing some of the Edward Bremer ransom cash, was drawn into a dispute his girlfriend was having with another woman in Pittsburg, Kansas. Doyle was hiding out with his sweetheart when she shot and critically wounded this other woman. He ran from the scene and his girlfriend was charged with attempted murder. Neither woman would talk about what happened or why. That night Doyle hid with people he knew in town. The police became aware of his presence and contacted the FBI. The two agencies set up a dragnet and the next day Doyle drove into it and had to come to a stop. Despite being outnumbered he quickly jumped out and took cover on the far side of his engine block where he opened fire. During the ensuing gun battle he suddenly jumped into his car, sped off, and successfully eluded the combined FBI/police posse. He made it 12 miles on a country side road before his engine conked out. Seven bullets from the lawmen had hit motor parts. Doyle walked to a farmhouse, called the Sheriff in Girard, Kansas, a couple miles away, volunteered his location, and waited to surrender. The incredible change in attitude from fierce warrior to abject capitulation indicates he had run out of ammo and had nothing left to fight with. When the Sheriff picked up Doyle, he ratted out the three people who had harbored him the night before and deputies quickly went to the residence to take them into custody. The three harborers were the couple who lived there and a woman who had escaped from a Missouri prison where she was serving a 20-year term for armed robbery. Edna Murray who was known as the "Kissing Bandit" was turned over to the FBI and charged as another ransom-money launderer in the Bremer abduction case. She then joined Doyle in squealing and turning state's witness in the upcoming Bremer kidnapping trial already described above.[173]

When FBI agents interrogated Jess Doyle about dispensing the Bremer ransom cash, he wrote and signed a confession. It was a surprising document because he not only voluntarily admitted this federal crime, but he also inexplicably revealed participating in the holdup of the Third Northwestern National bank in Minneapolis that led to the killing of two officers and a civilian. This case had long been adjudicated and closed, but he still volunteered this information about a local case the FBI agents did not even know about. Doyle said he had dressed in a chauffeur's uniform to drive the getaway car. He also claimed a seven-man team pulled off the bank robbery that included Lawrence Devol who was already serving life for the crime. Devol had yet to escape the asylum for a one-month spree before police killed him. Jess Doyle's confession was the first time that the Karpis-Barkers gang was implicated in this bank robbery. He claimed the heist was led by Karpis and the Barker brothers, Doc and Fred. He fingered the other two accomplices as paroled-lifer William Weaver who was still being sought for having been one of the four men who physically kidnapped Bremer, and Verne Miller, the supposed ringleader of the Kansas City Massacre who had since been slain by a Detroit organized crime gang.

Jess Doyle's confession exonerated the three men that Lawrence Devol had implicated three years earlier in his confession for the same bank robbery. Devol had accused Hankins, who had since been incarcerated, and two other suspects who had already been found not guilty. With this new information the FBI agents soon worked towards obtaining justice in the Hankins case but then reversed its efforts. Agents first notified Minneapolis police that they had determined Hankins was innocent but then agents refused to let detectives see Doyle's file. Since the agents gave the local detectives and courts no new evidence except their unsubstantiated opinion, no action could be taken to free him. The FBI's withholding of critical exonerating evidence kept Hankins in prison for another 16 years until the Minnesota Parole Board concluded Hankins was indeed innocent and the governor pardoned him.

Four years later the State Legislature acted to compensate Hankins for having spent 18 years in prison for a crime he did not commit. The Minnesota Senate passed a House bill authorizing a pension for the rest of his life of $300 monthly, a decent annual salary at that time. (It equals $29,000 a year in buying power today.) The Legislature also compensated part of the personal expenses of his sister and the Minneapolis attorney appointed to fight his case. His sister had worked diligently to free him all those years and spent everything she could afford on lawyers to fight for him. A news reporter was bestowed the National Pall Mall Award for his persistence in getting the "Big Story" by freeing this man.

Once Hankins was freed, his story became a heartwarming example of justice delayed but not denied. Ever since that time his wrongful conviction and unjustified long incarceration has been decried by crime historians, justice-advocacy groups, and various government agencies as one of the worst miscarriages of justice in the country's history, but no evidence supporting this conclusion of his innocence has ever been presented to the public. The FBI has never revealed why its agents at the time were confident Doyle was telling the truth about Hankins being innocent, and the Minnesota Parole Board's report and proceedings were unavailable to learn on what evidence they determined him to be innocent in order to recommend his pardon.

Because of this total lack of evidentiary support for Hankins innocence, this author conducted a cold-case examination of the known facts in his case. The conclusions follow because they raise serious questions about whether Hankins' case is indeed one of the most terrible miscarriages of justice as so many have long claimed, or it is instead one of the greatest flimflams of the legal-system ever perpetrated by a truly guilty man.

All of Hankins' defenders have ignored the most peculiar aspect of this case. Two career criminals confessed to a murder, an action they knew would result in an all-but-certain lifetime sentence; yet the two confessors identified having different accomplices. Such inconsistent confessions by professional lawbreakers in a murder case may be unprecedented in American jurisprudence.

Clearly one of these two criminals was lying, but which one? If the newest confession by Jess Doyle were indeed true, it meant Hankins was innocent making Lawrence Devol's earlier confession truly bizarre. It meant Devol hid the involvement of the Karpis-Barkers gang members from the police, and to accomplish this, he not only framed his two long-time partners in crime, but also his own brother with whom he lived. Devol certainly knew Karpis. Years before they had escaped from the Kansas Reformatory and had been caught together, but there is no reason to believe that Devol had any contact with, or loyalty to, Karpis after he was transferred to the Kansas State Prison. Indeed none of Hankins' defenders ever came up with an explanation of why Devol might have wanted to protect Karpis, nor why he destroyed the lives of the three people closest to him who would have been innocent if it is Doyle who told the truth. These gaping holes in the defense of Hankins' innocence were never addressed by any of his advocates.

While no one has been able to explain why Lawrence Devol would have falsely confessed to a guaranteed life sentence at hard labor, it is very understandable why Jess Doyle would have created a fictitious confession framing himself for three murders he had nothing to do with. He confessed two weeks before the Bremer kidnapping trial was to begin in which he was to be a defendant for passing some of the ransom money, and he faced a possible life sentence. By fingering fugitive Karpis who was Public Enemy Number 1 and other defendants who were awaiting trial, Doyle potentially upgraded his trial status from defendant to valuable state's witness. Jess Doyle was angling to get a deal from the FBI and he got it when he was made a witness for the prosecution. At the trial the Federal Prosecutor had all the state's witnesses testify and then rested his case. Before the defense began its case, the Prosecutor announced to the judge that he lacked enough witness testimony to connect the Bremer abduction to two defendants who had both testified as state's witnesses - Doyle and the Kissing Bandit. The Prosecutor asked his Honor to dismiss the charges against the pair, so Doyle's confession to three murders indeed got him a get-out-of-jail-free pass.

While plotting the Bremer abduction, the Kissing Bandit and Volney Davis, one of the Bremer abductors, had become lovers, and during breaks in the trial, newspaper photos show the pair sitting side-by-side making goo-goo eyes at each other. When the Bremer ransom-passing charges against the Kissing Bandit were dismissed the FBI returned her to the Missouri Women's Prison from where she had escaped. The FBI did bring her back to St. Paul to testify in the second Bremer-kidnapping trial and then returned her to Missouri to complete her 20-year armed-robbery term.

Soon after Jess Doyle was freed from the federal Bremer kidnapping case, he was serving time in an Oklahoma prison, but no records about this case were available. Unless another researcher locates more information about his Oklahoma incarceration, the following scenario is highly likely based on the known facts. It is improbable he was convicted in Oklahoma because that would have almost certainly been reported in the newspapers studied for this research, so the question is why did he plead guilty? When Doyle confessed to participating in the Northwestern bank robbery to the FBI he faced bank robbery charges in both Oklahoma and Minneapolis. FBI internal reports reveal local prosecutors in both cases admitted to agents that they lacked solid eyewitness identifications to convict Doyle. However the FBI learned this after the case had been turned over to the Federal Prosecutor, and he would have had no reason to comment to the state's witness about his outstanding local cases or assist him in any way after the sentencing deal had been cut. The operative factor in this case is that Doyle had confessed to the Minneapolis bank robbery that involved the murders of two policemen and a civilian. He undoubtedly assumed his confession would get him the death penalty, not knowing that Minnesota authorities were solidly committed to the opposing confession by Lawrence Devol and to the conviction of Leonard Hankins already affirmed by the Minnesota Supreme Court. The prime priority of America's court system is not the pursuit of justice but rather establishing certainty in cases. The courts may insist on many safeguards attempting to keep innocent people from being convicted, but once convicted courts are hesitant to reverse a decision because admitting mistakes destabilizes belief in the whole system. Doyle did not know the intricacies of the Minnesota charges against him and feared a death penalty prosecution for the bank robbery murders. Thus Doyle very likely requested transfer from federal custody to Oklahoma to plead guilty to bank robbery which meant he would remain alive and some day be free again. By the time he would be released back onto the streets, he expected the Minnesota murder charges would likely be too stale to be prosecuted. He was right. Even the exoneration of Hankins did not renew Minnesota's interest in him as a possible suspect despite his voluntary confession.

It is surprising that so many people accepted and defended Jess Doyle's confession exonerating Hankins without considering the serious implications of doing so. Doyle invalidated Lawrence Devol's confession, but no one has any explanation of why Devol would have lied. It also means that the 10 or so eyewitnesses who each positively identified one or more of the three suspects that Devol's confession fingered were all mistaken. Most amazing of all, not a single Hankins' defender looked at the sequence of events surrounding Doyle's confession to realize he had powerful motivation to lie and frame himself. The defenders included the FBI, the Minnesota Governor and Parole Board, and every crime and injustice historian who has written about this case. It seems like every one wore blinders to all facts surrounding the case except Doyle's confession.

It is important to note one other aspect of Jess Doyle's confession. His description of the bank robbery is not credible. He claimed he waited in the getaway car while six men robbed the bank even though the majority of witnesses saw only four enter. The seven men would have had difficulty squeezing into the stolen "large black Lincoln," and it would have been close to impossible for all seven, along with their stolen money bags, to have scrunched together in the "smaller green sedan" they were observed switching into at the park by two unrelated witnesses.

This cold-case examination should finally dispel the myth that Hankins' conviction was a travesty of justice because it was really a shocking mishandling of justice by everyone who became involved with his defense. A tragic number of innocent people have been incorrectly convicted and imprisoned by the justice system but the exonerated Hankins was not one of them.[174]

WHERE IN THE WORLD IS KARPIS?

After Karpis escaped the police pursuit in Atlantic City, he enjoyed a leisurely three-month sojourn in Reno, Lake Tahoe, and northern California. With his money running low, he returned to his old haunts in Cleveland where he looked up a friend who dealt blackjack at the Harbor Club. Freddie Hunter offered to hide Karpis at his residence, but the fugitive wanted to get out of Cleveland and Toledo where he was so well known. Hunter put him up in the Youngstown home of a friend. Clayton Hall was a sheet-metal worker. When Karpis said he needed to pull a heist for spending money, Hunter suggested robbing a big steel company payroll shipment that would be arriving by train in Warren, Ohio. Since this was Hunter's home town, he was afraid someone who knew him might recognize him so he did not participate. In fact Hunter never joined his pal in any crime, but Hunter become the constant companion of Public Enemy Number 1 in his misadventures on his fugitive run.

As Karpis' former associates were going through the dreary trial proceedings for kidnapping Bremer, the fugitive leader who was charged with them went back into action in Warren with his partner in crime, Harry Campbell. At the train station they robbed a mail truck messenger of payroll bags containing $72,000 in currency and $53,000 in registered U.S. bonds. The cash was part of the payroll for Republic Steel Corporation. As an aside, Republic Steel allowed its logo to be used on the helmets of the NFL Pittsburgh Steelers even though the company was headquartered at the time in the home town of the Steelers archrivals, the Cleveland Browns, the only NFL team ever nicknamed after its coach, Paul Brown.

For a second time in Karpis' criminal career, injustice reared its ugly head with the Warren train robbery. Neither Karpis nor Campbell was suspected, but two completely innocent men were. Both guiltless men were convicted, but they won an appeal for a new trial. At the second trial they were again convicted and were sentenced to serve 25 years. At both trials several state's witnesses mistakenly identified the pair because they resembled Old Creepy and Campbell. Both Federal Trial Juries believed the eyewitnesses over the truthful alibi witnesses, who testified that at the time the robbery occurred one defendant was 30 miles from the scene and the other 40 miles away.

FBI agents were always convinced they had gotten the guilty culprits, but Postal Inspectors had jurisdiction in the case because U.S. mail bags were robbed. To their credit they always suspected that the Karpis gang was actually responsible for the robbery despite the double convictions of the two other men. When these two men lost their appeal on the second conviction, Inspectors informed the Ohio U.S. Assistant Attorney General of their concern and he reopened the investigation into the crime. The FBI had no interest in reopening the case because Director Hoover focused only on conviction rate, not justice, and he slithered out of cooperating with the Justice Department's investigation by laying the crime at the doorstep of the Postal Inspectors. Fortunately they were dedicated lawmen who took their responsibilities seriously. The Postal Inspectors eventually proved that Karpis and Campbell were the real perpetrators leading President Roosevelt to grant unconditional pardons to the convicted innocent pair. From arrest to release they had spent 27 months in jail.

Ever since the AG had announced that Karpis was a suspect in the Bremer kidnapping 17 months earlier, the fugitive had frustrated the FBI. He successfully eluded Hoover's agents who rarely had any idea in what state he was residing or even if he was still in the country. Then Karpis boldly rubbed the FBI's futility into the Director's face by mailing him a handwritten letter from Dayton, Ohio. It announced that Public Enemy Number 1 was gunning for G-Man Number 1. Agents withheld any other details about his letter except that it was to avenge the agents' killing of his pal Fred Barker and his mother, but the timing was odd for this to be have been the fugitive's motive since it was sent eight months after they were slain.

A month later FBI agents closed in on two Bremer kidnapping associates - William Weaver and his girlfriend Myrtle Eaton. Earlier in his career Weaver had served six years of a life term for murder before being paroled from McAlester Oklahoma Penitentiary. A year later he was arrested in St. Paul for carrying a concealed weapon and posted $500 bond. When he failed to appear his bond was forfeited and his prison parole was revoked. For the three years since he had been on the run. During this time Weaver was one of the four men who had run up to Bremer's car and physically kidnapped him. Myrtle's record had three arrests for shop lifting, and the FBI wanted her for letting several of the Bremer-abduction perpetrators live in her apartment during the months they planned the snatch. The FBI had been searching for Weaver and Myrtle for more than a year.

Then the FBI located the couple staying at a chicken ranch seven miles south of Daytona Beach, Florida, but agents refused to reveal how they found their hideout. Agents swooped in and took them by surprise so they had no opportunity to resist. They had lived there for several months and avoided contact with locals. Four months earlier she had adopted the 2-year-old son of her destitute girlfriend to disguise their identity and make the couple appear to be respectable. As agents flew the couple to St. Paul for arraignment, a FBI clerical woman carried the baby. Two months later Weaver made the romantic gesture to plead guilty in return for having his girlfriend freed. This offer was endorsed by the Assistant Attorney Generals in both Florida and St. Paul where local authorities had custody of the baby. Hoover rejected the offer believing Weaver would change his plea when faced with the long sentence for actually participating in the abduction of Bremer.

Next the Director handed the press corp the following statement about finding the body of another Karpis-Barkers gang member. "We have established to our satisfaction that the body found in the burned barn at Ontarioville, Illinois, in January was that of William J. Harrison, member of the Karpis-Barkers gang and identified as one of the kidnappers of Edward G. Bremer of St. Paul." According to this statement the FBI had found the body a year after the kidnapping, but the FBI gave no reason why it hid this fact for the following 10 months. Hoover's refusal to make any comment made the FBI's action seem most curious.

Amidst the no comments an agent did point out that the Karpis' trail had been "hot" since Karpis mailed a death-threat letter to the Director almost three months earlier. This was typical Hoover bravado no matter how much it altered the facts. In reality the FBI had not received information about a single sighting of Karpis by anyone since receiving the threat.[175]

Three months after Karpis threatened Director Hoover's life, his machinegun-toting gang robbed an Erie Railroad mail train at the Garrettsville, Ohio station. When the two clerks in the train car saw the robbers' high-powered weaponry they skedaddled between the mail containers in the back. Karpis called out and ordered them to tell him where the big payroll bag was. When they remained hidden and silent he tossed a stick of dynamite in their direction without lighting it. Then he called out a warning that they had five seconds to come out or the next stick he threw would be ignited. They walked out of hiding with their hands in the air and were unharmed. The payroll Karpis was expecting was not on board, but he succeeded in stealing $34,000 in cash and $11,650 worth of bonds.

While criminals typically specialize in one type of crime, Karpis used his gun to rob banks and the mail and to kidnap wealthy victims. He also likely became the first to escape a major crime scene by flying away. He chartered a small plane in Garrettsville prior to the train mail robbery and had the pilot standing by at the landing field. The small plane had limited fuel capacity and Karpis did not want his gang recognized refueling in airports along the escape route. Thus he used a variation of his Bremer-kidnapping gas-can-refueling ploy that the pilot agreed to. Since the plane's engine used standard automotive gasoline, Karpis filled the plane's interior with many empty small gas cans. It is assumed the cans were empty because the tiny craft could not safely handle the weight of the additional gasoline. Then he had the pilot fly until running out of fuel when he would glide it onto an open farm field below. The pilot walked to the nearest road, hitch-hiked into the nearest town, and hired a local truck driver to deliver gasoline for his stalled plane. First the pilot and trucker drove out to the plane and loaded up all the small gas containers, and then they drove back to town and filled them up at a gas station. They returned to the plane, filled its tank, loaded the empty gas cans back into the plane, paid the truck driver, and took off again. Before reaching their destination, they had to refill the plane twice. Karpis is certainly the first and probably the only criminal to have escaped by leap-frogging across the country. While the FBI, Postal Inspectors, and local police continued their frantic search of the immediate area surrounding the robbery site in Ohio, the gang was comfortably settled back in their hideout and toasting their success in Hot Springs, Arkansas which was 900 miles distant the way a plane skips over the countryside.

In the 10 months since Karpis and Campbell had fled the Atlantic City police raid, the FBI had not had a hint about their whereabouts except when they committed a crime. Agents continued to search for them in Ohio because the two mail robberies in Warren and Garrettsville six months apart were just 18 miles from each other. Agents apparently thought the fugitives were holed up there or would soon return to the area for a third heist. The reality was that less than two months after pulling the first Ohio mail robbery the Karpis-Campbell gang moved their base of operations to Hot Springs. When they took their hop-scotching plane ride after the second mail robbery, they were heading back to their residences of almost five months.

Karpis and the other robbery gangs found safe havens from law-enforcement in three cities, but they used each city for a different purpose. Reno and Lake Tahoe were where they could disappear in geographical isolation when the heat was on at home or they were on the run. St. Paul was where they headquartered to launch most of their crimes, and Hot Springs was where they resided in obscurity for long periods as ordinary residents.

In Hot Springs the gang members resided quietly to remain unnoticed. Karpis and Cleveland friend Fred Hunter sometimes lived together and at other times near each other. Karpis described his girlfriend Grace Goldstein there as, "a peroxide blonde about thirty five [actually 29], and she ran the finest whorehouse in Hot Springs. ... She maintained great connections. The mayor had a big crush on her. She entertained all the top crooks who visited and all the top cops and politicians. Grace was a genuine big leaguer. ... She rented houses and cottages for me, ... When the feds started breathing closer to me, they latched on to Grace. They put her through some rugged times and, for the most part, she stood up to them with a lot of courage." Grace admitted in an FBI interview that Old Creepy was not much to look at but his bundle of cash made him appealing during the Great Depression. Fred lived with one of the prostitutes from Grace's Hatterie Brothel, Connie Morris. Karpis depended on Hunter and their two girlfriends to deal with the world in handling things like home rentals and car purchases so the wanted fugitive could remain out of sight.[176]

Hot Springs was a safe haven for major criminals for many years because Chief of Detectives Herbert "Dutch" Akers offered them protection for a price. He allowed wanted outlaws to reside in seclusion under false identities. Remember that it was Detective Akers who had given protection to Chicago-based fugitive Frank Nash to vacation in Hot Springs for three summers until FBI agents busted him as he was hanging out in crime boss Dick Galatas' White Front Cigar Store. Then Galatas promised Nash's wife he would free her husband, and Galatas obtained the FBI's railroad travel plans that made possible the Kansas City Massacre. The FBI's plans were almost certainly leaked by Detective Akers.

Three months after Karpis and Hunter arrived in Hot Springs, Campbell joined them in his own abode and one of Grace's girls moved in with him. The three fugitives took their girlfriends for a vacation at Dyer's Landing on Lake Hamilton seven miles south of Hot Springs. After the three couples checked out of their cabins and departed to steal a new bankroll in another state, Detective Akers assembled a group of reporters to announce that he discovered Karpis had been staying at the resort. Then he called the FBI Little Rock, Arkansas, Office to report Public Enemy Number 1's presence in Hot Springs in order to cover up his corrupt involvement. He also furnished the gang's license plate numbers and the aliases they had used. To the FBI it sounded like the same false sightings they had received from many other cities, but an agent was sent to investigate. This lead did not look promising because Akers emphasized he had not seen the suspects and no one at the resort could identify photos of Karpis. Since the trio had posed as Ohio gamblers, agents forwarded the aliases they had used to the Cleveland Office, but no one in the FBI had heard of these nonexistent identities. The agent who searched the cabins found three bottles of gonorrhea medicine and one was prescribed to Fred Hunter to treat a disease given him by his prostitute girlfriend. Hunter's prescription bottle included the only real name agents had but they did not send it on to Cleveland. His name had the potential to break the Karpis gang case wide open. As it would turn out, Karpis and Hunter would return and use Hot Springs as their home base for the next seven months. This means they either never heard about Detective Akers' press interview, or more likely, as they were leaving town he had warned them to quickly switch cars or at least change license plates to remain incognito. Thus he would have protected the fugitives' safety while distancing his association with them and embellishing his image as being an honest lawman.

Six months after Detective Akers had revealed Karpis had been in New Orleans, the FBI requested the nation's police and sheriff departments rush the prints of all arrested persons having mutilated fingertips to its Washington lab and refrain from releasing these prisoners until their prints were checked against Karpis'. The botched fingerprint job on Karpis by Doctor Moran had been performed two years earlier so it is unclear what led to this FBI's bulletin, but at this point Hoover's boys turned their focus on Public Enemy Number 1. Obviously the FBI Director was feeling some kind of political heat, but the Karpis-Campbell gang remained unconcerned because they knew his agents had no idea about their whereabouts. The Karpis-Campbell gang had satisfied themselves that the FBI was ineffectual by avoiding detection from agents for the 18 months since they were first accused of a federal crime as leaders of the Bremer kidnapping. This ineffectiveness was confirmed by FBI files showing agents dismissed two legitimate reports that Karpis was behind the two Ohio mail robberies. Karpis even publicly expressed his contempt for the FBI by taunting Director Hoover with a death threat, while at the same time displaying his respect for the Postal Inspectors by saying nary a word about that agency.

The Karpis gang was well aware Postal Inspectors were hot on their trail. After Inspectors solved the Warren mail truck heist and freed two innocent convicts, the Inspectors cracked the Garrettsville mail train robbery by showing the two fugitives' pictures to the train clerks. The Inspectors then quickly uncovered all the details of the heist and the Ohio-to-Hot-Springs plane ride that skimmed the surface of the countryside including occasionally bumping down for gas. The gang knew Inspectors were interviewing their contacts and obtaining all the details about their flight and hideaways. The Postal Inspectors' determined investigations stayed close enough on the heels of the gang's activities to greatly worry its members. Years later surviving gang members wrote or told reporters that they felt bird-dogged by the Inspectors. At the time the fugitives evidenced this concern with their routine of every few nights slowly driving around the downtown Hot Springs

Post Office looking for an infiltration of government cars that would indicate Inspectors were amassing in town to raid their residences. The heat caused by the Postal Inspectors' dedicated investigations caused Karpis to become distrustful of everyone except his closest associates and their girlfriends. He tried to cover up where he was staying from everyone else, and he frequently traveled between his Hot Springs hideout and a multitude of southern cities, rarely staying in one more than a few days and never over two weeks. He traveled with Fred Hunter and their Hatterie Brothel girlfriends.

Karpis' generalized fear that the Postal Inspectors were closing in on him turned out to be justified. They had learned that the fugitive had lived in Youngstown at the home of sheet-metal worker Clayton Hall. Inspectors targeted Hall because they thought he was the associate who would most readily crack from legitimate interrogation. He was not a career criminal, he had little loyalty to Karpis, and he could be threatened with prosecution in the Garrettsville mail-train robbery because he purchased the car used in the getaway and had harbored the ringleader in his home. While the Postal Service was assembling the final elements in its case against Karpis, the FBI had yet to generate a single clue in its year-and-a-half investigation about the whereabouts of the renegade.

Actually three informers had told FBI agents that Karpis employed Hall as a gofer, but this information was dismissed because agents could not conceive of the gangster being involved with a sheet-metal worker. At this point for some reason, Hoover stopped shrugging off the Karpis search to the Postal System and started a determined, almost desperate, hunt for Public Enemy Number 1. The FBI Director pressured Chicago SAC Connelley to finally come up with a lead. Connelley reviewed his past internal communications hoping something had been overlooked and came across a Cleveland Office report by an agent who stated he had surveyed Hall's Youngstown home and saw two Postal Inspectors there. Connelley telephoned the Cleveland SAC and asked him to send an agent to the sheet-metal worker's home. Hall was there and admitted he and Hunter were close friends and he also identified a photo of Karpis as "Ed King," a pal of Hunter. Hall agreed to meet SAC Connelley at the FBI Cleveland Office the next day, but he immediately phoned the Postal Inspectors he was already working with about the FBI agent's interview. Since Hall had assisted with one of the gang's mail robberies, he obeyed the Inspectors who told him not to show up at the FBI meeting. Then Hall stayed away from his house for the next three days as FBI agents repeatedly called on him. Notice the irony here that Hoover's boys' only lead came from trailing the Postal Inspectors' during their investigation.

The detectives of the Postal Service and the FBI operated by very different standards. Postal Inspectors investigated in a professional and quiet manner so their activities were rarely covered by the press, while Hoover took every opportunity to boast to reporters about his successes. In addition Postal Inspectors had cooperated fully with the FBI for almost a year by feeding agents all the information they learned about the whereabouts of Karpis and Campbell. Unbelievably this was the only information the FBI received about the two fugitives during that year. In contrast to the Inspector's cooperative spirit, the FBI never assisted or revealed anything to any other federal agency. In fact the FBI Director's memos to subordinates in numerous cases expressed his animosity and extreme distrust of the other federal law enforcement agencies. But Hoover was desperate. He needed to arrest Karpis to claim success against all four machinegun-toting Public Enemies to fend off mounting pressure. He needed to steal the Postal Inspectors' information to beat them to the punch in capturing the fugitive. Hoover had SAC Connelley humble himself by calling the Postal Service for help, but after a year of receiving no reciprocity, the Inspectors had no interest in offering further assistance. However informer Hall was in the driver's seat because neither detective force had any leads about where Karpis was situated except through him. He demanded verbal immunity from prosecution by both agencies and believed he could best get them to keep their words with the following ultimatum. He agreed to divulge all the details about Karpis' location to the Postal Service as planned but he insisted an FBI agent be present as well.

Both agencies were unhappy about having to work with the other, but Hall left them no choice. An FBI internal memo described their relationship. "Connelley drove to Youngstown and spent several hours closeted with Hall. Afterward he called Washington to say the frightened steelworker had given them everything, including the location of the house Karpis was renting seven miles south of Hot Springs. Connelley was already arranging a charter flight to Arkansas. With luck, he said, he could be on the ground there by noon the next day. He was obliged to take a group of inspectors along, he admitted, 'for the reason that the informant [Hall] is theirs, and it was only through their cooperation that we have the information at all.'"[177]

To make it possible for the FBI to find the hideout on a rural road, Hall drew a detailed sketch of the terrain surrounding the house. The next day SAC Connelley assembled the raiding party in town. He included an Arkansas Highway patrolman to help identify the correct house, and apparently a few Postal Inspectors, who were asked to block traffic on the road. Connelley consulted with Hoover by telephonic conferencing so the Director could claim he masterminded the bringing down of Public Enemy Number 1. The next morning at 6 a.m. the group of about 20 lawmen quietly surrounded the house ready for action. According to internal FBI reports the agents without warning launched massive firepower against the building, shooting out the windows and the door and starting a fire inside with tear-gas bombs. After this huge deluge of projectiles, agents discovered the house was unoccupied. They had riddled the building without any confirmation this was Karpis' hideout and with no idea who might be inside. The agents searched the perforated home to verify Karpis had lived there but he had departed with his belongings. The FBI may have had the right house but consider how horrific their depraved indifference would have been if the owner had since rented it to an innocent family when the fuselage whizzed through at upper-body level. This was a typical Hoover-Connelley raid - select a possible target, blow hell out of it, and sort out the facts and bodies only after making sure every one who might be inside is too incapacitated to fire back.

Instead of charging in like rampaging vigilantes the FBI should have staked out the home until they determined that Karpis was inside. But the Director demanded agents raid at 6 a.m. so he could announce the assassination early enough in the day to make the nation's evening papers. In a desperate bid for good PR, Hoover tossed out proper and responsible police procedure. Hoover gambled Karpis was there, but he was wrong. Unfortunately the FBI made the trusting innocent public the losers, because the fugitive, upon hearing about the failed raid, never returned, thus rendering the FBI's only lead worthless. Hoover's reckless, unprofessional, and irresponsible decision turned a great opportunity to accomplish a successful capture that he could have boasted about into yet another embarrassing miss. His agents slumped into their cars without commenting about the fiasco and sped away. The public might never have learned about this failed raid except a shocked and disbelieving Highway patrolman reported this botched raid he had witnessed to the press.

The FBI's search of Karpis' hideout yielded numerous tourist brochures from cities throughout the south leaving agents no way to select where the two couples were likely to be headed. The FBI was again without a lead as to Karpis whereabouts. The fugitive had planned to return to his hideout a couple days later, so if agents had properly staked-out surveillance of it, they would have gotten him. Instead the hunted killer was now headed to unknown destinations.

The FBI believed that Hot Springs Detective Chief Akers warned the fugitives about the pending raid and that is why they had taken a trip. While the agents were carrying out their raid, the three couples were visiting in Texas. When they heard about the devastating assault against their abode, Karpis and Hunter decided instead of returning to Hot Springs to take their girlfriends to New Orleans. There the two couples rented apartments a little distance apart.[178]

Chapter 10

HE SAID & HE SAID DIFFERENTLY

SKEWERING THE DIRECTOR

Director Hoover was obsessed with statistics, charts, and graphs that showed his detectives' high rate of solving each type of crime under the jurisdiction of the FBI. These quantified results were his only claim to fame. The Director regularly made bragging presentations about his great success record to the press and also periodically to Congress. The problem with his statistics was that he created them alone in the privacy of his office with no independent review by anyone. He could have given out any fabricated figures he wanted, and this is exactly what he seems to have done.

The most interesting crime to examine is kidnapping because the FBI's record is stellar. To keep these results in perspective, realize that kidnapping should have a very high conviction rate because it is the easiest type of armed robbery to solve. Other types of armed robberies are primarily random hit and run affairs, but kidnappers usually need to know inside information about the target's behavior, and abductors have to expose themselves to possible scrutiny twice – first when they collect the ransom money, and then when they pass the currency that is invariably marked by law enforcement. This is why the FBI mostly wiped out this crime in less than a four-year period after being given jurisdiction by Congress.

The problem here is not with the agents' performance in handling kidnappings, but rather the Director's many lies about what they accomplished. First off he cooked the numbers he presented. During the FBI's four-year concentrated effort against kidnapping he routinely gave out the number of crimes solved and the number of abductors arrested, convicted, and awaiting trial, but his numbers were not consistent over time. For example at the beginning of one six month period during which no kidnappings were reported in the country, he defended the FBI's record by claiming it had solved all 55 kidnapping cases since the Lindbergh Kidnapping Law had gone into effect making the crime a federal offense. This statement about 55 abductions was in response to seven convicted kidnappers going to the U.S. Supreme Court with a challenge to the constitutional overreach of the Lindbergh Law under the government's power to regulate interstate commerce. The Court rejected the criminals' contentions that the federal government did not have Constitutional authority to enforce this type of crime. Two months later the Director again announced the total of 55 kidnapping cases while reacting furiously against an announcement by aviator hero, Colonel Charles Lindbergh, almost four years after his 20-month-old son was abducted and had his skull crushed by a kidnapper despite having paid the ransom. Lindbergh told the world he had moved his family to England because of growing worries about the safety in the U.S. of his 3-year-old son, John. Hoover took this statement of Lindbergh's fear about lack of safety in America as a personal attack on his detective staff.

Two months later Hoover gave his next press conference and extolled the FBI's performance record against kidnappers by saying, "Every one of the 62 kidnappings perpetrated since the Lindbergh Law was passed in 1932 has been solved, and in each case, we've made it unhealthy and unprofitable for the kidnappers. … The underworld has learned, too, that kidnapping is not a paying racket. In every case handled by the Federal agents the victim has been returned unharmed; where ransom money was paid, most of it has been recovered; and the percentage of kidnappers and their aides who have escaped punishment is very small. None of them has yet got by with it." This statement contains multiple lies. First off he bragged that no new kidnappings had been attempted, and at the same time he claimed the total solved since passage of the Lindbergh Law had mystically risen from 55 to 62. Two months later the Director repeated the total of 62 kidnapping cases while testifying under oath before the U.S. Senate Appropriations Subcommittee. But just one week later he embellished his total again from 62 to 63 when publicly announcing the three-year old William Hamm Jr. kidnapping by the Karpis gang was finally solved. This very old abduction had been in his totals from the beginning of his kidnap record keeping. Other historians who have examined Hoover's statistical statements for other types of crimes have also found disturbing contradictions and outright lies.[179]

The other sentences in Hoover's quoted statement were also inaccurate. He always claimed every kidnapping had been solved, but this was always untrue until the kidnapping of Hamm was solved three years after the incident. His statistical numbers always showed every abductor was in custody, but the Bremer-snatching ringleaders, Public Enemy Number 1 Alvin Karpis and Harry Campbell, were still freely roaming the countryside. His statement said every victim was returned unharmed, but this was certainly not true in the most infamous kidnapping in history, the Lindbergh baby. Regarding recovery of the ransom money in every case, only negligible ransom money was recovered in the Bremer and Hamm kidnappings studied in this research. In addition the Director always gave his agents total credit for solving every one of these crimes, but as would soon become public, other agencies and concerned civilians solved many of them. This was true for the Lindbergh case, and Colonel Lindbergh was so disgusted with the performance of Hoover's boys he ordered them to get out of Hopewell, New Jersey. The Director routinely hid the serious flaws in his agents' performances by using misleading and dishonest statements, and many more examples might be discovered by researchers thoroughly examining each kidnapping that occurred during this four-year period no matter whether the total is 55, 62, 63, or some other number.

Less than two weeks after the FBI launched its firefight against Karpis' Hot Springs empty residence with no idea who might be inside, Hoover was finally forced to publicly account for some of his improper conduct and falsehoods due to a conflict with Democratic U.S. Senator Kenneth McKellar. The power struggle began when the Senator requested the Director to appoint a couple of his constituents as agents, but the tyrannical FBI leader who wanted autocratic control with no accountability to the U.S. government snubbed the Senator. However McKellar chaired the Appropriations Committee that controlled the Justice Department's budget, so the Senator complained directly to Hoover's boss, AG Cummings. An irate and vindictive Director struck back at the 20-year Senate veteran by arbitrarily firing without cause or justification three agents who heralded from McKellar's state of Tennessee.

Senator McKellar soon had the opportunity to exact vengeance when Hoover had to request a large increase in the FBI's annual funding to expand his staff to be able to implement the package of AG Cummings' anti-crime bills passed by Congress over the preceding two years. To obtain this funding Hoover had to appear before Senator McKellar's Committee. The furious but shrewd Chairman kept Hoover at the witness table for two days of private hearings and took him to task with every negative thing he had heard about him. A week later the Committee released a scathing written report containing the highlights of Hoover's chastising. This was far more than a personality or turf war. If McKellar won the conflict, the Senator might be able to ultimately get Hoover replaced as head of the federal secret police with a qualified law-enforcement official who could transform the FBI into a professional detective agency. But if Hoover won, the untrained and misdirected federal police force would continue unabated as would the Director's manipulation of Congress and the American people with his blackmailing political machine. The outcome of their battle would indeed impact the future of Hoover's career, and it would also transform his hunt for Karpis, America's most wanted.

The two-days of testimony centered on Hoover's FBI budget. It was already more than double what it had been eight years earlier, and now the Director asked to raise it another 21%. Concerning Hoover's claim he needed more funds, Senator McKellar said, "It seems to me that your Department is just running wild, Mr. Hoover. ... I just think that, Mr. Hoover, with all the money in your hands you are just extravagant." The Senator then systematically whittled away at the performance of the Director who publicized himself as the world's super-sleuth. McKellar debunked Hoover's carefully-tailored image with an embarrassing battery of questions. At the end of this two-day barrage, Senator McKellar got his Committee to vote a cut in Hoover's requested FBI budget increase from 21% to 16%.[180]

McKellar hit hard at Hoover's promotions of G-man magazine stories, movies, radio shows, and comic books. When the Director was not outright perjuring himself under oath, he was carefully mincing his words to give technically truthful answers that were totally misleading and false in the context of the question. To McKellar's question, "Have you any writers in your department?", Hoover replied "Not in the Bureau of Investigation." The Director left out that three high-salaried writers and press agents were on the staff of the parent Justice Department and much of their time was assigned to do Hoover's bidding promoting the FBI. Hoover lied again in this vein by denying any funds were being spent "directly or indirectly" to create advertising or publicity. Hoover repeatedly and falsely denied trying to influence the film industry, and also lied by testifying he officially objected to each one of the flood of G-men movies that frequently showed his picture. He specifically perjured himself by saying the FBI did not offer advice for movie and radio storylines or help write scripts.[181]

The Senator did not know that Hoover was involved with radio programs and comic books that announced being endorsed by, and having the cooperation of, the FBI; or McKellar's hearings would have exploded over the Director's lying testimony. Almost a year before Hoover testified, his collaboration with the radio show *G-Men* lasted three months before sponsors dropped it. The original episode began with the announcement, "This series of *G-men* is presented with the consent of the Attorney General of the United States and with the cooperation of J. Edgar Hoover, Director of the Federal Bureau of Investigation. Every fact in tonight's program is taken directly from the files of the Bureau. I went to Washington and was graciously received by Mr. Hoover and all of these scripts were written in the department building. Tonight's program was submitted to Mr. Hoover who personally reviewed the script and made some very valuable suggestions." A month after the Director testified, the first issue of *War on Crime* comic book was published and claimed to be "based on the official files" and produced "with the consent and cooperation of the Federal Bureau of Investigation." The storyline continuity was written by newspaperman Rex Collier, longtime publicist and friend of Hoover. Had the Senator known about this radio show and comic book, he probably would have been able to topple Hoover from his throne because of his grossly untrue testimony.

Senator McKellar went on to condemn the Director about several aspects of his leadership. He established that the most famous kidnappings which Hoover claimed to have solved were mostly due to breaks from tips by local police; concerned citizens such as taxi drivers, filling station attendants, and store clerks; and inside informants. He attacked the Director for claiming all the credit, but Hoover rebutted with the false claim he gave credit where it was due. Senator Joseph O'Mahoney of Wyoming asked the Director about the many complaints made by local police departments to Congress that the FBI did not cooperate, and Hoover replied agents did cooperate while claiming "that in work of our character, law enforcement, certain jealousies would be engendered." He went on to falsely claim the FBI cooperated "whenever we find that the local police are honest and will cooperate and will not give information to the press." McKellar then hit the Director's policy that publicity for arrests could only be released by his Washington Headquarters which lacked knowledge about the cases. The Senator also flatly asserted that SAC Purvis was forced to resign for getting more glory than Hoover. In addition Keller pointed out that other accused kidnappers besides Public Enemy Number 1 were still on the loose.

This is where the questioning became down and dirty, but every concern that Senator McKellar voiced was a serious one the other politicians were afraid to raise. After Hoover had proudly rattled off the FBI's arrests or killings of major bad man, the Senator challenged the necessity for assassinating eight criminals instead of arresting them. Hoover flatly denied ever having given a shoot to kill order even though he had stated this emphatically to the press and his agents in the Baby Face Nelson and Pretty Boy Floyd cases and strongly implied it in others. McKellar concluded like many of the FBI's other critics, "Even if a law enforcement officer knew a man was a murderer, he shouldn't have authority to kill him. We have courts to take care of that situation." The questioning even intimated that the Director's ill-planned, undisciplined shoot-outs were at least partly responsible for his four agents' deaths. This charge thoroughly enraged Hoover, but it was McKellar's final line of questioning that cut the Director to the core.

Senator McKellar hit Hoover with being unqualified by accusing him of having no law-enforcement schooling, training, or experience, and emphasized he had never even made an arrest himself. Hoover repeatedly dodged these painful realities by answering with descriptions of his length of leadership in the FBI and all the famous investigations he had headed. Senator McKellar finally nailed him with "I am talking about the actual arrests. … You never arrested them, actually?" Hoover tried to use the defense that the FBI had no right to carry guns and did not have the power of arrest until two years ago, but this just further made him sound like an untrained amateur who had been handed a badge he was ill-equipped to carry. Ultimately McKellar's repetitive focused questions forced Hoover to admit he had neither the education nor the experience for his position and responsibilities. Despite being unqualified for his job the Director continued to list himself in *Who's Who* as a criminologist.

As devastating as the Senator's demeaning of the Director was in the Committee's hearings, in the following days Hoover rallied the many senators he had already blackmailed with embarrassing personal information into backing him when the full Senate convened to vote. A combination of senators, who were either his dutiful lackeys, or who were afraid to vote against funding allegedly needed to fight crime, individually got up and sang his praises. The large legislative body then voted overwhelmingly to restore the 22% of his requested budget increase that had been cut by McKellar's Committee, and then also granted him an 11% salary boost to further reward his misdeeds.[182]

Back in his office Hoover exploded with a raging anger like never before. For the rest of his life he would rankle from Senator McKellar's thrashing. The Director's victorious Senate vote gave him little comfort because his manliness had been publicly impugned. He had been ridiculed for being America's top cop without ever having made an arrest. Worse his courage was in doubt because he was a commander who had never led or even joined his forces in battle. In an effort to build some respect for his badly tarnished image as the nation's leading law enforcer, he telephoned SAC Connelley with an order. The Director demanded maximum effort in locating Karpis ASAP. Hoover decided he had to personally lead the capture of Public Enemy Number 1. Karpis later wrote, "I enjoyed reading about Hoover's problems, but I had worse troubles of my own." Hoover was now gunning for him to protect his sagging political and public support, and to reinforce his shattered male pride, not exactly lofty motives for a lawman to kill a criminal.[183]

A MATTER OF MANHOOD

Days after the FBI carried out its ill-planned strike against the empty Hot Springs' residence of Karpis, he and Fred Hunter settled in New Orleans in different apartment buildings. Each was accompanied by his girlfriend. At this same time FBI interest in getting Karpis really heated up. First Senator McKellar dishonored Director Hoover before the Senate, and a week after this lambasting got underway, the FBI made simultaneous announcements from its Washington Headquarters and its Chicago Office by SAC D. M. Ladd that the three-year-old Hamm-kidnapping investigation had been concluded. Of the nine suspects named, two were dead, three had been incarcerated for the Bremer kidnapping, three had just been arrested, and Karpis alone was still at large. Four days after the FBI announced breaking the Hamm case, U.S. AG Cummings announced that the seven living suspects had been indicted by a St. Paul Federal Grand Jury. Karpis had been charged in the Bremer abduction more than two years earlier but he had successfully eluded the FBI manhunt since. Thus a frustrated AG Cummings placed a price on the head of Public Enemy Number 1. He offered $5,000 for information leading to Karpis' arrest in the Hamm and Bremer kidnappings and $2,500 for his sidekick Campbell. The only other two federal rewards ever offered were for John Dillinger and Baby Face Nelson, who had both been slain by FBI agents. A week later the Postoffice Inspection Service named both Karpis and Harry Campbell as the leaders of the train robbery at Garrettsville, Ohio six months earlier and added $2,000 to each fugitives' reward.[184]

The FBI continued searching for Karpis in his former city of residence, Hot Springs. Two days after the AG offered his reward for the fugitive, an agent went to the Hatterie Brothel looking for Madam Grace, but one of the girls said the boss was away and would be returning soon. The FBI believed they could pressure Grace into revealing Karpis' location, so Hoover ordered an agent to immediately pull a ruse to lure the Postal Inspectors out of Hot Springs. FBI files do not explain the nature of this ruse, but Hoover did not want to share any of the publicity from the possible bust of Public Enemy Number 1. This was the Director's thank you gift to the Inspectors who had supplied all the information the FBI was able to obtain on the whereabouts and activities of Karpis for the past year. In this regard a year earlier, Hoover had given a blunt speech on crime to the nation's police chiefs. In it he said, "The greatest ally of the criminally minded is looseness of method, bickerings between enforcement agencies, jealousies within organizations." This was a hypocritical statement by Hoover since his FBI was the most guilty violator of these types of transgressions, and he was now proving himself to also be a disloyal backstabber too.[185]

The day after the FBI agent had visited the Hatterie, two agents went back to bring Grace in for questioning, but Detective Chief Akers and his Hot Springs Police Chief had arrived earlier. After the agents parked and started walking toward the brothel, the two police officials walked out the front door with her in their custody. At the Police Department the two officials spent three hours interrogating her. They tried to pressure her to give up Karpis' location, but she divulged nothing, making her a regular "stand up gal." The police released her.

That evening FBI agents directed Clayton Hall, the sheet-metal worker who had harbored Karpis in Youngstown and was now an informer, to meet with Grace as a mutual friend of the fugitive. She trusted him and revealed that Karpis and Hunter had apartments in New Orleans where Hunter's prostitute girlfriend was undergoing syphilis treatment. This venereal disease was very difficult to eradicate until penicillin became available a few years later during World War II. Grace revealed everything she knew about Karpis except for withholding his residential address which the FBI had to have in order to be able to conduct a raid. Following this meeting the Director had agents begin to amass in New Orleans, as Hoover met with NBC radio network officials to plan two different shows describing how he personally led the capture of Public Enemy Number 1. He desperately wanted this personal capture action to counter the stinging criticism from Senator McKellar that revealed he had no police experience and had never made an arrest. While Hoover was developing his public propaganda campaign, agents arrested Grace as she walked along the street and subjected her to intense questioning. She steadfastly remained silent about her fugitive boyfriend's home address until agents threatened to prosecute her siblings who had helped her harbor Karpis. In return for a promise not to prosecute her family, Grace turned over the only address she had. It was not Karpis' apartment address but Hunter's. However Grace explained that Hunter and his infected girlfriend had Karpis join them for most meals.

Two agents surveyed Hunter's apartment building and selected a vacant house across the street to set up surveillance, as Hoover and his assistant Tolson flew to New Orleans aboard a chartered flight. The next morning agents watched as Karpis drove up to Hunter's building and walked inside. Soon Karpis and Hunter came out and drove off in two different cars. They returned 45 minutes later together in one vehicle. One agent went to a drugstore phone to notify SAC Connelley that the target was in place. Hoover, Tolson, Connelley, and 14 agents headed out to bust the fugitive. The plan was for Connelley to lead three agents to Hunter's apartment door as the remaining agents surrounded the building's exits. But their plan was disrupted. As two FBI cars approached the front of the building to be in position to take up pursuit if the two fugitives managed to escape from the pending raid, Karpis and Hunter prepared to leave the apartment again. It was hot out so Karpis did not put on a coat. Therefore he pulled his pistol from his belt and placed it under a sofa cushion. Hunter was also unarmed. Then the pair walked casually out of the apartment building to their car.

As Karpis settled behind the wheel and Hunter sat in the passenger seat, the two FBI cars pulled up and swerved to the curb to block the fugitives' parked car from both the front and back. As agents leaped out of the two cars, the agents hiding behind cover in the front of the apartment building charged the trapped unarmed men. The agents were carrying sawed-off shotguns, machineguns, and automatic rifles. Against these impossible odds, Hunter casually stepped from the car and began walking away from the scene at an unconcerned pedestrian's pace. Somehow in the confusion and the focus on Public Enemy Number 1, Hunter walked through the cordon of agents and appeared to be getting away, until someone yelled and pointed out a man headed down the street. An agent carrying a machinegun gave chase and used the weapon to point him back towards the car he had escaped from.

Three incidents marred the professionalism of this grand arrest by Hoover's boys. None of the agents who surrounded Karpis bothered to bring handcuffs, so one agent took off his necktie and bound the fugitive's hands. Hoover and Assistant Director Tolson got in the back of the car that carried Karpis in the front. They headed to the FBI Office in the Postoffice Building so the Director could be photographed walking Public Enemy Number 1 inside before giving an immediate press interview about his successful arrest. However, the Director's publicity plans were frustrated. The entire FBI staff in that car was made up of Hoover's out-of-town elite, and none had any idea where the local FBI office was located. However Karpis came to the rescue by offering to give them directions. Tolson asked the prisoner how he knew where their office was, and he replied, "We were thinking of robbing" the mail in the building. With this remark Karpis again showed total disdain for the Director and his detective staff. The fugitive might have been trussed up with an agent's necktie, but he let them know he did not consider their agency effective enough in their own office building swarming with agents to interrupt a robbery in progress or to stop the desperadoes from getting away. Actually Karpis was punking the FBI Director because he later wrote he never had any intention of robbing the building although he had surveyed it.

In Karpis' later writings he described the FBI's third inappropriate incident during the capture. He said an agent told him that if he and Hunter had not decided to walk out at that very moment, they would have been dead because agents planned to kick in his apartment door guns blazing and not stop firing until everyone inside was dead. This statement cannot be verified but America's secret police did machinegun to death the previous three Public Enemies Number 1 in such fashion. In addition Hoover would soon direct such an apartment door-busting shootout of another fugitive.

An hour after the arrests of the duo, Hoover stood before the press in the FBI New Orleans Office boasting about the successful capture of Public Enemy Number 1. Karpis' arrest culminated the FBI's two-year manhunt for the fugitive who eight months earlier had sent the Director a death-threat letter that still made him bristle. This was the Director's grandest moment, his first arrest, his opportunity to vindicate his courage and reestablish his stature as America's top cop. But pay attention to his statements for they seem to defeat this purpose, and they were filled with factual inaccuracies. With a slight smile, Hoover began, "I've got something interesting to tell you. We've captured Alvin Karpis." In describing the takedown, Hoover not only did not mention his role in the arrest, but he emphasized the overwhelming force covering the two fugitives. In addition the two fugitives were surrounded sitting in their car seats, but Hoover's following two statements describe the pair being taken down while walking out of the apartment building entrance to go to their car. Such a major inaccuracy about what happened at the arrest scene earlier that day made it sound like Hoover was not even present. "They had no opportunity to resist. Our men, who were concealed about the entrance to the place, were upon them before they could get into action. Six of the agents pointed sawed off shotguns at the pair and they gave up at once." "They were in the apartment on the first floor of the building and were leaving the house to enter an automobile when the agents surrounded them. The agents called upon them to surrender and they were taken without the firing of a shot." Hoover also falsely reported the coatless Karpis carried a pistol in his pants belt. This would have been aberrant behavior. In that era Citizens were not permitted to carry weapons openly, and the sight of the gun butt sticking out of his pants would have caused any concerned citizen who encountered the fugitive to call the police, exactly what Karpis was trying to avoid.[186]

At this point in his press conference, the Director bizarrely reversed his earlier and future public stance by saying, "Another thing, Karpis is not Public Enemy Number 1 to us." He declined to tell who had that ranking. His statement made no sense. The Director had given the fugitive this label after the slaying of Baby Face Nelson a year-and-a-half earlier, and then just nine days before the arrest Hoover had distributed circulars offering a $5,000 reward for Karpis, making him only the third man in history to be posted with a federal bounty. This was the first fugitive Hoover had found important enough to join in arresting, and he held this press conference for the sole purpose of bragging about bringing him down. Yet the Director tried to malign the prisoner's tough guy image. This was an illustrious takedown for Hoover, but instead of pumping up his role, his bruised ego made him play macho man and degrade the criminal stature of Karpis which also downgraded the importance of the arrest. After making all these put downs of Karpis at that victorious moment, the Director two decades later wrote in an autobiography, "Ma Barker and her sons, and Alvin Karpis and his cronies, constituted the toughest gang of hoodlums the FBI ever has been called upon to eliminate." Such inconsistency, contradiction, and flip-flops were a hallmark of Hoover.[187]

Hoover made another braggadocio statement about Karpis' capture with, "We have been on the trail of Karpis for two years. For the past two months he has been dodging in and out of New Orleans and we have been awaiting an opportunity to catch him here." This was to cover up that the FBI never had any idea where Karpis was during its whole two-year manhunt until he had already moved on to another unknown location. Hoover had not known about Karpis being in New Orleans until a couple days before the arrest as his agents scoured Hot Springs for him. This is why AG

Cummings had offered the reward a week before the capture because Hoover's efforts had been totally futile and he desperately needed the public's assistance.[188]

With Hoover's weird denial that Karpis was Public Enemy Number 1, it is relevant to look at the history of this sensational concept. The term "public enemies" had been created by the Chicago Crime Commission six years earlier. The Commission compiled the names of the city's 28 worst Public Enemies, attached a short criminal background of each, and sent this list to local law enforcement agencies and the newspapers in hopes the city's corrupt police department would start harassing them. One judge with reporters present issued a vagrancy warrant for each one. The first warrant was for the top name on the list and headlines branded Al Capone as "Public Enemy Number 1." This action generated unprecedented nationwide publicity against criminals and aroused citizen support for a war on crime. This led J. Edgar Hoover to plagiarize the Chicago Crime Commission's concept by declaring a succession of Public Enemies Number 1 throughout the 1930s. Then at the Karpis' arrest press conference Hoover pompously dismissed the importance of Karpis as Public Enemy Number 1, but the Director soon called in the press again to announce his new Number 1 as bank robber Maurice Denning. The FBI's website states that the term Public Enemy Number 1 "was used in speeches, books, press releases, and internal memorandum." Later Hoover morphed the public enemy concept into an FBI *Ten Most Wanted Fugitives List.*[189]

Following the New Orleans' press conference, Hoover, Tolson, and eight agents were all armed as they boarded a chartered plane to St. Paul to take Karpis for trial. Hoover's terrible fear of Karpis was obvious as the prisoner's hands and feet were handcuffed, and these two sets of handcuffs were then handcuffed together. Upon landing the next morning, Hoover gave another press conference that was filled with nasty, demeaning statements about the prisoner. Hoover said, "Karpis said he'd never be taken alive, but we took him without firing a shot. That marked him as a dirty, yellow rat. He was scared to death when we closed in on him. He shook all over – his voice, his hands and his knees." In contrast to Hoover's bluster, no agent or witness mentioned Karpis looking scared, but he certainly would have been justified given the situation. The fugitive was trapped unarmed in a car seat surrounded by shotguns and a fresh memory of the FBI's rash of assassinations of John Dillinger, Baby Face Nelson, Pretty Boy Floyd, Fred and Ma Barker, and a few other bank robbers he knew. After Hoover used the most insulting language he could muster about the prisoner, the Director and Tolson reboarded their chartered flight and headed for an evening of togetherness nightclubbing in New York City.[190]

Hoover's many falsehoods during the press conferences in New Orleans and St. Paul were intended to make him sound like a tough in-command cop. The following day Hoover phoned Headquarters to dictate his official version of the arrest events. This story was very different from his statements at the two early press conferences, and this became the tale that the FBI, and Hoover in his own writings, disseminated for countless articles and books from then until the present. This account made the Director the leader of the raid and the imposing hero in the center of the action. What is particularly odd about the sequencing in this evolving storyline is that in all the boasting at the New Orleans and St. Paul press conferences Hoover never once mentioned being involved.

The major discrepancies between the Director's statements in the first two press conferences compared to his official line from the time he landed in New York City has the fishy smell of Hoover and Tolson concocting this new brave tale while alone on the flight to the Big Apple after leaving Karpis in St. Paul. The Director's new version was a reversal because it now definitely defined Karpis as Public Enemy Number One, and it had SAC Connelley run from the FBI car in front of Karpis to the passenger's door, while Hoover rushed from the FBI car behind to the driver's door where he quickly grabbed Karpis by the collar to stop him from reaching into the backseat for a rifle. Not only did none of the internal reports by the agents who were present mention Hoover grabbing Karpis by the collar, not one acknowledged the Director's leadership or even presence at the scene. Other embellishments in the Director's new story to reporters on the second day included more demeaning of the prisoner with, "Stammering, stuttering, shaking as though he had palsy, the man upon whom was bestowed the title of Public Enemy Number One folded up like the yellow rat he is." In Hoover's new version as Karpis stepped out of the car with hands raised, the Director commanded, "Put the cuffs on him, boys." Remember it was actually an agent's necktie.[191]

Upon his return to Washington, Hoover was asked by a reporter waiting outside his office, "You led the raid in New Orleans, didn't you?" "I did," he answered, "but it was a 'we' job and not an 'I' job." From then on the FBI's official story and Hoover's books implied he was the lead action hero but it always placed him in groups of agents for each event such as "We nabbed them." Despite all of Hoover's bravado about the incident it was a simple arrest of two unarmed defenseless suspects trapped in car seats surrounded by an overwhelming force of high-powered weapons aimed at their heads.[192]

Two decades after the Karpis arrest, the Director wrote a magazine article about the events and then made them a key chapter in a book about G-Man Number 1. For his writings, Hoover concocted a new third version of the arrest events. The original press conferences had the fugitives at the buildings' entrance, his statements the next day had them in the car seat, and now his writings had them entering the car. In Hoover's written words, "Four assistants and I. … we moved out and hurried forward, demanding their surrender as the two men were entering the car. The last thing in the world that Alvin Karpis expected to see was the head G-man and a squad of what he had called 'sissy' agents! The tough hoodlum turned ashen. His expression was a curious mixture of amazement and fright. Neither he nor his shaking companion made an effort to resist." In this partial paragraph he wrote two lies because the agents trapped the fugitives sitting inside the car, and Karpis' unarmed companion not only resisted Hoover's cordon of heavily-armed detectives but almost escaped by simply getting out of the car and walking through them unnoticed because of the focus on Karpis.[193]

The nation's newspapers carried the initial accounts of Karpis' arrest based on statements by Hoover, his agents, and bystanders who witnessed it, but then for the next 35 years the only account available in books and magazine articles was the FBI's later revised version. This all changed when former Public Enemy Number 1 wrote his autobiography and described a far different arrest scene. Karpis wrote that after he had been taken into custody and his hands were tethered by an agent's necktie, "I could see that some of the men with the guns had turned their attention to another chore. They were looking over toward the corner of the building and they were waving their arms. I heard one guy shouting, 'We've got him. We've got him. It's all clear, Chief.' A couple of others shouted the same thing. I turned my head in the direction they were looking. Two men came out from behind the apartment" where they had been hiding to avoid stray bullets. One was Hoover and the other Tolson. Karpis explained why the Director was there. "The story of Hoover the Hero is false. He didn't lead the attack on me. He hid until I was safely covered by many guns. He waited until he was told the coast was clear. Then he came out to reap the glory." Karpis went on to deny he reached for a rifle on the backseat as Hoover had claimed for the first time in his third press conference on the day after the arrest. The model coupe Karpis was in did not have a backseat.[194]

For the rest of their lives, Karpis and Hunter expressed to people close to them their resentment about Hoover's false claims of being involved in the arrest of the pair. Karpis and Hunter wrote private letters to each other decades later complaining about Hoover taking credit for the arrests. Hunter's friends maintained he swore Hoover was nowhere in sight and his claim to being involved was phony. Late in Hunter's life he still got upset when shown newspaper pictures of Hoover on that day after the capture had been completed.

Two detailed accounts of the arrest events were written by participants, one by Karpis and the other by SAC Connelley, who headed the manhunt and bust. The SAC wrote an internal summary report of the episode 17 days after the arrest. His report states the Director was at the scene, but despite the great specifics Connelley presented about most aspects of the incident, he did not ascribe a single action or order to the Director. His comments about Hoover are unusually vague and do not indicate whether he was part of the initial charge or a bystander in hiding. However given the FBI's culture of paying homage to the Director, it is all but certain Connelley would have commended his boss for superb leadership and courageous action if Hoover's version were true. No agent's internal report and no eyewitness' account corroborated Hoover's assertion that he approached Karpis' car much less grabbed him by the collar. In addition no one else mentioned Karpis being anything but unarmed, which would not be the case if he was within arms reach of a rifle. While Connelley's official report confirms Karpis was sitting in a Plymouth coupe, it does not mention a rifle or any other gun in the passenger compartment which would be a major oversight and deviation from his otherwise detailed presentation. In the FBI inventory of items seized from Karpis' car were listed a .22 caliber Remington rifle, two .45 caliber pistols, two shoulder holsters, a hunting knife, and a tackle box, but the SAC surprisingly failed to mention where they were located, the trunk or passenger compartment. Given Connelley's penchant for detail in describing the scene, it is noteworthy that he did not mention where the weapons were stored as if he intentionally avoided contradicting Hoover's version by saying they were in the trunk. Just as today's CSI teams completely photograph an entire crime scene to later confirm exactly how the perpetrator left it, Connelley always wrote internal reports that routinely recorded if the culprits posed a threat, and the degree of danger they were to the agents involved. Yet there was no such mention in this report as the obedient SAC again avoided contradicting the Director's public version.

Crime historians have made the verbal dispute regarding Karpis' arrest between G-Man Number 1 and Public Enemy Number 1 a he-said she-said affair despite Hoover's seriously-compromised credibility on the subject. Hoover created three different versions that were contradictory and contained numerous proven falsehoods. In contrast, Karpis and Hunter continued to express frustration to associates about Hoover's lies decades after the arrest which would be expected given Karpis' description of the events in his book and the pals' personal letters to each other. But previous historians who have focused on Karpis and the other Great Depression bank robbers were unaware of important corroborating evidence from the gangster world that supported one version over the other. This additional aspect of Hoover's character makes it quite clear whether the lawman or the outlaw was telling the truth.[195]

CLOSETED COWARDICE

Three years after the arrest of Karpis, FBI Director Hoover made the fourth and final "personal" arrest of his career. His actions in this case revealed his real character when he was not in front of reporters and cameras spouting his tough-guy bluster and bravado. Unlike the Karpis arrest, the events in this case are indisputable because they were made public by one of the Director's few close associates who witnessed everything and Hoover even confirmed them.

The target in this takedown was Brooklyn gangster Louis "Lepke" Buchalter. His nickname is a shortened version of the word "Lepkelch" meaning "Little Louis." He ascended to gang leadership in the middle of Prohibition upon the murder of Lower East Side gang chieftain Jacob "Little Augie" Orgen. This thug's specialty had been producing muscle in union/management disputes for the party who paid the most. Although the Orgen murder was never solved, Lepke was the beneficiary, and after he took over the gang he expanded its activities into extortion of both unions and businesses to compete with Chicago's Al Capone as the nation's most powerful labor/industrial racketeer. During the late Roaring '20s Lepke used threats of violence and a number of killings to take control of New York City union locals that represented workers in several manufacturing industries as well as the truckers who transported these companies' products. When the Big Apple was the nation's fashion hub, Lepke had a stranglehold on the city's huge garment and fur businesses as well as bakery goods and flour. Upon taking control of these unions, Lepke plundered the treasuries; sold out the memberships by negotiating *sweetheart* contracts that reduced worker pay, benefits, and work rules in return for payoffs from their employers; took kickbacks from companies and individuals who wanted to handle the employees' health and pension plans; and extorted bribes from unionized companies through threats of strikes. He even extorted non-unionized businesses by creating sham trade associations that demanded monthly "protection" payments to deter vicious beatings of owners, managers, and truck drivers, and also bombings of stink, acid, and explosives against their plants' large valuable clothing or bakery inventories. His trade associations demanded every business that was a member adopt price schedules of half to double existing rates with Lepke getting the lion's share of these exorbitant increases. By eliminating pricing competition in these industries he forced the buying public to pay the brunt of his widespread extortions. He achieved these objectives by becoming one of the most murderous organized-crime leaders of his time.

Remember that Lepke also became involved with the Kansas City Massacre after the fact. He helped harbor Verne Miller during his fugitive flight when he was the prime suspect. Miller was the man who Frank Nash's wife had called to free her husband after he was taken into custody by the FBI, leading to this tragic slaying of lawmen. Lepke and wife Betty also took in Miller's wife, Vi Mathias, as their apartment guest and as their companion on a two-week vacation. FBI agents trailed the trio's travels trying to find Miller, but they failed to track him down before he was murdered gangland style in Detroit.

Lepke seemed impervious to law enforcement intervention as he viciously ruled over his racketeering empire. Arrested numerous times, he was never tried for anything. Then a decade after Orgen's murder, both U.S. AG Cummings and Manhattan DA Tom Dewey focused on Lepke's extortionist activities. This led to a most bizarre law-enforcement competition. On the one side, AG Cummings had initiated the War on Crime and his subordinate Hoover was hard at work establishing himself as America's top cop. On the other side, DA Dewey had his sights set on the Governor's Mansion in Albany, New York and then the White House in Washington, and he planned to win both positions by becoming the nation's formidable racket-busting prosecutor. In this competition Hoover and Dewey vied with each other to win the conservative Republican crown as the toughest law-and-order enforcer by stridently espousing harsh anti-crime rhetoric. In contrast Democrat AG Cummings, who had introduced crime fighting into the national political agenda, pursued Lepke through steady prosecutorial actions while avoiding the other two's pompous hyperbole.

AG Cummings went after Lepke for violation of the Sherman Antitrust Act by creating monopoly and price fixing in specific industries, while DA Dewey went after the gangster for violent extortion of individual businesses in these industries. The AG brought the first indictment, but both prosecutors ended up charging the gangster in multiple cases involving different crimes. The day Lepke was to appear at his trial for Federal Antitrust Law violations in the fur business, he instead jumped bail and went into hiding. Four months later AG Cummings offered a reward for the fugitive's apprehension, and his FBI Director signed the $5,000 wanted poster. Two years into Lepke's flight, DA Dewey was desperate to capture him. From hiding Lepke had ordered potential trial witnesses against him murdered, and three of the five shooting victims had died. This was terrifying other witnesses and weakening the pending cases. At that time Lepke's gang members were searching for a union official who had turned informer, but when they encountered a legitimate music-publishing-house executive who resembled their target, they mistakenly shot him to death. Three days later DA Dewey asked the city to offer a very large $25,000 reward for the fugitive, and upon receiving city approval the DA had the NYPD distribute one million "dead or alive" circulars through law enforcement agencies nationwide.

Lepke was now the prime target of the country's two most ambitious law enforcers - Manhattan DA Dewey and FBI Director Hoover. The two were locked in an intense political competition to be crowned America's preeminent crime-buster. Both were trying to achieve this status by using exaggerated, self-aggrandizing publicity releases, press conferences, and books. Both lawmen had futilely searched for Lepke for two years and each needed the bust to save face and a conviction to boost his racket-busting image.

As these lawmen intensified their efforts and publicity about Lepke, the fugitive had tired of living like a hermit in the isolated confines of a one-room apartment. He knew that DA Dewey's combined extortion charges amounted to life imprisonment, so the fugitive developed a plea-deal proposal to offer Hoover. Lepke agreed to surrender to the FBI but demanded two conditions - Hoover had to guarantee the fugitive would face only the narcotics-importing indictment with its maximum 15-year sentence, and also assure that he would be held in federal custody for the duration of his prison sentence protected from DA Dewey and state prosecution. Lepke knew his only chance to ever be free again was to serve his federal time and hope the New York charges would fade away during all the intervening years. However Lepke feared a verbal deal with the FBI Director would be meaningless. All of organized crime was well aware that three years earlier Hoover had violated the FBI's promise to give alien brothel madam Anna Sage residency in return for turning in John Dillinger. Thus Lepke decided to approach Hoover through an intermediary, who he hoped would publicize the Director's agreement to the nation and this public awareness would force him to keep his word this time.

Hoover lived in a tightly insulated world and was close to few people - a couple top aides, his PR man, and Walter Winchell, America's gossip king. He was the country's most read syndicated columnist with his *Walter Winchell on Broadway* and also the most listened to broadcaster with his Sunday evening national radio show. Through both venues Winchell supplied inside information and dirt about people of prominence. Almost daily he included a FBI-planted item praising "G-man Hoover" to turn the Director into a carefully crafted folk hero. In return the head of America's secret police supplied many embarrassing and damaging scoops about American citizens whom he personally disliked or whose political views or activities he disapproved. It would later become public that the Director illegally supplied Winchell many revelations from his confidential FBI blackmail files. Hoover also inappropriately supplied his valuable mouthpiece with an FBI agent protective escort, but the agent's real job may have been to record the spokesman's professional and personal conduct to make sure he would never embarrass the Director. Winchell's 3,908-page FBI file is larger than the folder for any gangster of his era and it is filled with agent summaries and evaluations of his syndicated newspaper columns and radio broadcasts. Hoover used these evaluations to advise Winchell about how to handle each scandal "properly" for his rumor-mongering broadcasts and columns. After Hoover's mother died in 1938, he usually spent Saturday afternoons at a New York racetrack and then dined at Winchell's permanently-reserved table at the Stork Club in midtown Manhattan. FBI agents' internal reports pointedly state "Winchell is on the Special Correspondent's List and, of course, is a long-time personal friend of the Director," making him a true untouchable.[196]

Winchell's columns and broadcasts were filled with fact, rumor, and editorial comment. Along with skewering the rich and famous and the politicians who displeased the Director, Winchell discussed national and international issues and problems from his and Hoover's rigid conservative perspective. Winchell was blunt and often mean-spirited. In his column he popularized the style of writing that features short comments interspersed by dots to make for fast-paced reading. On his radio show he delivered his remarks in a rapid almost hysterical barking machinegun-staccato style with a telegraph key tapping incessantly in the background like in a busy newsroom.

Lepke needed to have his surrender offer delivered to Winchell, so he snuck out to meet with Frank Costello. Costello operated elegant high-end illegal casinos that were fronted by fine restaurants in New York and New Orleans. He was politically influential and well acquainted with all of Manhattan's movers and shakers. Costello and Winchell occasionally shared common interests, and both went out nightly and patronized the same restaurants and nightclubs.

One evening soon after Lepke had met with Costello, he sat privately with Winchell and asked him to approach Hoover about a deal for the fugitive's surrender. Winchell readily agreed, but he wanted something in return. He would only do it if he could announce to his radio audience that he was in on the bust. The egotistical, self-serving Hoover must have been less than pleased with Winchell sharing in the capture of a public enemy, but after two years of futile searching, Hoover needed to arrest Lepke any way he could, especially with DA Dewey also bearing down on the fugitive.

Winchell presented the agreement he had reached with the fugitive to Hoover, but the Director also laid down a condition. He rejected Lepke's offer to voluntarily turn himself in at the New York FBI Office, and instead demanded the gangster play a role scripted by Hoover for a dramatically-staged capture by America's top cop. When the deal was sealed, Hoover documented the agreement in his internal Summarization about the case, "Mr. Winchell was authorized by the Director of the FBI, to publicly state that Lepke's civil rights would be respected and maintained should he surrender." Then Don Whitehead, a PR writer for the FBI penned, "As the FBI closed in on Lepke, Walter Winchell broadcast a radio appeal for the gang leader to surrender, with the promise that his civil rights would be respected by the FBI. ... The FBI got Lepke, and Winchell got an exclusive story." As the "capture" date grew close, Winchell in his usual brash, egotistical manner berated the gangster on his radio program - "Are you listening, Lepke? Are you listening? Come out, come out, wherever you are!"[197]

From the time DA Dewey issued his large wanted dead-or-alive reward, it took just two-and-a-half weeks for Lepke, Costello, Winchell, and Hoover to meet with each other, work out a deal, and conclude the fugitive's voluntary surrender arrangement. One evening without reporters, photographers, or witnesses present Lepke showed up at the site selected by Hoover and surrendered. Then the Director called a press conference at the New York City FBI Office. When the reporters assembled, the Director bragged that he had single-handedly brought in the fugitive, and then he uncharacteristically refused to give any details. He declined to describe his alleged heroic actions, to explain how he had "captured" the dangerous fugitive, or to even identify the location where he had picked him up. Hoover's secrecy seemed rather bizarre. His only admission about the circumstances was his revelation that the fugitive was unarmed, which sucked any drama out of the scene he was trying to create. Hoover's only other tidbit of information was that the fugitive had grown a mustache. The Director never explained why he kept everything secret leaving the reporters puzzled.

The rest of Hoover's statements were disingenuous. He falsely claimed he got Lepke through "FBI resources," and categorically denied having made any deal with the fugitive. The Director had no choice but to dutifully credit his pal Winchell with having made the successful contact with the gangster. Hoover emphasized that the NYPD and DA Dewey had no part in bringing the suspect into custody. This riled the local law enforcers because they had kept their part of an agreement to fully inform the FBI of their search for Lepke. However the Director iced the police out of his theatrically-staged capture just as he had stuck it to the Postal Inspectors who had given him so much assistance in the Karpis hunt.

Later Hoover scripted the FBI's official written version. It states that the Director walked the New York City streets alone during the darkness of evening to meet America's most-wanted fugitive and capture him without assistance. Hoover had finally created the illusion of himself as a media-style action-hero, but this story had that fishy smell. It failed to explain why Lepke was walking the empty business sidewalks alone at night, how Hoover knew he was going to be there, and why he did not have an assault team to ensure the capture of this dangerous killer.

Winchell later revealed what really happened at Lepke's surrender that night. As agreed to in their deal, the columnist waited at a specified sidewalk location unarmed. Lepke's car pulled up and he casually stepped out. Winchell frisked the cooperative fugitive to make sure he was also unarmed. Then the two men walked down the street to Hoover's parked armor-plated limousine. America's action hero was hiding inside the locked vehicle surrounded by two-dozen FBI agents protecting their boss from harm. Agents again frisked the fugitive and then cuffed him. Only when the prisoner was in custody and encircled by this contingent of heavily-armed agents did America's top cop dare stick his head out.

At Lepke's voluntary surrender, Hoover knew there would be no threat of harm to anyone. This fugitive desperately needed the Director's help to avoid a lifetime sentence by DA Dewey. Winchell, a columnist, demonstrated there was nothing to fear by standing alone and unarmed on an empty street to take the fugitive into custody. In fact Winchell reported to his radio audience that it was a jolly good adventure. Yet the Director hid like a quaking rat in a hole despite being surrounded by thick armor and an overwhelming detective contingent. Hoover's spineless hiding would have been unconscionable for anyone who had taken the oath to protect and serve, but for America's top cop it was the ultimate act of dishonor.

The Director's gutless actions in the surrender of Lepke make it easy to decide who was telling the truth about his leadership role in the earlier arrest of Karpis. In Karpis' case Hoover not only told proven untruths, but he also issued three different, contradictory versions of the event during the first 24 hours after it happened. Unlike the Lepke surrender, the Director had good reason to be concerned about the possibility of a violent confrontation in the capture of Karpis, a dangerous gunman with a record of aggressive shootouts against lawmen. In addition Old Creepy had mailed a letter threatening Hoover's life. It is inconceivable that America's top cop, who in the non-threatening Lepke voluntary surrender hid with cowardice in the extreme, did not avoid facing the capture of the dangerous Karpis by hiding behind the building out of firing range while his subordinates charged in and made the arrest.

It is interesting that throughout Hoover's long career he tried to cover up his severe fearfulness by presenting a tough bulldog cop image to the world. He also projected his most serious character flaw into his enemies' personalities whether they were cowardly or not. He always relished referring to major fugitives with disparaging words like "a dirty, yellow rat" to express his disgust with them, but while these dangerous criminals were indeed despicable men, not one was a coward like the Director.

Hoover not only concocted the so-called "arrest" of Lepke, but he also fabricated the effectiveness of the FBI's two-year worldwide search for him. Years later Hoover recorded on his stationary a Summarization of his detectives' extensive search for the fugitive as if it was a great drama. "A manhunt that encircled the continental United States and extended into Mexico, Costa Rica, Cuba, England, Canada, France, Puerto Rico and Carlsbad, Germany. Summary reports alone succinctly setting forth contacts of [lieutenant] Shapiro and Lepke, number over a thousand pages, to say nothing of the thousands of reports of Special Agents of the Federal Bureau of Investigation working in every section of the United States." Unfortunately Hoover again made his official records totally untruthful. Not only is this major organized-crime leader's whole file small at just 184 pages rather than the "thousands of reports of Special Agents," but worse the Director left out the most significant fact.[198]

The entire two years Lepke was supposedly "on the run" he actually lived in a rented furnished single room close to Brooklyn Police Headquarters and his family home. During his two years as a fugitive the FBI never had a clue of his whereabouts, but it would have always been simple to find him. Instead of having untold numbers of agents literally searching the world over, a single agent could have simply tailed his wife in a cherchez la femme. Every week she visited him at his rented room with $250 in cash for his living expenses taken from their two clothes-manufacturing companies. Later she was convicted of harboring her husband and sentenced to a year in federal prison.[199]

Hoover's so-called participations in the arrests of Karpis and Lepke were nothing more than fictional publicity creations. But soon after his first arrest of Karpis, the publicity about his false actions successfully turned the Director into a national action hero celebrated in newsreels, movies, and comic books. He had finally established an image as the epitome of top copdome. U.S. AG Cummings had begun the War on Crime three years earlier in response to the Kansas City Massacre, but it was concluded with the arrest of Karpis, causing the AG's role in policing America to soon be forgotten. Two days after the Karpis' arrest Hoover announced that Congressional funding was passed to increase his total agents by more than one-third from 600 to 825. It was clear the Director's image and his blackmailed Congressional coalition were both on an ascending trajectory. A few in Congress continued to object to Hoover's mismanagement of the country's secret police force, but they were now muted. Hoover had finally achieved independent operation of the FBI with accountability to no one.

A year after Hoover pulled the ruse to oust the Postal Service in the Hot Springs Karpis raid that had been made possible by Postal Inspectors, the nonpartisan Washington think tank, the Brookings Institute, published a report about the anti-crime crusade. It accused federal law-enforcement agencies with conflicts, jealousies, no cooperation, and conducting "feverish bursts of self-advertising." It covered all the agencies, but the FBI was singled out as the prime offender. It said both the FBI and the Postmaster General credited the arrest of Karpis to their own agency. It pointed out not only the "unwillingness on the part of one agency to give credit to another" but the "lack of cordial personal contacts among officials" and "indirect attacks" by one agency upon another. The Brookings' report cited the concern of another agency about the FBI. It involved a case months earlier of an "attempted investigation" by Secret Service agents of unspecified activities of the FBI. The report said, "The situation is generally recognized to be unwholesome and to militate against maximum efficiency."[200]

The situation with the Secret Service occurred because a top Roosevelt administration official asked the man in charge of the White House detail assigned to protect the President of the United States, Joe Murphy, to investigate what Hoover was up to. Soon Hoover fired a FBI agent, and Murphy had two Secret Service agents take the former FBI agent to a local tavern, ply him with drinks, and ask him for "dirt" on the Director. The former agent ran back to Hoover warning him what the Treasury Department's agents were up to and agreed to keep his mouth shut in return for getting his job back, thus successfully blackmailing the blackmailer in chief. Hoover went to his boss AG Cummings and demanded revenge, so the AG pressured the Secretary of the Treasury Henry Morgenthau Jr. to demote Murphy from assistant chief of the Secret Service and transfer him to the Los Angeles area even though he was being punished for carrying out orders from the

President's office. Murphy, who had an exemplary 37-year service record and was about to have been appointed to head the Secret Service, soon resigned. With this devastating spiteful strike against a separate department of the government and even the President's inner sanctum at that, the Director demonstrated that his sinister political blackmailing FBI juggernaut had collapsed the checks and balance system the Founding Fathers designed into the U.S. government. No one in Congress any longer had the backbone to stand up to Hoover, giving him complete autonomy as a sovereignty within, but separate from, the U.S. government. He was free to enforce his personal and political values on the governing elite and the people with impunity from interference by other federal law enforcement agencies, the courts, Congress, and the U.S. Constitution. For the next three decades of his life he would remain a politically-untouchable sinister power from within the government against dissent and nonconformity by the very people whose individualism and liberties he was supposed to protect and serve.[201]

WHAT DEAL?

Director Hoover kept his bargain with Lepke by keeping the prisoner isolated from everyone but his FBI agents, defense attorneys, and family members. Prosecutors from Manhattan DA Dewey's Office appeared at the jail several times requesting to talk with the prisoner, but the jailers always rebuffed them. Hoover and DA Dewey were already in an intense rivalry to become the country's top crime fighter, and this custody standoff over Lepke increased their friction. Since both Hoover and Dewey were astute political creatures, they refused any comment to the press about their mutual loathing, but each gave leaks about their animosity towards the other by having them attributed to anonymous sources.

Four months after surrendering, Lepke went on trial for the federal narcotic-smuggling charges and was convicted. He then pled guilty to the pending retrial of the rabbit-fur extortion charges, and he was given a combined 14-year sentence in Leavenworth. Right after Lepke's sentencing, DA Dewey applied in federal court for custody to try him on a bakery-and-flour-trucking labor-racketeering indictment. Hoover's surrender deal with the convict obligated him to appear at that court hearing to explain their surrender arrangement, but the FBI Director remained silent, breaking his solemn word. By denying this vital information to the Justice Department and to the U. S. Circuit Court of Appeals, the judges ruled a week later that Lepke had to be transferred forthwith from federal prison to stand trial in Manhattan's General Sessions Court.

Under the U.S. Appeals Court ruling Lepke was to remain in federal custody except when he was required to be at the Manhattan trial court sessions. Thus two U.S. Deputy Marshals transported him from and to his residence at the Federal House of Detention. At the conclusion of the trial the Manhattan jury convicted Lepke of bakery and flour industry extortion, and he was sentenced to 30-years-to-life in state prison. This sentence was to begin after he finished serving his 14 years with the feds, meaning he would remain in prison until he was at least 87.

In the meantime Brooklyn DA Bill O'Dwyer had arrested a number of Lepke's extortion-gang members on various unrelated felony charges. The DA systematically persuaded one member after another to turn state's witness against other members. He finally got some to turn on their former boss, and three months after Lepke's Manhattan extortion conviction, DA O'Dwyer obtained a first-degree murder indictment that imposed an automatic death penalty against Lepke and two lieutenants for killing Joe Rosen. He had been an independent garment trucker who had lost his business because of the gang's illegal monopolistic practices. As compensation Lepke had set up Rosen in a candy shop business, but Rosen became a potential informant for Manhattan DA Dewey against Lepke. One day Rosen was entering his candy store when assailants shot him dead. This happened four years before Lepke was indicted.

Four months after obtaining the indictment, DA O'Dwyer began trying to get Lepke transferred from the Federal Leavenworth Prison to face trial in Brooklyn for Rosen's murder. Hoover had given his word to Lepke that he would never be released from federal custody until he had served his prison time, but the Director dishonored himself and the country's justice system by remaining silent as the DA pushed to go ahead with his death penalty case. It took DA O'Dwyer more than seven months of wrangling before U.S. Deputy Marshals brought Lepke into a Brooklyn courtroom for arraignment. Seven months after that, Lepke and two lieutenants were convicted of Rosen's murder. Lepke was returned to Leavenworth to continue serving his federal sentence as he exercised his state and federal appeals of the Brooklyn first-degree murder charge. From the moment Lepke was convicted of murder, DA O'Dwyer said President Roosevelt must commute his federal sentence so custody could be turned over to the state for execution in the electric chair, but FDR quickly replied that he would not turn the convict over until all appeals had been exhausted and his guilt affirmed.

When the U.S. Supreme Court unanimously ruled in the final appeal that Lepke must die after the state court fixed a new execution date, the Brooklyn DA demanded U.S. AG Francis Biddle turn over custody of the Leavenworth convict. After three months of fruitless wrangling by the Brooklyn DA, the state's custody fight for Lepke was taken over by Dewey who was now Governor of New York. Both the Governor and the President used disingenuous arguments in their squabble for possession of the convict because he had become a pawn in the upcoming Presidential election. At the time Dewey entered the execution fray, FDR was a year away from facing voters for a fourth term as President, and his likely opposition was the New York Governor who had been elected a year earlier with the promise not to run for President which he soon broke. The cornerstone of Dewey's campaign for Governor had been his racket-busting image, a tactic credited with his victory. With the Republican Presidential primaries just months away, Dewey wanted Lepke dead to enhance his tough law-and-order reputation against his Republican opponents. Similarly FDR wanted to deny his prospective opponent this feather in his cap until after the general election was concluded.

The FBI Director served in office at the pleasure of the President of the United States and the Attorney General, and ironically both his bosses wanted a legitimate reason to maintain custody of Lepke. Hoover had such a reason because of his surrender-deal with the convict, but the Director had neither the integrity to live by his word nor the loyalty to his bosses to step forward and tell the truth. Thus Hoover sat silent in his office while his boss, the AG, unwittingly violated the Director's promise time and time again.

Governor Dewey mustered three arguments in his crusade to get custody of Lepke from the President, but all were fallacious. The first was that there could be no justice until the convict was executed even though it was guaranteed he would be executed upon completing his federal sentence. Dewey's sole purpose in speeding up the process was to expand his political base and garner votes, a rather macabre abuse of the justice system. Dewey's second argument was based on a manipulative political ploy. Even though he had Lepke's two codefendants in custody on death row in Sing Sing Prison, he refused to set an execution date for any of the three convicts. He proclaimed they needed to be electrified on the same day for reasons he never explained, but this was simply an irrelevant ruse to further his phony wailing about lack of justice in this case. The Governor's third argument was that he had to have the convict in custody before he could hold the clemency hearing required by law before conducting an execution. This was absolutely untrue as nothing in the law compelled the convict's presence at the hearing, and in fact, convicts never appeared before the clemency panel as these pleas were always made by their attorneys. The President had AG Biddle argue on his behalf that he could not pardon the convict until all the appeals including the Governor's clemency hearing had been concluded or the convict could end up going free. FDR's argument was also untrue as in similar cases in the past, Presidents had released convicts to states with the condition that the U.S. AG could revoke this action and order them returned to federal custody if any appeal rejected the execution penalty.

Dewey had no legitimate legal grounds on which to base his arguments so he conducted them primarily in the press for political gain, just as U.S. AG Biddle accused him of doing in a letter he sent to the Governor. Then the AG released this letter to the press. In it he said, "It is surprising to me that you should choose to communicate with the President or with me in this important matter through the medium of the press. The statements and implications in your public announcements that we are openly restricting your efforts to have Lepke's death sentence executed are totally unwarranted." Governor Dewey and his AG came back punching in the political arena by viciously accusing the President of protecting the imprisoned Lepke from punishment. For the next two months Dewey inflamed the electorate into a bloodletting passion, and as public pressure grew FDR decided this was a fight best not fought. The President retained custody over Lepke but turned him over to state authorities. Governor Dewey moved up the execution date to the first day after all the appeal impediments were removed. He had the trio executed in the Sing Sing electric chair one after the other. His rush to death as the GOP Presidential primary campaigns were beginning was rather ghoulish politics indeed.[202]

Lepke and his two associates certainly deserved to be executed. Each was a career criminal who had been involved in multiple murders. Their small Brooklyn gang become infamous as Murder, Inc. This supposedly huge nationwide contract-killing syndicate has became part of American mythology, but the real story has never been told. Because one of the gang's murders impacted the development of the early Las Vegas gambling resort industry, the whole unvarnished truth about the Murder Inc. saga will be detailed in the next volume of this series of historical books.

The surrender of Lepke became a milestone event in the FBI's history. It was the last of the Director's four personal arrests, and it was the Bureau's first major organized-crime arrest. Lepke became the first, and remains the only, major organized-crime leader ever executed in the U.S.

Unfortunately Hoover's misconduct in Lepke's case turned what he always claimed was one of his great successes into a hollow, actually disastrous, victory for American law enforcement. Because Hoover failed to keep his word to Lepke in their surrender deal, he would remain the FBI's only arrest of a major organized-crime leader for the next quarter century. Everybody involved with American gangland was deeply aware that Hoover had broken his word to not deliver Lepke to New York prosecutors, and also knew about the Director's failure to back up his SAC Purvis' promise to prevent the deportation of the Lady in Red in John Dillinger's case. American organized criminals' profound distrust of the lying FBI kept every single gang member across the country from ever considering turning state's witness no matter how serious the criminal charges they faced. Hoover's refusal to reveal his deal with Lepke to his two bosses, the President and the U.S. AG, was not only disloyal to them but also to the whole country he had sworn to protect. Adding to this woeful malfeasance, while the large Mafia gangs plundered and terrorized law-abiding citizens in major cities across the country, Hoover inexplicably ordered his FBI agents to sit on the sidelines of organized crime enforcement.

It needs to be noted that Hoover's sitting silently as Lepke was turned over to New York prosecutors did not increase the gangster's sentences but just their timing. If the Director had acknowledged his deal with Lepke, the gangsters life-sentence and death-penalty trials and his execution would have simply been delayed until after he had completed his federal sentence instead of during it. The nation lost so much and gained nothing. Hoover benefited by maintaining his personal arrest image instead of having to admit Lepke was a voluntary surrender, and Governor

Dewey got to enhance his crime-buster political image with an execution at the beginning of a Presidential election campaign.

Prosecutors find it extremely difficult to make a case against organized-crime leaders because they insulate themselves from the members who carry out their illegal orders. Thus it is almost impossible to successfully prosecute these leaders unless close accomplices, who have heard illegal orders issued, turn state's witnesses. Thus the Director's failure to keep his word to Lepke and the Lady in Red destroyed his agency's crucial organized-crime fighting weapon. He emasculated the ability of his police force to act against America's biggest and most dangerous criminals.

Chapter 11

CONCLUDING THE IMPROBABLE ASPECTS

ARRESTS NUMBER 2 & 3

A week after the FBI arrested Alvin Karpis in New Orleans, a nurse told agents in Toledo, Ohio that she had dated a friend of fugitive Harry Campbell, Karpis' long-time partner in crime. The nurse revealed Campbell was living with his wife in an apartment. FBI Director Hoover boarded a flight for Toledo to participate in his second personal arrest. Machinegun-carrying agents took up hiding places around the apartment building's entrances. At dawn Campbell limped out of the building's front door towards his car. Agents leapt out of hiding, quickly grabbed him, and snatched the pistol from his pocket in an uneventful takedown. Then Hoover came out from hiding along the side wall that contained no exit door so he was sheltered from Campbell bursting out of the building with a loaded gun in his hand. The witnesses described Hoover staying concealed and sheltered from harm during the agents' capture exactly as Karpis had claimed occurred in his arrest a week earlier.

Immediately after Campbell's arrest Hoover called a press conference and falsely incorporated nonexistent danger into the scene by saying, "Campbell showed a little resistance" to intimate his quarry reached for a gun. When the Director was asked if he led the raid like the one for Karpis, he replied, "I did both of them, but it was a 'we' job, not an 'I' job." To a question about assistance from Postoffice Inspectors, he lied. "I'll say this. We received no information and no cooperation of any kind from the Postoffice Inspectors … in capturing Karpis, Campbell, Hunter, or Coker."[203]

Toledo Police Chief Ray Allen asked why his men were not called in to join the Campbell raiding party, and Hoover blindsided him by revealing that Sheriff James O'Reilly had been friendly with Campbell for six months under the impression the gangster was "Bob Miller, a contractor." Hoover said, "The Sheriff has already admitted associating with this man for weeks. It seems to me that any one could have recognized Harry Campbell from his pictures which were plastered on nearly every wall in the country." Just five days earlier Hoover said the FBI would not cooperate with police fitting three categories, "Those who are dishonest, those who are overcome by the headlines of newspapers, and those who protect criminals." The Director totally avoided the fact that the Police Chief and Sheriff headed separate agencies, and the Sheriff with whom Hoover had a problem had no jurisdiction in the city of Toledo. The Director got away with an apples and oranges comparison. In effect he said I do not have to deal with him because I find a totally unrelated person to be unreliable.[204]

Agents shackled Campbell with leg irons and handcuffs, hurried him to a chartered plane in Toledo, and flew him to St. Paul. Agents later told reporters they kept Campbell in these manacles during four days of grilling but he told them nothing about the people who harbored him. The day after that Campbell, the last fugitive caught in the Bremer kidnapping, pled guilty and received a life sentence.

After the FBI's earlier arrests of Karpis and his gofer sidekick Fred Hunter in New Orleans, agents held Hunter in that city for a month until he pled guilty to harboring Karpis and received the maximum federal sentence of two years. Several Toledo and Cleveland residents also received two-year sentences for harboring Karpis and other gang members.[205]

Seven months after capturing Campbell, Hoover had the opportunity to join in his third personal arrest. This time it was a pair of bank robbers who hailed from Green Bay, Wisconsin. The hardcore criminal partner was Merle Vandenbush. He was assigned as an incorrigible to the Waukesha, Wisconsin Industrial School from the young age of 11 to 18. Two years after getting his freedom he was sentenced for forgery to the Green Bay, Wisconsin Reformatory. Upon his release he partnered with Harry Brunette who at 18 was four years younger. During the years Vandenbush had spent so much of his life incarcerated, Brunette had been a delinquent teenager and then became a librarian. It took the pair less than a year after Vandenbush's release to be convicted of car theft and assault in Toledo, Ohio. Both received sentences of 5 to 15 years at the Ohio State Penitentiary. They were eventually transferred to the London, Ohio Prison Farm, and more than five years into their sentence, the two pulled off an escape together. Ten days later the pair were parked in Mount Clemens, Michigan when three deputy sheriffs drove up to question the car's occupants. The records make it unclear whether the desperadoes held the peace officers at bay with guns, but it is possible the pair was unarmed and simply surprised the deputies and physically overpowered them. In any event, the duo stole the deputies' guns before escaping and used these weapons during the next three months to rob three banks in different Wisconsin cities for a total of $40,000.

Three days before the third bank robbery, the duo were driving near Somerville, New Jersey when a state trooper pulled them over for speeding. The pair, along with Brunette's girlfriend, kidnapped the trooper, a former U.S. Marine, probably to keep him from reporting their whereabouts. The gunmen threatened his life while driving him 45 miles west to Freemansburg, Pennsylvania where the desperadoes finally dumped him from their car. They added his gun to their law-enforcement collection. Because the kidnap victim had been taken across a state line the FBI was called in.

However, it was local police departments in three states who worked together to trace the two fugitives' whereabouts. After the desperadoes had let the abducted trooper out of the car, they turned south and drove 60 miles to Philadelphia, where late that afternoon they left the car in a garage. They never returned, and a few weeks later the garage owner informed local police about the abandoned car. Philadelphia police suspected this was the car used in the kidnapping of the New Jersey state trooper so they turned the investigation over to the victim's department even though it was in a different state. Vandenbush's fingerprints were found in the car, and the kidnapped trooper identified photos of Vandenbush and his partner Brunette as his kidnappers.

The car also contained a bill from a New York City garage. New Jersey troopers solicited the aid of the NYPD and the two departments from different states worked together on the investigation. They were informed by employees at the local garage that the bill was for repairs. Then the investigation disclosed that the car was owned by Vandenbush's younger partner Brunette, and it had been parked near the home of his girlfriend Arline LaBeau's parents where she lived. Officers put the home under surveillance until Arline was seen leaving with her sister. The kidnapped trooper immediately recognized her as being the girl with the pair of desperadoes who abducted him. However the surveillance team lost track of her, so they canvassed each apartment building in the area until they found a manager who recognized pictures of Arline and Brunette. The couple had rented an apartment two-and-a-half months earlier under an alias, and they had gotten married on Thanksgiving Day just two weeks before the surveillance was instituted.

NYPD detectives immediately began carefully studying the couple's first floor apartment in the five-story building to identify all means of escape. While the couple was away, detectives planted surveillance officers in another apartment in their building and also on the second floor of an apartment building that was across the street and a few doors away. This apartment's front window had a clear view of their building's front entrance. When the detectives had completed their plans to apprehend Brunette in the safest manner possible, they notified the FBI. NYPD detectives, New Jersey state troopers, and FBI agents met for an afternoon conference and all agreed how their joint capture would be conducted. It was decided to raid Brunette's apartment the next afternoon at 2 p.m. because the surveillance indicated he slept during the day and usually went out at night. Taking him in his sleep by surprise reduced the chance of bloodshed. In addition, it was possible Vandenbush, who was known to be in town and was clearly the more dangerous of the pair, might show up in the meantime and be captured too.

That night after midnight the surveillance team planted down the street in the empty apartment began rotating breaks. The two NYPD detectives walked to a nearby restaurant for coffee while the two New Jersey troopers continued to stand vigil. They observed as Hoover, who had just flown in from Washington, started deploying a contingent of 25 agents for an assault in violation of their multi-jurisdictional agreement. One trooper ran from the apartment to Hoover and asked why he had moved up the raid time, and the FBI director simply shrugged his shoulders. Even though Hoover had no idea about the physical layout of Brunette's apartment or the tactical issues involved, he kept on barking orders. The second trooper had run to get the NYPD detectives to try to bring some sanity back into the situation, but by the time the three officers reached Hoover, he had commenced the raid at 1:30 a.m.

This would be the closest Hoover would ever come to combat. In this situation he lacked the protection of either an armored-plated limousine or building walls, but he made sure he was insulated from the shooter by a barrier of machinegun-carrying agents. In the narrow hallway the Director remained standing near the entrance of the building well behind the 10 agents he had amassed together at Brunette's apartment door. Then Hoover had his remaining agents go to the apartment's rear window to try to "smoke" Brunette out by lobbing in teargas bombs. This completely took away the raiders' element of surprise. One of the bombs started a fire in a back room of the apartment, but the fugitive simply closed the door and then remained behind the apartment's front door defiantly yelling "Come in and get me!"

Smoke poured out of the apartment's back window bringing fire trucks, ambulances, and a bevy of police patrol cars. Firemen ran up to the roof of the adjacent building, jumped to the roof of the burning building, and ran down the stairs to be stopped by FBI agents pointing machineguns who ordered them to "stick 'em up." They scoffed at Hoover's boys as one pointed at his fireman's helmet and demanded, "Dammit, can't you read?" The firemen told the FBI agents that they had a job to do as they simply pushed the misguided agents aside. The firemen rushed to the door of the burning apartment with wrecking bars to pry it open, but the Director asserted authority by saying "there's a desperate man in there." Hoover overrode the firemen by instead ordering his men to machinegun off the lock. The only purpose this could have served was to cause the desperado inside to believe an assault was underway, thus forcing him to return fire. This in turn would have justified his agents continuing firing directly inside the apartment so Hoover, cowering far down the hallway, could avoid ever getting into the line of fire. As soon as his agents started shooting at the lock, Hoover who was alone near the building's front door gallantly led a retreat outside and quickly disappeared from sight. Unfortunately Hoover's boys had no more courage than he did, so when Brunette returned fire through the door with his pistol some ran up the nearby stairway to fire down from the second floor and the rest followed their boss by running out the building entrance. The agents ran to the apartment building across the street and up to its entrance stoop where they opened fire across the street, through the building's open front door, and down Brunette' hallway in case he stuck his head out of his apartment.[206]

Twenty families were trapped in their apartments on Brunette's floor and the ones above as smoke poured out his apartment window and FBI gunfire erupted down the first-floor hallway. Courageous fire fighters ignored the gunfire and expanded aerial ladders to the apartment windows on the upper floors to evacuate the residents in case the fire got worse. Flames consumed furniture and draperies in the room in which it had started, and smoke was seeping into the rest of the apartment. Suffering from the teargas and being overcome by the fire's smoke, Brunette ran into the hallway to quickly take cover in a nearby closet where he continued to hold off 25 machinegun-toting agents with his revolver. The agents continued firing down from upstairs and from across the street while all the families remaining in the apartments huddled in terror from all the gunfire as they choked on the fire's dispersing smoke. Soon after Brunette entered his closet refuge, the teargas and smoke drove his wife to run from their apartment into the hallway toward the fresh air out on the street. As she ran out an agent's machinegun burst grazed her leg but then the shooting stopped. Once she was outside and agents had her in custody, the fugitive was no longer a threat to any civilians. He was isolated from the families in the apartments and he had no hostage, yet the gunfight continued. He thrust his pistol out of the closet door firing blindly down the hallway as every FBI agent remained entrenched behind cover. One man with a revolver held off 25 agents with machineguns under the personal command of FBI Director J. Edgar Hoover for 35 minutes. Brunette did not stop the battle until he exhausted his ammunition. Just think how long this siege of the burning building might have lasted if he had been fortified with an arsenal of bullets. With nothing left to fight with he came out with his hands raised in surrender. As agents surrounded him, he sneered, "What a brave bunch of guys!"[207]

Agents cuffed Brunette, hurried him outside to a car, and encircled it while directing their machineguns his way. Only then did the Director finally come out of his hiding place to again take charge of the raid. Earlier Hoover had bolted out the front door to run down the block to duck behind cover between two buildings. Several machinegun-toting agents had dutifully followed and surrounded their boss safely ensconced behind protective walls. America's top cop now had to explain his spineless flight from the firefight he had just initiated. Thus he turned his cowardly holing up into a photo op with the pursuing newspaper cameramen by feigning being overcome by teargas exposure. An Associated Press photo in the *New York Times* showed Hoover's eyes closed with head collapsed against a wall and a caption stating, "He was slightly affected by tear gas used to drive the bandit from the building." It was actually impossible for him to have gotten the slightest whiff of aroma from the teargas, as he was far down the hallway from the suspect's closed apartment door when the gas was fired into the apartment's back room, and Hoover instantaneously bolted out the front door and ran in the opposite direction from the side of the building where agents had fired the gas and where a gun battle might ensue through the busted window.[208]

When the Director walked up to join the reporters assembled around the car containing Brunette and retook command of the unfolding drama, Hoover stoically declined any comment except to point out the NYPD and New Jersey troopers had cooperated in the arrest. He always stole the limelight when there was heroics, but he was already setting up the two groups of lawmen to take whatever criticism might ensue for what were exclusively his actions. The Director wanted to blame the other officers even though they had watched aghast from a distance at his amateurish, irresponsible, and reckless actions after they had first vehemently objected to his ill-conceived assault plan. Hoover then scurried along with his entourage and the fugitive to the Federal Building. Only after Brunette was finally in custody were the firemen able to go into the apartment and put out the blaze. Amazingly the fire was confined only to the one apartment but it was thoroughly burned out.

New York City officials quickly came up with a clever ploy to expose the atrocious behavior of Hoover and his boys without directly attacking the powerful Director of America's secret police. Republican Mayor Fiorello La Guardia, for whom the city's major international airport is named, demanded his Fire and Police Commissioners explain to him the role their men played in the melodramatic capture at the earliest possible date, and both dutifully wrote letters describing what had transpired. They released their letters about Brunette's capture to the newspapers later that day for scorching publication the following day. The Fire Commissioner wrote, "It occurs to me that members of the New York Fire Department are exposed to sufficient hazards in the line of duty without the added hazard of placing them in the line of gunfire and without adequate defensive equipment. I should say too that the use of a bomb capable of igniting the contents of a building is very short-sighted and should be given serious consideration in future activities. ... In the interest of public welfare and in the face of imminent peril created by the fire, it is my impression that a truce could have been declared, at least, by the Police Department until such time as the extinguishment of the fire and the prevention of its possible extension throughout the building had been effected." The Fire Commissioner also told reporters that "heroics" had dictated the FBI's capture, and "a couple of New York cops" could have taken him in peacefully. He pointed out that authorities did not know if people were sleeping in the building, and all the families inside were in danger if the fire got out of control. He said the FBI should have stopped firing to let the firemen put out the blaze. "I think even the gunman would have given the firemen that break. He was trapped in there too."[209]

The Police Commissioner wrote that the FBI's action "was taken without the consent, and as a matter of fact, contrary to plans carefully considered and agreed upon by the New York police, the New Jersey Troopers and the members of the Federal Bureau of Investigation, who were working with us on the case. These plans, if adhered to, I am convinced, would have resulted in the capture of the prisoner concerned without unnecessary danger to persons lawfully in the vicinity, law enforcement officials and the officers and men of the Fire Department. I have made it a rigid policy to prohibit melodramatic raids on the hiding places of criminals. They are unnecessary although they do bring bigger headlines in the newspapers. We are concerned with capturing lawbreakers and not with publicity. In a matter of departmental routine, members of our force frequently arrest criminals as desperate as Harry Brunette is alleged to be, yet always without fanfare, spectacular or unnecessary gunplay. ... These plans also precluded the spectacular, and guarded against any unnecessary danger to either persons who might have been in the vicinity or the arresting officers. However, this plan was ignored by the Federal men who, evidently without concern for the public welfare or for the many families residing in the large apartment house, with tear gas bombs and gunfire staged a raid over the protest of the New Jersey State Police and contrary to the agreement entered into by the three departments."[210]

Hoover tried to beat these officials to the punch by having letters delivered to all three that day expressing his appreciation for the "cooperation" of the police and firemen. He wanted to falsely include them in any criticism that might result from his actions. Then for the next five days he and his New York SAC, Rhea Whitley, denied every legitimate criticism leveled against the Director and his boys as untrue. Hoover falsely claimed there was no deal so he "never double-crossed anybody." He claimed it was a one-man show by the FBI from beginning to end even though FBI agents did not become involved until local police had Brunette staked out under surveillance. Hoover even scoffed at the NYPD complaints as "kindergarten stuff." For Hoover all that mattered was that he had captured "one of the most dangerous criminals" at large. Hoover's penchant for exaggeration soon took over as Brunette became "the toughest criminal I've seen." Every one of the statements by these two high-ranking FBI officials was a falsehood. For them to be true it would have meant that the New York City Fire Department, NYPD, New Jersey State Troopers, and the Philadelphia police, which were located in three different states, had created a giant conspiracy to falsely steal the thunder of the capture from the FBI. On the contrary they had refused to participate in the frighteningly improper action and had desperately begged the Director not to precede with what was clearly going to become a fiasco.[211]

Once in FBI custody Brunette quickly confessed all his crimes, implicated his partner Vandenbush in them, and even admitted his new wife was involved in the recent kidnapping of the New Jersey state trooper. Two days later a Newark Federal Grand Jury indicted him for abduction of the trooper, he pled guilty, and the Federal Judge immediately sentenced him to 15 years to life. He was subdued and told the judge he wanted to get the court proceedings over as soon as possible. The convict was then transported by car to Trenton. It was driven by U.S. Attorney John J. Quinn who was stopped by a New Jersey state trooper for speeding. The U.S. Attorney did not have his driver's license with him but was able to present a copy of the indictment against Brunette to get out of a ticket. Almost three months later Brunette pled guilty again, this time to threatening and assaulting the Director and 11 agents by firing at them. Ten years was added to his sentence meaning he would not be eligible for parole for 25 years.

After fleeing the burning building Mrs. Brunette was placed under guard in Bellevue Hospital in Trenton for three days to recover from her slight leg wound. Then she was arraigned for harboring a fugitive from justice, her husband. She remained silent at the hearing so the U.S. Commissioner entered a not guilty plea for her. Before coming to trial on the federal charge, she pled guilty in a local Somerville court to carrying concealed weapons because the Prosecutor did not think he had sufficient evidence to convict her of kidnapping the trooper. That trooper came to her defense by telling the Judge that her husband and Vandenbush were planning to kill him and would have without her intervening by begging for his life. His plea touched the Judge who gave her a lenient indeterminate term in the Clinton Reformatory for Women meaning she could be released by the Warden for good behavior. No further action on the pending federal harboring charge against her could be found.

Two months after the FBI's shootout capture of Brunette, his partner Vandenbush was back in action. He and a new partner dressed like car mechanics in khaki overalls with grease smears on their faces and walked into a bank in Katonah, New York. They pulled .38 caliber automatic pistols out of their pockets and announced "this is a stickup." They stole $17,600 without incident, but as they were about to leave the robbers told the three employees and three depositors lying face down in the vault that they intentionally did not lock a grill-gate so they could easily get out. Then the robbers ran out and down the street to a parked stolen car with New Jersey plates. The six robbery witnesses soon ran out to the sidewalk shouting, and someone at the Volunteer Fire Station next door pressed the siren alerting the villagers. No one could give a good description of the banditos or the escape car. From information learned later, the car was found not far away in a ditch on a dirt road where the robbers had a second getaway car waiting. At the time of their escape, the limited information about the two culprits and the car were teletyped to every police agency in Westchester County.

Twelve miles to the south of the robbery was the village of Armonk, New York with a four man police force. Route 22 ran through the village and a sergeant and two patrolman stood near their booth at a sharp turn stopping every approaching car. They had questioned the occupants of 40 cars when one of the patrolmen found a lone driver's answers about his job and reason for being there evasive. Curious he walked to the rear of the car and pulled up the turtle-back compartment lid to have pistols pushed into his side by two greasy-faced men in khaki overalls. He instantly let go of the lid which slammed shut as he shouted to his nearby fellow officers. It was never revealed whether the patrolman let go of the lid as a swift strategic response or simply out of shocked astonishment. When the patrolman shouted the driver started to bolt but the fist of an advancing policeman stopped him cold. That officer stood guard over him as the other two shouted to the pair in the trunk to drop their guns. When the officers heard the clank of metal objects they opened the lid, ordered the suspects out, and handcuffed them. In the trunk was a brown paper bag with all the bank loot. The trio was taken into custody 22 minutes after the robbery. At the police station Vandenbush gave an alias and false identity until he was about to be fingerprinted. In front of him on the wall was a FBI circular with his photo and fingerprints so he came clean. He had a poor hair-dye job that was part jet black and the rest chestnut. The two accomplices were cousins. One had a long rap sheet but the other had never been arrested. The inexperienced one was the driver of the second car, and he may never have faced a policeman's questions before. Three small-town cops took down the dangerous robber/kidnapper without a shot being fired in contrast to the FBI's dramatic shootout with his former less-experienced partner, Brunette. After the local arrest of Vendenbush, Hoover turned him into a celebrity by calling him "Public Rat Number 1."

The next day a Westchester County Grand Jury at White Plains, New York indicted the trio for first-degree robbery in the bank job. Vandenbush admitted he had robbed four banks and that the gun he had used in the bank robbery the day before had been stolen from the New Jersey state trooper he had kidnapped. Two weeks after the robbery the trio pled guilty. In passing sentence the Westchester County Judge took into account Vandenbush's criminal record and sentenced him to 45 to 70 years in Sing Sing Prison. The two men who committed the bank holdup were 29 and neither could be paroled before age 59.[212]

Hoover led his first three personal arrests to counteract the scathing lambasting about him not being a policeman by Senator McKellar during his Committee's hearings. Even though Hoover remained at a safely protected distance on all three raids, the Director incorporated his hollow action-heroics imagery into his agency's publicity. He no longer portrayed himself as the far-away Washington-based strategist of the anticrime crusade, but rather as the lead cop making arrests on raids just like the action-detective heroes in the movies, radio, and comic books. The FBI's publicity during the War on Crime had emphasized the agency, its professionalism, and its procedures, but with the advent of World War II, the publicity switched to highlighting the Director's leadership as the country's main defense against crime, sabotage, and espionage. Color stories were distributed about Hoover rather than the organization, and the action hero was turned into a celebrity of the Hollywood mold. His name regularly appeared in articles by celebrity columnists like Walter Winchell and Ed Sullivan. They discussed his favorite foods, pastimes, and interests. They showed him imbibing at the Stork Club, vacationing at Palm Beach, dining with movie stars, and socializing with the super rich who courted his favor.

TWO MORE KIDNAPPING TRIALS

After the first Bremer kidnapping trial had gotten underway the FBI captured three more perpetrators. Two were key players in the abduction and the third was a money handler. The mastermind behind the kidnapping plot was Harry Sawyer. He was born in Russia, and he compiled a long criminal record in the Midwest from his Nebraska base before moving to St. Paul where he became a bootlegger and then ran a nightclub. He assumed the throne of the St. Paul underworld after leader "Dapper Danny" Hogan was blown away by a bomb in an unsolved case. Sawyer directed the Bremer kidnapping for the Karpis-Barkers gang because a key St. Paul cop kept him informed about FBI investigations and raids. This police corruption led U.S. AG Cummings to brand St. Paul the "nation's poison spot of crime."

Sawyer was the person who selected Bremer as the second kidnap target, and the crime's planning was conducted at his home and also at Deafy Farmer's Bensenville, Illinois tavern. In the second Bremer-kidnapping trial the prosecution's chief witness was again Byron Bolton. He testified that when the gang assembled in St. Paul to pull off the kidnapping they wanted to abandon it in favor of holding up Bremer's bank, but Sawyer insisted they go through with his plan. After Sawyer was indicted with the other participants, he became a fugitive. He remained at large for 14 months until the FBI arrested him at a deluxe golfing resort in Pass Christian, Mississippi where he had been living for several months operating an illegal lottery.

The second participant in the Bremer kidnapping to be captured was Bill "Lapland Willie" Weaver. He was one of the four men who charged Bremer's car and drove off with him squished in the back floorboard. The other three men were Alvin Karpis, Doc Barker, and Harry Campbell. The third defendant in this trial was Havana-based ransom-money handler Cassius McDonald (see Chapter 8). Eight months after the first trial for the Bremer kidnapping a Federal Jury convicted all three. The judge quickly sentenced kidnap participants Sawyer and Weaver to life and the ransom handler to 15 years. It was almost two years since Bremer was kidnapped, and FBI agents continued their search for the six remaining indicted fugitives including Karpis and Campbell.[213]

The gang's first kidnap victim was William Hamm Jr., and three years after his abductors released him, the FBI finally announced it had solved the case. During this long period Director Hoover repeatedly lied to Congress and the American people that he had solved every kidnapping in the country. Even worse Hoover in all his glorious pronouncements about his great successes against kidnappers never mentioned how horribly the FBI had botched this investigation. Early on the Director and SAC Purvis built a court case to prosecute four Chicago gangsters who were innocent of this crime, but the Federal Jury saw through this obvious charade of injustice and acquitted them. Despite having persecuted these men who had no involvement, the Director continued to falsely maintain he had a perfect record against kidnappers.

The most reprehensible part of this first Hamm kidnapping miscarriage-of-justice prosecution is that Hoover and Purvis were flimflammed by the successor leaders of the Al Capone gang to prosecute a false case against the gang's archrivals and biggest criminal competitors. Interestingly the Caponites went to these extraordinary lengths to take down the competition because they feared this gang too much to ever challenge them in mortal battle. This first prosecution, with its gross travesty of justice, along with organized-crime's duping of America's two top cops into doing their illicit dirty work, will be the center piece of the next volume in this series of historical books because this criminal prosecution directly made possible two decades later the building of one of the Las Vegas Strip's greatest gambling resorts. The grand intrigue and amazing events that suckered the FBI into framing innocent men and the complex impact this had on the development of the booming Strip years later are indeed stranger than fiction.

When Hoover announced solving the Hamm kidnapping for the second time, he identified the nine actual perpetrators. Of these nine, two were dead - Fred Barker and Fred Goetz, who were killed by FBI agents and Cicero gangsters respectively. Three were already incarcerated for the Bremer kidnapping - Doc Barker, Elmer Farmer, and Byron Bolton. Karpis still remained a fugitive in the Bremer case, but he was arrested two weeks after Hoover's Hamm announcement. The three remaining accomplices in the Hamm kidnapping had not gone on to participate with the gang when they abducted Bremer seven months later. At the time of the Director's Hamm-kidnapping solution announcement these three suspects resided in different states, but agents swooped in and arrested them within a day of each other.

The modus operandi of the two kidnappings had one distinct difference. In the first one Hamm was not blindfolded during his captivity. This meant he could identify his captors, but it took the

FBI three years to determine who they were in order to show the victim the correct mug shots. The FBI finally uncovered what they believed was the two-story white frame house where Hamm had been held in a second-floor bedroom for three days. Ironically this meant Hamm and Bremer were held in bedrooms that were just two blocks apart in Bensenville after being abducted a few blocks apart in St. Paul. Hamm's bedroom prison was owned by Bensenville Postmaster Edward Bartholmey. Since Hamm did not recognize a picture of Bartholmey it was likely he had not seen the kidnap victim either. Thus the FBI came up with a clever ploy to get inside his home to determine whether it was indeed where Hamm was held captive without tipping its hand that he was under investigation. Two agents along with the victim knocked on the door of Postmaster Bartholmey' home and said they were Postoffice Inspectors so he welcomed them inside. Once in the living room Hamm surveyed the surroundings and nodded to the agents that he recognized them. With this the agents invited the Postmaster to join them for a social dinner. As soon as Bartholmey got in their car, the agents drove directly to a plane bound for St. Paul and his arraignment.

Bartholmey did not have a criminal background. He worked as a clerk in the yard offices of the Chicago, Milwaukee, St. Paul and Pacific Railroad for several years. He was injured in a railroad accident, and a few years later he used his influence as a Democratic precinct committeeman to get appointed as the town's postmaster. Immediately after the FBI's arrest became public, Postmaster General Farley announced that he had removed Bartholmey as Acting Postmaster. He added that his agency had not been informed of the arrest by the FBI. This was typical Hoover arrogance, always operating without consideration for anyone. As an aside, Bartholmey's wife was active in church societies and the Railway Ladies' Club. Upon her husband's arrest she claimed she had been away "on something like a visit" at the time Hamm was held captive in her home.

The Bensenville tavern operated by Deafy Farmer for about 20 years was central to bringing together the participants in the Hamm kidnapping. Farmer's tavern had become an out-of town hangout for the Karpis-Barkers gang, and Bartholmey met them because he also frequented the drinking hole after work. Bartholmey brought in another participant from the nearby Mohawk Country Club where he played golf. Fred Goetz possessed a club membership card when he was slain by Cicero gangsters nine months after the kidnapping. This odd collection of cohorts came together by happenstance in Bensenville, and they linked up because each recognized the others also had very dark sides.

The eighth suspect was Jack Peifer, owner of St. Paul's Hollyhocks Nightclub. He was arrested in adjacent Minneapolis. He was a native resident who had become a gambler and bootlegger with numerous arrests but no convictions. His most serious charge was the Northwest National Bank robbery in Milwaukee, Wisconsin. Given the corruption of the St. Paul police and judiciary, it is not surprising he successfully fought extradition and obtained release after just 10 days in custody. He was the gang member who set the Hamm kidnapping in motion by walking up to the victim on a St. Paul sidewalk and fingering him as the victim they sought. He was the mastermind and fingerman in Hamm's kidnapping just as Sawyer was in the later Bremer abduction. Each acted as the contact man between the kidnappers and the St. Paul Police Department in their respective abductions. It is important to note that despite all the gang informant testimony during the three trials, no state's witness ever mentioned seeing Ma Barker or heard of her being consulted at any time. Peifer and Sawyer were the architects behind the two abductions while Karpis and both Fred and Doc Barker were followers.

The final newly-arrested suspect was Charles Fitzgerald. He had a long police record, had served at least two prison terms, and was wanted for several bank robberies in Iowa and Nebraska. He had been posing as a businessman in Los Angeles for some time before the FBI arrested him there. Fitzgerald was the gang member who shook Hamm's right hand as two other goons poked guns in his ribs and pushed him into the backseat of the parked getaway car. Fitzgerald was also charged with another Karpis-Barkers gang crime by the Dakota County, Minnesota, Attorney. Two months after the gang kidnapped Hamm, Fitzgerald was the signal man in the South St. Paul payroll robbery in which Doc Barker killed a policeman.

Byron Bolton had pled guilty in Bremer's abduction and had been the star prosecution witness in both trials in that case, but he had never been sentenced for his Bremer plea pending his testimony in the Hamm trial. Even though Bolton was the chief witness in both Bremer trials he strangely did not inform on his associates in the Hamm case for almost two years while he was held in custody at the Ramsey County Jail in St. Paul. Four days after the FBI announced breaking the Hamm kidnapping, a St. Paul Federal Grand Jury indicted the seven suspects who were still alive based on testimony from Bolton, Bartholmey who waived immunity, and Hamm who had not been blindfolded.[214]

Two weeks after the Hamm indictments were issued, the FBI in New Orleans captured Karpis. They needed to transport him to St. Paul for trial because that is where both kidnappings were committed. Eight hours after Karpis' arrest, agents put him on a 14-passenger charter plane. He was kept heavily-manacled on the flight for the protection of Hoover and Tolson. They took off after midnight and did not arrive until morning because of two fueling stops. Once there Hoover gave his braggadocio press conference before leaving for New York and an evening of gaiety with Tolson.

Agents took Karpis to the St. Paul FBI Office, and kept him shackled as they grilled him. When they began the third degree Karpis had been up 24-hours. This inquisition continued non-stop around the clock for at least two more days during which Karpis was manacled in a single position in a chair and allowed no sleep. Agents proudly kept the press informed about their "secret" interrogation but gave no indication he told them anything. Years later, Karpis said upon his arrival in St. Paul, agents grilled him for four days without sleep while handcuffed to an office radiator. Its clear they got nothing out of him.

Upon the FBI's arrest of Karpis, West Plains, Missouri authorities clamored for him to be turned over for trial. They maintained they had a "hanging case" against Karpis for the callous killing of Sheriff C. R. Kelly more than four years earlier. The Sheriff had walked into a car garage investigating a crime they had not been involved with but Karpis had still shot him dead. Hoover was not concerned with justice or punishment but only adding a notch to his kidnapping statistical charts. It did not matter to the Director that his refusal to relinquish custody would preclude Public Enemy Number 1's execution and likely lead to his parole and freedom some day.

All the Hamm defendants initially pled not-guilty and then one after the other changed their plea to guilty. The first to switch was Bolton who again became the prosecution's star witness. Although he was one of the brutal thugs in both kidnappings, he sent 15 of his underworld pals involved in the two crimes to prison so the Federal Judge rewarded him with four three-year sentences that ran concurrently. With time already served of 20 months and then getting time off for good behavior, he had to serve only a few months. Fitzgerald was the next to plead. Then on the morning that the Hamm trial was to begin, Karpis also pled guilty to conspiracy in return for the kidnapping charges being dropped in both cases so he might be paroled some day. The next day the prosecutor was preparing to deliver his opening address to the jury when Bartholmey pled guilty and agreed to turn state's witness against the only remaining defendant, mastermind Jack Peifer.

During the trial Bolton testified about a personal experience with the case. Eight days after the gang released kidnap victim Hamm, Bolton, Peifer, his wife, and another woman took a flight from St. Paul to Chicago. The two men recognized a fellow passenger as Hamm and knew he had not been blindfolded. Bolton became so nervous that he got off the flight at Madison, Wisconsin and boarded a train headed for Chicago.

Before delivering sentence the Judge asked each defendant if he had anything to say. Karpis replied, "Jack Peifer is absolutely not guilty because I know the circumstances. He had nothing to do with the kidnapping." Fitzgerald also told the court that Peifer was "innocent" and that Bolton's testimony was "false." The Judge than gave Karpis and Fitzgerald life in prison. A week later the Judge gave Peifer a 30-year sentence and had him returned to his cell. The convict refused lunch, and the other prisoners reported that he seemed to be weeping before he fell back on his cot as if in convulsions. A physician assumed the gum found in his mouth was laced with poison.[215]

The first Hamm kidnapping trial also led to tragedy. Remember the four Chicago gangsters were clearly innocent of this crime but framed. While they awaited trial they were housed in the same St. Paul jail that Peifer and his codefendants would be for the second trial. One of the four innocent defendants, Willie Sharkey, was distraught by the injustice of the pending trial and the possible life sentence. In his cell he hung himself with a necktie. The Federal Jury soon found his three codefendants innocent just as Sharkey would have been. This innocent man committed suicide as a result of the false charges Hoover and Purvis turned over to the prosecutor as they functioned like tools for the successor leaders of the Capone gang carrying out their territorial-expansionist agenda. With the two guilty defendants' statements about Peifer's innocence, it is possible that Hoover had two innocent men prosecuted at separate trials for the Hamm kidnapping leading to the suicides of both.

The unsolicited statements that both Karpis and Fitzgerald had given to the judge about Peifer being innocent and about state's witness Byron Bolton committing perjury should have waved red flags. Before studying the specifics in this case it is important to examine the nature of confederate eyewitness testimony. A criminal who turns state's witness against associates is never motivated by any idealistic or public good. He simply wants a sentencing deal, and he knows the only way he can get it is to say what the prosecutor wants to hear no matter what the truth might be. In some cases criminal witnesses have manufactured testimony about events they were not present at. In other cases indicted underworld witnesses have falsely accused someone to settle a personal grudge against an enemy or to protect a friend. Thus it is often difficult to determine the veracity of a criminal accomplice's testimony, making the system dependant on perceptive, competent, and honest detectives and prosecutors to produce justice. However these officials have too often been men of less than stellar ability or character. As problematic as testimony by criminal associates can be, organized-crime gang members could rarely be convicted without such key inside-witness statements.

In the Hamm kidnapping case, part or much of Bolton's testimony may have been manufactured. Some of it seems unlikely, and part was supposedly told to him by his close associate Fred Goetz who had since been slain by Cicero gangsters. Thus Bolton could put any words he or the prosecutor wanted into Goetz' mouth, and the defense attorneys could not properly cross-examine Bolton because he admitted that he was not at the scene and that he did not know any details beyond what he claimed to have heard from Goetz.

This type of testimony is called hearsay evidence because Bolton did not see or participate in the events he described on the stand. Instead he claimed he was repeating information he had heard second hand from another person, in this case Goetz. Courts prohibit hearsay evidence in trials, but there is a major exception. Courts allow hearsay when both the witness giving the testimony, and the person who was the alleged source of the information, were involved together in the furtherance of a criminal conspiracy. When two people are either accomplices in a specific crime or members of the same gang, they are assumed to have a common goal or purpose, so courts deem that they speak for each other. This applies to any criminal behavior they might discuss even if it is about crimes they may not have participated in together. This is why Bolton, who was not involved in the Hamm kidnapping nor even a member of the Karpis-Barkers gang at that time, but who later joined the gang for the Bremer abduction, was allowed to testify about an alleged discussion he had with Goetz concerning the Hamm kidnapping. Under the hearsay exception rule regarding accomplices, this made Bolton part of the entire series of criminal conspiracies the gang was ever involved in, so if other members divulged anything about their own criminal behavior to him, Bolton was allowed to testify about it. This hearsay exception is why organized-crime leaders keep themselves so insulated from their gang members because any conversation an associate overhears can be included in their court testimony.

While perjured testimony is usually devastating to the pursuit of justice, in the Hamm case any lies or fabrications by Burton had no material effect on the jury's decision because his basic testimony was corroborated by other important state's witnesses that included victim Hamm, defendants Farmer and Bartholmey, and the wives of two other cohorts. Their combined testimonies make it extremely unlikely that the claims by Karpis and Fitzgerald about Peifer being innocent were truthful.

At the very moment Peifer was committing suicide in his cell, Karpis and Fitzgerald were being driven under guard to the entrance of Leavenworth Prison. There the guards ordered the two convicts out of the car, manacled them together, and pointed a machinegun at Karpis' back to walk them inside the gate. Once inside heavily-armed guards assembled the duo with Karpis' sidekick Harry Campbell and 17 other prisoners and marched them as a group into an iron-barred railway coach. The three-day journey took them to Oakland, California where they were placed on a launch for transport to their new home, Alcatraz Island Prison. The island had been home to hundreds of pelicans when it was first used as a military fortress named Isla de Los Alcatraces (Island of Pelicans) from which its current name was derived. Awaiting their arrival at the Prison was Doc Barker, but for the first four years Karpis was a resident, inmates were not permitted to talk to each other. Karpis' other associates on the Rock were Deafy Farmer and Volney Davis.

THE ST. VALENTINE'S DAY MASSACRE CONNECTION

Byron Bolton's confessions had other credibility problems, and his background was far more sinister than was indicated by his passive surrender to the FBI the evening he walked out unarmed and with hands in the air at the end of the raid in which agents shot to death Bremer-kidnapping fugitive Russell Gibson. The FBI arrested Bolton for living with the dangerous fugitive, but it does not appear that the FBI or any local jurisdiction had an arrest warrant out for Bolton. As soon as the FBI's arrest of Bolton made the newspapers, the Chicago Police Detective Bureau expressed interest in interviewing him because they had long suspected him in the six-year-old St. Valentine's Day Massacre in which seven Prohibition gangsters were murdered.

Although Chicago detectives had a long list of possible suspects in the atrocious slaughter, they developed strong evidence against only two. One was Bolton and the other was Fred "Killer" Burke. The two were known to be associates on that chilly St. Valentine's Day. Burke was a member of the notorious Egan's Rats in St. Louis, Missouri and Bolton was his chauffeur/bodyguard. Burke and Bolton were linked to Al Capone's Chicago South-Side gang through Rats' alumnus, Claude Maddox, who had become a division leader for Scarface. It is well-established that Maddox's Circus Café was the base where the St. Valentine's Day plot was hatched. His Café was wedged between Capone's two biggest North-Side enemies, the intended target of the Massacre, gang leader Bugs Moran, and the Little Sicily gang.

The roles of Burke and Bolton in the St. Valentine's Day Massacre become clear by understanding the planning and implementation of this horrific slaughter. Capone turned to these two out-of-town Egan's Rats killers because he did not want either his targets or witnesses to recognize the shooters as Caponites when they took out Moran and his key aides at a beer-truck garage that was a favorite meeting place of the gang leaders. Thus he had Bolton and a cohort rent the front apartment across the street from Moran's garage to watch for the gang leaders to rendezvous. For a week they observed each man who entered the garage and compared his facial features to a picture of Moran. Then one day seven of Moran's associates entered the garage individually. From the distance Bolton apparently mistook the seventh man as Moran so he telephoned the waiting seven-man assassination squad that the gang leader had arrived, and they swung into action.

The assassins had two black Cadillacs that were the same model the Chicago Detective Bureau used for its unmarked squad cars. They had equipped both cars with a clanging bell on the running board to look like the real thing. The two fake detective cars went in different directions to the garage so as not to attract undue attention by looking like a raiding team. One of the bogus detective cars carried two men who quietly positioned themselves in the alley behind Moran's garage to kill anyone who tried to run out of the building's back entrance. The other five men drove the other car towards the front entrance of the truck depot. The three who sat in the backseat wore suits like detectives, while the two in the front seat wore patrolman uniforms. One of the two men dressed like a patrolman was Burke who led the assault. When this replica detective car turned onto the street with Moran's garage, it sideswiped a truck, causing witnesses in that block to look at the occupants' faces and write down their license plate number. The five assassins did not slow down at the accident but continued driving directly to the front of the garage and parked outside its entrance. The three killers in suits remained sitting in the backseat waiting, as the two men dressed as patrolmen in the front seat got out and walked into the truck depot. At the moment these two bogus patrolmen were entering, intended target Moran was walking toward the garage. As he rounded the corner at the end of the block, Moran saw the two faux patrolmen go in and assumed he was looking at a standard Prohibition harassment police raid so he turned and walked back to his home a few blocks away.

The two bogus uniformed patrolmen ordered the seven men drinking coffee to line up facing the brick wall with their hands above their heads like this was a routine arrest and weapons' frisk. As Moran's men calmly complied, the three killers in the back seat of the car walked in, pulled out from beneath their overcoats two machineguns and a shotgun, and let go a withering fuselage of hundreds of bullets. One machinegunner sprayed the seven men from left to right while the other machinegunner went from right to left. One aimed at their heads, and the other at heart level. They reversed directions with one aiming at their butts and the other at their knees. The third killer fired a shotgun into the heads of two fallen victims who must have seemed to be still alive. Confident the victims were dead the five assassins walked away from the flowing river of blood towards their parked car. The three shooters in suits put their hands up in the air like they were under arrest as the two uniformed patrolmen took the machineguns and prodded the three in the back as if they were forcing them into the car. Then the five drove away. This was gangland's bloodiest slaughter, and it was quickly dubbed the St. Valentine's Day Massacre.

At the time of the Massacre, Burke was a fugitive running from bank robbery and murder charges in a half dozen states. After the horrific slaughter he eluded police for another two years until an amateur sleuth saw his picture in a detective-story magazine and notified Milan, Missouri police that Burke was living under an assumed name on the nearby farm of his wife's parents. In the middle of the night while everyone in the farmhouse was asleep, eight policemen armed with machineguns burst in and took him without resistance. In examining Burke's seized machineguns, it was found that one had fired some of the bullets taken from the Massacre victims so Chicago detectives showed his photo to witnesses. They identified him as one of the two fake uniformed patrolmen because of a missing front tooth. Of all the jurisdictions that wanted to prosecute Burke, Chicago had the preeminent claim because this was the most shocking slaughter in America's history. The Chicago Prosecutor offered to drop the death penalty if Burke would testify against the planners of the Massacre, but the prisoner rejected the deal. Instead of going ahead and trying Burke on a capital-murder charge as he had said he was going to do, the Chicago Prosecutor inexplicably and without explanation deferred his right to take Burke to trial to St. Joseph, Michigan authorities where he was wanted for killing a policeman during a routine traffic stop, a non-death-penalty case.

The only way to make sense out of the Chicago Prosecutor's inconsistency between his tough public posturing and his weird decision to give up the case is with the following scenario. First it was well known that successive Chicago Prosecutors had sold out their office to Capone because they never once successfully prosecuted any of his major gang members during their tenures. If we speculate for a moment that the Prosecutor's private meeting with Burke went as follows then all the facts fall into place. If the Prosecutor warned Burke that if he ever fingered their mutual employer, his office would institute a death-penalty prosecution against him, but if Burke would plead guilty in Michigan and keep his mouth shut, he would still have the possibility of winning parole some day. Whatever was actually said, within hours the Chicago Prosecutor relinquished his right to try Burke and the prisoner immediately pled guilty to killing the St. Joseph patrolman. Burke was sentenced to life at hard labor and died nine years later in Michigan's Marquette Prison from a heart attack at age 54 before he was eligible for parole. During those nine years of incarceration he never talked to anyone about any of his crimes.

After the Massacre, Chicago detectives learned that two men had rented an apartment across the street a week before to use as a vantage point. In the abandoned room they found a letter addressed to Byron Bolton bearing a postmark from Virden, Illinois. A Chicago detective went to the central part of the state and found Bolton's parent's living on a farm. The father turned over a picture of his son and Massacre witnesses identified him as one of the men who had rented the death-watch room. This was supported in FBI files by two redacted sources who said Bolton was the lookout who had given the gunmen the premature go-ahead to roll in their fake police car. Detectives also learned that Bolton had purchased a machinegun and after the slaughter had run back to his St. Louis base which is where he apparently became associated with the Karpis-Barkers gang after the Bremer kidnapping.

Chicago detectives knew Bolton was guilty in the St. Valentine's Day Massacre, but they claimed they did not issue an arrest warrant because they were afraid of driving the fugitive further underground. The FBI used the same rationale for keeping secret that key Karpis-Barkers gang members had been indicted in the Bremer kidnapping. But the FBI's strategy was effective as agents continued to quietly follow leads nationwide about the fugitives until they killed Gibson, arrested Doc Barker, and killed Fred and Ma Barker. In contrast, the Chicago detectives' silence gave them no way to search outside of Chicago so this subterfuge was a false way of trying to justify simply letting the case die. When the FBI arrested Bolton six years after the Massacre, the Chicago detectives and Prosecutor should have demanded the prisoner be turned over to them to face a capital-punishment case for the worst butchery of all time, especially since the FBI kidnap charges against Bolton involved neither physical harm to a victim nor the death penalty for the perpetrators. But Chicago law enforcement again remained silent. Three years after the FBI arrested Bolton, he was given federal parole for being a state's witness, but the Chicago detectives and Prosecutor failed to prosecute him because they did not want to risk upsetting their gangland masters. Capone's gang had evolved into new leadership but the key men who directed the Massacre were still in power. Capone's gang had bought and paid for this complete and appalling breakdown of the Chicago justice system.

An odd sense of justice in this case might be found in the fact that the Chicago detectives questioned 22 men suspected in connection with the slaughter and all but two of these died violent deaths. Unfortunately it is precisely these two that create the terrible sense of injustice because they were the only ones known for sure to be guilty, and they could have been convicted and executed at any time during this nine-year period. Instead Burke died in prison with parole possible if he had lived long enough, and Bolton lived the rest of his life a free man. Capone, the man who clearly initiated the slaughter, was never questioned because he was well-alibied in Miami when it occurred. Prosecutors could have only gotten to Scarface and his top aides by going through the two suspects they could have convicted with an executable offense – Burke and Bolton.

A major but short-lived battle raged in the press about whether Bolton had given the FBI a confession for the St. Valentine's Day Massacre. While both Director Hoover in Washington and Assistant FBI Director Harold Nathan in St. Paul quickly issued vigorous denials, it is clear they were desperate to win the Hamm and Bremer kidnapping trials and they needed Bolton's state's witness testimony to ensure this. These were powerful motives for these ambitious and unscrupulous FBI officials to quash a confession and terrify the prisoner to keep his mouth shut about other crimes by threatening to rescind his sentencing plea bargain. Challenging the FBI's denials were Chicago's Detective Bureau and diligent newspaper investigative reporters who rarely published false leads. This means they had almost certainly received leaked information from someone in the FBI, but that source's facts may have been inaccurate, or just wrong assumptions, about what Bolton said. It is impossible today to determine whether there was such a confession or not, but the information the detectives and reporters believed was in the confession contained major inaccuracies. This means if such a confession indeed existed and the facts in the newspapers were in it, then Bolton was a huge liar who would say anything about anyone to get off, as he ultimately did with some of his questionable testimony in the three trials for the kidnappings of Bremer and Hamm.[216]

A key participant in the Bremer kidnapping was Fred Goetz. It was his alleged admissions to associate Bolton that Bolton repeated as the state's witness in the two Bremer kidnapping trials to convict the Karpis-Barkers gang members. Goetz and Bolton were both from Illinois, but they got to know each other while working in St. Louis for St. Valentine's Day killer Fred Burke. Goetz started his career as an Army flyer in World War I and then attended the University of Illinois where he was campus director of the American Legion. Two years after graduation he quickly developed a bad arrest record. Employed for the summer as a Clarendon Beach life guard, he was arrested for the attempted rape of a 7-year-old girl. His parents posted a $5,000 bond which he forfeited when he fled. A year later he was sought for attempting to hold up a North Side doctor in his car in front of his home. When the doctor resisted, Goetz wounded him and killed his chauffeur. A Chicago gangster was caught and confessed to this crime, and he named Goetz as an accomplice. Three years later Goetz was charged as one of six robbers of $253,000 in cash and bonds from the Jefferson, Wisconsin Farmers and Merchants Bank and a $5,000 reward was placed on his head. One of the other fugitives in the case was Bugs Moran gangster Gus Winkler. When Chicago detectives began hunting for Goetz and Bolton as participants in the St. Valentine's Day Massacre, Goetz seemed to vanish from existence. Shortly after this a man named J. George Ziegler made his appearance in the underworld.

Goetz had actually begun converting to the alias Ziegler earlier. A year before the Massacre he was arrested in a Prohibition agents' raid of the Riviera Café on the Northwest Side of Chicago.

Under the name Ziegler he was not wanted for any crime so he was let go. For the five years after the St. Valentine's Day Massacre he was not charged with a crime, but late one night as he walked past a closed Cicero restaurant a car drove up to the curb and four shotgun blasts roared out. Goetz/Ziegler was struck in the head killing him instantly. One blast shattered the windows of the next door saloon narrowly missing the owner and several patrons. The car sped off toward Chicago. Whatever illicit business he was in apparently infringed on the Capone gang's territory. Detectives found he carried membership cards in a number of exclusive clubs, but he was only a member of the Mohawk Country Club in Bensenville, Illinois where the kidnapped Hamm and Bremer were held captive. His legitimate cover for neighbors and people he met socially was a card as a salesman for the Suburban Landscaping Company. The address actually belonged to his local gas station where the owner handled his mail delivery as a favor. Goetz possessed blank proxies for United States Steel Corporation shares made out in the names that he and his wife used as aliases. He also had forged American Express money orders. Concealed in the leather belt he wore were six slender but strong steel saw blades to cut through jail bars if arrested.

Then a third identity for Goetz/Ziegler appeared. He lived with his wife in an expensively-furnished lakeside apartment as a cultured gentlemen with sophisticated tastes. The building owner said, "They were fine people. Mr. Seibert seemed to me to be a very brilliant and handsome man. His wife was beautiful. They always seemed to have plenty of money." Under all three names he was always known to be courteous. As one FBI agent wrote in an internal memo, "His character was one of infinite contradictions. Well mannered, always polite, he was capable of generous kindness and conscienceless cruelty." It took a fingerprint check upon his death to prove what no one had ever suspected during his life - the college graduate, the desperado, and the investor were one and the same.[217]

THE IMPACT ON OTHER LIVES

The FBI went after the people who had harbored Karpis including the Hot Springs police. A year after the FBI assaulted Karpis' Hot Springs empty house, the city ousted its three top cops by dismissal or resignation. A year later a Little Rock Federal Trial Jury convicted the former Hot Springs Police Chief, former Chief of Detectives Akers, and his former Detective Lieutenant of harboring Karpis for a year while they were on active duty. In addition they convicted Madam Grace. The Jury fixed all sentences at the maximum of two years.[218]

The St. Paul police safe haven for criminals would be unraveled by state's witness testimony in the Hamm kidnapping trial for lone defendant Peifer. The prosecution's star witness Byron Bolton fingered St. Paul Detective Tom Brown. A decade earlier he had been Police Chief until he was indicted for Prohibition violations and suspended, but when the charges were quashed he was brought back as a detective. He was part of the detail that investigated the Hamm and Bremer kidnappings and also cornered and shot down Homer Van Meter, Dillinger gang lieutenant. Bolton testified that Detective Brown received $25,000 of the $100,000 Hamm kidnapping ransom for informing Peifer about police activities during the brewer's captivity. Immediately after Bolton's disclosures Public Safety Commissioner Gus Barfuss announced Brown would be suspended "without prejudice" pending outcome of the trial. Barfuss stated, "There have been rumors of the association of the police department with St. Paul kidnapping for some time. They have been checked with federal officials who were in a position to divulge information. Brown's name has been mentioned unfavorably in this trial." Since this testimony was presented at trial a month after the three-year statute of limitations expired on the Hamm kidnapping, the information could not be used to prosecute Brown as an accomplice but only fire him. Brown got off solely because FBI Director Hoover failed to do his job and go after a dishonest cop despite often proclaiming this was the most reprehensible of criminals. Hoover could have easily had charges brought against Brown in the kidnapping trial against Peifer, or he could have easily made Bolton and the other state's witnesses available for local officials to prosecute this dishonorable cop.[219]

Another witness against Detective Brown in the Peifer trial was former Police Chief Tom Dahill, who had recently resigned to follow an opportunity in the café business. He corroborated Bolton's testimony that the gang was tipped off on police movements by Detective Brown. The former Chief said, "I had my suspicions in the Bremer case before [U.S.] Attorney General Cummings made his remark [that St. Paul was the "nation's poison spot of crime"]. After I went to Washington my suspicions were strengthened." Dahill went on to explain that he had sent Brown to investigate a report of suspicious characters at a St. Paul address on the day kidnapped brewer Hamm was released. Brown went to the place and returned a half hour later to report that the occupants had no connection with the kidnapping. The former Chief later learned that the place was a hideout of Fred Barker and others of the gang. Bolton's testimony had backed this up when he said that Detective Brown had telephoned Peifer and told him to "get those people out of there."

The former Chief's testimony was followed by Detective Inspector Charles Tierney who was still in charge of the kidnap detail of which Brown was a member. The Detective Inspector told how he, Detective Brown, and Hamm's official ransom-contact man to the gang had gone to the Hamm brewery the night of the kidnapping to select a truck in which to deliver the ransom. The plan was for Detective Tierney to hide in the truck and fire on the kidnappers when they picked up the ransom. But the next day the kidnappers notified Dunn that they had new plans - the money was to now be delivered in a coupe with its doors removed. This testimony was further strengthened by Mrs. Gladys Sawyer, whose husband was already serving a life sentence in Alcatraz for the Bremer kidnapping. She overheard Peifer, who was drunk in Sawyer's saloon, tell her husband, "Me and Tom Brown just cut $36,000." Another gangster's wife testified Peifer encouraged her to take a trip to St. Paul by boastfully stating, "You don't have to be afraid. We've got police protection in St. Paul."

During the next two weeks detectives investigated the Hamm kidnapping trial testimony about Brown and found it all to be true. Detective Brown was fired for conspiring with both the Hamm and Bremer kidnapping groups. He was found to have disclosed confidential information on the movements of the Police Department to Harry Sawyer. Detective Brown was "discharged for inefficiency, breach of duty, misconduct, misfeasance and malfeasance." The St. Paul Police Department went after Detective Brown for protecting Karpis in that city just as the FBI had prosecuted and imprisoned Hot Spring's three top cops for harboring Karpis there. While Karpis' illegal activities caused the closing of two of the country's three fugitive safe havens, this does not mean that local crime bosses in these two cities did not continue to operate illegal gambling under the acquiescence of the new police leaders just as casinos were wide open in or near most other major cities during that era. The only criminal safe haven not taken down for catering to Karpis was Reno, but Graham and McKay were later undone by their own illegal enterprises (detailed in the third book in this history series).[220]

Karpis may have been facing a long prison term but life went on for all the legitimate people he had been close to. Despite his bad boy image and creepy appearance he was never without a woman. When Karpis got out of his earlier prison stretch he lived in Tulsa and married. His former wife later described their relationship. While others might have considered him creepy looking she said, "He was young and good looking and I fell for him hard when I met him at a nightclub. He told me he was a jewelry salesman and we ran off to Sapulpa, just west of here and were married. That was in December 1931. We went to Chicago. I left him after only a few months of married life. I never saw him after that." With a little bitterness she add, "It was in Chicago that I heard

Alvin boast to Freddie Barker that he never would be taken alive. After that he promised me he would 'go straight' but I guess he never did. I always thought that Freddie Barker was a bad influence on Alvin." Four years after their marriage she sued for divorce on the grounds of desertion to separate herself from the infamous Public Enemy Number 1, but she only accomplished making their marriage public knowledge. Two weeks later the business college where she was studying to become a stenographer kicked her out because of her choice in men. She took her maiden name and lived quietly in Tulsa after that but would not identify where she worked because of the stigma attached to her ex.[221]

While no evidence ever existed that Ma Barker was involved with any of her sons' criminal activities, it is clear that she was a doting-mother who enjoyed playing matchmaker. She liked a St. Paul girl named Dolores Delaney and introduced the young woman to her favorite pet, Alvin. Dolores traveled with Karpis for four years until he left her behind to be arrested as he escaped the Atlantic City police. Two weeks later she gave birth in a hospital with FBI agents walking the corridor, and the baby began life living with her in a jail cell. A few weeks later a Federal Court hearing was held in secret out of fear her fugitive boyfriend would attempt to free her during the proceedings. The Court sentenced her to five years in prison for harboring Karpis, and the baby was transported to the care of Karpis' parents. The fugitive had not visited his family during his five years on the run, but after the FBI delivered the him in St Paul for arraignment, his white-haired mother told reporters from their basement apartment that she and her husband planned to visit him within days. "Tell him we will bring his son Raymond along for him to see. He is getting to be a big boy and one to be proud of." The baby was 15-months old when Karpis' parents took him to raise until he was a young man.[222]

Karpis father, John, was a hard-working janitor at a Chicago apartment building. He and his wife Anna spoke broken English and could not read it so their three daughters read them the headline articles about their brother's exploits. The government gave the father his son's car but he could not afford to buy Illinois license plates to replace the ones on it from Arkansas. After three weeks of nonpayment he was fined $6, but no record of what happened to the car could be located. In the midst of this brouhaha, Anna filed a libel suit against *Time Magazine* seeking $100,000 damages for publishing, "Alvin Karpis is a product of Chicago's west side. His mother did time in Kansas, Missouri, and Oklahoma prisons." Her attorneys said she had never been in jail. Nine months later *Time* settled for $2,000 [$29,800 today].

While Karpis was spending his 23rd year in Alcatraz, his 24-year-old son Raymond made the Chicago press as a major thief. He was already on probation on a larceny charge when he and two associates were arrested. A number of tools that could be used in burglaries were found in their car so the next day detectives searched Raymond's apartment to find jewelry, furs, and cases of liquor valued at from $40,000 to $50,000 [today's value is $295,000 to $370,000]. Detectives also seized hundreds of keys that would fit the locks of virtually all autos in Chicago, many keys for turning off burglar alarm systems in stores and trucks, and fictitious license plates. During the seizure of the stolen goods detectives arrested Raymond's wife Nancy, age 22. Also found in the apartment was a letter by Karpis from Alcatraz to Raymond's mother, Dolores, that asked, "What is Raymond doing now? I'll bet he's sleeping all day and working all night." Raymond was charged with burglary but the next record that could be found for him was a year later when he was arrested for a $15,000 burglary of a fur coat, mink stole, and old coins from an expensive apartment when the building engineer identified a picture of Raymond as a man he saw walking in the building carrying a box. Detectives searched his apartment to find the stolen items and a list of addresses of 400 suburban homes which they assumed he had earmarked for burglaries. Detectives also suspected Raymond of another home robbery three days earlier in which $10,000 in furs and jewelry were taken along with a toy French poodle named Renee. The wife and two daughters were attached to the poodle and begged for his return. Raymond and his wife had a poodle themselves, but they refused to help locate the dog unless he were let go. Police were unable to find the pet. No disposition of Raymond's cases could be located.[223]

Both of Karpis' kidnap victims were said to have carried deep emotional scars from their horrifying and seeming endless captivities with each second passing slowly in their trapped confinement, but both lived long lives. Karpis' second kidnap victim, Bremer, lived for 31 years after he was kidnapped. He was swimming at his winter residence in Pompano Beach near Fort Lauderdale, Florida when he had a heart attack. Karpis was in the 29th year of prison confinement. His first kidnap victim, Hamm, lived 37 years after he was abducted. He had been ill for several weeks when he died at 87.[224]

Upon his release from captivity Hamm took legal action to recover his father's ransom money payment that could be traced. Hamm brought suit to recover $8,000 from a Waukegan safe deposit box owned by Fitzgerald and also sued to obtain a $1,000 bank note that Karpis had asked Miami's El Commodoro Hotel Manager Joe Adams to hold for him. Karpis signed an affidavit in Alcatraz contesting this claim by saying he had obtained the note legally. Records of the disposition of these two suits could not be located.

Karpis' 26 years in Alcatraz were the most time any prisoner ever spent on the Rock. He was transferred to McNeil Island Penitentiary in Washington for another seven years. He became eligible for parole 15 years into his term and he applied for parole every year from then on. However Hoover personally opposed each parole request. The U.S. Parole Board rejected Karpis' first 18 annual requests, but after serving 33 years of his life sentence he was finally paroled and deported at age 62. Guards took him directly from prison to an airport with plane tickets to his native Montreal. He was banned from returning to the U.S. unless he wanted to complete his sentence for parole violation.

Karpis had been sent to Alcatraz months after it opened and remained until months before U.S. AG Robert Kennedy ordered the island prison closed because it was costing $48,000 a year per inmate. This prompted Creepy Karpis to quip, "At that rate they could have put us up in hotel suites in San Francisco." The old fortress prison was then turned into a popular tourist attraction. During tours each visitor was allowed to stand in one of the small 5-by-9-feet concrete cells while the doors slammed shut and locked. This was stopped in 1981 after 50 visitors were trapped in the cells for six hours by a malfunction giving them a whole new appreciation for the concept of getting locked up. At least each visitor had his or her own metal toilet, but alas no toilet paper.[225]

Karpis had been a callus criminal but he seemed to have mellowed in that cramped cell over the years. Upon his release a prison official said at both prisons he had been a model prisoner and a good role model for the younger prisoners. The official said, "He straightened out a lot of punks both in the McNeil Prison and at Alcatraz." Karpis told reporters his sales pitch to the younger offenders was blunt, "I was Public Enemy Number 1. Look what it did for me." An editorial in the *Baltimore Sun* describes Karpis taking full responsibility for his actions. He told the reporter, "I picked up the gun because I had no better sense. I have no one to blame but myself." The editorial continued, "It is a remarkable statement to be made in these times. Karpis doesn't blame his parents or evil companions. He doesn't blame society or chromosomes or environment. He doesn't say his fate was predetermined by forces over which he had no control and that he was therefore the helpless victim of a malign fate. He says he became a criminal because he had no "better sense," and he takes – if we are to believe him – personal moral responsibility for the behavior for which he was punished." The killer of more than a half dozen people told a group of reporters that he avoided watching several of *The FBI* television-series programs because, "A lot of people I knew were in it and I didn't want to see them slaughtered."[226]

After Karpis settled in Montreal, he announced to the press that he and his gang had robbed a bank in Fort Scott, Kansas early in his career, and a man who had been jailed for it over the past 37 years was neither part of his gang nor involved in the holdup. Assuming Karpis was telling the truth the only justifiable reason he would have had for waiting so long was that he wanted to be pardoned and out of the reach of the U.S. judicial system before confessing to any more crimes. Frank Sawyer (no relationship to Harry Sawyer above) and three associates were arrested on the day of the bank robbery sitting in a car on the side of a road 20 miles east of Fort Scott across the state line near Nevada, Missouri. Sawyer was convicted and given a 20-to-100-year sentence. A year later he escaped from the Lansing Penitentiary in Kansas. Then he was arrested and convicted of murder in Oklahoma and after serving his time was turned over to Kansas to complete his sentence for the bank robbery. Based on Karpis' confession, the Kansas Board of Probation and Parole investigated Sawyer's case. Both the Governor's Pardon Attorney and the current Fort Scott Prosecutor said at the Parole Board hearing they believed Sawyer did not participate in the robbery and the Governor pardoned him. Sawyer walked out of prison at 70-years old. He may have been innocent but he was not a sympatric victim of injustice since he and the three other men sitting in the car were plotting to rob a bank in Rich Hill, Missouri 20 miles to the north. Had he not been arrested for the one bank heist, he admitted he would have robbed a different bank that day. This is just one more example of how difficult it is to accurately identify which crimes the various major bad men did and did not commit.[227]

Karpis lived in Montreal for four years and then moved to Torremolinos, Spain on the Costa del Sol (sun coast). He lived alone and quietly in an apartment for the next six years until he died at age 71 possibly from taking sleeping pills while drinking alcohol. He was looking forward to the publication of his second book *On The Rock*. The man J. Edgar Hoover called "a dirty yellow rat" had retorted bitterly, "I made that son of a bitch" when the Director falsely claimed he had led the arresting FBI team. To this day the name J. Edgar Hoover is boldly emblazoned over the entrance to the Washington FBI Office Building representing everything the FBI should never have been and should never become again.[228]

SWIMMING WITH DOC BARKER

A year before Karpis became an inmate at Alcatraz, Doc Barker had preceded him there. As Doc took the boat ride across the Bay from San Francisco to the Rock, he started devising an escape plan. From a few locations within the prison inmates saw a magnificent view of San Francisco. This tantalizing panorama led 36 men to try to escape during the federal prison's 29-year existence. Guards caught 30 of these on the solid-rock island, shooting 14 to death and quickly capturing the 16 others. Only one escaped and lived to tell about it. Wearing water wings made from blown up surgical gloves, he swam two-and-one-half miles southwest to Ft. Point near the Golden Gate Bridge. Upon reaching the rocky shore, the exhausted fugitive collapsed and lay shivering on the rough surface as police grabbed him and put him on a launch for a ride to solitary confinement. Still dressed in prisoner garb he was apparently hopeful of thumbing a ride across the Bridge out of the area because Ft. Point was a much longer swim from Alcatraz than Fisherman's Wharf which was one-and-one-half miles directly south of the prison.

One-and-one-half miles may not seem like an impossible distance for an athletic man to swim, but the Bay currents flowing out to sea under the Golden Gate were almost too powerful for the greatest of swimmers in top physical condition to overcome. In addition the water temperature fluctuated between the low and high 50s depending on the season and prisoners had no access to insulated wet suits. This is why five prisoners were never found. One pair tried it three years into the prison's existence and a trio attempted it a year before it closed. The fact no one ever heard from or about any of these five escapees makes it extremely likely their drowned bodies were floated out to the Pacific by the treacherous Bay currents. Had they lived, they probably would have been arrested for new crimes, been turned in by associates for plea bargains, or years later sold their escape stories to magazines or book authors As the first pair made their afternoon escape two years into Doc Barker's residency he watched their flight from a window. As they swam from the Rock, he saw them suddenly pulled underwater and lose hold of their empty five-gallon can buoys. Doc decided to repeat their escape route to the water's edge but he planned to traverse the difficult strait successfully. It would take him and his four cohorts a year of planning and preparing to be ready to go.

The prison assigned Doc Barker to work in the mat shop where convicts converted used tires into door mats. He developed loyalties with a few of the most dangerous prisoners working in the shop and while on the job they made their plans and preparations. To get away with this Doc established absolute rule over the operation of the shop. His gang used threats of violence to cower the other convict workers into silence. Despite their bullying Doc was concerned a few might squeal about his escape plans, so his gang members kept them in a state of terror until they requested transfers to other jobs. Doc could not stop them from talking, but he could keep them from learning any more about his plans.

The workers wore dust masks while cutting tires and the gang modified these into underwater breathing masks by adding a rubber tube to each one. Some of the used tires contained a rubber inner tube and these were converted into pairs of buoyant water wings. Each of the five plotters had to cut through several steel bars in his cell to make the opening wide enough to get his hips through them and then do the same with the other sets of bars that lay in their escape path. Each bar was about three-quarters of an inch in diameter. The schemers created a small pressure jack with concave round ends the width of the circular bars to forcibly press against each bar. They would place the jack between the target bar and the bar on one side to bend it in the opposite direction. Then they would place the jack between the target bar and the bar on the opposite side to bend the bar back in the opposite direction. They would repeat this back and forth maneuver over and over until the target bar cracked. Then they put the cut piece back in its original place, puttied the cut ends, and painted these patches the same color as the metal bars.

Since none of the prisoners were experienced swimmers they planned on building one large raft for the five of them to lay on and paddle with their arms. They intended to build the raft from the driftwood hitting against the edge of the rocks at the shoreline. Around the Rock, logs, boxes, old masts, and other flotsam drifted about. Warden James Johnston later said, "There is driftwood all the time. Sometimes there are large pieces, at other times only small bits. And there are prisoners who spend all their time thinking about escape." They planned to lash the pieces of wood together with cloth strips torn from their bed sheets. This raft was meant to help keep them afloat and also to keep most of each one's skin out of contact with the water to increase the amount of time before hypothermia would set in.[229]

When the five felons had everything prepared, they waited for a night with fog to help hide their movement on the Rock from the guard towers and roving spot lights. When that night arrived each laid quietly in bed until a guard completed D-Block's 3 a.m. bed check. Then the five plotters grabbed their bed sheets, let themselves through their cell bars, and opened the prepared sets of bars along the way to escape out of the building. As they ran along their path, they filled their sheets with lumber they had previously hidden from the shop. From the bluffs of the fog shrouded island they descended the steep rocky slopes to the water's edge. That early morning the tides supplied plenty of driftwood but they were small pieces making it harder to build a strong raft. Then they stripped off their prison garb, bundled up their clothing, and laid it atop their rafts. All they wore were their socks for a little protection against the hard sharp rocky ground surfaces.

When Doc had watched the two escapees a year earlier disappear under the water and never resurface he learned about the mighty undertow. But none of these five convicts was prepared for the powerful waves and really cold water. All five were stunned by what they encountered because none had ever walked on an ocean beach or dipped a toe into the surf. They had no choice but to push on because they knew they would probably never have a second chance. After building their raft they pushed off from the rock shore, but one escapee had a full-blown panic attack from the cold water and the bouncing rickety raft. He announced to the others that he did not know how to swim. When he went bonkers they were already half a football field out into the Bay. They rotated the raft and headed back to shore where they added more wood to increase the mass and stability of the raft. Then they boldly set off again. This time they got twice as far before the non-swimmer's renewed panic attack and desperate begging convinced the other four to return to further fortify their still unsound raft.

An hour had gone by and a guard was now conducting the 4 a.m. bed count. When he found five empty cells with severed bars he telephoned his Lieutenant. He flipped on the escape sirens and turned on the prison's powerful searchlights, but they could not penetrate far into the fog which was the thickest in years. The Warden described it as "like a mass of wool." He dispatched guards armed with rifles and machineguns from inside the Prison to spread out over the island. He also made calls to the Coast Guard and the San Francisco Police Department which rushed a police boat to the scene to join the prison launch in circling the island with their spotlights focused on the shoreline. Every effort to capture the escapees was badly hindered by the dense fog.

In the meantime, the butt naked convicts were hard at work strengthening their raft. The escape sirens were wailing, but the fugitives were oblivious because the sounds were drowned out by the roaring waves, bellowing wind, and blaring foghorn. Two convicts were diligently reinforcing the raft while the other three walked over the rocks searching for more wood to bring them.

Prison guards walking the Rock through the dense fog finally heard voices, and then the patrolling prison launch lit up the two escapees working on the raft. Guards riding the patrol boat ordered the pair to halt but the desperate escapees kept right on feverishly attaching more wood. The order to fire was given. Barker was shot in the forehead near his right eye and in the thigh, and the other escapee hit in both legs. After hearing the shooting, two more fugitives were suddenly scanned by the launch's searchlight and immediately surrendered. The only African-American escapee had separated from the others in his zeal to collect more pieces of driftwood. When guards on foot approached him, he tried to slide down the rock slope but he went over a cliff falling onto the rocks below. He laid sprawled near the water, and the bruised and cut escapee welcomed capture by the guards who descended after him. Guards loaded the two wounded escapees onto the launch which took them to the dock for medical treatment by the prison physician. The guards marched the other three escapees, naked except for their tattered socks, back up to the prison. None of these three was yet suffering from exposure so they were placed in dark isolation cells. Barker lost much blood from his thigh wound, but he also had a major brain hemorrhage indicated by a large amount of blood in his spinal fluid. Twelve hours after being shot he died and the official cause was listed as "Fracture of Skull." All four of Ma Barker's sons died by gunshot in separate instances and so did she near her son Freddie.

One document soon surfaced that made Alcatraz Prison officials look derelict in their duty. The Warden had received a letter outlining Doc Barker's planned escape. Across the top of the letter the Warden had written to a subordinate, "Check very carefully." Unfortunately prison officials made no record of the investigation. Here are the available facts. The letter was written by mat shop foreman Frank Gouker who was in prison for forgery, and he had obtained his position because the staff had confidence in him. He had written frequent letters to the Warden begging for an early parole, for a transfer to a prison closer to home, or for help for his wife and partner in crime, Anna, who was destitute in the Great Depression. In the letter about Barker's planned escape, most of it was devoted to begging for a transfer because his snitching was going to get him assassinated by the gang, and also to scary claims that the gang planned to cover their escape tracks by killing specific prison officials and African-American prisoners in the process. Crime historians who have mentioned this letter have left out the most significant fact - it was dated a year before the escape. Obviously during the following year these plotters had done nothing that aroused the staff's suspicions. Most notably the gang did not commit any of the violence Gouker feared was aimed at him, other prisoners, and prison officials. In addition one of the five escapees was African-American.[230]

THE LAS VEGAS STRIP CONNECTION

One more connection exists between these bank-robbing Public Enemies Number 1 and Nevada's casinos but to understand this the development of the Tommy Gun is relevant. This weapon was the World War I brainchild of General John T. Thompson who was U.S. Army Acting Chief of Ordinance. He wanted to develop an automatic rifle for trench fighting, but the war ended before he finished his weapon. Months before Prohibition began the Thompson Company began production of his weapon with the assistance of a financier. The intended market was the military and law enforcement, but its potential to spray nearby innocent civilians made it too powerful a weapon for law enforcement to use in trying to control crowds or in gun battles against pistols.

A third of the way through Prohibition, at the south end of Chicago, two small beer gangs were warring. One of the leaders was Ed "Spike" O'Donnell. One day he was standing and talking to a newsboy in front of a drugstore when a sedan pulled up. O'Donnell grabbed the boy and leaped to the pavement slamming the boy with him. From the sedan a machinegun sprayed the brick wall behind where both had just been standing. This weapon was a gangster's dream – light and concealable with awesome firepower. Soon the head of Al Capone's enforcement and bodyguard division made this his weapon of choice, and he quickly became infamous as "Machinegun" Jack McGurn. The first market for the Tommy Gun was some of the Prohibition gangs which forced local law-enforcement agencies to buy them to combat these goons. Eight years later the Kansas City Massacre caused the FBI to begin purchasing them. During the last third of Prohibition, which was also the first half of the Great Depression, Thompson's machinegun became the preferred weapon by a wave of Midwestern bank robbers making more law-enforcement departments carry them to match these criminals' firepower. The total criminal and law enforcement purchases were relatively small so the Thompson Company's initial inventory was not exhausted for two decades until World War II when the world's armies started buying the weapons in substantial quantities. After the War, sales again lagged until right-wing domestic extremists and foreign drug dealers became important markets.[231]

Public Enemies Number 1, Dillinger and Karpis, purchased the machineguns their gangs used to rob banks and shoot it out with lawmen from Chicagoan Joey Aiuppa. As a young man he had gone to work for Machinegun McGurn. He kept many of his shooters employed fulltime as bodyguards surrounding Capone in large rings. Aiuppa had the honor of standing near the notorious Scarface to hold his coat. McGurn transferred Aiuppa to work as an enforcer for division-leader Claude Maddox who headquartered at the Circus Café. This is where McGurn planned and directed the St. Valentine's Day Massacre plot while Capone was well-alibied at his Miami mansion. Aiuppa later rose to head the gang's gambling and vice operations in Cicero and Chicago's western suburbs. In 1956, Aiuppa and Maddox were convicted for the manufacture and distribution of gambling devices. Their Taylor Manufacturing Company of Cicero produced legal dice and roulette wheels but their crime was their proprietary Trade Booster that assisted illegal gambling on slot machines. This was an electronic device that could be attached to a legal free-play slot machine allowing it to record accumulated payoffs for cash, merchandise, or free plays without the attention-attracting noisy clang of payout coins into the machines' metal trays. Each of the retail outlets that used Trade Boosters also had a copy of a legal opinion upholding the device's legality signed by Illinois Attorney General Latham Castle. This document was used by proprietors to reassure suspicious police officers but as you might expect the AG's signature on it was forged.[232]

Three years after Aiuppa's Trade Booster conviction, the U.S. Senate Rackets Committee chaired by Democratic Senator John McClelland called him as a key witness. The hearings were about the Chicago-based International Hotel and Restaurant Employees and Bartenders Union and the powerful control exercised by the Chicago gang and specifically Aiuppa who was a behind-the-scenes leader. His role with this union began at the time Aiuppa was supplying machineguns to Karpis and Dillinger, when he had become head of the Cicero bartenders union local. During this period the gang forcibly took over a number of unions through threats of violence and the murders of a number of leaders. To counteract this violence by Capone's gang, some union officials lined up armies of bodyguards to fend off the gang's killers, and one of the union's hired guns just happened to be Baby Face Nelson before he became a Public Enemy Number 1 bank robber.

Over the years Aiuppa rose to top leadership in the International Union of hotel workers that represented most of the resort employees on the Las Vegas Strip. Aiuppa was questioned by the McClelland Committee's Chief Counsel Bobby Kennedy about plundering the union treasuries, demanding under-the-table kickbacks from unionized companies to avoid strikes and for sweetheart contracts that ripped off the members they represented in contract negotiations, and for violently extorting companies that were not unionized. To every question Aiuppa invoked the Fifth Amendment. Kennedy was most annoyed about Aiuppa's refusal to answer whether he had tried to drive over the Rackets Committee's Investigator James Kelly when he tried to serve a subpoena at the gangster's home. Kelly only survived Aiuppa's attack by leaping to the side of the oncoming car.

A little more than a decade after these hearings, Aiuppa became leader of the Chicago Mafia gang. He and Tony Accardo were about the last surviving members from Capone's Prohibition Era. While Aiuppa had been Scarface's coat holder, Accardo sat outside Capone's suite of hotel rooms with a machine gun cradled in his arms. As gang leader, Aiuppa with Accardo's approval directed the events that are depicted in the movie *Casino* (1995). But the many incredible untold stories about these events are for the next volume of this historical series.

It is finally time to study the Kansas City Massacre. All the pertinent facts that were developed by the local police, the FBI, and the press at that time, as well as crime historians since, have already been presented. However, there were a multitude of relevant facts available that no one until this research realized related to this case. These facts are assembled and analyzed in the following cold-case examination, and they reveal for the first time who actually ordered this slaughter of lawmen and who the three shooters were. The meaning behind the events in this case can only be understood by examining them in the political/criminal cultural context of Kansas City where they occurred. "And now for the rest of the story" circa Paul Harvey.

Chapter 12

WHO WERE THE MASSACRE SHOOTERS?

KANSAS CITY'S MAFIA GANG

The events surrounding the Kansas City Massacre cannot be understood without first examining the unique connection between the city's Mafia gang and the dominant Democratic political machine that was headed by the Pendergast family for three generations. In a number of other major American cities the governing Democratic or Republican political machine had close ties with the leadership of organized crime, but Kansas City was unique because the Pendergasts were actually under the direct influence of this Mafia gang.

Surprisingly the press and the public never talked about the existence of a Mafia gang in the city. The gang's leaders were referred to as *Party leaders* by the machine's Democratic supporters, and derogatorily as *Party Bosses* by the machine's Republican opposition. The newspapers invariably attached one of these two titles whenever mentioning the names of the Mafia gang's leaders as if their profession was politics instead of gangsterism.

This story has never been thoroughly told because the political historians who concentrated on Harry Truman's presidency lacked the background about the underworld to realize the political machine's leaders who put him into office were the local Mafiosi. Similarly crime historians who wrote about the Kansas City Massacre were not grounded in the city's political and law-enforcement chain of command. Since these historians lacked full knowledge of this whole interweaved political/criminal set up, they made incorrect assumptions about how, who, and why the Massacre occurred. It is now possible to finally solve this horrific crime by first understanding how the city's small Mafia gang and the dominating Pendergast political machine merged into a single entity.

The development of America's big-city crime gangs is related to the nation's immigration patterns. The vast majority of immigrants came to the United States seeking opportunity from political oppression or bad economic times, and they typically settled in low-income neighborhoods in large cities where the culture and language were familiar. They started their new lives working at the lowest paying jobs.

By the early 1800s adolescent delinquents in America's poor ethnic enclaves formed small tightly-knit professional street gangs. These career criminals preyed upon their fellow countrymen with a variety of crimes. These thugs profited from snatching purses, grabbing produce from street carts, shoplifting, burglary, strong-arm robbery, shakedowns of their fellow countrymen, extorting "protection" money from merchants, loan sharking, and operating gambling establishments and brothels. Some of these street gangs insulated themselves from criminal prosecution by paying bribes to police in the local precincts and doing the bidding of shady politicians in their district who had the power to tell the police and judges responsible for their areas to give a wink and a nod to favored criminals' activities. Many of these professional street gangs showed up en mass at polling stations in their districts and threatened those voters who objected to filling out their ballots while being observed in their private voting booths. Other gangs operated political clubs that assisted the neighborhood residents who had financial or job-related problems so the gang was able to deliver a large block of their fellow countrymen's votes on election day. In return the winning officials rewarded the gangs with law-enforcement immunity in their district during their term in office.

For a half century the biggest immigrant groups entering America every year were Germans followed by Irish. But beginning around 1890 and continuing for three decades East European Jews and Italians became the two largest groups of arrivals annually. In Kansas City, Missouri these mainland Italian and Sicily Island immigrants settled in Little Italy, also known as the Columbus Park area, in the northeast of town. In the early 1900s a small Sicilian Mafia gang formed in this area and committed the standard crimes.

With the advent of Prohibition, America's professional street gangs were handed the opportunity for unprecedented profits, but they had to either manufacture moonshine or import fine legitimate liquor from foreign countries. These small street outfits quickly expanded into major organized-crime gangs to operate their huge new liquor enterprises. The Mafioso who rose to lead the Kansas City Mafia gang during Prohibition was Johnny Lazia.

He had been named John Lazzio by his Italian immigrant parents who lived in Little Italy. He quit school after finishing the eighth grade to become a criminal. His juvenile arrests included petty theft and gambling. Then at age 18 an armed robbery got him a 12-year sentence at the Missouri State Penitentiary. Because America was facing the possibility it could be drawn into World War I that was raging in Europe, courts sometimes allowed selected prisoners to enlist and serve their country instead of serving time. Less than nine months after entering prison, Lazia was released to enter boot camp. Instead he headed back home to return to his life of crime.

Lazia went on to develop extensive gambling and Prohibition operations. The size of his rumrunning activities were made public a decade into Prohibition. Bribes insulated him from local police interference, but a large raid by Federal Prohi Agents and Deputy Marshals arrested Lazia and two dozen of his subordinates. Also arrested was Kansas City's Delinquent Tax Collector as she sat in her office at City Hall. This is where she kept the books for Lazia's illicit liquor trade and agents seized the complete set. They showed that the Mafioso controlled the city's wholesale liquor business supplying virtually every speakeasy, restaurant, and bootlegger in town. He also distributed to major retailers throughout the state and he delivered freight train car loads in six nearby states. As an aside Lazia manufactured ginger ale and anyone wanting to be in right with his Democratic organization in the North Side Italian district was a good customer for this brand.

Unlike many American Mafia gang leaders who lived unpretentiously and with a low profile, Lazia conspicuously displayed his success. He and his wife dressed expensively, and in addition to their luxurious apartment they had a fashionable home at Lake Lotawana 25 miles southeast of town. His demeanor was nothing like a movie-style thug but rather that of a respectable businessman. Claiming to be a soft-drink distributor, the trim 140-pounder had a mild, soft-spoken professional manner and wore thick rimless glasses to cope with glaucoma. The bespectacled Lazia had a deceptively benign appearance. With his illegal businesses doing well, he started developing political influence with his Little Italy neighbors, and this endeavor would cause him to bump heads with the city's well-established Democratic political machine.[233]

THE ULTIMATE POLITICAL DYNASTY

The Pendergast machine ranked among the country's most powerful. This Kansas City political dynasty was begun by Jim Pendergast whose Irish fellow countrymen had preceded the influx of Italian immigrants and established their imprint on the city's culture. Jim worked as a puddler in an iron foundry until 1881 when he bet on a long-shot racehorse named Climax. The nag won and paid handsomely so he quit his job and bought a saloon and a small hotel in the West Bottoms, west of downtown. This was the feeding place for the Kansas City Stockyards.

Jim Pendergast was a quiet, soft-spoken man who remained in the shadows and avoided personal publicity. He worked his way up the ranks of the Democratic Party in his district by turning out the votes. He advocated for the working man, helped people find jobs, and saw needy people had enough coal and food. A decade after buying the saloon Jim was elected Alderman for the West Bottoms. Less than a decade later at the turn of the century, "Pendergast controlled the mayor's office, the street and fire departments and dominated the police force. Pendergast named (specified the hiring of) 123 of the 173 police officers on the force."[234]

After Jim's brother, Tom, finished college he went to work at the saloon as a handy man and bouncer. Tom's size undoubtedly helped him keep the peace as his frame was shaped like a newspaper cartoonist's girthy-pear political boss. His figure also fit the image of the political powerhouse he would become. Older brother Jim taught Tom the advantages of controlling a large block of voters and how to get out the vote and to steal elections. Tom jumped passionately into grassroots politics, developed greater skills than his brother, and used them more ruthlessly. Tom kept receiving appointments to higher-ranking positions within the city's Democratic Party and then appointments to increasingly higher-paying local government jobs.

When elder brother Jim was dying in 1911, he turned over his liquor business and political mantle to his brother Tom who the year before had succeeded him as First Ward Alderman. Older brother Jim had carved his neighborhood into an important faction in city politics, but Tom soon expanded his influence into surrounding Wards and within five years was the most powerful Democrat in Kansas City. Tom won over his constituency by integrating their financial needs with his voting machine. As he explained it, "What's government for if it isn't to help people? They're interested only in local conditions - not about the tariff or the war debts. They've got their own problems. They want consideration for their trouble in their house, across the street or around the corner -paving, a water main, police protection, consideration for a complaint about taxes. They vote for the fellow who gives it to them. If anybody's in distress, we take care of them - especially in the poor wards. If they need coal or clothes, or their rent is overdue, we help them out - in and out of [political] season. We never ask about politics." The poor typically have much lower voting rates than the other economic demographic groups, but Tom turned them into a powerful loyal voting block as his ward heelers doled out whatever special assistance they needed including food baskets and help with medical bills. To this assistance program, Tom added his exceptional people skills. As he said, "I know all the angles of organizing and every man I meet becomes a friend. I know how to select ward captains and I know how to get to the poor. Every single one of my ward workers has a fund … and when a poor man comes to old Tom's boys for help we don't make one of those investigations like these city charities."[235]

Besides doling out assistance to the needy, Tom Pendergast and his ward heelers also dispensed thousands of city, county, and state patronage jobs, as well as special actions to favor seekers. Jobs became especially important during the Great Depression. By then Tom had his cronies were well entrenched in the state administration in Jefferson City. This allowed him to control Missouri's appointments to the statewide Federal Re-employment Program, Federal Work Relief Program, and Federal Civil Works Administration. Favored businesses received lucrative government contracts and tax breaks. Disgruntled businesses were restrained from complaining loudly because their property taxes might take a big jump. The beneficiaries of jobs and contracts became enthusiastic supporters at election time allowing Tom to maintain his power. He kept his unseemly conduct fairly well hidden so he actually achieved an image of respectability for his efforts to reinvigorate the economy during the Great Depression.

Tom helped many people and businesses, but he always saw to it that the companies he owned or controlled, like the Ready Mixed Concrete Company, were awarded all prime government building contracts. He was the most corrupt man in the history of Kansas City. During the Great Depression his machine ensured passage of a $40 million bond [$600 million today] for construction of civic buildings. The new buildings included a city hall, a Jackson County Courthouse, a Municipal Auditorium, the Kansas City Power & Light building, a Blue River flood-protection program, and parks improvements. He was the biggest beneficiary of this largess, but this program is also credited with helping the city survive the national financial collapse. In those tough times the unemployed lined up a long way to the entrance of his office daily to obtain a job referral to various agencies and projects.

Tom Pendergast became so powerful that many citizens cynically referred to the city as Tom's Town since everyone knew the actual seat of government was the Jackson Democratic Club in the modest office headquarters of Ready Mixed Concrete. This was the most important address in town. From this Mecca every morning Tom decided who would be governor, U.S. Senator, judge, and dog catcher. For these various elected offices, he controlled the Democratic Party's endorsement, campaign funding, and voter base. He also directed subordinates, dealt with businessmen, and dispensed to those needing favors.

Tom Pendergast helped many but his benevolence was always calculated to make him the ultimate beneficiary. He was ambitious, intimidating, and ruled with an iron hand that could be ruthless. The rotund former bouncer was known on occasion to use his fists to knock someone he disagreed with to the floor of his modest office. He demanded absolute loyalty from the candidates he supported and total devotion from his precinct workers who dealt daily with voters' concerns in their districts so they could ensure a large turnout for elections. Tom's large devoted constituency voted and demonstrated upon demand. At the height of Tom's power a Kansas City Federal Grand Jury issued a scathing report about the rotten conditions "under which individuals, and business firms as well, were afraid to oppose the machine for fear of being run out of business, closed up, intimidated in various ways, and even afraid of their lives." The Judge concurred.[236]

Despite having a solid voter base, Tom was never satisfied with a legitimate vote as he made a wretched mockery of democracy. On election days, his staff mobilized the flop houses by registering vagrants, giving them a hot meal, and showing them how to vote at the polls. Ward workers told their constituents to vote early and often. Then they drove them to the polls after giving them identities of the deceased from tombstones, of the incarcerated in prison, or of fictitious persons. A miraculous number of people rose from the dead to vote the Pendergast slate. Or as cynics said at election time, "Now is the time for all good cemeteries to come to the aid of the Party." Samplings of voting logs demonstrate that some people used their real names in voting over and over. Thugs and sometimes the cops prowled the voting booths intimidating honest voters and beating up those who resisted voting the machine's line. Republicans who were allowed to vote pencil marked their ballots as hard as they could to make it difficult for Pendergast's minions to rub them out and change their ballots. Pendergast overcame this by switching legitimate ballot boxes with fraudulent ones, or having his machine supporters who acted as election judges fill out falsified vote tallies.

Tom Pendergast's get-out-the-vote practices evolved into fraud, bribery, intimidation, and cases of murder. He did not pioneer any of these illicit techniques, but he was the nation's greatest practitioner of them. His ability to turn out the vote was phenomenal. Many wards approached 100% turnout, and some actually exceeded this number as so many ghost voters showed up. This allowed Pendergast to turn out winning margins of more than 100,000 votes in Jackson County for statewide candidates to give them victory. This made him the dominant political force in Kansas

City, the county, and the state. As unrealistic as these voting results were, many citizens were satisfied with the system because of his handouts.

Citizens who considered Tom Pendergast to be the biggest crook in town decried his control over Police Department appointments. They complained to successive Governors and to State Legislators. The state finally created a State Board of Police Commissioners to be appointed by the Governor to direct the Kansas City Police Department. This led Tom to expand into state politics in order to elect Governors who would appoint the Police Commissioners he selected. Then he had the police allow wide-open brothels in the city. It was years before Kansas City's municipal government would be returned to home rule of its Police Department. But it made little difference to Tom who controlled the appointments whether they were made by the Governor or the City Manager.

Under Tom Pendergast's rule, the 14 years of Prohibition came and went without anyone in Kansas City taking notice that Congress had either passed the Constitutional Amendment and law or then repealed them. Prohibition simply did not exist in the city as the bars remained open and the booze flowed unhindered. The Kansas City Federal Prosecutor was on Pendergast's payroll and he never prosecuted anyone for a felony under the Volstead Act. This led *Omaha Herald* Editor George Miller to remark, "If you want to see some sin, forget about Paris. Go to Kansas City."[237]

PARTNERSHIP OF A CRIME LORD & A POLITICAL KING

Pendergast's long-time North Side Ward Captain was fellow countryman Mike Ross. He had become the district's political leader when it was an Irish enclave, but the second generation of residents moved up the socio-economic ladder and out of the neighborhood as the Italians moved in when they became the country's newest large immigrant group. Eventually Ross also moved out of the neighborhood. This made him an absentee political boss relying on his Italian lieutenants to handle the problems of the area's residents.

After Mafia leader Lazia had established political influence with his fellow countrymen in Little Italy, he violently challenged Ross' leadership for the whole First Ward it was part of. As the 1928 election approached, Lazia threatened community leaders to force them to form political alliances with him, and he turned public opinion against the distant Ross. Then on election day Lazia ordered his gang to kidnap three of Ross' Italian lieutenants. A week into their captivity these lieutenants swore allegiance to Lazia, and Ross abdicated his throne, surrendering his North Side Democratic Club to the Mafia leader.

Pendergast was distressed by the violent overthrow of his long-time comrade, but it has long been said that politics makes strange bedfellows. Lazia was now in the position to deliver the North Side vote to whichever candidates he chose, so Pendergast embraced the Mafioso as his new Ward political leader and a major player in his machine apparatus. Their arrangement was simple. Lazia would continue to totally support Pendergast's candidates and political agenda but there was now a quid quo pro. Pendergast's political machine would become the law-enforcement protector of Lazia's Mafia criminal empire.

The Kansas City power structure became a triumvirate with Pendergast as the political kingmaker, his puppet City Manager Henry McElroy as the administrator, and Lazia as the totally insulated Mafia leader. Lazia agreed to stomp down on violent exploitive crimes by some of his gang members and other criminals in return for having unbridled right to wide-open Prohibition liquor, gambling, and brothels.

In what can only be described as a takeover of the Police Department, the City Manager appointed Lazia's chosen candidate as Police Chief. Through him the Mafia leader controlled who the police hired, promoted, and arrested, allowing him to control and direct all crime in Kansas

City. He staffed the Department with corrupt men and ex-cons setting the stage for the brazen attack on FBI agents at the Kansas City Massacre at Union Station. Similarly Pendergast through appointment or control of the ballot boxes put Mafia-sympathetic prosecutors and judges in office in Kansas City and Jackson County. Everyone in law enforcement knew not to interfere with the Mafioso's Prohibition and gambling operations. Lazia contributed something back to the arrangement. His gang members and associated thugs produced for the Pendergast machine some of the most corrupt and violent elections ever held in America.

Even before Lazia became involved with Pendergast, the political leader allowed a wide-open town where the alcohol flowed and gambling flourished by seeing that the ballots were cast to keep political allies in power who supported these policies. Reform elements despised Pendergast's corruption and control, and his critics accused him of allowing his areas of the city to become a hot bed of vice and crime. These criticisms escalated when Lazia became Pendergast's First Ward lieutenant. Detractors correctly claimed Lazia was the political kingmaker's direct link to the booming crime problem.

There was an interesting dichotomy in the Mafia leader's use of his police powers. On the one hand he made Kansas City a safe haven for fugitives on the run and for criminals who needed to hide out for awhile from heat at home. Any criminal wanting Lazia's protection had to inform him or his associates what his intentions for being in town were and how long he was planning to stay. On the other hand Lazia, no matter how great his power in both the town's underworld and overworld, considered major visiting hoods a potential threat. He had a small gang and a coveted, unprecedented position with political bossism giving him home rule over crime. Lazia realized a major gang from another city could have easily muscled and subordinated him, but he should have understood that it was all but impossible for an outside gang to eliminate and replace him. Organized crime cannot exist without the support of the local politicians and law enforcement, and the Kansas City lawmen, no matter how corrupt, were loyal to the city's power structure. They would have quickly exploded against an outside threat and with the power of the law behind them destroyed the intruding gang. This is why no criminal gang in American history has successfully entered a new city without first obtaining the support and approval of either the existing dominant criminal leader or the political and law enforcement establishment. Lazia made sure this did not happen in Kansas City by having the Police Chief drive out any criminal or gang members he did not feel comfortable having in his town.

Lazia's key gang members had two responsibilities – they ran the gang's criminal enterprises and they also turned out the vote for the political machine. This allowed Lazia to move transparently between all levels and facets of society. No one meeting him would have ever suspected he was a criminal let alone a gang leader. But the townspeople knew and this made him an intriguing figure. Adding to the American public's fascination with powerful criminal gang leaders, Lazia was a charismatic character. He was responsive to anyone who approached him, and he readily handed out money to the unemployed and people with hardships. A modest man, he was friendly and charming with a frequent smile. He had a good command of the language, told funny stories, but always chomped on gum.

Lazia set the town's crime policies, but he devoted most of his time acting as his precincts' political leader dealing with the problems of his legitimate constituencies. He also made friends and developed loyalties among the unemployed who ate in his soup kitchen during the day, and he hobnobbed with the high rollers who gambled in his swanky casinos in the evening. When the feds raided Lazia's Prohibition operations, the opposition newspapers referred to him not as a gangster or Mafioso but the most disparaging title they could install on him - the North Side Democratic

Boss. Whether Lazia and Pendergast were called Party Bosses or Party Leaders depended on which party the speaker supported.

Despite Tom Pendergast machine's awesome power, the 1934 election for Kansas City Mayor was hotly contested and became the darkest day of his reign. Tom's candidate was Incumbent Mayor Bryce Smith. His opponent Ross Hill warned Governor Guy Park, another Pendergast crony, that Pendergast's machine planned violence against the reformers on election day and asked him to call out the National Guard to protect the polling places. The Governor ignored this threat. The Police Department had been under home rule for two years and was completely corrupted under crime-lord Lazia's control. He ordered the police to avoid going near polling places that day as the machine violently ruled the election precincts. Election workers and voters were routinely intimidated, and dozens, including reporters, were injured in beatings. At the city's East Side polling places, political factional disputes led to four people being shot to death and 11 seriously wounded. The dead included a hardware store owner, a poll worker, a sheriff's deputy, and a machine thug. Tom's Mayor Smith was reelected, but this thuggery offended much of the public leading to the slow decline of the machine's power base.[238]

SOLVING THE MASSACRE COLD CASE

With this understanding of the unique political/criminal power structure in Kansas City, it is possible to conduct the first thorough examination of what happened on the evening before the Massacre and on that terrible morning in order to determine who the three shooters had to have been. Despite investigations by the FBI, investigative reporters at the time, and crime historians since, only one relevant fact has ever been established about this horrific slaughter. After Frank Nash was arrested by the FBI in Hot Springs, the prisoner's wife turned to his best friend, organized-crime associate Verne Miller who lived in Kansas City, seeking help in freeing her husband from custody.

It has always been assumed by those who studied this case that Miller then solicited two other killers to join him in attempting to free his pal, but the preceding analysis of the city's political/criminal power structure reveals a previously unconsidered fact that alters the course of a proper cold-case investigation. Miller lived anonymously in the safe haven of Kansas City for many years without interference from local police because he was under the protection and direction of the city's unofficial Police Chief, Mafia leader Lazia. He alone made every decision about crime and law enforcement in the city. Miller would not have dared commit any crime in town, let alone a major one, without first obtaining Lazia's approval. As a close loyal associate, Miller was well aware that an affront to Lazia's standing like this would have forced the Mafioso to retaliate in order to reestablish his dominance in the city. The Mafia leader would have at the least directed the whole police force to bring Miller down and most likely ordered gang members to eliminate him in a most brutal fashion.

Before trying to determine exactly what happened next, it is important to establish that the limited facts about this case always maintained by FBI Director Hoover were not only incredibly weak but also certainly untrue. The only evidence ever obtained by his agents were two contradictory second-hand stories about who did the Massacre shooting. These two underworld informants had no relationship to each other, and both were looking for sentencing deals. The first informant was Michael "Jimmy Needles" La Capra who claimed his brother-in-law, a member of Lazia's Mafia gang, had told him how the Massacre was carried out. Needles was looking to the FBI for witness protection from the gang because it had targeted him for death and had recently made two missed attempts on his life.

Needles' story contained the false claim that at the Massacre Pretty Boy Floyd was badly wounded in the shoulder from a ricochet bullet, but an autopsy proved he never had such an injury. More importantly Needles' version suffered from both a huge inconsistency and a whopper of a lie, either of which should have set off warning alarms to Hoover. The inconsistency resulted from Needles' claim that Lazia would not get involved with the Massacre because he feared heat from Kansas City detectives and this is why Miller chose Floyd and his partner Adam Richetti as shooters. But Needles then totally contradicted himself by stating the supposedly weary Lazia harbored and partied with the pair of bank robbers for the two evenings after the Massacre before personally escorting them out of town.

In addition to this unfathomable contradiction, La Capra's story had a glaring and fatal error, but Hoover failed to recognize this because he had no knowledge of Kansas City's political/criminal culture since he forbade his agents from investigating or even monitoring the nation's organized-crime members. Hoover and every crime historian who has studied this case has made the critical mistake of assuming Miller was the mastermind behind the Massacre because none knew Mafia leader Lazia alone made every decision about crime in the city. Thus Needles, who was a minor member of Lazia's gang, knew his statement to agents was a farcical fantasy, but the Director totally bought into it and directed his agents to find corroboration while ignoring other possibilities.

The second informant was Volney Davis who was a bank robber from Tulsa, Oklahoma. He was angling to get his life sentence at Alcatraz reduced. He was convicted of joining Alvin Karpis' gang in the violent kidnapping of St. Paul, Minnesota banker Edward Bremer. Davis claimed he and his girlfriend were told by Miller that the Massacre shooters were Miller and Floyd. However the couple's story does not hold together because the couple's statements said Miller and Floyd decided as they were leaving Miller's home that morning not to take Adam Richetti because he was too hung over from the night before to join them. The pair's story ends with Miller and Floyd driving to the Union Railway Station by themselves without offering any explanation where Miller found the third shooter or how he worked out the strategy with him in the little time before the train arrived.

At Richetti's Kansas City trial for the murder of the city's two detectives in the Massacre, the FBI supplied Needles' statement to the prosecutor, but agents kept Davis' statement hidden because it exonerated Richetti. It is a well-established principal in criminal law that the prosecution must turn over all exculpable evidence to the defense. This refers to all facts that clear the defendant of guilt such as Davis' statement because it is obviously improper for a prosecutor to put on trial or to convict anyone he knows to be innocent. But Hoover's secret-police force had become a law onto itself acting as police, prosecutor, judge, and at times executioner.

Needles and Davis hoped to benefit from their statements, but more importantly both lacked credibility. Needles and Davis claimed to FBI agents that Miller had told them separately who did the shooting, but Miller never talked to anyone about his criminal activity during his whole life. He was part of the first generation of American organized crime and this was an exceptionally tight-lipped breed. None of the major gangsters who came out of Prohibition ever talked about their activities to anyone including family, friends, associates, and the press. They could only protect their large criminal enterprises by keeping them secret, and they were too savvy to ever give another criminal information that the other criminal could use to barter with a prosecutor for a sentencing deal in return for turning state's witness, most especially nothing about an executable offense. Finally the gangsters of this era only trusted other gangsters who never talked about their own or anyone else's criminal and business activities because they knew anyone who talked about others' activities could not be trusted to keep anyone's confidences.

Miller was the epitome of the silent man who never discussed or admitted any crime to anyone. This is why law enforcement and the press never knew how he financed his lavish lifestyle. No one ever knew which types of crimes he specialized in, let alone which ones he had committed. In addition Miller was the darling of some of the most powerful Prohibition gang leaders. They only dealt with tight-lipped men and they were wary of anyone who had not taken a blood-oath initiation into their gang. Thus Miller had obviously passed close, cautious scrutiny of several of these leaders for New York gangster Lepke Buchalter to have harbored him after the Massacre and to have welcomed Miller's wife as the apartment guest and vacation companion of he and his wife.[239]

The fatal flaw in gangster Needles' Massacre story was the falseness of his fundamental premise. Needles claimed Miller only chose Floyd and Richetti, who first arrived in Kansas City that night, as shooters after Lazia told him he was afraid to have his Mafia gang become involved because it would cause "too much heat" from local police detectives. Of course this was utter nonsense since Lazia had personally selected, appointed, and controlled Police Director Eugene Reppert. In reality Lazia was confident his totally corrupted pawn of a Police Director would derail any investigation of his crimes, and the Director did not disappoint when he prohibited his detectives from investigating the Massacre case even though two of his own detectives had been murdered that morning.

Reppert had became Kansas City Police Director a year before this horrific slaughter of lawmen, when the state of Missouri transferred control of the Police Board from the Governor to the City Manager. Reppert was a wealthy car-dealership owner who had retired three years earlier. At age 46 he was named the first home rule Police Chief. He had not been identified closely with Pendergast's Democratic politics, but he had a close relationship with Lazia for reasons that never became public. As Police Director, Reppert let the Mafia leader select the new officers he hired so they typically had criminal records longer than their law enforcement resumes. The Kansas City police force had long been an extension of the Pendergast political machine, but the police now worked in lockstep with the local Mafia leader. Under Director Reppert's administration, cynics ruefully decried, "The easiest way to contact crime chief Lazia is to call the Police Department."

The horrendous Massacre of four lawmen was strictly a local crime because the shooters that morning violated no federal law, and the FBI at that time was still solely an investigative agency prohibited from carrying guns and making arrests. Even though the FBI had no jurisdiction and the Police Director was solely responsible for investigating the crime, Reppert shockingly told his surviving detective staff, "This is not a police matter, hands off. Have nothing to do with it." Next Director Reppert held a press conference and placed the blame squarely on the FBI by lying that the Nash arrest was a federal operation, when in fact his two slain detectives handled the fugitive's custody from the moment he arrived at Union Railway Station.[240]

Then Police Director Reppert accepted a request for a meeting from FBI's lead investigator Gus Jones who brought along two of his surviving three agents so the two agencies could coordinate their investigative efforts. It was at this meeting, according to an FBI memo, that Director Reppert told Agent Jones, "This is some mess you've gotten us into." When Jones offered to assist the police investigation, Reppert refused the offer with, "This is a [federal] government case and not a police matter." Reppert added he would not investigate the Massacre despite having two dead detectives and knowing the FBI by law had no jurisdiction whatsoever to investigate. By his actions Director Reppert completely disavowed his sworn oath to enforce the law and disowned any allegiance to his two slaughtered detectives. Reppert soon resigned.[241]

Director Reppert's Lieutenant explained the twisted loyalty of the Kansas City Police Department. The Lieutenant told two St. Louis, Missouri prosecutors about the Kansas City police operation in another case, "We have got to work for the good of the Democratic Party. I am in the employ of Kansas City, Missouri. Nevertheless I owe a greater duty to the organization there which is headed by Mr. Pendergast."[242]

Nine months after the Massacre during Kansas City's municipal election a non-partisan group charged that during Police Director Reppert's reign the man who actually controlled the Police Department was Lazia who the group described as a gambler and a powerful North Side politician. Eight months later a Kansas City Federal Grand Jury investigated the relationship between crime and politics in the city. It issued a report criticizing former Director Reppert for negligence in handling prisoner Nash's transfer from the train to the awaiting cars at Union Railway Station, and it indicted him for perjury for having denied under oath that he had told his officers they should not investigate the slaughter. Also indicted for perjury were his Lieutenant who denied under oath that he ever said his first loyalty was to Pendergast. The final police official charged with perjury was Reppert's Chief of Detectives. Although the three were certainly guilty the Federal Trial Jury acquitted.[243]

The Federal Grand Jury's report stressed two points about the Kansas City Police Department in rather fractured language. "On the date of the Massacre at the Union Station in June of 1933, it unquestionably was not as efficient or not as effective in the discharge of its duties as it should have been. In many respects this same situation applies during the whole period of time covered by our investigation. Criminal mobs and racketeers exist here composed wholly of men who permanently live in Kansas City." It also stated, "Unbridled gambling of major proportions in almost every conceivable form and in most numerous quarters has, according to positive testimony, been tolerated as a matter of general policy by more than one high official charged with the suppression thereof and is running in a most wide-open fashion."

This overwhelming mass of evidence confirms that Mafia boss/Police Chief Lazia alone possessed the power to decide how the Massacre would be handled, who the shooters would be, and prohibit the Detective Department from investigating the crime. He had several experienced shooters in his gang and he had close ties with leaders of tough gangs in a few other cities whose members Lazia could have imported if he were concerned that potential witnesses at Union Station might be able to recognize his local members' faces. The most obvious gang was Egan's Rats in St. Louis, Missouri. Al Capone used these notorious cold-blooded killers in Chicago's St. Valentine's Day Massacre so the members of the opposing Bugs Moran gang would not recognize them as Caponites. With St. Louis 245 miles east of Kansas City, it would have been an easy drive for Egan's shooters to be at the train station by morning. Lazia simply had no need for the unproven and untried Floyd and Richetti. Beside knowing nothing about their ability, Lazia had never met them and was intensely aware they had no loyalty to him. Lazia knew if Floyd or Richetti were ever caught for any major crime they could flip on him as their get-out-of-jail-free card. Lazia wanted killers who had taken blood oaths and who would never talk to the police or anyone else. He obviously found them because none of the actual participants ever talked about the slaughter.

New evidence that further confirmed Lazia's leadership of the Massacre surfaced 13 months after the slaughter during the investigation of another Kansas City gangland machinegun killing. Bullet comparisons revealed that the machinegun used to mow down this Mafioso had also been used earlier in the horrific slaughter of lawmen at Union Station. First this proved both crimes had been committed by the same shooters. Second the Mafioso's murder was definitely carried out by members of Lazia's Mafia gang (as detailed in the next chapter). Thus the Kansas City Massacre had to have been committed by these local Mafiosi shooters.

These bullet comparisons explain why not one of the multitude of witnesses to the Massacre, including the three surviving FBI agents during the two years leading up to Richetti's trial, could identify pictures of Miller, Floyd, or Richetti. None of these three suspects was at the slaying. The night before the Massacre, Richetti and possibly Floyd had a glass of beer at Miller's home. The two fugitives had gone to Miller because they needed permission from Mafia boss/Police Chief

Lazia to hide out in his town protected from the law for a few days and to make plans to party with the gangland leader the next night. Then the two wanted desperadoes left town with the machineguns they used throughout their long fugitive run. Ballistic tests later proved neither of their machineguns was used at the slaughter of the lawmen.

When the bank robbers met with Miller, Richetti felt he needed a small concealable weapon to carry at all times as well as toting his bulky machinegun in his desperate cross-country flight. It is clear that Miller either sold or gave him a pistol that night because when Richetti was arrested 16 months after the Massacre, the serial number on his pistol identified that it was part of a large burglary from the Kansas City National Guard armory. Other pistols taken in this theft were used by Lazia gang members and also criminals based in other areas of the country after they visited Kansas City with the approval of boss Lazia.

WHAT WAS THE MOTIVE FOR THE MASSACRE?

The FBI and crime historians have always assumed that the motive of the Massacre shooters was to free prisoner Frank Nash from custody. Everyone writing about this case has bought into this conjecture because the slaughter was initiated by Nash's wife and the plot was advanced by Nash's best friend, Miller. The goal of both of them was clearly to free him. But this scenario simply does not fit the way the slaughter was carried out.

At the Massacre scene, the assailant who shot downward from behind the prisoner's car watched from hiding as Nash was placed in the front passenger seat and then the visiting Police Chief and the two FBI agents squeezed into the back seat. A third agent was opening the driver's door by standing beside the backseat door when the shooting began. The attacker could have easily sprayed in a side-to-side direction in almost a straight line at the four lawmen without coming near the prisoner in the front seat. Instead the shooter killed the prisoner and the Police Chief sitting directly behind him by firing in a back-and-forth direction. If the usually-accepted scenario of freeing the prisoner from custody is correct it means this was an atrociously bungled and counterproductive shooting by a gang that literally could not shoot straight. However if the prisoner was the intended target, then the shooting was actually well performed to achieve the goal.

It is relevant to note that the two agents furthest from both the prisoner and the Police Chief were also shot. This was likely done by the shooter firing at that side of the car while the shooter from above did not even hit the agent sitting in the middle of the back seat right next to the Police Chief, reinforcing that this assailant sprayed in a back-and-forth manner.[244]

Most significant is the behavior of the assassins immediately upon felling all seven lawmen. Not one of the three shooters made any effort to rush over and find out the condition of the prisoner let alone make any attempt to rescue him. Instead all three immediately turned, ran to their getaway car, and sped away. This behavior was reported by the three surviving FBI agents and dozens of witnesses. If the goal was to free the prisoner, then the moment the gun clatter stopped at least some of the witnesses should have heard an "Aw shit!"

Not only does the shooters' behavior fit the scenario that Nash was really the intended target, but it makes a good deal of sense with what is known about the city's underworld culture. It is clear that once Miller got the phone call from Mrs. Nash pleading for help to free her husband from custody, Miller would not have dared to do anything without first getting the approval and direction of the city's crime lord, Mafia boss/Police Chief Lazia. While Miller may have sought to free his close friend, prisoner Nash meant nothing to Lazia who had no ties to him, never having met or dealt with the convict.

Lazia would not only have gained nothing by helping Nash, but the Mafia chieftain would have put himself in great jeopardy by doing so. The FBI was returning Nash to Leavenworth Prison to serve out the 18 years remaining in his 25-year sentence. If Lazia freed Nash, the fugitive would have gone back on the run. If he were captured again, Nash could have gotten a plea deal for his remaining long prison sentence by turning state's witness against the Mafia leader. While Nash would never have had any direct contact with the powerful Kansas City gang leader, Nash could have flipped on the three shooters who escorted him to freedom, and they in turn could have taken down Lazia for the Prosecutor. It was absolutely not in the crime lord's interest to have assisted Nash.

While there is no reason to believe the Mafia leader would have saved Nash, he may have had a good reason to target him. Lazia and Nash both had close ties to a number of organized-crime gang leaders in other cities. One or more of these gang leaders for whom Nash had committed violent acts might have feared the prisoner because if he was returned to Leavenworth he might have turned state's witness against him. Such a leader would have been most grateful to Lazia for eliminating this potential threat to his freedom.

In this regard it is very interesting who Nash's wife called first for help in freeing her husband from FBI custody. It was not his best friend Miller in Kansas City as has always been thought, but a Chicago associate of her husband, Louis "Doc" Stacci, proprietor of the O-P Inn speakeasy in Melrose Park 15 miles northwest of the Windy City. Nash may have been arrested by the FBI during his annual summer vacation in Hot Springs, Arkansas, but at that time he owned a Chicago Prohibition beer and slot-machine joint, meaning he had an arrangement with Al Capone's gang. Under these circumstances it is all but a certainty that Stacci notified his Capone-gang bosses about their comrade's capture. This gang was notorious throughout the years for killing many members and associates after they were charged with crimes that might lead to long sentences in order to eliminate the possibility of their turning state's witness.

All this evidence presented here also ties up the remaining loose fact in this case. Every analyst has assumed that Miller was the lead shooter in the Massacre without an iota of evidence, but if crime boss Lazia's intent was to silence Nash, the last thing he would have done was ask Nash's close friend to participate. If the Mafia leader's goal was to kill Nash, then it means Miller, just like Floyd and Richetti, was not involved that day. Thus this would make every one of the FBI Director's assumptions about this case wrong. Because Hoover used such bad judgment in analyzing this case, he incorrectly closed the slaughter case with the deaths of Floyd, Richetti, and Miller, preventing law enforcement from ever identifying or bringing to justice any of the three actual shooters, the getaway driver, or the mastermind behind it.

Over the years various crime historians have developed alternative hypotheses but each of these speculations has little evidentiary support. In addition none includes Kansas City's political/criminal cultural context that both greatly determined and limited what might or might not have happened that fateful day.[245]

Chapter 13

A STRUGGLE FOR JUSTICE

CONFLICT IN THE REALM

Kansas City Mafia boss/Police Chief Johnny Lazia built an unprecedented criminal, political, and law enforcement combine. On the surface it may have appeared impervious, but other gangs operated in other districts within the city. These gangland factions violently fought out their differences causing the town to suffer from a high murder rate. In addition a few concerned citizens had the courage to stand up and challenge Lazia's dominant combine. This was an unusual combination of reformers - two honest and dedicated judges, one local and the other federal; two independent and determined grand juries, one local and one federal; and a few powerful political-faction enemies from Lazia's own Democratic Party who each did their part in wreaking havoc on the city's powerful political/criminal machine.

At the very moment Mafia leader Lazia was directing the Kansas City Massacre, a Federal Grand Jury was investigating his income taxes. Political leader Tom Pendergast tried to fend off potential tax-evasion charges against his lieutenant by contacting everyone he had influence with in President Franklin Roosevelt's administration. Tom proposed to avoid criminal charges and a prison sentence for Lazia by having him pay appropriate back taxes, interest, and penalties in a civil settlement. The political kingmaker backed up his request with a threat to withhold Missouri Democratic-machine support for the President's upcoming and challenging reelection campaign.

Tom Pendergast's efforts were documented in a letter he penned to James Farley, who was appointed Postmaster General after his resounding victory as Roosevelt's 1932 election campaign manager. This letter became public. Tom told the Postmaster General that Lazia, "one of my chief lieutenants, has been in trouble with the income tax department for some time." He requested the Postmaster do his "utmost to bring about a settlement of this matter." The letter went on to say that Lazia would be accompanied by Jerome Walsh in Washington to see Farley about the income tax prosecution and added, "I think Frank Walsh spoke to the proper authorities about this." Frank Walsh was a Kansas City lawyer before practicing in New York where he was appointed by then Governor Franklin Roosevelt as Chairman of the New York Power Authority two years earlier. Pendergast argued Lazia was the victim of a political prosecution by saying he knew Lazia had been "jobbed (investigated) because of his Democratic activities" during Republican President Herbert Hoover's administration. President Hoover had indeed personally directed the IRS to attempt to prosecute two big-time Mafia-gang leaders, Lazia and Al Capone, who had totally corrupted the local police forces of Kansas City and Chicago respectively.

It never became public what influenced U.S. AG Cummings, but he instructed his U.S. Attorney in Kansas City to stop the criminal hearings before the Grand Jury concerning Lazia while the AG allowed the IRS time to negotiate a financial settlement that would leave the administration looking good with Pendergast's political machine. However the Grand Jurors were a group of concerned local citizens who opposed the rule of crime-lord Lazia. They had the courage to challenge the Federal Prosecutor by going directly to the Federal Judge who had impaneled them to ask if they had the authority to go into any matter they saw fit. When the Judge told them yes, they told him they were going into Lazia's taxes. Once the Jurors bolted and decided to proceed on their own, the AG ordered his U.S. Attorney to do the job right by leading the charge to examine Lazia's income taxes thoroughly. It turned out the crime leader had not only never filed an income tax return but he had left a trail of large unexplained bank account deposits. The Federal Grand Jury issued income-tax evasion indictments against the Mafia leader who the press referred to as the North Side political leader, or boss.

Just like the Federal Grand Jurors, the Jackson County Grand Jurors were an independently-minded group of concerned citizens. Over the objections of the County Prosecutor and with only one week left in their term, they decided to seriously investigate Lazia's big-time gambling operations. This did not allow them enough time to prepare indictments, but the Grand Jury did issue a scathing report about Kansas City being one of the nation's most wide-open cities and blamed police complicity. The report blasted police officials for testifying they had never seen a slot machine in operation despite general knowledge that about 2,000 slot machines dotted the town in hotels, speakeasies, social clubs, and drug stores where grammar school kids were encouraged to spend their lunch money on the "mechanical Santas." A Superior Court ordered 200 slots seized and confiscated. This led the town's unofficial police chief, Mafia-leader Lazia, to order all his gambling operations shut down until further notice. When the publicity ended, gambling burst into the open again.

Eight months after the Massacre, Lazia was convicted in Federal Court of failing to file income tax returns for two years. He was sentenced to a year in prison and immediately appealed. While he was free awaiting the decision, his subordinates and a rival gang started jockeying for the position he was likely to soon abdicate. Five months into his appeal, Lazia's wife was recuperating from an illness at the couple's vacation home at Lake Lotawana, Missouri, 25 miles southeast of the city. Lazia visited her there. He took along his lieutenant Charles Carollo as his driver and bodyguard. Late that night she decided she would feel better recovering at home in their luxurious apartment hotel, the Park Central. Carollo drove. She sat in the more spacious front seat and Lazia sat behind her. At 3 a.m. Carollo pulled into the Hotel's front driveway under a canopy, and Lazia got out to open the door for his wife. Two men were crouched behind a nearby clump of bushes in hiding. Without warning they stood up and opened fire with a machinegun and a shotgun. As the Mafia leader slumped to the ground, he yelled to Carollo to get his wife out of there. Carollo stepped on the gas and sped Lazia's wife to safety. Lazia was hit by eight slugs that fractured his jaw and broke his arm. It was the wound in his back that put him in critical condition. He was rushed to St. Joseph's Hospital where he was given three blood transfusions. Conscious in an oxygen tent, Lazia told his doctor he did not know who the shooters were or their motive. His last words were for his wife and a message intended for delivery to Boss Pendergast. "If anything happens to me notify Pendergast, my best friend, and tell him that I love him." This statement confirmed how close the two political manipulators were as newspapers referred to the criminal overlord as a local Democratic political leader. The 37-year-old Lazia died 11 hours after the shooting.[246]

Lazia's body lay in view at his sister's home. Thousands of people passed through. Then thousands surrounded the Holy Rosary Church during the service. Thousands more lined the funeral route to the cemetery taken by the procession of 120 cars and four trucks that carried flowers. His funeral crowd is generally considered to have been the largest in the city. All these people came to pay their respects to the powerful political figure who had helped so many throughout his career, while he at the same time violently turned Kansas City into a lawless town to plunder these same folks.

Kansas City detectives developed just two clues about Lazia's murder. A janitor who was in the basement of the Park Central Hotel during the shooting told police that just prior he had been in the alley in the rear of the building and had seen a car carrying three men drive in and park. The driver remained behind the wheel as the other two men got out carrying a machinegun and a shotgun. They walked alongside the building toward the front of the hotel. The janitor assumed the pair were police detectives trying to apprehend a dangerous suspect, so he went inside the back of the building where he did not hear the gunfire in the front. He was not able to identify this murderous trio, and at that early-morning hour there were no witnesses in front of the hotel. Lazia's killing was never solved.

This police investigation also uncovered the only piece of evidence ever found about the Kansas City Massacre. Bullet comparisons revealed that the machinegun used to mow down Lazia had also been used in the horrific slaughter of lawmen 13 months earlier. This means that whoever Lazia had ordered to commit the Massacre later turned the same high-powered weapons against him.

It is all but certain that Lazia's killers were his own blood-oath gang members. They are the only ones he would have trusted to carry out the high-profile Massacre. Whoever approached the leader's henchmen had to be very confident they would be agreeable to such murderous betrayal, or else they would have reported the proposal to Lazia who would have struck first. Lazia's lieutenant Carollo was the only person in a position to evaluate over time which gang members had the least loyalty and the most ambition, and he alone had the opportunity to slowly develop their allegiance through normal gang interactions. These and other circumstances made Carollo the only viable suspect. He alone benefited from Lazia's slaying because as his lieutenant Carollo immediately laid claim to his boss' triple crown of Mafia head, political leader, and unofficial Police Chief. In addition he was also the only person that night in a position to easily arrange the Mafia leader's slaying.

Whenever Lazia and Carollo went anywhere, they never told anyone where they were headed, so Carollo had to have been the person who tipped off the shooters about their plans and exactly where to hit his boss. As Lazia's driver that fateful night, Carollo knew his boss' itinerary and the approximate time he would likely arrive at each destination. He was the only person who knew Lazia's wife decided in the middle of the night to return to their apartment, and he probably telephoned the shooters from the vacation home just before they left to tell them approximately what time they should park along the route near the hotel to start tailing them after they passed by.

The Kansas City Police Director was Otto Higgins. He had replaced Eugene Reppert, who had been forced to resign for preventing his detectives from investigating the Massacre. Lazia had hand-picked Higgins as the replacement Police Director, and now it was Higgins' job to investigate Lazia's slaying. It had almost certainly been ordered by his lieutenant Carollo, but he had just succeeded the dead Mafioso as unofficial Police Chief making him Higgins' new boss. As the old saying about succession of royalty goes - the King is dead, long live the (new) King! Besides it would later be proven that from the time Carollo became Mafia boss, he paid a monthly bribe to Police Director Higgins.

Thus Police Director Higgins' so-called Lazia murder investigation deflected attention away from the only likely suspect Carollo. His detectives, who had been selected for appointment to their jobs by the dead Mafia boss, told the press they believed Lazia and Carollo might have been followed on their trip home by killers who waited until they got near the hotel to be sure where they were going and then sped ahead to arrive first. This creative fancy by the detectives has two serious flaws. First if the shooters had started following at the vacation home as the detectives proposed, it would have been simpler and safer for them to kill the unsuspecting Lazia as he walked out of his vacation home with his wife to the car. The assailants could have easily hidden near the home's walkway in the dark of night and no witnesses were outside in the quiet residential neighborhood at that hour. Second, only the Mafia leader and his lieutenant knew where they were going that night, so the stalkers would have had to tail them all the way from town and then back to town. In this alternative the trio could have simply pulled up beside them on any empty stretch of road, fired the machinegun and shotgun from the passenger seat and the seat behind, and then sped away leaving no witnesses or evidence.

The murderous trio clearly trailed Lazia's car to the apartment hotel, and Carollo was the only suspect who had a reason to delay the attack until they arrived there. If the shooting was done on the highway or at the vacation-home walkway, Carollo would have been close to Lazia and might have ended up in line of the deadly gunfire. At the hotel, Carollo sat in the car as Lazia got out to help his wife get out to walk her to their apartment to spend the night.

Police Director Higgins diverted suspicion away from Mafioso lieutenant Carollo by focusing the murder investigation on two other gangsters he elevated to prime suspects even though they gained nothing from Lazia's murder. The first was Lazia's ambitious political rival on the North Side, Joe Lusco. Minutes after the shooting police picked him up in his flower shop and then rounded up almost two dozen of his associates. Detective interrogations of Lusco and his henchmen elicited nothing. He lacked motive because the relative power balance between the two gangs remained in place with Carollo's succession of leadership.

Police Director Higgins' other suspect was Jimmy "Needles" La Capra. Soon after Lazia's slaying, Carollo had his underlings make two failed attempts on Needles' life. Based on the timing of these two attempts, FBI Director Hoover, and later crime historians, assumed that Carollo went after Needles out of vengeance over Lazia's killing, but Needles gained nothing from the slaying of Lazia. In contrast, Kansas City's investigative reporters wrote a more plausible explanation based on their gangland sources– Carollo targeted Needles because he was demanding a larger share in the profits of unspecified rackets of the gang. After the second attempt on Needles' life, he sought FBI protection by concocting the story about Pretty Boy Floyd and Adam Richetti being shooters in the Massacre.

This fictional Massacre account worked to Needles' benefit for some time, but three months after the FBI assassinated Floyd, agents had no further use for Needles as a witness. They released the addict from protective custody in the Sumner County Jail death cell. Needles continued to fear for his life so agents advised him to move to South America where he had family, but he chose to go to New York instead. Seven months later police found his bullet-riddled body on a highway outside Poughkeepsie.

The Kansas City police investigation of Lazia's murder yielded nothing because its futile efforts were directed by the new Mafia boss, Carollo, who was also the culprit. Even though Lazia was killed three months before the FBI assassinated Floyd, FBI Director Hoover ignored the ballistics finding that the machinegun used in the Mafia leader's murder had also been used in the Massacre. If the Director or his vaunted scientific lab had acknowledged this obvious strategic significance, his agents might have been able to solve both crimes – the Massacre and the murder of the Mafia leader. But Hoover stuck with Needles' concocted Floyd-Massacre story despite such powerful evidence to the contrary. The Director's bull-headedness to avoid admitting an error in judgment assured that the Massacre case would remain closed but actually unsolved, thus preventing bringing to justice the slaughterers of four peace officers including one of his own agents.

There was one other odd law-enforcement action in the Lazia case. Three months after the Mafia leader was murdered, U.S. AG Cummings was questioned by reporters at a press conference about his handling of Lazia's tax-evasion case that led to an indictment only because of an independently-minded runaway Grand Jury. Reporters asked the AG to reveal the corrupt politicians who had tried to shelter the Mafia leader from prosecution, but he stood behind what he said was the ancient rule of previous Attorney Generals to never disclose persons who sought paroles, pardons, or leniency for criminals. Reporters pointed out that the AG could and should smash combinations of the underworld and politicians by exposing them. He refused even though his inaction flew in the face of his heavily promoted anti-crime campaign. AG Cummings did admit, "I will say that a good many people have been inordinately interested in Mr. Lazia, but he is dead and gone now." When asked to reveal them, he said, "Oh, no, I couldn't do that. There would be no use in making the names public where the pleas are ineffective. In cases where the pleas win some leniency there might be more merit in the suggestion." He concluded, "We all know what Lazia's connections were and have known for some time." Ironically, the AG's subordinate, FBI Director Hoover, in a recent Chicago speech had urged state officials to make such disclosures. While this sounded like what a good law enforcer should want, Hoover failed to prosecute organized crime or the Mafia during the first four decades of his tenure until AG Robert Kennedy demanded he do so. Hoover's goal for the FBI was to uncover information about improper political influence not for the purpose of exposing or prosecuting the wrong doers, but to identify and blackmail them for their personal political support and to control their vote.[247]

THE GATHERING STORM CLOUDS
     And now the rest of the story about the fall of Kansas City's political/criminal dynasty. The ground work was laid in 1932 when Franklin D. Roosevelt assumed the Presidency. Roosevelt tried to distance himself from Pendergast's corrupt Democratic machine, but he had to work with Missouri's newly-elected Governor, Tom Pendergast protégé Guy Park. To be able to deal with Park, FDR had to ignore the popular name used for the Governor's mansion whenever one of Pendergast's hand-picked candidates occupied it - "Uncle Tom's Cabin." Governor Park was grateful to Boss Tom for being selected to run and be elected so he turned over many of the state level patronage jobs to Pendergast so he could disperse them to his loyal Kansas City supporters. The President, who had also received strong political support from this machine, grasped the reality of the state's power-structure so he bypassed the puppet Governor to turn over Missouri federal patronage jobs to the Kansas City powerbroker as well.
     Then a year into Roosevelt's term, Kansas City voters, who had long accepted the dominance of the Pendergast machine, began to rebel. This first surfaced with the bloody 1934 Kansas City municipal election when the town voted reform candidates onto the City Council. Four months later Lazia was slain. His key aide Charles Carollo succeeded him as both Mafia-gang leader and political lieutenant to Tom Pendergast, and these two men continued Lazia's close working political/criminal relationship. While the dynasty's operation had not altered, the surrounding political reality had. During Pendergast's career he had suffered occasional election defeats, but he always bounced back in the ensuing elections to reassert himself as top dog. However this time serious opposition continued to chip away at Tom's domain.
     Four months after the bloody Kansas City election, the Missouri statewide primary election was held. From the time the polls opened that day, voters poured into the Federal Building office of Kansas City U.S. Attorney Maurice Milligan to report voting irregularities. Every complainant reported that the Pendergast machine was throwing the election to fraudulently defeat the U.S. Attorney's brother, J. L. "Tuck" Milligan, as the Democratic candidate for the United States Senate. The U.S. Attorney quickly contacted the local FBI Office, and agents soon entered the voting precincts and questioned scores of voters who protested about illegal voting practices. These witnesses complained about being denied ballots after saying they were going to vote for Milligan, seeing repeat voters, and watching phony ballots stuffed into ballot boxes. Later complainants had observed the election judges, who counted the ballots after the polls closed, neglecting to count the majority of ballots cast for Tuck Milligan causing his defeat. U.S. Attorney Milligan had the

Federal Grand Jury recalled, but he lacked enough evidence to obtain convictions. An enraged U.S. Attorney Maurice Milligan was now the arch enemy of the Pendergast political machine, and as the local federal law enforcement leader, he became determined and prepared to act decisively against future voter fraud.[248]

Three months after the fraudulent statewide primary, a Jackson County Grand Jury spent seven weeks investigating the political/criminal partnership in Kansas City. The Jury returned no indictments but reported, "We find that Kansas City is infested with gambling, racketeering and other forms of lawlessness, and so dominated by intimidation and threats of reprisals by the underworld that citizens are afraid to tell the truth to the Grand Jury."

Two years later in the 1936 election, President Roosevelt ran for his second term, and millionaire Lloyd Stark ran to succeed Pendergast's retiring puppet, Governor Park. Stark had built his own statewide political base independently of the Kansas City powerbroker. As a successful apple grower he had the support of many farmers and other rural folks, and he had the endorsement of the St. Louis political establishment. When he approached Pendergast for his support, he was already the leading candidate so Boss Tom climbed aboard the bandwagon. When the Democratic campaigns were proceeding well in Kansas City, Pendergast decided to travel abroad. While he was away his followers aggressively increased their fraudulent voter tactics to help President Roosevelt win his second term and to propel Stark into the Governorship.

Thus soon after this election the machine's wholesale vote fraud was exposed by the *Kansas City Star* which published detailed evidence of massive illegal registration of voters. Even though the two key beneficiaries were President Roosevelt and Governor Stark, neither had any personal ties to Pendergast. They merely aligned with him in Missouri out of political necessity, but both found the Boss' lack of ethics repugnant. Thus it was easy for both to start retreating from associating with him, and then they teamed up to limit the abusive power of their recent backer's machine. Their efforts began when the Governor privately secured approval from the President for the Governor to publicly request a federal probe of the voter fraud accusations, and then the President directed his Justice Department to respond with a Grand Jury investigation in Kansas City. A Federal Judge admonished the Jurors, "We can't surrender the ballot boxes to thugs, gangsters, and plug-uglies. We can't stand that any longer." Under the direction of Kansas City U.S. Attorney Maurice Milligan, the Grand Jury found Pendergast's machine had piled up Democratic majorities as great as 100,000 and thus carried statewide elections for Governor and U.S. Senator. Two months after the election, the Grand Jury indicted 36 people for voter fraud. This was a violation of the Civil Rights Act by miscounting votes for federal positions. Most of those charged were election officials including key members of Pendergast's Democratic machine but a surprising number of Republicans were involved as well. Prosecutor Milligan continued this Grand Jury voter fraud investigation and over time charged many more participants.[249]

President Roosevelt was well experienced with this type of political/criminal machine. In New York City the Democratic Party was headquartered in Tammany Hall. The city had the country's largest population and more than half of the nation's wealthiest people resided in Manhattan. Tammany Hall was an extremely corrupt political machine and it was under the influence of the nation's largest Mafia gang. Roosevelt had become New York's Governor from whence he launched his presidential bid. As Governor, FDR always kept his distance from the stigma of Tammany Hall. He refused to compromise with its leaders to accomplish things for the city, but he also avoided antagonizing this powerful machine by only taking action to restrain Tammany's local affairs when disgraceful scandals hit the newspapers. Although his efforts to control Tammany's worst excesses were limited, these still led to enough animosity inside this large political organization for it to refuse to support him at the 1932 Democratic presidential nominating convention. In fact Tammany's leaders openly and aggressively lobbied other state delegations to defeat FDR's bid. While lack of backing from a candidate's home-state delegation is usually the kiss of death, Tammany had a bad reputation for corruption with the rest of the nation so these politicians' opposition probably improved his image with the other state's delegations who nominated Roosevelt as the Democratic candidate on the fourth ballot.

Interestingly in the first presidential election of the Great Depression, the desperate economic times did not cause more people to vote than had voted four years earlier, but voters switched parties to make it a landslide for challenger Roosevelt as they wanted a change from incumbent Republican President Herbert Hoover. Four years later President Roosevelt ran for reelection and the voting pattern changed again. While the total votes for the Republican challenger remained about the same as four years earlier, FDR's vote total increased by almost 22% as new constituencies, who liked his popular New Deal economic-stimulus job-creation policies, came out to the polls.

During President Roosevelt's first term, he had worked well with Pendergast out of political necessity, but he had no more liking for dealing with the Kansas City machine than he had had for working with Tammany Hall. During FDR's second term, with newly-elected Governor Stark wanting to distance himself from the Pendergast fraudulent voting scandal, the pair aligned to minimalize Boss Tom's power. The Governor took back control over state-level patronage jobs from Pendergast, and the President shifted authority over federal New Deal funds and patronage jobs from Boss Tom to the Governor. Stark also began building a competing Kansas City Democratic Party organization faction to represent he and the President in the next election.

Then the two new allies went a step further. Many Kansas City residents had pled with former Governor Guy Park to use the state police to reinstitute law and order in their city, but the puppet leader refused out of obedience to Pendergast. However Governor Stark was his own man and he laid in readiness for the right opportunity to go after the corrupt, organized-crime-dominated Pendergast machine. In solidarity with the Governor was the President who remained ready to direct the Justice Department to proceed at the right moment against the machine that had helped put both men in office. The opening for these two united leaders to strike against the political/Mafia machine occurred when an old criminal case exploded into scandalous headlines.

AN OLD CASE FANS THE FLAMES

The old criminal case that would ignite a prosecutorial firestorm against the Pendergast political/criminal machine had been directed by crime leader Lazia. Two months after he ordered the Kansas City Massacre, Lazia targeted Chicago gangster Ferris Anthon for murder. He was a moonshine manufacturer in the Illinois towns of Aurora and Batavia, both 40 miles west of Chicago, and distributed a half million gallons of his product yearly to other states. Kansas City, Kansas, separated by a state boundary line from Kansas City, Missouri, was such a major market for Anthon that he became known in Chicago as Kansas City Tony. Anthon had begun operations about the time Lazia came to power. Five years into production, Federal Prohi Agents built a case against Anthon and six associates. The moment the indictment was announced in Chicago, the fugitive gangster disappeared from that city and entered Lazia's safe haven where he was allowed to operate across the state line.

Anthon operated in Kansas City on the Kansas side where he was arrested multiple times for Prohibition violations, and he once turned state's witness causing several city officials to resign. Lazia allowed Anthon's operations until he expanded into the Mafia chieftain's Missouri territorial boundaries; then Lazia sent four henchmen to wipe out Anthon. This competitor and his wife lived at the Cavalier Apartments in the Missouri-side midtown apartment hotel district. The physical location of the Cavalier on its street block is relevant to understand what was about to occur. The building was on the south side of Armour Boulevard near the east end of the block at Forest Avenue which ran north and south. That night the four assassins parked their car down the block facing the front of the apartment building so they could observe Anthon if he walked in or out. Thus the assassins car was facing east toward Forest Avenue.

The targeted Chicago fugitive had taken his wife, her 7-year-old brother, and her mother out that evening to watch the wrestling matches at the International Arena and then to his nightclub that was adjacent to the Arena. Around 1 a.m. the foursome returned to the Cavalier Apartments. Anthon drove past the assassin's parked vehicle and also his apartment building to park at the curb in front of the next building which was on the corner, the Steuben Club. As the family of four got out of their parked car, the assassins car pulled up beside them, and the two gunmen in the back seat leaped out and let go with a burst of pistol fire hitting Anthon eight times. He collapsed on the sidewalk and died. But then their getaway plans were disrupted.

While the four assassins were still parked watching Anthon's apartment front entrance, Jackson County Sheriff Thomas Bash had been attending a social ice-cream lawn party with his wife and a 15-year-old neighbor girl who was to spend the night at the Sheriff's home. The three party guests then headed home in the Sheriff's patrol car driven by a deputy sheriff. The deputy headed south on Forest Avenue and was approaching Armour Boulevard just as the assassins opened fire on Anthon around the right corner and across the street. The four occupants in the Sheriff's car heard an "almost deafening" bark of gunfire from the intersection followed by a woman screaming, so the deputy slowed so he could turn right onto that street and flipped on the red light. As soon as the pair of desperadoes waiting in their car saw the flashing red illuminating the night sky to their left beyond the corner of the cross street, the getaway driver stepped on the gas and pulled far into the intersection as if he were trying to escape, and then he hung a sharp Ueeee to head back towards the front driver's side of the Sheriff's car. As the two desperadoes charged toward the deputy driving they fired pistols at him from outside their open windows.

The moment the getaway driver reversed direction towards the Sheriff's car, the deputy stopped about 75 feet from the intersection, the Sheriff reached for the riot gun racked in the ceiling of the car, and both lawmen leaped out to confront. The Sheriff aimed his riot gun at the windshield of the attacker's car and fired twice killing both men in the front seat. As the driver slumped, his car continued rolling forward hitting head-on into the side of the Sheriff's patrol car. The sharp-shooting Sheriff hit his targets because he practiced and hunted regularly, but some of the killers' shots went through apartment windows without injuring any occupants. The dead men's revolvers lay on the floor of the car in front of their bodies. One reporter summed up the scene by saying, "The extraordinary thing about the Anthon murder was not the murder, but the fact that for once, in their swift getaway, the assassins ran smack into the path of a sheriff equipped with a riot gun, a cool head, steady eye and plenty of courage."[250]

As the two lawmen surveyed the two dead killers in the car in front of them, they were looking southeast so they had no idea that the two shooters of Anthon were still at the murder scene to the southwest because this was behind the lawmen's right shoulders and out of their field of vision. When the Sheriff shot their cohorts, both killers started running across the street toward the lawmen, but at the nearest corner they split up running in different directions. One of the assassins, Charles Gargotta, came running down the sidewalk in the darkness towards the unsuspecting Sheriff and opened fire with his pistol. The surprised Sheriff turned right towards the direction of the renewed gunfire and aimed his riot gun at the approaching man. Gargotta stopped shooting because he had emptied his automatic pistol, but in this tense situation the Sheriff could only assume that the desperado had run out of ammo. Sheriff Bash later testified, "I started to shoot. Then I thought it would be unfair to shoot a defenseless man. I kept moving in. I put my gun's muzzle to his stomach," causing the assailant to drop his empty gun to the ground as he fell to his knees sobbing for mercy, "For God's sake don't shoot! Don't shoot me."[251]

After the two Anthon shooters had run across the intersection and Gargotta had continued heading toward the unsuspecting Sheriff, the other shooter turned to the right at the corner to run across the intersection down Armour Boulevard, the street where the victim had been killed. As he fled across the intersection, he heard Gargotta's shots at the Sheriff and twisted his torso opening fire wildly at the deputy who returned fire. This desperado ran up the terrace of the northeast corner home and disappeared into the rear. The deputy was too far behind to give chase to the assailant who had a maze of escape routes between the homes, so the deputy ran over to assist the Sheriff with the shooter he had captured. The deputy picked up the gun Gargotta had dropped, put it in his pocket, cuffed him, and turned him and his dropped gun over to two Kansas City policemen who arrived at the scene because of calls by neighbors about ongoing gun battles in the neighborhood.

As the deputy took charge of the arrest, the Sheriff ran back to his patrol car to see if his wife and the young neighbor girl were alright, and they were. Mrs. Bash later described what it was like to watch her husband kill two gangsters in their car, while they were shooting bullets at him, and then to see powder flashes light up the sky as the two running shooters fired from different directions. "The whole world was on fire. Shots seemed to be coming from all points. It seemed to me the shots were clipping the trees all about me."[252]

At the hectic shooting scene, the deputy had not had time to search Gargotta who had dropped his gun in front of the Sheriff for additional weapons before turning him over to police. In the squad car, the policeman who sat next to the handcuffed prisoner later testified, "I felt a hard object in Gargotta's clothes. Then he told me it was another pistol, and to take it." This second .45 caliber automatic pistol was loaded and cocked. Gargotta had not dared to draw it to continue his duel with the Sheriff because he had dead aim on him.[253]

The two dead gangsters in the getaway car operated nightclubs in town with the Mafia chieftain's permission. The wife of one of these dead men filed a lawsuit against his life insurance company for failing to pay double indemnity on her husbands $2,000 policy. The jury ruled his death was not accidental because he started shooting at the Sheriff first so the double indemnity clause did not apply.

The two killers who shot Anthon were enforcers for Mafia boss Lazia, and the captured thug, Charles Gargotta, was a chief lieutenant in the gang. He had a two-page police record during the 14 years prior to the murder of Anthon that included payroll and bank holdups in which witnesses were willing to testify against him. However Gargotta was never tried for these arrests because the Mafia leader controlled the police department, the prosecutor, and some judges. The only punishment Gargotta ever received for his crimes was fines for violating Prohibition laws and for vagrancy.

The second Anthon killer, the man who escaped on foot that night, was Thomas "Tano" Lococo. Minutes before the slaying a witness had seen him casing the layout outside Anthon's apartment building. The night before the murder, two patrolmen were cruising and noticed two men sitting in a car parked near the Arena Buffet, officially licensed as a soft-drink stand to cover for the nightclub and speakeasy, in which victim Anthon was a partner. The patrolmen recognized Lococo as a gangster so they searched the two men and the vehicle but they found no weapons and let them go. After Anthon's slaying the two patrolman saw newspaper pictures of murderer Gargotta and recognized him as the man sitting with Lococo in the car the night before the murder. They immediately began searching for Lococo and arrested him as he walked out of a restaurant. Police questioned Lococo but he was never charged by the Lazia-controlled Kansas City law-enforcement apparatus. Lazia further rewarded Lococo for keeping his mouth shut by ordering his extensive criminal record removed from the files at Police Headquarters.

Regarding his criminal past, newspaper articles reported that a decade before Anthon's murder Lococo's Ringside Athletic Club was blown up. He had also once been charged in Kansas City, Kansas with placing a chemical bomb in the Pershing Theater during strife between movie-theater projectionists and theater owners. Ironically at the time of the attempted murder of Sheriff Bash, Lococo and a partner operated a filling station across the street from the courthouse where the Sheriff and his deputies fueled their patrol cars on Sundays when the gas supply ran low in the county pumps. The Sheriff abruptly terminated the policy of using that gas station. Lococo, like the other three assassins, was a member of Lazia's North Side Democratic Club. The witnesses could not identify Lococo, but the County Prosecutor charged Gargotta with the first-degree murder of Anthon, the attempted murder of the Sheriff, and carrying concealed weapons.[254]

THE BIZARRE PROSECUTIONS IN THIS OLD CASE

Eight and a half months after Anthon's slaying, Gargotta went on trial for murdering him. The prosecution's evidence was compelling. The four witnesses in Sheriff Bash's car saw two men drive away from the murder scene directly toward them firing as they came until the Sheriff shot them dead. Then they saw Gargotta and another man run around the corner from the direction of the slaying while firing at the Sheriff and his deputy.

Next two 18-year-old boys testified that just prior to the shooting, they and their girlfriends had left their apartment in the Cavalier to get a late-night meal. The foursome walked out the building's front entrance and turned left to the west alley where the two teenagers' motorcycles were parked against the wall. One of the boys testified that after he had mounted his cycle, "I heard first about five shots, then a scream, then two or three more shots. I started my motorcycle out onto Armour Boulevard, but the motor died. I saw a man walking from Anthon's car, with a pistol in his hand." He headed for Armour Boulevard where the red light was flashing on the Sheriff's car. As the pair followed him, they past the victim's wife who was cradling her dead husband's head in her lap. After the suspect rounded the corner, both teenagers heard gunfire and when the two youthful witnesses rounded the corner they saw the Sheriff arresting this man. Both young men positively identified defendant Gargotta as both the gun totter they had seen at the scene and the prisoner who was soon taken into custody by Sheriff Bash.[255]

Then two policemen further tied Gargotta to the homicide by testifying they had questioned Gargotta the evening before the murder because he was sitting in a parked car observing the victim's place of business. Finally the state's ballistics expert identified the smoking gun. Anthon had been shot eight times with five wounds in the chest, two in the left arm, and one in the right hand, as he apparently threw up his arms to try to fend off the bullets from his torso. Seven of the eight bullets had passed through Anthon's body, and the coroner testified the only remaining bullet was taken from the front unions of his collarbone. The ballistics expert testified that this .45-caliber bullet was a perfect match with a bullet he test fired from the .45 caliber automatic pistol that Gargotta had emptied at Sheriff Bash before dropping it at his feet while begging for mercy. Given this overwhelming evidence, everyone was stunned when the jury's murder verdict found Gargotta not guilty.

During the long legal process of the preliminary hearing, defense depositions, and trial, Gargotta's attorneys focused on just three issues when cross-examining state's witnesses. The defense's main concern was the gun that their client dropped in front of Sheriff Bash. Thus Gargotta's attorneys seemed to undermine their case when they offered their own ballistic expert to testify for the prosecution that yes indeed the bullet from Anthon's body came from the gun in evidence. However from the beginning the defense argued that this was not the gun that Gargotta had dropped at the Sheriff's feet, which seemed like a pointless position until the prosecution called at trial a Kansas City Detective to affirm the police's chain of custody for Gargotta's dropped weapon. Kansas City Detective L. L. Claiborne testified that at the murder scene Sheriff Bash handed him custody of the gun that the assassin who escaped from the scene had dropped between two buildings while making his getaway. When the Detective read this gun's serial number it shocked everyone in the courtroom because this serial number was the one the prosecution claimed belonged to Gargotta's gun. This revelation made it appear that the police had misidentified the two guns, meaning the shooter of the one bullet found in the victim was the fourth assassin who escaped and not Gargotta.

Three witnesses quickly approached the prosecutor offering to refute Detective Claiborne's jolting testimony as a lie. Both the state's ballistic expert and his wife then testified that the Detective had shown up at their home a few days before he testified in court. The Detective falsely claimed to the couple that he was in a jam because the Sheriff had given him Gargotta's gun, and he failed to write down the serial number that he needed for his pending testimony. The expert assisted Claiborne by turning over the number of Gargotta's gun. When the Detective testified in court, he told the truth that the Sheriff had given him the gun of the escaped assassin. But he then perjured himself by reading the serial number of Gargotta's gun while falsely claiming it was the number of the assassin's gun the Sheriff had given him. Following this couple's testimony Sheriff Bash retook the witness stand to emphatically state that the gun he gave to the Detective was the escaped assassin's, and that Claiborne had never seen Gargotta's gun so he could not have legitimately obtained its serial number because the Detective arrived at the scene after both Gargotta and his gun had been turned over to two other police officers. Regarding Gargotta's gun, Sheriff Bash stated, "It has been in my possession constantly, and Claiborne never had had his hands on it. The weapon he testified about which I turned over to him was the other weapon." The two police officers who had already testified that they had been given custody of both Gargotta and his gun by the Sheriff reaffirmed this. Finally two FBI agents testified to the proper procedure the Sheriff and the Kansas City police had taken in tagging and keeping identified the five separate weapons taken from the four shooters – two in the getaway car, two from Gargotta, and one along the path of the escaped assassin. The FBI had carefully investigated the four .45 caliber automatic pistols recovered in these ongoing shootouts because they had been stolen from a National Guard arsenal used by United States Army members. The FBI was in the process of preparing federal criminal charges over these stolen weapons.[256]

After the shocking not guilty verdict, reporters went to the 12 jurors' homes and asked each one why he found Gargotta innocent. The number one reason was that the prosecution's chain of custody for the guns did not seem complete, but these jurors should have seen through Detective Claiborne's lie. With all the credible witnesses discrediting the Detective, it should have been obvious to the jury that Claiborne obtained the serial number of Gargotta's gun that he presented at trial from the ballistics expert and not because he had ever handled the weapon. However a number of jurors told reporters after the trial that they were confused by the way the bullet testimony was handled.

In contrast to these murder-case jurors, U.S. Attorney Maurice Milligan was incensed by Detective Claiborne's fraudulent testimony, and the Federal Prosecutor quickly hauled him before a Federal Grand Jury to explain his testimony about the two guns and their serial numbers. Under oath Claiborne had to tell the same story he had in court so he claimed Sheriff Bash gave him the gun dropped by the escaped assassin, and then the Detective said he placed a red tag on it for identification. U.S. Attorney Milligan then presented evidence that the Kansas City police did not use that type of tag until two months after Claiborne took the gun into custody, and the Federal Grand Jury indicted the Detective for perjury. Just two months after the Anthon murder jury acquitted Gargotta based on the Detective's lie, a Kansas City Federal Jury readily convicted Claiborne for perjury. He received a 4-year sentence that was delayed a year until a Federal Appeals Court affirmed his guilt. The court issued an order for Claiborne to surrender to U.S. Marshals, but he arrived 10 days earlier then specified to begin his sentence because he said, "I want to get it over with." He served almost 2 years of his sentence at Leavenworth, Kansas Penitentiary before being paroled.[257]

By failing to properly cross-examine Detective Claiborne, the Prosecutor let him get away with perjury and let Gargotta get away with murder. The federal perjury indictment roused public opinion against Jackson County Prosecutor W. W. Graves for failing to have taken action on this evidence himself. Prosecutor Graves gave a number of empty excuses for his inaction. These included the claim he had searched for the tag but learned the defense attorneys had stolen it from the evidence table, and that he had insufficient funds to conduct an investigation.

Several American newspapers in the 1900s featured outstanding investigative reporters who exposed much of the wrongdoing by the local political machines and organized-crime gangs. In Kansas City the investigative reporters for the *Star* and the *Times* did an excellent job of revealing the corruption of the Pendergast machine and the crimes of Lazia's Mafia gang. However during Gargotta's trial for murdering Anthon, these reporters failed to realize that Jackson County Prosecutor Graves had undermined his own prosecution of what should have been an open and shut case. For example, the only gun that was relevant in this case was the one that shot the sole bullet remaining in the victim. Prosecutor Graves had no reason to call Detective Claiborne about the gun of a criminal who was not on trial, but he needed Claiborne's false testimony to assist Gargotta's primary defense. Beginning with the preliminary hearing Gargotta's attorneys claimed the Sheriff and police misidentified the guns even though they had no evidence whatsoever to back up this assertion. This would have been a pointless strategy unless these attorneys were already in cahoots with both the Detective and the Prosecutor. It is certainly easy to believe both law-enforcement officials may have been corrupt. Not only was Detective Claiborne a key member of Mafioso Lazia's personally-selected Kansas City police force, but newly-elected Prosecutor Graves was a Pendergast loyalist who would soon exhibit a consistent pattern of protecting from prosecution Gargotta and the other Mafia gang members.

Prosecutor Graves malfeasance in Gargotta's trial involved much more chicanery than just joining in with the perjury scheme of the Detective and defense attorneys. At critical times in questioning witnesses, and in giving arguments before the Judge, the Prosecutor left out vital points of law. For example, Graves failed to instruct the jury that it did not matter whose gun fired the bullet into Anthon, because anyone who is involved in a felony that results in the death of anyone, no matter whether it is an innocent victim or a fellow criminal, is guilty of that person's murder. Gargotta was unquestionably at the Anthon murder scene carrying a gun, and he also attempted to murder Sheriff Bash. Prosecutor Graves should have also tried Gargotta for the murders of his two associates who were killed by Sheriff Bash. In addition Prosecutor Graves failed to remind the jury that the bullet retrieved from Anthon's body was just one of eight fired into him that night. Since the eyewitness testimony makes it certain that Gargotta was one of the two shooters who pumped those eight slugs into the victim, the identity of which gun fired any one of those bullets was totally irrelevant. It is a travesty that Detective Claiborne was called as a witness and that both the Prosecutor and the Judge allowed such irrelevant testimony to be introduced before the jury.

The juror's later told reporters their second problem with the Prosecutor's case was his failure to present a motive for the murder. Mafia gang leader Lazia's hand-picked Kansas City Police

Department never developed a motive even though local newspaper investigative reporters printed that they had learned from their underworld sources that Anthon was expanding into Lazia's territory on the Missouri side of Kansas City. This would have been easy for detectives to have learned from their informants if they had bothered to ask them, especially since weeks before Anthon's murder, one of the two men Sheriff Bash killed in the car escaping the slaying scene had gotten into a fist fight with the victim as tensions between the two gangs was building.

Many jurors said their third reason for having reasonable doubt was confusion remaining about various aspects of the case. This resulted from the Prosecutor failing to challenge the defense attorneys and witnesses when they contradicted the facts established by so many credible state's witnesses, and the Prosecutor not clarifying issues and placing them in their proper context to counteract all the contradictory testimony.

Gargotta's defense case consisted of three witnesses. The first was a woman who lived at the Cavalier Apartments and was his alibi. Nancy Thomas testified that on the night Anthon was murdered Gargotta was in her apartment for three hours. He took off his coat, but she saw no pistol or holster. She recalled the precise time he left, which was right after the shooting took place in front of the building even though they did not hear the shots in the apartment. She remembered every detail about that evening with Gargotta, but under cross-examination she could not recall anything about their alleged first flirtatious meeting a month earlier. She had lived in Kansas City for four years but had never worked because her father sent her a monthly allowance. He lived in Tempe, Arizona and was also unemployed. Not exactly a believable story, but it laid the groundwork for Gargotta's follow-up fraudulent testimony.

When Gargotta testified about his activities that evening, he also remembered leaving Nancy's apartment at 1:18 a.m. after Anthon had been murdered. Then he contradicted the testimony of the four witnesses in Sheriff Bash's car, the two teenagers at the murder scene, and the two police officers who had seen him stalking Anthon's business the night before. Gargotta claimed he was unarmed, never fired on anyone, and was not running from the murder scene. He also said the Sheriff advanced on him pointing a riot gun. The only admission Prosecutor Graves got from Gargotta was that he knew the two gangsters killed by Sheriff Bash as "acquaintances" rather than friends. It was well known that the dead gangsters were Gargotta's companions so the Prosecutor was forced to raise the issue of his relationship to them, just as Gargotta dared not deny knowing them. The jurors' stated that their fourth problem with Prosecutor Graves' case was that he never countered Gargotta's testimony by showing the defendant had worked in concert with the other assassins, like four known associates at a murder scene carrying and firing guns was not enough.

The final defense witness was the victim's widow who traveled from Milwaukee, Wisconsin to testify on behalf of her husband's killer. The former Mrs. Anthon testified under the name Evelyn Hats. Like Gargotta she contradicted the prosecution's witnesses and evidence by claiming there was only one shooter, not two. She also said that even though he "had a handkerchief over the lower part of his face," it was definitely not Gargotta who she said she had known for two and a half years. She claimed there was no trouble between her husband and the defendant, but he would not have discussed his Prohibition underworld conflicts with anyone, including his wife. She clearly lied about what happened to protect her husband's killer, and it can only be assumed that she was well paid. Graves did not challenge her about all the contradictions between her account and the established evidence. The jurors' fifth problem with the Prosecutor's case was that he had not challenged the widows testimony, and this made her seem more believable than all the consistent statements by the many other eyewitnesses.[258]

After the not guilty verdict was read in court, Prosecutor Graves' comment to the press was, "The verdict indicates the jury believed Gargotta's story, and if they believed it, they must have believed the evidence presented by the state was perjury." Prosecutor Graves' admission that the strong and consistent testimonies by his state's witnesses did not seem believable to the jurors is an indication of just how muddled he had made these strong and straightforward issues.

It would later come out that Prosecutor Graves systematically undermined the criminal justice system in hundreds of felony cases. A fresh examination is presented here of Gargotta's legal maneuvers prior to the trial. They demonstrate that the Prosecutor's malfeasance had to have been planned even before he entered office. This is the only way to explain why Gargotta's attorneys worked so hard to keep delaying his trial even though it meant their client languished in jail for eight and one half months because a death-penalty charge was not a bailable offense. The Sheriff had arrested Gargotta at the scene of the slaying, and his attorneys kept asking for delays until Prosecutor Graves won election and assumed office. His attorneys first used pointless technical continuances that would obviously be rejected. Then to make their postponement scheme less obvious, his attorneys added another lawyer to the team who was a Pendergast loyalist and a member of the State Legislature. By law, attorneys could not be forced to try their cases so long as the Legislature was in session which it was until newly-elected Jackson County Prosecutor W. W. Graves took office.

From the moment the Legislature adjourned, Prosecutor Graves started arguing for continuances on the basis that he needed to familiarize himself with the case. However this made no sense because the new Prosecutor had no trial experience, while his two assistants were capable prosecutors who had been ready to go to trial for months. Graves' argument to the court was that the case was so important that he wanted to handle it himself, despite the fact that he was the only amateur on the prosecution team. Even though Prosecutor Graves' requests for continuance were unwarranted, the defense attorneys wholeheartedly endorsed each one because every Gargotta hearing was conducted by a different Judge. When the fifth Judge took charge, both Prosecutor Graves and the defense attorneys immediately announced they were ready to proceed. During the trial Prosecutor Graves questioned every witness and made every legal argument before the Judge to muddle the jury, while he turned over the prosecution's opening and closing statements to a qualified assistant to handle in a professional manner.

The juror's deliberations were very contentious. They had to take 15 ballots before reaching unanimous agreement for acquittal, but this still only took them five and a half hours. Throughout the trial, the courtroom had been packed with Gargotta's fellow Mafiosi and Lazia's North Side Democratic Club members. When the Bailiff read the not guilty verdict the crowd burst into deafening cheers as Gargotta immediately shook the hands of selected jurors telling them, "I thank you a million times." Then in a most unusual expression of gratitude Gargotta shook the hand of Prosecutor Graves who had sought his death by execution. Several of the Mafiosi also shook jurors' hands congratulating them on their "good," "fine," or "just" verdict.

Gargotta walked out free of the Anthon murder charge after he had posted bond to face a still pending charge for assault to kill Sheriff Bash. The next day Kansas City U.S. Attorney Maurice Milligan ordered a contingent of lawmen made up of FBI agents, U.S. Marshals, and Sheriff Bash with his deputies to arrest Gargotta as he walked out of his political club. He was charged with possession of two Army pistols stolen along with 73 other guns from the Kansas National Guard armory 10 months before the murder of Anthon. U.S. Attorney Milligan presented all the relevant witnesses from the Anthon murder trial to prove Gargotta had two guns in his possession when Sheriff Bash took him into custody. They were marked on one side with the words "Model 1911, U.S. Army" and on the other side "United States property." Gargotta's attorney did not cross-examine a single witness and did not present a defense case except to point out that Army guns bearing these words were frequently sold for $25 to Army officers for private use, and these officers could pass them on to others. U.S. Judge Merrill E. Otis immediately replied much of the evidence proved the defendant knew the guns were stolen. For example Gargotta denied to law enforcement from the time of his arrest that he ever owned these or any other pistol. The Judge argued that if he did not have guilty knowledge they were stolen, he would not have denied they were in his possession, and that if he had obtained them legally, he would not have been afraid to admit ownership. It took the Federal Trial Jury 31 minutes to find Gargotta guilty of concealing and possessing the two stolen U.S. Army pistols, and the Judge sentenced him to 3 years in prison.

Eleven months later Gargotta's stolen-gun possession conviction was reversed by a 2-to-1 U.S. Circuit Court of Appeals vote. The majority may have ruled correctly that the prosecution had not produced evidence that Gargotta knew the pistols were stolen, but the majority offered an interesting caveat. While preparing their ruling, these two judges admitted finding it difficult to keep "from reverting to the fact the defendant was with gangsters and was using one of the pistols in a deadly assault on the Sheriff. It may be a gangster today, while tomorrow it may be a first citizen." The Court could have separated the gangsters from legitimate, or first, citizens by ruling that the prosecution must produce evidence that the possessor of a stolen gun either knew it was stolen or used it in an armed crime. The Court could have made use of an untraceable gun in a violent crime prima fascia evidence the perpetrator had to know it was stolen because the nature of the crime meant his intent was to use it as a throwaway weapon. The dissenting vote presented a different solution by arguing that Gargotta's denial he ever possessed the guns, and his refusal to offer an explanation of how he might have come by them innocently, meant that "the duty of the court was to let the jury decide." This Court reversal of Gargotta's conviction left him facing just the one remaining charge of attempting to murder Sheriff Bash. The Mafioso remained free on bail awaiting trial as the cases involving he and Prosecutor Graves became even stranger. Eventually gangster Gargotta would go on to become an embarrassment for the White House.[259]

THE ULTIMATE BETRAYAL

Gangster Gargotta had been found not guilty of murdering Anthon by the Jackson County Jury, and he won his appeal of the federal stolen-gun possession conviction. He still faced one remaining indictment from that fateful night, the attempted murder of County Sheriff Bash. But the Pendergast political/criminal machine protected the Mafioso from facing trial by simply directing their puppet County Prosecutor Graves to request a postponement of each trial date as it approached. Of course Gargotta's defense attorneys were most obliging with the Prosecutor in filing a joint written stipulation asking each trial date be continued until the court's next term as this allowed their client to remain free on bail.

The Gargotta case demonstrates how the local political/criminal machine rendered the Kansas City Police Chief and the Jackson County Prosecutor completely ineffective against Lazia's blatant gang violence even when it was directed against local lawmen. With this information in hand, it is time to examine the FBI's Kansas City Massacre case one final time. The Gargotta case proves that FBI informant "Needles" La Capra's statement to agents that Mafia leader Lazia feared the local police was a perverse mockery of the truth because Lazia had absolute control over the Kansas City Police Department, the County Prosecutor, and some Judges. Yet FBI Director J. Edgar Hoover relied on this one totally false statement from informant La Capra to construct all his erroneous conclusions and misguided actions in the Kansas City Massacre murder case of four peacekeepers. Hoover made this horrendous slaughter case falsely appear solved and thus blocked its possible solution resulting in justice denied.

Returning to Gargotta's attempted murder charge of Sheriff Bash, each Jackson County court term lasted about two months. On the first day of each term, a judge called each pending case on the criminal docket and named the judge and scheduled the trial date. Every time the Gargotta case for the attempted murder of Sheriff Bash was called, Prosecutor Graves, with the connivance of defense attorneys, asked the judge to continue it until the next court term. Prosecutor Graves received approval of 27 such requests in a row until the killing of Anthon and the attempted murder charge of Sheriff Bash were five years and four months old. The Sheriff had since retired and become president of the Federal Engineering and Construction Company.

Prosecutor Graves played his delaying game until he thought enough years had transpired for everyone to forget about the attempted murder of the former Sheriff. Then when a new judge was assigned the case, the Prosecutor asked that the charges against Gargotta be dismissed on the grounds that the defendant had already been acquitted by a jury for the murder of Anthon, and the state had no additional evidence to present in the attempted-murder case. The Prosecutor's assertion about lack of evidence was absolutely false. In the Anthon slaying no one had witnessed Gargotta fire a gun, but in the pending attempted-murder case, Graves had truly overwhelming evidence. Six witnesses were in very close range as the gangster emptied his pistol at the Sheriff before falling to his knees to beg for his life. These six were the former Sheriff and his wife, his deputy, a neighbor girl, and two teenagers who lived in victim Anthon's apartment building. All were eagerly awaiting the opportunity to positively identify Gargotta as the shooter against the former Sheriff.

The conniving judge who had taken over Gargotta's case tried to cover up the great miscarriage of justice he and Prosecutor Graves were perpetrating by delivering a lengthy lecture to the Prosecutor with carefully crafted words that made it sound like a stern condemnation when it really concealed the truth about the nature of the case for the official court record. The nation's newspapers carried shortened summaries of his lecture that made it sound like a distraught judge had no choice but to dismiss for which he admonished Prosecutor Graves, "You have let this case become synonymous with the lack of law enforcement in Kansas City. Your activities in this case have put everybody connected with law enforcement in a bad light."[260]

In contrast the local Kansas City newspapers carried a detailed account of the judge's harsh criticism which actually delivered exactly the opposite impact. In reality the judge was not angry that Prosecutor Grave's was dismissing the case, but instead that he had not dropped it four years ago when the judge had admonished him to do so. The judge went on to condemn "your stubbornness and refusal to listen to anyone" by continuing the case. The judge then deceitfully claimed it had always been a weak case by presenting a revisionist history - "In that [Anthon] case Gargotta might have had a motive but he had no motive in the Bash case. As I remember, Bash happened on the shooting, and when Gargotta recognized him he ran toward Bash begging for mercy." Then the judge gave false accolades about Prosecutor Graves' performance in office. "In looking over my docket I see your office in this term of court, has sent 30 prisoners to the penitentiary for a total of 140 years. I am not bragging as to the length of time those persons have been sentenced, but it speaks for good work in your office." Prosecutor Graves left the courtroom without saying a word to the press. As usual neither Gargotta nor his attorney were present even though defendants always appeared when their case was called. A totally disgusted former Sheriff Bash who had been there ready to testify clenched his jaws as he said, "I have no comment."[261]

After the Gargotta dismissal Prosecutor Graves returned to his office where he quickly learned his assumption about the public having a poor memory was wrong. His action incited immediate outrage in the community. Governor Stark and President Roosevelt decided this was the type of major political scandal they had been privately waiting for as they had sealed a pact to work in concert to try to clean up Kansas City's political/criminal machine two years earlier when the Federal Grand Jury issued its first massive voter-fraud indictments.

The afternoon of Gargotta's dismissal Governor Stark was in Washington, where he launched the opening salvo against corruption in Kansas City. Governor Stark denounced the Prosecutor's dismissal action to the press by saying it was a "disgrace to the law enforcement agencies of Missouri. Any law enforcement agency that was a party to that is not fit to be a part of the law enforcing machinery of Missouri. … The spectacle of the man who had attempted the murder of the able and courageous sheriff being let off scot free by the very law enforcing authorities who should have used every possible effort to punish him to the full extent of the law, is revolting to every honest and patriotic citizen of Missouri. The only reason this sheriff escaped death was because of the poor marksmanship of this man who had fired five shots at him at close range. This type of absolute lack of law enforcement is what has given Kansas City, according to recent press reports, the highest murder and homicide rate than the fifteen largest cities in the United States. All of this results from the combination of politics and crime."[262]

The Governor followed this public barrage four days later by delivering a strongly-worded letter to Missouri AG Roy McKittrick directing him to launch an inquiry to fight the breakdown of law and order in Kansas City as authorized under the state's Constitution. The Governor ordered the AG to send his assistants into Jackson County to investigate and prosecute law violations, and to file ouster proceedings against any law enforcement officer who had failed to perform his duties or who refused to cooperate with this cleanup.

The Governor's letter to the AG detailed the city's criminal problems. "In Kansas City it is charged that unrestrained violations of the law are openly and notoriously committed and that there is a definite breakdown in law enforcement; that such serious crimes as homicide go unsolved and the perpetrators go unpunished; that rackets of various types flourish openly in defiance of law and order; that open and notorious gambling dens and vice brothels exist; and that the state's liquor laws are violated openly with impunity. Information from reliable sources shows that the gambling racket is carried on openly in defiance of law and without protest from any official heads of the city's government, that houses of prostitution flourish within the very shadow of the courthouse and city hall and the inmates solicit openly, unashamed, and unafraid of official authority. Gangsters and racketeers, unmolested by officials, ply their trade and prey, through violence and intimidation, upon citizens and business men. Our citizens living outstate and in other states are an especial prey of petty thieves and other criminals of this city." The AG, a Pendergast loyalist, replied that if the investigative funds were authorized he was ready to become a racket buster. The Governor responded by seeing to it that the AG was adequately funded.[263]

Kansas City was known as one of the most politically corrupt cities in the country. Even the *Christian Science Monitor* called it "wilder open than any place outside Reno" and attacked its residents for being "astonishingly complacent about it all." The comparison with Reno, the domain of casino partners Graham and McKay, was strong because Nevada was the only state that had legalized any of three sinful vice pleasures of casinos, brothels, and 24-hour liquor sales, and the state boasted about having all three. In addition Nevada offered the quickest divorces, and Reno accommodated the wives of the rich and famous at fine dude ranches where handsome cowboys showed them the surrounding beautiful natural environment while these women met the residency requirement. Thus Reno had a well-established reputation in the rest of the country as the armpit of the nation.[264]

On the same day that Governor Stark wrote the letter to his AG, President Roosevelt's Justice Department roared into action. Missouri U.S. Attorney Maurice Milligan had the Kansas City Federal District Judge order the Federal Grand Jury to continue its investigation of the 1936 election-vote fraud. In a little more than two years, Milligan prosecuted 19 trials against political/criminal machine workers for voter fraud during that election and convicted 257 without a single acquittal. Governor Stark also reduced the machine's voter-fraud abuses by appointing a non-political election board in Kansas City that removed 60,000 illegal voter registrations from the rolls.

Under direction from President Roosevelt's Justice Department, Federal Prosecutor Milligan next introduced evidence to the Judge about wide-open gambling in Kansas City. An IRS agent had visited half of the city's 100 or more gambling operations and talked with each operator. The IRS agent posed as a casino investor and said he would like to open a joint. Every operator informed him he would have to meet with the "Big Man." The Judge ordered the Grand Jury to go after this Big Man of Kansas City gambling without mentioning Mafia-gang leader Carollo by name. These state and federal drives quickly closed the flourishing gambling business and it remained shuttered for at least a year due to all the heat. At the same time the Jackson County Special Grand Jury took up an investigation of crime and rackets in Kansas City.

When one political party has control of all key government positions, wrong-doing is rarely investigated as party members typically protect each other. Checks and balances only work when government offices are divided between political parties. In Missouri during the Great Depression all the key players were Democrats, but a factional feud developed as individual party members, who were fed up with the excessive influence and corruption of Pendergast, used the power of their positions to challenge the Boss' fiefdom.

Governor Stark's order to investigate the break down of law enforcement in Kansas City was quickly championed by crusading State Judge Allen C. Southern, who was an arch foe of Boss Pendergast and of illegal gambling. Judge Southern realized that even the Grand Jury pools of prospective jurors had been tampered with by the political/criminal machine. He found almost one-quarter of the members in prospective jury panels were city or county employees beholden to the machine for their jobs, so he had the Kansas City Lawyers Association make sure government employees did not make up a disproportionate percentage of future jury panels. Judge Southern knew the Special Grand Jury that was in session would dissolve in five weeks with the end of the court term, so he directed them to immediately start a broad inquiry into alleged "unrestrained violations of law" and return indictments against criminals and errant public office holders before adjournment.

County Prosecutor Graves planned to control and undermine the Special Grand Jury's efforts. He asked AG McKittrick to assist him in the presentation of witnesses, but Judge Southern saw through this masquerade. Since both prosecutors were political allies of Pendergast, Judge Southern blocked the pair from testifying in an effort to keep the Grand Jury sacrosanct from partisan manipulation. Simultaneously with the Judge's actions, Governor Stark denounced Prosecutor Graves' continued efforts to circumvent justice, asked that he be immediately ousted from office, and expressed hope the Grand Jury would investigate his official actions and misconduct. The Governor proclaimed that Graves "should be removed from office because of his failure to prosecute ghastly felonies." Reacting quickly County Prosecutor Graves went into court to claim the proceedings were illegal and got them halted. This kicked the legality issues to the Missouri Supreme Court for a decision. Within two weeks the Court ruled that Graves could not stop the investigation, but the Court did affirm the right of both the Prosecutor and the AG to appear before the Grand Jury. McKittrick later appeared, but Graves claimed illness to remain absent from the Grand Jury proceedings. The County Prosecutor did not dare risk perjuring himself under oath with false claims that he was not guilty of malfeasance.[265]

By the time the Missouri Supreme Court had ruled on Prosecutor Grave's Grand Jury illegality claim, it left the jurists just three weeks to investigate the political/criminal hotbed and to bring indictments. These jurors were unbelievably dedicated and effective. Taking control of their inquiry, they indicted 166 persons representing every corrupt aspect of the political/criminal machine. They reindicted Gargotta for assault with intent to kill Sheriff Bash because this five-and-a-half-year-old crime carried no statute of limitations. They indicted many high-ranking public officials who were henchmen of Pendergast. Heading the list was Prosecutor Graves and the head of the county commission whose official title was County Presiding Judge. Both were charged with neglect of duty. Also accused was the County Buildings Supervisor who saw to it that kingmaker Pendergast and Mafia leader Carollo got the most valuable government construction contracts. Immediately after the Judge had instructed the Special Grand Jury to investigate crime, Mafia leader Carollo ordered his extensive gambling operations to go dark to avoid antagonizing the jurors. This massive closure did not stop the jurors from indicting Carollo for operating a casino. Many other gangsters, gamblers, and tavern owners were also charged. The Grand Jury's final report said it attempted to examine city financial records "and gave up its intention only when, after three days of effort, the sheriff's office was unable to find any one in authority on whom they could serve subpoenas." As the Jury was turning in its report, the police finally started doing their job by rounding up 90 persons in a raid on an illegal racehorse book.

Remember that the Prosecutor, the dismissing judge, and machine supporters had all made false claims that the state had no attempted-murder case against Gargotta. But three months after being indicted a second time the Mafioso recognized he was facing a truly overwhelming eyewitness prosecution. Thus Gargotta approached AG McKittrick and offered to plead guilty to the attempted murder of Sheriff Bash in return for a 3-year sentence. The AG was holding a virtually airtight case so he had no legitimate reason to accept such a light slap on the wrist, but he still accepted it. AG McKittrick defended his action to the judge by lying that he was having difficulty assembling the witnesses even though two days earlier the main four had sat in a court hearing ready to testify. The AG told the judge that former Sheriff Bash was in favor of the deal, and afterward Bash inexplicably told reporters, "That's a relief." AG McKittrick was part of the Kansas City political/criminal machine, and he had obviously sold out just as the Jackson County Prosecutor had been doing for more than five years.

Gargotta seemed to be very upset about the reality of facing prison time. Two days before he pled guilty, he was at a hearing about his upcoming trial. Gargotta restlessly walked in and out of the courtroom proceedings and wandered about the building. Then within minutes after the judge accepted Gargotta's guilty plea, the life seemed to drain out of him. He slumped against the defendant's table, his eyes dulled and he seemed to grow older. A decade after Gargotta pled guilty, the U.S. Senate Committee studying organized crime's influence on politics in American cities was chaired by Senator Estes Kefauver who said of the killer, "If ever a human being deserved the title of 'mad dog' it was Gargotta."[266]

Governor Stark would have almost certainly seen to it that Gargotta serve every day of his sentence, but Stark was prohibited by law from running for reelection. He was succeeded as Governor by Forrest Donnell who was a Republican, but his ambition was to become U.S. Senator so he sold out to the Kansas City's Mafia leader to obtain the support of his Democratic political machine. In return Governor Donnell pardoned the vicious killer just five weeks after Gargotta had served half of his three-year sentence. The Governor also restored the admitted attempted-murderer's civil rights. The Governor's action followed the corrupt Prosecutor's score of delays and dismissal of the case against Gargotta, so this was one more official insult heaped on former Sheriff Bash who had so valiantly risked his life standing up for law and order. Governor Donnell pardoned Gargotta on the recommendation of his Parole Board after its members had rejected a strong protest by the legitimately-appointed Kansas City Police Chief. The Board ignored his complaint that Gargotta was a hard-core violent criminal who had been arrested 40 times in Missouri during the past 25 years. Despite this awful criminal pardoning action, Governor Donnell went on to win election as U.S. Senator from Missouri.

As soon as Governor Donnell gave Gargotta his freedom, he returned to his life of crime and became the lieutenant of Kansas City Mafia leader Charles Binaggio. In the ensuing years Gargotta was arrested a few times for armed robbery, but the County Prosecutor never took him to trial despite having witnesses who were ready to testify. Other than these arrests Gargotta conducted his illicit businesses in obscurity until he burst into the headlines again. These articles would cause embarrassment for a Jackson County, Missouri politician who had ascended to the White House. They revealed Gargotta's association with President Harry Truman, but these revelations are presented later in the misadventures of the Kansas City political/criminal machine.

JUSTICE DELAYED & MANIPULATED

Returning to the chronology of events surrounding the offenses committed by Prosecutor Graves and gangster Gargotta, two weeks after the County Special Grand Jury reindicted the Mafioso for the attempted murder of Sheriff Bash, Governor Stark made a surprise appearance before the Missouri Legislature. He asked the legislators to return the Kansas City Police Department to state control under a bipartisan board of four members who would be appointed by the Governor. He said, "Your plain duty is to emancipate the Police Department, to free it from political slavery. … The Police Department of Kansas City has become a signal of notorious failure. As a police department it has virtually ceased to function. It has become the instrumentality of politicians." Three months later the Legislature complied by passing a law returning the Kansas City Police Department to state control, and Governor Stark appointed an anti-political-machine board that hired a new Police Chief who in turn fired half the force for corruption.[267]

Less than two months after reestablishing state control over the Kansas City Police Department, Governor Stark directed AG McKittrick to file a suit in the Missouri Supreme Court to oust corrupt Jackson County Prosecutor Graves from office with a charge of neglect of duty. Graves had already been indicted criminally by the County Special Grand Jury for neglecting his duty, and the County's indictments came to trial before the Supreme Court ruled. Prosecutor Graves' two trials were presided over by Circuit Court Judge Marion Waltner who, like Graves, was a loyal henchman of the Pendergast/Mafia machine. Judge Waltner was determined to protect the Prosecutor from ever facing a jury, so the Judge turned both proceedings into travesties of justice.

In one trial Prosecutor Graves was charged with failing to act against the obviously wide-open gambling operations in Kansas City. Judge Waltner sat back as Assistant AG Olliver Nolen presented the state's case that Graves knew of five illegal gambling establishments but made no effort to close them. Then Judge Waltner turned to the defense attorney who made a motion to dismiss the charge. The Judge instantaneously sustained the dismissal before the Assistant AG had any time to object. The Judge defended his capricious decision by concluding "since there is no allegation of personal corruption," meaning no evidence the Prosecutor accepted money, no crime had been committed. The Assistant AG combatively objected to the Judge's misinterpretation of the law by presenting well-reasoned Missouri Supreme Court decisions which established the only relevant issue was dereliction of official duty. They clearly stated that motive was not a consideration whether it was for personal gain or not. Among the precedents presented by the Assistant AG was, "In the case of the State versus Wymore, it was indirectly held that when a matter is so open that the newspapers and public know of it, that knowledge has previously come to the prosecutor." Judge Waltner countered with deceitful, tortured, and irrelevant arguments to falsely claim Prosecutor Grave's actions were exceptions to all applicable Missouri law. When the Judge realized he was losing to the Assistant AG's cogent arguments, His Honor summarily silenced the prosecuting attorney by pointing out that further discussion was futile since he had previously disposed of the case before hearing the Assistant AG's objections.[268]

Prosecutor Graves' other trial was for neglect of duty by "willfully and corruptly" dismissing the case against Gargotta for the attempted murder of Sheriff Bash. Judge Waltner conducted this trial in the same manner. He first allowed the Assistant AG to present his case to the jury, and then the Judge agreed with defense attorney motions that no mention had been made that money changed hands. A payoff was just as irrelevant in this trial because the charge was purely about failure to perform no matter what the motive. Next Judge Waltner allowed the defense attorney to lie that the Prosecutor's evidence against gangster Gargotta in the attempted murder of the Sheriff was no better than in the murder of gangster Anthon that had earlier resulted in acquittal by jury. This was an atrocious revision of history as seven months earlier Gargotta had pled guilty and admitted he had attempted to kill the Sheriff rather than face the prosecution's overwhelming witness case. Despite the defense's outrageously untrue arguments, the Judge ordered a directed verdict of acquittal that automatically dismissed the indictment and allowed no appeal under law. Judge Waltner was one of the political/criminal machine's puppets who regularly allowed continuances, reduced charges, gave minimum sentences, and dismissed cases for members of the Mafia gang.

Waltner's improper decisions in both of Prosecutor Graves' neglect of official duty trials left Jackson County without further legal authority to act against his shameful misconduct. The only hope for justice now resided with the Missouri Supreme Court which was just beginning to hear the ouster petition evidence against the corrupt Prosecutor. This is when Prosecutor Graves vindictively retaliated against three courageous public-spirited Pendergast critics with outlandish County Grand Jury felony indictments whose sole purpose was to blacken these men's fine reputations. Graves chief target was legitimate Police Chief Lear Reed appointed by Governor Stark. His alleged crime was oppression in office by photographing and fingerprinting arrestees before they were convicted of a crime. The State Police Board that had been appointed by the Governor promptly paid the Chief's $1,500 bond and expressed their confidence in him. The other two legitimate citizens had also worked to bring down Pendergast's corrupt machine. A judge soon tossed these malicious, ridiculous charges against all three men.

The Missouri Supreme Court appointed a Special Commissioner to review volumes of records from the Criminal Circuit Court involving cases prosecuted by Graves. The Commissioner's conclusions about the Gargotta case for the attempted-murder of Sheriff Bash was at all times "eyewitnesses were ready and willing to testify to the charge," but Graves refrained from bringing the case to trial. The Special Commissioner charged that Prosecutor Graves did "without any cause, justification or excuse, unlawfully dismiss said case, well knowing that there was sufficient material and legal evidence available to convict the defendant of the crime charged against him." The Special Commissioner continued that Gargotta's guilty plea proved the strength of the case against him, and pointed out that the reason the case was dismissed was because defendant Gargotta and the Prosecutor were political friends and members of the same political organization.[269]

The Special Commissioner spent seven months investigating Prosecutor Graves actions and sent a detailed report to the Missouri Supreme Court which issued an eight-page ruling categorizing the many laws Prosecutor Graves either violated or failed to enforce. The Court concluded, "A prosecuting attorney has no arbitrary discretion in dismissing criminal proceedings pending in the courts of his county." Without mentioning Judge Waltner's name the Supreme Court made it clear that the Judge was wrong in dismissing the neglect of duty criminal charges against Prosecutor Graves because the prosecution does not have to show any corrupt motive to convict for criminal neglect of official duty.

The Court then dealt with Prosecutor Graves' many forms of dereliction of duty in hundreds of separate cases. During his almost seven years in office, many murderers, armed robbers, burglars, car thieves, and other assorted criminals were given endless continuances and either illegal dismissals or reduction of felonies to misdemeanors resulting in mostly minor fines. He also routinely dismissed armed robbers despite having witnesses ready and willing to testify. Prosecutor Graves even once failed to follow a court order directing him to destroy the gambling equipment of Mafia gang leader Frank Carolla seized in a police raid of his Fortune and Snooker Clubs.

Regarding the wide-open gambling houses, sale of Prohibition liquor, and brothels with girls soliciting passersby on the sidewalk that Prosecutor Graves failed to investigate and prosecute, the Missouri Supreme Court established that the prosecution does not need to prove a prosecutor had personal knowledge of specific criminal wrongdoing but just newspaper articles or other general information that "an ordinary reasonable and prudent man would have known" that wrongdoing was going on. The Supreme Court emphasized the following distinction regarding the use of this type of general evidence. "Of course these newspaper articles would be inadmissible for the purpose of showing the truth of the statements therein contained," but they prove "such conditions were generally known in the county and that the prosecuting attorney made no bona fide effort to investigate such conditions or to institute proceedings to combat evils described."

During Prosecutor Graves' tenure all the prosecutions for voter fraud, corruption by political leaders, gambling, and Prohibition booze were brought by Kansas City U.S. Attorney Maurice Milligan. The Missouri Supreme Court said that the huge number of people who pled guilty to federal voter fraud in the 1936 election proved it was widespread, and U.S. Attorney Milligan prosecuted in the elections for federal offices. However Prosecutor Graves was responsible to prosecute in the elections for state officials, but he failed to investigate or "even choose to discuss the matter with the federal prosecutor." During the Special Commissioner's investigation, the *Kansas City Star* pointed out, "Many of the vote criminals are still in federal prison; but Tom Graves, the man who ignored the whole business, is still the prosecutor of Jackson County."[270]

The Missouri Supreme Court concluded that all these examples "established a failure or refusal of attorney to perform his duties under law, which would cause a forfeiture of his office." Based on the powerful mass of evidence, and after confirming its admissibility, the Missouri Supreme Court unanimously voted to oust Jackson County Prosecutor Graves from office immediately. This was mostly a symbolic action because his term had just four months to go, but this humiliating public censure prevented him from successfully running for office again.

Governor Stark not only ousted the Prosecutor and reformed the corrupted Kansas City Police Department, but he also dismantled the Pendergast machine's patronage power at the state level. Pendergast had controlled the Work Progress Administration jobs and its contracts in Missouri, but the Governor took charge. He terminated state employees who had been appointed on behalf of Boss Tom, and also reduced the share of state patronage jobs going to Kansas City residents.

In the middle of Governor Stark's term he got into a major political fight with Pendergast. The Governor had appointed James Douglas to fill a Missouri Supreme Court vacancy, and Justice Douglas soon cast the deciding vote against Pendergast's position in an insurance-rate case. This infuriated Boss Tom who retaliated by recruiting James Billings to become an opponent and challenge Douglas' upcoming reelection campaign. Every Pendergast politician and loyalist rallied to the cause of the machine's candidate, and Stark countered by touring the state proclaiming a vote for his incumbent Justice was also a vote to end bossism. Pendergast's Jackson County delivered the usual 100,000-vote majority, but the rest of the state voted so overwhelming for the Governor's candidate that it gave a resounding defeat to Pendergast and his judicial candidate.

This Missouri Supreme Court election campaign exposed the public to an unsettling fact - the state's judges were handpicked by political machines to do their judicial bidding. This revelation set off a major political debate about how to fix this problem, but this has never been adequately resolved in Missouri or by any other state. When elected politicians - no matter whether the governor, legislature, or an appointed commission - are given the authority to appoint judges, they typically select allies who share their partisan biases, but when the public is given the power to vote for judges, the electorate cannot make an informed decision because the voters know virtually nothing about the quality of the decisions the incumbent judges have rendered. In addition most campaign donations for judicial candidates come from the law firms and special interest groups that anticipate having clients or associates appearing in lawsuits or criminal proceedings before the judges during their term of office. Thus it is a difficult balancing act trying to obtain good judges. In these judicial elections there is only one certainty – if criminal defense attorneys endorse a judge because he or she utilizes "cutting edge" sentencing, it is all but guaranteed that the judge is on the take by running a let 'em go mill. Tough judges who act in the public interest are not endorsed by defense attorneys. Some states have committees of non-criminal attorneys rate judicial candidates for the voters, and some of these panels have produced good results.

This Supreme Court election campaign also led to a major public debate about government patronage jobs that are awarded to political loyalists versus a merit system of professional tenured employees who cannot be replaced at the whim of every new administration. In the spoils system, government jobs lasted only if an employee's politician-sponsor was reelected. Employees knew they owed their employment to their bosses or party and they worked in the interest of their bosses and not for the people. Employees knew they had to campaign for their boss in order to keep their jobs. Most state employees had to donate to their boss' campaign fund to hold on to their jobs.

During this Supreme Court election campaign Governor Stark used the same spoilage-system tactics as his Pendergast-machine predecessors. He gave state employees leaves of absence to campaign for his Supreme Court candidate and forced many to contribute 5% of their annual salary to his campaign. The public found all this conduct to support an incumbent Supreme Court Judge rather unseemly. This patronage versus merit public debate was picked up in many states. The establishment of merit systems was the biggest single blow to the power of the political machines. It removed the primary reward for paying homage to a machine's leadership.

However, it is difficult to maintain an effective balance for good government. While the patronage system results in unqualified and partisan government employees, permanent employees under the merit system too often become far too close to the very businesses and individuals they are supposed to monitor and control, and these corrupted but tenured employees are difficult to terminate. Thus merit employees can too easily turn their government agencies into self-serving enterprises that are outside the control of not only the electorate but also the administration.[271]

Chapter 14

THE DYNASTY TOPPLES SOMEWHAT

TAKING DOWN THE POWER KINGS

The Kansas City Pendergast political/criminal machine was challenged over the years by a succession of reformers, but none were big enough to have much impact. Ironically the machine's leaders would ultimately be toppled by two candidates they helped put in office. While Governor Lloyd Stark kept up his unrelenting attacks, it was the New Deal Democratic administration that would inflict the lethal blows. President Roosevelt's election victory was a landslide resulting from the country's economic collapse of the Great Depression so he could afford the political risk and inevitable backlash of trying to topple his Democratic Party's powerful Pendergast machine in Missouri. President Roosevelt directed AG Cummings to expand the voter-fraud criminal probe by Kansas City-based U.S. Attorney Maurice Milligan. While Pendergast's all pervasive machine had been able to override the will of the legitimate voters in Kansas City and the state, the federal government could aim devastating blows for income-tax evasion. Prosecutor Milligan brought in IRS agents to target the machine's leaders one after the other, just as Roosevelt's predecessor, Herbert Hoover, had used the IRS to bring down Mafia leaders Al Capone in Chicago and Johnny Lazia in Kansas City.

The tax-evasion prosecutions began when Prosecutor Milligan caught Tom Pendergast with his hand in the cookie jar. This occurred when the insurance companies raised their rates for fire coverage in Missouri by 16%. The state countered by stopping the companies from charging policyholders the increased amounts and by impounding the additional $9.5 million in premiums they had already collected until the State Insurance Superintendent could negotiate a settlement with the companies that was acceptable with Governor Stark. Under the back-room direction of Pendergast, the Insurance Superintendent reached an agreement with the companies that returned a paltry 20% of the money to the policyholders and gave the rest to the companies that set aside 30% of their share to cover anticipated court and litigation costs. An intermediary handled the negotiation, and the insurance companies paid him almost $450,000 for his services in two installments, one shortly before the agreement was reached and the second a few weeks after its signing.

Federal Prosecutor Milligan decided to trace these funds. When he inquired where the money went, the intermediary revealed he had shared the two payments by giving $315,000 to Pendergast and $62,500 to the Insurance Superintendent while pocketing $72,500 for himself. Upon learning of this an angry Governor Stark ousted the Superintendent from office, but he could not have either the Superintendent or Pendergast prosecuted because their corrupt dealings did not violate state law. However, Prosecutor Milligan found both bribe recipients had failed to report these payments as income to the IRS and presented this information to a Federal Grand Jury. Soon President Roosevelt's administration conveyed strong symbolic public support for U.S. Attorney Milligan's actions against the Pendergast machine by having new U.S. AG Frank Murphy visit Kansas City and applaud the Grand Jury's investigation as "greatly significant" by involving "some big politicians." U.S. Attorney Milligan soon indicted Pendergast and the Insurance Superintendent for tax-evasion on these bribes.

Two months later Pendergast was scheduled to go to trial, but the day before, he pled guilty to dodging income taxes in return for a reduction in the total number of charges. Prosecutor Milligan accepted this deal expecting the Federal Judge to impose a prison sentence appropriate for the group of crimes in the original indictment. Instead Pendergast was given a 15-month sentence and his cohort Insurance Superintendent received one year. While Pendergast was in prison he offered a $340,000 settlement for the IRS's tax claims against him of $444,000 so he could be paroled early. He was pardoned after a year, but most of this time he had spent in the prison hospital due to a series of heart attacks. America's most powerful kingmaker left Leavenworth Penitentiary broken in health and spirit.

Ironically, it was horseracing, then the country's most popular spectator sport by far, that both founded and then toppled the Pendergast political dynasty. Brother Jim launched the empire with a long-shot win, and brother Tom lost it by taking a bribe to support his addiction to the Sport of Kings. On any afternoon he could bet $50,000 on the ponies ($750,000 today). Except for Tom's passionate attendance at the races, he rarely ventured out in public from the seclusion of his mansion, and he led a circumspect life. Tom did not drink, went home from work early every evening to be with his family, and attended Mass religiously. Tom's probation had a provision he abstain from politics for five years after release. As this provision was nearing expiration, Tom died in the hospital at age 72. His political machine went on, but it was seriously weakened, becoming a minor faction in Kansas City.[272]

Federal prosecution against the Kansas City political/criminal machine was starting to coalesce. Just 10 days after the tax-evasion indictment was returned against Pendergast, U.S. Attorney Milligan also indicted his North-Side lieutenant, Mafia leader Charles Carollo. This was three months after Prosecutor Milligan had asked the Federal Grand Jury to investigate the Big Man in Kansas City gambling. The charge was mail fraud for muscling out the two owners of the Fortune Bingo Parlor in Kansas City. It was opened by Joseph Zermansky of California and Barney Morris of Reno. Carollo first used threats of violence to make them give him half interest and then forced them to sell him the remaining half for $1. The mail fraud charge in this case was unusual and was possible because the gangster who ruled Kansas City's large wide-open gambling enterprises sealed the deal by mailing bills of sale to the pair for their remaining interest after he had sent them packing back west. The Justice Department claimed it had jurisdiction in prosecuting this case because the game of bingo was subject to federal lottery laws.

Carollo's mail fraud indictment was followed by two federal perjury indictments. He had been born in Italy and when he was two his parents moved to New Orleans and then Kansas City. One perjury count was for falsely stating in his citizenship application as an adult that he had never made any gambling profits. The second perjury charge was for his answers to IRS agents' questions about his income when he again denied making any profit from gambling. Besides these three pending federal charges, he was convicted by a Jackson County Trial Jury for running a gambling operation. Then the IRS indicted Carollo for income-tax evasion of his gambling profits. The next day the blustering 240-pound thug who had a big head, bulging neck, and fat cheeks was arrested. He told reporters, "I don't owe the government a cent. All the money I got went to the other guy. They're not prosecuting me, they're persecuting me."[273]

Three months later Carollo went on trial for committing perjury to IRS agents by claiming he never made any profit from gambling. A long line of witnesses testified that they had paid him monthly for the right to operate gambling in Kansas City. Then Carollo got up on the witness stand and admitted collecting monthly from around 100 gambling spots until a state-federal drive closed the flourishing business earlier in the year. The Mafia gang leader claimed all the payments were campaign contributions that he turned over in their entirety to Pendergast. His denial was consistent with his answers to the IRS agents' questions. He testified, "Mr. Pendergast told me to take over the campaign collection and so I did. I don't owe the government nothin'." Based on the testimony of many witnesses and his own pathetic lies, the Federal Jury convicted him.[274]

The next day Carollo faced a federal mail-fraud trial that could lead to his third felony conviction along with his convictions by the feds for perjury and the County for gambling. This would permit the Immigration and Naturalization Service to deport him back to his native Italy. When reporters asked after the perjury conviction if he believed the government would try to deport him, he replied, "All I know is what I read. I've lived in Kansas City since I was a 2 year old kid. This is my country. I'm not a foreigner. What the hell would I do in Italy?" Carollo also again denied that he owed back taxes, but overnight he reversed this position. The next day before his mail-fraud trial was to begin, Carollo pled guilty to not only using the mail fraudulently to muscle into a bingo parlor but also to tax evasion. The following day the Big Man of Kansas City gambling was sentenced for perjury, mail fraud, and tax evasion to a total of 8 years, but the Judge specified two years would be reduced from his sentence for payment of delinquent taxes. Before he was sentenced, Prosecutor Milligan said Carollo "was the notorious link between politics and the underworld." At Leavenworth Penitentiary he was charged with helping smuggle in narcotics and was sent to Alcatraz to finish out his sentence.[275]

Mafia leader Carollo's selected Police Director, Otto Higgins, had resigned earlier in the year when the IRS started indicting the Mafioso's political and criminal cohorts. Then a week after Carollo pled guilty to tax evasion, a Kansas City Federal Grand Jury indicted Higgins for failing to pay income taxes on a monthly bribe stipend during the five years Carollo had headed the Mafia gang. The bribes were to ensure the police left the Mafioso's gambling empire alone. As the benevolent North-Side political leader, Carollo had donated the bribes intended for Higgins to the police benefit fund, which took care of widows and children of officers who died or were killed in the line of duty. However Higgins used the money for his own purposes. Upon entering his plea, the Judge immediately sentenced the former Director to two years and he was transported directly from the courtroom to Leavenworth.[276]

Along with the federal toppling of political kingmaker Pendergast and Mafioso Carollo, Governor Stark had the state retake control of the Kansas City Police Department from the Mafia. He named former FBI agent Lear Reed as the new Police Chief. He was a Georgian who had served in the FBI in Kansas City where he had seen first hand the dirty alliance between Police Director Higgins and Carollo's gambling and vice empires. The new Chief told a businessmen's group about the web of corruption he had inherited from the hands of the machine. He revealed, "We found among other things a list of names of certain men not to be arrested under any circumstances." He quickly fired most of the cops and made the remaining officers swear on questionnaires how much they had been required to pay annually to the corrupt political machine in order to keep their jobs. This included campaign donations, dues to a club they were not allowed to use, and supposedly voluntary good-will gifts. Reed revamped the Department based on the merit system.[277]

City Manager Henry McElroy had controlled the local government agencies on behalf of Tom Pendergast during the last 13 years of his powerful reign. After Pendergast entered Leavenworth, McElroy resigned under fire. The suspicious Mayor ordered an audit of Kansas City's books. The citizenry had a rude awakening with the discovery that their city was $20 million in debt due to the waste and corruption of the cronies of the kingmaker's political/criminal machine. While McElroy had portrayed himself as a cost cutter and had trimmed some public employees' salaries, he actually created a special city emergency fund and deposited $8 million from his cost-cutting savings into it.

He spent some of this money for legitimate purposes, but he developed a reputation as a philanthropist by donating large amounts to charities, the largest one being himself. A County Grand Jury indicted him for misuse of public funds by embezzlement but ill health protected him from going to trial. Three months after he was charged he died.[278]

THE DYNASTY AIMS FOR THE WHITE HOUSE

When the Kansas City political/criminal machine leaders were under attack by Federal Prosecutor Maurice Milligan, they marshaled their strong political influence to try to thwart this threat. They enlisted the aid of a man who would later become the President of the United States, Harry S Truman - there is no period after the S because he had no middle name. Truman grew up on the family's Missouri farm working with his father to make a modest living. When the U.S. entered World War I, Truman's National Guard artillery battery was ordered into combat against Germany in France. Captain Truman led this unit at age 33. After returning to civilian life in Kansas City, he invested his war-service savings in a new downtown haberdashery. Three years into its operation it went under because of a recession that caused a downturn in the nation's farm economy. It took Truman many years but he ultimately paid off his debts.

Truman returned to working on his grandmother's mortgaged farm. Since he blamed the fall in farm prices that had ruined his business on Republican monetary policies, he became a Democrat and prepared to enter politics because he had several campaign strengths. He was well-known in Jackson County surrounding Kansas City and had relatives living throughout the rural precincts. He belonged to organizations that gave him political appeal like the Legionnaires, Masons, and Baptists. In addition a member of Truman's former National Guard unit, Jim Pendergast, just happened to be the nephew of Boss Tom Pendergast. Jim solicited his uncle to throw his political machine's support behind his military buddy's candidacy. Truman had a spotless record so Tom Pendergast sponsored his first foray into politics, and Truman remained forever a loyal minion of the Boss.

Truman's first campaign was for judge of the County Court and he was elected. This was not a court of law but a three-member administrative body most often called a county commission in other states. Two years later he was defeated for reelection by an insurgent Democratic political faction that had some successes against the dominant machine. Boss Tom kept Truman on the County payroll by having him appointed overseer of oiling the secondary road system. The loyal County Court members made sure the oil for these roads was purchased from Pendergast's Eureka Petroleum Company. Two years later Truman ran for election again but this time it was as Presiding Judge, or chairman, of the three member County Court, or commission. He won and was reelected to serve a total of eight years before he decided to move on.

Truman always maintained he voted independently of Pendergast, but how could this have been? It was well known the Boss demanded absolute loyalty from his hand-picked candidates. While Pendergast liked to boast he never exacted promises from candidates before elections, he once clarified this in an interview. "If a candidate hasn't got sense enough to see who helped him win and hasn't sense enough to recognize that man's friends, there is no use asking for favors from that candidate in advance."[279]

The County Court had one fine success during Truman's tenure as Presiding Judge and he claimed credit for this during future campaigns. It was a $10 million County highway building program because Pendergast always encouraged his minions to push building projects to keep his Ready Mixed Concrete Company and paving and construction companies busy. Pendergast may have been the beneficiary of these construction contracts, but this project remained cost effective because it was directed by a bipartisan board of prominent engineers who prohibited Truman and the Boss from meddling in their developmental plans.

Truman enjoyed a good reputation as an able administrator, and he was never accused of wrong doing. However he appointed the men Pendergast told him to appoint and approved the contracts he was told to approve. A few years after Truman left the County Presiding Judge position, the *Kansas City Star* exposed the misdeeds carried out by some of the men Truman had appointed on behalf of Pendergast.

The one action Truman personally undertook for Pendergast was to try to expand the Boss' power over County government by going to the Legislature in Jefferson City to advocate for tax reform and reorganization. He proposed big savings by abolishing five elective county offices and placing their authority under his County Court. The legislators ignored his request because they had fallen for this Pendergast ploy years earlier when they passed a new charter to create a City Manager system in Kansas City. This plan was supposed to have produced fine nonpartisan and nonpolitical government but all it accomplished was to make it easier for the Boss to consolidate and control the whole City administration under one loyal political hack.

During Truman's final two years as Presiding Judge, President Roosevelt launched his New Deal programs, and Boss Tom had the administration appoint Truman the director of both the Federal Re-employment Program and the Federal Civil Works Administration in Missouri. These programs produced an enormous number of jobs and contracts, and Truman followed the Boss' bidding to hand these out as patronage to the machine's political loyalists.

As Presiding Judge, Truman regularly spoke to clubs preaching frugal government spending while actually permitting Pendergast to indulge in wasteful and extravagant excesses. Truman allowed no accounting of the County's books and even denied access to them by the nonpartisan, independent Civic Research Institute. Most records from Truman's tenure were destroyed in a fire. Under his administration, the County far outspent its income and acquired such a large debt that the Missouri Legislature passed a budget law forbidding counties from spending more than they took in. Under Truman's leadership the County's credit rating became so bad the debt sold for less than half its value. Two years after Truman left as Presiding Judge, Pendergast bought up the County's debt for 40 cents on the dollar, and then he awoke his mass of ghost voters to pass a bond issue providing the funds to pay off the debts at 100% of face value giving the Boss a two-and-half-times return on his investment, courtesy of the County taxpayers.

After Truman departed office, it came out that 4,600 properties were not listed on the tax books, and hundreds of parcels were listed as unimproved even though they contained buildings. Under Truman's tenure, hustlers approached businessmen offering to cut their property taxes for a percentage of the reduction, and his County Court approved these tax decreases.

Pendergast's chosen successor to replace the retiring Truman as Presiding Judge also carried out the Boss' orders. Five years into his tenure he resigned during an investigation into spending public funds to repair his son's building. Then Governor Stark appointed a Democrat who was a Pendergast foe. This leader was able to continue all County services despite dramatically cutting both operating and construction costs by eliminating the massive boondoggles of Pendergast and his patronage employees. It took the County almost a decade to dig out of the financial hole left by Truman and his successor.

Late in Truman's final term as Presiding Judge the next election was approaching. He went to Boss Tom and requested appointment as County Collector for the IRS because it was a higher-paying position with the salary based partly on fees. The Boss shook his head frowning. "No, Harry, the best I can do for you now is a United States senatorship." Pendergast saw to it that his favorite politician won with massive Kansas City voter fraud, but a great deal more political calculation and effort went into Truman's selection and state-wide victory than just ghost ballots.[280]

The Democratic primary for U.S. Senator looked like a pathetic mismatch to Missouri's political observers. The other three candidates held state-level offices while Truman had only his experience in the rural county. Historians typically consider Truman to have been an obscure and unprepared candidate, but it is important to remember that his dubious performance as Presiding Judge did not become public knowledge until later in his career. The reality was that Pendergast had learned a hard lesson when it came to statewide campaigns. He could only resurrect so many cemetery voters, and this large ghostly band could not overcome the number of real voters in the rest of the state when the St. Louis Democratic politic leaders endorsed an opposition candidate and the rural folks rejected having another Kansas City machine puppet at the state level. Pendergast had carefully groomed Truman to bring these three constituencies together. Truman remained far distanced from city politics to avoid being associated with the Kansas City machine, and Pendergast had also developed his protégé as a positive force in the state by having puppet Governor Park assign him high-profile state roles during the two years leading up to the election.

The Governor had Truman present a petition in Washington for federal relief in Missouri and to head the state's Re-employment Service requiring him to appear in the Jefferson City Capital more than once a week to meet the huge number of people who benefited from this Depression-era program as did the state's political powers. On behalf of the Governor, Truman spoke during the spring leading up to the election in 35 counties on behalf of a $10 million statewide bond to improve the penal and charitable institutions.

In the year leading up to the campaigning, crime had been a major issue locally and in the country. The city's still unsolved Massacre of lawmen that shocked the public's sensibility had been followed by the infamous bloody Kansas City municipal election and then came the machinegunning of Pendergast's political lieutenant and local Mafia leader Lazia. In addition trigger-happy bank robbers were rampaging the Midwest with the FBI just beginning to effectively confront these gangs, and there had been many high-profile kidnappings for ransom. Through it all Truman was never associated with any of Pendergast's unseemly election and political tactics and had never been touched by scandal. On the contrary, Truman had an undeserved good reputation as a county administrator.

When it came to the Senatorial campaign Pendergast had his machine lead the effort in Kansas City as did the powers in St. Louis. At the same time Truman took his strong grass roots appeal directly to the rural residents across the state. He was unassuming and genial, talking in a folksy language rather than like a statesman. He could be blunt and brusque when determined or irritated. At the height of the Great Depression, his personal experiences were a reflection of the difficult times. He had grown up with the hardships of farming and had also failed as a small businessman. Since he continued to pay down his debts a decade later, he drew admiration from working men and businessmen alike.

Truman belonged to several organizations respected by many voters, and the most beneficial was his presidency of the Missouri County Judge Association. This kept him in close contact with the state's 342 county judges, or commissioners. They often held important political party posts, and the Democrats helped spread the word all over the state about Truman's Jackson County and statewide accomplishments.

Truman conducted a determined Democratic primary campaign. He tirelessly traveled the rural areas averaging four speeches a day for two months. All these factors came together to give him a resounding victory for the nomination, but he still needed a highly-inflated machine-contrived vote in Kansas City to pull off this win. The strongest candidate in the four-man primary was respected

House Representative John J. Cochran of St. Louis. "In the election, Cochran swept St. Louis and most of Missouri's counties, but Truman won the nomination because of a tremendous block of votes counted for him in Kansas City. The official returns in Kansas City were: Truman 120,180 and Cochran 1,221." This vote differential in Kansas City gave Truman a 119,000 vote edge with 99% of the total vote, which was obviously impossible, to more than offset his 79,000-vote deficit in the rest of the state. After the general election a local Federal Judge ordered the Election Commission to remove fraudulent names from the voter-registration books to protect future elections. The 50,000 fictitious voters removed was greater than Truman's 40,000-vote primary winning margin over second-place finisher Cochran. The most unbelievable results were in the First and Second Wards under the control of Mafia and political leader Charles Carollo. Slightly more people cast ballots in these two Wards than their combined populations that included all those under age 21 who were prohibited by law from voting. This Pendergast assault on democracy turned a county administrative chairman into the Democratic Party's U.S. Senatorial candidate. Truman went on to beat the Republican candidate in the general election by 262,000 votes meaning the fraudulently-nominated candidate likely won that election. He was carried by the Democratic landslide produced by the popularity of President Roosevelt's New Deal program proposals during his first two years in office.[281]

After winning the election Truman was generally regarded as a puppet of the Boss and was referred to as "the senator from Pendergast." As Truman prepared to go to Washington to be sworn in, Pendergast's parting words to his newly-elected Senator were "Work hard, keep your mouth shut and answer your mail." During his six-year term Truman followed this advice by saying little and drawing scant attention. When he did speak, he made it simple, coherent, forceful and brief.[282]

Truman had campaigned as a New Deal Democrat in support of President Roosevelt, and he voted loyally in the Senate for FDR's measures that included the creation of Social Security. Truman assigned all his Washington-based job and contract patronage authority to Pendergast back in Kansas City, and he defended this by saying he offered the Boss a little to save a lot. He always claimed he voted according to his conscience even when pressured by his benefactor, but his record must be evaluated to determine the veracity of his statement.

The most significant part of Truman's first six-year term in Washington was the bitter infighting that went on between local Democratic leaders in Kansas City. Truman remained totally committed to Boss Tom, and stood beside him against the reformers and opponents who challenged his dominating machine. The problem for the Senator was that Pendergast was deeply involved with crime through election fraud, bribery, corruption of the police department, and his tight-knit relationship with his political lieutenants, Lazia and successor Carollo, who headed the city's Mafia gang.

In stark contrast U.S. Attorney Maurice Milligan was an exemplary prosecutor who convicted 254 Pendergastites in 19 trials for voter fraud in the 1936 election, and three years following it, he convicted political Boss Tom Pendergast, Mafia leader Carollo, and Police Director Otto Higgins for tax evasion to badly wound the strength of the powerful Kansas City political machine. Of all the influential people in Kansas City, Milligan stands out as the big-time hero. Yet even heroes have flaws and Milligan's was that he was also a political animal. Milligan and Truman competed for leadership of the Missouri Democratic Party. Both men may have had legitimate or personal reasons for hating each other, but Truman tarnished his career in Washington as Senator, Vice President, and President of the United States by focusing on destroying the career of this exceptional Prosecutor, who had so effectively done his job, in order to punish him for bringing down Truman's thoroughly corrupted patron and his cohorts.

The Truman-Milligan feud began with the 1934 U.S. Senate Democratic primary election. Prosecutor Maurice Milligan's brother, Jacob "Tuck" Milligan, was one of the three other candidates who opposed Truman in the race, and he had a distant third-place finish. With the general election for Missouri U.S. Senator just three days away, Prosecutor Maurice Milligan's Federal Grand Jury issued a scathing report about Kansas City mob activities, racketeering and "unbridled gambling," and the Jurors also charged the city's three top cops with perjury for false statements about the police investigation of the brutal Massacre. Incumbent Republican U.S. Senator Roscoe Patterson quickly attacked the corrupt, lawless Pendergast machine and pointed out that Truman was its hand-picked challenger against him. Given the pace of the Federal Grand Jury's hearings, there is no reason to believe that Prosecutor Milligan timed the report and indictments to help the Republican incumbent but the loathing between the two Democrats was cast. This made Senator Truman an extreme critic of the effective Prosecutor's many successful crime-busting victories when the Senator from Pendergast should have been extending his highest commendations.

Four years into Truman's first term, Prosecutor Maurice Milligan's first term expired. He was racking up massive convictions against the 1936 election crooks, and he was building strong cases against the leaders of the Pendergast machine who he was a year away from imprisoning. Milligan was originally appointed after a Washington meeting with AG Cummings who explained to him that the administration regarded Kansas City as a hot spot for crime and was looking for a new U.S. Attorney who would prosecute vigorously. Milligan was living up to expectations at great personal risk. Throughout the long series of trials, Milligan followed the FBI's advice and kept a .45 caliber revolver beside his bed. Milligan understood better than anyone that he was fighting far more than a zealot political organization. He was battling a dangerously violent political/criminal gang.

Senator Truman planned a strategy to take down dedicated Prosecutor Milligan during a visit with Boss Tom. Truman exposed his subservient role by going to Pendergast's business office rather than having the political kingmaker come to his senatorial office in the Kansas City Federal Building. Pendergast was adamant that the Prosecutor was a serious threat to him and had to be removed from office. Truman intended to exercise his Senatorial rights and single-handedly block the renomination in his state from being considered for approval, but he feared two consequences if he took any action beyond publicly denouncing him. First President Roosevelt warned Truman that he was ready to fight for fine Prosecutor Milligan who was diligently carrying out the President's mandate to cripple the corrupt Pendergast machine. If Truman had blocked the nomination, Roosevelt would never have selected him as his Vice President, and Truman would never have become President of the United States. Second Truman was worried he would not survive his upcoming election two years hence under the withering Missouri press' denunciation that would have inevitably resulted from punishing crime-busting Prosecutor Milligan for doing his job so well.

Thus two weeks later when President Roosevelt's nomination to reappoint the Prosecutor was read to the assembled Senate, Truman immediately rose and bitterly smeared and demeaned with blistering language Prosecutor Milligan and the two Federal Judges who orchestrated the Kansas City cleanup. Truman hysterically made false claims that Prosecutor Milligan was unqualified professionally and morally. Truman went on to accuse the two Kansas City Federal Court Judges as the most "violently partisan judges" since Jefferson's administration. "I say to the Senate, Mr. President, that a Jackson County, Missouri, Democrat has as much chance of a fair trial in the Federal District Court of western Missouri as a Jew would have in a Hitler court or a Trotsky follower before Stalin. ... Because the President asked for him, I have not attempted to exercise the usual senatorial prerogative to block his confirmation. I think, however, I would not be doing my public duty if I did not tell the Senate just what is going on."[283]

New Hampshire Republican Senator Styles Bridges interrupted Truman with a strong rebuttal. "I have in my hand a tabulation of figures of comparative registrations showing in 1936 from the various Kansas City wards a registration of 263,934, and a registration in 1938 two years later of 177,506. After the vote fraud prosecutions the registrations dropped very materially as a result of the excellent action of Mr. Milligan and the two Judges who so honestly and fearlessly did their duty." The Senator then showed one Kansas City election ward had 30% more registered voters than its total population including minors. After this impassioned debate, the Senate voted unanimous approval of Prosecutor Milligan with the exception of Truman's lone no vote.[284]

A year later Tom Pendergast and his closest cohorts went to prison. His nephew, Jim, Truman's World War I comrade, took over control of the machine, but it was badly weakened. Its candidates were defeated by Democratic reformers in local elections the next year and again two years later. In the first of these two elections, the year after Pendergast went to Leavenworth, Senator Truman came up for reelection. With Missouri's enemies of the machine circling around him, he should have been an easy target, but the two biggest political opponents of Pendergast both challenged Truman in the Democratic primary. Prosecutor Maurice Milligan had a personal score to settle after Truman tried to end his distinguished career, and Governor Stark, who was prohibited by law from running for reelection, not only wanted the more prestigious position of the U.S. Senate but had dreams of using it as a stepping stone to the presidency. Both men proudly proclaimed in their campaigns that they had done their part in bringing down Boss Pendergast but neither would step aside to assure the other victory.

The feisty Truman launched a tireless and combative campaign. He also garnered the strong support of St. Louis Democratic Committee Chairman Robert Hannegan. He helped push Truman over the top to narrowly defeat the Governor by 8,000 votes as both men grabbed 40% of the vote. Milligan took the remaining 20% to split the anti-Pendergast vote majority allowing Truman to edge through in the Democratic primary. In the U.S. Senate general election Truman won by 44,000 votes, or 2.5%, against the Republican challenger. Four years later Hannegan from St. Louis would become Democratic National Committee Chairman and broker the deal that would make Senator Truman the Vice Presidential candidate on Roosevelt's fourth and final presidential ticket.[285]

MACHINE-MADE PRESIDENT

Truman's second senatorial term began almost a year before the attack on Pearl Harbor. The nation was preparing for war and the rearmament program was getting into full swing. Rumors circulated that defense contracts suffered from favoritism and influence, so a deeply-concerned Truman drove his car for tours of the major defense plants and projects. His 30,000-mile trip was equivalent to crossing the country 10 times. Truman was disturbed by what he found and proposed to the Senate Military Affairs Committee that a special preparedness subcommittee be created to ensure defense contractors delivered to the nation quality goods at fair prices. The Senate appointed a Special Committee to Investigate the National Defense Program composed of seven men. It became known as the Truman Committee because he was chairman and this brought him into national prominence. He immediately began bold investigations of every aspect of military procurement, attacked every bad actor involved no matter how politically powerful or connected, and corrected the abuses. He tackled fraud and mismanagement, the excessive amounts paid industrialists and demanded by union leaders, and inefficient operations like the rationing of fuel oil and gasoline. He exposed shortages in critical materials and manpower and proposed practical common-sense solutions. He was especially concerned with excessive drafting of farm workers that he feared endangered the food program badly needed in the European War theater as well as domestically. He even presented a scathing expose that the President's unpaid military-industrial-company advisors, known as dollar-a-year men, were garnering an inordinate proportion of the major contracts. Truman's revelations about, and stern warnings against, waste and corruption helped President FDR develop an efficient war-production machine. Truman demanded military court martials and civilian criminal prosecutions for those the Committee identified as guilty of inappropriate conduct, and his threats may have deterred others from becoming involved with fraud. His cost-saving measures were credited with saving the taxpayers billions of dollars. Truman's determined hard work, firm but fair and impartial leadership, and tough pointed questioning of the nation's most powerful men raised the stature of the Senator from Pendergast to one of great respect by his fellow Senators, the White House, and the nation. He was voted by Washington's political reporters as the civilian who "knew most about the war" except for President Roosevelt, and two years into the War, Truman made his first appearance on the cover of *Time Magazine.*

Midway in Truman's second term, President Roosevelt began planning his 1944 reelection campaign. His Vice President Henry A. Wallace was considered too liberal for current public sentiment, and FDR looked for an alternative among Democratic Senators and Governors. At the Chicago Convention a bitter conflict developed between the Party's conservatives and liberals, who had played such a prominent role in the administration's New Deal agenda. Truman became a logical compromise candidate because of a combination of traits. Politically he was a centrist; he was not closely identified with unions like Wallace; he was moderate on civil rights unlike the Southern segregationist candidates; he was recognized nationally as being very knowledgeable about the War effort; he had always been a loyal party man to the President's programs as well as to Pendergast; and he had no major enemies. However, Truman had bumped heads with FDR over the Pendergast machine and U.S. Prosecutor Milligan. It was at this point that St. Louis attorney Robert Hannegan stepped in. He had supported Truman in both Senate campaigns, and the Irish Hannegan had made the difference in Truman's closely-contested reelection Democratic primary especially in the Catholic neighborhoods. Since then Hannegan had been appointed IRS Commissioner by President Roosevelt who then backed him for National Democratic Committee Chairman. At the Convention Hannegan lobbied tirelessly with FDR and finally brokered the deal to make Truman the vice presidential candidate. Truman never knew he was being considered until Hannegan met with him to say it was a done deal. Truman was in such disbelief he demanded a phone call from the President to confirm Roosevelt really did want him. With Truman listening in on the conversation, Hannegan telephoned FDR. Hannegan said, "He's the contrariest Missouri mule I've ever dealt with." The President replied, "Well, you tell him if he wants to break up the Democratic party in the middle of a war, that's his responsibility."[286]

During Truman's campaign for Vice President of the United States, opponents revealed the Senator had made at least three badly-flawed appointments in his first Senate term. Soon after he took the oath of office Truman recommended and pushed through the appointment of Kansas City Director of Public Works Matthew Murray to be WPA Administrator for Missouri over strong protests about his appropriateness by the Democratic National Committee Vice Chairman. Murray was a Tom Pendergast minion who collected his salary from Kansas City even though he was on a leave of absence and also being paid for his actual job of handing out federal relief jobs to 10,000 workers. He dispensed these jobs on a purely political basis and the Boss' loyalists got all the supervising positions. Murray awarded all the millions of dollars in public-work contracts to Pendergast by improperly and deviously making each work order for less than $2,000 to avoid the competitive bidding requirement. Murray drew both salaries for five years until the IRS convicted him of failing to pay taxes on $50,000 in bribes from Pendergast and his General Contractor. He received a two-year prison sentence.[287]

Truman also got a Pendergast minion appointed as WPA District Director for 20 Northwest Missouri counties where he had control over 9,000 employees. He resigned three years later before his indictment and conviction for payroll padding that led to a six-month jail sentence.[288]

Another Truman appointee was his gofer, Fred Canfil, who served Truman from the time he was first elected County Presiding Judge. At that time Presiding Judge Truman appointed Canfil as Director of Public Buildings even though no legal authority for that position existed. Canfil is the man who so bloated all County public-building expenditures for operations and construction during Truman's eight-year tenure. When Truman moved to Washington, Canfil was caught back home directing a wrecking crew to demolish the old unoccupied Jackson County Courthouse to sell the valuable scrap. Pendergast's County Court members quickly ratified Canfil's so-called deal in order to protect him. However, he was discovered having spent $10,200 in County money to remodel property owned by Truman's successor, Presiding Judge Long who was handpicked by Pendergast. The investigation forced both Canfil and Long to resign. Governor Stark replaced Presiding Judge Long with George Montgomery who soon cut courthouse operating expenses in half while maintaining all services.

Senator Truman rewarded the unemployed Canfil by quickly recommending him for appointment as Kansas City U.S. District Marshal, which would have given him custody of all of Prosecutor Milligan's impounded evidence against Pendergast and his cohorts. The resulting FBI investigation reported Canfil was unfit for public office, and the U.S. AG's office rejected Senator Truman's recommendation. Despite Truman's vehement objections to the rejection, President Roosevelt reappointed the respected incumbent. Truman's next move was to give his dishonest gofer a job on his Senate Committee investigating war expenditures. Four year's later, the U.S. Marshal's term again expired, and Truman again recommended Fred Canfil. This time the Justice Department, the White House, and the Senate approved Canfil's nomination because FDR was preparing for another election. Canfil spent most of his time as Marshal promoting the candidacy of Truman for Vice President of the United States. Despite these serious flaws, the Roosevelt-Truman ticket was well received and they defeated Thomas Dewey in the election.[289]

A year before Truman's reelection campaign, Boss Tom Pendergast had been sentenced to prison, and the Senator responded to the news of his downfall by saying, "I won't desert a ship in distress." Then five years later Boss Tom Pendergast died. This was just nine days after Truman was sworn in as the Vice President, and he shocked many when he flew in an Army bomber to Kansas City from Washington to attend the funeral. Truman brushed aside the criticism by saying, "He was always my friend and I have always been his." Truman was the only elected official of the machine to pay his respects to the disgraced patron who had made all their careers. Then Truman reboarded the bomber to make a speech in Philadelphia. Truman proved he was a very loyal man but unfortunately it was too often to greedy, dishonest vested interests rather than for the good of his country.[290]

The President's long battle with polio had badly weakened him physically, and the disabled leader was no longer up to the strenuous effort of campaigning. It was up to vice presidential candidate Truman to single-handedly represent the Democratic ticket and he vigorously stumped the nation.

Roosevelt easily won his fourth term over Republican New York Governor Thomas Dewey. Then less than three months into Truman's vice presidency, he received a call in the Congressional offices telling him that he was urgently needed at the White House. He rushed into the second-floor study to meet with Eleanor Roosevelt. She stepped towards him and wrapped her arm across his shoulders. She told him her husband had suddenly died, and he was now President of the United States. He was stunned and could think of nothing to say. Finally fighting off tears he asked her if there was anything he could do for her. The former First Lady with her usual empathy replied, "Is there anything *we* can do for *you?* For you are the one in trouble now." Truman would go on to become the most corrupt President in history by being the only one to ever sell out to organized crime.[291]

THE MOBBED-UP WHITE HOUSE

In every elected position Truman ever held he responded to the demands of the Kansas City political/criminal machine. One of his first acts as President was to demand the resignation of Kansas City U.S. Attorney Maurice Milligan who had brought down corrupt kingmaker Pendergast. To replace him Truman nominated a political supporter and machine crony, the Missouri Democratic Party State Chairman. However the campaign of vengeance Truman conducted to punish the dedicated Prosecutor who he had dismissed boomeranged. The Justice Department immediately rehired Milligan to another position that increased his pay by one third because he had established such a stellar prosecutorial record fighting lawlessness and reestablishing democratic voting rights in Kansas City.

During all the years he was Vice President and President, Truman consistently turned over his patronage to the political organization of Jim Pendergast, his old Army buddy who had been so instrumental in beginning his political career. Upon becoming President, Truman also appointed Jim's brother, Francis, as a commercial analyst of the U.S. Office of Inter-American Affairs. Francis had been one of the original chairmen of the Truman for Senator Club when he first ran for federal office, and Francis had received the lion's share of the city's insurance business when his uncle, Boss Tom, ruled as Democratic overlord.

The first Christmas of Truman's Presidency he flew on the Presidential plane Sacred Cow to his Independence, Missouri home for a three-day visit. From there he flew to a five-day New Year's yachting on the Williamsburg in the Potomac River and Chesapeake Bay. The Trumans were accompanied by Jim Pendergast with his wife and daughter. Pendergast proudly displayed in his office a picture of President Truman that was inscribed to Jim as "friend, comrade and adviser," and Jim was a frequent visitor at the White House.[292]

Despite Truman's continuing warm connections with his Kansas City base the political situation had changed at home. During the long rule of Jim Pendergast's uncle, Boss Tom, the two successive Mafia leaders, Johnny Lazia and Charles Carollo, had been Tom's loyal political-machine lieutenants. But when Boss Tom and Mafioso Corolla both went to prison for tax evasion, their successors were different sorts of men. Boss Tom's nephew Jim Pendergast was a mild leader and he inherited a badly weakened political faction. Complicating the status quo was new Mafia gang leader Charles Binaggio who was more politically astute and ambitious than his two predecessors. Little is known about Binaggio's background because he always avoided the limelight and deliberately obscured his criminal activities and rise to gangland power. Throughout his career he gave different stories about where he grew up, his date of birth, and his supposed legitimate occupations. During the time his predecessor had controlled the Kansas City Police Department, Binaggio's criminal record disappeared from the files. He had a juvenile police record, and he was arrested many times as an adult. His only recorded conviction was for auto theft with another man in August 1927, and both received two years probation. He was arrested in Denver in 1930 for carrying a concealed weapon according to FBI records, and Missouri highway patrolmen arrested him while gambling in a casino in 1945 for which he paid a $50 fine.

Illegal gambling operations were the main source of income for all three consecutive Mafia bosses. In fact Binaggio started his gangland career in Kansas City working in a Lazia gambling parlor. The low-profile Binaggio first came to public attention at Lazia's funeral where he and Charles Gargotta were pallbearers. Lazia was succeeded as Mafia leader by his lieutenant Charles Carollo, and when he went to prison five years into his reign Binaggio assumed the mantle with Gargotta as his lieutenant in crime.

Soon after Binaggio's arrival in Kansas City he had begun a sideline to his criminal career by working in the political arena for his gang boss Lazia as a ward heeler and slowly moved up the ladder in stature. When Binaggio assumed the Mafia toga he began to covertly and systematically build his own political organization from within Pendergast's structure. He started at the precinct level where he gathered young, ambitious, energetic men who did not carry the taint of extensive police records. Over time he developed control over a majority of the votes in 11 precincts in the First Ward. As Binaggio rose to political power he became physically trim and erased the traces of his criminal life. No thug in appearance he was polite, quiet spoken, almost self effacing. While he could be gracious he could also be vehement in his opinions. Dapper in his expensive but conservative dark blue suits and tinted glasses to shade his piercing black eyes, he has been described as a "man of lethal calm." He worked in his office at the First District Democratic Club practically every day and was usually accessible to visitors. At his home he lived in refined luxury but avoided the ostentatious.[293]

After five years of organizing his own political structure Binaggio was ready to challenge Pendergast for control of his faction of the city's Democrat Party. Before making his move Binaggio expanded his sphere of influence by creating an alliance with the disgruntled Irish political leader of the Second Ward, a former justice of the peace and saloonkeeper, and formed another bond with the Jackson County Assessor who had the power to keep the city's businessmen in line with property-tax rewards and punishments. Binaggio made his independent move to launch a political coup in the 1944 local election by endorsing a separate slate of candidates from Pendergast for the Democratic primaries. Faring well Binaggio was now an important independent political player.[294]

This made the Mafioso and the political kingmaker arch rivals a year before Truman was elected Vice President and then ascended to the presidency. Thus interwoven with Truman's many momentous achievements as President was an occasional quiet intervention to mediate the conflicts between these two men in his home political base. Truman wanted to protect his old buddy from the Mafioso out of personal loyalty, and he also wanted the pair to work together to further his Congressional political agenda by backing Missouri candidates who espoused the President's positions. Throughout Truman's many years in elected offices his numerous improprieties had been done to honor the requests of either Tom or Jim Pendergast, but now the President crossed over the line by eliciting Mafioso Binaggio to illegally reintroduce voting fraud into the Kansas City election system to produce a more friendly Congress. As former Prosecutor Milligan later wrote about these serious political hijinks, "We gave Pendergastism an exciting funeral, but the corpse has made a notable recovery. The revival is more menacing than ever because it has, at least, the good will of the President of the United States."[295]

After the 1936 election Prosecutor Milligan had convicted 257 vote stealers but a decade later most had finished serving their time. President Truman had pardoned 22 of the worst of these Pendergast machine criminals from prison to make his nefarious scheme work. He needed their services to purge Kansas City Representative Roger Slaughter from Missouri's 5th District in the 1946 Democratic Primary election because as a member of the House Rules Committee he regularly voted and spoke out against Truman's policies. The President informed a press conference that he had summoned Jim Pendergast to Washington to personally demand he work for Slaughter's defeat in the Democratic primary, and on election day Truman flew to Kansas City to campaign for his handpicked challenger. The President was successful in defeating the incumbent, but the *Kansas City Star* conducted an investigation of the primary election records and uncovered wholesale vote buying, voting by non-existent persons, and voter coercion so common a decade earlier. Truman's challenger lost in every ward except for the four controlled by the Pendergast/Binaggio political machine. In two of these precincts not a single vote was cast for his incumbent opponent. This incensed the city's voters so Truman's winning primary candidate went on to lose the general election to his Republican opponent who ironically was the son of the Federal Judge who had sent so many Pendergast henchmen to prison for vote fraud a decade earlier.

Nine months after the primary election a Jackson County Grand Jury returned 81 indictments for vote fraud and stated in its report that the defeated incumbent Representative Slaughter had actually won the relatively close primary election. The Grand Jury also asked U.S. AG Tom Clark to direct his Justice Department and FBI to enter the investigation, but Truman's AG kept both his agencies muzzled by outright lying. He announced, "Where fraud and irregularity are not shown to nullify the vote for federal candidates, neither the department nor the federal courts has the power to prosecute or punish." Not only in this case had the fraudulent votes changed the outcome, but there was no such prosecutorial prohibition under the law. The AG could have investigated at any time because the Jackson County Sheriff had impounded all the ballots from the Binaggio wards that proved the election had indeed been stolen. These ballots were secured in the Election Board Office in the Jackson County Courthouse. The night before AG Clark was to appear before a U.S. Senate Subcommittee to explain why he had shackled the FBI from investigating these violations of federal law the Mafioso's henchmen broke into the Courthouse, dynamited the Election Board's safe door, and stole the ballots from the worst offending precincts that were the evidence against the 81 election stealers making conviction impossible. At the moment this bombing and crime against democracy were being committed, the mastermind behind it all, the President of the United States, was sound asleep five blocks away in a Kansas City hotel. Once the evidence had disappeared, the U.S. Attorney chosen by President Truman to represent Kansas City finally convened a Federal Grand Jury because there was no longer anything to investigate.[296]

After the President purged U.S. Representative Slaughter in the Kansas City Democratic primary election by initiating massive voter fraud, Truman's AG Tom Clark had the successors to Al Capone's Chicago gang commit voter fraud in that city's general election on behalf of Democratic U.S. House candidates. The U.S. AG had earlier been approached by this Mafia gang to arrange for President Truman to pardon its five imprisoned leaders. Even though these convicts were undoubtedly America's most dangerous and vicious gangsters, AG Clark took a cash bribe and had the President sign their pardons, undoing the determined efforts of President Roosevelt's anti-crime administration that had diligently put the five behind bars for the maximum time permitted by law. There is no evidence that Truman personally profited or was even involved in the plot by his AG and Federal Parole Board, but from the moment the scandal broke, Truman had his administration stonewall in what became nine months of hearings by the U.S. House Committee On Expenditures, attempting to prove huge bribes had been paid to top administration officials. The Committee publicly berated and embarrassed the AG and the Parole Board members for their many lies while testifying under oath and for placing the public in extreme jeopardy by freeing these domestic criminal terrorists.

With money-grabbing AG Clark denying everything, the Committee had no way to tie Truman to the Chicago gang's cash bribe, but its hearings exposed a political gift the gang gave the President in return for the pardons. In the general election Chicago Republican candidates were highly successful except in the five Italian wards where the gang ruled supreme. Political observers were struck by the sudden switch of voter sentiment to Democratic candidates, and the mysterious failure of Republican leaders to campaign in these wards from the moment word went out that the gangsters might be paroled. Rumors circulated in these neighborhoods that the Republicans delivered their votes "so the boys can get out on parole." As a *Chicago Tribune* editorial said, "The Capone gang is known to control the Republican Committeemen in a number of Chicago wards, but these are the wards that pile up some of the biggest Democratic majorities."[297]

It is difficult to believe that this late condition of vote stealing in return for approval of the paroles was not conceived by the President because he was the only beneficiary. To put Truman's actions into perspective, when Roosevelt was elected President early in the Great Depression, the Democrats took majority control of both the U.S. Senate and the U.S. House and held on to these until this election when the Republicans took control of both chambers as the public moved away from the Progressive policies of Roosevelt and Truman. The President directed Mafia gangs to commit massive voter fraud in the Kansas City primary and the Chicago general election to try to stave off losing control of the House of Representatives but Republicans still assumed the majority. Despite AG Clark's horrible offenses against the most basic principles of American democracy by vote stealing and pardoning America's most dangerous criminals, Truman rewarded his corrupt official by appointing him as a U.S. Supreme Court Justice to interpret the Constitution he had so fundamentally violated.[298]

Chapter 15

A MAFIOSO & A PRESIDENT RUMBLE

A MAFIOSO EMBARRASSES THE WHITE HOUSE

On the November 1948 evening that Truman celebrated winning a second term as President he had no inkling that the election in his home state of Missouri that day was about to change the political landscape in a way that would deeply affect the rest of his presidency. Truman's problem was ambitious Kansas City political/criminal leader Charles Binaggio who was intent on expanding his illegal empire. His goal had been to control the governor because he named the police commissioners for both Kansas City and St. Louis. Thus Binaggio had boldly expanded his political power base statewide and had led a strong campaign to get gubernatorial candidate Forrest Smith elected. During the campaign Binaggio and his associates had told many people that he planned to turn both Kansas City and St. Louis into wide-open gambling centers. In Kansas City gambling had been forced underground by the reform faction that had taken office eight years earlier following the death of Boss Tom Pendergast, and the Democratic political factions of both Binaggio and Pendergast had been unable to wrest back control of city government. In this election Binaggio's other "must win" candidate was for County Assessor because he was in a position to reign a halter on business leaders to silence any criticism or opposition. On election day the candidates supported by Binaggio and his Irish political ally swept into office, and after the ballots were counted that evening the pair, flush with victory, celebrated together around town.[299]

For the next five months Binaggio's puppet Governor Smith quietly and slowly moved forward laying the groundwork for the Mafioso's grand design for wide-open gambling. But then Binaggio's two roles collided when a decision as the Mafia chieftain disrupted his carefully calculated plans as political leader. This occurred when a gangster in Binaggio's ranks challenged his monopoly on crime. The defiant underling was Wolfgang "Wolf" Rimann who was known in the community as the manager and golf pro at the city's Hillcrest Country Club. But anyone in the business community who wanted to have a juke box or pinball machine in his establishment knew Wolf's Western Specialty Company had exclusivity in these fields in the city that was backed up by force under the orders of Mafia leader Binaggio. Wolf also owned several bars but it is when he obtained a statewide wholesale liquor license that he overstepped his bounds. This infuriated Binaggio because he was a silent partner in Duke Sales Company that had a monopoly on Schenley liquor products in western Missouri. Binaggio warned his underling not to try to compete but Wolf naively ignored the threat. Wolf thought he could get away with this brazen challenge because he was a good friend of Jackson County Sheriff Jacques "J. A." Purdome, and was even commissioned as a special deputy which allowed him to carry a gun and have his car equipped with a siren and red lights. One afternoon after Wolf had made application for the wholesale liquor license he walked out to his car parked at the curb. As he got inside two men in a black sedan rounded the corner behind him and drove up to stop beside him. The passenger opened fire from his seat and continued firing as he leapt out and ran up to Wolf and placed the pistol muzzle against his head for the final shot. Wolf was fatally hit in the skull, neck, and chest. The slain gangster was 43 and his wife

Esther 40. A year after Wolf's slaying, Sheriff Purdome divorced his wife to marry the widow of his late gangster friend.[300]

Even though Kansas City detectives never identified or arrested a suspect for this murder, Binaggio's violence as Mafia chief cost him dearly in his role as political kingmaker. The ongoing Kansas City police and Jackson County Grand Jury investigations about Wolf's murder generated massive negative publicity that forced puppet Governor Smith to stop initiating Binaggio's ambitious political scheme to open up Kansas City and St. Louis to wide-open gambling.

The ongoing bad publicity about Wolf's murder was not Binaggio's only political problem. Despite having spent the last six years wresting control of the four key downtown wards that had furnished the bulwark of votes to the Pendergast faction, Binaggio's power was not yet secure. He still had to divide up the patronage jobs getting only those from the state and county for his wards. The city jobs were still in the hands of the reform administration that had taken power away from the Pendergast regime eight years earlier, and President Truman continued to turn over federal patronage jobs for disbursement by his close friend Jim Pendergast. The President remained deeply loyal to his old war buddy and illustrated this by maintaining his membership in Pendergast's Jackson County Democratic Club. In addition Truman was deeply disturbed by Mafioso Binaggio's bad press coverage for the Democratic Party and wanted the gangster to move into the background behind the political image of Pendergast like the Kansas City political/criminal machine had been structured for decades. However both Pendergast and Binaggio refused to reconcile their competitive differences.

At that time there was a false belief held by the U.S. Justice Department and many local law enforcement agencies that Al Capone's successors in the Chicago gang and Frank Costello of New York City were getting ready to introduce illegal gambling in some major cities around the country. Costello had an imposing image. He was the biggest political kingmaker in the Big Apple; he owned America's premier nightclub, the Copacabana; he and some of his close associates operated elegant illegal casinos in a number of American cities; and he was one of the country's biggest bookmakers. With FBI Director J. Edgar Hoover holding his agents on the sidelines as organized crime flourished across the country, no one in law enforcement understood that each casino operator worked independently in each locale by corrupting local law enforcement and by cutting in for a share any powerful crime syndicate in the locale. Several mayors across the country had heard false rumors that Costello was planning to move into their cities and they called upon U.S. AG James McGrath to move against gamblers and hoodlums. Although false, this worry gave Truman the reason he had been looking for to stomp on Binaggio's rebellious politics in Kansas City. The President announced that he had directed his AG to have IRS agents investigate the criminal and business interests of gangsters in the complaining mayors' cities and to present their findings to local Federal Grand Juries. However AG McGrath later admitted that no special IRS crime investigations had been undertaken anywhere but Kansas City, meaning Truman only took action to embarrass his home base opposition Democratic political faction.[301]

While Binaggio's taxes were being scrutinized, Republican Missouri U.S. Senator Forrest Donnell was facing a reelection campaign. The Truman-Pendergast faction endorsed a candidate, and Binaggio recruited a different candidate to run against him in the Democratic Primary. This further infuriated the President who took this as a slap in the face. Missouri's newspapers reported the two political factions were negotiating to resolve their differences. The *St. Louis Star-Times* reported Binaggio was trying desperately to make political peace with the President possibly because of the developing IRS case before the Federal Grand Jury, but the two sides wanted different solutions to end their conflict. While Binaggio wanted both sides to agree on a third compromise candidate, Truman simply wanted the gangster to get out of politics, and there is some indication the Mafioso was actually considering this.[302]

Two weeks after Wolf Rimann's murder a Terminal Cab driver decided to take a breakfast break at Gehr's Café. At 4 a.m. he parked near Binaggio's First District Democratic Club and as he walked past the eastside of the building toward the diner across the alley he heard water running inside the closed offices. He walked on to the Café where he telephoned police, and two patrolmen responded to the Democratic Club. They found the front door slightly ajar and as they swung it open and started to walk into the darkened lobby they were just about to stumble over a body sprawled on the floor when their flashlights illuminated the slumped form. Their search further inside discovered another body in a chair at a desk in the rear of the room. Both men had been shot four times in the head. The two corpses were the Club's political leader, Mafioso Binaggio, and his lieutenant, Charles Gargotta.[303]

Detectives carefully studied the crime scene and recorded every relevant detail. The next day detectives traced Binaggio's activities for the previous 12 hours before his slaying at about 1 a.m. Then they developed from the multitude of assembled facts a scenario of what must have happened in the Democratic Club that night. The gangster/political leader had spent the afternoon tying up rose bushes in his yard and then had dinner with his family before leaving home about 7 p.m. His wife told police he had showed no sign of worry. She relayed that he had told her he was "just going down on the boulevard for a while. He wasn't afraid of anything." His father-in-law said he was in good spirits and added that Binaggio frequently went out on business at night but rarely told family members where he was headed.[304]

Binaggio had been driven by his bodyguard/chauffeur to the Last Chance Tavern, the city's most controversial casino operation because the building straddled the state line between Missouri and Kansas. The crap tables floated back and forth from the front to the back of the building into whichever cities' police jurisdiction was most amenable to illegal gambling at the moment. The two corrupt police forces never coordinated their raids to enter both ends of the building at the same time, trap the dice operators red-handed, and put them out of business. The morning after the two murders, Kansas City police visited the Last Chance to follow through on the bodyguard's timeline information, but hours before neighbors had seen all the gambling equipment loaded into a truck that was long gone.

When Binaggio had visited the Last Chance he had been joined by his lieutenant Gargotta, a gunsil who saw to it that others followed his boss' orders. Gargotta was a specialist in violence and known as The Enforcer or sometimes The Executioner, but that night he was unarmed. At the Last Chance the two top Mafiosi met with Homer Cooper, a casino operator for them in Council Bluffs and Carter Lake in Iowa. About 8 p.m. Binaggio received a phone call from a person who detectives were never able to identify, and then Binaggio and Gargotta huddled in a private powwow for a few minutes. Afterwards Gargotta asked Cooper to "let me borrow your car." Cooper told detectives he had lent him his car several times before. Binaggio's bodyguard/chauffeur got up to put on his coat to drive them, but Binaggio said, "You don't need to come, Nick. We'll be back in 15 or 20 minutes." At that moment a woman friend of Gargotta called him about getting together, and he informed her he had some business to take care of first, "but it shouldn't take more than 30 or 40 minutes" before he would join her. The two Mafiosi's expectation that their meeting with the killers would be so short indicates this was not intended to be an involved discussion of either business or politics. It may have been to shake hands on a deal that was completed through intermediaries or for a financial payoff, but this payoff was delivered in bullets instead of cash. The unknown caller to Binaggio lured him to his death at his own empty clubhouse. Detectives conjectured Binaggio would not have met with anyone in that isolated location who he did not trust and he would have taken his bodyguard if he had any suspicion there could be trouble. The bodyguard/chauffeur waited until 4 a.m. for the pair to return and then went home. Police found Cooper's car still parked on the street in front of the Democratic Club and found the keys close to Gargotta's body.[305]

The Detectives' thorough examination of the scene found just one scenario fit the facts. The victims were obviously killed by different shooters because the .32-caliber slugs taken from the two bodies had distinctly different ballistics patterns. Nothing indicated Binaggio had sensed any type of threat until one visitor suddenly opened fire. Detectives concluded Binaggio awaited the arrival of his two guests sitting at a desk in a railed-off area in the rear of the large main lobby rather than in his office. Gargotta let the two guests in the front door and then walked them to the back. Binaggio's body was found seated in a swivel chair perpendicular to the desk as if he was greeting someone who was standing right in front of him. That is when the pair drew their guns and one opened fire at Binaggio while the other went after Gargotta. Binaggio was shot up close because all four bullet wounds had heavy powder burns. One bullet entered the forehead above the left eye, and then the shooter circled Binaggio with two hitting in front of the left ear and the final shot was to the back of his head. Binaggio's head was found bent back hanging limply over the top of the chair. Police found his head was caked with blood, and blood had also dripped to the floor where it had pooled and clotted. His suit and colorful tie were untouched, but his hat, long cigarette holder, and spectacles were scattered on the floor near his feet. One of Binaggio's shoulders was sprinkled with cigarette ashes and a cigarette butt was under his chair, probably a memento from the shooter.

As soon as this first shooter had pulled his gun and started firing at Binaggio, Gargotta had turned from the scene and run for his life towards the glass-paneled double doors at the entrance with the second shooter in hot pursuit. Gargotta reached out to open a door when the second shooter fired into the back of his head. Gargotta fell backwards away from the glass door while clawing at some slats of a Venetian blind covering it. When he hit the floor, this shooter leaned over him to fire three closely-spaced slugs near his left eye. These three wounds had heavy powder-burn marks whereas the first wound to the base of the skull was shot from at least a foot away because it had no powder burns. Police found Gargotta's body with his head lying in a large pool of blood and his hat on the floor near him.

It is clear that Binaggio and Gargotta knew their killers well and had great trust in them because they arranged to meet them in an empty building after midnight unarmed and without Binaggio's constant bodyguard/chauffeur protecting him. This was in stark contrast to Binaggio's ever-present precautions. He was reticent to meet with any stranger, and he never met with anyone, not even reporters, without gang associates observing from close at hand according to investigative reporters who followed his career.

Police immediately ruled robbery out as a motive because Gargotta had $2,401 in his wallet and Binaggio still wore his expensive diamond-studded wrist watch. This was clearly a professional hit but with one unusual feature, no weapons were found in or around the club. Organized-crime members typically toss untraceable guns without fingerprints at the scene in case they are arrested during their getaway. The police investigation did identify the sound of the running water that had alerted the taxi driver. A plugged toilet in the hotel upstairs had overflowed and water was dripping down from the Club's ceiling to the floor where it had spread out to within a few inches of Binaggio's feet.

For Binaggio's funeral there were 56 dishonorary pallbearers including two current Kansas City Police Board Commissioners, the sheriffs for both Kansas City and St. Louis, former Missouri AG Roy McKittrick who cut the sweetheart plea deal with Charles Gargotta for the attempted murder of Sheriff Bash, former Kansas City Police Director Eugene Reppert who refused to investigate the Union Station Massacre 17 years earlier, judges, Democratic politicians, gamblers, gangsters, and gunmen. This list clearly illustrated the sordid alliance between political leaders, law enforcers, and Mafia bosses in Kansas City and Missouri.

Thousands of voters from the four political wards Binaggio controlled passed his pier at the funeral home. Binaggio's favors to constituents had been numerous. At the requiem high mass, a priest read a statement instead of giving a sermon. It said that Binaggio was granted a Roman Catholic funeral because "recently he was seen receiving the sacraments and attending Sunday mass." It further stated, "As Catholics we abominate and we condemn syndicated crime and vice. It is as despicable as it is evil. … We are gathered here this morning in the presence of the Savior who was not ashamed to be found in the company of sinners. To Him we recommend the soul of the individual whose remains are about to be consigned to the grave." A procession of 105 cars followed Binaggio's casket from the church to the cemetery.[306]

After conclusion of the services Binaggio's 28-year-old widow spoke about her gangster husband to the press. She stated he enjoyed embroidering and had stitched his baby's clothes. He also liked working in his basement workshop and the garden. She claimed she had no idea why anyone would want to kill the "kindhearted man who was a soft touch for anyone in need." She said he was gentle, kind, and one who had "done nothing but good in all the 41 years of his life. It's about time he received some credit for the good things he did."[307]

Truman may have hated the political opposition of Binaggio but after his death the mobster single-handedly maintained the President's Senate majority. While Binaggio's Democratic primary candidate for U.S. Senator eked out a 4,132 statewide vote victory over the Truman-Pendergast candidate by strongly capturing his home base in St. Louis County, the gangsters' candidate then went on to handily defeat incumbent Republican Senator Donnell with a 7.25% margin. This was the only Senatorial seat the Democrats picked up in this midterm election as they lost a net of five seats to barely hold on to the majority with 49 to 47 seats.[308]

Two days after the slaying of Binaggio, the *Kansas City Star* came out with a strong editorial attacking Governor Smith for deriving his main political support from a gangster. The editorial said that soon after Smith took his oath Binaggio became a regular visitor at the Governor's office as "the underworld came out of its exile to reap its rewards." The *Star* opposed the return of political protection for gambling, prostitution, and crime. Its editorial accused the Governor of making "friendly alliances" with gangsters, "condoning" a setting for gang murders, weakening the Kansas City police, and permitting a return of gambling and gang killings. It demanded that the Governor "crush this ominous rising power." The editorial noted there had been 23 gang murders in Kansas City during the past three years, and the Governor had been in office for the last half of this period. While illegal gambling was not wide open like it was under Mafioso Johnny Lazia in the 1930s it had been increasing under the Governor's administration. It added that the Ministerial Alliance made up of 122 Protestant churches had just supplied police with a list of 20 open casinos and bookie joints. The *Star* expressed worry for the future by pointing out the Governor gave half the spots on the election board to Binaggio underlings, and he sought Binaggio's approval before appointing two men to the Kansas City Police Board. The editorial stated, "A considerable number of men formerly dismissed from the department have been restored to jobs" which had a demoralizing effect on the exiting police force as did statements by Binaggio's criminal henchmen. They frequently told police officers that their boss would soon have the power to "make or break" them.[309]

Everybody related to this scandal began political grandstanding by pointing the finger at others' alleged misconduct while defending their own actions as virtuous. These are the facts. The Kansas City Police Board was composed of four members appointed by the Governor. Two appointees of the previous governor were anti-Binaggio so when their terms ended Governor Smith replaced them. The Governor selected as the new Chairman his long-time friend and Kansas City campaign manger J. L. "Tuck" Milligan. Tuck was the brother of former U.S. Attorney Maurice Milligan, but his ties to Binaggio's political faction put him on the other side of the law. The press reported that Tuck had traveled in the same Pullman car as Binaggio to attend the Washington inauguration of President Truman, but Tuck brushed this off as a pure coincidence. The press revealed a more disturbing association. Both of the Governor's Police Board appointees were listed as dishonorary pallbearers at the funeral of gangster Binaggio. Tuck dismissed this as someone mistakenly placing his name in the funeral list. Tuck claimed the only time he met Binaggio was soon after he was appointed Chairman. Tuck explained the dead gangsters' approach this way, "Binaggio came to me and asked about opening up gambling. I told him that all the laws would be enforced." Governor Smith's second appointee was an outspoken advocate for wide-open illegal gambling.[310]

Even Kansas City's long-time reform Mayor was attacked for his role as the ex-officio fifth member of the Police Board because he had attended just eight of the 184 meetings since becoming Mayor. However he had attended the really important hearing. This is when Governor Smith's two appointees had just taken office and their first move was to try to replace the police chief with a man recommended by Mafioso Binaggio. The Mayor appeared specifically to join the two holdover members in blocking new Chairman Milligan's corrupt proposal with a three-to-two vote.

Kansas City leaders' publicly requested Governor Smith to investigate the city's crime and police problem. He not only rejected this by falsely claiming everything was fine, but then he summarily removed from office the two holdover Police Board members without justification so he could bring in new appointees. Both of these replaced fine public servants had demonstrated their integrity by voting against Binaggio's agenda and by reporting the following events to Governor Smith shortly after he took office. Binaggio in his role as a political leader had requested a private meeting with each man at which he had thrown a large amount of cash into the police official's lap in a bribery attempt to open up the city to wide-open gambling and other unspecified crimes. Both men reported that they had indignantly tossed the cash back "like a hot rivet." These dedicated officials said further that Binaggio had also made it clear he planned to move on St. Louis because he wanted to become the statewide crime czar. Both men later testified about their experiences with Binaggio and the Governor before the Kefauver Committee.

The four honest Police Board members Governor Smith replaced had issued an honorary gold-plated police badge to President Truman, but Governor Smith's newly-appointed Board members invalidated this privilege to symbolically demonstrate that Binaggio's successor political/criminal leader Tony Gizzo and his puppet Governor were going to continue challenging the President and his friend Jim Pendergast's political faction. This action made it obvious that Governor Smith planned under the new gang leadership of Gizzo to inaugurate Binaggio's scheme to have the police protect the Mafia's criminal empire. However the resulting public indignation forced Governor Smith to instead dismiss the two new board members he had appointed. Later the Kefauver Committee's Preliminary Report stated that more than a "passing connection" existed between Governor Smith's appointment "of two members to the Kansas City Police Board who favored a 'wide-open' town and Binaggio's support during the election." The Report also revealed that Binaggio had offered former AG McKittrick a bribe to withdraw from the Gubernatorial race so the gangster could further his gambling interests through Governor Smith. It was almost a year after Governor Smith's dismissal of the honest Police Board members, that the U.S. Senate Kefauver Committee would begin hearings across the nation that would create a public uproar for reform that would stomp out wide-open illegal gambling not only in Kansas City but virtually every other city.[311]

WHAT SEEMS OBVIOUS MAY BLUR REALITY

In the murders of Binaggio and Gargotta detectives failed to come up with a likely suspect or even a possible motive. This gave investigative reporters free reign to speculate about the reason, and the day after the double homicide their favorite scenario was presented in a *St. Louis Star-Times* copyrighted story. Based on nothing but a vague rumor the popular belief was that Binaggio had arranged for out-of-state illegal gambling associates to donate large sums to elect Governor Smith to ensure they would be able to participate in the explosion of wide-open casinos that was sure to follow. After Governor Smith's election victory he was clearly politically indebted to the Mafioso political kingmaker, but Binaggio's own misjudgments hindered his grand scheme. His mistake in St. Louis was agreeing with Governor Smith to appoint as head of the Police Board a man who had never been politically active. For some reason the Mafioso thought he could handle him, but the *St. Louis Star-Times* reported that this official instead became a "stubbornly righteous man – almost a reformer."

This article went on to say it had learned Binaggio had been threatened with a death sentence in a hotel room in St. Louis three months before his slaying because he had failed to turn the city wide open. Then five days before he was slain Binaggio had supposedly made another trip to St. Louis to meet with these unidentified associates and they allegedly demanded he persuade the reformist St. Louis Police Board Chairman to resign. The article alleged they threatened Binaggio if he failed to keep his campaign promises. In response to this article Binaggio's widow told reporters, "He wasn't afraid of anything. This talk about his having been given a death warrant somewhere around St. Louis – that's ridiculous." However he never told her anything about his business and someone certainly did sentence him to death whether or not they ever threatened him beforehand, so her statement is really not illuminating.[312]

In Kansas City it was Binaggio's murder of interloper Wolf Rimann that slowed down the Governor's move for casino development. While some new casinos had opened since Governor Smith had taken office they operated in the shadows and were nowhere near as big or wide open as under former Mafia boss Johnny Lazia during the Great Depression. Thus the popular conjecture was that Binaggio had been murdered because his unidentified St. Louis or out-of-state associates were supposedly angry and retaliated for having invested in what turned out to be empty promises about both cities' futures.

It is amazing that such vague gossip gained traction with the press and public because popular rumors about gangland invariably identify the name of the alleged group or the leader who supposedly perpetrated the crime. In this case no evidence ever surfaced that Binaggio had needed or raised either campaign contributions or bribes from another gangster. The organized crime leaders of this generation were not Neanderthals who used violence willy nilly to vent frustration as is so often depicted by organized crime novelists and Hollywood films. These criminals used violence for three specific purposes – to defend themselves when threatened, to intimidate potential victims in their financial crimes, and to knock out their boss to ascend the throne.

Binaggio's supposed enemies gained nothing from his death, but they lost his valuable potential assistance. This powerful political/gang lord had strong influence over the Governor; was slowly acquiring control of the Kansas City Police Board; directed a large and loyal voting constituency to put friendly politicians, prosecutors, and judges in office; and offered a secure hide out under police protection for the nation's gangsters whenever they felt the heat bubbling up at home.

The tidbit of gossip that was the foundation for this supposition about why Binaggio was murdered lacked two other important standard elements. It offered no explanation why the successful Binaggio needed to go to outside sources for election funding and why he was not able to pay it back from the profits produced by his criminal empire. Even if we surmise he did not have all the cash on hand to reimburse the contributions, it is standard practice in organized crime to let people pay off debts with installment payments plus interest. In fact Binaggio was known to offer people who lacked immediate cash resources such deals, so he certainly would have proposed this as a solution when surrounded by gunsils in a St. Louis hotel room.

As an example Binaggio offered such an installment deal to an errant casino manager down on his luck. This situation developed when Binaggio decided to invest in building a new legal gambling resort on the Las Vegas Strip about the same time Ben Siegel was constructing his Fabulous *Flamingo*. His investment involved Bob Carnahan who had managed illegal casinos for three successive Kansas City Mafia gang leaders - John Lazia, Charles Carollo, and Binaggio. Over the years Carnahan had operated the city's largest casino, the Twelfth Street Recreation Parlor, the Blue Hills Country Club, and some downtown places. Carnahan was slated to be the casino manager of the new *Thunderbird Hotel* on the Strip and a partner to owner Marion Hicks who was born in Joplin, Missouri. Carnahan was from Wichita, Kansas and continued to operate in that city when he was not managing in Kansas City. Hicks needed additional investment capital, so Carnahan arranged for Mafioso Binaggio to invest as a silent partner. Carnahan was to be an owner of record fronting both his and Binaggio's interests. He was to share his take of the profits by slipping cash to Binaggio under the table. Their total investment was $1 million ($9 million today), most of it Binaggio's. Carnahan arrived in Las Vegas with the cash in hand and held on to it until construction was to begin.

In the meantime Bob Carnahan became bored bidding his time so he began drinking in the various casinos during the evenings. It was only while drinking that he ever gambled, and the various casinos were glad to extend the inebriated man large amounts of gambling credit because he had a fine reputation for integrity. Several nights in a row he lost between $100,000 and $300,000 until the whole cash investment was gone. This delayed construction of the *Thunderbird* because Hicks had to scramble for a new casino manager who was able to invest the needed capital. Another glitch that delayed construction was a new federal post-war prohibition against non-essential building projects in order to give proper maintenance to the country's infrastructure that had been ignored during the war.

The now broke Carnahan had to return to Kansas City to face Binaggio about his costly irresponsible conduct. If this was a movie the audience would already know that Carnahan was a dead man walking, but this was reality not Hollywood. Binaggio got no benefit from killing Carnahan so he cut a deal to get his lost investment back over time. The Mafioso told Carnahan to return to Las Vegas, get a job as a casino manager, and pay him a percentage of his income every year for the rest of his life. When the money Carnahan had lost was paid off the future payments would constitute interest for what had now become a loan.

Carnahan was competent and he returned to Las Vegas where he went on to become a very successful Strip casino manager. He became a pioneer of the Strip casino-junket programs of the 1960s and 1970s. Strip resorts chartered planes from specific cities each week and filled them with high-rollers whose expenses were borne by the resorts. This included all airfare, room, food, and beverage charges. These free gambling trips did not include wives because they might observe their husbands' losses and complain to slow them down. Some resorts had one or more flights arriving and leaving on Sundays and Thursdays to keep their rooms continuously filled with the country's biggest players. Later in his life Carnahan became an outstanding casino host with an extensive book of high rollers' phone numbers from all over the country. He would occasionally call each one to inquire how he was doing and if he could do anything for him. These players called Carnahan to set up all their accommodations and arrangements when they wanted to come out and gamble.

During the many years I conducted my historical research I would occasionally make the rounds of the Las Vegas casinos to see what was going on at each one. When I would walk through the *Tropicana* during the evening and see Bob Carnahan on the casino floor alone with no customers around, I would sit with him and we would discuss what was going on at the various casinos. He was a very pleasant and knowledgeable elderly man who still had to work to pay his living expenses and his old debt to Kansas City. One evening Bob told me about his gambling losses, but he never wanted to talk about them again. He would not tell me how much he owed or what percentage of his income he was still paying 23 years later because he said, "I get sick today realizing how much I threw away."[313]

Binaggio could have cut a similar time-payment deal with the unidentified gangsters who had supposedly supported Governor Smith's campaign. The press usually reported the total amount contributed by other gangsters at $200,000 ($1.8 million today). Because of Binaggio's many illegal and legal enterprises, he could have easily paid back $100,000 a year for five years which would have included total interest of 150%. The IRS investigation President Truman ordered before Binaggio's death uncovered his many Kansas City holdings including nearly a dozen gambling operations, the local outlet for the national horseracing wire service to bookies, the policy racket or lottery that he had stolen from the neighborhood operators "by sheer muscle," a nightclub, and a retail fur store operated by his wife and some partners.

Binaggio's horseracing wire service was named the Harmony Publishing Company. Because of the Mafioso's clout as a political kingmaker his wire service operated under a Jackson County Circuit Court Judge's temporary but indefinite injunction against interference by the police. However another court issued an injunction that prevented the Western Union Telegraph Company from supplying Harmony racing information from Chicago's Continental Press, the nation's only horserace information supplier. Continental operated in Missouri under the name Midwest News Service. After reading the terms of this injunction Binaggio and his supplier humorously tried a gambit. They reopened Harmony under the name Standard News Service and had Continental supply them under a different name, General News Service. Two of the partners later testified to the McFarland Senate Interstate Commerce Subcommittee that to their surprise nobody stopped them because neither name was listed in the injunction. One of the partners who testified was Thomas "Tano" Lococo. He was the fourth assailant who murdered Ferris Anthon, the one who shot at Sheriff Bash as he ran between residences to escape, although he was never identified by the police. He and Gargotta, the second shooter of Anthon who charged the Sheriff and eventually pled guilty, were partners with Binaggio in the racing wire service. Eight months after President Truman ordered the IRS to go after Binaggio and his Mafiosi, it charged Lococo with income tax evasion, and four months later, he pled guilty and received a two-year prison sentence.

The Duke Sales Company in Kansas City distributed Canadian Ace Beer from a Chicago plant controlled by the successors to Al Capone. The two official local owners of Duke Sales testified before the Federal Grand Jury investigating Binaggio's tax returns that they gave half their net profits to Binaggio and his close associate, Tony Gizzo, in exchange for the Mafia boss' influence in marketing their beer. Virtually every Kansas City bar kept it on tap and every retail liquor outlet offered it in bottles to stay in the good graces of the powerful political kingmaker. Another of Binaggio's associates headed the wholesale Superior Wine and Liquor Company and likely had a similar arrangement to share his profits in return for the Mafioso preventing competition in town, as Wolf Rimann learned when the lead started flying.

The Kansas City Federal Grand Jury interim report said the tax-fixing racket in the County Assessor's office was "the most sordid and vicious situation existing in Jackson County." The Mafia gang extorted local businesses by threatening to jack up property and business taxes and actually did it to those who refused to pay. An even larger scheme was to have tax adjusters double or triple assessments on properties and when the owners complained to the Assessor he would remove the properties from the tax rolls in return for cash bribes depriving the community of vast sums of money. Binaggio's political machine had put the Assessor in office and Binaggio received a cut of the Assessor's tax extortion and bribery racket.

One of the 14 partners in one of the city's biggest gambling operations, the Town Recreation, was an Assistant County Prosecutor, according to the Kansas City Federal Grand Jury interim report. The evening of the report's release the County Prosecutor summarily fired his wayward subordinate. The former Assistant defended his relations with gamblers by claiming that they occurred solely in his role as an attorney, apparently meaning he was the defense attorney for the very criminals he was supposed to be prosecuting. The Grand Jury report also stated the Last Chance Tavern that straddled the Kansas-Missouri state line had been operated by two partners until one refused to take in Binaggio as a partner and was murdered. Then the surviving partner welcomed Binaggio, Gargotta, and three of their henchmen. The Jury pointed out the coincidence that both the slain Last Chance partner and Binaggio were killed with four bullets to the head. This leads to the possibility that the shooter Binaggio ordered to take out the defiant casino-owner victim was also the shooter who was later used to eliminate Binaggio.[314]

Besides the profitable enterprises uncovered by the IRS, Binaggio also had other lucrative ventures. For example when he failed to create wide-open gambling in Kansas City he spread out to other areas of the country. He encountered Davie Berman in Council Bluffs, Iowa. As a youth Davie had become hired muscle in the Midwest. He rode shotgun for Prohibition convoys; beat up casino players behind on their debts; and robbed banks, post offices, and private poker games. Then he kidnapped two New York City Prohibition partners for $20,000 ransom and wound up serving almost eight years in Sing Sing Prison. Upon release Davie joined his brother Chickie to operate illegal casinos in Minneapolis, Minnesota. When Pearl Harbor was attacked the 37-year-old Davie joined the Canadian Army and distinguished himself fighting with the Allied forces liberating France. When the war in Europe ended, Davie moved to the tiny town of Las Vegas to join New York friends who had run Ben Siegel's illegal gambling operations. This was before Siegel contemplated building his fabulous *Flamingo* resort on the Las Vegas Strip. When he purchased the *El Cortez Hotel Casino* downtown he brought Davie in as casino manager and a partner.

Davie's brother Chickie continued to operate their illegal casinos in Minneapolis and he joined two Omaha, Nebraska associates to buy the upscale Stork Club dinner restaurant with its attached unlawful casino across the river in Council Bluffs, Iowa. Binaggio in Kansas City supplied Council Bluffs the horserace wire service and he had his eyes set on the Stork Club too. One night after the casino closed and Chickie and a partner were counting the cash win, Binaggio's goons burst in. While some of the thugs held Chickie at gunpoint in the casino the others took his partner to a cornfield and pressed a pistol to his temple. Both victims refused to sign away their interests in the Stork Club. The kidnappers held the pair like this for 12 hours before calling Davie in Las Vegas to tell him, "If you don't get your brother out of here, we'll kill him." Davie convinced Chickie to comply.[315]

Next Binaggio expanded to the North Shore of Lake Tahoe close to the California border by leasing the shuttered *Nevada Tahoe* casino. At that time Lake Tahoe was strictly a summer vacation spot because of the difficult winter snow and icy highway conditions. Binaggio opened the *Nevada Tahoe* for the 1949 summer season managed by Sam Termini to whom Binaggio was the literal godfather in the baptismal sense. Because of Termini's successful summer season Binaggio made plans during the winter to invest in a major upgrade to give his operation national recognition, but that spring the gangster was killed in his Democratic Club and Termini could not fund the bankroll to reopen for the upcoming summer season. The again shuttered *Nevada Tahoe* was later sold at a bankruptcy auction.

All these profitable businesses demonstrate Binaggio had solid income to buy himself out of his dilemma with the alleged gangsters to whom he had supposedly promised wide-open gambling, but no evidence was ever uncovered that these gossiped gangsters ever existed. The local newspaper investigative reporters were never able to pull from their many political and underworld sources the identity of who these whispered criminals might be or even if any gangsters had actually contributed cash for use to elect and/or pay off Governor Smith.

A GOLD-FILLED POT OR A MIRAGE

In the month after the double murders of the Kansas City political/criminal leaders, various newspapers substantiated an enormous amount of diverse facts about Binaggio's recent criminal and political activities and they uncovered an extensive number of successful financial investments most illegal. Amazingly not one of the many reporters and authors who have written about this case over the years ever bothered to search out all this relevant information. For the first time all these facts are assembled in the new cold-case investigation that follows. It provides a remarkable view into the inner workings of Binaggio's criminal/political empire and the ominous threats he was facing. It demonstrates the pair was not murdered because of the popularly believed rumor about a broken promise over wide-open illegal gambling. That often repeated story was nothing more than false gossip. More importantly this analysis finally reveals the actual motive and identity of the killers of Mafiosi Binaggio and Gargotta.

First this examination eliminates an obvious person of interest as a possible suspect. Right after the double homicides Kansas City detectives questioned Mafia-gang member Charles Carollo who 16-years earlier had been the lieutenant when political/crime boss Johnny Lazia was murdered. Not only did Carollo succeed Lazia as head of the Kansas City Mafia but it was widely believed Carollo had orchestrated his boss' killing that night. Actually as shown earlier the evidence is overwhelming that he was the only person who could have arranged the killing that fateful night. Later Carollo went to prison for tax evasion and he voluntarily turned leadership over to Binaggio. Since Carollo had been released from Alcatraz four years before Binaggio's murder, it was thought he might have harbored ambitions of reassuming leadership. However at the time of Binaggio's killing Carollo was facing a serious threat of deportation because he had never become a citizen and he had been convicted of multiple felonies. It would take another four years for deportation legalities to play out, but as expected the U.S. finally put Carollo on a ship bound to his native Sicily.

Not only did Carollo's pending deportation make him an unlikely candidate for leader, but an interesting coincidence a week after Binaggio and Gargotta were slain further weakened his suitability. Carollo was at a residence just a mile from that bloody scene when he was arrested by a dozen agents of the Kansas City Federal Alcohol Tax Unit. They swooped in on a two-story home equipped with steel front and back doors and a conveyor belt that ran up and down to the basement. Carollo and three other men were unloading a truck filled with 1,135 cases of Bourbon, Scotch, and Champagne. They were charged with wholesaling liquor without having the required occupational tax stamp and not making federal tax payments. This bust and Carollo's pending deportation ended his influence in gangland.[316]

The leadership of Binaggio and Gargotta had been facing a very real threat for some time, but it was from the ongoing IRS investigation instigated by President Truman. Details about its progress became public three weeks after their slayings, when the Kansas City Federal Grand Jury hearing the IRS agents' tax-evasion case against the pair released its interim report. This revealed the Grand Jury was on the verge of indicting Binaggio and Gargotta, and soon after Binaggio's death the IRS did place a large lien against his estate, leading a gang member to tell a reporter, "Some guy with a pistol just beat Uncle to the draw."

The Grand Jury's report also exposed the character of Gargotta, the cold-blooded killer who had cowardly knelt and begged for mercy when facing Sheriff Bash's riot gun. He had become an informant to the IRS and disclosed the names of his partners and associates in the city's gambling operations and horserace news wire service. Gargotta's Mafia associates likely had inside information about what went on in the Federal Grand Jury's closed hearings, but it must have been obvious to them that a very high-ranking member in their criminal enterprise was snitching. Out of the 185 witnesses the IRS subpoenaed to appear before the Federal Grand Jury 90% were law violators, and the agents who questioned them had detailed knowledge about their illicit business connections.

During the drawn-out IRS investigation both Binaggio and Gargotta had met frequently with agents, both had testified before the Grand Jury, and both were under subpoena to testify again 11 days after their slayings. If these upcoming Grand Jury appearances, pending tax-evasion prosecutions, and leaked gang-insider information had not thoroughly unnerved the two Mafia leaders' associates, Binaggio added to their consternation by letting it be known that he wanted to step down from political and gang leadership in Kansas City, move to another state, and go into a legit business. By doing so he would have severed his criminal ties with his gang associates, distanced his personal relationships with them, and possibly disengaged his loyalty to them.[317]

Binaggio's next move to extricate himself from the mounting prosecutorial and gangland pressure would lead to one of the most bizarre episodes in the history of the White House and more embarrassment for President Truman. Oddly it would result from events transpiring in the Cold War with the Soviet Union. Their first atomic bomb test shocked U.S. nuclear scientists and intelligence officials because they thought the first detonation was at least several years away. The American people reeled from the horrifying reality that this ominous expansionist enemy now possessed such a powerful weapon. Many Americans considered building bomb shelters in their back yards stockpiled with the food and water needed to survive underground for the first few weeks after a nuclear holocaust until they hoped it would be safe to surface. These discussions ignored the reality of the world the survivors would reemerge into. The handful of gasoline refineries would have evaporated so there would be no transportation, no food or other critical supplies, and no drugs or medical treatment for injuries, radiation poisoning, or illnesses. Hollywood had not yet spawned its genre of movies about the horrifying realities of life above ground in a radioactive Apocalypse that would have imbedded itself in the country's population centers and then drifted over and contaminated America's hitherto fertile farmlands and pure water supplies.

Prior to the Soviet's first nuclear test, the U.S. Atomic Energy Commission (AEC) had begun the search for building materials that would shield structures from radiation. The AEC had contracted with the University of New Mexico (UNM) for a year-long study of the possible benefits of pumice, a volcanic ash, as a concrete building material for AEC construction in the southwest. Just two months into their research five UNM professors in the Civil Engineering and Geology Departments became convinced of the value of pumice so they filed 17 claims near Los Alamos. Five months later they formed Pantheon Corporation and distributed a prospectus to potential investors based on their confidential but unclassified research findings. When UNM learned about their professors' personal use of research information, it dismissed two professors and gave letters of reprimand to the other three.

It was just two days after the research team submitted its final report to the AEC highly recommending the use of pumice that the Soviets detonated their first atomic bomb. The head of this research project was an Albuquerque civil engineer who had become a true believer that pumice possessed insulation qualities against nuclear radiation so he had become VP of Pantheon. He was convinced building blocks made of pumice concrete would resist heat and retard the penetration of gamma radiation by dispersing it. This engineer spent the next four months trying to convince the officials he dealt with at the AEC to conduct another study of pumice concrete as a defensive counter to nuclear warfare. The engineer envisioned constructing new homes out of pumice concrete blocks and for existing homes either to build underground backyard bomb shelters or to line their walls with these blocks. Finally in exasperation he sent letters about his beliefs and recommendations to the highest levels of the AEC and to the government including President Truman. The AEC quickly wrote back to the engineer that pumice did not adequately protect against a blast so testing its shielding qualities would serve no useful purpose. However the AEC had no reason to notify President Truman about one more fruitless research result. Thus Truman, like the head of the research project, moved ahead with his own private business project to take advantage of these alleged research findings.

The President quickly organized a group of men who were also enthralled with the marketing potential of pumice concrete. The possibility of this new business opportunity was about to strangely bring together Kansas City's two bitter warring political antagonists, President Truman and political/criminal leader Binaggio. A few days after the President received the engineer's letter he attended a dinner and reception held in his honor at the showcase farm of Blevins Davis near Truman's hometown of Independence, Missouri. Davis was a wealthy New York theatrical producer and intimate friend of Truman and his family and frequently hosted them at social functions.

At this event the principals selected for this entrepreneurial enterprise met. The President had reached out to his long-time senatorial colleague from New Mexico, Democrat Dionisio "Dennis" Chavez Sr., and asked him to identify a local politically savvy man as the proposed company's president. The Senator recommended Roy Cook, Democratic politician and former postmaster of Albuquerque, who attended the dinner. A deal was struck. Davis invested $100,000 to capitalize the company for a 51% interest, and Cook received the remaining 49% share to be president. Also in attendance was the youngest brother of Truman's wife, David Wallace. He became the company treasurer, the bomb-shelter architect, and the boss over Cook because Davis gave him power of attorney to vote his controlling majority stock shares.

In the four years prior to becoming a Senator, Chavez had served as Chairman of the House Committee on Indian Affairs. During the three months after Truman's dinner his administrative assistant and son Dennis Jr. helped Cook negotiate a mining lease through the Interior Department for 1,920 acres of pumice land on the Santa Clara Indian Reservation near Santa Fe. At the same time they merged their venture with two local companies, one to mine the pumice and the other to manufacture building blocks. The Senator's son-in-law became the agent for the enterprise.

This is when Mafioso Binaggio heard in his high-echelon Democratic political circles about Davis' promising New Mexico pumice investment, and he wanted to buy into what sounded like a dream opportunity. Since Davis was very close to Truman who despised Binaggio, the gangster decided to buy his interest through a front man who would never mention his name when dealing with the principals. Interestingly the investors never asked the front man where the money behind him came from because they were so anxious to get the needed financing. The only principal who knew was Dennis Jr., and he was not worried about the association because he knew Binaggio was a major Democratic political leader in Missouri, the President's home state. Binaggio also needed someone who knew the pumice business to represent his interest so he had a former Probate Court Clerk introduce him to the Kansas City sales representative for the General Pumice Corporation. Binaggio hired him as his emissary and sent him to Albuquerque to meet with Dennis Jr. for assistance in surveying the business sites and in buying a large $200,000 share of the business from Davis and Cook. A Washington lobbyist who had a long association with Binaggio also attended some of these meetings and planned to invest several hundred thousand dollars more. Binaggio's emissary spent 10 days in Albuquerque and returned to Kansas City with positive information about the prospects of pumice, so the Mafioso planned to go back with him to finalize the deal. But two days before their scheduled date of departure Binaggio was murdered. The fact Binaggio had at least $200,000 in cash available to invest in the pumice business should finally put to rest any consideration that he was unable to settle with the supposedly unknown out-of-town gangsters in the highly-doubtful story that they invested this amount in the Governor's campaign and that they killed him because he could not pay them back.

With Binaggio's slaying his planned $200,000 investment evaporated so Truman's brother-in-law Wallace had to turn to the federally-backed Reconstruction Finance Corporation (RFC), a New Deal-era agency charged with providing government loans to struggling businesses. Wallace requested a $50,000 loan to continue developing the company's sites. However to get this loan the firm needed to show a viable business contract. Thus the company managed by Cook and Wallace had their concrete plant make a bid to furnish 1.8 million volcanic-cinder blocks, for an 800-unit housing and apartment project to house personnel at Walker Air Force Base near Albuquerque. They made a ridiculously-low bid that had no possibility for profitability. Their goal was to bid well under the legitimate competitors, and they won a $350,000 Air Force contract. With this document in hand the President's brother-in-law Wallace was able to secure the RFC loan. The moment the company obtained this money it canceled the Air Force contract before having delivered even 10,000 blocks and the next highest bidder completed the project based on the realistic bid it had submitted.

Seven months after Wallace's RFC loan was approved the U.S. Senate Banking Subcommittee took President Truman to task for giving underhanded aid to secure Davis' pumice company's RFC loan. Even though Senator Bill Fulbright [Arkansas] was a Democrat he went after the leader of his party because of his gross financial misconduct, and because the Senator wanted leverage in his efforts to replace the five man RFC Board of Directors with a single Administrator who would be easier to manipulate. The Committee exposed that Truman had placed two Missouri couples, who were his friends and also close with each other, in key government positions. When Truman was Senator he had made Mrs. Loretta Young his personal stenographic secretary and her husband E. Merle Young a messenger. The Senator also got Donald Dawson into the RFC as Director of Personnel, and he placed his wife Alva in charge of its files. Dawson then brought Merle Young in as an RFC examiner before moving him up to loan expediter assisting persons desiring loans. When Truman became President, he brought Dawson into the White House as his personal adviser making him the key man in most Presidential appointments.

Fulbright's Senate Committee report was signed by every member, the four Democrats as well as the two Republicans. The Committee accused three of the five RFC Directors of yielding improperly to outside influence in granting several loans. Just two had refused to sign the $50,000 loan to the enterprise of Mrs. Truman's brother David Wallace because it contained statements they considered improper. The Committee was never able to untangle the involved misfortunes of Pumex that went bankrupt and never repaid its RFC loan. The company's collapse led President Cook to bring a lawsuit against investor Davis and the President's brother-in-law Wallace.

The pumice company loan was relatively small, but Truman's RFC appointees' also participated in far more gross misconduct. For example E. Merle Young arranged $37 million in loans for Lustron Corporation, then resigned the RFC to become VP at Lustron which went broke leaving the taxpayers holding the bag on these huge loans. Adding insult to injury another RFC loan applicant testified under oath he lent E. Merle Young $9,500 so the RFC official could purchase a pastel mink coat for his wife Loretta who was President Truman's personal secretary. The Committee's report also charged two White House staff members of using their influence to swing RFC loans in favor of friends. Truman's personal adviser Dawson and the Democratic National Chairman both wrote influence letters to the RFC members. Dawson sent 100 and the Chairman 50. The Committee ignored the 850 influence letters that had been written by members of Congress. Once the Senate had done its job of investigating and exposing the administration's wrongdoing it became the responsibility of Truman's Justice Department to build and prosecute the criminal cases against its own administrative branch of the government. However in every Congressional investigation of Truman's corrupt administration the President stonewalled. He always refused comment, made his appointees and documents unavailable, and kept the Justice Department from investigating or launching criminal proceedings.[318]

THE STRANGE DEMISE OF A MAFIOSO

Binaggio's efforts to sneakily acquire a secret interest in a private business partnership of the man who was both his sworn political adversary and the President of the United States seems strange indeed. Surprisingly Binaggio was close to pulling off his subterfuge in this deal when he was slain. He had wanted into the deal simply because it was the best investment he could find to carry out his intended plans to move to another state and go into a legitimate business and way of life. He had told a number of people about his desire to go legit. For example Binaggio's emissary in the pumice-deal explained to detectives investigating his homicide, "Binaggio said he wanted to get out of Kansas City and was looking for some kind of legitimate business to get into." A Kansas City based Federal Bureau of Narcotics agent later testified before the Kefauver Committee that Binaggio had told him shortly before his murder that he planned to move to New Mexico, where he had acquired some mining interests. In this regard Binaggio's widow told a reporter a week after his slaying that she had pushed him for a long time to get out of "his business. Then he told me he was quitting. In a few more days he would have quit and gone away with me, just gypsy style with no definite idea of where we were going." Obviously she did not know about his specific business plan but she did understand how he wanted to change his career and lifestyle.[319]

The Kansas City investigative reporters who so effectively penetrated and revealed such a great deal about the political and criminal intrigue in their town and state for decades could learn nothing about Binaggio's late-life efforts from their many inside political and criminal sources who readily exposed others in hopes of more favorable reporting about themselves. The best these investigator reporters could come up with was that Binaggio was running from some criminal or political upheaval. Binaggio's desire to voluntarily abdicate his dominating political and criminal power and large income in Kansas City to start a completely different way of life across the country as an unconnected newcomer is unique in the annals of American organized crime. It simply made no sense to anyone who investigated this case because no other gang leader ever voluntarily relinquished his throne because of pending prosecution unless he had a deal with his successor that he and his family would be satisfactorily provided for. All the other gang leaders who have become vulnerable or endangered invariably struggled to consolidate their power to better maintain control over their members and to confront outside threats. But Binaggio had done something never done by any other gangster. He had politically challenged and personally angered the President of the United States, who in retribution had directed a determined IRS unit and Federal Prosecutor to put him behind bars.

Binaggio knew he was about to be tried for felony tax evasion and realized he would likely be convicted. He also understood he had but one chance to avoid going to prison and that was to throw himself to the mercy of Truman by demonstrating he was forever withdrawing from Kansas City and Missouri politics and would never again be an antagonist to the President's agenda. By moving to another state and going into a legitimate business to support his family, he hoped to obtain the goodwill of the President who might tell the IRS to settle his outstanding tax liability for the amount owed along with interest and appropriate fines in lieu of criminal prosecution. After all Truman's predecessor, President Roosevelt, had a decade and a half earlier told his AG to back off prosecuting Kansas City Mafia gang leader Johnny Lazia in return for an IRS settlement until a reformist Grand Jury disrupted that proposal by moving ahead on it own with indictments. Binaggio was trapped in a corner with no other options, and he had a ray of hope with Truman. The President may have been well known as a bare-knuckle political fighter, but he also had another side. He had a soft spot for the underdog and sometimes in victory he had been merciful toward the vanquished.

Another factor came into play. Truman's administration suffered an unprecedented political scandal over the IRS when it was revealed many agents had accepted bribes to reduce tax payer's obligations or assessments or to drop their prosecutions. Some agents even extorted bribes by threatening tenacious but unjustified prosecution. President Truman had inherited this long-time problem. It resulted from Senators who choose comrades who lacked scruples as appointees for the top IRS offices in their states. They too often ignored the transgressions of their patron Senator's friends while harassing his enemies. Truman ordered AG J. Howard McGrath to investigate the IRS situation but his botched efforts led to Republican political charges of a whitewash so the President demanded his resignation. Truman or his appointees had been involved in so many scandals that he had to fire his AG to separate himself from the one scandal he was innocent of. Truman replaced McGrath as AG with James McGranery who effectively went after the offenders. He dismissed 166 IRS officials for taking bribes and convicted almost a dozen. Truman also pushed through Congress a bill that restructured the IRS and placed virtually all top officials under civil-service merit promotion rather than political appointment.

Knowing all these facts about Truman's presidency gave Binaggio cause for optimism. He thought that if he could get the pending federal prosecution off his back, he was set because he was finalizing what he believed was an excellent investment opportunity in pumice in Albuquerque. Of course with hindsight we know he would have lost almost his whole investment and would have been a new guy in town with no gang members, no police contacts, no political allies, and possibly little savings with which to rebuild his life.

This leaves one remaining pertinent question about Binaggio's murder. Who were his killers? Only one man benefited from the slayings of Binaggio and Gargotta, Tony Gizzo, the third in command in the gang's hierarchy. He assumed Binaggio's Mafia and political toga, but the detectives and the press barely mentioned his name in the murder investigations. Gizzo should have been the primary suspect because he gained so much and also because of his gang background. As a young man during Prohibition Gizzo had moved from New York City to Chicago where he became closely aligned with leaders in Al Capone's gang especially Charlie Fischetti, the cousin of Scarface. Then Gizzo moved to Kansas City to work for Mafia leader Johnny Lazia. By the time Lazia's successor, Charles Carollo, went to prison and Binaggio took over the gang, Gizzo was Binaggio's equal partner and manager of his gambling and liquor enterprises. Thus when Binaggio was murdered Gizzo not only ascended to gang leader but also took over Binaggio's business holdings, thus over night doubling his net worth. Binaggio and Gizzo both had close personal ties with Chicago gang leaders, and the pair wholesaled Chicago's Canadian Ace Beer.

The Chicago gang was notorious throughout the years for killing many members and associates after they appeared before Grand Juries or were charged with felonies that might lead to long prison terms because of fear they might turn state's witness. This trend was also a hallmark of the Kansas

City Mafiosi. Remember 16 years earlier Kansas City Mafia leader John Lazia had been machinegunned as his tax-evasion-conviction appeal neared a decision that he was expected to lose. Then in the three years prior to the murders of Binaggio and Gargotta, Kansas City had had 21 other gangland-style killings. Three of these victims, including a local fur store woman partner of Binaggio's wife, plus Binaggio and Gargotta had been subpoenaed to testify before the Federal Grand Jury before their deaths. Thus both the Chicago gang and lieutenant Gizzo had plenty of motive to kill Binaggio and Gargotta. There were the Grand Jury appearances with more still pending, soon-to-be issued federal felony indictments, gang informant leaks, and separation anxiety over Binaggio's early retirement. Thus the criminal associates of Binaggio and Gargotta were greatly worried that one or both might cut a deal and become a state's witness.[320]

Only Gizzo profited from the murders of Binaggio and Gargotta, and every known motive fit the modus operandi of both Gizzo and the Chicago gang to whom Gizzo had a long loyalty. Gizzo was the only person Binaggio and Gargotta trusted enough to show up in an isolated location unarmed and without bodyguards. Thus Gizzo was undoubtedly the unknown telephone caller who lured the two victims to the Democratic Club that fateful night. Gizzo later testified to the Kefauver Commission that Binaggio's wife telephoned him the morning after her husband was slain to seek his help. She told him her late husband had left the evening before with $12,000 in his pocket that the police did not find on him. This was certainly a share of the profits intended for Gizzo from one of the illicit businesses they partnered together in, and that is why both Binaggio and Gargotta were confident it would be such a short get-together. This wad was probably sitting on the desk in front of Binaggio which is why Binaggio had $24 in his pocket and Gargotta $2,401. Since Gizzo would have gotten this payment owed him whether or not he killed the pair, robbery is still ruled out as a motive since nothing else was taken. The killers certainly had plenty of time to search the bodies for valuables because no one was in the vicinity of the building to hear the indoor gun shots.

THE SENATE INVESTIGATES A MURDER

The murders of Binaggio and Gargotta had tremendous impact on the national political scene both at the federal and local levels. In the five years after World War II ended the American people increasingly expressed concern about the growth of powerful organized-crime syndicates and the resulting gang warfare in the nation's larger cities. Democratic Senator Estes Kefauver (Tennessee) tapped into the public's growing worry by introducing a resolution to authorize a nationwide Senate investigation into the impact of organized crime in interstate commerce and its corruptive influence on local governments. This set off a political tug-of-war between opposing factions in the U.S. Senate. Two-and-a-half months into this ongoing maneuvering the killing of the two Kansas City criminal-political leaders right beneath the President's portrait quickly made it the centrally debated issue.

To fully understand this Senate political wrangling and its serious ramifications, Kefauver had aimed his proposal primarily at the big gambling syndicates that had grown out of the Prohibition gangs because they were the most visible and easiest type of crime to uncover. Kefauver focused especially on Frank Costello of New York and the successors of Chicago's Al Capone gang because officials in Miami, New Orleans, and Los Angeles had complained they were trying to move in on their cities' politics when the truth was they were simply partnering with the already-established criminal gangs in those cities.

Kefauver's proposal called for the investigation to be conducted by the Senate Judiciary Committee because he was a member, but this set off a jurisdictional battle with the Interstate and Foreign Commerce Committee. It had the experienced Investigating Subcommittee staff, and one of its members, Republican Joe McCarthy (Wisconsin), had already proposed an investigation of crime syndicates having "too much influence in municipal elections." Kefauver anticipated the jurisdictional conflict so he offered the compromise of using the Investigating Committee's established staff in his proposed Judiciary Subcommittee inquiry because his only purpose was to build national recognition for himself as its chairman. Both Kefauver and McCarthy were freshman senators who coveted the national spotlight afforded by this chairmanship because both dreamt of one day occupying the White House. Thus Kefauver and McCarthy continued quiet, behind-the-scenes manipulation for this advantageous leadership position.

The Congressional leaders of both parties were weary of allowing such an investigation because both parties possessed powerful big-city political machines with close ties to local organized-crime and Mafia gangs who could get out the votes in their territories. While both parties feared exposure of their very dirty hands, both parties also relished the thought of controlling the direction of such an investigation in order to tarnish the other party in the forthcoming elections later in the year. Thus the battle over whether there would be an organized-crime investigation, and if so over who would control it, became one of the most furious ever fought in the U.S. Senate.

Kefauver was able to have his resolution referred to the Judiciary Committee, but the Democratic Chairman Pat McCarran (Nevada) feared any investigation would target his state's legalized casino industry that was regularly tarnished by the press over gangster involvement in certain Las Vegas Strip resorts. Also U.S. AG J. Howard McGrath feared the hearings would focus on the Kansas City political/criminal machine, the country's most corrupt, that supported President Truman. Thus Senator McCarran and the AG combined to get Kefauver's proposed funding cut in half to reduce its potential impact before it was approved by both the Judiciary and Rules Committees. Then Senator McCarran and the AG kept Kefauver's bill bottled up without a vote by the full Senate.

The anti-organized crime bill remained dormant until headlines announced the two gangland murders in Kansas City. This instantly changed the nation's political climate because Binaggio and Gargotta were the gangster leaders of the First District Democratic Clubhouse on Truman Road, a main artery to the President's hometown of Independence, Missouri. Accompanying the articles were photos of Binaggio's body sprawled out in a chair under a five-feet-high enlarged portrait of President Truman. The next day Missouri's Republican Representative charged in the House that gangster Binaggio was slain because he opposed the Senate candidate endorsed by President Truman and Kansas City's Pendergast machine. "Mr. Binaggio was in the way. So what happened? He is bumped off." The Representative went on to claim Truman had been elected to the Senate by vote frauds perpetrated by Pendergast and denounced his machine as "one of the most dastardly, dirtiest, corrupt, diabolical, ruthless political machines in the history of this country, that takes its toll from bawdy houses and gambling dens, and will not stop short of murder." Short's accusations against the President were applauded by both the GOP members on the floor and the Party's supporters in the galleries. Chiming along with the Missouri Representative in the House was a New York Republican Representative who said, "Binaggio and his henchman were killed beneath the portrait of President Truman in the Kansas City Democrat headquarters. When gangland murder touches associates of the White House, it is certainly time for action." Republicans followed this with a wild clamor in both the Senate and House for a nationwide crime investigation beginning at Truman headquarters in Kansas City. Amidst this hullabaloo Democratic Congressmen sat tight lipped as they watched the proposed investigation brewing into a witch-hunt. The White House also kept mum except for falsely saying the President had had no political associations with the slain gangster/political leaders. This statement totally ignored the reality that President Truman had pardoned Binaggio's election-vote thieves and had directed Binaggio to stuff the ballot boxes in the

Democratic Primary reelection of Representative Slaughter that led to the bombing of the Kansas City Election Board's safe to destroy the criminal evidence.[321]

The following day the *Chicago Tribune* jumped into this erupting political scandal with a blistering editorial about how the old Capone gang members had been pardoned by Truman. The editorial pointed out the Chicago gang was one of the suspects in Binaggio's murder, but "The Chicago mob is in Truman's corner. It delivered needed support to the Arvey political machine in 1946, and in recompense four of its leaders, doing federal time for extortion, got out of jail just as fast as the law would permit. That job came straight from the White House. It could not have been engineered without the intervention of some of Mr. Truman's personal friends and action by his AG, Tom Clark, now on the U.S. Supreme Court." Thus the editorial ended with the cynical conclusion "An investigation of a national crime syndicate, which the Binaggio killing may force on the administration, would be a lulu in the field of whitewashing. The Truman administration would be investigating itself." While it is likely true that President Truman caused Binaggio and Gargotta to be murdered, it was because of the legitimate and unrelenting IRS prosecutorial pressure he unleashed against the two Mafiosi rather than connivance with their killers.[322]

In the midst of all this Republican outcry for a Senate investigation, Missouri Democratic Governor Smith, who had acted as Binaggio's puppet, and officials in Kansas City asked the FBI for help in tracking down the killers of the two leaders of the city's political machine and criminal gang. This put Truman in a difficult position because he absolutely did not want the FBI investigating his filthy laundry, but at the same time he definitely wanted to avoid the appearance of a cover-up. In this conflicted situation the best he and his AG could do was remain mute to these requests for FBI assistance.

Then Missouri Republican James Kem turned up the heat by charging from the Senate floor that there was an "unholy alliance" between Kansas City crime and politics and demanded the President order the FBI to investigate the murders of Binaggio and Gargotta. The Senator pointed out both men had testified before a Federal Grand Jury and were under subpoena to appear again. Regarding this he read a federal statute making it a criminal offense to "impede" a witness in a Federal Trial and then coyly demanded to know whether a dead witness was an "impeded" one. This clever attack forced the President to respond the next day at a press conference, but he refused to answer most questions about the two political/gangster murders, and claimed he had not talked to the AG or anyone else about them because they were not within the President's jurisdiction. To this a reporter asked whether in the President's opinion, the murder of the two witnesses could be construed as tampering with a Federal Jury. Truman replied disingenuously that he was no legal expert and couldn't say. He said the questioner could draw his own conclusions. This was a most unhelpful answer from the man who had the ultimate authority to decide whether the FBI would or would not investigate.

With the Republicans clamoring for a comprehensive investigation of interstate organized crime in an election year, Democrats feared the Republican focus in such an inquiry would be the President's obvious ties to major gangsters. But with the Kansas City political-machine homicides still in the headlines the Democrats dared not continue blocking the anti-crime investigation from moving forward. Thus the Democratic leadership decided to restructure the Kefauver investigation proposal to make it repugnant to Republicans. Since the Democrats had already cut Senator Kefauver's requested expenditure budget in half they further limited its scope by allowing it to operate for just two months until July 1, 1950 when the election campaigns would be heating up. Kefauver's original plan called for the 11-man Judiciary Committee to conduct the inquiry, but this included the Senate's two ace investigators – Republicans Homer Ferguson [Michigan] and Forrest Donnell [Missouri]. Former Judge Ferguson was Congress' most effective and devastating investigator. Donnell had detailed knowledge of Missouri's criminal/political situation of which Truman was an active member and he also had a personal stake in this debate. Senator Donnell was running for reelection later in the year, and Truman had selected the Democratic candidate who opposed him. Thus Democratic Senate Majority Leader Scott Lucas [Illinois] desperately wanted to keep these two effective Republican investigators off the Committee's membership, and he quickly came up with a bit of legislative legerdemain to rig the enacting legislation to exclude them. Lucas proposed merging both the Judiciary and the Interstate Commerce Committees this one time to create a special five-member Joint Subcommittee comprised of members from both major Committees. Lucas also proposed this Subcommittee have three Democrats and two Republicans with the members named by Vice President Alben Barkley, and suggested Kefauver be Chairman. With all the Republican Senators on both major Committees to choose from the Democratic VP could easily bypass the two dreaded Republican investigators. Republican Senators immediately hollered foul. They continued to endorse a nationwide crime inquiry by the Senate Judiciary Committee as Kefauver originally proposed and strenuously opposed the creation of a Special Joint Subcommittee. Republicans rightly claimed the move "is largely for the purpose of eliminating those [Senators] who know most about it and have shown the most interest." They argued it was patently unfair for the Democrats to pick the Republican membership for committees.[323]

In addition to the Republican outcry Democratic Senate Judiciary Chairman Pat McCarran vocally objected to taking the investigation out of his Committee because he wanted control over the Kefauver Committee members to protect Nevada's unique legalized casino industry. The only major industries in his state were tourism from gambling along with mining and ranching so McCarran was in a position to trade his vote on the vast majority of issues that came before the Senate to garner votes to protect his pet businessmen at home. It took two days for Senate Majority Leader Lucas to bring the Democratic Chairmen of the Judiciary and Interstate Commerce Committees around to his position. Both Chairmen approved Senator Kefauver drafting a new resolution authorizing VP Barkley to select the proposed Joint Committee's five members in hopes this toxic pill would muffle the Republicans' demand for an organized-crime investigation. Once Senator Lucas had his negative strategy in place he took no further action on the bill, but two weeks later unrelated forces heightened public pressure for an anti-crime inquiry.

Democratic Senator Ernest McFarland (Arizona) had his Senate Interstate Commerce Subcommittee begin hearings over two anti-gambling bills proposed by U.S. AG McGrath. One was to ban the interstate transmission of racehorse gambling information to bookmakers and the other was to prohibit the interstate shipment of slot machines except to locales where they were permitted by state law. McFarland's hearings were not in competition with Kefauver's proposal because his was a much broader study to determine whether organized crime and gambling syndicates were operating in interstate commerce, and if so to learn how they operated, who was connected with these operations, and to what extent they were a corrupting influence on local politics and governments. It was already obvious to much of the public that local politicians allowed crime gangs to operate booming wide-open gambling in their jurisdictions, but no one knew the extent of their elected officials' involvement. Since most organized crime operated within state boundaries the U.S. Justice Department knew little about it except that the various casino operators and bookmakers seemed to be well acquainted with each other. Thus the Justice Department developed an hypothesis without any factual basis that the nation's gangs, at least in the area of wide-open gambling, were centered under Frank Costello of New York City and the successor leaders of Al Capone's Chicago gang. McFarland's Subcommittee finally opened the veil shielding the immensity of illegal gambling when its members questioned Frank Costello and he forthrightly testified under oath about his New York and New Orleans elegant high-end casino operations, his slot routes that placed machines in various retail stores, and his nationwide bookmaking operation. He was not concerned that his honest admissions under oath might lead to criminal prosecution because he violated no federal laws and the local voters, politicians, and police supported his operations because of the tourism and well-paying, high-tipped jobs they created. Costello's candid revelations astounded the public.

Just two days after Costello's testimony was covered by the nation's press, a Kansas City Federal Grand Jury further shocked the public with a scathing interim report detailing the many nefarious criminal activities and corruption by Binaggio's Mafia gang and Democratic political machine. This information resulted from the IRS investigation President Truman had instigated against political-faction opponent Binaggio nine months earlier. This scandalous expose forced the Senators in both parties to quickly support an anti-crime bill to avoid accusations of a cover-up. Six days later the full Senate considered Kefauver's proposed bill. With this kind of public momentum no Senator wanted to vote against an anti-crime investigation, but the two parties were still jockeying about the contents of the bill for political gain. The first vote was on a Republican amendment that two of the five members on the Committee must be from the GOP and they were to be nominated by the Republican Senate Minority Leader. This was defeated by a party line vote 39-31. The next vote was for the Democratic amendment that said Vice President Alben Barkley was to appoint all five Committee members without regard to party, meaning he could appoint five Democrats and investigate only Republican districts across the country. Senator Ferguson rose and made a fiery speech complaining that the Republicans would not be allowed to select their own representatives because the selection was to be made by the executive branch through the VP. Four Democrats voted against this amendment so the result was a tie 35-35, and VP Barkley cast the tie-breaking vote to empower himself. Senator Kefauver had shrewdly arranged for the vote to be held on a day when powerful Nevada Democratic Senator Pat McCarran was absent because he sided with the Republicans out of fear the investigation would become a damaging assault against his state's unique legalized casino industry. An amendment to triple Majority Leader Lucas' expense authorization received strong bipartisan support since Senators now had to appear to support the anti-crime investigation. Then came the vote for final approval of the U.S. Senate Special Committee to Investigate Organized Crime in Interstate Commerce based on Majority Leader Lucas' proposal. The Republican Senators hated the unfairness of this bill but they were afraid to vote against an anti-crime investigation so it was 69-1 in favor with only Missouri Senator Donnell continuing to object loudly to the unjust Democratic politics. A week later VP Barkley named the Committee's three Democrats and invoked the time-honored Senate principal of seniority to justify selecting the senior Republican on both the Judiciary and Interstate Commerce Committees to exclude both Senators Ferguson and Donnell from membership.

The Democratic leaders thought the legislation they pushed through gave them control over the Committee's actions, but VP Barley made a critical mistake. He appointed as a member the bill's introducer, Senator Kefauver, and assumed he would be a party loyalist. However as soon as the ambitious Kefauver was elected Chairman by the other four members it quickly became obvious he had promoted the organized-crime investigation not only to make a national name for himself but to smear the President's reputation. From the onset Kefauver made Truman, his political machine, and his criminal associates the Committee's primary target as Kefauver had his sights set on the White House in the election two years hence. The Kefauver Committee first held three days of closed executive hearings in Kansas City that were supposed to be off-the-record. Before leaving town Kefauver graciously told the press the city's gambling and prostitution seemed pretty well closed up. The Committee's staff was given two months to validate the witnesses' statements for perjury and then the five members returned to town for three days of open public hearings questioning the same public officials and many more Mafiosi about gangster control of local politics including the President's political machine. The testimony was not earthshaking but it further tarnished Truman's already tawdry corrupt image.

During the Kefauver Committee's 15 months of hearings it questioned or corresponded with many hundreds of crime-gang leaders, mayors, police chiefs and sheriffs, district attorneys, state attorneys general, and newspaper editors and crime reporters throughout the country to elicit their knowledge and hear their views. The wide-open gambling operations the Committee focused on were well-known by most residents in each community, but the headline-making exposes about the cozy alliances between the gambling operators and both local police officials and politicians was a shock to the public. These revelations led to local reform movements that shut down wide-open illegal casinos and bookmaking in every city where the Committee held hearings and practically every other city in the rest of the country as well. These closures caused the rapid development of the early Las Vegas Strip because the shuttered owners had the capital saved from their illicit profits to build new legally-licensed gambling resorts, the knowledge of how to successfully market and operate a gambling enterprise, and a large list of former devoted players who no longer had an outlet in their home locale to enjoy their passion for gambling.

The Kefauver Committee produced the greatest crime investigation in history by identifying the leaders of the major criminal gangs and divulging how their illegal enterprises operated. The Committee investigation produced a treasure trove of information about the nation's organized-crime gangs that specialized in illegal casinos and/or bookmaking during the three decades beginning with the onset of Prohibition in 1920. The testimony by and about the top gambling criminals of the mid 1900s contained in the Committee's many volumes has been of immense assistance in this author's research.

At the same time Kefauver's efforts earned much deserved criticism. For starters he preached moralistic intentions but was a phony hypocrite. During the Las Vegas hearings Kefauver espoused that "Big time gambling is amoral. Gambling produces nothing and adds nothing to the economy or society of our nation." This from a politician who was known to be fond of gambling. In addition his road-show hearings across the country stayed out of his home-state of Tennessee and the four states represented by the other members of his Committee. As one gangster of the era told this author in an interview, "Kefauver closed down the whole country, except for Tennessee. It didn't have a major gambling center; but it had lots of little places, like the rest of the country." From the beginning Kefauver's Senate resolution and proposals promised to investigate organized crime in all its facets, but his Committee focused almost exclusively on illegal gambling while completely ignoring the many types of crimes that far-more-sinister and violent criminals used to prey on innocent victims. The justification for Congressional investigations is to allow the lawmakers to obtain expertise about pending bills. But this Committee's long 15-month investigation produced just one anti-crime law and it was trivial. It required bookmakers to buy an annual $50 betting-tax stamp but this law proved to be unenforceable because these illegal operators handled wagers with their players in private and individually with no witnesses present. The Committee made a recommendation to the U.S. AG that he convene special Federal Grand Juries in big cities all over the country every year to investigate local crime conditions, but one year later new AG James McGranery announced he was junking these plans. He explained he did it because of a cool reception by some Federal Judges but it was really because J. Edgar Hoover refused to cooperate and provide the necessary detective work. In fact Hoover flatly rejected having his FBI agents conduct organized-crime investigations for all 17 AGs who were his bosses except for Robert Kennedy. He alone had the clout and resolve to force Hoover and his FBI to actually do their job and delve into organized crime, but this only lasted during Robert Kennedy's short three-and-a-half-year reign. Thus the Kefauver Committee revelations produced no important lasting law-enforcement effects but it rapidly hastened the building of Las Vegas Strip gambling resorts.[324]

The biggest disappointment of the Kefauver Committee was its conclusion about the nature of organized crime in its final report of more than 11,000 pages. Because of the lack of knowledge and cooperation by Hoover's FBI detectives, the Committee had no hard knowledge about organized crime except the testimony they elicited and this was all about local crime activities that did not cross state lines. Thus the Committee relied on the long-held false belief of the Justice Department that there were two national organized-crime syndicates with both having corporate-style organizational structures. The Committee came to this conclusion because much testimony showed that organized-crime figures in different cities often knew each other, cooperated in areas of mutual benefit and protection, and sometimes partnered. Kefauver and the Justice Department never understood that all crime is local to each city. The police and politicians take bribes only from people they know and who are local and under their thumb so they can be trusted to keep their mouths shut about their indiscretions. In any crime enterprise involving partners from various cities, the local cohort is always the sole managing partner, and the distant criminals merely silent investors.

According to the Justice Department one of the two national organized-crime syndicates was supposedly headquartered in Chicago and was led by close associates of the deceased Al Capone - Tony Accardo, Jake Guzik, and Charlie Fischetti. There is no question that Chicago developed very close ties of mutual interest with the Mafia gangs in Kansas City, St. Louis, Milwaukee, Cleveland, Los Angeles, and Dallas as well as with some of the Las Vegas Strip resort owners. The other syndicate was allegedly based in New York and was made up of Frank Costello, Joe Adonis, and Meyer Lansky with Charlie Luciano somehow sitting above the others. These four New York hoods were certainly highly respected by criminals across the country including the Chicago gang, but admiration and influence are far different from power and control. While belief in a national organized criminal conspiracy by Kefauver and the Justice Department may have been unfounded, it was J. Edgar Hoover's total denial of localized organized criminals and Mafia gangs that was truly absurd. The existence of organized crime and Mafia gangs was known by every big city police department and newspaper, and it would be proven by the FBI after the Director's death with extensive convictions of numerous members in many cities.

Kefauver was an opportunist who turned the Committee's hearings into a mammoth personal publicity machine with his name always in the forefront. Kefauver gave a press conference before every session and often took strategically-timed breaks from testimony to hold conferences early enough to make the evening newspapers. An increasing number of Americans were buying their first black and white television sets and many of the Committee's hearings were shown by the networks live to large daytime and sometimes early evening audiences. The hearings became a sensation because this was the first time America had been able to watch its government in action or to observe the nation's most infamous hoods either talk about their illicit activities or else repeatedly take the Fifth Amendment to avoid incriminating themselves. A Detroit television station even preempted the popular children's show *Howdy Doody* to broadcast senators grilling local mobsters. The highlight of the hearings was the appearance of the nation's most notorious gambler, Frank Costello. He refused to testify unless the cameras were taken off him, so the lenses focused strictly on his hands. It made for riveting viewing to hear the senators bark questions and the gangster reply defiantly while the audience stared at the nervous agitation of his hands. This changed the American culture as families stayed indoors gathered in the eerie half-light of their living rooms completely transfixed on a single matter. All this exposure accomplished Kefauver's real goal of successfully transforming himself from an obscure freshman Senator into a popular heroic crusader against dangerous criminals and corrupt politicians making him a serious White House contender.[325]

KANSAS CITY PENETRATES THE STRIP

After Gizzo had Binaggio and Gargotta murdered he reigned for three years as Kansas City's Mafia chieftain until he was stricken with a fatal heart attack at age 52, and Nick Civella ascended to his throne. Civella had been Gizzo's chauffeur and bodyguard, the man who Gizzo most trusted to protect his life and to keep his secrets. Nick Civella and his brother Carl along with their relatives and associates lived in a plush North Side enclave dominated by Nick's residence. Four years after assuming power Civella attended the conference of America's Mafia leaders who convened in Apalachin, New York. During the ensuing local police raid he was observed fleeing but he always denied attending. Three years following his Apalachin escape the Nevada Gaming Commission instituted a Black Book of men who the state's casinos were required to keep off their premises under threat of gaming license revocation. On the original list of 11 undesirables were Nick Civella and his brother Carl.

Nick Civella as leader of an influential Democratic political faction worked closely with many prominent residents of Kansas City on goals of common interest. He developed an especially close relationship with Roy Williams who was high in the hierarchies of the Teamsters International Union and Pension Fund. Civella used both his friendship with Williams and his long-time ties with the much larger and more powerful Chicago gang to create much clout with the Teamsters Pension Fund. Then he convinced the Pension Fund to finance gambling resort purchases on the Las Vegas Strip when ownerships were undergoing rapid changes.

Sales of so many Strip gambling resorts within a few-year period can be understood by looking back a half century to the beginning of Prohibition in 1920. Most of the gang leaders who came to power during this era were young Turks (meaning ambitious, physically strong, and testosterone raging) around 20 years old when this Grand Experiment began. After Prohibition was ended the leaders of the most successful fine liquor importing gangs used their established corrupt police protection to operate illegal, but wide-open, elegant casinos across the country during the 1930s and 1940s. When local reform movements began shutting these high-end operations down the operators moved to Las Vegas and built gambling resort hotels along the Strip. They operated their establishments during the great Golden Era of Strip gambling with its superstar and grand production entertainment from the late 1940s through the late 1960s. But by then these gangland owners were around 70 years old and they began retiring, selling out, or passing on. Traditional financial institutions considered Nevada's underworld-infested casino industry to be a tainted business and refrained from investing. Civella saw the opportunity to fill this financing void by tapping into the Teamsters Pension Fund. As each Strip gambling resort went on the sale block Civella had the Pension Fund finance its purchase by people he was associated with.

Nick Civella began his new money-finder career assisting Frank Caroll who had moved from Kansas City to Las Vegas to build shopping centers. Caroll had gone busted during early construction of the *Landmark* casino resort on the Strip, and Civella came to his rescue with a Teamsters Pension Fund loan for which the black-listed gangster was officially paid a finder's fee. Later in construction Caroll sold the *Landmark* to tycoon Howard Hughes who opened it as one of seven casino operations he owned in Nevada for the remainder of his life.

Three years after arranging the *Landmark* loan, Civella and 17 other men took a charter flight from Kansas City to *Caesars Palace* where Sheriff Ralph Lamb had the group arrested for vagrancy but the charges were dismissed. The Nevada gaming regulators did not want Black Book figure

Civella anywhere near the state's licensed casinos, but they could not uncover or block his continuing behind-the-scenes influence over the Teamsters Pension Fund.

Civella's next foray into financing was his biggest. He was instrumental in arranging $160 million in Teamsters Pension Fund loans for Allen Glick, front man for Civella's Chicago gang friends, to buy the *Stardust* resort on the Strip, the *Fremont Hotel Casino* in downtown Las Vegas, and other hotel-casino interests. These events inspired the movie *Casino* (1995).

Next Civella went into cahoots with St. Louis criminal defense attorney Morris Shenker. He had represented Teamster Union President Jimmy Hoffa and other organized crime figures while heading the St. Louis Crime Commission. This is just one more unhealthy example of Missouri's strange relationships between the Mafia and law enforcement. Shenker had also raised money for Democratic candidates and worked in cooperation with Civella's Kansas City political/criminal machine in elections for statewide offices. Shenker had purchased blocks of stock in the public company that owned the *Dunes* until he became the largest stockholder. As the dominating force in the *Dunes,* Shenker welcomed a visit by his friend Civella to the resort under an assumed name as a VIP guest. He gave the Black Book member a complimentary suite, his favorite liquor, flowers, and casino cage credit upon demand. When the gaming authorities learned of this the Nevada Gaming Commission fined the *Dunes* $10,000 for allowing him to stay there. Two months later the Gaming Commission approved Shenker to turn the resort into a private company using a $40 million Teamsters Pension Fund loan courtesy of Civella. Five months after Shenker acquired the *Dunes* his most famous client, Jimmy Hoffa, vanished.

The IRS soon brought a $16 million lawsuit against the *Dunes* for allegedly skimming off profits. Defense attorney Shenker employed the nation's two top tax law firms to represent the *Dunes.* These attorneys hired me as their sole expert witness to make their case because I instructed the pioneer course *Casino Management* for the College of Hotel Administration at UNLV and was the author of the classic book for succeeding in the gaming industry, entitled *Casino Management.* When they hired me they stated that if I could get them off with a $1 million fine I would be their hero. I replied that if I found the case to be as they had represented it to me, the *Dunes* was innocent under the law and should be exonerated. They explained that in big-money high-profile cases the IRS always demanded some bone of admission of at least accounting errors to justify their actions, or they would continue to harass the target with ever-increasing legal defense fees and the possible threat of conviction.

For months I organized all the Federal Grand Jury testimony by a multitude of *Dunes* executives and employees. These volumes of transcripts were piled in stacks from the floor to eye level in one part of the office of Chairman of the Board Shenker. I had to be waiting in the lobby every weekday before the offices closed precisely at 6 p.m. because I had no key to the offices complex. Shenker would get out of his office chair to leave for the evening, and I would settle into it to work a 12-hour shift until the cleaning crew arrived at 6 a.m. with their noisy vacuum cleaners and banging of waste baskets to empty them in garbage bins. It never seemed quite right to me to sit in another man's still-warm seat night after night. I was amused that I had no key when Shenker and his attorneys trusted me alone all night with all their most sensitive documents. Standing beside my left was Shenker's imposing thick-walled vault with the door always left open. I did not need to leave because every afternoon Shenker had a large platter of exquisite fresh fruit sent up, and he left most of it untouched in the tray to my right. That gorgeous variety of fruit, cheeses, and crackers is what I snacked on during those long nights of studying and comparing testimony statements. When I finished my analysis, Shenker's tax law firm submitted it to the IRS and the case was dropped. Of course it was impossible to prove no uncounted cash had disappeared, but I effectively presented what a "Rube Goldberg" approach to stealing money resulted by integrating the many separate

Grand Jury testimonies. I demonstrated that no one would ever use such a complex system that involved so many employees who had to be paid off and kept silent when there were much simpler ways to accomplish this illicit deed. Most importantly it was clear a jury would never believe it.

While Civella was helping Shenker finance his takeover of the *Dunes,* Civella decided to get into the Nevada casino business himself. He had his front man, Joe Agosto, start plotting a takeover of the *Tropicana* a mile further south on the Las Vegas Strip. In an incredible coincidence, *Tropicana* casino host Bob Carnahan was still there when Mafia boss Binaggio's successor, Civella, became the hidden majority interest holder of the gambling resort. Thus Civella's company paid Carnahan's salary, and after paying income taxes he gave the percentage he had agreed to with Binaggio to Civella three decades after he had gambled away the $1 million *Thunderbird* investment.

While Civella was financing casino resorts on the Las Vegas Strip and secretly owned the *Tropicana,* he was conducting political/criminal business as usual in Kansas City. This was revealed eight years into Civella's Mafia reign by a Jackson County Grand Jury criminal investigation that intensively questioned known criminals and police officers before releasing a blistering report. Testimony established that when Civella took over in 1953 he made a pact with the Kansas City Police Department to permit gambling, prostitution, and liquor law violations in return for a pledge that no major exploitive or violent crimes would be committed in town. Because the voting public no longer tolerated wide-open gambling his operations were small back-door affairs, so Civella turned Kansas City into a major fencing center for goods stolen by criminals from all over the Midwest. Some of Civella's gang members specialized in hijackings and thefts of goods in surrounding Midwestern states according to state and federal investigations. A week prior to the County Grand Jury issuing its report it indicted Police Chief Bernard Brannon and two high ranking officers for perjury and for willful misconduct for not filing selected crime reports in department records.

If this criminal/police arrangement sounds familiar so was Civella's political influence as he continued to control the gang's traditional election wards. The reformers still held onto power in Kansas City, but the political/criminal factions controlled the Jackson County government with its many patronage jobs giving them their power base. This machine continued to elect governors and also enough state legislators who held seniority positions to allow them to bottleneck effective anticrime legislation. The man who took over the Pendergast political machine was Alex Presta who led the Metropolitan Democratic Club, formerly Binaggio's Club where he was slain. This Club once again dominated the city's other political factions. Presta was always closely associated with Civella having partnered with him in an illegal casino before he became Mafia leader. Presta was prohibited from voting because of three federal Prohibition convictions decades earlier and President John Kennedy refused his request for a pardon. Presta wanted the pardon in hopes of ending the joke that came up every election. "Presta is the man who cannot vote but can deliver thousands of other people's votes." On most work days Presta was seen visiting governors, legislators, county officials, and judges.[326]

This completes the careers of the five successive Kansas City Mafia political leaders from John Lazia during Prohibition through Charles Carollo, Charles Binaggio, and Tony Gizzo in the illegal-casino period to Nick Civella who arranged the financing for the second wave of Las Vegas Strip underworld casino owners. This second group of gangsters fanned out in the Strip gambling resorts at the same time wealthy entrepreneurs Howard Hughes and Kirk Kerkorian and major public corporations led by Hilton Hotels first ventured into the Las Vegas Strip casino business. As the involvement of the second wave of hoods continued producing scandalous media coverage about their Strip operations, these respected private investors and corporations started giving this industry its first aura of legitimacy and uprightness.

The second book in this historical series covers the early careers of the first wave of underworld leaders before they moved to Las Vegas to pioneer the development of the great gambling resorts of the fantastic early Strip. This was the three-decade era of their careers that the Kefauver Committee investigated in 1950, but while the Committee exposed a great deal about the specific businesses of the major gangs, its conclusions about how these localized gangs interrelated were based on nothing but suppositions and were totally wrong. This second book is based on almost a half century of research investigating massive documentation and the only extensive in-depth interviews ever conducted of these crime leaders and their associates, and it describes for the first time how organized crime began, how each of the key gangs were structured, and how the various local territorial gangs interacted with each other across the nation.

The second book also details the careers of seven leaders of the three gangs that were far and away the largest fine liquor importers during Prohibition and then became the most successful operators of wide-open, but illegal, elegant gambling casinos across the country catering to the wealthy. These seven leaders totally dominated the leadership and direction of organized crime during these three decades.

All seven of these men had a close working relationship with the Chicago gang beginning with Al Capone during Prohibition and then with each of his successors during the illegal gambling and early Las Vegas Strip eras. Chicago always supported these seven leaders in the surprisingly complex politics of the underworld that more than once drew the major gangs across the country into wars that drove the members into secret hideouts. Chicago also allied its strong overworld political base with the three dominating groups' powerful big-city political machines to further their mutual national interests. In addition Chicago repeatedly partnered with the seven leaders of the three premier organized-crime groups in both legal and illegal businesses and on the Las Vegas Strip. Also included are the careers of the first six leaders of the Chicago gang who have never been revealed before since historians and crime writers have focused primarily on Scarface.

The second book ends when one of these seven crime leaders, Ben Siegel, convinced his six pals and Chicago that the future of gambling laid along a barren strip of land outside the city limits of a tiny desert town in Southern Nevada. Siegel moved to Las Vegas a decade before the Kefauver Committee's shocking exposés led to local reform movements that closed down illegal casinos in cities across the nation. Before this happened Siegel's persuasiveness had led his buddies to began planning gambling resorts along the Strip. Thus these seven crime leaders and their associates built 80% of the fabulous Las Vegas Strip resorts during its Golden Era from the opening of the *Flamingo* in 1946 to the opening of *Caesars Palace* in 1966. This is when the Strip was the world's gambling and entertainment mecca, the greatest adult playground ever created.

The media and local Las Vegans have long used the term "the mob that built the Strip." They were merely referring to the licensed owner/operators of these marvelous gambling resorts. No one in Las Vegas ever had the slightest suspicion that there might actually be an interrelated criminal mob hidden behind the scenes calling all the shots in the vast gambling-tourism industry along the Strip. Then 20 years into this research project the seven men and their associates directing everything had finally built up enough trust to finally let me into their inner sanctum so I could write the whole amazing story of what actually occurred and how it all worked. In the second book these leaders of the early Las Vegas Strip will be revealed for the first time. But you can already read a summation of these seven men's incredible story and their huge impact on American culture at www.FriedmanSpeaksVegas.com on the Home and Untold Stories navigators. This second manuscript is already completed and being prepared for publication.

UPCOMING BOOKS & AUTHOR'S SPEECHES

TO LEARN ABOUT THE PUBLICATION

OF UPCOMING BOOKS IN THIS

NEVADA GAMBLING INDUSTRY & ORGANIZED CRIME

HISTORICAL SERIES

PLEASE CHECK OUT:

www.FriedmanSpeaksVegas.com

YOU CAN ALSO FIND OUT ABOUT BILL FRIEDMAN'S

NEVER BEFORE TOLD

ENTERTAINING, NOVEL, & HUMOROUS STORIES

COVERING THE HISTORY OF

THE NEVADA CASINO INDUSTRY & ORGANIZED CRIME -

HIS SPEECH WILL BE THE HIGHLIGHT

OF YOUR LAS VEGAS CONVENTION OR MEETING

ENDNOTES, TIMELINES, & BIBLIOGRAPHY

HOW THE SOURCE DOCUMENTATION IS PRESENTED

The historical research for this series of books was conducted over almost five decades by rigorously collecting the available facts about the backgrounds, careers, interrelationships, values, and lifestyles of the men who built the Nevada casino industry and, for this book, also the Kansas City political and criminal hierarchies. Following this, the political and sociological dynamics surrounding these men's careers was exhaustively analyzed. These endnotes provide three types of support information for the material in the text.

1- The information in the text was found in a variety of sources, which are identified in these notes to assist historians interested in further study or to confirm the accuracy of their use in this text. For every quote, the name of the person who said it and the source where it was found are identified either in the text or in these notes. Quotes taken from gambling-industry pioneers who contributed to my research are listed as "my interview." Facts contained in most consecutive sentences in the text are from different sources, so a complete documentation would require a book much longer than this one. The simple but effective solution was to not identify the specific newspaper sources because most information was obtained from the combined reportage of six daily newspapers from 1930 on - the *New York Times,* the *Chicago Daily Tribune,* the *Los Angeles Times,* the *Las Vegas Review Journal,* the *Las Vegas Sun,* and Reno's *Nevada State Journal.* Also valuable sources for this book in this series were the following two daily newspapers from 1923 through 1950 - the *Kansas City Star* and the *Kansas City Times.* Historians, scholars, interested readers, and critics can easily obtain more detailed information about each issue by going to these newspapers or other local papers for the multitude of dates listed in the notes below. The importance of newspapers in crime investigations is described in the Introduction.

In addition to these newspaper sources, many documents were used, and each is identified either in the text or in these endnotes. They include Congressional hearings, FBI files, legislative and court records, books and magazines, and unpublished documents. In the text these are cited by type – for example, "in testimony before the U.S. Senate Kefauver Committee."

2- The names of people who appear only briefly in a single incident are listed just in these endnotes in order to be available to historians, without cluttering, complicating, or slowing reading of the text. These people are clearly identified in the text according to their relationship to the event. For example "an eyewitness" or "his girlfriend."

3- Dates in the text are replaced with the length of time in days, weeks, or months between pairs of related events to make the time frame clear. The dates for all major events are presented in the endnotes, and the key dates for related events are listed in chronological order to create clear historical timelines. These groups of related dates will be an invaluable research resource and validation aid to historians who may wish to quickly look up the event and study specific facts in more detail. I wish such timelines had been available to me, but I had to search out each individual incident. Historians can look up every event in the eight listed newspapers that were repeatedly used or in other local papers. Usually, the stories appear on the day after the date of an incident in the morning editions but occasionally on the same day as the event in the evening editions.

When the FBI releases document pages under the Freedom of Information Act, it usually redacts (blacks out) the names of everyone except the file subject. Thus, quotes of FBI documents in the text and in the endnotes may contain five small x's in quotes ('xxxxx') to indicate a redacted name was in the quote of an FBI document.

Notes
INTRODUCTION

THE EXTENSIVE NEWSPAPER RECORDS
i- The two quotes by Bob Cahill are from my June 4, 1968 interview.

Notes Chapter 1
CASINOS, BABY FACE, & DILLINGER

THE BABY-FACED KILLER
1- The comparison between the buying power of the present value of the dollar and its value on these historic dates was calculated by using the official U.S. average Consumer Price Index (CPI) for the given calendar year. This index, calculated since 1913, represents changes in prices of specified goods and services purchased for consumption by urban households with 1913 used as the base of $1. In the text, the value of the U.S. dollar's buying power that is presented in every example is the amount that could be bought in 2009 compared to the amount in the year specified. In this example, $29,000 could be bought in 2009 compared to $3,600 in 1955 based on a ratio of the dollar at $8.01 to $1. The home page of the official U.S. Consumer Price Index is www.bls.gov/cpi/, and the ratios used here were produced at www.USInflationCalculator.com.

2- Nelson was born on December 6, 1908. He was sent to a boy's home in 1922 and paroled in April 1924. He was returned to the boy's school in September 1924 and paroled in July 1925. He was returned again to the boy's home in October 1925 and was paroled on July 11, 1926. The Sausalito rumrunners were Joseph Parene and Hans Strittmatter; the driver was Joseph Raymond "Fatso" Negri; and the armed guards were Nelson and John Paul Chase. Chase and Negri became Nelson's closest and most trusted associates. Nelson married Helen Wawrzyniak on October 30, 1928. Nelson's Chicago trio began their robbery spree with the home invasion of Charles Richter on January 6, 1930. Nelson robbed the Itasca State Bank in Wheaton on October 3, 1930 and the Hillside State Bank on November 22, 1930. Nelson was convicted of the Hillside robbery on June 25, 1931 after cohort Harry Lewis turned state's witness and accomplice Stanton Randall possessed the pistol stolen from the bank. The saw blades were discovered on July 9, 1931, and Nelson escaped from prison guard R. N. Martin on February 17, 1932 after being convicted of the Itasca robbery.

DEFIANCE WITHOUT PURPOSE
3- The quote by Delbert Hobson at 89 is from the March 13, 1994 Chicago Tribune. Hobson was two years younger than Dillinger and considered him his best friend.

4- Dillinger was born on June 22, 1903 and signed up with the Navy in 1923. The assault and robbery was on September 6, 1924 and he was sentenced on September 15, 1924. The grocer was Frank Morgan and Dillinger's accomplice was Ed Singleton. Dillinger was transferred to Michigan State Prison on July 15, 1929. The Deputy Warden who objected to Dillinger's parole and was fired for it was H. William Claudy. Dillinger was paroled on May 22, 1933 and his first robbery was on June 10, 1933. Dillinger tossed three guns into Michigan City Prison on September 10, 1933, and 10 convicts escaped on September 26, 1933. Dillinger was arrested visiting girlfriend Mary Longnaker on September 22, 1933 and he was freed from the Lima jail on October 12, 1933. The Sheriff's killers were Harry Pierpont, Charles Makley, and Russell Clark. Dillinger's gang hit the police stations in Auburn, Indiana, on October 14, 1933 and in Peru, Ohio, on October 20, 1933, followed by the Greencastle bank robbery on October 23, 1933. Staying in the apartment with Dillinger was girlfriend Evelyn "Billie" Frechette and with Pierpont was Mary Kinder. Dillinger escaped the Chicago Police trap outside the office of Doctor Charles H. Eye on November 15, 1933, and robbed the American Bank and Trust company of Racine, Wisconsin, on November 20, 1933. Dillinger led the Chicago bank robbery on December 13, 1933. The Public Enemies list was issued on December 28, 1933 and the roadhouse robbery was on December 31, 1933. Dillinger slaughtered Detective Patrick O'Malley in the January 15, 1934 East Chicago robbery. The quotes by Dillinger and Bank Vice President Edward Steck during the East Chicago robbery are from the January 16, 1934 *Chicago Tribune*.

5- The letter to the editor quote is from the August 9, 1964 *New York Times*.

6- The Dillinger quote is from the January 31, 1934 *Chicago Tribune*.

7- Nelson's entire FBI file of 225 pages concerns just the first robbery of the Peoples Savings Bank in Grand Haven, Michigan, for $14,000 on August 18, 1933. He then robbed the First National Bank in Brainerd, Minnesota, for $32,000 on October 23, 1933. Homer Van Meter was paroled from Michigan City Prison on May 18, 1933. Dillinger drove from Chicago on January 15, 1934, arrived in Reno on January 18, 1934, and left for Tucson on January 21, 1934.

A WOODEN GUN

8- The Dillinger quote is from the January 31, 1934 *Chicago Tribune*.

9- Dillinger's quote is from a statement by Sheriff Holley in the March 6, 1934 *Chicago Tribune*.

10 The quote by U.S. AG Homer Cummings is from the March 8, 1934 *Chicago Tribune*. Youngblood was killed in Port Huron, Indiana, on March 16, 1934.

11 Dillinger's Attorney Piquett's investigator was Arthur O'Leary and the convict was Meyer Bogue. Dillinger's long-time girlfriend was Billie Frechette.

12- The quote by former Judge Martin J. Smith is from the March 5, 1934 *Chicago Tribune*. The quote of Cahoon is from prisoner James Posey in the March 11, 1934 *Chicago Tribune*. Posey was given leniency for assisting the County Grand Jury, and his testimony was backed up by at least one guard.

13- The first Dillinger quote is from the January 26, 1934 *Chicago Tribune* and the second from the May 10, 1934 *Chicago Tribune*.

14- Dillinger arrived in Tucson on January 22, 1934 and he and his three henchmen were arrested on January 25, 1934. His photo with the prosecutor appeared in the January 31, 1934 *Chicago Tribune* and Dillinger's hand was posed similarly in another photo of the same scene in the October 9, 1938 edition. This article also contains a photo of a happy Dillinger wearing a suit and hat and posing with the infamous wooden pistol in one hand and a machinegun in the other. Dillinger escaped from the Crown Point Jail on March 3, 1934. The Jail Warden was Lew Baker, the garage mechanic and hostage was Edward Saager, and the mail-truck driver was Robert Volk.

Dillinger's letter to his sister and wooden gun was hand delivered on March 19, 1934. Dillinger's letter to Ford was mailed on May 6th, 1934 from Minneapolis, Minnesota. The information about the two alleged Dillinger letters possessed by Ford is from an excellent investigation and analysis. It explains the interesting discovery of the legitimate letter in the Henry Ford Museum and the reasons why the second letter is clearly a fraud including historical contradictions. This Matt Hardigree article is on jalopnik.com. Some of this information is from *Public Enemy*.

Notes Chapter 2
THE FBI DEVELOPS INTO A DETECTIVE AGENCY

GENESIS OF A NATIONAL POLICE FORCE

15- Daugherty was AG from March 4, 1921 to April 6, 1924. Two years later two juries deadlocked over whether he received funds in the sale of American Metal Company assets seized during WWI. In the second trial just one juror was unconvinced of his guilt. Daugherty's successor, Stone, was AG from April 7, 1924 to July 3, 1925, and he became Chief Justice of the Supreme Court in 1941. Hoover was appointed director of the DOJ's Bureau of Investigation in May 1924 and started his fingerprint lab in 1925, opening his national crime lab to local law enforcement on November 24, 1932. The quote by Stone is from *Robert Kennedy and His Times* by Arthur M. Schlesinger, Jr. New York: Ballantine Books, a division of Random House 1978.

16- The quote by Sherley, a Kentucky Representative from 1903 to 1919, is from *J. Edgar Hoover: The Man and His Secrets*.

17- The first quote is from *Advances in Fingerprint Technology Second Edition* edited by Henry C. Lee and R. E. Gaensslen CRC Press 2001, and the second quote is from FBI.Gov. Some information is also from *Weighing Fingerprints As Forensic Evidence* CBS News May 4, 2008; *FBI Admits Fingerprint Error, Clearing Portland Attorney* by David Heath and Hal Bernton in the *Seattle Times* May 25, 2004; *"That's Not My Fingerprint, Your Honor" Lawyer Saved By The Spanish National Police From FBI Terrorist Frame-Up* by Hans Sherrer in *Justice:Denied* magazine Summer 2004; *Do Fingerprints Lie?* by Michael Specter in *The New Yorker* May 27, 2002. Jennifer L. Mnookin authored *The Validity Of Latent Fingerprint Identification: Confessions Of A Fingerprinting Moderate* and also *Law, Probability and Risk, Forthcoming* at the UCLA School of Law 2007 and *Scripting Expertise: The History Of Handwriting Identification Evidence And The Judicial Construction Of Reliability* at the University Of Virginia School of Law December 2001. The PBS American Experience – *People & Events: The Rise of the FBI – Public Enemy #1* (Dillinger).

18- Congress passed the National Motor Vehicle Theft Act, or Dyer Act, on October 29, 1919. Charles Augustus Lindbergh Jr. was kidnapped on March 1, 1932; his body was discovered on May 12, 1932; and Congress passed the Lindbergh Law on June 17, 1932.

TRAGEDY AT A TRAIN STATION

19- FDR was inaugurated on March 4, 1933.

20- Nash was convicted of murdering his friend Nollie "Humpy" Wortman in 1913. The train robbery was on August 20, 1923 and Nash escaped from Leavenworth on October 19, 1930. Nash assisted prisoners escape from Leavenworth on December 11, 1931 and from Kansas State Penitentiary on May 31, 1933. The FBI captured bank robbers Francis Keating and Tom Holden on July 7, 1932 but agents and Police Chief Otto Reid did not capture Nash until June 16, 1933. Some of the info about Nash is also from EncyclopediaOfArkansas.net and ASUHerald.com (The Herald of Arkansas State University 9-28-2010).

21- The Kansas City Massacre occurred on June 17, 1933. Killed that day along with the prisoner were FBI Agent R. J Caffrey; McAlester, Oklahoma Police Chief Otto Reed; and Kansas City Police Detectives W. J. Grooms and Frank Hermanson. FBI Agent F. Joseph Lackey was seriously wounded by three bullets and Agent-in-Charge Reed E. Vetterli was shot in the left arm. Some of this information is also from FBI.Gov

A GOVERNMENT WAR ON CRIME

22- The quotes from Roosevelt's speech, the "Only Thing We Have to Fear Is Fear Itself," on March 4, 1933 are from his text on HistoryMatters.GMU.edu.

23- The Kansas City Massacre occurred on June 17, 1933. FDR ordered AG Cummings to prepare a war against crime on July 26, 1933, and the AG announced he was launching the war on July 29, 1933. Congress authorized FBI agents to make arrests and carry firearms on June 18, 1934. The FBI's original name was the Bureau of Investigation which was changed to the Division of Investigation before Hoover finally changed his agency's name to the Federal Bureau of Investigation on July 1, 1935. Some of this info is from the PBS American Experience series *People & Events: The Rise of the FBI – Public Enemy #1 (Dillinger)*

J. EDGAR'S WAR AGAINST DEMOCRACY

24- The quote by Doris Lockerman, former confidential secretary to Agent-in-Charge Melvin Purvis, is from her October 7, 1935 *Chicago Tribune* article.

25- The three quotes in these two paragraphs are from the Ray Tucker article in the August 19, 1933 *Collier's Magazine*.

26- The *New York Time's* obituary for Hoover was published on May 3, 1972.

27- The two quotes are from the Ray Tucker article in the August 19, 1933 *Collier's Magazine*.

28- Sullivan's two quotes are from the May 15, 1973 *Los Angeles Times*. Tom Bishop headed the FBI's Crime Records Division, and his quote is from the Senator Church Committee hearings about the FBI's conduct under Hoover in November and December 1975.

29- The quote by the anonymous FBI agent is from the March 3, 1968 *Washington Post*.

Notes Chapter 3
DILLINGER THWARTS THE EARLY FBI

THE FBI JOINS THE FRAY

30- The quotes by Hoover are from his memos to Assistant Pop Nathan and to SAC Purvis on March 6, 1934.

31- The quote by the Director is from his March 7, 1934 telegraphic wire ordering his entire force to go after Dillinger.

A BREAK IN THE CASE

32- The apartment owner was Mrs. Ed Goodman. The quote "shoot him" was by the FBI's Inspector W. A. Rorer according to Agent Ed Notesteen's memorandum on the FBI's execution of Green.

33- The quote by Hamilton's sister's son, Charles Campbell, is from the April 22, 1934 *Chicago Tribune*. Hamilton's sister, Mrs. Anna Steve, was sentenced for harboring on June 7, 1935.

34- Nelson killed driver Theodore W. Kidder in Minneapolis on March 4, 1934. Dillinger and Nelson robbed the Security National Bank & Trust Company in Sioux Falls, South Dakota, on

March 6, 1934 and the First National Bank in Mason City, Iowa, on March 13, 1934 when Judge John C. Shipley shot two of them. The FBI raided Dillinger's apartment on March 31, 1934. The apartment manager was Mrs. Daisy Coffee, and the two FBI agents were Rosser "Rusty" Nalls and Rufus Coulter and the detective was Henry Cummings. The FBI assassinated Eugene Green on April 3, 1934. The Dillinger family reunion was on April 8, 1934, and Dillinger escaped the FBI trap at the Tumble Inn but Billie Frechette was arrested on April 9, 1934. Dillinger robbed the police-station arsenal on April 14, 1934. Dillinger stayed with Hamilton at his sister's home the night of April 17, 1934.

A QUIET VACATION

35- The quote by owner Emil Wanatka is from the April 24, 1934 *Chicago Tribune*.

36- The Little Bohemia Lodge escape was on April 22, 1934. The slain man was 35-year-old Eugene Boisoneau, a specialist at the Civilian Conservation Corps (CCC) at Mercer. The two survivors were John Morris age 59, a cook at the CCC camp, and 28-year-old driver John Hoffman, an oil station attendant in Mercer. The fugitive trio hijacked the car of employee Robert Johnson at the resort owned by E. J. Mitchell. The trio stole the car on the highway near St. Paul Park from Roy Francis, his wife, and baby. Hamilton's body was buried on April 24, 1934. Hamilton's death was first reported by Van Meter's girlfriend on December 21, 1934 and Hamilton's body was dug up on August 28, 1935.

37- At Birch Lodge owned by Alvin Koerner, Nelson murdered FBI Agent W. Carter Baum and wounded Agent J. C. Newman and Spider Lake Constable Carl C. Christensen.

BACKLASH TO A DEBACLE

38- The two Republican U.S. Senators who castigated the FBI were Thomas Schall of Minnesota and Arthur Robinson of Indiana. The Michigan Public Safety Commissioner was Oscar G. Olander. Will Rogers quote is from the April 24, 1934 *Washington Times*.

39- The April 24, 1934 *Chicago Tribune* article was datelined April 23, 1934 from Washington D.C. Keenan's quote is from the May 7, 1934 *Time Magazine*.

40- AG Cummings quotes are from the April 25, 1934 *New York Times*.

41- Senator Copeland's quotes are from the April 25, 1934 *New York Times*.

42- The anticrime bills were signed by the President on May 18, 1934 including bank robbery, and Congress passed more anticrime legislation on May 22, 1934 and June 18, 1934.

43- The quote is by Moe Dalitz from my October 11, 1969 interview. He was the closest thing Las Vegas ever had to a Godfather and one of the most influential men in the history of American organized crime.

Notes Chapter 4
THE HUNT FOR DILLINGER

LIFE & THE LAW AFTER BOHEMIA

44- Dillinger stole the license plates of Dr. E. E. Shelly of Freeport, Illinois the evening of April 23, 1934. The abandoned car was found on May 2, 1934. Dillinger had dinner at a restaurant with the two women on April 26, 1934. Dillinger disarmed three Bellwood policemen on April 30, 1934. The two quotes were by Patrolman Harry Wayland and Lieutenant Joseph Hagneister from the May 1, 1934 *Chicago Tribune*. The third officer was Patrolman Gus Nendze. Dillinger's gang was indicted with sheltering charges on May 2, 1934.

45- The three Dillinger gang members' women were freed on May 26, 1934. Hoover appointed Agent Cowley to head the Dillinger case on June 2, 1934. Van Meter's girlfriend dropped from sight on June 14, 1934.

46- Purvis' three quotes are from the April 30, 1934 *Chicago Tribune.*

47- Purvis' statement are from the May 29, 1934 *Chicago Tribune.*

48- East Chicago, Indiana Detectives Lloyd Mulvihill and Martin O'Brien were murdered on May 24, 1934. Five states offered a reward for Dillinger's capture on May 25, 1934, and the AG did so on June 23, 1934.

WHICH BANK ROBBERIES?

49- Van Meter robbed the Villa Park bank on April 27, 1934 and then the Fostoria bank on May 3, 1934. The Bank President was Andrew Emerine and the VP was A. E. Mergenthaler. Cashier Frances Billyard notified Police Chief Frank Culp and patrolman Louis Stagger. The retired policeman was Ed Walters, the farmer was Roy Feasel, and the bystander was Robert Sheilds. The cashier was R. W. Powley. The hostages were bookkeeper Ruth Harris and assistant cashier William Daub. The local sign painter was Bud Boyher. Some info is also from the January 15, 1981 *Fostoria Review Times* column *Welcome to Potluck* by Paul Krupp; the July 3, 1967 *Fostoria Review Times* obituary for banker Emerine; and the January 2, 1991 USA Today.

50- The quote by assistant cashier Ralph Barbour is from the May 4, 1934 *Los Angeles Times.*

51- The first quote by Krupp is from his column in the January 15, 1981 *Fostoria Review Times,* and the second quote by Ernie Duffield is from the January 2, 1991 *USA Today.*

52- The South Bend, Indiana bank robbery was on June 30, 1934. The slain traffic officer was Howard Wagner, 32; the wounded bank VP was Perry Stahley; and the cashier was Delos Coen. The two pursuing patrolmen were Harry Henderson and Harry McCormick. The motorist shot in the eye was Samuel Toth. The metal manufacturer near death in the hospital was Jacob Solomon.

53- Dr. Laird's quote was from the July 2, 1934 *Chicago Tribune.*

54- The Kosciusko County Sheriff was Harley Person.

THE DEVIL'S DISCIPLES

55- Attorney Piquett's investigator was Arthur O'Leary. Dr. Wilhelm Loeser did the surgery and Dr. Harold Cassidy handled the anesthesiology. Arrangements for the operations were made on May 15, 1934; Dillinger's surgery was on May 28, 1934; and Van Meter's on June 3, 1934.

56- Prohis arrested Mayor Raleigh Hale, Police Chief James Regan, and Detective Chief Zarkovich on August 16, 1929 and they were found guilty on January 17, 1930.

A GANGSTER MOVIE BECOMES TOO REAL

57- Dillinger was killed on July 22, 1934. Purvis quote is from the July 23, 1934 *Chicago Tribune.* Some of this information is also from www.FBI.Gov.

58- The two innocent women shot by the FBI were Mrs. Etta Natalsky and Theresa Paulus.

59- The two quotes by Sage are from the September 29, 1935 *Chicago Tribune.*

60- The quote by Purvis is from the July 23, 1934 *Chicago Tribune.*

61- The quote by Cowley is from the July 24, 1934 *Chicago Tribune.*

62- The quote of the Inquest Jury's findings are from the July 24, 1934 *Chicago Tribune.*

63- The three Chicago patrolman at the scene were Frank Slattery and Edward Meisterheime in street clothes and Michael Garrity in uniform. The quote by Officer Slattery is from the July 23, 1934 *Chicago Tribune.*

64- The quote by AG Cummings is from the July 24, 1934 *Chicago Tribune.*

65- Zarkovich's gun sold at auction on February 23, 1998, and O'Neil's gun was auctioned in July 2009.

66- The quotes by the Director are from the July 23, 1934 *Chicago Tribune.*

67- The first quote by the AG Cummings is from the July 23, 1934 *Chicago Tribune,* and his second is from the July 24, 1934 *Chicago Tribune.*

BETRAYED BY THE DIRECTOR

68- AG Cummings announced payment of the rewards on October 4, 1934.

69- Anna Sage testified in Federal Court on September 28 and 29, 1935. Purvis' first quote is from the October 1, 1935 *Chicago Tribune* and his second quote is from the October 4, 1935 edition.

70- The Judge Barnes court ruling quote is from the October 17, 1935 *Chicago Tribune.* The quote of the Court of Appeals ruling is from the April 7, 1936 *Chicago Tribune.* Anna Sage's quote is from the April 17, 1936 *Chicago Tribune.*

71- Controller General J. R. McCarl ruled against paying the hospital expenses on October 13, 1934.

A DETECTIVE IN TROUBLE AGAIN

72- Zarkovich was promoted to Detective Chief on May 20, 1939 and to Police Chief on November 8, 1947. The malfeasance indictments were returned on May 1, 1951. The private meeting of the Judge and defendant Zarkovich was exposed on June 22, 1951. The Lake County Judge was William Murray and the Prosecutor was David Stanton. Judge Murray's quote is from the June 23, 1951 *Chicago Tribune.* The Judge ruled Zarkovich's indictment was improper on April 18, 1952 and Zarkovich resigned on May 1, 1952. The Indiana Supreme Court ruled against the Judge on October 21, 1952 but the Judge was reelected on November 6, 1952.

DEFENDING THE INDEFENSIBLE

73- Probasco plunged to his death on July 26, 1934. The man he narrowly missed landing on was R. J. Lambert of Maywood, Illinois. The Probasco inquest was conducted by Deputy Coroner Jacob Schewel.

74- The two quotes of Inspector Cowley in the previous two paragraphs are from the July 27, 1934 *Chicago Tribune.*

75- Probasco's sister was Mrs. Louise Hamilton. His funeral was on July 30, 1934 and the quote is from the *Chicago Tribune's* editorial of that date.

76- FBI agent quotes are from Galatas' motion to suppress presented in Bryan Burrough's *Public Enemies.*

PROSECUTING THE HARBORERS

77- Piquett was found innocent of harboring Dillinger on January 14, 1935, but Piquett was found guilty of harboring Van Meter on June 25, 1935. Dr. William Loeser was remanded to Leavenworth. Dr. Harold Cassidy committed suicide on July 30, 1946.

THE REST OF THE GANG

78- Van Meter was convicted of car theft in 1924 and convicted of train robbery in 1925. He was paroled from Michigan City Prison on May 18, 1933 and he was killed on August 23, 1934.

79- Pierpont and Makley attempt to escape on September 22, 1934, and Pierpont was executed on October 17, 1934.

Notes Chapter 5
THE SEARCH FOR PRETTY BOY FLOYD

HUNTING THE KANSAS CITY SUSPECTS

80- The Massacre was on June 17, 1933. The FBI chased Vi Mathias from Lake Placid on July 22, 1933 to Newark on August 7, 1933. The FBI failed to capture Miller at Vi Mathias' apartment on November 1, 1933, and the critical FBI report was written by Assistant Director Vincent Hughes. Miller's body was found on November 29, 1933. The FBI Summary Report memo about the agents' interview of Lepke Buchalter on November 28, 1933 was written by New York Agent F. X. Fay to the Kansas City SAC on November 29, 1933. Buchalter's criminal career and the story of Murder, Inc. are the subject of Chapter 8 in the author's upcoming book about the mob that built the Las Vegas Strip. Information about the possible existence of Murder, Inc. did not surface until six years after the FBI's interview of Lepke when he was alleged to head the national murder-for-hire organization.

FLOYD BECOMES ENSNARED

81- The first four quotes are from internal FBI memos on September 24, 1934. The first of these is from Hoover to his Assistant Ed Tamm. The next three are from Tamm to Hoover about his orders to New Orleans Agent R. G. Harvey. The final quote is from Harvey to Hoover on September 26, 1934.

82- The two quotes by Purvis' former Secretary Doris Lockerman are from the October 16, 1935 and October 7, 1935 *Chicago Tribune* respectively.

83- The FBI compared the fingerprints from Miller's beer glasses on March 14, 1934. President Roosevelt signed the Crime Control Laws that lifted restrictions preventing federal agents from making arrests and carrying arms on May 18, 1934. Lazia was machinegunned on July 10, 1934. La Capra talked to FBI agents on September 1, 1934. Vi Mathias was paroled and then kidnapped by the FBI on September 18, 1934, and the FBI arrested Galatas on September 22, 1934 after his photo was recognized in the September 15, 1934 *Liberty Magazine*. Hoover accused the Massacre trio on October 10 1934. Some of this information is also from FBI.gov.

WHO WAS THIS PRETTY BOY?

84- Floyd robbed the St. Louis payroll on September 11, 1925 and his first arrest was on September 16, 1925. He was released on March 7, 1929. Floyd was arrested in the Sylvania, Ohio bank robbery on May 20, 1930 and was sentenced on November 24, 1930. Floyd killed Bowling Green, Ohio Patrolman Ralph "R. H." Castner on April 16, 1931. Oklahoma's Bankers called on the Governor to get Floyd on January 14, 1932. Floyd killed the Governor's investigator, Ervin Kelly, at Ben Hargraves' farm on April 9, 1932. They robbed the Stonewall bank of $600 on April 21, 1932 and kidnapped cashiers Furman Gibson and Ed Salle and driver Estelle Henson. Floyd robbed the Sallisaw State Bank on November 1, 1932 where the farmer was Bob Fitzsimmons and the kidnapped assistant cashier was Bob Riggs. At the Boley bank on November 23, 1932 the murdered President was D. J. Turner, and the heroic cashier who killed Birdwell was H. C. McCormick. The African accomplice who was also killed was Charles Glass while the European C. C. Patterson was seriously wounded. Floyd and Richetti kidnapped Polk County Sheriff Jack Killingworth in Bolivar on June 16, 1933. Some of this info is also from the Oklahoma Historical Society's Encyclopedia of Oklahoma History & Culture at Digital.Library.OKState.edu/Encyclopedia; from the Carnegie Public Library in East Liverpool, Ohio at Carnegie.Lib.Oh.; and from FBI.gov.

AN ASSASSINATION TEAM AT WORK

85- The first quote is from Hoover's memo to Assistant Tamm on June 23, 1934, and the second quote is from Hoover's memos to Assistants Nathan and Tamm on June 28, 1934.

86- The quote is from the October 24, 1934 *Chicago Tribune*.

87- Floyd's emissary forwarded his offers to surrender to the FBI in early June 1934. Floyd was not seen by anyone from the night before the Kansas City Massacre on June 16, 1933 until he escaped the pheasant farm shootout on October 11, 1934. He then robbed a bank in Tiltonsville on October 19, 1934 and shot Police Chief John Fultz on October 21, 1934. Floyd was killed on October 22, 1934 and buried on October 28, 1934. Widow Ellen Conkle made Floyd dinner and Mr.

and Mrs. Stewart Dyke were driving him. Arthur Conkle called East Liverpool Police Chief Hugh McDermott. The Headquarters' call to Purvis was from official Bob Newby who reported it in his memo dated October 24, 1934. Richetti was convicted on June 17, 1935 for the murder of Kansas City Detective Frank Hermanson and was executed on October 7, 1938. The eight conspiracy defendants were indicted in the Massacre conspiracy on October 24, 1934. The two who became state's witnesses were Frank Nash's widow Frances and Miller's widow Vi Mathis. The Federal Jury convicted the other six on January 4, 1935 - Mr. and Mrs. Dick Galatas, Mr. and Mrs. Herbert "Deafy" Farmer, "Doc" Louis Stacci, and Frank Mulloy. Some of this info is also from the Oklahoma Historical Society's Encyclopedia of Oklahoma History & Culture at Digital.Library.OKState.edu/Encyclopedia; from the Carnegie Public Library in East Liverpool, Ohio at Carnegie.Lib.Oh; and from FBI.gov.

Notes Chapter 6
NELSON STILL ON THE RUN

BABY FACE AFTER LITTLE BOHEMIA
88- After Nelson's Little Bohemia escape on the evening of April 22, 1934, he arrived at Ollie Catfish's shack at Lac du Flambeau on April 23, 1934. Nelson stole the car of mailman Adolph Goetz at Lac du Flambeau on April 26, 1934 and bought a car in Marshfield on April 28, 1934.

89- Purvis quote about the new Public Enemy was from the October 23, 1934 *Chicago Tribune.*

90- The quote of Walker Lake resort proprietor Mrs. John Benedict is from the April 4, 1935 Reno *Nevada State Journal.*

91- The quote by Nelson's sister, Mrs. Juliette Fitzsimmons, is from the August 14, 1934 *Chicago Tribune.*

92- The three quotes by Nelson's mother, Mrs. Mary Gillis, and sister, Mrs. Juliette Fitzsimmons, are from the August 14, 1934 *Chicago Tribune.*

93- SAC Guinane learned Nelson had been in California on August 15, 1934 according to his FBI report written three days later. Sausalito Police Chief Manuel Menotti took Chase's girlfriend, Sally Backman, into custody on October 6, 1934 and she told the FBI what she knew on October 8, 1934. Sally was flown to Chicago on October 23, 1934. The FBI interviewed Lake Como Inn owner, Hobart Hermanson, on November 4, 1934.

A CROSS-COUNTRY PURSUIT
94- Chase's message was in the October 11, 1934 *Reno Evening Gazette.* Chief Kirkley's quote is from the December 29, 1934 Reno *Nevada State Journal.*

95- FBI agents flew into Reno on October 10, 1934 because police had spotted Chase's car. SAC Guinane showed the suspect's photos on October 11, 1934. The two quotes of SAC Guinane are from the March 29, 1935 Reno *Nevada State Journal.*

96- Cochran's testimony quote at his trial for harboring Nelson about the Sheriff's statement is from the April 3, 1935 Reno *Nevada State Journal.*

97- Cochran's two testimony quotes at his trial for harboring Nelson are from the April 3, 1935 Reno *Nevada State Journal.*

98- Nelson and Chase stole the V-8 Ford on November 26, 1934. Negri's quote is in his harborers' trial testimony from the March 27, 1935 *Nevada State Journal.*

DESTINATION CHICAGO
99- The quote by Agent John Medallie about passing but not recognizing Nelson's car is from the November 28, 1934 *Chicago Tribune.*

100- The two quotes by Chase are from the March 23, 1935 *Chicago Tribune,* and the quote by Agent William Ryan is from the March 20, 1935 *Chicago Tribune.* Both are testimony from Chase's trial for murder.

101 The first two Agents to encounter Nelson on November 27, 1934 were at Lake Como - C. B. Winstead and James Metcalfe. They later testified at Chase's trial for killing the two FBI officials. The second pair of Agents failed to recognize Nelson, but soon after they called the Chicago Office from the Barrington Hospital where Hollis had been taken. The Agents refused to give reporters their names, but they told their Office over the phone who they were – John Medallie and La France. The third set of Agents who ran from the gunfire were William Ryan and Thomas McDade.

102- The quote by Agent Thomas McDade at Chase's trial for murder is from the March 20, 1935 *Chicago Tribune.*

103- The quote by Chase is from the March 23, 1935 *Chicago Tribune.*

104- The quote by Cowley's civilian target P. W. Sherman is from the November 28, 1934 *Chicago Tribune.*

105- The first quote by Chase is from the March 23, 1935 *Chicago Tribune.* The second quote is by gas station operator Mrs. Frances Kramer from the November 28, 1934 *Chicago Tribune* and *New York Times.*

106- The quote by Mrs. Frances Kramer at Chase's trial for murder is from the March 21, 1935 *Chicago Tribune.*

107- The station attendant with the rifle was Alfred Trestik. The targeted civilian was P. W. Sherman, and his three quotes are from his testimony at Chase's trial for murder from the March 21, 1935 *Chicago Tribune.* The Highway Policeman was William Gallagher and his quote of Cowley's whisper is from the November 28, 1934 *Chicago Tribune.*

108- Purvis' first quote is from the November 28, 1934 *Chicago Tribune.* His second quote and headline are from the November 28, 1934 *New York Evening Journal.* FBI Agent John Madala's quote of Cowley's alleged statement to Purvis at the Coroner's Inquest is from the December 1, 1934 Reno *Nevada State Journal.*

109- Doctor Morgan Carpenter's quote was at Chase's trial for murder from the March 21, 1935 *Chicago Tribune.*

110- Hoover's memo to file was dated November 28, 1934 the day after the Nelson shootout.

111- The FBI's leak to the *Chicago American* was published on December 5, 1934. AG Cummings banned the FBI from commenting on cases on December 6, 1934.

112- Nelson was machinegunned on November 27, 1934. The Doctor's quote was at Chase's trial for murder from the March 21, 1935 *Chicago Tribune.* Cowley's mother's quote is from the November 29, 1934 *Chicago Tribune,* and Cowley's wife's quote is from the November 30, 1934 *Chicago Tribune.* Hollis' wife's quote is from the December 1, 1934 *Chicago Tribune.* Some info in this section is also from FBI.gov; *J. Edgar Hoover: The Man and His Secrets* by Curt Gentry New York: W.W. Norton & Company 1991; and *Public Enemies: America's Greatest Crime Wave and the Birth of the FBI, 1933-34* by Bryan Burrough New York: The Penguin Press 2004.

THE FINAL SEARCH

113- The Catholic Priest was Reverend Philip Coughlin. The two quotes of Chase's testimony at his trial for murdering an FBI official is from the March 23, 1935 *Chicago Tribune.*

114- Nelson told his associates to transfer his robbery loot to McKay in July 1934.

115- Chicago's Chief of Detectives was John L. Sullivan.

CLOSING THE CASE

116- Helen Gillis was sentenced for parole violation on December 7, 1934, and given probation for harboring her husband on December 13, 1935.

117- Chase worked at the fish hatchery in 1928, and he was arrested for drunkenness in 1931. The Mount Shasta Police Chief was A. L. Roberts. Chase's quote is from the December 30, 1934 *Chicago Tribune*.

118- Chase was found guilty on March 26, 1935 and entered Alcatraz on March 31, 1935. Chase was paroled on October 31, 1966, and he died on October 5, 1973.

119- Nelson's harborers were convicted on April 5, 1935.

THE SILENCING OF PURVIS

120- Purvis resigned on July 12, 1935, and his first three short quotes are from the July 13, 1935 *New York Times*. The quote in the article about Hoover's FBI is from the June 21, 1936 *Chicago Tribune*. The last two quotes Lockerman wrote in her October 19, 1935 and October 7, 1935 *Chicago Tribune* articles.

121- The two quotes in Purvis first Post Toasties ad are from the May 10, 1936 *Chicago Tribune*.

122- The quote of Richard Gid Powers is from his *G-Men: Hoover's FBI in American Popular Culture*.

123- Some info in this section is also from *J. Edgar Hoover: The Man and His Secrets* by Curt Gentry New York: W.W. Norton & Company 1991, and from *G-Men: Hoover's FBI in American Popular Culture* by Richard Gid Powers Southern Illinois University Press 1983.

Notes Chapter 7
IMAGERY VERSUS LAW ENFORCEMENT

COMPETING ANTI-CRIME CAMPAIGNS

124- AG Cummings hired Henry Suydam of the *Brooklyn Eagle* on August 29, 1934, and the AG held his crime conference in mid December 1934.

125- AG Cummings quote is from the October 27, 1934 *Chicago Tribune*.

126- The quote about former SACs is by Curt Gentry in his *J. Edgar Hoover: The Man and His Secrets*.

127- Pegler's 1941 quote is from *The Nation Magazine* October 18, 1958 *Special Issue: The FBI* by Fred J. Cook.

128- The quote by the FBI administrative assistance is from *J. Edgar Hoover: The Man and His Secrets* by Curt Gentry.

129- Hoover's quote is from his obituary in the May 3, 1972 *New York Times*.

130- The quote is by Richard Gid Powers in his *G-Men: Hoover's FBI in American Popular Culture*.

131- Gould started the *Dick Tracy* comic book in 1931. *G-Man* comic came out in October 1935 and *The Feds* comic came out in December 1935 but folded in September 1937. Hoover launched *War on Crime* comic book on May 18, 1936. Some info in this section is also from *G-Men: Hoover's FBI in American Popular Culture* by Richard Gid Powers Southern Illinois University Press 1983.

FEMINIZATION OF MINCING

132- The first quote is from the Walter Trohan article in the June 21, 1936 *Chicago Tribune,* and the second by Chief Justice Stone is from the May 3, 1972 *New York Times*.

133- The quote is by reporter Walter Trohan in the June 21, 1936 *Chicago Tribune.*

134- The first quote is by attorney Guy McGaughey, Chairman of the Section on Criminal Law of the Illinois Bar Association, in the December 1, 1934 *Chicago Tribune.* The two quotes by Chicago Crime Commission President Frank Loesch and the quote by Cook County Circuit Judge Harry Fisher are from the February 15, 1935 *Chicago Tribune.* The fifth quote by resident David Cupp in a letter to the editor dated November 30, 1934 is from the December 3, 1934 *Chicago Tribune.*

135- In these three paragraphs the five quotes are by reporter Walter Trohan in the June 21, 1936 *Chicago Tribune.*

136- The two quotes by Walter Trohan are from his *Political Animals: Memoirs of a Sentimental Cynic* Doubleday 1975.

137- Hoover's 1943 letter quote is from the September 13, 1999 *Philadelphia Inquirer* article *Couples Hoover and Tolson Used Tactics to Push FBI to New Highs, Lows* by Patricia J. Foster at Philly. com, and from *Internal Affairs: Were J. Edgar Hoover and Clyde Tolson lovers?* by Beverly Gage November 11, 2011 at Slate.com

138- Nichols quote is from an interview by author Curt Gentry for *J. Edgar Hoover: The Man and His Secrets.*

139- Hoover's first obscene letter to all SACs was sent on March 24, 1925 and the second on March 29, 1966.

140- The quote about Hoover's male companion is from the March 11, 1940 *Time Magazine.*

141- The quotes by Warren Olney III, who headed the FBI's Criminal Division from 1953 through 1957, are in the December 7, 1964 *Newsweek Magazine.* Some info in this section is also from *J. Edgar Hoover: The Man and His Secrets* by Curt Gentry; *From The Secret Files of J. Edgar Hoover* edited with commentary by Athan Theoharis; *Official and Confidential: The Secret Life of J. Edgar Hoover* by Anthony Summers; *J. Edgar Hoover: The Man In His Time* by Ralph de Toledano; and *Robert Kennedy and His Times* by Arthur M. Schlesinger, Jr.

142- Hoover's quote is from his memo to Commissioner of Immigration Anthony Caminetti January 22, 1920. Hoover's second memo was also to Caminetti on February 2, 1920.

143- Hoover's quote is from his memo to his boss U.S. AG Palmer on January 28, 1920.

144- Hoover's quote is from his October 18, 1924 memo to Assistant AG, Criminal Division, William Donovan.

145- Hoover's quote is from his memo to his assistants on April 23, 1969.

146- Hoover's quote is from his speech *Fifty Years of Crime: Corruption Begets Corruption* before the National Fifty Years in Business Club on May 20, 1939 in *Vital Speeches.* Japan had previously invaded China on July 7, 1937, and had killed 300,000 in the Nanking Massacre on December 13, 1937. The U.S. had complained to Japan about its occupation of China on October 6, 1938, and Japan had proclaimed its New Order in Northeast Asia on December 22, 1938. Germany would invade Poland and set off World War II on September 1, 1939.

147- Some info about Hoover and the FBI in this chapter is also from *J. Edgar Hoover: The Man and His Secrets* by Curt Gentry 1991 New York: W.W. Norton & Company; *From The Secret Files of J. Edgar Hoover* edited with commentary by Athan Theoharis 1991 Chicago; *G-Men: Hoover's FBI in American Popular Culture* by Richard Gid Powers 1983 Southern Illinois University Press; and Ivan R. Dee; *Official and Confidential: The Secret Life of J. Edgar Hoover* by Anthony Summers 1993 New York: G. P. Putnam's Sons.

Notes Chapter 8
BANK ROBBERIES & KIDNAPPINGS

BIRTH OF THE KARPIS-BARKERS GANG

148- Herman Barker killed Deputy Arthur Osborn on August 1, 1927, and Herman Barker killed himself on August 29, 1927. Lloyd Barker went to prison in 1921, was released from Leavenworth on October 29, 1938, and his wife killed him on March 14, 1949. Karpis was born on August 10, 1909 and he went to the reformatory in 1926. He escaped with Lawrence Devol and the pair was arrested as fugitives on March 23, 1930. Karpis was transferred to the State Penitentiary on May 19, 1930. Karpis and Fred Barker were released in early 1931. Karpis was arrested in Tulsa on June 10, 1931 and he was sentenced on September 11, 1931. Karpis killed West Plains Sheriff C. R. Kelly on December 19, 1931. Doc Barker and Volney Davis were falsely convicted for killing night watchman Thomas Sherrill on August 16, 1921 and entered prison on February 10, 1922. Doc was pardoned on September 10, 1932. The gang's supposed Minneapolis robbery and murders of policemen Ira Evans and Leo Gorski were on December 16, 1932.

EXPANSION INTO KIDNAPPING

149- Karpis' quote is the opening line in his book *The Alvin Karpis Story* written with Bill Trent New York: Berkley Medallion Books 1971

150- SAC Ladd's quote is from the August 7, 1936 *Chicago Tribune*.

151- Hamm was kidnapped on June 15, 1933 and released on June 18. The official who handled Hamm's ransom payment was William Dunn. Karpis and Fred Barker killed his stepfather Arthur Dunlap in early July 1933 but his body was not discovered until later. Fred Barker distributed the Hamm ransom on July 24, 1933. The Karpis-Barkers gang robbed the Kansas bank on July 26, 1933 and then robbed the South St. Paul payroll and postal receipts on August 30, 1933. The gang robbed the Chicago bank on September 22, 1933 and then killed Patrolman Miles Cunningham. Related to two of these robberies, the FBI raided Doc's apartment on January 8, 1935 and released the results of the machinegun and ballistic test on March 12, 1935. The gang spent October and November 1933 in Reno. They kidnapped Bremer on January 17, 1934; his father's appeal was on February 3; the ransom was delivered on February 6; and the victim was released on February 8, 1934. The doctor who treated Bremer while he was a captive was H. T. Nippert, and the contractor who handled Bremer's ransom payment was Walter Magee. The AG announced that Karpis and Doc Barker were the Bremer kidnappers on March 22, 1934, while Karpis and Fred Barker were vacationing in Reno with their car parked in Cochran's garage. The FBI discovered the Bensenville apartment where Bremer was held on January 20, 1935.

152- Dr. Moran was convicted of abortion in November 1928, paroled on April 7, 1930, and finally freed on December 15, 1931. Doc Moran disappeared in June 1934 and his body was found in September 1934. The FBI had his body exhumed in August 1936. Agents interviewed harboring defendants on June 10, 1937 and announced his body was identified on July 21, 1937.

THE RANSOM-CASH TRAIL

153- McLaughlin's quote is from the April 29, 1934 *Chicago Tribune*.

154- Bremer-ransom passer Bill Vidler was arrested on April 26, 1934 and both bartender Phil Delaney and McLaughlin were arrested on April 27, 1934. McLaughlin possessed bonds from a Loop mail robbery committed on December 6, 1932. The day the Loop robbery indictment was released on October 6, 1933, 225 Night Club owner Edgar Lebensberger committed suicide and street thug and vice operator Gus Winkler was killed three days later. The details of Detective Harry Lang's December 19, 1932 attempted assassination of Nitti on behalf of Newberry are detailed in Chapter 15 of the volume in this series about the development of American organized crime.

Assistant Director Nathan flew into Chicago on April 28, 1934. McLaughlin pled guilty to the Bremer ransom cash on November 2, 1934.

155- Heller's two quotes are from the February 4, 1935 *New York Times.*

156- The three Karpis-Barkers gang girlfriends were arrested in Cleveland on September 5, 1934. Karpis fled from Havana to Florida on December 3, 1934. The two Miami suspects were arrested and indicted with four others on January 31, 1935 for having harbored Karpis in Havana from September 1934 until December 3, 1934. The *Ahora* newspaper article was published on February 6, 1935, and the U.S. indicted Heller on February 9, 1935 and Cuba released him to the FBI on February 11, 1935.

157- McDonald and five other people were indicted in Miami for harboring Karpis on February 9, 1935. McDonald was arrested in Detroit on September 26, 1935, convicted on January 24, 1936, sentenced on February 1, 1936, and released on June 6, 1940.

GIBSON WAS THE FIRST TARGET

158- Gibson was arrested in Oklahoma and became a fugitive in 1929. Karpis and Doc Barker escaped Connelley's Cleveland trap in September 1934. Gibson was fatally wounded in Chicago on January 8, 1935. The inquest for Gibson's shooting was held on January 10, 1935. Agents machinegunned and tear gassed the apartment of civilian J. H. Twitchell. His quote is from the January 10, 1935 *Chicago Tribune.* The Town Hall police officers were Lieutenant William Blaul in the front of the building and Sergeants Everett Mullaney, Martin Walsh, and Fred Leckie in back.

GOING AFTER THE BARKERS

159- The FBI learned about Doc's marriage in Toledo on December 3, 1934, the same day an agent found Bremer ransom money in Havana. Doc Barker was captured on January 8, 1935. His quote is from History.com and NotFrisco.com.

160- The two quotes of Woodbury and the one by Connelley are from FBI records in Bryan Burrough's *Public Enemies: America's Greatest Crime Wave and the Birth of the FBI, 1933-34,* and the second Woodbury quote is also from the January 17, 1935 *New York Times.*

161- The neighbor's quote is by Mrs. A. F. Westberry from the January 17, 1935 *New York Times.*

162- The FBI killed Ma and Fred Barker on January 16, 1935. The U.S. Senate past the House's bill to reimburse damages to the owner's home on August 7, 1937.

A DANGEROUS LITTLE OLD LADY

163- The *New York Times* article quote was from January 17, 1935 the morning after the killings.

164- Hoover's first quote is from *Persons in Hiding* by J. Edgar Hoover Boston: Little, Brown, & Co. 1938. His remaining four quotes are from *The FBI In Action* by J. Edgar Hoover with Ken Jones New American Library 1957.

165- The first quote is from *The Alvin Karpis Story* by Karpis, and the second quote is from *Robbing Banks Was My Business: The Story of J. Harvey Bailey, America's Most Successful Bank Robber* Canyon, Texas: Palo Duro Press 1973 and also from Bailey's interview in *Run the Cat Roads: A True Story of Bank Robbers in the Thirties* by L. L. Edge W.W. Norton & Co. 1981.

Notes Chapter 9
WHERE IS OLD CREEPY?

THE FBI'S HUNT FOR KARPIS

166- Dr. Horace Hunsicker was kidnapped by Karpis and Campbell and his two quotes are from the January 22, 1935 *New York Times.*

167- The girlfriends of Karpis and Campbell arrived in Atlantic City from Florida on January 11, 1935; Karpis and Campbell checked in on January 19, 1935; and the pair escaped the Atlantic City Police raid on January 20, 1935. The Patrolman who found their car was Elias Saab and the Detectives at the hotel were Edward Mulhern, George Brennan, and Arch Witham who was shot in the cheek. The three uniformed Patrolmen at the garage were Sergeant Joseph Florentino, and James Campbell who had joined Elias Saab. Karpis and Campbell kidnapped the Doctor about midnight on January 20, 1934 and released him in Ohio at 9 pm on January 21, 1934. Karpis and Campbell robbed the Illinois bank on January 23, 1935. Karpis' machinegun was found in the Truckee River at the beginning of March 1935.

THE BREMER KIDNAPPING TRIAL

168- The two quotes by defendant Wilson are from the May 9, 1935 Chicago Tribune. The two FBI agents were Ralph Brown and John Madala. Agent Madala had previously testified on behalf of Purvis' false statement about Cowley at the Chicago Coroner's Inquest over the killing of Baby Face Nelson.

169- The busy FBI night taking down five Bremer-kidnapping suspects was on January 8, 1935 and 22 people were indicted for the crime by a St. Paul Federal Grand Jury on January 24, 1935. The first Bremer-abduction trial began on April 15, 1934 and the Federal Trial Jury returned its verdicts on May 17, 1935. William Vidler and Phil Delaney were acquitted. The sentencing was on June 7, 1935.

LUCK OF THE HIGHEST ORDER

170- The quote by Aurora tavern owner Ted Smith is from the February 9, 1935 *Chicago Tribune.*

171- Doc Barker and Volney Davis were falsely convicted for killing night watchman Thomas Sherrill on August 16, 1921 and entered prison on February 10, 1922. Doc was pardoned on September 10, 1932. Davis was granted a leave of absence from prison on November 3, 1932 until July 1, 1933. Davis escaped FBI custody on February 6, 1935. The pilot was Joseph Jacobson, the farm owner was E. L. Matlock, and his neighbor was William Ford. Davis was recaptured on May 31, 1935 and sentenced on June 7, 1935.

JUSTICE DELAYED, DENIED, OR BUNGLED?

172- Devol's quote is from the July 9, 1936 *Daily Journal-World* in Lawrence, Kansas. In the December 16, 1932 Minneapolis bank robbery the two patrolman killed were Leo Gorski and Ira Evans and the murdered civilian car passenger was Oscar Erickson. The three other suspects fingered by Lawrence Devol were Clarence Devol, Robert Newbern, and Leonard Hankins. Lawrence Devol pled guilty and was sentenced on January 10, 1933. Devol escaped on June 7, 1936 and Police killed him on July 8, 1936. The bar owner was Jim O'Neal. In the tavern Patrolman Cal Palmer was killed and Patrolman Ralph Knarr was seriously wounded. Assistant Chief of Police Lelon Coyle had his finger shot off, and civilian L. J. Edwards was slightly grazed. The other officer involved in the pursuit was Lester Dash.

173- Mrs. Vinita Stacey, age 32, was the girlfriend of Doyle, age 34, who critically shot Mrs. Frances Taylor, age 27, in his Kansas City hideout on February 6, 1935. The couple who harbored

Doyle in Pittsburg, Kansas, were Mr. and Mrs. H. C. Stanley. Doyle turned himself into Girard Sheriff Leon Delamaide on February 7, 1935.

174- The Minnesota Supreme Court affirmed Hankins conviction on February 1, 1935. Jess Doyle confessed and exonerated Hankins on March 30, 1935; the Bremer kidnapping trial began on April 14, 1935; the Prosecutor moved to dismiss the charges against Doyle on May 6, 1935; and the Jury ruled on May 17, 1935. Doyle clearly perjured himself on the witness stand because he had nothing to do with the Northwestern Bank robbery, but the Bremer kidnapping evidence against the defendants was overwhelming without his false testimony. Hankins was pardoned in 1951 and the Minnesota Legislature awarded him a pension on April 13, 1955. Hankins sister was Mrs. Della Hankins Lowery; his attorney was John J. Kelly, and the award-winning newspaperman was Jack Mackay. Some info in this section is also from the Police Officers Federation of Minneapolis in MPDFederation.com; the Minnesota Law Enforcement Memorial Association in MNLEMA.org; the Minnesota Supreme Court's ruling denying the appeal of Leonard Hankins on February 1, 1935 in FindACase.com; WesternKYHistory.org; VictimsOfTheState.org; Terrible Injustices in GeoCities.com; and HoratioAlger.org

WHERE IN THE WORLD IS KARPIS?

175- Hoover announced on October 16, 1935 the finding of Harrison's body the previous January. Hoover's statement quote is from the October 17, 1935 *New York Times.*

176- Karpis' quote is presented by Richard Kudish, crime historian and author, from his *Alvin Karpis: Pursuit of the Last Public Enemy* on TruTV.com.

177- The quote is from Cleveland FBI SAC P. E. Foxworth internal memorandum to Director Hoover dated March 28, 1936.

178- Karpis' gang robbed the mail truck at the Warren, Ohio, train station on April 24, 1935. Ohio U.S. Attorney Emerich B. Freed reopened the Warren robbery investigation. The presidential pardon for Tony Labrizetta and George Sargent for the Warren mail robbery was on July 21, 1935. Karpis threatened Hoover's life in early August 1935. Weaver had been paroled by Oklahoma on June 30,1931 and arrested by St. Paul police on August 2, 1932. Detective Akers reported Karpis' Hot Springs presence to the FBI after he left Lake Hamilton in early September 1935. The investigation report by FBI Agent B. L. Damron was completed on October 17, 1935. The FBI captured Weaver on September 1, 1935 and rejected his guilty-plea offer on November 9, 1935. The Karpis-Campbell gang robbed the mail train at Garrettsville, Ohio, on November 7, 1935. The FBI's mutilated fingerprint request was on March 11, 1936. Cleveland FBI Agent E. J. Wynn interviewed Hall at his home on March 25, 1936, and Chicago SAC Connelley interviewed Hall on March 28, 1936. The FBI bungled its raid for Karpis in Hot Springs on March 30, 1936.

Notes Chapter 10
HE SAID & HE SAID DIFFERENTLY

SKEWERING THE DIRECTOR

179- Charles Augustus Lindbergh, Jr., 20-month-old son of the famous aviator was kidnapped on March 1, 1932, and his decomposed body with a crushed skull was found on May 12, 1932. The Lindbergh Kidnapping Law was passed on June 22, 1932. Hoover claimed the FBI had solved all 55 kidnappings since then on November 2, 1935 when kidnappers challenged the law's constitutionality, and repeated this total when Lindbergh announced his family had moved to England for safety on December 23, 1935. Even though there had been no kidnappings since these two statements, Hoover's quote from a press conference defending the FBI's kidnapping record of solving all 62 kidnappings is from the February 16, 1936 *New York Times,* and the Director repeated this total in a hearing before the U.S. Senate Appropriations Subcommittee on April 10, 1936. When Hoover announced the solution to the William Hamm Jr. kidnapping on April 19, 1936, he increased the total kidnappings perpetrated and solved to 63, even though this kidnapping had occurred in June 15, 1933 and was included in the total when he began keeping kidnapping records. Some of this info is also from CharlesLindbergh.com.

180- Senator McKellar's quote is from *J. Edgar Hoover: The Man and His Secrets* by Curt Gentry.

181- The Senator McKellar and Hoover quotes are from the Senate Appropriations' hearings in the April 17, 1936 *Chicago Tribune.*

182- The Senate Appropriations Committee had Hoover testify on April 10 and 11, 1936, and the Committee's written report was released to the public on April 16, 1936. The FBI's 1928 budget was $2,250,000, and in 1936 it was $5,000,000, when Hoover requested an increase for 1937 of $1,025,000, or 21%, and Senator McKellar's Committee cut this increase back by $225,000, or -22$, to $800,000, or 16%. Some info in this section is also from *J. Edgar Hoover: The Man and His Secrets* by Curt Gentry New York: W.W. Norton & Company 1991; from *In Brief Authority* by Francis Biddle New York: Doubleday 1967; and from Richard Gid Powers *G-Men: Hoover's FBI in American Popular Culture.*

183- Karpis' quote is from his book *The Alvin Karpis Story.*

A MATTER OF MANHOOD

184- The FBI announced three arrests in the Hamm kidnapping on April 18, 1936. The Hamm kidnapping indictments and the AG's reward for Karpis were issued on April 22, 1936.

185- Hoover's speech quote was before the International Association of Chiefs of Police convening from 600 cities at the Hotel Ambassador in Atlantic City on July 9, 1935.

186- Hoover's first and third quotes are from the May 2, 1936 *New York Times,* and his second quote is from the May 2, 1936 *Chicago Tribune.*

187- Hoover's first quote is from the May 2, 1936 *Chicago Tribune,* and his second quote is from *The FBI In Action* by J. Edgar Hoover with Ken Jones New American Library 1957.

188- Hoover's quote is from the May 2, 1936 *Chicago Tribune.*

189- The FBI quote is from FBI.Gov/wanted/TopTen/ten-most-wanted-fugitives-FAQ.

190- Hoover's statement to the press is from the *New York Times, Chicago Tribune, New York Evening Journal,* and *Chicago American* on May 2 and 3, 1936.

191- Hoover's two quotes are from the May 2, 1936 *New York Evening Journal.*

192- Hoover's quote is from the May 8, 1936 *New York Times.*

193- Hoover's quote is from the chapter *The Toughest Mob We Ever Cracked* in *The FBI In Action* by J. Edgar Hoover with Ken Jones New American Library 1957.

194- Karpis two quotes are from his book *The Alvin Karpis Story.*

195- The Hot Springs ruse for the Postal Inspectors is from the internal memo Fletcher sent Connelley on April 25, 1936. The NBC broadcast negotiations are from the internal memo Assistant Director Clyde Tolson sent Hoover April 27, 1936 and from Hoover's reply to Tolson entitled "Proposed broadcast of the capture of Alvin Karpis." The FBI captured Karpis on May 1, 1936. Hoover phoned in his official version of events to T. D. Quinn who prepared a memo to file on May 2, 1936. SAC Connelley's internal report about the Karpis arrest was dated May 18, 1936. The Chicago Crime Commission's Public Enemy list was published on April 23, 1930, and Municipal Judge John Lyle issued his first mass gangster vagrancy warrants on September 16, 1930. Hoover announced Denning as Public Enemy Number 1 on July 20, 1936. The FBI began the Ten Most Wanted Fugitives list on March 14, 1950. Some info is also from History.com,

AlcatrazAlumniAssoc.org, Karpis' autobiography writer Robert Livesey at LittleBrick.com, Richard Kudish at TruTV.com, MaBarkerAncestorsAndDescendants.BlogSpot.com, NotFrisco.com, *The Alvin Karpis Story* by Alvin Karpis with Bill Trent, and *On the Rock* by Alvin Karpis as told to Robert Livesey Beaufort Books, Inc 1980.

CLOSETED COWARDICE

196- The quote about Winchell is from a FBI Headquarters Internal Memo May 24, 1960.

197- Whitehead's quote about Winchell's involvement in the Buchalter arrest is from his book *The FBI Story, A Report to the People* Random House 1956 with a forward by J. Edgar Hoover. Winchell's quote is from his radio broadcast on August 20, 1939 four days before Buchalter surrendered.

198- Hoover's quote about the FBI's fugitive hunt for Buchalter was taken from his Headquarters' Internal Summarization, but the date is unclear. The document contains information that indicates it was written in late 1947, and it was misfiled in the FBI file of Ben Siegel.

199- Orgen was killed on October 16, 1927. A Federal Jury found Buchalter guilty of Antitrust Law violations of New York's rabbit-fur dressing trade on November 8, 1936 and he received a two-year sentence. DA Dewey indicted Lepke for extortion of the garment industry on March 1, 1937, and then on March 8, 1937 a U.S. Circuit Court sent the fur case back for retrial due to insufficient evidence to link Lepke with the crime. On the retrial of the fur business for Antitrust Law violations Buchalter failed to appear in court on July 6, 1937. U.S. AG Cummings offered a $2,500 reward for information about Lepke on November 8, 1937. FDR appointed Frank Murphy AG on January 2, 1939 replacing Homer Cummings who resigned at age 68, and on January 4, 1940 appointed Murphy to the U.S. Supreme Court. FDR appointed Francis Biddle AG on September 5, 1941. Music publishing executive Irving Penn was murdered on July 25, 1939 because he resembled union official Philip Orlovsky, and DA Dewy offered a $25,000 reward for Buchalter on August 7, 1939. Fugitive Lepke surrendered to the FBI on August 24, 1939, and Beatrice Buchalter was convicted for harboring her husband on November 6, 1939. While Lepke was a fugitive he was indicted for narcotics importing and a Federal Jury convicted him on December 20, 1939 resulting in a 14-year sentence.

200- The Brookings Institute report was published on September 28, 1937, and the six quotes are from the next day's *New York Times*.

201- Joe Murphy retired from the Secret Service on December 31, 1936.

WHAT DEAL?

202- Buchalter challenged his transfer for trial in New York for the bakery industry-extortion case, but lost his appeal to the U.S. Circuit Court on January 10, 1940. A Manhattan Grand Jury indicted Lepke anew for garment-industry extortions on January 16, 1940. DA Dewey prosecuted Buchalter for the bakery extortion and obtained a guilty verdict on March 2, 1940. Brooklyn's indictment of Lepke for the murder of Joe Rosen on September 13, 1936 was made public on May 27, 1940. DA O'Dwyer began trying to get Buchalter from the feds on September 20, 1940 and succeeded in arraigning him in Brooklyn on May 9, 1941. Lepke and lieutenants Emanuel "Mendy" Weiss and Louis Capone were convicted of first degree murder on November 29, 1941. Special Prosecutor Dewey was elected Manhattan DA in 1937. Then he was the Republican nominee for New York Governor in four elections, losing in 1938 and winning in 1942, 1946, and 1950. The U.S. Supreme Court decided the final appeal in the Buchalter case on June 1, 1943. Governor Dewey formally demanded President Roosevelt surrender Lepke to the state on September 1, 1943. U.S. AG Biddle's letter dated November 29, 1943 was published in the November 30, 1943 *New York Times.* Lepke joined his two associates in the Sing Sing death house block on January 22,

1944; all three were executed on March 4, 1944; and the Republican convention was held in late June 1944.

Notes Chapter 11
CONCLUDING THE IMPROBABLE ASPECTS

ARRESTS NUMBER 2 & 3

203- Hoover's first quote is from the *Chicago Tribune* and his next two quotes are from the *New York Times,* both papers dated May 8, 1936.

204- Hoover's first quote is from the May 9, 1936 *Chicago Tribune* and his second quote is from the May 3, 1936 *New York Times.*

205- Karpis left New Orleans after midnight on May 1, 1936. The FBI arrested Campbell on May 7, 1936 and he pled guilty to the Bremer kidnapping on May 12, 1936. Hunter pled guilty to harboring Karpis on May 27, 1936.

206- The fireman's quote is from the December 26, 1936 *Newsweek Magazine.* Hoover's quote was reported by New York Fire Chief McElligott in the December 17, 1936 *New York Times.*

207- Brunette's quote is from the December 15, 1936 *New York Times.*

208- The AP photo of Hoover allegedly "slightly affected by tear gas" is from the December 16, 1936 *New York Times.*

209- The quote from Fire Commission McElligott's letter and his three quotes to reporters are from the December 17, 1936 *New York Times.*

210- The quote from Police Commissioner Valentine's letter is from the December 17, 1936 *New York Times.*

211- Hoover's first and third quotes are from his letter in the December 16, 1936 *New York Times.* His second quote is from the December 20, 1936 *New York Times,* and his fourth quote is from the March 10, 1937 *New York Times.*

212- Vandenbush was in the Industrial School from 1918 to 1925, and in the Reformatory from 1927 to 1930. Vandenbush and Brunette were sentenced for car robbery on April 25, 1931 and escaped from the Prison Farm on July 21, 1936. They robbed the three Mount Clemens deputy sheriffs on July 31, 1936. Vandenbush and Brunette held up three Wisconsin banks - the Seymour State Bank on August 17, 1936, the Ripon State Bank on October 2, 1936, and the Citizens Bank of Monroe on November 14, 1936, after having kidnapped State Trooper William A. Turnbull near Somerville, New Jersey on November 11, 1936. The FBI shoot out with Brunette was on December 15, 1936. The New York City Fire Commissioner was John McElligott and the Police Commissioner was Lewis Valentine. Brunette pled guilty to firing at the Director on March 9, 1937, and Mrs. Brunette was sentenced on June 22, 1937. Vandenbush robbed the Northern Westchester Bank of Katonah and was captured on February 25, 1937. His two accomplices were George and Anthony Rera; and the arresting officers were Sergeant John Hergenhan and Patrolmen Gerald Hendricks and William Orman. Vandenbush pled guilty on March 11, 1937.

TWO MORE KIDNAPPING TRIALS

213- Sawyer was arrested in Mississippi on May 3, 1935. The second Bremer trial convictions were on January 24, 1936

214- Hamm was kidnapped on June 15, 1933. Roger "Terrible" Touhy and his three associates were acquitted of the Hamm kidnapping on November 28, 1933. Bartholmey had been appointed Postmaster on April 1, 1935, and the FBI announced three arrests in the Hamm case on April 18,

1936. Peifer had been charged with the February 7, 1925 Milwaukee bank robbery. The Hamm kidnapping indictments and the AG's reward for Karpis were issued on April 22, 1936.

215- Peifer was convicted in the Hamm kidnapping on July 25, 1936 and sentenced on July 31, 1936. Bolton was sentenced on August 25, 1936.

THE ST. VALENTINE'S DAY MASSACRE CONNECTION

216- The St. Valentine's Day Massacre was on February 14, 1929, and Chicago issued Massacre arrest warrants for Burke on April 2, 1929. Burke's live-in companion was Viola Brenneman who told police he was away from their residence the day of the Massacre. Burke killed a Michigan patrolman on December 14, 1929. Burke's photo was recognized by 30-year-old truck driver Joe Hunsacker, and the fugitive was captured on March 26, 1931. Burke pled guilty to the St. Joseph, Michigan patrolman's murder on April 28, 1931 and he died on July 10, 1940. Bolton was arrested and Gibson fatally wounded on January 8, 1935.

217- Goetz was charged with rape in 1925. He was sought for wounding Dr. Henry R. Gross and killing Barney Hernandez in 1926 after accomplice Roger Bessmer identified him as an accomplice. Goetz was charged with robbing the Jefferson, Wisconsin Farmers and Merchants Bank in 1929. Ziegler was arrested in a Chicago Prohibition raid on June 9, 1928. Goetz-Ziegler-Siebert was killed in Cicero on March 20, 1934. The first quote by apartment owner Mrs. Leonora Smith about Siebert is from the March 23, 1934 *Chicago Tribune*. The second quote by an FBI agent is from *Public Enemies* by Bryan Burrough.

THE IMPACT ON OTHER LIVES

218- The Little Rock Federal Jury convicted four on October 29, 1938 for harboring Karpis in Hot Springs and these included former Police Chief Joseph Wakelin and former Detective Lieutenant Cecil Brook.

219- Chief Brown was indicted and suspended in 1926. Barfuss' quote is from the July 18, 1936 *Chicago Tribune*.

220- The quotes by Chief Dahill and Gladys Sawyer are from the July 21, 1936 *Chicago Tribune*. The quote of Georgette Winkler, widow of Gus Winkler, slain Capone lieutenant, is from the July 22, 1936 *Chicago Tribune*. Some of this info is also from *In The '30s, St. Paul Was The Hideout Of Choice For America's Most Infamous Gangsters* by Tim Brady in the April 2007 MinnesotaMonthly.com

221- Karpis married Dorothy Slayman in October 1931 and she sued for divorce on October 3, 1935. Her two quotes are from the May 2, 1936 *Chicago Tribune*.

222- Delaney gave birth to Raymond on February 2, 1935 and she was sentenced in late February 1935. The quote by Anna Karpavicz is from the May 3, 1936 *Chicago Tribune*.

223- Karpis' mother filed the suit on August 13, 1936 over the May 4, 1936 issue of *Time* and settled on January 11, 1937. Karpis son, Raymond was arrested on October 10, 1959 again for the home burglary on December 24, 1960.

224 Bremer died on May 4, 1965 and Hamm died on August 20, 1970.

225- Karpis' quote is from the February 19, 1984 *Chicago Tribune*.

226- Karpis was released from McNeil Prison on January 14, 1969. The quote by the unidentified prison official and the first quote by Karpis are from the November 29, 1968 *New York Times*. The *Baltimore Sun* editorial was reprinted in the January 29, 1969 *Chicago Tribune*. Karpis final quote is from the January 15, 1969 *New York Times*.

227- The Fort Scott, Kansas bank robbery was on June 17, 1932. Frank Sawyer was pardoned on September 17, 1969. The Kansas Governor was Robert Docking, the Governor's Pardon Attorney was Robert Ochs, and the Fort Scott Prosecutor was Frank O'Brian.

228- Karpis died on August 26, 1979.

SWIMMING WITH DOC BARKER

229- The Warden's quote is from the January 14, 1939 *New York Times*.

230- Convicts Ted Cole and Ralph Roe disappeared from the island prison on December 16, 1937. Doc Barker was killed in the Alcatraz escape attempt on January 13, 1939 and kidnapper Dale Stamphill was shot in both legs. The pair who surrendered as soon as approached were bank robber Henri Young and bank robber and kidnapper Rufus McCain. The escapee guards had to search for was post-office robber William Martin. Inmate John Paul Scott swam to the rocky San Francisco Ft. Point shore just months before the prison was closed. Some of this info is also from NotFrisco.com and History.com.

THE LAS VEGAS STRIP CONNECTION

231- Production of the Tommy Gun began in 1919 and O'Donnell was shot at in June 1925. Some of this info is from *The Gun That Made the Twenties Roar* by William J. Helmer Macmillan Publishing Company 1969.

232- Aiuppa, Maddox, and three associates were convicted for gambling violations on January 26, 1956. Aiuppa appeared before the McClelland Committee on July 18, 1958.

Notes Chapter 12
WHO WERE THE MASSACRE SHOOTERS?

KANSAS CITY'S MAFIA GANG

233- The Prohi raid against Lazia was on May 26, 1931. Kansas City's Delinquent Tax Collector was Rosemary Lyons. Some info is also from the Kansas City Public Library's biography *John Lazia: Crime Figure 1896-1934* by Daniel Coleman; and from *Johnny Lazia: Law Of The Land* by Allan R. May 2000 at AmericanMafia.com

THE ULTIMATE POLITICAL DYNASTY

234- The quote is from the Kansas City, Missouri Police Officers Memorial at KCPoliceMemorial.com. Jim Pendergast was elected Alderman for the West Bottoms in 1892.

235- Tom Pendergast's two quotes are from the Missouri Secretary of State Archives & Records in *It All Adds Up: Reform and the Erosion of Representative Government in Missouri, 1900-2000* by Missouri State Archivist Kenneth H. Winn at SOS.MO.gov.

236- The Grand Jury quote is from its October 27, 1939 report.

237- Miller's quote is from Ken Burns in *Kansas City, a Wide Open Town* from *Jazz* on PBS 1997.

PARTNERSHIP OF A CRIME LORD & A POLITICAL KING

238- The bloody Kansas City municipal election was on March 27, 1934. Some info in this and the previous section are also from the Missouri Secretary of State Archives & Records in *It All Adds Up: Reform and the Erosion of Representative Government in Missouri, 1900-2000* by Missouri State Archivist Kenneth H. Winn at SOS.MO.gov; the University of Missouri-Kansas City at UMKC.edu; and the Kansas City, Missouri Police Officers Memorial at KCPoliceMemorial.com. Some is from the Kansas City Public Library's biographies including *John Lazia: Crime Figure 1896-1934* by Daniel Coleman 2007; *James Francis Pendergast: Kansas City Alderman 1856-1911* by Nancy J. Hulston; *Thomas Pendergast: Business Owner and "Political Boss" 1873-1945* by Susan Jezak Ford; and *Bryce B. Smith: Mayor of Kansas City 1930-1940* by Nancy J. Hulston. In addition some is from *Tom's Town* by William M. Reddig 1947 Philadelphia: J. B. Lippincott Co.; and *Johnny Lazia: Law Of The Land* by Allan R. May 2000 at AmericanMafia.com

SOLVING THE MASSACRE COLD CASE

239- A third gangster came forward 38 years after the Massacre with a third second-hand story in his autobiographical book. In the 1971 *Alvin Karpis Story,* Karpis told his biographer Bill Trent that Floyd had admitted to him that he was a Massacre shooter. It is important to note Karpis made many false claims in both his books in hopes of generating bigger sales. It is unlikely Karpis ever met Floyd, and if he did it was certainly no more than a superficial pass by. Karpis was the only person to claim Floyd had talked about the Massacre, but Floyd like Miller never talked to anyone about his crimes. This is why the law, press, and crime historians have always been uncertain about which robberies he did and did not commit. In addition the families of both Floyd and Richetti always maintained the two men vehemently denied involvement in the Massacre. Most significant, if Karpis had indeed obtained this information from Floyd, he would have used it to turn informant to finally close out that case when he was convicted of kidnapping to get a reduction in his sentence. It is not reasonable to assume that Karpis facing a life sentence kept his mouth shut for a man he met no more than once and was already deceased. As it turned out Karpis ended up serving 33 years and spent the most time of any convict in Alcatraz.

240- Reppert's quote is from the November 5, 1934 *Chicago Tribune.*

241- Both the first quote by Agent Jones and the second quote by Police Director Reppert are from an FBI internal memo by Agent A. G. Harvey on February 15, 1935.

242- Police Director Reppert's Lieutenant was George Rayen and his quote is from the November 5, 1934 *New York Times.*

243- The Kansas City Municipal election was in March 1934. The Grand Jury Report and Police Director Reppert's indictment were issued on November 3, 1934, and it was Detective Sergeant B. H. Thurman who testified Reppert made the quoted statement. The third police officer charged with perjury was Detective Chief Thomas Higgins.

WHAT WAS THE MOTIVE FOR THE MASSACRE?

244- The positioning of the victims at the Massacre is described in the surviving FBI agents' reports and at FBI.Gov.

245- Until now speculation has run rampant in the Massacre case. It has even included the possibility that the gunfire was set off by a FBI agent, who accidentally did all the shooting inside the car with a shotgun he was inexperienced in handling and thus initiated return fire from the three assailants. This is presented by Robert Unger in *The Union Station Massacre: The Original Sin of J. Edgar Hoover's FBI* Kansas City Star Books 2005.

Notes Chapter 13
A STRUGGLE FOR JUSTICE

CONFLICT IN THE REALM

246- Lazia's quote of last words are from the July 11, 1934 *Los Angeles Times.*

247- FDR was Governor when he appointed Walsh in 1931. Pendergast's letter to Farley was dated May 12, 1933. Lazia was indicted for tax evasion in September 1933, and he was convicted of tax evasion on February 14, 1934. Lazia was killed on July 10, 1934. AG Cummings refused to identify political manipulators on October 18, 1934, and his three quotes are from the October 18, 1934 *Chicago Tribune.* "Needles" La Capra talked to FBI agents on September 1, 1934. La Capra was released from protective custody in January 1935 and was killed on August 21, 1935. Some of this info is also from *Johnny Lazia: Law Of The Land* by Allan R. May 2000 at AmericanMafia.com.

THE GATHERING STORM CLOUDS

248- The bloody Kansas City municipal election was held on March 27, 1934. The fraudulent Missouri statewide primary election was on August 7, 1934.

249- The quote by Federal Judge Albert Reeves is from January 1935 and was reported in the January 10, 1937 *New York Times.*

AN OLD CASE FANS THE FLAMES

250- The quote is by the reporter who wrote the article in the May 6, 1934 *Kansas City Star.*

251- Sheriff Bash's testimony quote at Gargotta's murder trial of Anthon is from the May 3, 1934 *Kansas City Times.*

252- Mrs. Bash's quote at Gargotta's defense attorney's deposition is from the May 3, 1934 *Kansas City Times.*

253- Police Sergeant John Harrington's quote at Gargotta's preliminary hearing is from the August 21, 1933 *Kansas City Star.*

254- Anthon was indicted in Chicago on September 29, 1932, and he was killed in Kansas City on August 12, 1933 after which the gunfight between Sheriff Bash and Gargotta ensured. The two slain gangsters were Gus Fasone and Sam Scola, who was the brother-in-law of James "Jimmy Needles" La Capra who claimed Sam was his source for the fable that Floyd and Richetti joined Miller as the Kansas City Massacre shooters. Lococo was a partner in the Ringside Athletic Club that was blown up on November 19, 1922. The Deputy Sheriff who was driving was Lawrence Hodges, and the neighbor girl was Melva Taylor. The wife of dead gangster Scola lost her life insurance lawsuit on March 8, 1936.

THE BIZARRE PROSECUTIONS IN THIS OLD CASE

255- Delivery boy Jerome Kissick testified to the same facts at both Gargotta's preliminary hearing and trial for murder. Kissick's quote was at the hearing from the August 21, 1933 *Kansas City Star.* His friend who testified to the same facts was Wendell Harris.

256- Sheriff Bash's testimony quote is from the May 5, 1934 *Kansas City Star.*

257- Former Detective Claiborne's quote is from the July 16, 1935 *Kansas City Star.*

258- Anthon's widow's quote at Gargotta's murder trial is from the May 8, 1934 *Kansas City Times.*

259- Anthon was slain on August 12, 1933, and Gargotta was charged with first-degree murder on August 16, 1933. Gargotta's attorney who was a Kansas City member of the Missouri Legislature was Edgar Keating. Prosecutor Graves took office at the beginning of January 1934. Gargotta's trial for Anthon's murder began on April 30, 1934 and he was found innocent on May 9, 1934. The judge who presided at his trial was Emory H. Wright, and the Assistant Prosecutor presenting the opening and closing arguments was John V. Hill. The state's ballistic expert was Merle A. Gill. Mafioso Gus Fasone had a fistfight with murder victim Anthon weeks before being killed by Sheriff Bash. Former Detective Claiborne was convicted of federal perjury on July 25, 1934; he surrendered on July 16, 1935 and was paroled on July 1, 1937. The Kansas National Guard armory was burglarized on October 23, 1932. Gargotta was convicted of possessing stolen pistols on June 20, 1934, and this verdict was reversed on appeal on May 10, 1935. The Gargotta majority opinion was written by Judge James A. Donohue and the dissent was by Judge J. W. Woodrough.

THE ULTIMATE BETRAYAL

260- Judge Brown Harris' quote to the Prosecutor is from the December 24, 1938 *Chicago Tribune.*

261- County Judge Brown Harris' three quotes and Sheriff Bash's quote are from the December 19, 1938 *Kansas City Star.*

262- Governor Stark's quote is from the December 21, 1938 *Kansas City Star.*

263- The quote from Governor Stark's letter is in both the December 24, 1938 *Chicago Tribune* and the January 1, 1939 *New York Times.*

264- The two 1938 quotes in the *Christian Science Monitor* are from the Kansas City, Missouri Police Officers Memorial at KCPoliceMemorial.com.

265- Governor Stark's quote is from the March 5, 1939 *Kansas City Star.*

266- Senator Kefauver's quote about Gargotta is from *The Mafia Encyclopedia: From Accardo to Zwillman* by Carl Sifakis 1987 New York: Facts On File Publications, Inc.

JUSTICE DELAYED & MANIPULATED

267- Governor Stark's quote to the Legislature was from the March 24, 1939 *Chicago Tribune* and *New York Times.*

268- The quotes of Judge Waltner and Assistant AG Nolen are from the January 24, 1940 *Kansas City Times.*

269- Special Commissioner Leon Embry's two quotes are from the September 25, 1939 *Kansas City Star.*

270- The *Kansas City Star* quote was on January 24, 1940

271- Roosevelt was reelected on November 3, 1936. The Kansas City vote fraud indictment was on January 9, 1937. The Missouri Supreme Court Douglas versus Billings election battle was in 1938. Prosecutor Graves had County Judge Harris dismiss Gargotta's attempted murder charge on December 19, 1938. Governor Stark issued his Kansas City clean-up order to AG McKittrick on December 23, 1938. That day Federal District Judge Albert L. Reeves resumed the Grand Jury's vote fraud investigation, and he ordered the Grand Jury to go after the Kansas City gambling Big Man on January 24, 1939. The Jackson County Special Grand Jury was also to begin on that date, but it was delayed until the Missouri Supreme Court ruling about Prosecutor Graves testifying so the Grand Jury took up its investigation of crime and rackets on February 4, 1939. Its final indictments were on March 11, 1939. Among the indictees were County Presiding Judge David Long and County Buildings Supervisor J. W. Hostetter. Governor Stark asked the Legislature to return the corrupted Kansas City Police Department to rule by the Governor on March 23, 1939. The County Grand Jury reindicted Gargotta for attempted murder on March 4, 1939; he pled guilty on June 14, 1939; he entered prison on June 19, 1939; and Governor Donnell pardoned Gargotta on January 28, 1941. AG McKittrick filed suit with the Missouri Supreme Court to oust Prosecutor Graves on May 10, 1939. County Judge Waltner dismissed the four neglect of duty charges against Prosecutor Graves on January 20 and 23, 1940. Prosecutor Graves got County Grand Jury indictments against Police Chief Reed, Attorney Paul Barnett, and Walter Bliss on March 9, 1940. The Missouri Supreme Court hearings on Prosecutor Graves' ouster proceedings began under Special Commissioner Leon Embry on January 29, 1940 and the court ruled to oust him on September 3, 1940 from his position that would have terminated on December 31, 1940.

Some of the info in this section is from the Kansas City Fraternal Order of Police at KCFOP.org; the Kansas City, Missouri Police Officers Memorial at KCPoliceMemorial.com; *It All Adds Up: Reform and the Erosion of Representative Government in Missouri, 1900-2000* by Missouri State Archivist Kenneth H. Winn from the Missouri Secretary of State Archives & Records at SOS.MO.gov; and Judging Illinois Judicial Selection: An Analysis on the Need and Method for Reform by the University of Illinois Civic Leadership Practicum 2009-2010 at CivicLeadership.Illinois.edu.

Notes Chapter 14
THE DYNASTY TOPPLES SOMEWHAT

TAKING DOWN THE POWER KINGS

272- Tom Pendergast and State Insurance Superintendent R. Emmet O'Malley were indicted for tax evasion on April 7, 1939. Pendergast entered Leavenworth Prison on May 29, 1939, and he died on January 26, 1945.

273- Carollo's quote is from the July 23, 1939 *Chicago Tribune.*

274- Carollo's quote is from the October 19, 1939 *Chicago Tribune.*

275- Gambling was closed down in Kansas City in January 1939. Carollo was indicted for federal mail fraud on April 17, 1939 and then for tax evasion on July 21, 1939. Already convicted of running a gambling place by the County, Carollo was convicted of perjury in federal court on October 18, 1939. Carollo pled guilty to tax evasion and mail fraud on October 19, 1939. Carollo's quote is from the October 19, 1939 *Chicago Tribune* and Prosecutor Milligan's quote is from the October 21, 1939 *Chicago Tribune.*

276- Former Police Director Higgins pled guilty on November 3, 1939.

277- Chief Reed's quote is from the November 29, 1939 *Fair Enough* column by Westbrook Pegler in the November 30, 1939 *Los Angeles Times.*

278- Some of the info in this section is also from articles in the *Kansas City Star* and the *Kansas City Times* from June 9, 1923 to March 24, 1966 that were supplied by the Interlibrary Loan/ Document Delivery Department of the Kansas City Public Library. Additional info is from the Kansas City Fraternal Order of Police at KCFOP.org; the Kansas City, Missouri Police Officers Memorial at KCPoliceMemorial.com; *It All Adds Up: Reform and the Erosion of Representative Government in Missouri, 1900-2000* by Missouri State Archivist Kenneth H. Winn from the Missouri Secretary of State Archives & Records at SOS.MO.gov; and *The Mafia And The Machine: The Story Of The Kansas City Mob* by Frank R. Hayde at AmericanMafia.com.

THE DYNASTY AIMS FOR THE WHITE HOUSE

279- Pendergast's quote is from the September 13, 1944 *Chicago Tribune.*

280- Pendergast's quote is from the September 16, 1944 and April 13, 1945 *Chicago Tribunes.*

281- The quote is by reporter Carl Wiegman in the September 16, 1944 *Chicago Tribune.*

282- Pendergast's quote is from KCPoliceMemorial.com.

283- The speech of U.S. Senator Truman is quoted from the September 18, 1944 *Chicago Tribune.*

284- The speech of U.S. Senator Bridges is quoted from the September 18, 1944 *Chicago Tribune.*

285- Truman mustered out of war service in 1919, and he was elected Jackson County Judge in 1922 and Presiding Judge in 1926 and again in 1930. Missouri's Legislature transformed Kansas City to a City Manager system in 1924. Truman was followed as Jackson County Presiding Judge by David E. Long in 1934, and Governor Stark appointed George S. Montgomery as Long's replacement in 1939. Truman was elected to the U.S. Senate in 1934. Truman visited Tom Pendergast's office about Prosecutor Milligan's reappointment on January 31, 1938, and Truman's condemnation speech was on February 15, 1938. Truman was reelected to the Senate in 1940.

Some info in this section is also from the Kansas City, Missouri Police Officers Memorial at KCPoliceMemorial.com; Harry S. Truman in the NewWorldEncyclopedia.org; Harry S. Truman Presidential Library and Museum at TrumanLibrary.org; the University of Virginia's MillerCenter.org; *Harry S. Truman And The Pendergast Machine* by Gene Schmdtlein in the Midcontinent American Studies Journal from the University of Kansas Libraries at

Journals.KU.edu; *Missouri's Nonpartisan Court Plan From 1942 To 2005* by Charles B. Blackmar from the University of Missouri School of Law at law.Missouri.edu/LawReview; and election results from USElectionAtlas.org.

MACHINE-MADE PRESIDENT

286- The quotes by Hannegan and FDR are from Truman's *New York Time's* obituary by Alden Whitman reprinted on May 8, 2010.

287- Truman's recommendation of Murray was challenged by the former Democratic National Committee Vice Chairman, Mrs. Emily Newell Blair, who at that time headed the National Recovery Administration's Consumers Division in 1935.

288- Truman had A. R. Hendricks appointed as WPA District Director for Northwest Missouri.

289- Henry Dillingham was the incumbent Kansas City U.S. District Marshal.

290- Truman's first quote is from the September 18, 1944 *Chicago Tribune,* and Truman's second quote if from *Harry Truman* by David M. Oshinsky in *The American Presidency* by Alan Brinkley and Davis Dyer 1004 Boston, MA: Houghton Mifflin.

291- Truman succeeded to the presidency on April 12, 1945. Eleanor Roosevelt's quote is from TrumanLibrary.org. Some info in this section is also from the NewWorldEncyclopedia.org; Harry S. Truman Presidential Library and Museum at TrumanLibrary.org; and MillerCenter.org of the University of Virginia.

THE MOBBED-UP WHITE HOUSE

292- Milligan was appointed by President Roosevelt in 1934 and fired by President Truman in 1945. President Truman nominated Samuel Wear as Kansas City U.S. Attorney on May 3, 1945. Truman appointed Francis Pendergast to Inter-American Affairs on October 19, 1945. Truman flew to his New Year's yachting on December 28, 1945.

293- The quote about Binaggio is from *Charles Binaggio: Politician, Gangster 1909-1950* by David Conrads, a 1999 summary of available source materials by the Kansas City Library.

294- The Second Ward boss was Henry McKissick, and the Jackson County Assessor was George R. Clark who allied with Binaggio.

295- Maurice Milligan's quote is from his book *Missouri Waltz* published by Charles Scribner's Sons 1948.

296- Truman's press conference opposing Representative Slaughter was on July 18, 1946. The Democratic Primary scandal against Representative Slaughter occurred in August 1946 when he was defeated by Pendergast candidate Enos Axtell who lost to Republican Albert L. Reeves Jr. AG Clark's quote is from the May 26, 1947 *Chicago Tribune,* and the safe was blown on May 27, 1947

297- The editorial quote is from the April 11, 1950 *Chicago Tribune.*

298- The Chicago gang delivered needed voter support to the 1946 U.S. House election for the political machine of Cook County Democratic Party Chairman Jake Arvey to help President Truman. Chicago gangsters Paul Ricca, Louis Campagna, Philip D'Andrea, Charles Gioe, and John Rosselli were paroled on August 13, 1947, and the U.S. House's nine months of hearings were from September 25, 1947 to June 21, 1948. Truman appointed Clark AG in 1945 and to the Supreme Court in 1949. A discussion of the Chicago gang's bribe payoff to AG Clark was overheard in a bugged conversation by the FBI in 1964 from *J. Edgar Hoover: The Man and His Secrets* by Curt Gentry 1991 New York: W. W. Norton & Company

President Truman's shameful sordid pardoning of these Chicago gang leaders is detailed in the next book in this series that covers the history of the four top Prohibition gangs who would build the Las Vegas Strip resorts during its Golden Era from the *Flamingo* in 1946 to *Caesars Palace* in 1966. This book presents the three decades before these four gangs arrived in Las Vegas when they dominated Prohibition and then operated wide-open high-end illegal casinos across the country that were more elegant and glamorous than any Las Vegas Strip resort casinos of today.

Notes Chapter 15
A MAFIOSO AND A PRESIDENT RUMBLE

A MAFIOSO EMBARRASSES THE WHITE HOUSE

299- Binaggio's other must win candidate in the 1948 election was Joseph T. Lenge for county assessor.

300- Rimann was murdered on March 24, 1949.

301- The IRS went after Binaggio and Gargotta in September 1949.

302- In the 1950 Democratic primary for U.S. Senator the Truman-Pendergast faction endorsed State Senator Emery W. Allison and Binaggio supported U.S. Representative Thomas C. Hennings, Jr. of St. Louis.

303- Binaggio and Gargotta were murdered on April 6, 1950. The taxi driver was Walter Gambill.

304- The quote by Binaggio's widow is from the April 14, 1950 *Chicago Tribune.*

305- Binaggio's chauffeur bodyguard was Nick Penna, and Gargotta's woman friend was Blanche Howard. Her quote is from the April 14, 1950 *Kansas City Star.* Cooper's quote and the two quotes by Gargotta and Binaggio that Penna gave to police are from the April 6, 1950 *Kansas City Star.*

306- The Catholic Church's statement is from the April 11, 1950 *Chicago Tribune.*

307- The two quotes by Binaggio's widow are from the April 14, 1950 *Chicago Tribune.*

308- In the 1950 Democratic primary for U.S. Senator Binaggio's candidate U.S. Representative Thomas C. Hennings, Jr. of St. Louis beat the Truman-Pendergast faction candidate State Senator Emery W. Allison who had been unpopular with the state's African-Americans because he bottled up Missouri legislation that would have permitted them to attend the state university. Allison was a big supporter of the President's Fair Deal policies but he was the antithesis of Truman when it came to racial equality.

309- The six editorial quotes are from the April 8, 1950 *Kansas City Star.*

310- Milligan's quote is from the April 12, 1950 *Kansas City Star.*

311- Kansas City's long-time reform Mayor was William Kemp. Governor Smith appointed Tuck Milligan and Sheridan Farrell who supported gambling to the Kansas City Police Board on May 3, 1949. The *Kansas City Star* editorial came out on April 8, 1950, and on May 2, 1940 Governor Smith removed the two Kansas City Police Commissioners he had not appointed, Hampton Chambers and Robert Cohn who brought suit for reinstatement that the Missouri Supreme Court dismissed in early July 1950. The Kefauver Committee's Preliminary Report was released on February 28, 1951.

WHAT SEEMS OBVIOUS MAY BLUR REALITY

312- Governor Smith appointed William Holzhausen as St. Louis Police Board Chairman. The quote made by the *St. Louis Star-Times* was in an April 7, 1950 article. The quote by Binaggio's widow is from the April 14, 1950 *Chicago Tribune.*

313- Hicks purchased the land for the *Thunderbird* on March 4, 1946. Carnahan suffered his Las Vegas casino loses at the end of August and the beginning of September 1946. The *Thunderbird* opened on September 2, 1948. Carnahan's quote is from the author's March 6, 1969 interview.

314- Harmony Publishing reopened as Standard News Service in January 1949, and partners Lococo and Eddie "Spitz" Osadchey testified before the McFarland Committee on May 4, 1950. Lococo pled guilty to tax evasion on September 11, 1950. The operators of liquor distributor Duke Sales Company in Kansas City were Max Ducov and his brother-in-law, Nathan Bassin, who testified before the Federal Grand Jury. The info about Assistant County Prosecutor Sam Hayden being a partner in Town Recreation is from the Kansas City Federal Grand Jury interim report released on April 29, 1950. He was fired that night by County Prosecutor Henry H. Fox Jr., a Democrat serving his first term. Last Chance Tavern partner Fred Renegar was slain in January 1947. Surviving partner John Goulding joined the Binaggio combine.

315- Chickie Berman bought the Stork Club in 1945 with partners Al Abrams and Cy Silver. Later that year Berman and Abrams, who was taken to the cornfield, relinquished their rights but Silver continued to operate it with four new partners associated with Binaggio. The info about this incident is from the Kansas City Federal Grand Jury interim report released on April 29, 1950, and also from *Easy Street: The True Story of a Mob Family* by Susan Berman 1981 The Dial Press. She compiled this event from the FBI's file on her father, Davie Berman, and comments made to her by her father and his brother Chickie.

A GOLD-FILLED POT OR A MIRAGE

316- Carollo was arrested for wholesaling liquor on April 14, 1950 along with his son-in-law Mike Arnone, Tony Marcella, and Sam Tortorice. Carollo was deported on January 7, 1954.

317- The quote by the unidentified gang member is from the April 6, 1950 *Kansas City Star*.

318- The North Atlantic treaty was signed on April 4, 1949 and ratified by the Senate on August 14, 1949, and then the Soviet Union exploded its first atomic bomb on August 29, 1949. The AEC's pumice research project began at UNM on July 7, 1948; the five professors filed their claims in October 1948; the Pantheon prospectus was dated March 23, 1949; and their final report was submitted to the AEC by project head and engineer Walter E. Gay on August 31, 1949. Gay sent a letter to President Truman on December 20, 1949, and Davis' dinner reception for Truman was on December 26, 1949. Dennis Chavez Sr. served in the U.S. Senate from 1936 until his death in 1962. Davis' venture merged with two existing companies that organized as New Mexico corporations under the names Pumex Corporation in January 1950 and the Superlite Materials Corporation in May 1950. The Indian Reservation lease was approved on March 28, 1950. The Washington lobbyist who wanted to invest with Binaggio was Al Marshall. The RFC loan to Wallace for Davis' Superlite Material Corporation was authorized on June 26, 1950. Cook brought a receivership suit again Davis and Wallace over Pumex Corporation on January 20, 1951. Senator Fulbright's Banking Subcommittee issued its report on February 2, 1951. The Democratic National Chairman was William Boyle. The *Chicago Tribune* ran an outstanding investigative four-part series by Paul Homes in late November 1950 that exposed all the elements in this pumice deal, and the *Kansas City Star* uncovered the involvement of Binaggio and his emissary Clyde Lockwood who was introduced to Binaggio by former Probate Court Clerk James Cleary.

THE STRANGE DEMISE OF A MAFIOSO

319- The quote by Binaggio emissary Clyde Lockwood is from the May 4, 1950 *Kansas City Star*. The Bureau of Narcotics agent was Claude A. Follmer. The quote by Binaggio's widow is from the April 14, 1950 *Chicago Tribune*.

320- The IRS began its investigations of Binaggio and Gargotta in September 1949. The Kansas City Federal Grand Jury was called on March 14, 1949 and it released its interim report on April 29, 1950. Binaggio's wife's slain business partner was Mrs. Irene Sarno.

THE SENATE INVESTIGATES A MURDER

321- Missouri Republican Representative Dewey Short's two quotes and New York Republican Representative M. K. Macy's quote are from the April 7, 1950 *Chicago Tribune*.

322- The two *Chicago Tribune* editorial quotes were on April 8, 1950.

323- The quote by Republican Policy Committee Chairman Robert A. Taft [Ohio] is from the April 12, 1950 *Nevada State Journal*.

324- Kefauver's quote is from the *American Experience People & Events* at PBS.org. The quote by Vincent "Jimmy Blue Eyes" Alo, a Prohibition and illegal casino partner and close friend of Charlie Luciano and Meyer Lansky, is from the author's June 12, 1997 interview.

325- U.S. Senator Kefauver introduced a resolution calling for an investigation of big-time illegal gambling operators on January 23, 1950. Costello testified before the McFarland Interstate Commerce Committee on April 27, 1950, and the Kansas City Federal Grand Jury interim report was released on April 29, 1950. U.S. VP Barkley broke the tie vote for the Kefauver Committee on May 3, 1950, and President Truman signed it into law on May 17, 1950. In between those two dates VP Barkley appointed five Senate members to the Kefauver Committee on May 10, 1950 – they were Democrats Kefauver of Tennessee, Herbert R. O'Conor of Maryland, and Lester C. Hunt of Wyoming, along with Republicans Charles W. Tobey of New Hampshire and Alexander Wiley of Wisconsin. The Kefauver Committee held closed hearings in Kansas City on July 18 through 20, 1950, and then questioned these people in public hearings on September 28 through 30, 1950. Kefauver was the Committee's initial chairman until he relinquished it on April 30, 1950 after releasing its final report on April 17, 1951, and Senator O'Conor replaced him until the Committee folded on September 1, 1951. AG McGranery ended annual organized-crime Special Grand Juries on September 7, 1952. Some information in this section is also from Senate.gov and from *American Experience People & Events* at PBS.org.

KANSAS CITY PENETRATES THE STRIP

326- Gizzo died on April 1, 1953. The Apalachin Mafia meeting was on November 14, 1957. The Nevada State Gaming Control Board announced the Black Book on April 3, 1960. The Jackson County Grand Jury issued its report about Civella on May 4, 1961. The Teamsters loan to the *Landmark* was in August 1966 and Hughes opened it on July 1, 1969 after Civella was rousted at *Caesars Palace* in May 1969. The Nevada Gaming Commission approved Glick in the *Stardust* and *Fremont* in April 1974. Civella was a guest at the *Dunes* in September 1974 and the fine was ordered in December 1974. The Gaming Commission approved Shenker in the *Dunes* in February 1975 as Civella's man Agosto started taking over control of the *Tropicana*. Hoffa disappeared on July 30, 1975. Roy Williams was Teamsters International President from May 15, 1981 to April 14, 1983. The IRS charged the *Dunes* with skimming profits in October 1972, and the IRS made a back-taxes claim of $16.5 million in May 1974. The IRS dropped the *Dunes* skimming charges in August 1976.

ABOUT THE AUTHOR

Bill Friedman is president of the Friedman Management Group, which specializes in solving casino marketing, design, and operations problems. He has consulted for forty years to casinos throughout the United States and in England, South Africa, Monaco, Australia, Russia, Canada, and several Caribbean Islands.

Friedman was president and general manager of the Castaways Hotel and Casino and the Silver Slipper Casino in the heart of the Las Vegas Strip for thirteen years. He transformed them from perennial losers into super successes, consistently in the top of Nevada's highest profit-per-square-foot performers.

Friedman is author of the groundbreaking research work *Designing Casinos to Dominate the Competition* published by the University of Nevada Reno. He is also author of the seminal book for succeeding in the casino business *Casino Management.* He taught the pioneer course in casino management for the University of Nevada Las Vegas's College of Hotel Administration in the early years during the decade of the 1970s.

The saga about Friedman's 45-year historical investigation methodology is presented on the Research page at www.FriedmanSpeaksVegas.com.

CPSIA information can be obtained at www.ICGtesting.com
Printed in the USA
BVOW06s1846220914

367874BV00011B/142/P

9 781494 9581